Dedication & Special Thanks

This book is dedicated to Alexa & Sam, who make everything possible.

I'd also like to recognize my interns who helped with the format, content, and corrections of this book.

Sasha Norman
Jordan Walker
Edgar Woods

I also want to thank my students who often reviewed sections, offered suggestions, lent their names for word problems, and inspired me to write this book.

I'd Like to Hear from You

I'm always happy to talk to students and parents. I can be reached through my website: www.thetestguy.com/contact or you can email me at Jacob@thetestguy.com.

Found a mistake in the book? Drop me a line at jacob@thetestguy.com

Navigating the Book

The Table of Contents starts on the next page, but here's an overview.

The beginning section of the book is all about *how to take the test, what mistakes to avoid, and how to use this book based on different score levels & preparation times.*

The end section of the book is *strategy*. Every math topic has it's own strategy notes, but at the end of the book, you'll find discussion of some of the more useful and broadly applicable strategies.

The middle sections are *math*. It's broken down into sections like you'd see in school: pre-algebra, elementary algebra, intermediate algebra, coordinate geometry, plane geometry, and trigonometry.

Each of those sections has a pre-test. Start there, and then go to the topics you need to cover.

Each topic has a question set specifically written for it. Those problems are really useful, and the solutions are right after the question set.

Videos

I really encourage you to check out the videos that go with the sections. They're listed on the *Wrap Up* page of each section.

You can find them on my website: www.thetestguy.com/videos

Table Of Contents

Elementary Algebra

Intermediate Algebra

Coordinate Geometry

Plane Geometry

Trigonometry

Strategy

How to Use This Book

The ACT is a standardized test, but your preparation *needs* to fit you individually. Everyone is different. Your goals, needs, experience, days/weeks before you take the test, and time you have available to prepare are unique.

I designed this book to help you with the content of, and the strategies for, the math section. Use actual ACTs to work on timing. The ACT publishes a book of tests, and you can also find ACT's annual booklet, which contains a test, online.

Take the Pre-Tests

Each section has a pre-test that covers each topic and the most common problem types. They are very thorough and will give you a good idea of what you need to work on. *I wouldn't set time limits while taking the test.* You can really on either *accuracy* or *speed*—it's hard to work on both.

Dig into the Pre-Tests

After you finish each pre-test, check your answers and look up the solutions of the questions you missed. Dig into the solutions and really understand the questions you missed *and* the questions you weren't very comfortable on. Really, really dig into the solutions.

Strategize

After you've gone over the pre-test, make a list of the sections you need to cover. Prioritize based on the importance of the sections. It's best if you go through every section, but be realistic about how much time and motivation you have.

How do I Get the Most from this Book?

When I teach students, I work hard to meet them where they are. I don't know you, unfortunately, but I wanted to give you some ideas of how you should use this book best. I'm using two criteria: time and your current score. If you haven't taken the ACT yet, convert your PSAT Math score using an online table (just Google) or take a full practice section of the Math ACT (again you can find one by a quick Google search).

In general, you should follow the steps on the previous page: start with the pre-tests, dig into each of those tests, and make a list of what you need to cover. *Then follow the steps below.*

I've got a ton of time

Review the strategy chapter (at the back of the book) and then start with pre-algebra and work your way through. You can skip around if you'd like, but it's best to start with *pre-algebra* and *elementary algebra.* Those skills are foundational.

I've got 6 weeks or less

Review the strategy chapter (at the back of the book). Work through each section where you missed or guessed on a pre-test question. It's best to start with *pre-algebra* and work your way through the sections you found difficult. You may end up backtracking to skills you didn't "need" to review; I encourage you to do so.

I'M ALMOST OUT OF TIME!

Review the strategy chapter (at the back of the book), and work through as many sections as you can. Focus on sections that show up the most: *key skills*, then *multiple times per test*, then *100% of tests,* and so on. *Don't burn yourself out. It's all about quality, not quantity.*

My Math Score is under 23

Spend extra time working on the key skills and sections that show up on every test; be thorough. There are many sections you can pick up points that can bleed over to other question types. If you automatically turn to *guess and check* or *testing answers*, use the strategy section and **deliberate practice** to break yourself of the habit.

My Math Score is between 23 and 27

You've got gaps in your math knowledge and/or you're not recognizing when to apply some skills. Make sure that you understand the questions you answered correctly on the pre-test but that you felt unsure on. If you don't have time to go through the material for each section, try and do all the problem sets. Working several problems on the same topic will help you recognize problems, firm up your math skills, and make you comfortable with applying strategies.

My Math Score is 28 or greater

> Once you get into the tail of the score curve, a question or two is a point on your score. For example, the difference between a score of 28 and a score of 30 is three correct questions. So, *small things count.* Spend time on the smaller topics. Most importantly, be flexible in your approach. Consider practicing without a graphing calculator (if you use yours a lot); you'll become a more creative problem solver. Don't neglect pre-algebra: it's often a weak spot for high scorers.

How to Prepare for the ACT

First, I want to discuss two terrible ways to prepare for the ACT.

The Martyr

I regularly have students come to me and say something like, "I'm not working and I'm not in school right now, so I'm going to study eight or ten hours a day." I grimace and then talk them out of it.

The ACT requires you to think at a high level; it's not a test of rote memorization. You've got to pick up on the nuances and complexities of the test while solving problems quickly and creatively. That's not something your brain, or any brain, can do all day long. Studying all day will wear you down. You'll pass from enthusiasm, to frustration, to misery, to dejected apathy.

The Machine Gunner

Another harmful preparation method is *question only.* It's not uncommon to see a student who has completely worked problem book after problem book but hasn't had their score go up. You have to spend time figuring out why you missed things, why you got them right, and why you were unsure. *Quality practice matters much more than quantity.*

Deliberate Practice

If you only get one concept out of this book, this is what I want you to walk away with: "expertise" and "genius" are the product of deliberate practice.[1] Deliberate practice is the *single best way to improve your ACT score.*

Intentional

> *You've got to be motivated to spend effort and time to practice.* Eliminate distractions; put your phone on airplane mode, turn off Netflix, etc.

Designed for your Skill Level

> *You need to pick up after a brief period review and be able to answer questions.* That's why the book is structured into self-contained topics. It takes time to improve—give yourself permission to be wrong—especially at the beginning. Wrong answers are opportunities for improvement.

Immediate feedback

> *You absolutely have to review problems right away.* If you want, stop partway through the pre-tests and check your answers and review the material. It's not enough just to check your answers. You have to dig into the questions that gave you trouble while they're fresh in your mind.

Repetition

> *You've got to drill what you've covered.* Use the problem sets in this book to reinforce what you're reviewing. It's not about the number of problems you do each day; it's about taking each problem seriously.

---

[1] Deliberate practice is the brainchild of K. Anders Ericcson, a Florida State University professor of psychology. The importance of quality practice & expertise has become a popular topic, and there are some great books out there by Angela Duckworth, Malcolm Gladwell, & others.

The Score Report

If you've taken an ACT, or ACTs, use your score report to give you some insight on what you need help on. It's not a perfect fit because the categories on the score report are pretty expansive and somewhat arbitrary. Let's start by talking about the big categories.

Integrated Essential Skills + Preparing for Higher Math = ACT Math

The ACT breaks all problems into Integrated Essential Skills and Preparing for Higher Math. On the next page you'll find the score report categories and which book section(s) correspond to those categories. Here's how the ACT describes the three main divisions:

Preparing for Higher Math (57 – 60%)
This category captures the more recent mathematics that students are learning, starting when students begin using algebra as a general way of expressing and solving equations....[2]

Integrating Essential Skills (40 – 43%)
These questions address concepts typically learned before 8th grade, such as rates and percentages; proportional relationships; area, surface area, and volume; average and median; and expressing numbers in different ways. You will solve problems of increasing complexity, combine skills in longer chains of steps, apply skills in more varied contexts, understand more connections, and become more fluent.[1]

Let me try and translate: Preparing for Higher Maths is the stuff from Algebra 1 on. Integrating Essential Skills is Pre-Algebra, some basic algebra, and some of the simpler geometry (area of a rectangle, perimeter, etc.). *Preparing for Higher Math* is divided into five categories that are covered on the next pages.

Modeling (>25%)
Modeling questions are also *Integrating Essential Skills* or *Preparing for Higher Math* questions. Remember, IES + PHM = ACT Math, so *Modeling* is a double count on some questions. *Modeling* questions are about mathematical models and are often word problems. I'm sorting the ACT score report categories and simplifying them to make things manageable.

Preparing for Higher Math (57 – 60%)

Number & Quantity (7 to 10%)

Real & Complex Number Systems	**Pre-Alg: Numbers**
	Int Alg: Complex Numbers
Integers	**Pre-Alg: Numbers**
Rational Exponents	**Elem Alg: Exponents**
Matrices	**Int Alg: Exponents**

Algebra (12 to 15%)

Solving Linear Equations	**Elem Alg: Operations**
	Elem Alg: Inequalities
Graphing Linear Equations	**Coord Geo: Line Equation**
Solving Polynomial Equations	**Elem Alg: Quadratics**
	Int Alg: Rational Expressions
Graphing Polynomial Equations	**Coord Geo: Functions**
Radical Equations	**Int Alg: Radical Expressions**
Exponential Equations	**Elem Alg: Exponents**
	Int Alg: Logs
Systems of Equations	**Int Alg: Systems of Equations**

Functions (12 to 15%)

Function Definition	**Int Alg: Functions**
Function Notation	**Int Alg: Functions**
The Graphs of Functions	**Coord Geo: Functions**

---

[2] Preparing for the ACT 2016-2017

Geometry (12 to 15%)

Triangles	**Plane Geo: Triangles**
	Plane Geo: Right Triangles
	Trig: Find the Side
Circles	**Plane Geo: Circles**
Other Shapes	**Plane Geo: Four Sided Shapes**
	Plane Geo: Other Polygons
	Plane Geo: Combo Shapes
Surface Area & Volume	**Plane Geo: 3D Geometry**
Congruence & Similarity	**Plane Geo: Angles**
	Plane Geo: Triangles
Trigonometric Ratios	**Trig: Find the Side**
	Trig: Find the Angle
	Trig: The Unit Circle
	Trig: Identities

Statistics & Probability (8 to 12%)

Measures of Central Tendency	**Pre-Alg: Mean, Median...**
	Pre-Alg: Data
Data Collection Methods	**Pre-Alg: Data**
Bivariate Data	**Pre-Alg: Data**
Calculate Probabilities	**Pre-Alg: Probabilities**

<u>**Integrating Essential Skills (40 – 43%)**</u>

Percentages	**Pre-Alg: Percentages**
Rates	**Pre-Alg: Rates & Units**
Proportion	**Pre-Alg: Ratios**
Area	**Plane Geo: 4-Sided Shapes**
	Plane Geo: Triangles
Surface Area	**Plane Geo: 3D Geometry**
Volume	**Plane Geo: 3D Geometry**
Average	**Pre-Alg: Mean, Median...**
Median	**Pre-Alg: Mean, Median...**
Simplification/Equivalence	**Pre-Alg: Fractions**
	Pre-Alg: Decimals
	Elem Alg: Operations

<u>**Modeling (>25%)**</u>

You'll find modeling questions in most sections, and they also fit into either *Preparing for Higher Math* or *Integrating Essential Skills*. If your modeling score is low, spend time on problems that have a real world connection—typically word problems.

From the Other Side: The Limits of Writing an ACT

I don't write the ACT, I never have, and I probably never will. But I think a lot about the ACT, and I think about it from the perspective of the men and women who write the test. There are a few things about how they *have* to do their job that can make your job (taking the test) easier.

1. **There are only so many topics.**

    The ACT has a list of math topics that are fair game. Anything that's not on the list doesn't get tested.

2. **The weights are pre-defined.**

    Each section (pre-algebra, trig, etc.) is a defined percentage of the ACT. That means there is a pretty tight range of the number of questions for each section. For example, the trig section is between 5 and 10% of the total test. That translates into 3 to 6 questions. By the way, there are usually 4 trig questions.

4. **Questions can only take 60 seconds**

    The ACT Math is 60 questions in 60 minutes—60 seconds per question. The questions can't be too involved or have too many steps. When questions do have a lot of steps, there's almost always a shorter way. They *have* to build in shortcuts on longer questions.

5. **Questions don't require a calculator**

    The ACT doesn't require a calculator so the questions can't require one either. The arithmetic needs to be relatively simple. More importantly, it means that the ACT tends to test concepts more than calculations.

6. **You can't have too many people get the question right nor too many miss.**

    To keep scores consistent test after test, year after year, the distribution of scores needs to be about the same. For example, on every test in the official ACT book, a math score of 25 means you got between 37 and 40 questions right.

    What does that mean? The test makers know what percent of people miss a particular question type, and they can anticipate that beforehand. They really, really don't want any surprises. They use the same questions over and over; they just change them slightly. They don't get to experiment much at all.

Speed vs. Accuracy

The ACT is a fast test; the limited time per question ups the difficulty of the entire test. You need to think about speed, and practice speed, but don't get obsessed with speed.

Better to Guess than Rush

I'd rather you run out of time with a few questions (five or less) left than rush through the section. Rushing makes you misread questions, misread answers, and causes careless errors. You'll do better guessing on the last few problems (which are hard problems, by the way) than rushing through the entire section. *Every question counts the same, so make sure you get all the easy points.* That said, you don't want to guess on the last 15 questions, so you need to develop a fast pace. The good news is, most students aren't fairly close to a good pace.

You Can't Train Speed & Accuracy at the Same Time*

*Unless you're putting the finishing touches on your prep.

If you're having trouble with concepts or question types, don't time yourself. Work on getting questions right. Maximizing the number of correct responses should always be your first priority. **This book is designed to help you get every question right.** You can, if you want, time yourself on the pre-tests, but don't guess or rush when you run out of time. Instead, focus on giving a thorough attempt to each question. That way you'll be able to accurately diagnose your weaknesses.

How to Work on Your Speed

Use actual ACT exams to work on your speed. Online, you can find actual ACT exams, and I encourage you to buy the latest version of the *Real ACT Guide*. It's got practice tests as well as explanations. Start your timed work with 10 questions at a time. The ACT gives you 60 seconds per question. In general, you can expect that the first 10 or 20 questions will take you less than 60 seconds per question and the last 10 – 20 questions to take longer. Work your way up to 20 or 30 questions at a time. You can, if you want, to entire sections at a time, but don't tackle longer problem sets until close to your test date.

The 6 Biggest ACT Math Mistakes

1. **Hugging your calculator**

   Don't run to your calculator like it's a security blanket. Graphing calculators can't solve most problems, and running to your calculator will confuse you. If you don't have your question set up right, you won't notice when your calculator spits out a bad answer. The ACT writes trap answers for calculator mistakes.

2. **Thinking & not writing**

   Don't try to power your way through the section. The more you can automate things by setting questions up, the fewer mistakes you'll make. You'll also save "gas" in your mental tank for harder questions and later sections of the ACT.

3. **Not using the answer choices**

   The answer choices are your allies. Use them, it will help you start problems, and keep you from taking questions too far, or going down a wrong path.

4. **Jumping to plugging-in answers**

   Jumping to plugging-in is the polar opposite of the previous mistake. Plugging-in answers works great on some questions, and it's a good last resort, but it can't be your go-to strategy. On most problems, plugging-in doesn't work unless you've already set the problem up—in which case you can just solve.

5. **Getting lost in the question**

   It's easy to get lost in really long (or really short questions). There's either too much or too little to start with. Reading and re-reading and re-re-reading a question wastes time, makes you anxious, and gets you nowhere.

6. **Not using or drawing diagrams**

   Not drawing diagrams when the problem describes a shape leads to conceptual and calculation errors. You can garble your inputs, have trouble finding where to start, and solve for the wrong measure.

Pre-Algebra

According to the new way the ACT breaks down questions, *pre-algebra* is more of an *Integrating Essential Skills* category, but *numbers, combinations & permutations, probability, mean, median & mode*, and *Data* will be in *Preparing for Higher Maths*.

Pre-Algebra is 20 to 25 percent of the ACT Math section. That translates into between 12 and 15 questions per test. Here's how often each topic appears and where you'd find it on your score report. (Check out more).

Numbers	0 – 2 questions	**PHM/IES: Num. & Quantity**
Decimals	0 – 2 questions	**Integrating Essential Skills**
Factors[key skill]	1 – 2 questions	**PHM: Num. & Quantity**
Fractions[key skill]	0 – 2 questions	**Integrating Essential Skills**
Percents[key skill]	2 – 3 questions	**Integrating Essential Skills**
Probability	2 – 3 questions	**PHM: Statistics**
Ratios[k]	1 – 3 questions	**Integrating Essential Skills**
Rates[k]	1 – 3 questions	**Integrating Essential Skills**
Mean, Median...	2 – 3 questions	**PHM: Statistics**
Data	1 – 3 questions	**PHM: Statistics**
Comb. & Perm.	1 – 2 questions	**PHM: Statistics**

IES: Integrating Essential Skills
PHM: Preparing for Higher Math
MOD: Modeling

A detailed explanation of the math score report is covered at the beginning of the book in the **Score Report.** There are five key skills in *Pre-Algebra*, and the importance of those topics is bigger than their question count.

Strategies

There are a lot of key skills here, pick them up. You'll find a higher question density per topic in the Pre-Algebra topics than anywhere else. So, I would spend a little extra time on this stuff.

Setup, Setup, Setup
> By-in-large, most pre-algebra questions are word problems. Word problems always benefit from setup. You have to understand the elements and their relations clearly.

Use Formulas
> Use formulas for percent, average, and probability and turn tough word problems into plug-in problems. Lean on these formulas when you can't figure out what to do.

If You're Stuck, Test Answer Choices
> If you can't get the problem to "work right," but you can "see" how the calculations work, test answers. Sometimes, like on GCF & LCM, it's best to test answers.

Have a Game Plan for Calculator Use
> Before you test, think a little on what situations you want to use a calculator and practice those skills. You can waste a lot of time, and end up redoing problems if you aren't decisive about your calculator use.

Pre-Algebra: Pre-Test

1. When a is a rational number which *must be false*?

   A. a is a complex number
   (B.) a is an integer
   C. a is natural number
   D. a is a fraction
   (E.) When squared, a is a negative number.

2. James bikes $6\frac{5}{6}$ miles in one day and $10\frac{4}{9}$ miles the next day. How many miles does he bike in total?

   A. $16\frac{11}{36}$

   B. $17\frac{11}{36}$

   (C.) $17\frac{5}{18}$

   D. $16\frac{5}{18}$

   E. $16\frac{11}{18}$

   (handwritten work)
   $6 + 10 = 16$
   $\frac{5}{6} + \frac{4}{9}$
   $\frac{15}{18} + \frac{8}{18} = \frac{23}{18}$
   $1\frac{5}{18}$
   $17\frac{5}{}$

3. Solve for x when $3x - \frac{1}{3} = \frac{1}{2}$.

   A. $2\frac{1}{3}$

   B. $2\frac{1}{2}$

   (C.) $\frac{5}{18}$

   D. $\frac{1}{6}$

   E. $1\frac{1}{6}$

   (handwritten work)
   $\frac{2}{6} \quad \frac{3}{6}$
   $3x = \frac{5}{6}$
   $x = \frac{5}{6} \div \frac{5}{1}$

4. What is the greatest common factor of 18, 54, and 90?

   A. 54
   (B.) 18   *9*
   C. 9
   D. 3
   E. 1

5. What is the least common multiple of 8, 10, & 12

   A. 12
   B. 24
   C. 60
   D. 80
   (E.) 120

6. Pork shoulder roasts require fifty minutes of cooking time for each pound of weight. How long should a 7 and ½ lb. pork shoulder cook for?

   A. 504 minutes
   B. 540 minutes
   (C.) 375 minutes
   D. 450 minutes
   E. 340 minutes

   (handwritten work)
   $\frac{50m}{1\,lb} = \frac{xm}{7.5}$

7. Dale Jr. leaves home to drive to Daytona. He drives 220 miles in four hours then stops for lunch. He then drives 15 miles per hour faster and reaches Daytona three hours later. How far does Dale Jr. drive in total?

   A. 210 miles
   B. 265 miles
   C. 573 miles
   D. 540 miles
   (E.) 430 miles

   (handwritten notes)
   55 mph
   70 mph

8. Iron Chef Morimoto only has 60 minutes to prepare four servings of soup for the chairman and judges of a competition. If it takes the Iron Chef 90 seconds to chop the ingredients, five minutes to sauté the ingredients, and 5/6th of an hour to simmer the soup, how much time will he have remaining to plate his dish?

A. 4 minutes
B. 3.5 minutes
C. 56.5 minutes
D. 9.5 minutes
E. 50.5 minutes

9. Duchess Katherine's dinner party begins promptly at 7:00 p.m. The Cornish games hens require 10 minutes to clean, two hours to marinate, and one hour and fifteen minutes to roast. The chef, sensibly, wants to have the hens out of the oven 5 minutes early to rest. What time should the kitchen staff begin to clean the hens?

A. 4:30 p.m.
B. 3:30 p.m.
C. 4:35 p.m.
D. 3:35 p.m.
E. 3:35 p.m.

10. A Boeing 747 at cruising speed burns one gallon of fuel per second. There are one thousand gallons of fuel remaining on board the aircraft, which is at its cruising speed of 567 miles per hour. Approximately how many miles can the 747 travel before it exhausts its fuel supply?

A. 158 miles
B. 9,450 miles
C. 34 miles
D. 863 miles
E. 257 miles

11. Seventeen of the 30 students in an AP calculus class are female and the rest are male. What is the ratio of female to male students?

A. 17 : 30
B. 13 : 30
C. 30 : 13
D. 17 : 13
E. 13 : 17

12. There are 24 pre-algebra/elementary algebra questions, 18 algebra II/coordinate geometry questions, and 18 plane geometry/trigonometry questions on a particular ACT math section. The ACT math section consists *only* of those categories. What is the ratio of pre-algebra/elementary algebra questions to total math questions?

A. 3 : 10
B. 10 : 3
C. 2 : 5
D. 15 : 6
E. 1 : 3

13. For every 33 students at Test Guy Polytechnic 3 are graduate students and the rest are undergraduates. Students are *either* graduate students or undergraduate students. What fraction of students are undergraduate students?

A. $\frac{10}{11}$

B. $\frac{1}{11}$

C. $\frac{1}{10}$

D. $\frac{11}{10}$

E. $\frac{10}{33}$

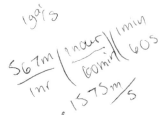

14. Harper is constructing a scale model of the Empire State Building. The Empire state building is 1,454 feet tall. Harper is building the model on a scale of 1 foot of building equals $\frac{1}{16}$ inch.

Approximately how tall, in inches, will the model be?

   Ⓐ   91 inches
   B.   65 inches
   C. 23,264 inches
   D.   64 inches
   E.   912 inches

15. A car is priced at 14,000 dollars. The sales tax on the purchase of the car is 7%. What is the total price of the car, including tax?

   Ⓐ $14,980
   B. $13,020
   C. $23,800
   D. $23,980
   E. $17,980

16. A projector is on sale for 25% off and has a sale price of $300. What was the original price of the projector?

   Ⓐ $400
   B. $225
   C. $75
   D. $1,200
   E. $600

17. If 10 is 20% of a number, then what is 200% of that number?

   A. 200
   Ⓑ 100
   C. 80
   D. 50
   E. 40

$$\frac{10}{x} = \frac{20}{100}$$

$$20x = 1000$$
$$x = 50$$

$$\frac{10}{50} \qquad \frac{50}{50} = 100\%$$

18. The revenue of the Test Guy's hoverboard business has dramatically increased in the last three years. Every year, revenue has grown by 40%. If the hoverboard business had 10 million in revenue in the first year, what was the revenue in the third year?

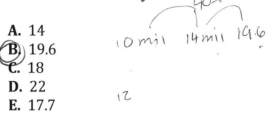

   A. 14
   Ⓑ 19.6
   C. 18
   D. 22
   E. 17.7

19. Test Guy Labs is filing a patent for a super soldier serum the lab developed. In the patent paperwork they detail the results of a trial involving 1,000 volunteers. There was no effect in 70% of the volunteers. Of volunteers that experienced an effect, 20% had enhanced endurance. How many volunteers received enhanced endurance?

   A. 140
   B. 50
   C. 60
   D. 35
   E. 300

20. A number of high school juniors join the Future Math Book Writers of America (it's really cool). Among these members 10% are elected to the executive committee and 2% of the executive committee are elected to four national offices. How many juniors are members of the club?

   A.   300
   B.   200
   C.   400
   D. 1,000
   E. 2,000

21. Sam grew from 20.5 inches to 23 inches. Approximately, what was the percent change in her height?

A. 12%
B. 89%
C. 112%
D. 32%
E. 61%

22. The Test Guy is outfitting his utility belt. He has 4 black markers, 1 green, 1 blue, 1 can shark repellant, and 1 Batarang. If the Test Guy randomly selects any item from his utility belt, what are the odds that the selected item is a black marker?

A. $\frac{2}{3}$

B. $\frac{1}{3}$

C. $\frac{1}{2}$

D. $\frac{4}{7}$

E. $\frac{3}{4}$

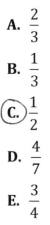

23. John is rolling three six-sided dice simultaneously and needs to get sixes on all three rolls. What is the probability that John will roll three sixes?

A. $\frac{1}{6}$

B. $\frac{1}{12}$

C. $\frac{1}{36}$

D. $\frac{1}{72}$

E. $\frac{1}{216}$

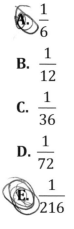

24. Aydan rolls a six-sided dice two times. What are the odds that his second roll matches the first?

A. $\frac{1}{6}$

B. $\frac{1}{36}$

C. $\frac{1}{12}$

D. $\frac{1}{4}$

E. $\frac{5}{12}$

25. There are 10 cards in a deck, 4 blue cards and 6 red cards. Jimmy draws a card and, without replacing the first card, draws a second. What is the probability that *both* of the cards that Jimmy draws are blue?

A. $\frac{4}{25}$

B. $\frac{2}{5}$

C. $\frac{3}{5}$

D. $\frac{2}{50}$

E. $\frac{2}{15}$

26. The probability of discrete random variable a is shown in the table below. What is the expected value of a?

a	Probability
1	0.3
2	0.15
3	0.2
4	0.05
5	0.3

A. 0.2
B. 0.3
C. 1.5
D. 2.9
E. 3

27. When the Test Guy selects an outfit for the day, he picks a pair of jeans from 6 pairs of jeans, a shirt from 10 t-shirts, a pair of socks from 8 pairs of socks, and shoes from 4 pairs of shoes?

   A. 28
   B. 60
   C. 240
   D. 680
   E. 1,920

6 jeans
10 shirt
8 socks
4 pairs of shoes

28. How many distinct permutations are there of the letters in the word *batter*?

   A. 360
   B. 120
   C. 480
   D. 630
   E. 720

permutations

29. There are eight runners in the final track heat of the state championship. The first three finishers win gold, silver, and bronze medals. How many ways can the winners finish?

   A. 6
   B. 36
   C. 336
   D. 1,080
   E. 40,320

30. Duncan has five exams in his AP US history course. He has taken four and his grades have been a 93, 82, 91, and 89. What will Duncan need to make on his fifth exam to have a 90 average in the course?

   A. 90
   B. 92
   C. 93
   D. 95
   E. 100

31. Thirty students took a survey as part of a study on the use of social media. The time students use social media per week is shown below.

Time	Number of Students
3 hours	1
7 hours	9
11 hours	13
13 hours	7

Approximately, what is the average length of time students use social media per week?

300 / 30

   A. 7.5 hours
   B. 8.0 hours
   C. 8.5 hours
   D. 9 hours
   E. 10 hours

32. Four homes are for sale at $130,000, $90,000, $210,000, and $150,000. If a fifth house is added to the dataset, which price will result NOT in a median *less* than the median of the four houses?

   A. $60,000
   B. $100,000
   C. $110,000
   D. $130,000
   E. $160,000

33. The Test Guy conducts a survey of 225 students to determine their college preferences. Students were asked whether they preferred small colleges or large universities. They were also asked whether they preferred in state or out of state schools. The results are shown on the table below.

	Small College	Large University	Total
In State	70	65	135
Out of State	40	50	90
Total	110	115	225

Based on the results, what is the likelihood that a randomly selected student wants to attend a small college given that they prefer in state schools?

A. $\dfrac{4}{11}$

B. $\dfrac{14}{27}$

C. $\dfrac{14}{45}$

D. $\dfrac{14}{45}$

E. $\dfrac{8}{45}$

34. The class size of 30 courses in a college's political science department is shown by frequency below. Which class size interval is the median of the data?

Class Size Interval	Frequency
under 10	3
10 - 30	6
30 - 50	4
50 - 100	5
100 - 150	9
150 +	3

A. 10 - 30

B. 30 - 50

C. 50 - 100

D. 100 - 150

E. 150+

35. A survey of 15 high school juniors asked the number of times the students had taken the ACT. Their responses are shown below. What, approximately, is the average number of attempts?

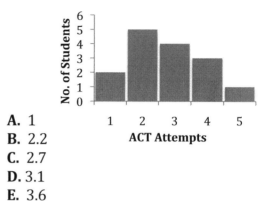

A. 1

B. 2.2

C. 2.7

D. 3.1

E. 3.6

36. Erin is running for student government president and wants to do a poll to see what percent of the student body plans to vote for her. She surveys everyone in her homeroom. Which of the following describes Erin's poll?

A. Randomized census

B. Nonrandomized census

C. Randomized experiment

D. Randomized survey

E. Nonrandomized survey

37. $\dfrac{4.2\times10^{12}}{8.4\times10^{9}}=?$

A. 5×10^{4}

B. 5×10^{3}

C. 5×10^{2}

D. 5×10^{-2}

E. 5×10^{-3}

.5 × 10³
5 × 10²

38. A bacteria measures 6.08×10^{-7} meters. If a colony of bacteria is 3,000 bacteria wide, what is the width of the colony?

A. 1.824×10^{-2}

B. 1.824×10^{-3}

C. 1.824×10^{-4}

D. 1.824×10^{-5}

E. 3.041×10^{-4}

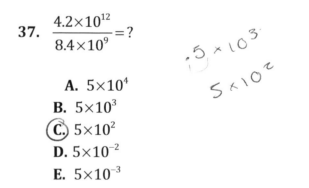

Pre-Test Answers

1.	E ✓	Numbers	
2.	C ✓	Fractions	
3.	C ✓	Fractions	
4.	B ✓	Factors	
5.	E ✓	Factors	
6.	C ✓	Units	
7.	E ✓	Units	
8.	B ✓	Units	
9.	B ✓	Units	
10.	A ✓	Units	
11.	D ✓	Ratios	
12.	C ✓	Ratios	
13.	A ✓	Ratios	
14.	A ✓	Ratios	
15.	A ✓	Percents	
16.	A ✓	Percents	
17.	B ✓	Percents	
18.	B ✓	Percents	

19.	C	Percents	
20.	E	Percents	
21.	A	Percents	
22.	C	Probability	
23.	E	Probability	
24.	A	Probability	
25.	E	Probability	
26.	D	Probability	
27.	E	Combinations	
28.	A	Combinations	
29.	C	Combinations	
30.	D ✓	Mean & Median	
31.	E ✓	Mean & Median	
32.	E ✓	Mean & Median	
33.	B	Data	
34.	C	Data	
35.	C	Data	
36.	E	Data	
37.	C ✓	Decimals	
38.	B ✓	Decimals	

Numbers
> 50% of Tests

Introduction
This is where I'm covering the definitions of different types of numbers. You can, and often do, apply some strategies. But, the key to *numbers* problems is the definitions.

What You Need to Know
- ✓ The definition of prime numbers and some of the smaller primes
- ✓ The definition of natural numbers & integers
- ✓ The definition of rational & irrational numbers
- ✓ The definition of complex numbers
- ✓ Know how to determine if a number is divisible by 3

Definition: Prime Numbers

> **Prime numbers** are **integers** that are only divisible by 1 and the integer itself. With the exception of 2, prime numbers are odd.

List: Primes Worth Memorizing

2	17	41
3	19	43
5	23	47
7	29	
11	31	
13	37	

These are the primes under 50.

These are useful, but it's not strictly necessary to memorize them.

Definitions: Complex Numbers, Irrational Numbers, Rational Numbers, Integers, & Natural Numbers

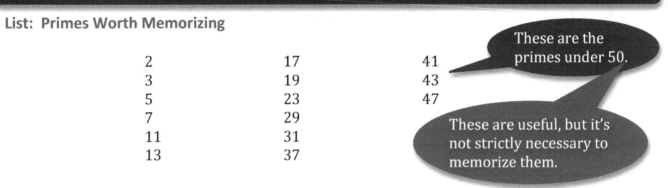

All numbers are subsets of *complex numbers*.

There's a *video* on *Numbers*.

Complex Numbers

> **All numbers are complex numbers**, we just don't think of them that way. Complex number are written as $a + bi$. i is the square root of -1, and is an *imaginary number*. Real numbers can be written like this, but b will be 0.

Real Numbers
$3 + 0i = 3$
$\pi + 0i = \pi$

Imaginary Numbers
$3 + i = 3 + i$
$\pi + 2i = \pi + 2i$

Real & Imaginary Numbers

Real numbers are all numbers that aren't imaginary. Positive or negative, integer or decimal.

Imaginary numbers have *i*. If you square the number and the result is negative, it's imaginary.

<u>Real Numbers</u>

$3^2 = 9 = 3$

$\pi^2 = \pi^2$

<u>Imaginary Numbers</u>

$(3i)^2 = -9$

$\sqrt{-16} = 4i$

Fractions, Integers, & Natural Numbers

Fractions are rational numbers that aren't integers. They have a decimal or are a non-reducible fration.

Integers are a number with no fractional part.

Natural numbers are **positive integers.** They're the numbers we'd expect to see in nature (we don't usually see negative numbers in nature).

<u>Fractions</u>	<u>Integers</u>	<u>Natural Numbers</u>
$\frac{3}{2} = 1\frac{1}{2}$	-8	1
	0	5
$\frac{1}{2} = \frac{1}{2}$	1,300	9

> These are nice to know, but don't stress over them.

Odd & Even

<u>**Operations with Odds & Evens**</u>

odd + odd = even	odd x odd = odd	odd – odd = even
even + odd = odd	odd x even = even	even – odd =odd
even + even = even	even x even = even	odd – even = odd
		even – odd = odd

Divisibility Rules

<u>**Divisibility Rules**</u>

A number is **divisible by 3** if its digits add up to a multiple of three

$21 \rightarrow 2 + 1 = 3$. 21 is divisible by 3.

A number is **divisible by 4** if its last two digits are divisible by 4.

$408 \rightarrow 08 \rightarrow 8$ is divisible by 4, so 408 is divisible by 4.

A number is **divisible by 6** if it's even & divisible by 3.

> Three is the most useful of all divisibility rules.

> There are other divisibility rules, but these are the most useful.

1. When *a* is a rational number which *must be false*?

   A. *a* is a complex number
   B. *a* is an integer
   C. *a* is natural number
   D. *a* is a fraction
   E. When squared, *a* is a negative number.

Solve

This is a standard setup for a numbers question. It's a definition question, and to solve it, we'll mark-off. Whenever the question is *must be false*, we mark-off answer choices **that could be true.**

A. *a* is a complex number
   All numbers are complex numbers. So a has to be a complex number.

B. *a* is an integer
   This could be true; a can be an integer but it doesn't have to be.

C. *a* is natural number
   This could be true; a can be a natural number but it doesn't have to be.

D. *a* is a fraction
   This has to be true; a is either going to be a fraction or an integer. Integers can be expressed as fractions.

E. When squared, *a* is a negative number.
   This can't be true. The only numbers that are negative when squared are imaginary numbers.

Wrap Up

What You Need to Know
   ✓ The definition of prime numbers and some of the smaller primes
   ✓ The definition of natural numbers & integers
   ✓ The definition of rational & irrational numbers
   ✓ The definition of complex numbers.
   ✓ Know how to determine if a number is divisible by 3.

Videos
   Numbers

The Strategies
   ✓ You'll need to mark-off on most problems.
   ✓ Occasionally you'll need/want to pick numbers
   ✓ It all comes down to knowing your definitions. Be comfortable with them.

Key Skill
   ✓ Fractions

   ✓ Quadratics (factoring)

   ✓ Rational Expressions

   ✓ Roots & Exponents

Pre-Algebra: Numbers

1. What is the sum of the prime numbers between 20 and 40?

    A. 83
    B. 89
    C. 52
    D. 120
    E. 104

    handwritten: 23, 27, 29, +

2. Which of the following statements about integers is *never* true?

    F. The square root of an integer is a rational number.
    G. The square root of an integer is irrational.
    H. The quotient of two integers is a rational number.
    J. The quotient of two integers is irrational.
    K. The product of a rational number and an irrational number is irrational

3. In the equation $-3(6 \oplus 2)+(8 \oplus 4)^2 = -5$, the circle $\bigcirc$ can represent any arithmetic operation. Which operation(s) is it?

    A. addition & multiplication
    B. addition
    C. subtraction
    D. subtraction & division
    E. division

    handwritten:
    $-3(6+2)$
    $-18-6$
    $8-4$ 16
    $(8-4)(8-4)$
    $-3(3)+4$ $64-32-32+16$
    $-9+4$

4. What is the value of 233 + 219 + 613 rounded to the nearest ten?

    F. 1,060
    G. 1,070
    H. 1,100
    J. 1,000
    K. 1,065

5. Which of the following is can be FALSE about odd & even numbers?

    A. odd x odd = odd
    B. even + even = even
    C. $\dfrac{even}{even} = even$
    D. even + odd = odd
    E. even x odd = even

6. A number is accidentally divided by 3 when it should have been multiplied by 4. What operation will give the intended result?

    F. multiply by 4
    G. multiply by 7
    H. multiply by 12
    J. divide by 4
    K. divide by 12

    handwritten: ·3·4

7. For every integer *a*, what could be false?

    A. *a* is a natural number
    B. *a* is a rational number
    C. *a* is a real number
    D. *a* is a rational number
    E. *a* is a complex number

1. What is the sum of the prime numbers between 20 and 40?

Correct Answer D

There's not really a short way to do this problem, unless you know your prime numbers. It's a problem that can be worked efficiently by using your pencil and a good setup. Start by listing your numbers from 20 to 40. I'm going to skip all of the *even* numbers (because the only even prime number is 2).

21	31
23	33
25	35
27	37
29	39

Pick a place to start marking-off the remaining numbers. You can get rid of the 5's first.

21	31
23	33
2̶5̶	3̶5̶
27	37
29	39

Now get rid of the multiples of 3. Remember that if the digits in a number sum to a multiple of 3, that number is divisible by 3.

Now, any number you aren't sure on, test some other numbers (like 7 or 13). In this case, however, these are the primes. We need to add the primes to finish the question.

$$23 + 29 + 31 + 37 = 120$$

Answer choice **D** is correct.

<u>What You May Have Done Wrong</u>

    A. You left off a prime (37).
    B. You left off a prime (31).
    C. You left off two primes 31 & 37.
    E. This is a calculator or conceptual error. Check your primes and your calculation.

2. **Which of the following statements about integers is *never* true?**

Correct Answer J

This is a mark-off question that depends on definitions. The integers are whole numbers that can be negative (we usually think of whole numbers as natural numbers, starting at 0 and going positive).

This is a question where you'll probably be able to mark-off several answers before you even test numbers. I'm going to show testing numbers. For questions that ask *never* true, we want to mark off answer choices by proving that they *could be true*.

~~F.~~ *The square root of an integer is a rational number.*

There are square roots that aren't rational numbers, $\sqrt{2}$ for example. But perfect squares have rational square roots $\sqrt{4} = 2$.

~~G.~~ *The square root of an integer is irrational.*

We showed in **F** that this could be true, $\sqrt{2}$. Actually, *the square root of every prime number is irrational*.

~~H.~~ *The quotient of two integers is a rational number.*
This is *always true*. Rational numbers are defined as numbers, which can be expressed as the ratio (fraction) of two integers. We can test this. ½ is the ratio of two integers, 1 & 2, and is a rational number.

J. *The quotient of two integers is irrational.*
This is the opposite of the previous answer and it can't be true. Rational numbers are numbers that can be expressed as a ratio of two integers.

~~K.~~ *The product of a rational number and an irrational number is irrational.*

This can be true $2 \cdot \sqrt{2} = 2\sqrt{2}$. In fact, it is true unless the rational number is zero.

Answer choice **J** is correct.

3. **In the equation** $-3\left(6 \bigcirc 2\right) + \left(8 \bigcirc 4\right)^2 = -5$**, the circle** $\bigcirc$ **can represent any arithmetic operation. Which operation(s) is it?**

Correct Answer E

Testing operations is the only way to solve this problem. The answer choices represent four operations: addition, subtraction, multiplication, & division. Start by testing an operation that appears in multiple answer choices (don't test multiplication). I'll start with addition.

Addition

$$-3\left(6+2\right) + \left(8+4\right)^2 = -5 \quad \rightarrow \quad -24 + 144 = -5 \quad \rightarrow \quad 120 \neq -5$$

We can mark off answer choices **A** & **B**.

Subtraction

$$-3\left(6-2\right) + \left(8-4\right)^2 = -5 \quad \rightarrow \quad -12 + 16 = -5 \quad \rightarrow \quad 4 \neq -5$$

We can mark off answer choices **C** & **D**. Even though we know the answer is *division* only, let's take a look.

Subtraction

$$-3\left(6 \div 2\right) + \left(8 \div 4\right)^2 = -5 \quad \rightarrow \quad -9 + 4 = -5 \quad \rightarrow \quad -5 = -5$$

Answer choice **E** is correct

4. What is the value of 233 + 219 + 613 rounded to the nearest ten?

Correct Answer G

This is another definition question. First, add the numbers.
$$233 + 219 + 613 = 1,065$$

Now determine which digit is the 10's place.

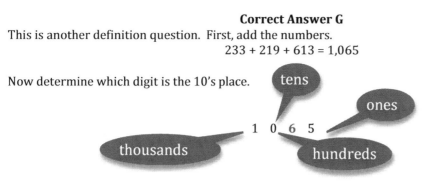

To round the tens place, we either round the ones place up or we round the ones place down. We round 5 and any integer greater than 5 up. It looks like this:

Round Down	Round Up
0	5
1	6
2	7
3	8
4	9

We round up the five.

$$1,065 \rightarrow 1,070$$

Answer choice **G** is correct.

What You May Have Done Wrong:
    F. You rounded down instead of up.
    H. You rounded up the hundreds place.
    J. You rounded down the hundreds place
    K. You forgot to round; this is the halfway answer.

5. Which of the following is can be FALSE about odd & even numbers?

Correct Answer C

This is a tougher problem to test. It's difficult to test for *can be false*; because that requires you to mark-off answer choices by proving they *must be true*. We don't have the time, or ability, to test every number to see if they must be true. We can think a little bit before we pick numbers to test, and test a second pair if we need to.

    A. odd x odd = odd is always true, 1 x 3 = 3 & 3 x 5 = 15.

    B. even + even = even is always true, 2 + 4 = 6 & 4 + 6 = 10

    C. $\dfrac{even}{even} = even$ **can be false**, $\dfrac{4}{2} = 2$ **but** $\dfrac{6}{2} = 3$

    D. even + odd = odd is always true, 2 + 1 = 3 & 3 + 2 = 5

    E. even x odd = even is always true, 2 x 1 = 2 & 2 x 3 = 6

Answer choice **C** is correct.

6. A number is accidentally divided by 3 when it should have been multiplied by 4. What operation will give the intended result?

Correct Answer H

You can do this problem algebraically, but it's easier to do by *picking a number*. Remember, whenever the question is about relationships (here it's division & multiplication) and the answer choices are about relationships (again division & multiplication), picking numbers works well. I'm going to pick a number that, when divided by 3; the quotient (answer) is an integer. I'll use 3. Let's look at our statements.

Statement 1: a number is accidentally divided by 3.

$$\frac{n}{3} = \frac{3}{3} = 1$$

Statement 2: it should have been multiplied by 4.
$$4n = 4 \cdot 3 = 12$$

So, the answer we got is 1, and the answer we should have gotten is 12. To make 1 equal to 12, we'll need to multiply 1 by 12.

Answer **H** is correct.

What You May Have Done Wrong
   F. This is true if we hadn't divided by 3 first.
   G. You added the "divided by" and the "multiplied by" together.
   J. This is a conceptual error. Review your steps.
   K. This is a conceptual error. Review your steps.

7. For every integer *a*, what could be false?

Correct Answer A

This is a mark-off question that's built on definitions. If you don't know all of the definitions, you'll have to use your gut.

   A. *a* is a natural number
      All natural numbers are integers *but* not all integers are natural numbers. Natural numbers are the numbers we'd see in nature and we wouldn't see negatives in nature. Integers, on the other hand, are all whole numbers both positive & negative.

   B. *a* is a rational number
      All integers are rational numbers. Rational numbers can be expressed as a ratio (fraction) of two integers. Regardless of the integer, we can set it over 1.

   C. *a* is a real number
      All integers are real numbers. Real numbers are numbers that aren't imaginary. So, *a* is a real number.

   D. *a* has no decimal component.
      a will never have a decimal component, because integers are whole numbers.

   E. *a* is a complex number
      Ok, this is the confusing bit. All numbers are complex numbers, but the *i* term of real numbers has a coefficient of zero. Check out the *Intermediate Algebra: Complex Numbers* for more information.

Factors
Key Skill

Introduction
Factors are numbers that you can multiply to arrive at another number. Factor problems are somewhat common, and it's a critical skill. You'll need factors to handle many pre-algebra, algebra, geometry, *and* trig problems.

What You Need to Know
- ✓ How to factors numbers and algebraic expressions.
- ✓ How to find the prime factors of a number.
- ✓ How to find the Least Common Denominator & Greatest Common Factor.

Definitions: Factors

Factors are components of a number. A number is a multiple of its factors and there can be many factors for a given number.

Example: Factors
1. The factors of 8
   $8 \times 1 = 8$
   $4 \times 2 = 8$
   $2 \times 2 \times 2 = 8$

   > Factors are assumed to be positive unless otherwise stated.

2. The factors of x^4
   $x^4 \cdot 1 = x^4$
   $x^3 \cdot x^1 = x^4$
   $x^2 \cdot x^2 = x^4$

   > The exponents don't need to *multiply* to 4; they need to *add* to 4.

Definitions: Prime Factors & Factorization

Prime factors are just that, factors that are prime numbers. Prime Factorization is breaking down a number entirely into prime numbers.

Example: Prime Factorization
1. What are the prime factors of 6?

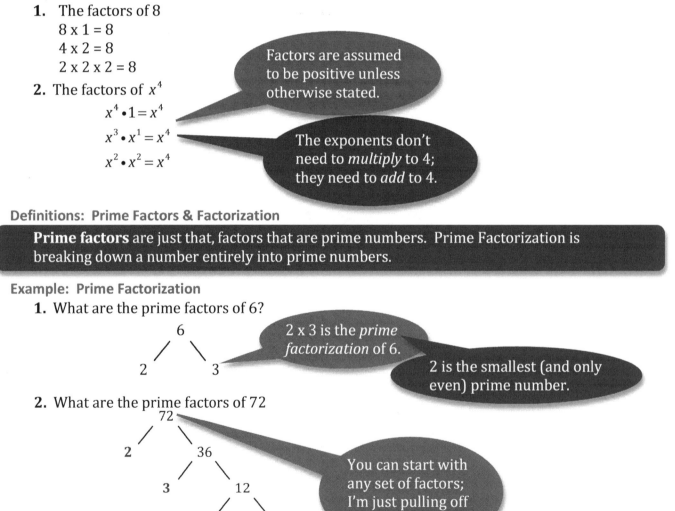

   > 2 x 3 is the *prime factorization* of 6.

   > 2 is the smallest (and only even) prime number.

2. What are the prime factors of 72

   > You can start with any set of factors; I'm just pulling off the primes as I go.

The *prime factors* are 2 & 3, the unique prime factors of 72. The *prime factorization* of 72 is
2 x 2 x 2 x 3 x 2 = 72

> One of each factor

-28-

The **greatest common factor** is the largest number that will divide evenly into a set of numbers.

Examples: Greatest Common Factor

1. What is the greatest common factor of 20 and 30?

Solve

There are a few ways to handle these questions. Let's look at *prime factorization.*

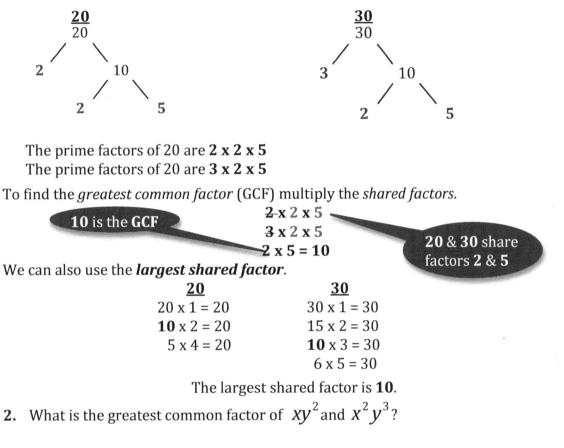

The prime factors of 20 are **2 x 2 x 5**
The prime factors of 20 are **3 x 2 x 5**

To find the *greatest common factor* (GCF) multiply the *shared factors.*

$$2 \text{ x } 2 \text{ x } 5$$
$$3 \text{ x } 2 \text{ x } 5$$
$$2 \text{ x } 5 = 10$$

10 is the **GCF**

20 & 30 share factors **2 & 5**

We can also use the *largest shared factor.*

20	30
20 x 1 = 20	30 x 1 = 30
10 x 2 = 20	15 x 2 = 30
5 x 4 = 20	**10** x 3 = 30
	6 x 5 = 30

The largest shared factor is **10**.

2. What is the greatest common factor of xy^2 and x^2y^3?

Solve

When we have variables, the lowest exponents of each variable make the GCM.
Let's look at the factors to see why:

$$xy^2 = x \bullet y \bullet y$$
$$x^2y^3 = x \bullet x \bullet y \bullet y \bullet y$$

xy^2 and x^2y^3 share the common factors $x \bullet y \bullet y = xy^2$ is the GCF.

In this problem, the GCF is our *smaller* number

Rules of the Road: GCF on the ACT

Steps to Solving

1. Try the *smallest* number in the set.
2. Test answers starting from the *the answer choice that is the smallest number in the set,* finding the largest common factor, <u>or</u> prime factor.

Check out the *video* on *GCF on the ACT*

1. What is the greatest common factor of 18, 54, and 90?

    A. 54
    B. 18
    C. 9
    D. 3
    E. 1

Solve

This is a common setup for a GCF question. I really recommend that you start by testing the answer choice that is the *smallest number in the set* (18). The *smallest number in the set is the largest the GCF can ever be.*

Testing Answer Choices

$$\frac{18}{18}=1, \frac{54}{18}=3, \frac{90}{18}=5$$

> About 50% of the time the answer will be the smallest number in the set.

18 is our GCF

    ~~**A.**~~ 54 ← The GCF can *never* be larger than our smallest number.
    B. 18 ← Every number is divisible by 18, so this is our GCF
    C. 9
    D. 3
    E. 1

> This is my preferred method for solving.

> If we work from *largest* to *smallest* we can **stop** when all our numbers are divisible by an answer choice.

Finding the Largest Shared Factor

We can factor each number and find the *largest factor* all numbers have in common.

18	**54**	**90**
18 x 1 = 18	54 x 1 = 54	90 x 1 = 90
9 x 2 = 18	27 x 2 = 54	45 x 2 = 90
6 x 3 = 18	18 x 3 = 54	30 x 3 = 30
	9 x 6 = 54	18 x 5 = 18
		10 x 9 = 90

> It helps if you know your *divisibility rules.*

Prime Factoring

We can find the *prime factors* of each number and multiply the *shared* factors to get the GCF.

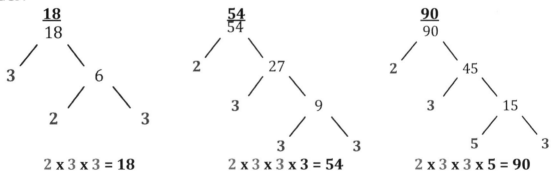

2 x 3 x 3 = 18   2 x 3 x 3 x 3 = 54   2 x 3 x 3 x 5 = 90

The shared factors are 2, 3, & 3, so the GCF is **2 x 3 x 3 = 18.**
Answer Choice **B** is correct.

The **least common multiple (LCM)** is the *smallest* number that has each of the given numbers as a factor.

Examples: Least Common Multiple

1. What is the least common multiple of 20 and 30?

Solve

Match the Multiples

One of the easiest ways to find the LCM is to **match of the multiples** of each number.

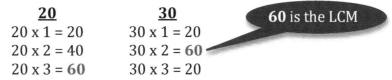

20	**30**	
20 x 1 = 20	30 x 1 = 20	
20 x 2 = 40	30 x 2 = 60	**60** is the LCM
20 x 3 = 60	30 x 3 = 20	

Prime Factors

We can also find the **prime factors** of each number.

Look for the most frequent occurrence of each prime factor.

2: appears twice in 20 (**2** x **2** x 5 = 20)
3: appears once in 30 (2 x **3** x 5 = 30)
5: appears once in 20 & once in 30 (2 x 2 x **5** = 20) & (2 x 3 x **5**)

Now, multiply the number of maximum occurrences together.

$$2 \times 2 \times 3 \times 5 = 60$$

Example: Least Common Multiple

2. What is the least common multiple of xy^2 and x^2y^3?

Solve

In algebra problems the **highest exponents make the LCM**. Let's look at the factors to see why.

$$xy^2 = x \bullet y \bullet y$$
$$x^2y^3 = x \bullet x \bullet y \bullet y \bullet y$$

Look for the most frequent occurrence of each factor.

***x*:** appears twice in $x^2y^3 = x \bullet x \bullet y \bullet y \bullet y$

***y*:** appears three times in $x^2y^3 = x \bullet x \bullet y \bullet y \bullet y$

Now, multiply the number of maximum occurrences together.

$$x \bullet x \bullet y \bullet y \bullet y = x^2y^3$$

In this problem, the *largest number is the LCM*

The **highest exponents** make the LCM

Steps to Solving
1. Try the *largest* number in the set.
2. Test answers starting with the *largest number in the set,* match the multiples of each number, *or* prime factor.

ACT Example: Least Common Multiple on the ACT

1. What is the least common multiple of 8, 10, & 12

    A. 12
    B. 24
    C. 60
    D. 80
    E. 120

On **LCM** we try the *largest* on **GCF** we try the *smallest.*

Greatest with **least** and **least** with **greatest**

Solve

<u>Test Answers</u>

Start with the answer choice that matches your largest number and then *work your way up.* Test answer by dividing the choice by 8, 10, & 12. Use common sense to eliminate some answers before calculating.

    ~~A.~~ 12 ← isn't divisible by 8 or 10. Also, since 10 is a factor, the answer choice will have to end in 0.
    ~~B.~~ 24 ← isn't divisible by 10. Also, since 10 is a factor, the answer choice will have to end in 0.
    ~~C.~~ 60 ← isn't divisible by 8.
    ~~D.~~ 80 ← isn't divisible by 12.
    E. 120 ← **is divisible by 8, 10, & 12**

<u>Match the Multiples</u>

We'll have to run through a bunch of multiples, but we can multiply to find the LCM.

8	**10**	**12**
8 x 1 = 8	10 x 1 = 10	12 x 1 = 12
8 x 2 = 16	10 x 2 = 20	12 x 2 = 24
8 x 3 = 24	10 x 3 = 30	12 x 3 = 36
8 x 3 = 32	10 x 4 = 40	12 x 4 = 48
8 x 3 = 40	10 x 5 = 50	12 x 5 = 60
8 x 3 = 48	10 x 6 = 60	12 x 6 = 72
8 x 3 = 56	10 x 7 = 70	12 x 7 = 84
8 x 3 = 64	10 x 8 = 80	12 x 8 = 96
8 x 3 = 72	10 x 9 = 90	12 x 9 = 108
8 x 3 = 80	10 x 10 = 100	12 x 10 = 120
8 x 3 = 88	10 x 11 = 110	
8 x 3 = 96	10 x 12 = 120	
8 x 3 = 104		
8 x 3 = 112		
8 x 3 = 120		

This problem shows the **drawback** of **matching multiples**.

Prime Factors
    We can also find the **prime factors** of each number.

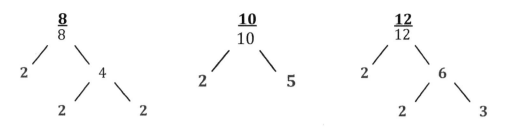

    Now we multiply each unique factor by the maximum number of times it appears.
        2: appears three times in 8 (**2 x 2 x 2**)
        3: appears once in 12 (2 x **3** x 5)
        5: appears once in 10 (2 x 3 x **5**)

$$2 \times 2 \times 2 \times 3 \times 5 = 120$$

Answer Choice **C** is correct.

Wrap Up

What You Need to Know
    ✓ How to factors numbers and algebraic expressions.
    ✓ How to find the prime factors of a number.
    ✓ How to find the Least Common Denominator & Greatest Common Factor.

Videos

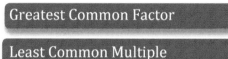

The Strategies
    ✓ For LCM test the smallest answer choice and work up.
    ✓ For GCF, test the largest answer choice and work down.
    ✓ You'll need to know how to factor for other problems.

Key Skill
    ✓ Fractions

    ✓ Quadratics (factoring)

    ✓ Rational Expressions

    ✓ Roots & Exponents

1. What is the least common denominator for the fractions $\frac{1}{4}, \frac{1}{5}, \frac{1}{6}$, and $\frac{1}{8}$?

    A. 60
    B. 80
    C. 120
    D. 240
    E. 480

2. What is the least common multiple of 15, 135, and 45?

    F. 135
    G. 150
    H. 270
    J. 180
    K. 405

3. What is the greatest common factor of 7, 56, and 84?

    A. 1
    B. 2
    C. 3
    D. 7
    E. 14

4. What is the greatest common factor of 24, 108, and 156?

    F. 3
    G. 6
    H. 8
    J. 12
    K. 16

5. If a^3b^2 and a^2b have a greatest common factor of 48, what could b equal?

    A. 2
    B. 3
    C. 4
    D. 9
    E. 16

$$a^2b = 48$$

$$b$$

1. What is the least common denominator of the fractions $\frac{1}{4}, \frac{1}{5}, \frac{1}{6}$, and $\frac{1}{8}$?

Correct Answer C

In this case, our largest number (8) won't be the answer. You can approach this problem in two ways. You can do it the "proper" way by using prime factorization. Or you can do it the easy way by testing answer choices, with **LCM start with the smallest answer choice.**

<u>The Proper Way</u>

We find the prime factors of all the denominators:

$$4 = 2 \times 2$$
$$5 = 5 \times 1$$
$$6 = 2 \times 3$$
$$8 = 4 \times 2 \rightarrow 2 \times 2 \times 2$$

Find which number (4, 5, 6, 8) has the greatest occurrence of each factor.

$$2 = 3 \text{ times } (8 = 2 \times 2 \times 2)$$
$$3 = 1 \text{ time } (6 = 2 \times 3)$$
$$5 = 1 \text{ time } (5 = 5 \times 1)$$

Multiply those factors together.

$2 \times 2 \times 2 \times 3 \times 5 = 120$

<u>The Easy Way</u>

A. 60 ← does not work with 8
B. 80 ← does not work with 6
C. 120 ← Works with everything.
D. 240
E. 480

We can stop testing, because the other answer choices are *larger*.

Answer choice **C** is correct.

2. What is the least common multiple of 15, 135, and 45?

Correct Answer F

The smallest the LCM can be is the *largest number in the set*. The *smallest* the LCM can ever be is the largest number in the set. In this case, 135 is divisible by both 15 & 45, making 135 our answer. If you didn't get that, you could solve it the "proper" way or the "easy" way. I'm just showing the easy way.

<u>The Easy Way</u>

Start at the lowest answer choice, 135, and test the answer choices.

135 is divisible by 15 & 45, and is our lowest answer. Therefore 135 is correct.

Answer choice **F** is correct.

<u>What You May Have Done Wrong</u>

G. This isn't divisible by 45 or 135 (it's also greater than the LCM)
H. This is greater than the LCM
J. This isn't divisible by 135 (it's also greater than the LCM)
K. This is divisible by all three numbers, but it's not our LCM.

3. **What is the greatest common factor of 7, 56, and 84?**

Correct Answer D

The largest the GCF can be is the smallest number in the set. Always check it first. In this case, 7 *is* a factor of 56 & 84. We can also do it the *proper* way or the *easy* way.

<u>The Proper Way</u>

We find the prime factors of each number and then multiply all the shared factors.

$$7 = \mathbf{7} \times 1$$
$$56 = 7 \times 8 \rightarrow \mathbf{7} \times 2 \times 2 \times 2$$
$$84 = 42 \times 2 \rightarrow 21 \times 2 \times 2 \rightarrow \mathbf{7} \times 3 \times 2 \times 2$$

The only shared factor is seven, and our answer is 7.

<u>The Easy Way</u>

Test each answer in order. **Start with the largest answer choice that *does not* exceed the smallest number in the set.** We can mark off 14 because it's bigger than 7. We're looking for the largest number that divides evenly into 7, 56, and 84. Answer choice **A** is a factor, but it's awfully small (1 is a factor of everything). **B** & **C** are not factors of all the numbers in the set.

Answer choice D is correct

<u>What You May Have Done Wrong</u>

A. This is a common factor, but it's not the greatest common factor.
B. This isn't a factor of 7.
C. This isn't a factor or 7 or 56.
E. This is larger than our smallest number, 7.

4. **What is the greatest common factor of 24, 108, and 156?**

Correct Answer J

Always check the smallest number (24) to see if it's a common factor of the larger numbers. The smallest number is the *largest* the GCF can be. 24 is not a common factor, so we'll have to work this problem. We can do it the *proper* way or the *easy* way.

<u>The Proper Way</u>

We find the prime factors of each number and then multiply all the shared factors.

$$24 = 8 \times 3 \quad \rightarrow \mathbf{2} \times \mathbf{2} \times 2 \times \mathbf{3}$$
$$108 = 12 \times 9 \quad \rightarrow \mathbf{2} \times \mathbf{2} \times \mathbf{3} \times 3 \times 3$$
$$156 = 12 \times 13 \rightarrow \mathbf{2} \times \mathbf{2} \times \mathbf{3} \times 13$$

Each number shares two 2's and a 3 as common factors. Multiply them to get the GCF.

<u>The Easy Way</u>

Test each answer in order (start with the biggest) to find the largest number that divides evenly into 24, 108, and 156.

F. 3 ← is a common factor, but isn't the GCF
G. 6 ← is a common factor, but isn't the GCF
H. 8 ← is not a common factor.
J. 12 ← *is a common factor, and is the largest common factor.*
K. 16 ← is not a common factor.

Start with **K** (the largest) and work down.

You should have started with the biggest answer choice (16) and worked your way down. Once you hit a common factor (12) you can stop.

Answer choice J is correct.

5. If a^3b^2 and a^2b have a greatest common factor of 48, what could b equal?

Correct Answer B

This is a tricky problem. We're given a number and two expressions and we have to find a possible value for b. a^3b^2 & a^2b have a GCF of 48, we can find what the GCF is in terms of a and b. Factor each expression:

$$a^3b^2 \leftarrow a \cdot a \cdot \cancel{a} \cdot b \cdot \cancel{b}$$

$$a^2b \leftarrow a \cdot a \cdot b$$

The greatest common factor of a^3b^2 and a^2b is a^2b. The question tells us that, numerically, the GCF is 48.

$$a^2b = 48$$

Now we factor 48 to find what will work, we'll be interested in *all* of the factors of 48, not just the prime factors.

Factors of 48

48 x 1	16 x 3
24 x 2	12 x 4
	6 x 8

We'll need a set of factors where one factor is a perfect square. There are two options, 16 x 3 and 12 x 4. We can set up two equations to show this relationship:

$$a^2b = 16 \times 3$$

-OR-

$$a^2b = 12 \times 4$$

The perfect square term has to be a, because the a term is squared. Either $a = \sqrt{16}$ or $a = \sqrt{4}$. That gives us two possible b values of 3 or 12. Let's take another look at both equations.

$$a^2b = \left(\sqrt{16}\right)^2 \times 3$$

-OR-

$$a^2b = \left(\sqrt{4}\right)^2 \times 12$$

Since 3 is an answer choice and 12 is not, 3 is our answer.

Answer choice **B** is correct.

<u>What You May Have Done Wrong</u>

A. This is an acceptable value of a.

C. This is another acceptable value of a (or a^2)

D. This is a conceptual or calculation error.

E. This is an acceptable value of a^2.

Introduction

Most decimals problems test your ability to work with scientific notation. There can also, from time to time, be questions that compare decimals and fractions. Don't be intimidated by scientific notation, there's not that much to it.

What You Need to Know

✓ How to work with scientific notation

✓ How to compare decimals & fractions

There's a video on Scientific Notation

Definitions: Scientific Notation

Scientific notation is a way to easily express very large or very small numbers.

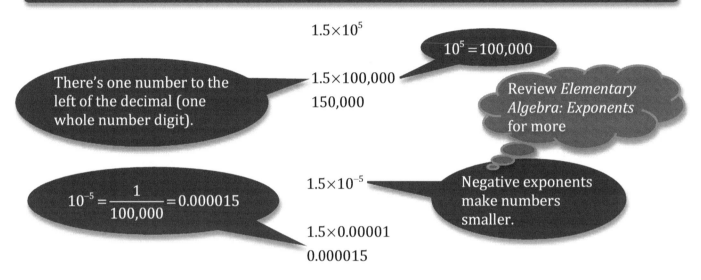

1.5×10^5

$10^5 = 100,000$

There's one number to the left of the decimal (one whole number digit).

$1.5 \times 100,000$

$150,000$

Review Elementary Algebra: Exponents for more

$10^{-5} = \dfrac{1}{100,000} = 0.000015$

1.5×10^{-5}

Negative exponents make numbers smaller.

1.5×0.00001

0.000015

Rules of the Road: Scientific Notation

Positive exponents make numbers bigger. We use positive exponents to put **big numbers in scientific notation**.

Negative exponents make numbers smaller. We use negative exponents to put **small numbers in scientific notation**.

To solve, move decimals or use your calculator.

ACT Examples: Scientific Notation

1. $\dfrac{4.2 \times 10^{12}}{8.4 \times 10^9} = ?$

    A. 5×10^4

    B. 5×10^3

    C. 5×10^2

    D. 5×10^{-2}

    E. 5×10^{-3}

Solve

You can solve this using your calculator. Just enter the numbers and solve. Be careful to put the numerator and denominator in parentheses or your order of operations may get goofed up. And it's probably faster to work it by hand.

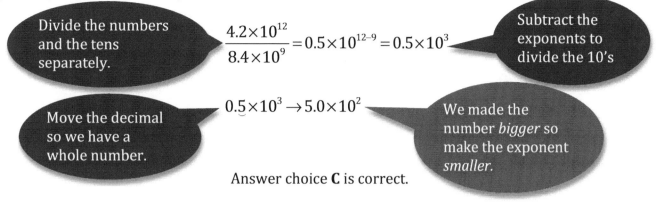

Divide the numbers and the tens separately.

$$\frac{4.2\times10^{12}}{8.4\times10^{9}}=0.5\times10^{12-9}=0.5\times10^{3}$$

Subtract the exponents to divide the 10's

Move the decimal so we have a whole number.

$$0.5\times10^{3}\rightarrow5.0\times10^{2}$$

We made the number *bigger* so make the exponent *smaller*.

Answer choice **C** is correct.

2. A bacteria measures 6.08×10^{-7} meters. If a colony of bacteria is 3,000 bacteria wide, what is the width of the colony?

    A. 1.824×10^{-2}
    B. 1.824×10^{-3}
    C. 1.824×10^{-4}
    D. 1.824×10^{-5}
    E. 3.041×10^{-4}

Solve

This is another problem that's pretty easy to do in your calculator. You can also do it by multiplying the exponents.

$$6.08\times10^{-7}\cdot3,000$$
$$6.08\times10^{-7}\cdot3.0\times10^{3}$$
$$18.24\times10^{-7+3}\rightarrow18.24\times10^{-4}$$
$$1.824\times10^{-3}$$

You're making the number *smaller* so the exponent gets *bigger*

Answer choice **B** is correct.

Wrap Up

What You Need to Know
    ✓ How to work with scientific notation
    ✓ How to compare decimals & fractions

Videos
    Scientific Notation

The Strategies
    ✓ If you have trouble with these problems, use your calculator. Be careful to use parentheses around each term.

Related Skills
    ✓ Fractions
    ✓ Unit Conversions

Pre-Algebra: Decimals

1. If there are 1.2×10^3 bacteria in a milliliter of water, how many milliliters will have 9.6×10^9 bacteria?

- **A.** 8×10^6
- **B.** 8×10^3
- **C.** 8×10
- **D.** 1.25×10^5
- **E.** 1.25×10^{-6}

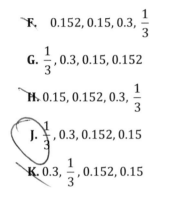

$$\frac{1.2 \times 10^3}{1 mL} = \frac{9.6 \times 10^9}{x mL}$$

4. The concentration of harmful bacteria in a lake was 1.6×10^7 bacteria per liter. After an initial treatment, the concentration of bacteria is 1,000 times less. What is the concentration of bacteria after the initial treatment?

- **F.** $1.6 \times 10^{\frac{4}{3}}$
- **G.** $1.6 \times 10^{\frac{7}{3}}$
- **H.** 1.6×10^3
- **J.** 1.6×10^4
- **K.** 1.6×10^{10}

1.6×10^6

2. Which inequality orders $0.15, 0.152, 0.3, \& \frac{1}{3}$ from greatest to least?

$\frac{1}{3}$

- **F.** $0.152, 0.15, 0.3, \frac{1}{3}$
- **G.** $\frac{1}{3}, 0.3, 0.15, 0.152$
- **H.** $0.15, 0.152, 0.3, \frac{1}{3}$
- **J.** $\frac{1}{3}, 0.3, 0.152, 0.15$
- **K.** $0.3, \frac{1}{3}, 0.152, 0.15$

5. Approximately 682,000 gallons of water goes over Niagara's Horseshoe Falls every second. Approximately how much water goes over Horseshoe Falls in three hours?

- **A.** 4.09×10^7
- **B.** 2.4552×10^9
- **C.** 7.3656×10^9
- **D.** 1.227×10^8
- **E.** 5.3726×10^9

$6.82 \times 10^5 /s$

3. When 9,320,000 is multiplied by 10^x, the result is 9.32, what is the value of x?

- **A.** -8
- **B.** -7
- **C.** -6
- **D.** 6
- **E.** 7

9.32×10^6

Decimals: Solutions

1. If there are 1.2×10^3 bacteria in a milliliter of water, how many milliliters will have 9.6×10^9 bacteria?

Correct Answer A

This is a division problem. There's two ways to do it, by hand or by calculator. I think by hand is probably faster, but it's up to you.

<u>TI Graphing Calculator</u>

Using the *mode* button change the mode from NORMAL to SCI. Enter 9.6×10^9 in that form. Or enter 9.6E 10 using 2nd EE (it's the comma button). Hit the division button and enter 1.2×10^3 using the same method. ENTER will give you your answer.

<u>By Hand</u>
First, divide 9.6 by 1.2 (using your calculator). $\dfrac{9.6}{1.2} = 8$

Now, divide the exponents $\dfrac{10^9}{10^3} \rightarrow 10^{9-3} = 10^6$

> When we divide exponents with the *same base* (10), we **subtract** the exponents.

Answer choice **A** is correct.

<u>What You May Have Done Wrong</u>
  B. You divided the exponents instead of subtracting.
  C. You made an exponent error; review your steps.
  D. You flipped your division, dividing the 1.2 term by the 9.6 term.
  E. You flipped your division, dividing the 1.2 term by the 9.6 term.

2. Which inequality orders 0.15, 0.152, 0.3, & $\dfrac{1}{3}$ from greatest to least?

Correct Answer J

This is a *which* question, so you'll want to mark-off. Be careful, you'll most likely want to start with the *least* but the question wants you to start with the *greatest*.

The greatest is $\dfrac{1}{3}$, which has a decimal of $0.3\overline{3}$.

> You can convert fractions into decimals by entering the fraction as division in your calculator.

We can mark-off **F, H, & K**. Since we're left with two answers (**G & J**), it makes sense to look at each and find the mistake in one of them.

  ~~**G.**~~ $\dfrac{1}{3}$, 0.3, 0.15, 0.152

> 0.152 is **greater** than 0.15

  J. $\dfrac{1}{3}$, 0.3, 0.152, 0.15

Answer choice **J** is correct.

<u>What You May Have Done Wrong</u>
  F. This is ascending (least to greatest) order and there's a mistake.
  G. This is descending order (greatest to least) but there's a mistake.
  H. This is ascending order (least to greatest).
  K. This is descending order (greatest to least).

3. When 9,320,000 is multiplied by 10^x, the result is 9.32, what is the value of x?

Correct Answer C

This is a scientific notation question, but it doesn't really look like one. Let's turn the question into an equation.

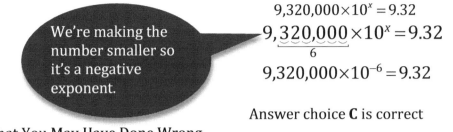

$$9,320,000 \times 10^x = 9.32$$

$$\underbrace{9,320,000}_{6} \times 10^x = 9.32$$

$$9,320,000 \times 10^{-6} = 9.32$$

We're making the number smaller so it's a negative exponent.

Answer choice **C** is correct

What You May Have Done Wrong
  A. This would result in 0.0932.
  B. This would result in 0.932.
  C. This would make 9,320,000 *larger*.
  D. This would make 9,320,000 *larger*.

4. The concentration of harmful bacteria in a lake was 1.6×10^7 bacteria per liter. After an initial treatment, the concentration of bacteria is 1,000 times less. What is the concentration of bacteria after the initial treatment?

Correct Answer J

This question is operations with scientific notation. You can do this in your calculator or you can do it by hand.

TI Graphing Calculator

Using the *mode* button change the mode from NORMAL to SCI. Enter 1.6×10^7 in that form. Or enter 1.6E 10 using 2nd EE (it's the comma button). Hit the division button and enter 1,000. ENTER will give you your answer.

By Hand

First convert 1,000 into a power of 10. $1,000 = 10^3$

Now divide 1.6×10^7 by 10^3.

$$\frac{1.6 \times 10^7}{10^3} \quad \rightarrow \quad 1.6 \times 10^{7-3} \quad \rightarrow \quad 1.6 \times 10^4$$

When we divide exponents with the *same base* (10), we **subtract** the exponents.

Answer choice **J** is correct.

What You May Have Done Wrong:
  F. You divided the exponents; you should have subtracted them. You also made a mistake with your exponents.
  G. You divided the exponents; you should have subtracted them.
  H. You probably made an arithmetic error, changing 1,000 to a power of 10.
  K. You multiplied by 1,000 instead of dividing. There is *1,000* times less, not more.

5. 682,000 gallons of water goes over Niagara's Horseshoe Falls every second. How much water goes over Horseshoe Falls in three hours?

Correct Answer C

This is an involved problem with a bunch of steps and some big numbers. Because the numbers are so big, it's easiest to convert to scientific notation at the outset.

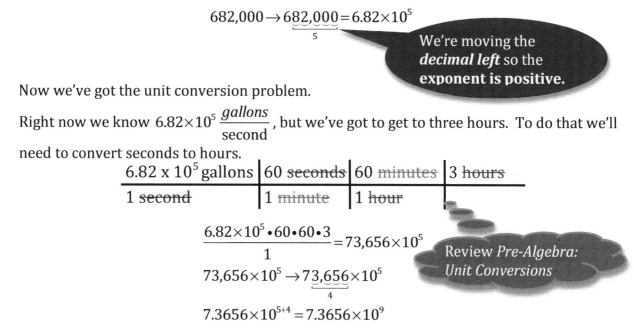

$$682{,}000 \rightarrow \underbrace{682{,}000}_{5} = 6.82 \times 10^5$$

We're moving the **decimal left** so the **exponent is positive.**

Now we've got the unit conversion problem.

Right now we know $6.82 \times 10^5 \dfrac{gallons}{second}$, but we've got to get to three hours. To do that we'll need to convert seconds to hours.

$$\dfrac{6.82 \times 10^5 \text{ gallons} \mid 60 \text{ seconds} \mid 60 \text{ minutes} \mid 3 \text{ hours}}{1 \text{ second} \quad \mid 1 \text{ minute} \mid 1 \text{ hour}}$$

$$\frac{6.82 \times 10^5 \cdot 60 \cdot 60 \cdot 3}{1} = 73{,}656 \times 10^5$$

Review *Pre-Algebra: Unit Conversions*

$$73{,}656 \times 10^5 \rightarrow \underbrace{73{,}656}_{4} \times 10^5$$

$$7.3656 \times 10^{5+4} = 7.3656 \times 10^9$$

In three hours 7.3656×10^9 gallons go over Horseshoe Falls.

Answer choice **C** is correct.

<u>What You May Have Done Wrong</u>
    A. This is the amount of water for one minute
    B. This is the amount of water for one hour.
    D. This is the amount of water for three minutes
    E. This is a calculator error; review your steps.

Introduction

Fractions are numbers that represent division and fractions are ratios. Fraction problems are on nearly every test, and sometimes more than once. More importantly, you'll need to understand operations with fractions to solve ratios/proportions, unit problems, some algebra problems, rational expressions, similar triangles, & trig problems.

What You Need to Know

- ✓ How to add, subtract, multiply, and divide fractions.
- ✓ How to simplify fractions by cancelling factors.
- ✓ How and when to cross-multiply.
- ✓ How do deal with linear equations containing fractions.

> Video on fraction operations

Multiplying Fractions

> Fractions are simple to multiply. You **multiply the numerator by the numerator and the denominator by the denominator.** *Multiply straight across.*

Example: Multiplying Fractions

1. $\dfrac{1}{2} \cdot \dfrac{1}{2} = \dfrac{1 \rightarrow 1}{2 \rightarrow 2} = \dfrac{1 \cdot 1}{2 \cdot 2} = \dfrac{1}{4}$

> Multiply the *numerator* by the *numerator* & the *denominator* by the *denominator*.

> When we multiply fractions less than 1, the product (answer) is smaller than the multiplied fractions.

2. $\dfrac{1}{3} \cdot \dfrac{2}{5} = \dfrac{1 \rightarrow}{3 \rightarrow} \cdot \dfrac{2}{5} = \dfrac{1 \cdot 2}{3 \cdot 5} = \dfrac{2}{15}$

> We don't need a common denominator. It doesn't matter if the *denominators match.*

Dividing Fractions

> Fractions are simple to divide, but it feels complicated. **Flip the second, or bottom, fraction & multiply.**

Example: Dividing Fractions

1. $\dfrac{1}{2} \div \dfrac{1}{2} = \dfrac{1}{2} \cdot \dfrac{2}{1} = \dfrac{1 \cdot 2}{2 \cdot 1} = \dfrac{1}{1} = 1$

> flip means take the **reciprocal**

> Flip the **second ½** and **multiply**.

> When we **multiply** fractions **less than 1**, the answer is **larger** than the fraction we started with.

2. $\dfrac{\dfrac{1}{4}}{\dfrac{1}{9}} = \dfrac{1}{1} \cdot \dfrac{9}{4} = \dfrac{9}{4}$

> When we have 1 as a *numerator*, dividing by a fraction results in the *reciprocal* of that fraction.

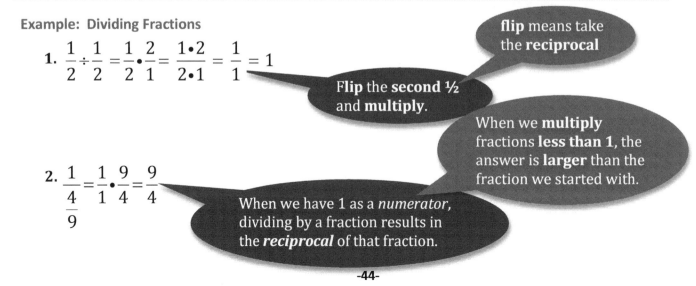

Adding & subtracting fractions is more difficult than multiplying/dividing, because you need a *common denominator*.

Examples: Adding & Subtracting Fractions

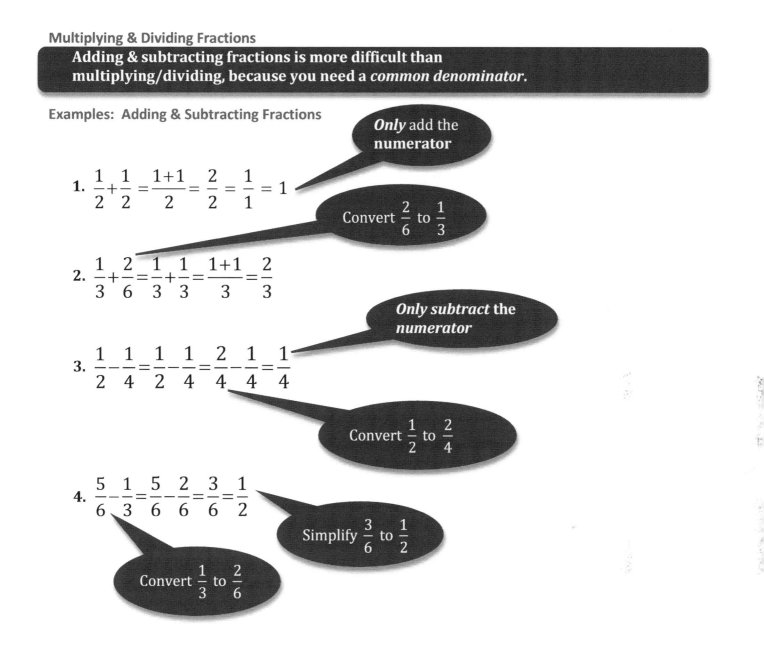

1. $\dfrac{1}{2} + \dfrac{1}{2} = \dfrac{1+1}{2} = \dfrac{2}{2} = \dfrac{1}{1} = 1$

***Only* add the numerator**

Convert $\dfrac{2}{6}$ to $\dfrac{1}{3}$

2. $\dfrac{1}{3} + \dfrac{2}{6} = \dfrac{1}{3} + \dfrac{1}{3} = \dfrac{1+1}{3} = \dfrac{2}{3}$

***Only subtract* the numerator**

3. $\dfrac{1}{2} - \dfrac{1}{4} = \dfrac{1}{2} - \dfrac{1}{4} = \dfrac{2}{4} - \dfrac{1}{4} = \dfrac{1}{4}$

Convert $\dfrac{1}{2}$ to $\dfrac{2}{4}$

4. $\dfrac{5}{6} - \dfrac{1}{3} = \dfrac{5}{6} - \dfrac{2}{6} = \dfrac{3}{6} = \dfrac{1}{2}$

Simplify $\dfrac{3}{6}$ to $\dfrac{1}{2}$

Convert $\dfrac{1}{3}$ to $\dfrac{2}{6}$

Finding a Common Denominator

Find a factor or multiple that both denominators share. You can do this by finding the Least Common Multiple, or multiply the denominators together.

Examples: Adding & Subtracting Fractions

1. Find the common denominator of $\dfrac{1}{2}$ & $\dfrac{1}{6}$.

   2 is a factor of 6 (2 x 3) so the Least Common Multiple is 6. We can also multiply the denominators together 2 x 6 = 12.

2. $\dfrac{1}{3}+\dfrac{2}{5}=?$

   The two denominators have *no* factors in common. So, the easiest way to find a common denominator is to multiply the 3 & 5

   $$3 \times 5 = 15$$

   We've got to multiply each denominator by the missing factor to get the common denominator. **But we've also got to multiply the numerator by that number or we'll change the fraction.**

   $$\frac{1}{3}\left(\frac{5}{5}\right)+\frac{2}{5}\left(\frac{3}{3}\right)=\frac{5}{15}+\frac{6}{15}$$

   $$\frac{5}{15}+\frac{6}{15}=\frac{11}{15}$$

   > Multiply by the missing factor of the common denominator

Simplifying Fractions

Fractions need to be in the simplest possible form.
The *only* way to simplify fractions is to cancel out common factors.

Example: Simplifying Fractions

1. $\dfrac{32}{64}\rightarrow\dfrac{8\cdot4}{8\cdot8}\rightarrow\dfrac{\cancel{8}\cdot4}{\cancel{8}\cdot8}=\dfrac{4}{8}\rightarrow\dfrac{4\cdot1}{4\cdot2}\rightarrow\dfrac{\cancel{4}\cdot1}{\cancel{4}\cdot2}=\dfrac{1}{2}$

   > There's usually more than one way to simplify. We could have factored out 2's or 4's

Why Just Factors?

Simplification doesn't change the fraction; it just expresses it in its simplest terms.

1. $\dfrac{2+3}{3+3}\rightarrow\dfrac{5}{6}$

   But, if we tried to cancel the 3's... $\dfrac{2+\cancel{3}}{3+\cancel{3}}\rightarrow\dfrac{2}{3}$

   > $\dfrac{2}{3}\neq\dfrac{5}{6}$

ACT Example: Fractions

1. James bikes $6\frac{5}{6}$ miles in one day and $10\frac{4}{9}$ miles the next day. How many miles does he bike in total?

A. $16\frac{11}{36}$

B. $17\frac{11}{36}$

C. $17\frac{5}{18}$

D. $16\frac{5}{18}$

E. $16\frac{11}{18}$

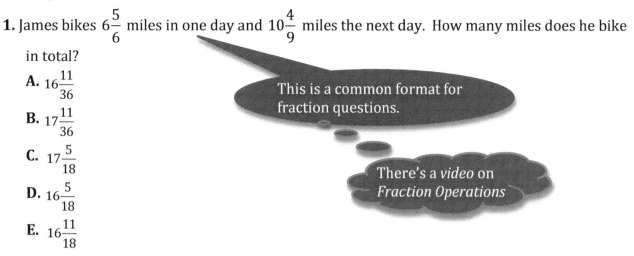

This is a common format for fraction questions.

There's a *video* on *Fraction Operations*

Solve

This is a common setup for a fraction question. We've got to add the fractions to get the total distance James rides. Let's ignore the whole numbers for a minute while we find a common denominator.

$\frac{5}{6}$ & $\frac{4}{9}$ can be rewritten as $\frac{5}{2\cdot3}$ & $\frac{4}{3\cdot3}$ but neither one of the fractions can be *simplified*.

One way you can find the common denominator is to run through the *multiples* of 6 and 9 and look for a shared multiple

6 x 1 = 6	9 x 1 = 9
6 x 2 = 12	9 x 2 = 18
6 x 3 = 18	

We can use 18 as our common denominator. I prefer to leave the whole numbers whole, and not convert them into the numerator of the fraction. It's easier, particularly at the end when we need to simplify. Let's do the math.

$$\frac{5}{6}\left(\frac{3}{3}\right)+\frac{4}{9}\left(\frac{2}{2}\right)=\frac{15}{18}+\frac{8}{18}=\frac{23}{18}\to1\frac{5}{18}$$

$$6+10+1+\frac{5}{18}=17\frac{5}{18}$$

I like leaving the whole numbers out. It's easier and we won't have to simplify difficult fractions.

We could also find the common denominator by multiplying 6 & 9. There's absolutely nothing wrong with that approach and if it works best for you, go for it.

We can simplify this fraction

$$\frac{5}{6}\left(\frac{9}{9}\right)+\frac{4}{9}\left(\frac{6}{6}\right)=\frac{45}{54}+\frac{24}{54}=\frac{69}{54}$$

$$\frac{69}{54}\to\frac{23\cdot3}{18\cdot3}\to\frac{23\cdot\cancel{3}}{18\cdot\cancel{3}}=\frac{23}{18}=1\frac{5}{18}$$

$$6+10+1+\frac{5}{18}=17\frac{5}{18}$$

Answer Choice **C** is correct.

Calculators

Calculators can solve many of these problems, but that's not the point. **You absolutely need to know how to do these problems without a calculator** because they aren't always numeric, we'll have fractions involving variables as well.

Let's use the last example to look at how to handle these problems on a Texas Instruments graphing calculator.

Example: Addition of Fractions

1. James bikes $6\frac{5}{6}$ miles in one day and $10\frac{4}{9}$ miles the next day. How many miles does he bike in total?

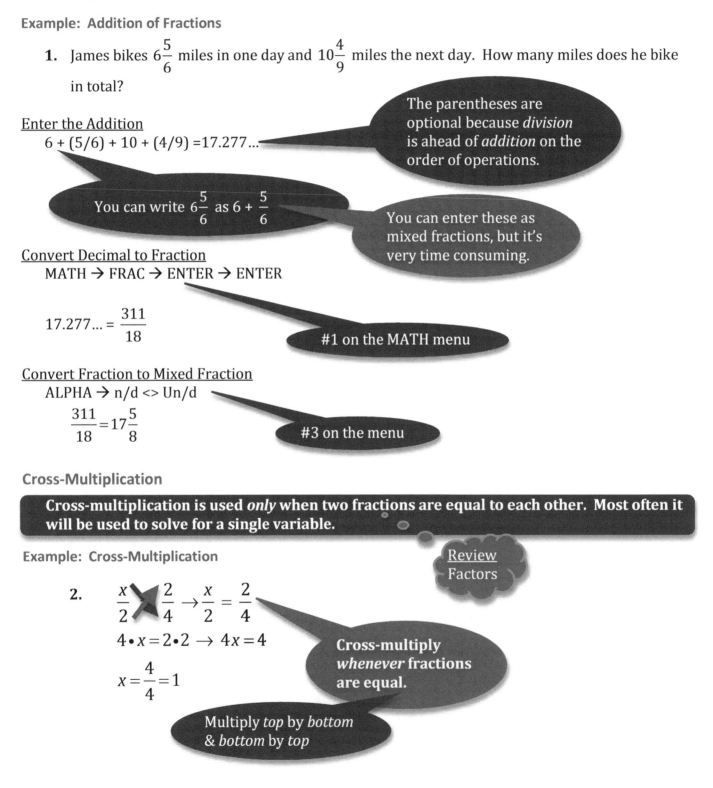

Enter the Addition
$$6 + (5/6) + 10 + (4/9) = 17.277...$$

The parentheses are optional because *division* is ahead of *addition* on the order of operations.

You can write $6\frac{5}{6}$ as $6 + \frac{5}{6}$

You can enter these as mixed fractions, but it's very time consuming.

Convert Decimal to Fraction
MATH → FRAC → ENTER → ENTER

$$17.277... = \frac{311}{18}$$

#1 on the MATH menu

Convert Fraction to Mixed Fraction
ALPHA → n/d <> Un/d

$$\frac{311}{18} = 17\frac{5}{8}$$

#3 on the menu

Cross-Multiplication

Cross-multiplication is used *only* when two fractions are equal to each other. Most often it will be used to solve for a single variable.

Example: Cross-Multiplication

2. $$\frac{x}{2} \times \frac{2}{4} \rightarrow \frac{x}{2} = \frac{2}{4}$$

$$4 \cdot x = 2 \cdot 2 \rightarrow 4x = 4$$

$$x = \frac{4}{4} = 1$$

Review Factors

Cross-multiply *whenever* fractions are equal.

Multiply *top* by *bottom* & *bottom* by *top*

ACT Example: Linear Equations with Fractions

1. Solve for x when $3x - \dfrac{1}{3} = \dfrac{1}{2}$.

A. $2\dfrac{1}{3}$

B. $2\dfrac{1}{2}$

C. $\dfrac{5}{18}$

D. $\dfrac{1}{6}$

E. $1\dfrac{1}{6}$

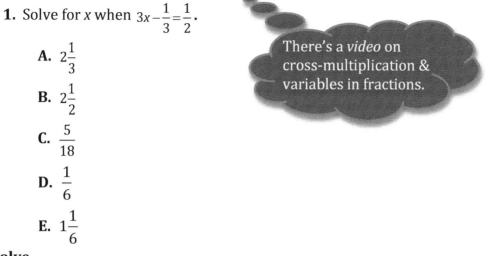

There's a video on cross-multiplication & variables in fractions.

Solve

This is a linear equation that's made confusing by the presence of fractions. First, isolate the $3x$.

We need a common denominator, 6 in this case.

$$3x - \frac{1}{3} = \frac{1}{2} \;\rightarrow\; 3x = \frac{1}{2} + \frac{1}{3}$$

$$3x = \frac{1}{2}\left(\frac{3}{3}\right) + \frac{1}{3}\left(\frac{2}{2}\right) \;\rightarrow\; 3x = \frac{3}{6} + \frac{2}{6} \;\rightarrow\; 3x = \frac{5}{6}$$

Dividing by 3

$$3x = \frac{5}{6} \;\rightarrow\; x = \frac{5/6}{3}$$

$$\frac{5}{6} \cdot \frac{1}{3} = \frac{5}{18}$$

Cross-multiplying

$$3x = \frac{5}{6} \;\rightarrow\; \frac{3x}{1} = \frac{5}{6}$$

$$18x = 5 \;\rightarrow\; x = \frac{5}{18}$$

Answer Choice **C** is correct.

Wrap Up

What You Need to Know

- ✓ How to add, subtract, multiply, & divide fractions.
- ✓ How to simplify fractions.
- ✓ How to cross-multiply.
- ✓ How to solve linear equations with fractions.

Videos

> Fraction Operations

> Cross-Multiplying & Solving Linear Equations

The Strategies

- ✓ Know how to do fraction operations, don't just rely on your calculator.
- ✓ Use cross-multiplication whenever fractions equal each other.
- ✓ Treat linear equations with fractions like any other equation.

Key Skill

- ✓ Decimals
- ✓ Rational Expressions
- ✓ Percents & Probability

Pre-Algebra: Fractions

1. Jared ran $7\frac{1}{3}$ miles on Monday and $5\frac{4}{5}$ miles on Tuesday. How many miles did he run in total?

   A. $13\frac{2}{15}$

   B. $12\frac{2}{15}$

   C. $12\frac{1}{3}$

   D. $12\frac{1}{5}$

   E. $13\frac{4}{15}$

2. $x + 2\frac{3}{4} = 6\frac{5}{12}$, what does x equal?

   F. $9\frac{5}{12}$

   G. $4\frac{2}{3}$

   H. $3\frac{1}{3}$

   J. $3\frac{2}{3}$

   K. $3\frac{5}{12}$

3. A road is $12\frac{1}{4}$ miles long. Town A and B are on that road such that Town A is $2\frac{5}{16}$ miles from one end of the road and Town B is $3\frac{5}{8}$ miles from the other end of the road. How far are Town A and Town B from each other?

   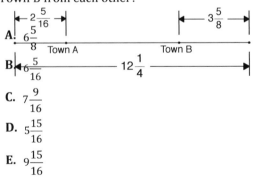

   A. $6\frac{5}{8}$

   B. $6\frac{5}{16}$

   C. $7\frac{9}{16}$

   D. $5\frac{15}{16}$

   E. $9\frac{15}{16}$

4. $\frac{3}{5} \cdot \frac{2}{3} \div \frac{1}{2} = ?$

   F. $\frac{3}{15}$

   G. $\frac{9}{20}$

   H. $\frac{9}{10}$

   J. $\frac{4}{5}$

   K. $2\frac{1}{10}$

5. $\frac{7}{8} - \frac{1}{4} \div \frac{2}{3} = ?$

   A. $\frac{15}{16}$

   B. $\frac{1}{2}$

   C. $\frac{5}{12}$

   D. $\frac{17}{24}$

   E. $\frac{2}{3}$

Pre-Algebra: Fractions

1. Jared ran $7\frac{1}{3}$ miles on Monday and $5\frac{4}{5}$ miles on Tuesday. How many miles did he run in total?

Correct Answer A

This is a fraction addition question. We've got two days to add, and the distances for those days have different denominators.

$$7\frac{1}{3}+5\frac{4}{5}=?$$

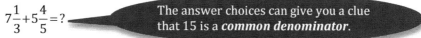

The answer choices can give you a clue that 15 is a *common denominator*.

We need a common denominator. We can look for the LCM by multiples of each denominator, but it's likely you can already tell it's...

$$3 \times 5 = 15$$

I'll set aside the integers and add them at the end. I think it's much easier than making an improper fraction.

$$\frac{1}{3}+\frac{4}{5} \to \frac{1}{3}\left(\frac{5}{5}\right)+\frac{4}{5}\left(\frac{3}{3}\right) \to \frac{5}{15}+\frac{12}{15}$$

$$\frac{5}{15}+\frac{12}{15}=\frac{17}{15}=1\frac{2}{15}$$

$$7+5+1+\frac{2}{15}=13\frac{2}{15}$$

Answer choice **A** is correct.

<u>What You May Have Done Wrong</u>
   B. You probably did everything right, except you forgot to add the one from the improper fraction.
   C. When you found the common denominator, you forgot to multiply the numerator.
   D. You made an error converting to 15ths
   E. This is a calculation error. Review your steps.

2. $x+2\frac{3}{4}=6\frac{5}{12}$, what does x equal?

Correct Answer J

This is a bit of an algebra problem, but the tricky part is subtracting fractions. To subtract fractions, we'll need a common denominator. First, re-arrange the equation.

$$x+2\frac{3}{4}=6\frac{5}{12} \to x=6\frac{5}{12}-2\frac{3}{4}$$

Because 12 = 4 x 3 four is a factor of 12. Therefore, the least common multiple (and a common denominator) is 12. **Let's do the fractions first, and leave the integers to the end**.

$$\frac{5}{12}-\frac{3}{4}\left(\frac{3}{3}\right) \to \frac{5}{12}-\frac{9}{12}$$

$$\frac{5}{12}-\frac{9}{12}=-\frac{4}{12}$$

Now our problem looks like this:

We can rewrite **4** as $3+\dfrac{12}{12}$.

$$x=6-2-\frac{4}{12} \quad \to \quad x=4-\frac{4}{12}$$

$$x=3+\frac{12}{12}-\frac{4}{12} \quad \to \quad x=3\frac{8}{12} \to 3\frac{2}{3}$$

Answer choice **J** is correct.

<u>What You May Have Done Wrong</u>
   F. You *added* the fractions, you should have subtracted.
   G. You forgot to subtract the 1 to deal with the -4/12
   H. You didn't subtract the fractions properly.
   K. This is a compound error. Review your steps.

3. A road is $12\frac{1}{4}$ miles long. Town A and B are on that road such that Town A is $2\frac{5}{16}$ miles from one end of the road and Town B is $3\frac{5}{8}$ miles from the other end of the road. How far are Town A and Town B from each other?

Correct Answer B

This is a fraction subtraction problem that looks a lot tougher than it is. Let's mark-up our diagram:

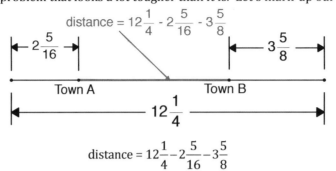

$$\text{distance} = 12\frac{1}{4} - 2\frac{5}{16} - 3\frac{5}{8}$$

We'll need a common denominator. 4 and 8 are factors of 16, so we can use 16 as our common denominator (it happens to be the least common denominator). Let's deal with the fractions first.

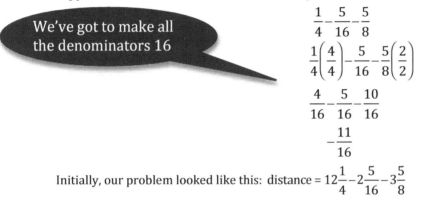

We've got to make all the denominators 16

Initially, our problem looked like this: $\text{distance} = 12\frac{1}{4} - 2\frac{5}{16} - 3\frac{5}{8}$

After we subtracted our fractions, we're left with this:

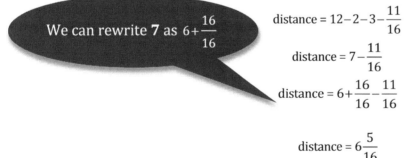

We can rewrite **7** as $6 + \frac{16}{16}$

$$\text{distance} = 12 - 2 - 3 - \frac{11}{16}$$

$$\text{distance} = 7 - \frac{11}{16}$$

$$\text{distance} = 6 + \frac{16}{16} - \frac{11}{16}$$

$$\text{distance} = 6\frac{5}{16}$$

Answer choice **B** is correct

<u>What You May Have Done Wrong</u>
    A. You may have made an arithmetic error, or made a calculator mistake (probably a conversion).
    C. This is a compound error. Review your steps.
    D. You added the distances from the ends of the road to the towns, instead of subtracting them from the total distance of the road.
    E. This is a halfway answer. You subtracted $2\frac{5}{16}$ from the total distance of the road.

4. $\dfrac{3}{5} \cdot \dfrac{2}{3} \div \dfrac{1}{2} = ?$

Correct Answer J

This is a straightforward operations problem. *Multiplication & division* have the same "rank" in the order of operations. Generally, we move from left to right, but we can do either first. I think it's easier to do the multiplication first.

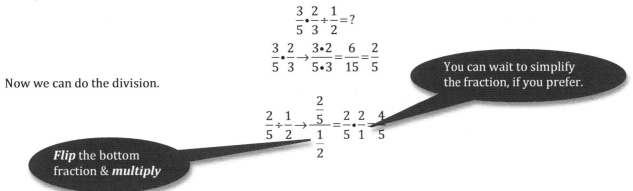

$$\dfrac{3}{5} \cdot \dfrac{2}{3} \div \dfrac{1}{2} = ?$$

$$\dfrac{3}{5} \cdot \dfrac{2}{3} \rightarrow \dfrac{3 \cdot 2}{5 \cdot 3} = \dfrac{6}{15} = \dfrac{2}{5}$$

You can wait to simplify the fraction, if you prefer.

Now we can do the division.

$$\dfrac{2}{5} \div \dfrac{1}{2} \rightarrow \dfrac{\frac{2}{5}}{\frac{1}{2}} = \dfrac{2}{5} \cdot \dfrac{2}{1} = \dfrac{4}{5}$$

Flip the bottom fraction & multiply

Answer choice **J** is correct.

What You May Have Done Wrong:
    F. You didn't flip your fraction when dividing.
    G. You cross-multiplied *and* you didn't flip your fraction when dividing.
    H. You cross-multiplied.
    K. You cross-multiplied.

5. $\dfrac{7}{8} - \dfrac{1}{4} \div \dfrac{2}{3} = ?$

Correct Answer B

This is about the order of operations as much as it is fractions. We've got *subtraction* and *division*. The order of operation is PEMDAS, and division is a higher "rank" than subtraction, so we need to deal with the division first.

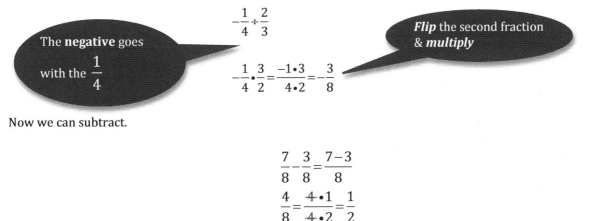

$$-\dfrac{1}{4} \div \dfrac{2}{3}$$

The negative goes with the $\dfrac{1}{4}$

Flip the second fraction & multiply

$$-\dfrac{1}{4} \cdot \dfrac{3}{2} = \dfrac{-1 \cdot 3}{4 \cdot 2} = -\dfrac{3}{8}$$

Now we can subtract.

$$\dfrac{7}{8} - \dfrac{3}{8} = \dfrac{7-3}{8}$$

$$\dfrac{4}{8} = \dfrac{4 \cdot 1}{4 \cdot 2} = \dfrac{1}{2}$$

Answer choice **B** is correct.

What You May Have Done Wrong
    A. You subtracted first; you need to divide first.
    C. You subtracted first *and* you forgot to flip your fraction when dividing.
    D. You forgot to flip your fraction when dividing.
    E. This is a calculation error. Review your steps.

Introduction

Ratios describe relationships. They tell us how the quantity of one thing relates to the quantity of another thing. Ratios are a **fundamental skill** for ACT success. Not only are they directly tested, but also they are helpful or necessary on many types of word problems, unit conversions, similar triangles, and trig functions.

What You Need to Know

- ✓ How to set up a ratio as a fraction.
- ✓ The difference between *part*-to-part and *part* to *whole* ratios.
- ✓ Convert text to ratios & proportions.
- ✓ How to properly set up proportions & cross-multiply to solve.

There's a video on ratios.

Definition: Ratios

Ratios describe relationships. Ratios are relative, not absolute. Ratios represent the *minimum* quantity of each thing, not necessarily the quantity itself. This allows ratios to represent any number of things or any unit.

I have three apples for every four oranges

3 apples : 4 oranges *-or-* 4 oranges : 3 apples.

Example: Part to Part Ratios

1. On a baseball team, three of the batters are right-handed. Six of the batters are left-handed. What is the ratio of right-handed to left-handed batters?

Right-Handed	:	Left-Handed
3	:	6

Order matters in ratios!

Part to Whole Ratios

Ratios take two forms. *Part to part* ratios compare two or more items (apples to oranges or right-handed to left-handed batters).

Part to whole ratios consider a part (component) to the whole it belongs to. For example, right-handed batters to team or apples to fruit salad.

1. On a baseball team's starting lineup, three of the batters are right-handed. Six of the batters are left-handed. What is the ratio of right-handed batters to the team?

Right-Handed	:	Team
3	:	9
1	:	3

Always label your ratios when working problems.

Always simplify ratios.

2. If fruit salad only contains 3 lbs. of apples and 4 lbs. of oranges, how many ounces of apples are in 7 ounces of fruit salad?

Apples	:	Fruit Salad
4 oz	:	7 oz

It doesn't matter that we switched from pounds to ounces. The ratio stays the same in any unit.

But, we have to keep the same units within the ratio.

1. Seventeen of the 30 students in an AP calculus class are female and the rest are male. What is the ratio of female to male students?

    A. $17:30$
    B. $13:30$
    C. $30:13$
    D. $17:13$
    E. $13:17$

Solve

This question gives us a *part to whole* ratio and asks us to find the missing part to make a new ratio.

$$\underline{\text{Female Students}} : \underline{\text{Total}}$$
$$17 \qquad\quad : \quad 30$$

Every student that isn't female is male. So we can say...
$$male = total - female \rightarrow male = 30 - 17 \rightarrow male = 13$$

Now, we just set up the ratio we're looking for:

$$\underline{\text{Female Students}} : \underline{\text{Male Students}}$$
$$17 \qquad\quad : \qquad 13$$

Answer Choice **D** is correct.

2. There are 24 pre-algebra/elementary algebra questions, 18 algebra II/coordinate geometry questions, and 18 plane geometry/trigonometry questions on a particular ACT math section. The ACT math section consists *only* of those categories. What is the ratio of pre-algebra/elementary algebra questions to total math questions?

    A. $3:10$
    B. $10:3$
    C. $2:5$
    D. $15:6$
    E. $1:3$

Solve

In this problem we are given all of the parts, and we'll need to find the whole.

Pre/Algebra		Alg. II/Coord.		Plane/Trig		Total/Whole
24	+	18	+	18	=	60

We don't need the Alg. II/Coord. and Plane/Trig. numbers anymore.

Pre/Algebra	:	~~Alg. II/Coord~~	:	~~Plane/Trig~~	:	Total/Whole
24	:	~~18~~	:	~~18~~	:	60

The ratio of pre-algebra/elementary algebra to total is $24:60 \rightarrow 6:15 \rightarrow 2:5$

Answer Choice **C** is correct.

Ratios are Fractions

Ratios can be written as fractions. We see this most frequently with *part to whole* ratios, but *part to part* ratios can be expressed as fractions. Most ratio & proportion problems require converting ratios into fractions.

Let's look at some examples.

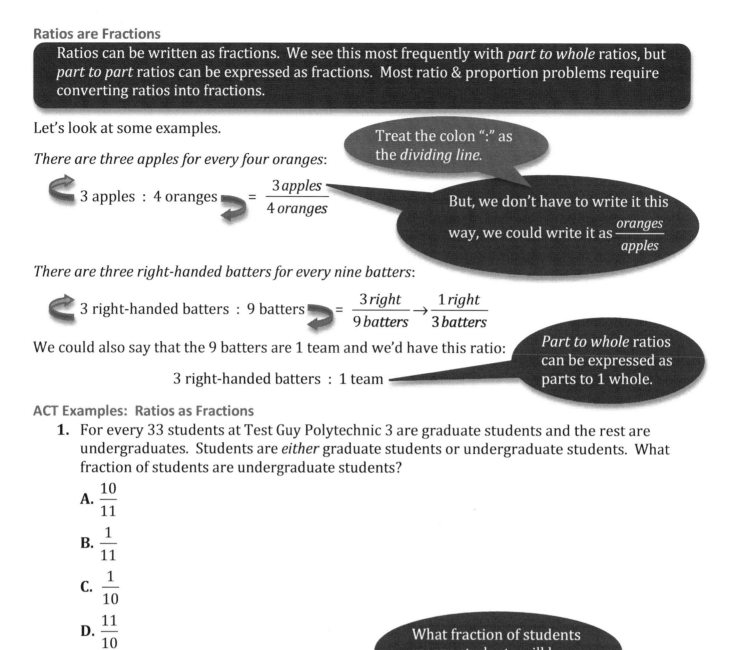

There are three apples for every four oranges:

$$3 \text{ apples} : 4 \text{ oranges} = \frac{3\,apples}{4\,oranges}$$

Treat the colon ":" as the *dividing line*.

But, we don't have to write it this way, we could write it as $\dfrac{oranges}{apples}$

There are three right-handed batters for every nine batters:

$$3 \text{ right-handed batters} : 9 \text{ batters} = \frac{3\,right}{9\,batters} \rightarrow \frac{1\,right}{3\,batters}$$

We could also say that the 9 batters are 1 team and we'd have this ratio:

$$3 \text{ right-handed batters} : 1 \text{ team}$$

Part to whole ratios can be expressed as parts to 1 whole.

ACT Examples: Ratios as Fractions

1. For every 33 students at Test Guy Polytechnic 3 are graduate students and the rest are undergraduates. Students are *either* graduate students or undergraduate students. What fraction of students are undergraduate students?

   A. $\dfrac{10}{11}$

   B. $\dfrac{1}{11}$

   C. $\dfrac{1}{10}$

   D. $\dfrac{11}{10}$

   E. $\dfrac{10}{33}$

   What fraction of students means students will be the *denominator*

Solve

We're dealing with a *part to whole* ratio. Start by setting up the ratio we're looking for. We don't have the number of *undergraduate* students, so we'll have to calculate it from the *total students* and *graduate students*.

Graduate Students		Undergraduate Students		Total
3	+	undergrads	=	33

$$total - graduates = undergraduates \rightarrow 33 - 3 = undergraduates$$
$$undergraduates = 30$$

$$30 \text{ undergraduates} : 33 \text{ students} = \frac{30}{33} \rightarrow \frac{10}{11}$$

Answer Choice **A** is correct.

Definition: Proportions

The majority of ratio questions are proportion questions.

> Proportions are two equal ratios. They are changes in quantity, dimension, or measure.

Rules of the Road: Solving Proportions

> **The steps to solving proportions:**
> 1. Set up your ratios. You'll have only one missing term and place a variable there
> 2. Make fractions from your ratios.
> 3. Set your fractions equal, cross-multiply, and solve.

There's a video on proportion

Example: Proportions

1. At the Test Guy's Famous Fruit Emporium there are three apples for every four oranges. If there are 120 apples, how many oranges are there?

Solve

In proportion problems, we need three of the four components of the ratios. We have one complete ratio (3 apples : 4 oranges) and one incomplete ratio (120 apples : x oranges) and we know that they should be equal. First, let's set up our ratios.

Step 1: Set up your ratios

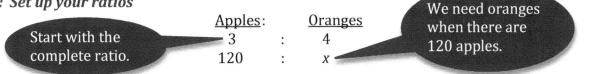

Start with the complete ratio.

Apples:		Oranges
3	:	4
120	:	x

We need oranges when there are 120 apples.

The ratio of 3 apples : 4 oranges will equal the ratio of 120 apples : x oranges.

Step 2: Make fractions from your ratios

To solve, we have two options. **We can create fractions from our columns (vertically), or we can create fractions from our rows (horizontally).**

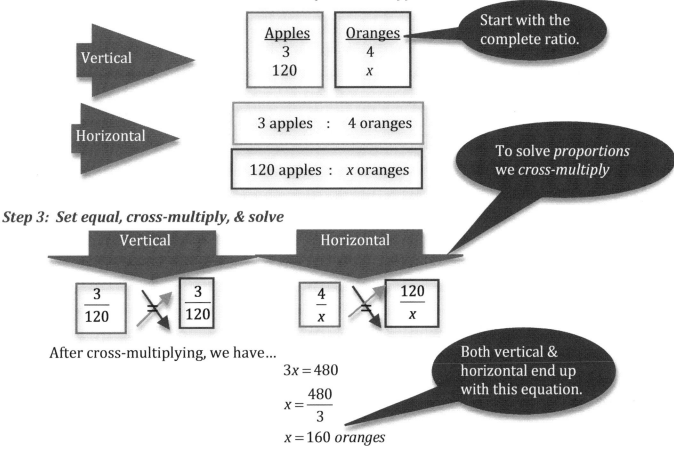

Step 3: Set equal, cross-multiply, & solve

After cross-multiplying, we have...

$$3x = 480$$

$$x = \frac{480}{3}$$

$$x = 160 \ oranges$$

Both vertical & horizontal end up with this equation.

1. Harper is constructing a scale model of the Empire State Building. The Empire state building is 1,454 feet tall. Harper is building the model on a scale of 1 foot of building equals $\frac{1}{16}$ inch. Approximately how tall, in inches, will the model be?

    A.   91 inches
    B.   65 inches
    C. 23,264 inches
    D.   64 inches
    E.   912 inches

Check out Pre-Algebra: Rates, Units, & Time for more

Solve

This problem is a unit conversion that can be solved as a proportion.

Step 1: Set up your ratios

Feet		Inches
1	:	1/16
1,454	:	x

Start with the complete ratio.

Step 2: Make fractions from your ratios

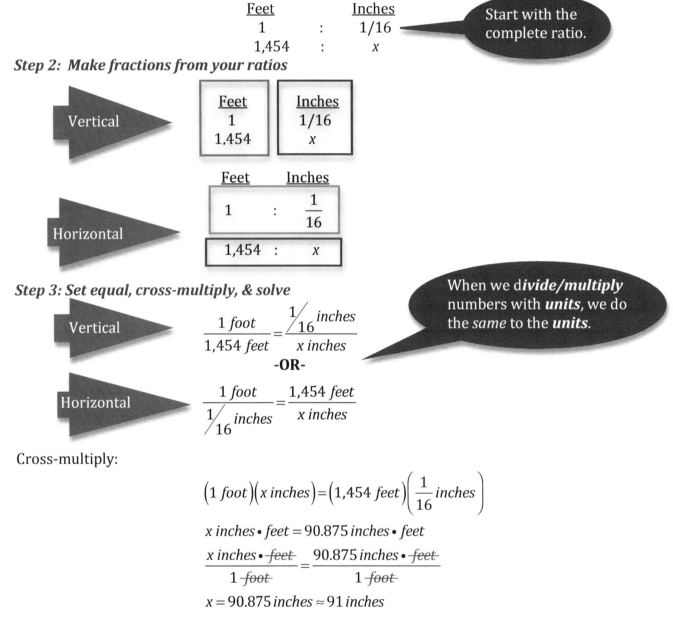

Vertical

Feet	Inches
1	1/16
1,454	x

Horizontal

Feet	Inches
1 :	$\frac{1}{16}$
1,454 :	x

Step 3: Set equal, cross-multiply, & solve

Vertical

$$\frac{1\ foot}{1,454\ feet} = \frac{\frac{1}{16}\ inches}{x\ inches}$$

-OR-

Horizontal

$$\frac{1\ foot}{\frac{1}{16}\ inches} = \frac{1,454\ feet}{x\ inches}$$

*When we **divide/multiply** numbers with **units**, we do the same to the **units**.*

Cross-multiply:

$$\left(1\ foot\right)\left(x\ inches\right) = \left(1,454\ feet\right)\left(\frac{1}{16}\ inches\right)$$

$$x\ inches \cdot feet = 90.875\ inches \cdot feet$$

$$\frac{x\ inches \cdot \cancel{feet}}{1\ \cancel{foot}} = \frac{90.875\ inches \cdot \cancel{feet}}{1\ \cancel{foot}}$$

$$x = 90.875\ inches \approx 91\ inches$$

Answer Choice **A** is correct.

What You Need to Know
- ✓ How to set up a ratio as a fraction.
- ✓ The difference between *part* to *part* and *part* to *whole* ratios.
- ✓ Convert text to ratios & proportions.
- ✓ How to properly set up proportions & cross-multiply to solve.

Videos

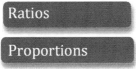

The Strategies
- ✓ Remember that ratios are fractions, and recognize part-to-part and whole-to-whole.
- ✓ Use a formal setup for proportions and label your categories. The most common mistake on these problems is to flip something.
- ✓ Keep an eye out for ratios in other places.

Key Skill
- ✓ Unit Conversions

- ✓ Fractions

- ✓ Trig Functions

- ✓ Similar Triangles

1. Five of the 12 members of a club are female and the rest are male. What is the ratio of males to females in the club?

   A. 7:5
   B. 8:4
   C. 5:7
   D. 4:3
   E. 9:3

2. The ratio of 2.5 to 32 is the same as the ratio or 0.25 to x. What is the value of x?

   F. 51.2
   G. 12.8
   H. 3.2
   J. 7.2
   K. 6.4

3. The price of a chicken is directly proportional to its weight. If a 4-pound chicken costs $6.00 then how much does a 3.25-pound chicken cost?

   A. $4.88
   B. $7.38
   C. $1.50
   D. $6.34
   E. $4.65

4. There are two kinds of animals up for adoption, cats and dogs. There are two cats for every five dogs, and there are 18 cats up for adoption. How many animals, in total, are up for adoption?

   F. 7
   G. 25
   H. 27
   J. 45
   K. 63

5. The ratio of j to k to l to m is 5 to 4 to 3 to 2. If j = 60, what is the value of m?

   A. 150
   B. 48
   C. 24
   D. 36
   E. 57

6. After working for nine months Jim earned 6 days of vacation time. How many days will he have earned after working for two years?

   F. 16 days
   G. 36 days
   H. 24 days
   J. 2 days
   K. 26 days

7. A punch recipe calls for three parts juice to two parts soda. In order to make 30 quarts of punch, how many quarts of soda should I use?

   A. 10
   B. 12
   C. 15
   D. 20
   E. 75

8. Many years ago, the dental amalgam used to fill cavities was composed of 4:2:1 parts tin, silver, and mercury, respectively. If Billy discovers one ounce (28 grams) of amalgam in Ghost Town's abandoned dental office, how many grams will be silver?

   F. $\dfrac{1}{2}$
   G. 1
   H. 8
   J. 2
   K. 4

Ratios & Proportions: Solutions

1. **Five of the 12 members of a club are females and the rest are males. What is the ratio of males to females in the club?**

Correct Answer A

We're looking for *males : females*, but we aren't given males. We'll have to use total to calculate males.

$$males + females = club$$
$$club - female = males$$
$$12 - 5 = 7 \; males$$

Order matters in ratios, ***be careful***

$$
\begin{array}{ccc}
\underline{Males} & : & \underline{Females} \\
7 & : & 5
\end{array}
$$

Answer choice **A** is correct.

<u>What You May Have Done Wrong</u>

   B. You've got the wrong numbers involved. Review your steps.
   C. You've got your ratio backwards, make sure you label it!
   D. You've got the wrong numbers involved. Also, it's not possible to get a ratio of 4:3 with a total of 12.
   E. You've got the wrong numbers involved. Also, this ratio would reduce to 3:1

2. **The ratio of 2.5 to 32 is the same as the ratio or 0.25 to *x*. What is the value of *x*?**

Correct Answer H

This is a proportion problem, and there's a great trick to it (if you see it). I set up my proportions vertically because I prefer it.

Step 1: Setup your ratios

$$
\begin{array}{ccc}
\underline{Small} & : & \underline{Large} \\
2.5 & : & 32 \\
0.25 & : & x
\end{array}
$$

> I'm using small & large to label my ratio. ***Always*** label your ratio.

Step 2: Make your fractions & set equal

$$\frac{2.5}{0.25} = \frac{32}{x}$$

Step 3: Cross-multiply & solve

> 0.25 is 2.5 with a decimal shifted one place.

$$2.5x = 8 \rightarrow x = \frac{8}{2.5} \rightarrow x = 3.2$$

There's a trick on this problem, let's take a second look at our fraction.

$$\frac{2.5}{0.25} = \frac{32}{x}$$

> If we move a decimal over on 32, we'll get 3.2

Answer choice **H** is correct.

<u>What You May Have Done Wrong</u>

   F. You jumbled your proportion, flipping one ratio.
   G. You divided 32 by 2.5, which works, but you didn't multiply by 0.25.
   J. This is a calculation error or a guess.
   K. This is a calculation error or a guess.

3. The price of a chicken is directly proportional to its weight. If a 4-pound chicken costs $6.00 then how much does a 3.25-pound chicken cost?

Correct Answer A

This is a relatively straightforward proportion problem. If you're comfortable with proportions, this one should be a breeze.

Step 1: Setup your ratios

Pounds		Cost
4	:	$6.00
3.25	:	x

Step 2: Make your fractions & set equal

$$\frac{4}{3.25} = \frac{6.00}{x}$$

Step 3: Cross-multiply & solve

$$4x = 19.50 \rightarrow x = \frac{19.50}{4} \rightarrow x = 4.875 \approx \$4.88$$

Answer choice **A** is correct

What You May Have Done Wrong

    B. This is the price *per* pound, not the price of the chicken

    C. You flipped your proportion or multiplied straight across

    D. This is probably a calculator error.

    E. This is a calculator error or a guess.

4. There are two kinds of animals up for adoption, cats and dogs. There are two cats for every five dogs, and there are 18 cats up for adoption. How many animals, in total, are up for adoption?

Correct Answer K

This question has two parts. First, we need to find the number of dogs up for adoption. Then we have to find the total (sum) of the animals

Step 1: Setup your ratios

Cats	:	Dogs
2	:	5
18	:	x

Step 2: Make your fractions & set equal

$$\frac{2}{18} = \frac{5}{x}$$

Step 3: Cross-multiply & solve

$$2x = 90 \rightarrow x = 45$$

Now we need to find the *total* number of animals up for adoption.

$$cats + dogs = total \rightarrow 18 + 45 = total \rightarrow total = 63$$

Answer choice **K** is correct.

What You May Have Done Wrong:

    F. You reversed cats & dogs, flipping the 2 and the 5. You also forgot to add the cats (18).

    G. You reversed cats & dogs, flipping the 2 and the 5

    H. You *subtracted* the cats from the dogs (you should add).

    K. This is the number of dogs, a halfway answer.

5. The ratio of *j* to *k* to *l* to *m* is 5 to 4 to 3 to 2. If *j* = 60, what is the value of *m*?

Correct Answer C

This is a problem with a bunch of extraneous (extra) information. We're comparing a part (*j*) to another part (*m*). It's a straight *part-to-part* proportion.

Step 1: Setup your ratios

$$j : \cancel{k} : \cancel{l} : m \qquad\qquad j : m$$
$$5 : 4 : \cancel{3} : 2 \quad\rightarrow\quad 5 : 2$$
$$60 : \quad : \quad : x \qquad\qquad 60 : x$$

> We have no values for *k* & *l* here, and we don't need them.

Step 2: Make your fractions & set equal

$$\frac{5}{60} = \frac{2}{x}$$

Step 3: Cross-multiply & solve

$$5x = 120 \rightarrow x = \frac{120}{5} \rightarrow x = 24$$

Answer choice **C** is correct.

<u>What You May Have Done Wrong</u>
   A. Your proportion was correct, but you multiplied straight across.
   B. You used *k*'s ratio and not *m*'s.
   D. You used *l*'s ratio and not *m*'s.
   E. This is probably a calculator error.

6. After working for nine months Jim earned 6 days of vacation time. How many days will he have earned after working for two years?

Correct Answer F

Before we set up our proportion, we'll need to either convert 9 months to years (I wouldn't because it would give us a fraction) or convert two years to months.

$$2 \text{ } years \cdot 12\frac{months}{year} = 24 \text{ } months$$

Step 1: Setup your ratios

Time Working	:	Vacation Days
9	:	6
24	:	*x*

Step 2: Make your fractions & set equal

$$\frac{9}{24} = \frac{6}{x} \rightarrow 9x = 144 \rightarrow x = 16$$

Answer **F** is correct.

<u>What You May Have Done Wrong</u>
   G. You either flipper your proportion or multiplied straight across.
   H. You set up your proportion incorrectly; you probably used 6 twice.
   J. You set up your proportion incorrectly or multiplied straight across. It also doesn't make sense that after two years Jim would have less vacation time.
   K. You probably made a calculation error.

7. A punch recipe calls for three parts juice to two parts soda. In order to make 30 quarts of punch, how many quarts of soda should I use?

Correct Answer B

This question asks about a *part : whole* ratio. Before we set up the ratio, we need to add a column. We need a whole, or total, column.

Step 1: Setup your ratios

$$\text{Three Parts Juice} + \text{Two Parts Soda} = 5 \text{ parts punch}$$
$$3 \text{ quarts} + 2 \text{ quarts} = 5 \text{ quarts total}$$

Now we can set up our ratio. We needed the juice to calculate the total, but now it is extraneous information and can be discarded.

~~Juice~~ :	**Soda** :	**Total**
~~3~~ :	**2** :	**5**
	x :	30

Step 2 & 3: Make your fractions, set equal, cross-multiply, & solve

$$\frac{2}{x} = \frac{5}{30} \quad \rightarrow \quad 5x = 60 \rightarrow x = 12$$

Answer choice **B** is correct.

<u>What You May Have Done Wrong</u>
- **A.** You divided the number of quarts by the amount of juice.
- **C.** You divided the number of quarts by the amount of soda.
- **D.** You had your proportion flipped, or you multiplied straight across.
- **E.** You did not set up the *total* column. You did a part-to-part proportion.

8. Many years ago, the dental amalgam used to fill cavities was composed of 4:2:1 parts tin, silver, and mercury, respectively. If Billy discovers one ounce (28 grams) of amalgam in Ghost Town's abandoned dental office, how many grams are silver?

Correct Answer H

This problem isn't any different than the *part to whole* problems we've seen so far, but it feels a lot more complicated. Start by setting up your ratio. We'll need a total column, so we can the 28 grams of amalgam to a calculated total.

Step 1: Setup your ratios

<u>Tin</u> :	<u>Silver</u> :	<u>Mercury</u> :	<u>Total</u>
4 :	2 :	1 :	7
-- :	x :	-- :	28

We don't need *tin* & *mercury* now that we've calculated the total.

~~Tin~~ :	**Silver** :	~~Mercury~~ :	**Total**	
~~4~~ :	**2** :	~~1~~ :	7	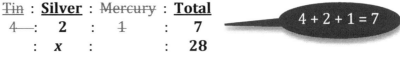 4 + 2 + 1 = 7
:	x :	:	28	

Steps 2 & 3: Make your fractions, set equal, cross-multiply, & solve

$$\frac{2}{x} = \frac{7}{28} \quad \rightarrow \quad 7x = 56 \rightarrow x = 8$$

Answer choice **H** is correct.

<u>What You May Have Done Wrong</u>
- **F.** You multiplied straight across or flipped your proportion.
- **G.** You used mercury instead of silver.
- **J.** You only used the amount of silver in seven grams.
- **K.** You used the amount of silver in 14 grams (you probably made a proportion error).

Introduction

Rate questions show up on every ACT and usually multiple times. In addition, rates are important to solving some algebra, geometry, and other word problems. You can also expect time and units to be on every ACT math section. They're closely related to rates and reward a systematic approach.

What You Need to Know

- ✓ How to find rates
- ✓ When and how to use proportions to solve rates
- ✓ How to deal with time problems by unit conversion & counting
- ✓ How to do multiple unit conversions

Definition: Rates

Rates are a measure, quantity, or a frequency (how often something happens) compared to a different measure, quantity, or frequency.

Rates are ratios that compare things with different units.

> Review *Pre-Algebra: Ratios*

Examples: Rates as Ratios

- miles *per* hour → miles : hour
- liters *per* flush → liters : flush
- beats *per* minute → beats : minute
- feet *per* second → feet : second

> The *per* becomes the colon

Rates are Fractions

To work with rates, we've got to convert them into fractions. *Per* becomes the dividing line between numerator & denominator.

$$\text{miles } per \text{ hour} \rightarrow \frac{miles}{hour} \qquad \text{beats } per \text{ minute} \rightarrow \frac{beats}{minute}$$

$$\text{liters } per \text{ flush} \rightarrow \frac{liters}{flush} \qquad \text{feet } per \text{ second} \rightarrow \frac{feet}{second}$$

Rules of the Road: Working with Rates

Rates problems take many forms, but here are some guidelines.

1. **Convert rates into fractions**, **units** are incredibly important in rates. Keep your eye on them.
2. **Simplify the fractions**. It's ideal if your denominator is 1.
3. **Decide** whether you need to solve by using proportion, modifying the rate, or unit conversion.

Examples: Rates as Proportions

We can use proportion to solve rates questions *if* we've got a consistent relationship. Let's look at a couple of examples.

1. James runs at 6 miles an hour. Kate runs the same pace, how long will it take Kate to run 15 miles?

Solve

We can use proportion here because James & Kate are going at the same *rate*.

> More in *Pre-Algebra: Ratios & Proportion*

$$\frac{6\,miles}{1\,hour} = \frac{15\,miles}{x\,hours}$$

> Cross-multiply & solve

$$6x = 15 \quad \rightarrow \quad x = 2.5$$

2. Sophie earns $100 a for an 8 hour shift as an expert alligator wrangler. If Taylar earns twice as much per hour as Sophie, what does Taylar earn per hour?

Solve

We ***can't*** use proportion here because we don't have the same rate. Taylar earns more money than Sophie and so Sophie ≠ Taylar. Instead, we'd find Sophie's rate and double it.

$$\frac{\$100}{8\,hours} = 12.50\,\frac{dollars}{hour}$$

$$Taylar = 2 \cdot Sophie \quad \rightarrow \quad Taylar = 2 \cdot 12.50 = 25.00\frac{dollars}{hour}$$

ACT Example: Rates as Proportions

1. Pork shoulder roasts require fifty minutes of cooking time for each pound of weight. How long should a 7 and ½ lb. pork shoulder cook for?

    A. 504 minutes
    B. 540 minutes
    C. 375 minutes
    D. 450 minutes
    E. 340 minutes

Solve

This is a proportion style rate question. We've got a time and a weight, and we'll solve this just like a proportion problem.

Step 1: Set up the ratios & convert to fractions

$$1\text{ lb. : }50\text{ minutes} \rightarrow \frac{1\,lb.}{50\,minutes} \qquad 7.5\text{ lbs : }x\text{ minutes} \rightarrow \frac{7.5\,lb.}{x\,minutes}$$

Step 2: Set equal, cross-multiply, & solve

$$\frac{1\,lb.}{50\,minutes} = \frac{7.5\,lb.}{x\,minutes}$$

$$x \text{ minutes} \cdot \text{lbs.} = 375 \text{ minutes} \cdot \text{lbs.}$$

$$\frac{x \text{ minutes} \cdot \cancel{lbs.}}{\cancel{lbs.}} = \frac{375 \text{ minutes} \cdot \cancel{lbs.}}{\cancel{lbs.}} \rightarrow x = 375 \text{ minutes}$$

Answer choice **C** is correct.

Using rates

The most common type of rates question requires you to use or calculate a rate to find another quantity. In these problems, we'll simplify the rate to its lowest possible fraction (usually with 1 in the denominator).

ACT Example: Rates as Proportions

1. Dale Jr. leaves home to drive to Daytona. He drives 220 miles in four hours then stops for lunch. He then drives 15 miles per hour faster and reaches Daytona three hours later. How far does Dale Jr. drive in total?

   A. 210 miles
   B. 265 miles
   C. 573 miles
   D. 540 miles
   E. 430 miles

We need at least 1 equal quantity to use proportion.

Solve

In this problem, we don't have two rates equal to each other. Dale Jr. travels different speeds, for different lengths of time, and we don't *know* that he travels the same distance (it's possible). The question depends on finding how fast Dale Jr. travels *after* lunch, so we need to find how fast he travels *before* lunch.

$$\frac{220\,miles}{4\,hours}=55\,\frac{miles}{hour}$$

Now we can find how fast Dale Jr. goes after lunch.

$$55\,\frac{miles}{hour}+15\,\frac{miles}{hour}=70\,\frac{miles}{hour}$$

He travels at that rate for three hours.

$$70\,\frac{miles}{hour}\cdot 3\,hours=210\,miles$$

Add the distance before lunch and the distance after lunch.
$$220\,miles+210\,miles=430\,miles$$

Answer Choice **E** is correct.

Time

Time problems require us to convert multiple time units to a single unit or require us to add/subtract to find a specific time. Let's look at an example of each.

ACT Examples: Time

1. Iron Chef Morimoto only has 60 minutes to prepare four servings of soup for the chairman and judges of a competition. If it takes the iron chef 90 seconds to chop the ingredients, five minutes to sauté the ingredients, and 5/6th of an hour to simmer the soup, how much time will he have remaining to plate his dish?

   A. 4 minutes
   B. 3.5 minutes
   C. 56.5 minutes
   D. 9.5 minutes
   E. 50.5 minutes

Use your answer choices to determine what unit to convert to.

There's a video on time.

Solve

We've got three units: seconds, minutes, and hours. We'll need to convert to a single unit to answer the question and you should use minutes because that's the unit in the answer choices.

$$\text{Time left} = 60 \text{ minutes} - 90 \text{ seconds} - 5 \text{ minutes} - \frac{5}{6} \text{ hour}$$

First, let's convert seconds to minutes.

$$\frac{90 \text{ seconds}}{1} \cdot \frac{1 \text{ minute}}{60 \text{ seconds}} = \frac{90 \, \cancel{\text{seconds}} \cdot \text{minute}}{60 \, \cancel{\text{seconds}}} \rightarrow 1.5 \text{ minutes}$$

Now, let's convert hours to minutes.

$$\frac{5 \, hour}{6} \cdot \frac{60 \text{ minutes}}{1 \, hour} = \frac{300 \, \cancel{hour} \cdot \text{minutes}}{6 \, \cancel{hour}} \rightarrow 50 \text{ minutes}$$

Time left = 60 minutes – 1.5 minutes – 5 minutes – 50 minutes = 3.5 minutes

Answer Choice **B** is correct.

ACT Example: Time

2. Duchess Katherine's dinner party begins promptly at 7:00 p.m. The Cornish games hens require 10 minutes to clean, two hours to marinate, and one hour and fifteen minutes to roast. The chef, sensibly, wants to have the hens out of the oven 5 minutes early to rest. What time should the kitchen staff begin to clean the hens?

   A. 4:30 p.m.
   B. 3:30 p.m.
   C. 4:35 p.m.
   D. 3:35 p.m.
   E. 3:35 p.m.

Solve

We've got almost everything in the same units, but since we're looking for a specific time, it's easier *not* to do unit conversions. Be careful using your calculator on these questions (it can be done but usually isn't worth it). Let's set up the problem, we'll work backwards from the start time.

7:00 p.m. – 2 hours – 1 hour & 15 minutes – 10 minutes – 5 minutes

Start with hours

7:00 p.m. – 2 hours – 1 hour = 4:00 p.m. We can mark-off *A* & *C*.

Now do minutes

4:00 p.m. – 15 minutes – 10 minutes – 5 minutes = 4:00 p.m.
4:00 – 30 minutes = 3:30

Answer Choice **B** is correct.

Unit Conversions

In many ways *rate* problems are unit conversion problems. But on the ACT, we'll often be given more than two numbers and more than two units to work with.

Organization is critical for ACT math success. These problems can be unwieldy and it's easy to flip a rate or miss a step. Under ACT conditions, you'll often miss your mistake and, as a result, miss the question.

Rules of the Road: Solving Unit Conversions

> **The steps to solving unit conversions:**
> 1. **List the given quantities & their units. Convert rates into fractions.** Also list the units you're answer will be in.
> 2. **Find how to cancel all the units except those you need in your answer.**
> 3. **Solve**.

Dimensional Analysis

All of you chemistry lovers, and haters, have spent some time doing dimensional analysis. It's an organized way to solve these problems and I prefer it because it always works and severely limits the likelihood of error.

To use dimensional analysis, we create a grid with two rows and as many columns as we need.

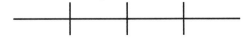

We fill in the grid with the units we have. To cancel units, we place the unit in the opposite box in the next column. If it's in the top, we put it in the bottom of the next column, and vice versa.

Unit 1	Unit 2	Unit 3	
	Unit 1	Unit 2	
~~Unit 1~~	~~Unit 2~~	Unit 3	Unit 3
	~~Unit 1~~	~~Unit 2~~	

There's a video on Unit Conversions.

The answer will be in terms of unit 3.

Example: Dimensional Analysis

1. Alexa made 100 posts on the Test Guy's Instagram. She makes an average of 1.5 posts per day. She spent an average of two hours per week on the posts. How many hours did it take to make all 100 posts?

Solve

This is a common format for an ACT unit conversion problem. We're given two *rates* and a quantity in single units. Start by listing your quantities and their units

Step 1: Make a list of your quantities and their units. Convert rates to fractions.

$$100 \text{ posts}, \frac{1.5 \, posts}{1 \, day}, \frac{2 \, hours}{1 \, week}, ? \, hours$$

Rates usually have the number in the numerator and 1 as the denominator.

Step 2: Make a grid and fill in your units to cancel.

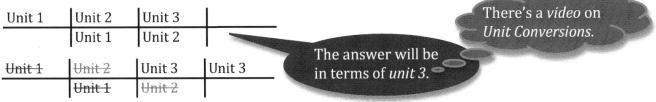

The rate is flipped so posts will cancel.

This rate isn't in the problem. We needed to convert days to weeks.

We can multiply all the way across the top & bottom, or do it step-by-step.

Step 3: Solve

Multiply Across

100 ~~posts~~	1 ~~day~~	1 ~~week~~	2 hours
	1.5 ~~posts~~	7 ~~day~~	1 ~~week~~

Multiply Across

$$\frac{100 \text{ posts}\;|\;1\text{ day}\;|\;1\text{ week}\;|\;2\text{ hours}}{\;\;\;\;\;\;\;\;\;\;\;|\;1.5\text{ posts}\;|\;7\text{ day}\;|\;1\text{ week}} = \frac{100 \times 2}{1.5 \times 7} = \frac{200}{10.5} = 19.05 \; hours$$

It will take Alexa ~19 hours to make the Instagram posts.

Dimensional analysis is not the only way to solve these problems. Some students "see" these problems right away and have no trouble. You may, however, consider this method or a similar formal setup. It's the best way to avoid confusion and missed points.

ACT Example: Units

1. A Boeing 747 at cruising speed burns one gallon of fuel per second. There are one thousand gallons of fuel remaining on board the aircraft, which is at its cruising speed of 567 miles per hour. Approximately how many miles can the 747 travel before it exhausts its fuel supply?

   A. 158 miles
   B. 9,450 miles
   C. 34 miles
   D. 863 miles
   E. 257 miles

Solve

We'll need to fill in a couple of conversions on this problem because we need to get from hours to seconds (or seconds to hours). I'm doing the problem by converting *miles per hour* to *miles per second*.

Step 1: Make a list of your givens with units

$$1 \frac{gallon}{second}, \; 1,000 \; gallons, \; 567 \frac{miles}{hours}$$

Step 2: Make a grid and fill in your units

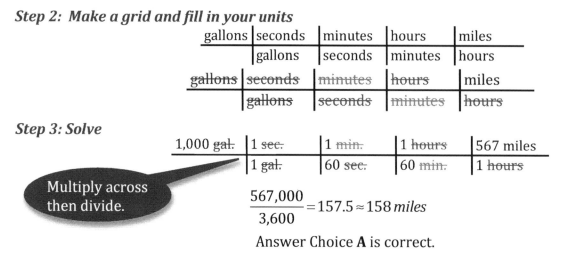

Step 3: Solve

1,000 ~~gal.~~	1 ~~sec.~~	1 ~~min.~~	1 ~~hours~~	567 miles
	1 ~~gal.~~	60 ~~sec.~~	60 ~~min.~~	1 ~~hours~~

Multiply across then divide.

$$\frac{567,000}{3,600} = 157.5 \approx 158 \; miles$$

Answer Choice **A** is correct.

Wrap Up

What You Need to Know
- ✓ How to find rates
- ✓ When and how to use proportions to solve rates
- ✓ How to deal with time problems by unit conversion & counting
- ✓ How to do multiple unit conversions

Videos

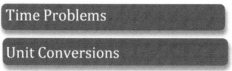

The Strategies
- ✓ Use a formal setup. Every second you spend on setting up the problem is two saved in solving it, not to mention the points you'll save.
- ✓ Approach time questions carefully and piece by piece.
- ✓ Set your rates as units in a fraction.

Related Skills
- ✓ Fractions

- ✓ Proportions

- ✓ Make an Equation

- ✓ Geometry word problems

1. Mario employs one person in his plumbing business, his brother Luigi. Luigi is a salaried employee, earning $40,000 per year in a 220-day work year. If Luigi calls in sick, Mario has a plumber from a temp agency fill-in for $100 for the day. If Luigi takes an unpaid sick day, and the temp fills in, how much money does Mario save?

   A. $109.58
   B. $9.58
   C. $81.82
   D. $181.82
   E. $100.00

2. One tablet of anti algae treatment treats 30 gallons of water. Each week the pond loses water to evaporation and must be refilled with 75 gallons of water and the new water must be treated. How many tablets would be a one-year supply?

   F. 104 tablets
   G. 52 tablets
   H. 365 tablets
   J. 130 tablets
   K. 21 tablets

3. Matt travels 20 miles in four hours and Norman travels twice as fast for six hours. How far did Norman travel?

   A. 15 miles
   B. 20 miles
   C. 30 miles
   D. 60 miles
   E. 120 miles

4. A pump fills a gallon swimming pool at 18 gallons per minute. If the pump requires six hours and 43 minutes to fill the pool, what is the capacity of the pool?

   F. 7,254 gallons
   G. 11,574 gallons
   H. 5,706 gallons
   J. 3,224 gallons
   K. 5,144 gallons

5. A Honda Civic averages 40 miles per gallon on the interstate. Alexa is driving the speed limit of 70 mph. The Civic has a 12-gallon gas tank. Approximately, how many hours does Alexa drive if her tank was full and she stops for gas with ¼ tank remaining?

   A. 15.75 hours
   B. 7 hours
   C. 6 hours
   D. 5 hours
   E. 21 hours

6. Half-hour broadcast television programs have a length of 18 minutes. The rest of that time is filled with commercials, and each commercial is 30-seconds in length. How many commercials are broadcast during two 30-minute television programs?

   F. 24 commercials
   G. 36 commercials
   H. 48 commercials
   J. 60 commercials
   K. 72 commercials

7. A kayak rental is charged by the hour or any part thereof. The first hour costs $5.50, the second hour costs $4.25, the third hour costs $3.75, and all subsequent hours cost $3.00. If Lenny rents a kayak at 10:03 a.m. and returns it at 4:14 p.m., how much does the rental cost?

   A. $21.00
   B. $22.50
   C. $18.00
   D. $25.50
   E. $28.50

8. There are 16 ounces in a pint, two pints in a quart, and four quarts in a gallon. If a gallon of milk costs $3.45 how much does milk cost per ounce, rounded to the nearest cent?

   F. $0.11
   G. $0.08
   H. $0.07
   J. $0.06
   K. $0.03

1. Mario employs one person in his plumbing business, his brother Luigi. Luigi is a salaried employee, earning $40,000 per year in a 220-day work year. If Luigi calls in sick, Mario has a plumber from a temp agency fill-in for $100 for the day. If Luigi takes an unpaid sick day, and the temp fills in, how much money does Mario save?

Correct Answer C

This is a rate problem that can be set up as a proportion, but because the ratio of Luigi's pay does *not* equal the temp's pay, you'll have an extra algebra step, it would look like this

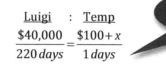

Solvable but there's an easier way

$$\underset{\dfrac{\$40,000}{220\,days}}{\text{Luigi}} = \underset{\dfrac{\$100+x}{1\,days}}{\text{Temp}}$$

__The Easy Way__

We're already given the rate of pay for the temp, $100\,\dfrac{dollars}{day}$.

We can find Luigi's daily rate by dividing his annual salary by the number of days he works.

$$\frac{40,000\,dollars}{220\,days} = 181.82\,\frac{dollars}{days}.$$

Subtract to find how much Mario will save.

$$181.82\,\frac{dollars}{day} - 100\,\frac{dollars}{day} = 81.82\,\frac{dollars}{day}$$

Answer choice **C** is correct.

__What You May Have Done Wrong__

A. You calculated Luigi's earnings based on a 365-day year & you forgot to subtract $100 to find the difference.
B. You calculated Luigi's earnings based on a 365-day year.
D. You correctly calculated Luigi's earnings, but you forgot to subtract $100.
E. Calculator error, check your inputs.

2. One tablet of anti algae treatment treats 30 gallons of water. Each week the pond loses water to evaporation and must be refilled with 75 gallons of water and the new water must be treated. How many tablets would be a one-year supply?

Correct Answer J

We can do this problem by dimensional analysis, or we could find the number of tablets per week (2.5) and multiply it by the number of weeks in a year (52). First, write up your givens and their units.

$$30\,\frac{gal.}{tablet},\ 75\,\frac{gal.}{week},\ 52\,\frac{weeks}{year}$$

__Mathematically__

We're looking for the number of tablets in a year, so find the number of tablets per week.

$$\frac{75\,gal./week}{30\,gal./tablet} = 2.5\,tablets/week\ \rightarrow\ 2.5\,\frac{tablets}{week}\cdot 52\,\frac{weeks}{year} = 130\,\frac{tablets}{year}$$

__Dimensional Analysis__

Arrange the units so they will cancel, multiply across both the top & bottom and then divide the top by the bottom.

$$\left.\begin{array}{c|c|c}\dfrac{75\ \cancel{gal.}}{1\ \cancel{week}} & \dfrac{1\ tablet}{30\ \cancel{gal.}} & \dfrac{52\ \cancel{weeks}}{1\ year}\end{array}\right| \ \rightarrow\ \frac{75\bullet 52}{30} = \frac{3,900}{30} = 130\,tablets$$

Answer choice **J** is correct.

__What You May Have Done Wrong__

F. Check your inputs, this is probably a calculation error.
G. You probably guessed, or multiplied then divided by 30 gallons.
H. Review your steps, you may have tried to convert to days instead of weeks.
K. You flipped your fraction, inputting so that each tablet treated 75 gallons instead of 30 gallons.

3. Matt travels 20 miles in four hours and Norman travels twice as fast for six hours. How far did Norman travel?

Correct Answer D

We'll need to use Matt's rate to find Norman's rate (speed) and then multiply Norman's speed by how long he travels (6 hours) to find how far Norman travels.

Matt's speed = $\dfrac{20\,miles}{4\,hours}=5\,\dfrac{miles}{hours}$

Norman's speed = $5\,\dfrac{miles}{hours}\cdot 2=10\,\dfrac{miles}{hours}$

Norman's distance = $10\,\dfrac{miles}{hours}\cdot 6\,hours=60\,miles$

Answer choice **D** is correct

<u>What You May Have Done Wrong</u>

    A. You may have had Norman traveling at *half* of Matt's speed, 2.5 mph.

    B. That's Matt's distance. Norman travels *twice* as fast and for a different length of time.

    C. You either made a mistake with the length of time Norman traveled or you used Matt's speed, 5 mph.

    E. You used Matt's distance as Norman's rate.

4. A pump fills a gallon swimming pool at 18 gallons per minute. If the pump requires six hours and 43 minutes to fill the pool, what is the capacity of the pool?

Correct Answer F

You can solve this problem in a few ways. You can use a *proportion* because the ratios of gallons/time should equal gallons/time. You could also use *dimensional analysis* (it's trickier though).

<u>Dimensional Analysis</u>

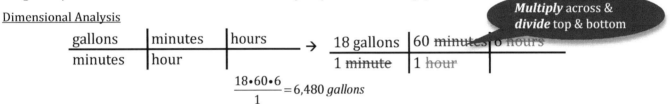

Multiply across & *divide* top & bottom

$\dfrac{18\cdot 60\cdot 6}{1}=6{,}480\ gallons$

We'll have to add a second grid, to cover the 43 minutes. The 43 minutes is added, and dimensional analysis is incapable of working with addition. You could, however, convert hours to minutes ahead of time.

$\dfrac{18\ gallons}{1\ \cancel{minute}}\ \bigg|\ \dfrac{43\ \cancel{minutes}}{}$ → 774 gallons.

6,480 gallons + 774 gallons = 7,254 gallons

<u>Proportion</u>

I think this is the much easier way to solve the problem. You will, however, have to convert hours to minutes first.

$6\ hours\cdot 60\ \dfrac{minutes}{hour}=360\ minutes$

For proportion, we'll need to **convert hours to minutes first**

360 minutes + 43 minutes = 403 minutes

Set up your ratios:

    <u>Minutes</u> : <u>Gallons</u>

        1   :   18

     403 : x

Make fractions, set equal, and cross-multiply:

$\dfrac{1}{403}=\dfrac{18}{x}$ → $x=7{,}254$

Answer choice **F** is correct.

<u>What You May Have Done Wrong:</u>

    G. You made an input error. You set it up as 100 minutes per hour.

    H. You made a math error. You correctly calculated that 6 hours = 360 minutes but you subtracted the 43 minutes when you needed to add.

    J. You made a math error. Check your gallons per minute.

    K. You made a math error. Check your gallons per minute *and* your ours to minutes conversion.

5. A Honda Civic averages 40 miles per gallon on the interstate. Alexa is driving the speed limit of 70 mph. The Civic has a 12-gallon gas tank. Approximately, how many hours does Alexa drive if her tank was full and she stops for gas with ¼ tank remaining?

Correct Answer D

This is a unit conversion problem. We've got to get to *hours* and we'll have to start with *gallons*. The trick to this problem is to make sure you get the right amount of gas used. Alexa starts with a full tank and she stops with 1/4ᵗʰ a tank, so she uses ¾ᵗʰˢ of a tank.

$$1\,\text{tank} - \frac{1}{4}\,\text{tank} = \frac{3}{4}\,\text{tank} = 9\,\text{gallons}$$

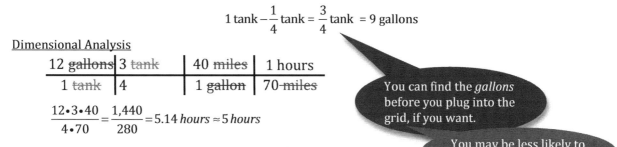

Dimensional Analysis

12 ~~gallons~~	3 ~~tank~~	40 ~~miles~~	1 hours
1 ~~tank~~	4	1 ~~gallon~~	70 ~~miles~~

$$\frac{12 \cdot 3 \cdot 40}{4 \cdot 70} = \frac{1{,}440}{280} = 5.14\,hours \approx 5\,hours$$

You can find the *gallons* before you plug into the grid, if you want.

You may be less likely to make an error that way.

Answer choice **D** is correct.

What You May Have Done Wrong
  A. You multiplied 70 by 9, which would give you how far Alexa would drive in 9 hours. Essentially, you flipped your 40 and your 70.
  B. You used 12 gallons (the full tank) instead of 9 gallons.
  C. You either made a calculator error or rounded up.
  E. You flipped your 40 & 70 *and* also used a full tank.

6. Half-hour broadcast television programs have a length of 18 minutes. The rest of that time is filled with commercials, and each commercial is 30-seconds in length. How many commercials are broadcast during two 30-minute television programs?

Correct Answer H

You can solve this problem by *proportion* (just remember to double your answer) or by *dimensional analysis*.

Proportion
  Before you started you'll need to find how much time, per half hour, is commercials.
$$30\,minutes - 18\,minutes = 12\,minutes$$

  You'll also need to do a unit conversion, turning 12 minutes into seconds.
$$12\,minutes \cdot 60 \frac{seconds}{minutes} = 360\,seconds$$

  Now we can set up the proportion.
$$\frac{1\,commercial}{30\,seconds} = \frac{x\,commercial}{360\,seconds}$$

Or you could say 2 commercials *per* minute

  Cross-multiply, solve, and then double the result (to account for both shows).
$$360\,seconds \cdot commercial = 30x\,seconds \cdot commercial$$
$$x = 24\,commercials$$
$$24\,commercials \cdot 2 = 48\,commercials$$

Dimensional Analysis
  We can run the whole problem through dimensional analysis. This is a great problem for dimensional analysis.

1 commercial	60 ~~seconds~~	12 ~~minute~~	2 ~~shows~~
30 ~~seconds~~	1 ~~minute~~	1 ~~shows~~	

$$\rightarrow \frac{60 \cdot 12 \cdot 2}{30} = \frac{1{,}440}{30} = 48\,commercials$$

Answer **H** is correct.

What You May Have Done Wrong
  F. This is one show, not two.
  G. You used 18 minutes instead of 12 *and* you didn't find the value for two shows.
  J. This is a calculator error.
  K. You used 18 minutes instead of 12.

7. A kayak rental is charged by the hour or any part thereof. The first hour costs $5.50, the second hour costs $4.25, the third hour costs $3.75, and all subsequent hours cost $3.00. If Lenny rents a kayak at 10:03 a.m. and returns it at 4:14 p.m., how much does the rental cost?

Correct Answer D

This is a counting problem. We've got to count the hours, match those to the prices, and add the costs. I like to solve these by just counting up the hours, it's simple and it's hard to make an error. First, count up your hours:

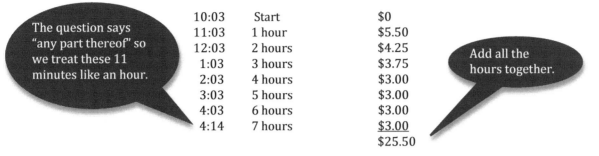

10:03	Start	$0
11:03	1 hour	$5.50
12:03	2 hours	$4.25
1:03	3 hours	$3.75
2:03	4 hours	$3.00
3:03	5 hours	$3.00
4:03	6 hours	$3.00
4:14	7 hours	$3.00
		$25.50

The question says "any part thereof" so we treat these 11 minutes like an hour.

Add all the hours together.

Answer **D** is correct.

What You May Have Done Wrong
- **A.** You used $3.00 an hour for all of the hours.
- **B.** You left off the last hour. Every part of an hour is treated like an hour.
- **C.** You used $3.00 an hour for all of the hours *and* you only counted six hours.
- **E.** You counted too many hours (8) instead of seven.

8. There are 16 ounces in a pint, two pints in a quart, and four quarts in a gallon. If a gallon of milk costs $3.45 how much does milk cost per ounce, rounded to the nearest cent?

Correct Answer K

This is a lengthy unit conversion problem and is best done using *dimensional analysis*.

$$\frac{3.45 \text{ dollars}}{1 \text{ gallons}} \cdot \frac{1 \text{ gallons}}{4 \text{ quarts}} \cdot \frac{1 \text{ quarts}}{2 \text{ pints}} \cdot \frac{1 \text{ pints}}{16 \text{ ounces}}$$

$$\frac{3.45}{4 \cdot 2 \cdot 16} = \frac{3.45}{128} = \$0.027 \approx \$0.03$$

Answer **K** is correct.

What You May Have Done Wrong
- **F.** You used one quart instead of two. Meaning, you made 1 quart = $3.45
- **G.** This is a calculation error, review your steps.
- **H.** This is a calculation error, review your steps.
- **J.** You doubled the cost. Most likely you miscalculated the number of ounces in a gallon as 64 instead of 128.

Introduction

Every test has at least one (and usually two or more) percentage problem *and* percentages are a key skill because they show up in other question types. For the most part, percentages are straightforward, but the ACT can write some devilishly difficult percentage questions. ***Percent problems reward solid setup.***

What You Need to Know

- ✓ The fundamental percent formula
- ✓ How to translate word problems into actionable steps
- ✓ How to find percent, part, and whole
- ✓ How to deal with discounts and increases
- ✓ How to do multiple-step word problems
- ✓ The percent change formula

Definition: Percents

Percentages are a rate, amount, or number in terms of 100.

$$percentages = \frac{rate, amount, or number}{100}$$

> *Per* is a dividing line.

Percent means *per hundred*. There are a 100 years in a **cent**ury, and 100 **cents** in a dollar.

Percents can be greater than 100 unless we're dealing with a ***portion*** or a ***probability***. Portions & probability are between 0% & 100%.

We **can't** have 150% of high school juniors
We **can't** have a 200% chance of rain.

Percents can only be ***negative*** when we're dealing with ***percent change***.

We **can** have a -8% change in sales from last year to this year
We **can't** have a -25% of high school juniors. -40% chance or rain.

The Percent Equation

There are three ways to write the equation, but I like this one best.

$$part = percent \bullet whole$$

The trickiest part for most test takers is telling *part* from *whole*.

Telling Part from Whole

The Whole

The ***whole*** is *multiplied* by the ***percent***. When looking for a percentage the ***whole*** is the *denominator*. Think of the ***whole*** as ***before*** the ***percent*** is applied. Here's some common phrases that indicate ***whole***.
- ✓ "whole" was before
- ✓ of "whole" ← past tense verb
- ✓ total

There's a video on *percent word problems*

Examples: Using the Percent Formula
  1. 10% of 50 is what number?
      part = % x *whole*
      part = (0.10)(50) → *part* = 5

  2. 40 is 50% of what number?
      part = % x *whole*
      $40 = (0.50)(whole) \rightarrow whole = \dfrac{40}{0.50} \rightarrow 80$

Discounts & Increases

Often the ACT has "real world" problems where we deal with discounts and increases.

> Words like *sale, discount, decrease,* and *off* indicate a **discount.**
> Words like *increase, grows, tax,* or *expands* indicate an **increase.**

The formula and the math don't change, but we have to be pickier about percent. Let's look at an example:

Examples: Using the Percent Formula
  1. The official Test Guy bomber jacket was $100 before it was placed on sale for 20% off. How much does the jacket cost?

Solve
  You'll see we've got a couple of the phrases that indicate *whole*. $100 is **whole.**
              *Jacket **was** $100 **before***

Let's look at percent. 20% off means we discount the original price by 20%. We can do this in one or two steps.

The One-Step Method
  We find the percent increase or decrease based on 100%. For this problem, we have a 20% discount, so we subtract (we add for increase).

$$100\% - 20\% = 80\%$$

  Now we just plug into the formula and solve.
  $part = percent \cdot whole \quad \rightarrow \quad part = 80\% \cdot \$100$
  $part = \$80$

I much prefer this method. Not only does it save a step, but also the "two-step" method doesn't work on some problems.

The Two-Step Method
  This is the most common way people solve this problem. We find the amount of the discount and then subtract that from the original price. If it were an increase, we'd find the amount of the increase and then add it to the original value.
  $part = percent \cdot whole \quad \rightarrow \quad part = 20\% \cdot \$100$
  $part = \$20$

$$\$100 - \$20 = \$80$$

ACT Example: Discounts & Increases

1. A car is priced at 14,000 dollars. The sales tax on the purchase of the car is 7%. What is the total price of the car, including tax?

   A. $14,980
   B. $13,020
   C. $23,800
   D. $23,980
   E. $17,980

Solve

This is an increase question. We've got a *tax,* which is in *addition* to the price of the car.

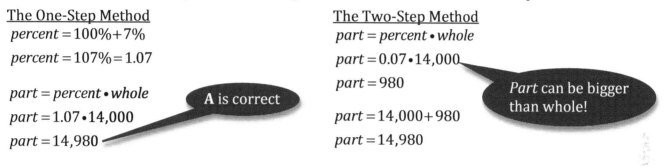

The One-Step Method

$percent = 100\% + 7\%$

$percent = 107\% = 1.07$

$part = percent \cdot whole$

$part = 1.07 \cdot 14,000$

$part = 14,980$

A is correct

The Two-Step Method

$part = percent \cdot whole$

$part = 0.07 \cdot 14,000$

$part = 980$

Part can be bigger than whole!

$part = 14,000 + 980$

$part = 14,980$

ACT Examples: Discounts & Increases

2. A projector is on sale for 25% off and has a sale price of $300. What was the original price of the projector?

   A. $400
   B. $225
   C. $75
   D. $1,200
   E. $600

Solve

This is a *discount* question because the projector is on sale. It's also a question where we need to find the whole.

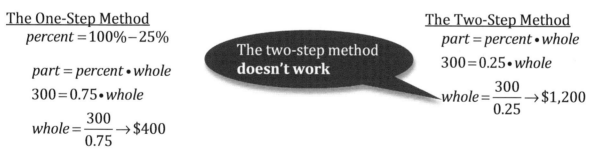

The One-Step Method

$percent = 100\% - 25\%$

$part = percent \cdot whole$

$300 = 0.75 \cdot whole$

$whole = \dfrac{300}{0.75} \rightarrow \$400$

The two-step method **doesn't work**

The Two-Step Method

$part = percent \cdot whole$

$300 = 0.25 \cdot whole$

$whole = \dfrac{300}{0.25} \rightarrow \$1,200$

Answer Choice **A** is correct.

Two-Step Percent Problems

The ACT likes percent questions with two parts. In general, best to do one part and then the second. The trick is knowing which part to start with and then doing both parts correctly.

Rules of the Road: Two-Part Percent Problems

<u>Steps to Solving</u>
1. **Figure out where to start.** Start where you have *two of three components: part, whole, &/or percent.* Don't hesitate to break the question down into **statements**.
2. **Complete the first step.**
3. **Setup the second step using the first step's answer.** Be careful, *part* can become *whole* and *whole* can become *part*

ACT Example: Two-Part Percent Problems

Setup is incredibly important

1. If 10 is 20% of a number, then what is 200% of that number?

   A. 200
   B. 100
   C. 80
   D. 50
   E. 40

Check out the *video* on *two-step % problems*

Solve

Let's find where we have two numbers. To do that, let's break down the question into statements.

Statement 1: If 10 is 20% of a number...

There are two numbers here. So this is where to start.

Statement 2: ...then what is 200% of that number?

There's only one number and two missing components

<u>Starting with statement 1:</u>

Statement 1: If 10 is 20% of a number...

$$part = percent \cdot whole$$

"10 is" is the *part.*

$$10 = 20\% \cdot whole \quad \rightarrow \quad whole = \frac{10}{0.20} \rightarrow 50$$

Statement 2: ...then what is 200% of that number?

$$part = percent \cdot whole$$

"what is" means we're looking for *part.*

$$10 = 200\% \cdot 50 \quad \rightarrow \quad part = 2.0 \cdot 50 \rightarrow 100$$

Answer Choice **B** is correct.

2. The revenue of the Test Guy's hoverboard business has dramatically increased in the last three years. Every year, revenue has grown by 40%. If the hoverboard business had 10 million in revenue in the first year, what was the revenue in the third year?

A. 14
B. 19.6
C. 18
D. 22
E. 17.7

On word problems like this, it's often easiest to make a diagram.

This problem will need to be done in two steps. The **part** in the first step becomes the **whole** of the second.

Solve

First, let's look at the statements.

Statement 1: Every year revenue has grown by 40%!

Statement 1 tells us that revenue *increases* by 40% from year 1 to year 2 **and** another 40% from year 2 to year 3.

Statement 2: ...the hoverboard business had 10 million dollars in revenue in the first year.

Now, we know the hoverboard business had 10 million in revenue *before* it grew by 40% in the second year. That means 10 million will be a *whole* in our first equation. Because revenue "had", revenue will be our *whole*.

Statement 3: ...what was revenue in the third year?

The question wants to know the revenue in the third year. To do that, we'll first need the revenue from the second year.

Let's make a diagram:

+40%   +40%

First Year ➤ Second Year ➤ Third Year
10 million

This is an *increase problem*, so we'll want to add 40% to 100% and use that as our percent.

$$percent = 100\% + 40\% \quad \rightarrow \quad percent = 140\%$$

First Year → Second Year

$$part = percent \cdot whole$$
$$part = (100\% + 40\%) \cdot 10$$
$$part = 1.4 \cdot 10 \rightarrow 14$$

The most commonly made mistake is to add another 4 million to get year 3. The starting point (the **whole**) of years 2 → 3 is 14, not 10

Second Year → Third Year

+40%   +40%

First Year ➤ Second Year ➤ Third Year
10 million   **14 million**

The **part** from the last step is the **whole** here.

The **percent** is the same

$$part = percent \cdot whole \quad \rightarrow \quad part = (100\% + 40\%) \cdot 14$$
$$part = 1.4 \cdot 14 \rightarrow 19.6$$

Depending on your math knowledge, you may have a different way to solve the problem. **When percent increases/decreases are the same over time you can use exponential growth/decay.** Exponential growth/decay is used to calculate compound interest, but can be used anytime the growth or decay rate remains constant over time periods.

$$part = whole \cdot (percent)^{time\ periods} \quad \rightarrow \quad part = 10 \cdot (1.40)^2 = 19.6$$

While it's a great way to solve problems, don't bother memorizing it if it's unfamiliar to you. This particular type of problem isn't common enough to warrant memorizing something else.

Answer Choice B is correct.

ACT Example: Two-Part Percent Problems (part of a part of a part)

3. Test Guy Labs is filing a patent for a super soldier serum the lab developed. In the patent paperwork they detail the results of a trial involving 1,000 volunteers. There was no effect in 70% of the volunteers. Of volunteers that experienced an effect, 20% had enhanced endurance. How many volunteers received enhanced endurance?

    A. 140
    B. 50
    C. 60
    D. 35
    E. 300

Solve

This is a really longwinded problem that requires us to find a part from a part. This question involves multiple statements; let's take a look:

Statement 1: ...a trial involving 1,000 volunteers.
    Statement 1 provides the *whole*. *All* of the individuals tested equaled 1,000.

Statement 2: In 70% of the volunteers there was no effect.
    Statement 2 tells us that of the volunteers (1,000) that there was no effect. Since we are interested in the individuals that had an effect this is a ***discount*** percentage.

Statement 3: Of volunteers that experienced an effect, 20% had enhanced endurance only.
    Statement 3 tells us that of all the volunteers that had an effect (the *part* of the previous question) 20% had enhanced endurance.

Let's diagram it, start with volunteers and calculate the number of volunteers affected.

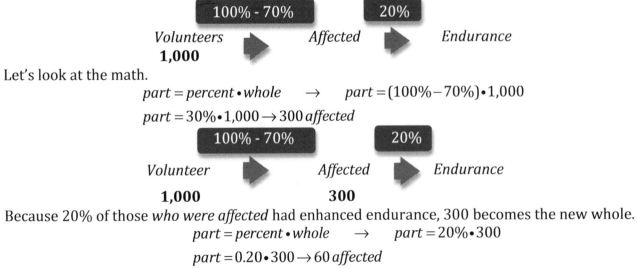

Let's look at the math.

$$part = percent \cdot whole \quad \rightarrow \quad part = (100\% - 70\%) \cdot 1,000$$
$$part = 30\% \cdot 1,000 \rightarrow 300\ affected$$

Because 20% of those *who were affected* had enhanced endurance, 300 becomes the new whole.

$$part = percent \cdot whole \quad \rightarrow \quad part = 20\% \cdot 300$$
$$part = 0.20 \cdot 300 \rightarrow 60\ affected$$

Answer choice C is correct.

4. A number of high school juniors join the Future Math Book Writers of America (it's really cool). Among these members 10% are elected to the executive committee and 2% of the executive committee are elected to four national offices. How many juniors are members of the club?

    A. 300
    B. 200
    C. 400
    D. 1,000
    E. 2,000

Solve

    Again, we have multiple statements so let's examine each statement.

Statement 1: A number of high school juniors join....
    Statement 1 is an early indication that we will be looking for total membership in the club. Generally, but not always, the phrase "a number" refers to something that we will need to solve for.

Statement 2: Among these members 10% are elected to the executive committee.
    We are given a percentage but no part or whole. We can't solve here. We can summarize this as, *10% x members = executive committee.*

Statement 3: 2% of the executive committee are elected to four national offices.
    Statement 3 finally gives us two components to work with. "2% of" tells us the executive committee is the *whole* and needs solved for.

We're working backwards, from national officers to total members (from *part* of a *part*, to *part*, to *whole*), but I would still organize the diagram from large to small.

10%   **2%**

Members      *Executive Committee*   *National Officers*
                                                     4

<u>Executive Committee → National Officers</u>
    Because *national officers* are a *part* of the *executive committee*, 4 is our part.

$$part = percent \cdot whole \quad \rightarrow \quad 4 = 2\% \cdot whole$$

$$whole = \frac{4}{2\%} \rightarrow \frac{4}{0.02} \quad \rightarrow \quad whole = 200$$

10%   **2%**

Members   *Executive Committee*   *National Officers*
                       200   **4**

<u>Executive Committee → National Officers</u>
    Because the *executive committee* are a *part of the members*, 200 is our *part*.

$$part = percent \cdot whole \quad \rightarrow \quad 200 = 10\% \cdot whole$$

$$whole = \frac{200}{10\%} \rightarrow \frac{200}{0.10} \quad \rightarrow \quad whole = 2,000$$

Answer choice **E** is correct.

Percent Change

Percent change often shows up on the ACT. You've probably used it in lab sciences, but students have a hard time remembering it. I think it's better to know the percent change formula, but you can use the other method.

Rules of the Road: The Ways to Calculate Percent Change

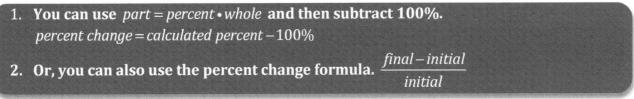

1. **You can use** $part = percent \cdot whole$ **and then subtract 100%.**
   $percent\ change = calculated\ percent - 100\%$

2. **Or, you can also use the percent change formula.** $\dfrac{final - initial}{initial}$

ACT Example: Percent Change

1. Sam grew from 20.5 inches to 23 inches. Approximately, what was the percent change in her height?

   A. 12%
   B. 89%
   C. 112%
   D. 32%
   E. 61%

   There's a video on percent change

Solve

This is a straightforward percent change problem. She grew *from* 20.5 inches, making 20.5 the *initial*. Her *final* height is 23.

$$\frac{23 - 20.5}{20.5} \rightarrow \frac{2.5}{20.5} \rightarrow 12.2\%$$

Or, we can calculate *what percentage* 23 is of 20.5

$$part = percent \cdot whole \quad \rightarrow \quad 23 = percent \cdot 20.5$$

$$percent = \frac{23}{20.5} \rightarrow 112.2\% \quad \rightarrow \quad 112.2\% - 100\% = 12.2\%$$

Subtract the 100% from the percent calculated.

Answer choice **A** is correct

<u>Wrap Up</u>

What You Need to Know
- ✓ The fundamental percent formula
- ✓ How to translate word problems into actionable steps
- ✓ How to find percent, part, and whole
- ✓ How to deal with discounts and increases
- ✓ How to do multiple-step word problems
- ✓ The percent change formula

Videos

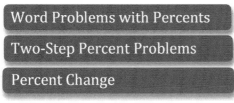

Word Problems with Percents

Two-Step Percent Problems

Percent Change

The Strategies
- ✓ Use a formal setup, especially with word problems.
- ✓ Break complicated questions down into statements.
- ✓ Rely on your basic formulas; don't muscle your way through.

Key Skill
- ✓ Probability
- ✓ Decimals
- ✓ Fractions

1. 35 is 90% of what number?

    A. 38.89
    B. 31.50
    C. 35.90
    D. 38.50
    E. 32.50

2. An inkjet cartridge costs $22.00. It is on sale for 20% off. How much does the ink cartridge cost?

    F. $18.60
    G. $17.60
    H. $4.40
    J. $26.40
    K. $110.00

3. Tuition at US colleges increases at a rate of 10% per year. Justin is a freshman and his first year tuition is $25,000. What will his tuition be for his junior year?

    A. $30,250
    B. $27,500
    C. $30,000
    D. $31,250
    E. $28,500

4. After taxes, Alexa won a million dollar on Jeopardy. She paid taxes of thirty percent. Approximately how much were her winnings before taxes?

    F. $700,000
    G. $3,333,000
    H. $1,645,000
    J. $1,420,000
    K. $1,300,000

5. In psychological licensing, students must pass a written exam and students who pass the written exam then take an oral exam. 70% of students pass the written exam. 30% of students who pass the written exam pass the oral exam. In a sample of 100 students how many can you expect to pass both the written and the oral exam?

    A. 70
    B. 9
    C. 0
    D. 21
    E. 43

6. 35% of Stark Enterprise's Avengers budget is capital expenditures. Of this portion 15% goes to the frequent repair and periodic improvement of Stark Tower. If Tony Stark spent 10 million dollars on repairs and improvements to Stark Tower last year, how much is the total Avengers budget?

    F. 18.10 million
    G. 190.48 million
    H. 66.67 million
    J. 23.33 million
    K. 4.28 million

7. Last year, the population of Athens, a town of 1,021 acres, was 1,024 people. This year the population is 924 people. By what percentage did the population change?

    A. -9.5%
    B. 9.8%
    C. 9.5%
    D. -9.8%
    E. 0.3%

8. Sales of widgets increased from 5,000 units to 7,000 units in one year. The next year they increased from 7,000 to 8,500 units. What was the average percent change?

    F. 30.7%
    G. 70%
    H. 35%
    J. 20%
    K. 61.4%

Percentages: Solutions

1. **35 is 90% of what number?**

Correct Answer A

The trick of this problem is realizing that 35 is the *part* not the whole. Remember, "is" and other present tense verbs usually indicate *part*. 35 *is* 90% means that 35 *is part*.

$$part = percent \cdot whole \quad \rightarrow \quad 35 = 90\% \cdot whole$$

$$whole = \frac{35}{0.90} = 38.89$$

Answer choice **A** is correct.

<u>What You May Have Done Wrong</u>
- **B.** You treated 35 as the *whole*.
- **C.** You added 0.9 to 35 or made a calculator error.
- **D.** You added 10% of 35 to 35, making 110% of 35, which is not the same as 35 *is* 90%. This is the most common error.
- **E.** You probably made a calculator error

2. **An inkjet cartridge cost $22.00. It is on sale for 20% off. How much does the ink cartridge cost?**

Correct Answer G

This is a discount problem. We've got to find out how much the cartridge costs after the discount.

First, let's change the percent.

$$100\% - 20\% = 80\%$$

I'm only showing this in one-step, because you need to learn the method.

Now that we've changed the percent, we can plug in $22.00 for the *whole* and 0.80 for the *percent*.

$$part = percent \cdot whole \quad \rightarrow \quad part = 80\% \cdot 22.00$$
$$whole = 17.60$$

The sale price of the printer cartridge is $17.60

Answer choice **G** is correct.

<u>What You May Have Done Wrong</u>
- **F.** You probably made a calculation error.
- **H.** You calculated 20%, but this is a *discount* of 20%.
- **J.** You went the wrong direction, increasing the price by 20%
- **K.** You divided $22.00 by 20%.

3. Tuition at US colleges increases at a rate of 10% per year. Justin is a freshman and his first year tuition is $25,000. What will his tuition be for his junior year?

Correct Answer A

This is a multiple percentage problem. We've got to show the increase in tuition from freshmen to sophomore year and then from sophomore year to junior year. It's also an increase problem.

Two-Step Method

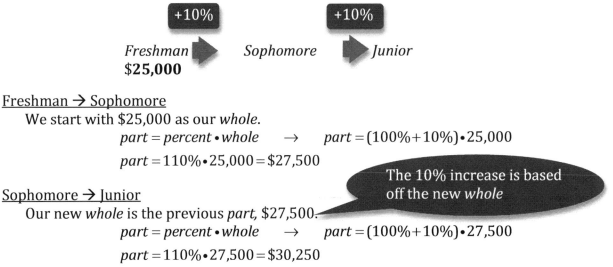

Freshman → Sophomore
We start with $25,000 as our *whole*.
$$part = percent \cdot whole \quad \rightarrow \quad part = (100\% + 10\%) \cdot 25,000$$
$$part = 110\% \cdot 25,000 = \$27,500$$

The 10% increase is based off the new *whole*

Sophomore → Junior
Our new *whole* is the previous *part*, $27,500.
$$part = percent \cdot whole \quad \rightarrow \quad part = (100\% + 10\%) \cdot 27,500$$
$$part = 110\% \cdot 27,500 = \$30,250$$

One Step Method

We can do this problem in one step. Multiple percentages can be dealt with by multiplying the percents together.

College Tuition increases 10% per year
The change is +10% per year, or 110%

We're concerned with two years, so we can write our formula like this.
$$part = percent \cdot whole \quad \rightarrow \quad part = (110\% \cdot 110\%) \cdot whole$$
$$part = (110\% \cdot 110\%) \cdot 25,000 \quad \rightarrow \quad part = 121\% \cdot 25,000 \rightarrow \$30,250$$

Exponential Method

Whenever the change in percents is the same (here it's +10% for both years), we can raise the percent to a power.
$$part = percent \cdot whole \quad \rightarrow \quad part = (110\% \cdot 110\%) \cdot whole$$
$$part = whole \cdot (percent)^{time} \quad \rightarrow \quad part = 25,000 \cdot (110\%)^{2} \rightarrow \$30,250$$

Answer choice **A** is correct

We can rewrite this as $(110\%)^2$

What You May Have Done Wrong
- **B.** This is the halfway answer; it's sophomore year's tuition.
- **C.** You added the initial increase $2,500 twice. The second 10% increase will be based on $27,500.
- **D.** You may have read the answer choice carelessly or made a calculator error.
- **E.** This is a calculation error; review your steps.

4. After taxes, Alexa won a million dollar on Jeopardy. She paid taxes of thirty percent. Approximately how much were her winnings before taxes?

Correct Answer J

This is a straightforward percent problem. The first step is identifying whether 1 million is the *part* or the *whole*. Because it's "after taxes" 1 million will be the part. This is also a discount problem. Taxes are a discount; they reduce value. We'll need to treat the percentage properly. Now we can plug-in and solve.

I drop the zeroes to make the math

$$part = percent \cdot whole \quad \rightarrow \quad 1 = (100\% - 30\%) \cdot whole$$

$$1 = 70\% \cdot whole \quad \rightarrow \quad whole = \frac{1}{0.70} \rightarrow 1.42 \quad \rightarrow \quad whole = 1,420,000$$

Answer choice **J** is correct.

<u>What You May Have Done Wrong:</u>
   F. You treated one million as the whole.
   G. You used 30% as the percent, which would be a tax rate of 70%
   H. This is a calculation error.
   K. You found 30% of a million and added it to 1 million.

5. In psychological licensing, students must pass a written exam and students who pass the written exam then take an oral exam. 70% of students pass the written exam. 30% of students who pass the written exam pass the oral exam. In a sample of 100 students how many can you expect to pass both the written and the oral exam?

Correct Answer D

This is a multiple percentage problem and it's really wordy so it can be pretty confusing. We're given a total and we'll have to find a part of a part. In this problem, we don't need to change the percents.

Two-Step Method

Students	70%	Written Test	30%	Oral Exam
100				

<u>Students → Written Test</u>
   Students will be the *whole*.
$$part = percent \cdot whole \quad \rightarrow \quad part = 70\% \cdot 100 \rightarrow 70$$

<u>Written Test → Oral Exam</u>
   The students who passed the written exam is our *whole*. The *part* from the last step has become the *whole*.
$$part = percent \cdot whole \quad \rightarrow \quad part = 30\% \cdot 70 \rightarrow 21$$

One Step Method
   Even though the percents are different, we can still multiply them together to make this a one step problem.
$$part = percent \cdot whole \quad \rightarrow \quad part = (70\% \cdot 30\%) \cdot 100 \quad \rightarrow \quad part = 21\% \cdot 100 \rightarrow 21 \, students$$

Answer choice **D** is correct.

<u>What You May Have Done Wrong</u>
   A. This is the halfway answer, the number of students who passed the written exam.
   B. You set it up so that 30% of students pass the written exam (100% - 30%)
   C. You subtracted 70 & 30 from 100. The *part* of 30% is not based on a *whole* of 100.
   E. You divided 100 by 70%.

6. 35% of Stark Enterprise's Avengers budget is capital expenditures. Of this portion 15% goes to the frequent repair and periodic improvement of Stark Tower. If Tony Stark spent 10 million dollars on repairs and improvements to Stark Tower last year, how much is the total Avengers budget?

Correct Answer G

This is a really convoluted problem and it's a good example of why diagramming is so helpful. Let's take a look.

This problem is a *part* of a *part* but we're working backwards.

Two-Step Method

<u>Capital Expenditure → Repair & Improvement</u>

We need to get 10 million *is* 15%, so 10 million *is* a *part*.

$$part = percent \cdot whole \quad \rightarrow \quad 10 = 15\% \cdot whole$$

$$whole = \frac{10}{0.15} \rightarrow 66.67 \, million$$

<u>Capital Expenditure → Repair & Improvement</u>

66.67 million *is* 35% of the budget, so 66.67 million *is* the *part*.

$$part = percent \cdot whole \quad \rightarrow \quad 66.67 = 35\% \cdot whole$$

$$whole = \frac{66.67}{0.35} \rightarrow 190.48 \, million$$

One Step Method

Doing it in one step feels tricky, but it's actually the same steps we always follow to do a multiple percentage problem in one step.

$$part = percent \cdot whole \quad \rightarrow \quad 10 = \left(15\% \cdot 35\%\right) \cdot whole$$

$$10 = \left(5.25\%\right) \cdot whole \quad \rightarrow \quad whole = \frac{10}{0.0525} \rightarrow 190.48 \, million$$

Answer **G** is correct.

<u>What You May Have Done Wrong</u>

F. You subtracted the percents and divided 10 million by 85% and 65%.

H. This is the halfway answer, the capital expenditures budget.

J. You multiplied by 35%, instead of dividing.

K. You multiplied by 15%, instead of dividing.

7. Last year, the population of Athens, a town of 1,021 acres, was 1,024 people. This year the population is 924 people. By what percentage did the population change?

Correct Answer D

There's an extra piece of information in the problem. We've got how many acres are in the town, 1,021 acres. We don't care about the size of the town. This is a good example of why you should either break out your quantities (I prefer this) or underline the quantities you'll need to use. You can calculate percent change in two ways.

You can use *part = percent • whole* to find what percent 924 is of 1,024.

$$part = percent \cdot whole \quad \rightarrow \quad 924 = percent \cdot 1,024$$

$$percent = \frac{924}{1,024} \rightarrow 90.2\%$$

To complete the problem, we have to subtract 100% from our *final* percentage, 90.2%.

$$90.2\% - 100\% \approx -9.8\%$$

I prefer using (and learning) the percent change formula.

$$\frac{final\ value - initial\ value}{initial\ value} \quad \rightarrow \quad \frac{924 - 1,024}{1,024} \quad \rightarrow \quad \frac{100}{1,024} \approx -9.8\%$$

Answer choice **D** is correct.

<u>What You May Have Done Wrong</u>
  A. You used the acreage of the town (1,021) instead of the initial population.
  B. You have the correct percent, but the percent change in this problem is negative
  C. You used the acreage of the town (1,021) instead of the initial population. You also calculated a positive percentage.
  E. You calculated the percentage using the acreage of the town (1,021) divided by the initial population.

8. Sales of widgets increased from 5,000 units to 7,000 units in one year. The next year they increased from 7,000 to 8,500 units. What was the average percent change?

Correct Answer F

This is another percent change problem, but it's got an extra step. We'll have to average the two percent changes together.

<u>First Year to Second Year</u>

$$\frac{final - initial}{initial} \rightarrow \frac{7,000 - 5,000}{5,000} \rightarrow 40\%$$

<u>Second Year to Third Year</u>

$$\frac{final - initial}{initial} \rightarrow \frac{8,500 - 7,000}{7,000} \rightarrow 21.4\%$$

Now we average the two together.

$$average = \frac{sum}{number} \quad \rightarrow \quad average = \frac{0.40 + 0.214}{2} \rightarrow 30.7\%$$

Answer choice **F** is correct.

<u>What You May Have Done Wrong</u>
  G. You found the percent change over both years, not the average.
  H. You found the percent change over both years, and then divided by 2.
  J. That's percent change for the first year you then divided it by 2.
  K. You added the two percent changes together but you didn't divide.

Introduction

Probability is the likelihood of an event occurring. It tells us what fraction, or percent, of favorable outcomes to total outcomes. It shows up frequently on the ACT and takes several forms. While the questions can be pretty different, the underlying principles are the same.

What You Need to Know

- ✓ How to calculate probability, and correctly assign your numerator and denominator.
- ✓ How to compute compound probabilities of *independent* events
- ✓ How to find the dependent probability of *dependent* events

Definition: Probability

- ▪ Probability is a percent that can't be less than 0 or greater than 1.
- ▪ Probability represents the likelihood of any single trial has the desired outcome. You could also say that probability is how many desired outcomes you can expect out of 100 trials.

Alexa wins 75% of poker games she plays.

75% change that Alexa will win any one poker game

-OR-

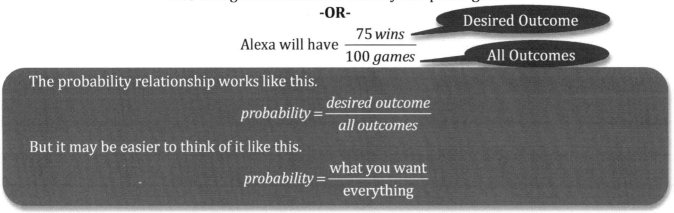

Alexa will have $\dfrac{75\ wins}{100\ games}$ — Desired Outcome / All Outcomes

The probability relationship works like this.

$$probability = \frac{desired\ outcome}{all\ outcomes}$$

But it may be easier to think of it like this.

$$probability = \frac{what\ you\ want}{everything}$$

ACT Example: Probability

1. The Test Guy is outfitting his utility belt. He has 4 black markers, 1 green, 1 blue, 1 can shark repellant, and 1 batarang. If the Test Guy randomly selects any item from his utility belt, what are the odds that the selected item is a black marker?

Check out the video on
Simple Probabilities

- **A.** $\dfrac{2}{3}$
- **B.** $\dfrac{1}{3}$
- **C.** $\dfrac{1}{2}$
- **D.** $\dfrac{4}{7}$
- **E.** $\dfrac{3}{4}$

Solve

This is a standard setup for a probability question. We've got to find the numerator and denominator and then simplify them (if applicable).

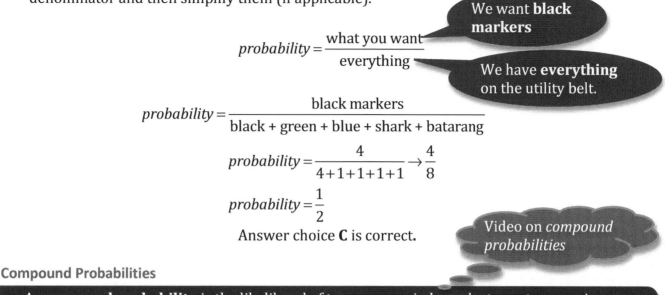

We want **black markers**

We have **everything** on the utility belt.

$$probability = \frac{what\ you\ want}{everything}$$

$$probability = \frac{black\ markers}{black + green + blue + shark + batarang}$$

$$probability = \frac{4}{4+1+1+1+1} \rightarrow \frac{4}{8}$$

$$probability = \frac{1}{2}$$

Answer choice **C** is correct.

Video on *compound probabilities*

Compound Probabilities

A **compound probability** is the likelihood of two or more *independent* events occurring. Compound probabilities are always calculated by multiplying the probability of each event together.

Independent events are events that aren't affected by what happened in the past (past events). Coin flips and dice rolls are example. A coin flip isn't more or less likely to be heads if the last flip was heads, or does it matter if we flip more than one coin at once. A dice roll isn't affected by what came up on the previous roll or by rolling other dice at the same time.

Rules of the Road: Compound Probabilities

Steps to Solving
1. Make sure you have two events with specific outcomes.
2. Calculate the probability of each independent event.
3. Multiply the probabilities.

Example: Compound Probabilities

1. Aydan flips a coin twice. What is the probability that his first flip is heads is and the second flip is tails?

Solve

Step 1: Make sure that you're dealing with a compound probability.

This is a *compound probability* because we want *exact results* from each flip and the events don't affect each other.

Step 2: Find the probability of each flip.

Probability the first flip is heads: $probability = \frac{what\ you\ want}{everything} \rightarrow \frac{1}{2}$

Probability the second flip is tails: $probability = \frac{what\ you\ want}{everything} \rightarrow \frac{1}{2}$

Step 3: Multiply the probabilities.

Probability of flipping heads *then* tails: $\frac{1}{2} \cdot \frac{1}{2} = \frac{1}{4}$

Let's look at a diagram to see *why* it works this way.

Our first toss gives us two possibilities, heads or tails.

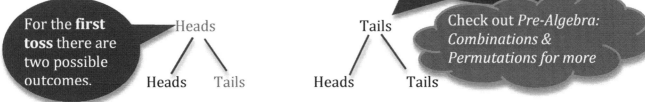

We still have **heads/tails** (2 outcomes) but after the first toss we have *4 possible results from two coin tosses.*

For the **first toss** there are two possible outcomes.

Heads

Heads   Tails

Tails

Heads   Tails

Check out *Pre-Algebra: Combinations & Permutations for more*

ACT Example: Compound Probabilities

1. John is rolling three six-sided dice simultaneously and needs to get sixes on all three rolls. What is the probability that John will roll three sixes?

   A. $\frac{1}{6}$

   B. $\frac{1}{12}$

   C. $\frac{1}{36}$

   D. $\frac{1}{72}$

   E. $\frac{1}{216}$

Video on compound probabilities

Solve

Step 1: Make sure you have two events with specific outcomes.

This is a *compound probability* because we want *exact results* from each toss and the events don't affect each other. It doesn't matter that the events happen at the same time, the probabilities are still independent and still compound.

Step 2: We need to find the probability of each roll.

Probability that dice 1 is six: $probability = \dfrac{\text{what you want}}{\text{everything}} \rightarrow \dfrac{1}{6}$

Probability that dice 2 is six: $probability = \dfrac{\text{what you want}}{\text{everything}} \rightarrow \dfrac{1}{6}$

Probability that dice 3 is six: $probability = \dfrac{\text{what you want}}{\text{everything}} \rightarrow \dfrac{1}{6}$

Step 3: Multiply the probabilities.

The probability of rolling three sixes is $\frac{1}{6} \cdot \frac{1}{6} \cdot \frac{1}{6} = \frac{1}{216}$

Answer Choice **E** is correct.

Fake Compound Probabilities

It's not uncommon to see a problem that *appears* to be a compound probability. In these problems it looks like we need a specific value for the first event, but we really don't.

ACT Example: Fake Compound Probabilities

1. Aydan rolls a six-sided dice two times. What are the odds that his second roll matches the first?

    A. $\dfrac{1}{6}$

    B. $\dfrac{1}{36}$

    C. $\dfrac{1}{12}$

    D. $\dfrac{1}{4}$

    E. $\dfrac{5}{12}$

Solve

It actually doesn't matter what Aydan gets on the first roll. It only matters what Aydan gets on the second roll. Let's take a look.

First Roll	What We Want for Second Roll	Probability of Second Roll Matching
1	1	1/6
2	2	1/6
3	3	1/6
4	4	1/6
5	5	1/6
6	6	1/6

We don't have to multiply probabilities. We only have one event—the second roll.

No matter what Aydan gets on his first roll, he has a 1/6 chance of matching it on the second roll.

Answer Choice **A** is correct.

Dependent probabilities change from event to event. If we select things and don't put them back in the pool, we change the probability. That will change the denominator of the probability (and often the numerator).

ACT Example: Dependent Probabilities

1. There are 10 cards in a deck, 4 blue cards and 6 red cards. Jimmy draws a card and, without replacing the first card, draws a second. What is the probability that *both* of the cards that Jimmy draws are blue?

   A. $\dfrac{4}{25}$

   B. $\dfrac{2}{5}$

   C. $\dfrac{3}{5}$

   D. $\dfrac{2}{50}$

   E. $\dfrac{2}{15}$

Solve

We're going to use the same method to solve this problem as we would an *independent compound probability*.

Step 1: Make sure that you have two events with specific outcomes.
There are two events. Jimmy has to draw one blue card and then a second blue card.

Step 2: Find the probability of each event.
Unlike our *compound probabilities* example, we'll have **different probabilities for each event.**

Probability that the first card is blue: $probability = \dfrac{\text{what you want}}{\text{everything}} \rightarrow \dfrac{4}{10}$

Before we look at the second card drawn, let's think about what's left in the deck.

Since we took one blue card out and didn't put it back, our deck now looks like this:

Number of blue cards: $4 - 1 = 3$
Number of total cards: $10 - 1 = 9$

We took one blue card away

Probability that the second card is blue: $probability = \dfrac{\text{what you want}}{\text{everything}} \rightarrow \dfrac{3}{9}$

There are no longer 10 cards in the deck; Jimmy removed one.

Step 3: Multiply the probabilities:

$$\text{probability of drawing two blue cards} = \dfrac{4}{10} \cdot \dfrac{3}{9}$$

$$\text{probability of drawing two blue cards} = \dfrac{2}{5} \cdot \dfrac{1}{3} \rightarrow \dfrac{2}{15}$$

Answer Choice **E** is correct.

Expected Value

When we have a set of outcomes that are discrete (they exist as individual items), each outcome can have a different likelihood of occurring. The expected value is a weighted average of all the outcomes & their probabilities. **It's a probability weighted average**.

ACT Example: Expected Value

1. The probability of discrete random variable a is shown in the table below. What is the expected value of a?

   A. 0.2
   B. 0.3
   C. 1.5
   D. 2.9
   E. 3

a	Probability
1	0.3
2	0.15
3	0.2
4	0.05
5	0.3

This is the most common format of expected value questions.

Review Weighted Average in Pre-Algebra: Mean & Median

Solve

This is a standard setup for expected value questions. We've got a table that gives us the value of a and the likelihood (probability) of that value. One way to find weighted average is to multiply the portion (percent or probability) by the value.

$$probability_1 \bullet value_1 + probability_2 \bullet value_2...$$

a	Probability	$a \times p$	$a \times p =$
1	0.3	1 x 0.3	0.3
2	0.15	2 x 0.15	0.3
3	0.2	3 x 0.2	0.6
4	0.05	4 x 0.05	0.2
5	0.3	5 x 0.3	1.5

I like to do these calculations next to the table to keep things neat.

Now, we just add them up to find the weighted average of the probabilities.

$$0.3 + 0.3 + 0.6 + 0.2 + 1.5 = 2.9$$

Answer choice **D** is correct.

Check out the video on Expected Value

Wrap Up

What You Need to Know

- ✓ How to calculate probability, and correctly assign your numerator and denominator.
- ✓ How to compute compound probabilities of *independent* events
- ✓ How to find the dependent probability of *dependent* events

Videos

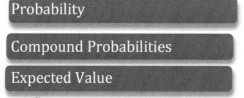

- Probability
- Compound Probabilities
- Expected Value

The Strategies

- ✓ Use a formal setup, it's easy to make a setup error.
- ✓ Be careful with compound probabilities. Make sure you use the right number of events.
- ✓ Be comfortable with weighted averages.

Related Topics

- ✓ Percents
- ✓ Data
- ✓ Central Tendency

1. Harvey Dent flips a lucky coin whenever he has a difficult decision to make. With Batman, Robin, and Alfred captive, he is faced with three difficult decisions. Harvey wants his last two tosses to match his first. What are the odds that Harvey's last two tosses match his first toss?

    A. $\frac{3}{8}$

    B. $\frac{1}{4}$

    C. $\frac{1}{8}$

    D. $\frac{1}{16}$

    E. $\frac{3}{2}$

2. Harper has a bag containing dog treats. She has 5 Milk Bones, 8 Beggin' Strips, and 7 Pupperonis. How many additional Milk Bones must she add to make the probability of randomly drawing a Milk Bone 50%?

    F. 5

    G. 10

    H. 7

    J. 20

    K. 15

3. In a gumball machine the ratio of gumballs is 5 yellow gumballs to 4 red gumballs to 6 blue gumballs. What is the probability that any gumball from the machine is NOT blue?

    A. $\frac{2}{5}$

    B. $\frac{2}{3}$

    C. $\frac{3}{5}$

    D. $\frac{4}{15}$

    E. $\frac{1}{3}$

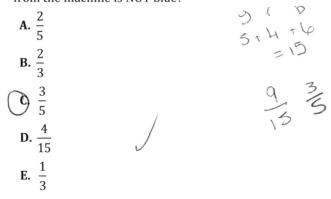

4. To win a game of Trivial Pursuit, Alex calculates he must roll a 6 on a single six-sided dice, answer the question correctly, and then roll a 5. Assuming Alex knows he will answer the question correctly, what are his odds of making both of those rolls?

    F. 16.67%

    G. 33.3%

    H. 13.8%

    J. 2.77%

    K. 83.33%

5. 90 cards are numbered 00 through 89 in a thoroughly shuffled deck. Sean draws one card at random from the deck. Without replacing the card in the deck, Sean draws a second card randomly. Sean wins if both of his cards end in the same digit (0,1,2,3,...). Sean's first card is 01. What are his odds of winning?

    A. 11.11%

    B. 8.89%

    C. 10.11%

    D. 17.78%

    E. 8.98%

6. The probability of a discrete random variable v is shown in the table below. What is the expected value of v?

    F. 2.54
    G. 10
    H. 13.25
    J. 15.25
    K. 22.5

v	Probability
5	0.15
10	0.3
15	0.1
20	0.25
25	0.2

7. During the holidays, LaGuardia airport experiences heavy flight delays. The airport predicts the probability of specific percentages of flights being delayed on a single day. If 500 flights are scheduled on a given day, what is the expected number of flights that will be delayed?

Percent Delayed	Probability
0.30	0.26
0.45	0.18
0.55	0.31
0.60	0.12
0.75	0.13

    A. 275
    B. 250
    C. 260
    D. 214
    E. 375

8. The probability of a discrete random variable, x, is shown below. What is the probability that x has a value less than 9?

    F. 3.4%
    G. 23.0%
    H. 64.5%
    J. 35.5%
    K. 77.0%

x	Probability
3	0.034
6	0.196
9	0.415
12	0.217
15	0.138

1. Harvey Dent flips a lucky coin whenever he has a difficult decision to make. With Batman, Robin, and Alfred captive, he is faced with three difficult decisions. Harvey wants his last two tosses to match his first. What are the odds that Harvey's last two tosses match his first toss?

Correct Answer B

This is a *compound probability* problem. Every coin flip is an *independent event*, the odds of a coin coming up heads or tails isn't changed by the previous coin flip. The probability of heads or tails in any fair coin flip is ½.

The trick is that we only need to calculate the probability of *two* independent events. It doesn't matter what Harvey's if Harvey's first toss is heads or tails, only that the second two tosses match it.

Heads	**Tails**
Heads $\frac{1}{2}$	Tails $\frac{1}{2}$
Heads $\frac{1}{2}$	Tails $\frac{1}{2}$

Whenever we are looking at the probability of independent events occurring, we multiply probabilities.

$$\frac{1}{2} \cdot \frac{1}{2} = \frac{1}{4}$$

Answer choice **B** is correct.

What You May Have Done Wrong

    A. You added numerators and multiplied denominators for 3 tosses.

    C. This is the probability of 3 tosses turning up a specific way.

    D. You went too far, calculating four coin flips not two.

    E. You added the probabilities of three tosses together; probability can never exceed 100%.

2. **Harper has a bag containing dog treats. She has 5 Milk Bones, 8 Beggin' Strips, and 7 Pupperonis. How many additional Milk Bones must she add to make the probability of randomly drawing a Milk Bone 50%?**

Correct Answer G

This is an intimidating question, but it's not as bad as it appears. It does, however, require some algebra. Let's start with the fundamental percent formula.

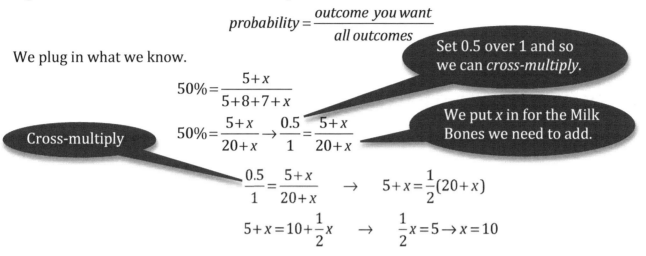

$$probability = \frac{outcome\ you\ want}{all\ outcomes}$$

We plug in what we know.

> Set 0.5 over 1 and so we can *cross-multiply.*

$$50\% = \frac{5+x}{5+8+7+x}$$

> We put x in for the Milk Bones we need to add.

> Cross-multiply

$$50\% = \frac{5+x}{20+x} \rightarrow \frac{0.5}{1} = \frac{5+x}{20+x}$$

$$\frac{0.5}{1} = \frac{5+x}{20+x} \quad \rightarrow \quad 5+x = \frac{1}{2}(20+x)$$

$$5+x = 10 + \frac{1}{2}x \quad \rightarrow \quad \frac{1}{2}x = 5 \rightarrow x = 10$$

That's the best way to handle this problem. You could, however, count up the treats. Write all of the treats in a list, and then write the Milk Bones in a second column or row.

M, M, M, M, M, M, M, M, M, M, M, M, M, M, M

B, B, B, B, B, B, B, B, P, P, P, P, P, P, P

The red M's are the Milkbones I need to add. I figure out that I need 10 additional Milkbones by counting them. Because you don't have a red pen on the ACT, you'll want to circle them or indicate them in another way.

There are drawbacks to this method. First, it works really neatly with 50%, but if we had something like 35% or 28% it is messier. Second, it only works well if you have a manageable number of items. For example, if Harper had 200 treats then this is impractical.

I show it here, but I recommend you be comfortable with solving these algebraically.

Answer choice **G** is correct.

What You May Have Done Wrong
  F. Every Milk Bone added also adds to the total number of treats.
  H. This is a calculation or conceptual error, review your steps.
  J. It's likely you calculated what percentage the Milk Bones represented originally (25%) and then divided the number of Milk Bones by that percentage.
  K. You may have assumed that you just needed to add one Milk Bone for every one of the other types of treats. This actually works, but you forgot about the 5 original Milk Bones.

3. In a gumball machine there are 5 yellow gumballs for every 4 red gumballs and every 6 blue gumballs. What is the probability that any gumball from the machine is NOT blue?

Correct Answer C

This problem really tests setup—whether or not you can find the right numerator and denominator. Make sure you draw a box, or otherwise mark your NOT, it's the single biggest error on these questions.

$$probability = \frac{outcome\ you\ want}{all\ outcomes} = \frac{NOT\ Blue}{All\ Gumballs} \rightarrow \frac{Yellow + Red}{Yellow + Red + Blue}$$

$$probability = \frac{Yellow + Red}{Yellow + Red + Blue} \rightarrow \frac{5+4}{5+4+6}$$

$$probability = \frac{5+4}{5+4+6} \rightarrow \frac{9}{15} = \frac{3}{5}$$

Answer choice C is correct

<u>What You May Have Done Wrong</u>
  A. This is the probability of *blue* gumballs.
  B. This is the probability of *red + blue* gumballs.
  D. This is the probability of *red* gumballs.
  E. This is the probability of *yellow* gumballs.

4. To win a game of Trivial Pursuit, Alex calculates he must roll a 6 on a single six-sided dice, answer the question correctly, and then roll a 5. Assuming Alex knows he will answer the question correctly, what are his odds of making both of those rolls?

Correct Answer J

This is a compound probability question. We've got two separate events, the dice rolls, and we'll have to find the probability that *both* dice rolls turn out the way that Alex wants.

Rolling a particular number on a six sided dice is *always* a $\frac{1}{6}$ chance.

$$probability = \frac{outcome\ you\ want}{all\ outcomes} = \frac{1}{6}$$

The numerator won't be 5, because 5 is the *value* not how many times it shows up on a dice.

Alex has the same probability of rolling six.

$$probability = \frac{outcome\ you\ want}{all\ outcomes} \rightarrow \frac{1}{6}$$

Now, we multiply the probabilities together to find our compound probability.

$$probability\ of\ 5\ then\ 6 = \frac{1}{6} \cdot \frac{1}{6} = \frac{1}{36} = 2.77\%$$

Answer choice J is correct.

<u>What You May Have Done Wrong:</u>
  F. This is the probability of having a single roll turn out correctly.
  G. You added the probabilities together. The likelihood of two events occurring independently will *always* be less than a single event.
  H. You calculated the odds of the first roll as 5/6. Five is the value, not the number of times it occurs.
  K. You used the *value* of the dice to calculate the probabilities as 5/6 and 6/6.

5. **90 cards are numbered 00 through 89 in a thoroughly shuffled deck. Sean draws one card at random from the deck. Without replacing the card in the deck, Sean draws a second card randomly. Sean wins if both of his cards end in the same digit (0,1,2,3,...). Sean's first card is 01. What are his odds of winning?**

Correct Answer B

This is a tricky problem to setup. First, the problem *seems* to be a compound probability, but it's not. Sean has to draw two cards and he's already drawn the first. The probability is the likelihood of drawing a second winning card.

$$probability = \frac{outcome\ you\ want}{all\ outcomes}$$

$$probability = \frac{card\ ending\ in\ 1}{90\ cards}$$

The question tells us there are 90 total cards.

We'll need to find our numerator and it's easiest to do that by making a list of the cards ending in 1.

01, 11, 21, 31, 41, 51, 61, 71, 81

We've already drawn card **01** and we don't replace it, so we won't count it.

0̶1̶, 11, 21, 31, 41, 51, 61, 71, 81

There are 8 cards left that end in 1. So the probability is $probability = \frac{8}{90} = 8.89\%$

Answer choice **B** is correct.

What You May Have Done Wrong

    A. You used 10 as the numerator.
    C. You used 9 as your numerator *and* 89 as your denominator.
    D. You used 16 as your numerator, you probably misunderstood the problem.
    E. You either read your answer choices carelessly or divided 8 by 89.

6. **The probability of discrete random variable v is shown in the table below. What is the expected value of v?**

Correct Answer H

Expected value questions are *weighted average questions*. To find the expected value we multiply the value of v by the probability of that value of v. Do that for each possible value of v.

v	Probability	v × p	v × p =
5	0.15	5 x 0.15	0.75
10	0.3	10 x 0.3	3
15	0.1	15 x 0.1	1.5
20	0.25	20 x 0.25	5
15	0.2	15 x 0.2	3

I like to do these calculations next to the table to keep things neat.

Now we just add all of the products of $v \times p$

$$0.75 + 3 + 1.5 + 5 + 3 = 13.25$$

Answer choice **H** is correct.

Review *Pre-Algebra: Mean & median* for more

What You May Have Done Wrong:

    F. This is a calculator or conceptual error. Review your steps.
    G. You picked the value of v with the highest probability.
    J. You selected the median value of v. Expected value is a weighted average, not a median
    K. You averaged 20 & 25. Review your steps.

7. During the holidays, LaGuardia airport experiences heavy flight delays. The airport predicts the probability of specific percentages of flights being delayed on a single day. If 500 flights are scheduled on a given day, what is the expected number of flights that will be delayed?

Correct Answer B

This is a really wordy and somewhat confusing question. But it boils down to calculating the expected value (finding the weighted average). In this case the expected value is the percent of flights delayed. To find the expected number of flights we'll multiply that expected percentage by 500. Let's find the expected value:

Percent Delayed	Probability	% × p	% × p =
0.30	0.26	0.30 × 0.26	0.078
0.45	0.18	0.45 × 0.18	0.081
0.55	0.31	0.55 × 0.31	0.1705
0.60	0.12	0.60 × 0.12	0.072
0.75	0.13	0.75 × 0.13	0.0975

I like to do these calculations next to the table to keep things neat.

Add each term together.

$$0.078 + 0.081 + 0.1705 + 0.072 + 0.0975 = 0.499$$

To find the number of flights, multiply the expected percentage (0.427) by the number of flights (500).

$$0.499 \cdot 500 = 249.5 \approx 250$$

Answer choice **B** is correct.

What You May Have Done Wrong

A. You used the *middle* percentage, which also has the highest probability.
C. You used the first percentage (30%). Review your steps.
D. You averaged the percents without weighting them.
E. You used the last percentage (0.75). Review your steps.

8. The probability of a discrete random variable, x, is shown below. What is the probability that x has a value less than 9?

Correct Answer G

This is a really straightforward problem that looks really tough. The question wants to know the probability that x is less than 9. If x is less than 9, x is either 3 or 6. We can add the probability that x is 3 and the probability that x is 6 to find the probability that x is less than 9.

x	Probability
3	0.034
6	0.196
9	0.415
12	0.217
15	0.138

Let's add the probabilities

$$0.034 + 0.196 = 0.23 = 23\%$$

Answer choice **G** is correct.

What You May Have Done Wrong:

F. This is the probability that $x = 3$.
H. This is the probability that x is less than *or equal to* 9.
J. This is the probability that x is greater than 9
K. This is the probability that x is greater than or equal to 9.

Introduction

Combinations & permutations are how many ways things can happen. Most problems in this topic are *combinations* problems, but permutations show up often enough to warrant knowing how to do them.

What You Need to Know
- ✓ How to tell whether you're dealing with a combination or a permutation
- ✓ How to calculate combinations
- ✓ How to calculation permutations

> There's a video on *combinations*

Definition: Combinations

Combinations are how many ways something can be arranged if **order doesn't matter.** Some combinations have repetition (the same thing more than once) and some do not.

Example: Combinations

1. Plain Phil's lunch shop only offers 2 soups, tomato and chicken noodle and 2 sandwiches, ham and turkey. How many different lunches including a soup and a sandwich can a customer get at Phil's?

2 x 2 = 4

It doesn't matter which is selected first, the soup or the sandwich. There would still be four possible lunches. Another way to think about is we're picking one from each of a set of categories (like soups & sandwiches).

Calculating Combinations
When we calculate combinations, we just multiply the size of each category together (number of soups x number of salads).

ACT Example: Combinations

1. When the Test Guy selects an outfit for the day, he picks a pair of jeans from 6 pairs of jeans, a shirt from 10 t-shirts, a pair of socks from 8 pairs of socks, and shoes from 4 pairs of shoes?

A. 28
B. 60
C. 240
D. 680
E. 1,920

> This is the most common format of *combination* questions

> There's a *video* on combinations.

Solve

This is a standard setup for combination questions. We're selecting one from each of several categories. It doesn't matter what order we select them; I could build my outfit around my socks, my shoes, etc.

Jeans	Shirts	Socks	Shoes
6	10	8	4

We pick one of 6 pairs of jeans, meaning that we have 6 options. For each of those jeans, we could wear any of the 10 shirts. For each of those combinations of shirts and jeans we could wear any of 8 pairs of socks.

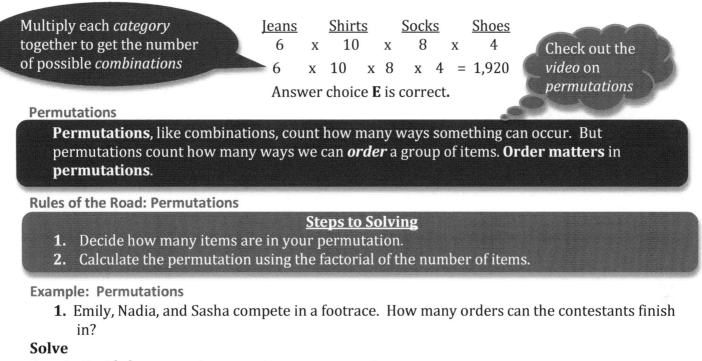

Multiply each *category* together to get the number of possible *combinations*

Jeans		Shirts		Socks		Shoes
6	x	10	x	8	x	4

6 x 10 x 8 x 4 = 1,920

Answer choice **E** is correct.

Check out the *video* on *permutations*

Permutations

Permutations, like combinations, count how many ways something can occur. But permutations count how many ways we can **order** a group of items. **Order matters** in **permutations**.

Rules of the Road: Permutations

Steps to Solving
1. Decide how many items are in your permutation.
2. Calculate the permutation using the factorial of the number of items.

Example: Permutations
1. Emily, Nadia, and Sasha compete in a footrace. How many orders can the contestants finish in?

Solve

Step 1: Decide how many items are in your permutation
  We've got three runners, and each could finish in 1st, 2nd, or 3rd.
  So, we've got three runners and three slots.

Step 2: Calculate the permutation.
For this example, let's look at a sample race to see why permutations work the way they do.

Winner: Sasha
2nd : _____
3rd : _____

Now that the Sasha has won she can't finish second or third. Only Nadia and Emily can finish second and third. Let's say that Nadia finishes second.

Winner: Sasha
2nd : Nadia
3rd : _____

Neither Sasha nor Nadia can finish third, leaving only Emily.

Winner: Sasha
2nd : Nadia
3rd : Emily

Let's review: there were three options for the winner, but after someone has won, only two options for second. After the second person places, there is only one contestant left to finish third.

This is a *factorial*

$3 \times 2 \times 1 = 6\ orders$

These are **distinct permutations** because each order is unique & does not repeat.

Let's take a look at all of the possible outcomes to get a better idea.

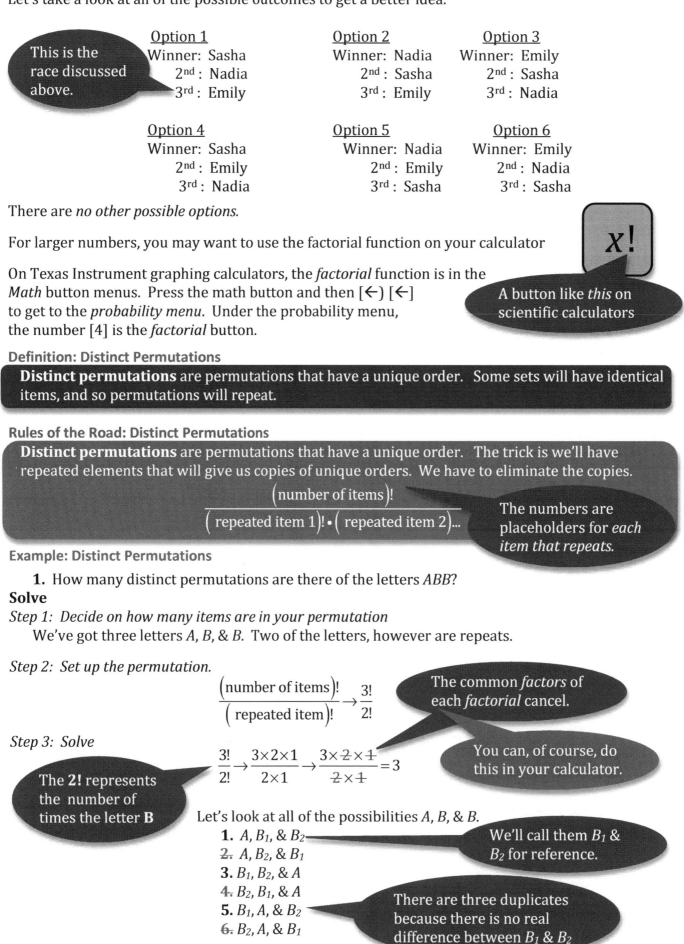

Option 1
This is the race discussed above.
Winner: Sasha
2nd : Nadia
3rd : Emily

Option 2
Winner: Nadia
2nd : Sasha
3rd : Emily

Option 3
Winner: Emily
2nd : Sasha
3rd : Nadia

Option 4
Winner: Sasha
2nd : Emily
3rd : Nadia

Option 5
Winner: Nadia
2nd : Emily
3rd : Sasha

Option 6
Winner: Emily
2nd : Nadia
3rd : Sasha

There are *no other possible options.*

For larger numbers, you may want to use the factorial function on your calculator

$x!$

A button like *this* on scientific calculators

On Texas Instrument graphing calculators, the *factorial* function is in the *Math* button menus. Press the math button and then [←] [←] to get to the *probability menu*. Under the probability menu, the number [4] is the *factorial* button.

Definition: Distinct Permutations

Distinct permutations are permutations that have a unique order. Some sets will have identical items, and so permutations will repeat.

Rules of the Road: Distinct Permutations

Distinct permutations are permutations that have a unique order. The trick is we'll have repeated elements that will give us copies of unique orders. We have to eliminate the copies.

$$\frac{\left(\text{number of items}\right)!}{\left(\text{repeated item 1}\right)! \cdot \left(\text{repeated item 2}\right)...}$$

The numbers are placeholders for *each item that repeats.*

Example: Distinct Permutations

1. How many distinct permutations are there of the letters *ABB*?

Solve

Step 1: Decide on how many items are in your permutation
We've got three letters *A*, *B*, & *B*. Two of the letters, however are repeats.

Step 2: Set up the permutation.

$$\frac{\left(\text{number of items}\right)!}{\left(\text{repeated item}\right)!} \rightarrow \frac{3!}{2!}$$

The common *factors* of each *factorial* cancel.

Step 3: Solve

$$\frac{3!}{2!} \rightarrow \frac{3\times2\times1}{2\times1} \rightarrow \frac{3\times\cancel{2}\times\cancel{1}}{\cancel{2}\times\cancel{1}} = 3$$

You can, of course, do this in your calculator.

The **2!** represents the number of times the letter **B**

Let's look at all of the possibilities *A*, *B*, & *B*.
1. *A*, B_1, & B_2
2. *A*, B_2, & B_1
3. B_1, B_2, & *A*
4. B_2, B_1, & *A*
5. B_1, *A*, & B_2
6. B_2, *A*, & B_1

We'll call them B_1 & B_2 for reference.

There are three duplicates because there is no real difference between B_1 & B_2

ACT Example: Distinct Permutations

1. How many distinct permutations are there of the letters in the word *batter*?

- **A.** 360
- **B.** 120
- **C.** 480
- **D.** 630
- **E.** 720

This is the most common format of distinct permutation questions.

Solve

Step 1: Decide on how many items are in your permutation

There are six letters in the word *b-a-t-t-e-r*. There is one duplicate item; there are two *t's*.

Step 2: Set up the permutation.

$$\frac{(\text{number of items})!}{(\text{repeated item})!} \to \frac{6!}{2!}$$

There's a video on Selecting from a Set

Step 3: Solve.

$$\frac{6!}{2!} \to \frac{6\times5\times4\times3\times2\times1}{2\times1} \to \frac{6\times5\times4\times3\times\cancel{2}\times\cancel{1}}{\cancel{2}\times\cancel{1}} = 360$$

Answer Choice **A** is correct.

Permutations: Selecting from a Set

Some problems require us to find the number of ways we can order items selected from a set. *When order matters, it's a permutation.*

To calculate how many ways we can select a group of items from a set:

$$_NP_K = \frac{n!}{(n-k)!} \to \frac{(\text{number of items})!}{(\text{number of items} - \text{number selected})!}$$

You can also think about it this way:

Start your factorial, but stop when the number of terms you are multiplying equals the number of terms you are selecting.

Example: Selecting from a Set

1. Five candidates are running for two city council spots. The winner with the highest vote total becomes mayor, and the other winner becomes deputy mayor. How many ways can the candidates finish?

Solve

Step 1: Decide on how many items are in your permutation

We have five total items in the permutation. We're selecting two.

Step 2: Set up the permutation.

$$\frac{(\text{number of items})!}{(\text{number of items} - \text{number selected})!} \to \frac{5!}{(5-2)!} \quad \textbf{-OR-} \quad 5\times4 = 20$$

Start the permutation & stop when we get two numbers (for our two items)

Step 3: Solve.

$$\frac{5!}{(5-2)!} \to \frac{5\times4\times3\times2\times1}{3\times2\times1} \to \frac{5\times4\times\cancel{3}\times\cancel{2}\times\cancel{1}}{\cancel{3}\times\cancel{2}\times\cancel{1}} = 20$$

ACT Example: Selecting from a Set

1. There are eight runners in the final track heat of the state championship. The first three finishers win gold, silver, and bronze medals. How many ways can the winners finish?

    A. 6
    B. 36
    C. 336
    D. 1,080
    E. 40,320

Solve

Step 1: Decide on how many items are in your permutation
    We have 8 total items in the permutation. We're selecting 3.

> Start the permutation & stop when we get 3 numbers (for our 3 items).

Step 2: Set up the permutation.

$$\frac{(\text{number of items})!}{(\text{number of items} - \text{number selected})!} \rightarrow \frac{8!}{(8-3)!} \quad \textbf{-OR-} \quad 8 \times 7 \times 6 = 336$$

Step 3: Solve

$$\frac{8!}{(8-3)!} \rightarrow \frac{8 \times 7 \times 6 \times 5 \times 4 \times 3 \times 2 \times 1}{5 \times 4 \times 3 \times 2 \times 1} \rightarrow \frac{8 \times 7 \times 6 \times \cancel{5} \times \cancel{4} \times \cancel{3} \times \cancel{2} \times \cancel{1}}{\cancel{5} \times \cancel{4} \times \cancel{3} \times \cancel{2} \times \cancel{1}} = 336$$

Answer Choice **C** is correct.

Wrap Up

What You Need to Know
- ✓ How to tell whether you're dealing with a combination or a permutation
- ✓ How to calculate combinations
- ✓ How to calculation permutations

Videos

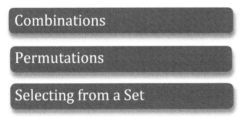

The Strategies
- ✓ Be careful when deciding combination or permutation.
- ✓ On permutations, remember to cancel repeating items.

Related Topics
- ✓ Probability

Pre-Algebra: Combinations & Permutations

1. Harper knows how to make four kinds of cupcakes. Each of the types of cupcakes can be topped a single frosting, buttercream, cream cheese, or buttermilk icing. To garnish, she uses one of three colors of sprinkles. How many combinations of cupcakes can Harper make?

    A. 10
    B. 9
    C. 24
    D. 36
    E. 72

2. Alexa has the Test Guy on a diet. For lunch he has a choice between 6 different kinds of salad, three vegetable based drinks, 4 pieces of fruit, and a boiled egg *or* cup of fat free cottage cheese. How many options do I have for lunch?

    F. 15
    G. 72
    H. 36
    J. 144
    K. 256

3. Six students drop by Test Guy World Headquarters (somewhere on the bottom of the Atlantic Ocean). The Test Guy can only see one student at a time. How many different orders can these students be called in?

    A. 21
    B. 120
    C. 480
    D. 720
    E. 46,656

4. Alex, Lucy, Cal, and Jackie are going to a movie and will sit together in the group. Cal has to sit on either end of the group. How many unique orders can the group sit in?

    F. 10
    G. 12
    H. 24
    J. 48
    K. 64

5. Wendy is having a dinner party for 8 people, including herself and her husband, Gary. If Wendy and her husband occupy both ends of the rectangular table and three guests are seated per side, how many ways can she seat the remaining guests?

    A. 720
    B. 40,320
    C. 640
    D. 1,440
    E. 36

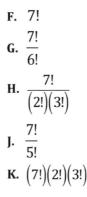

6. Which expression gives the number of distinct permutations of the letters in the word BANANAS?

    F. $7!$

    G. $\dfrac{7!}{6!}$

    H. $\dfrac{7!}{(2!)(3!)}$

    J. $\dfrac{7!}{5!}$

    K. $(7!)(2!)(3!)$

7. Which expression gives the number of permutations of 18 objects taken 6 at a time?

    A. $\dfrac{18!}{(18-6)!}$

    B. $\dfrac{18!}{6!}$

    C. $(18!)(12!)$

    D. $12!$

    E. $6(18!)$

Combinations & Permutations: Solutions

1. Harper knows how to make four kinds of cupcakes. Each of the types of cupcakes can be topped a single frosting, buttercream, cream cheese, or buttermilk icing. To garnish, she uses one of three colors of sprinkles. How many combinations of cupcakes can Harper make?

Correct Answer D

This is a pretty common format for combination problems. To make it more complicated they force you to extract the information. I'm a big fan of problem setup and organization (and hopefully you become one if you aren't already) and I like to make tags for each category and write their values below.

Cupcakes	Frosting	Sprinkles
4	3	3

You **always** do better on word problems with a formal setup. The math on this problem, once setup is complete, is straightforward:

Cupcakes		Frosting		Sprinkles	
4	x	3	x	3	= 36 combinations

Answer choice **D** is correct.

<u>What You May Have Done Wrong</u>
   A. You added the cupcakes, the frosting, and the sprinkles.
   B. You may have just multiplied the amount of frosting and sprinkles.
   C. You probably added the frosting and sprinkles (3 + 3) and *then* multiplied.
   E. This is a conceptual error or calculation error, review your steps.

2. Alexa has the Test Guy on a diet. For lunch he has a choice between 6 different kinds of salad, three vegetable based drinks, 4 pieces of fruit, and a boiled egg or cup of fat free cottage cheese. How many options do I have for lunch?

Correct Answer J

This is another classic setup for a *combination* question. There's a bit of a wrinkle, "boiled egg *or* cut of fat free cottage cheese" can trip students up. You treat it just the same as any of the other choices (4 pieces of fruit for example).

Salad		Drinks		Fruit		Egg/Cottage Cheese	
6	x	3	x	4	x	2	= 144 lunches

Answer choice **J** is correct.

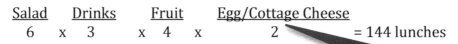 There are 2 options, egg *or* cottage cheese.

<u>What You May Have Done Wrong</u>
   F. You added the options together instead of multiplying them.
   G. You may have missed multiplying the egg or cottage cheese.
   H. You probably missed the fruit, or divided somehow. Review your steps.
   K. This is a conceptual or calculation error. Review your steps.

3. Six students drop by Test Guy World Headquarters (somewhere on the bottom of the Atlantic Ocean). The Test Guy works with each student once and one student at a time. How many different orders can these students be seen in?

Correct Answer D

This is a *permutation* problem. Once I see a student, they won't be seen again (they aren't replaced in the pool). Order matters, according to the question and we don't have replacement and that lets us know we've got a *permutation* problem.

Permutation problems are solved by factorials.

You can either enter **6!** into your calculator, or do it by hand.

$$6! = 720$$
$$6 \times 5 \times 4 \times 3 \times 2 \times 1 = 720$$

Answer choice **D** is correct

<u>What You May Have Done Wrong</u>
    A. You added $6 + 5 + 4 + 3 + 2 + 1 = 21$. You should have multiplied.
    B. You calculated 5! ($5 \times 4 \times 3 \times 2 \times 1$)
    C. This is a calculation or conceptual error.
    E. You treated the problem like a combination, multiplying
       $6 \times 6 \times 6 \times 6 \times 6 \times 6 = 46,656$

4. Alex, Lucy, Cal, and Jackie are going to a movie and will sit together in the group. Cal has to sit on either end of the group. How many unique orders can the group sit in?

Correct Answer G

This is a *permutation problem*. Once a person sits in a seat, they can't sit in a second seat. So, once they sit down they are *removed* from the pool. This is a fairly tough problem and you really ought to draw a diagram. Let's take a look:

We've got two options because "Cal has to sit on either end of the group." That puts Cal out of the permutation, because he can't sit anywhere he likes. It *also* tells us that we'll end up doubling our permutation.

Each of these is a *3!*

So we've got to find *3!* (for Alex, Lucy, and Jackie) and then double it.
$$3! = 6 \rightarrow 6 \times 2 = 12$$
$$3 \times 2 \times 1 = 6 \rightarrow 6 \times 2 = 12$$

Multiply by **2** to account for Cal

Answer choice **G** is correct.

<u>What You May Have Done Wrong</u>
    F. You added $4 + 3 + 2 + 1$
    H. You calculated 4!. Cal's seat is restricted, so he's not included in the factorial.
    J. You probably calculated 4! And then doubled it. It should be 3! x 2
    K. This is a calculation or conceptual error, review your steps.

5. Wendy is having a dinner party for 8 people, including herself and her husband, Gary. If Wendy and her husband occupy both ends of the rectangular table, how many ways can she seat the remaining guests?

Correct Answer D

Either Wendy or Gary sits at the left head of the table, and the other sits at the other end. Along the sides of the table are six seats. We don't care about the rows, or anything about the seats other than the fact that they are unoccupied and can be filled by any of the guests who are not Wendy or Gary. We can mark up the diagram provided.

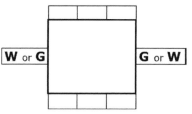

There are two possible setups for the dinner party. In one, Wendy sits on the left and Gary on the right. In the other, Gary sits on the left and Wendy sits on the right.

Where the guests sit doesn't matter. They can sit in any order on any side. We don't care   about order or side.

There are six guests, so we're dealing with a permutation of 6.

$$6! = 720$$
$$6 \times 5 \times 4 \times 3 \times 2 \times 1 = 720$$

We need to double 720, to count both of the possibilities where Wendy & Gary sit.
$$720 \times 2 = 1,440$$

Answer choice **D** is correct.

What You May Have Done Wrong

A. You forgot to double the permutation to account for Wendy and Gary being able to sit at either end.

B. You calculated *8!*. Gary & Wendy don't fall into the permutation because where they sit is restricted.

C. This is a calculation or conceptual error.

E. You added 8 + 7 + 6 + 5 + 4 + 3 + 2 + 1. When we talk about combinations & permutations we always multiply.

6. **Which expression gives the number of distinct permutations of the letters in the word BANANAS?**

Correct Answer H

Distinct permutations are how many unique ways (no duplicates) we can order a set of things. To remove duplicates we have to account for the letters that appear more than once.

Step 1: Decide on how many items are in your permutation
There are seven letters in the word *b-a-n-a-n-a-s.* There are two duplicate letters, two *n*'s and three *a*'s.

Step 2: Set up the permutation.

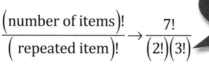

We *divide* by the repeated items to remove duplicate orders.

$$\frac{(\text{number of items})!}{(\text{repeated item})!} \rightarrow \frac{7!}{(2!)(3!)}$$

Answer choice **H** is correct.

<u>What You May Have Done Wrong:</u>
    F. This is the number of ways that bananas ordered, but we'll have repeats/copies.
    G. You multiplied 3! & 2!, but 3! x 2! = 12 and that does *not* equal
        6!, which equals 720.
    H. You added the denominator. You can't combine factorials in this way.
    K. You multiplied 3! and 2! when you should have divided.

7. **Which expression gives the number of permutations of 18 objects taken 6 at a time?**

Correct Answer A

This problem is about *selecting from a set.*

Step 1: Decide on how many items are in your permutation
    We have a set of 18 objects and we're selecting 6 of them.

Step 2: Set up the permutation.

$$\frac{18!}{(18-6)!}$$

If you want to work it that way, we'll have some extra work.

-OR-

$18 \times 17 \times 16 \times 15 \times 14 \times 13$

If you work it by counting down the permutation you'll have to check your answer by calculator (really long). The better way to do it is look at what factors will cancel in each answer choice. Overall, it's best to know the formula above.

Answer choice **A** is correct.

<u>What You May Have Done Wrong</u>
    B. This would be the expression if you were picking 12 items. We've got to cancel up to
        the number we need.
    C. You multiplied where you should have divided. Remember, we're going to make the
        number of orders *smaller*, not larger.
    D. This is picking 12 items of a group of 12 items.
    E. This is a conceptual error. Review your steps.

Mean, Median, & Mode
Multiple Times per Test

Introduction
Every test has *multiple* questions about mean, median and mode. Almost all of these questions are about mean (average) or median (middle number).

What You Need to Know
- ✓ The differences between mean, median & mode
- ✓ The fundamental average formula & how to use it to solve *missing component* problems.
- ✓ How to find weighted averages.
- ✓ How to find median for a dataset.
- ✓ How to find median for a frequency table.
- ✓ The definition of mode & unique mode.

Definitions: Mean, Median, & Mode
Mean is the **average** of a set of numbers.
Median is the **middle number** of a dataset.
Mode is the **most frequently** occurring number.

Mean
It's absolutely critical you know the fundamental average formula. Most likely, you already do, but you don't think of it as a formula.

$$average = \frac{sum\ of\ all\ terms}{number\ of\ terms}$$

Example: Mean
1. What is the average of 2, 4, 6, and 12?

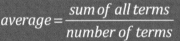

$$average = \frac{sum\ of\ all\ terms}{number\ of\ terms}$$

$$average = \frac{2+4+6+12}{4} \rightarrow \frac{24}{4}$$

$$average = 6$$

There's a *video* on *mean*

Rules of the Road: Mean on the ACT
Mean questions on the ACT can require you to find something other than the average.

Steps to Solving
1. **Set up your formula.**
2. **Plug-in** what you know and decide what is missing. *There will only be one missing component!*
3. **Solve.**

ACT Example: Mean

1. Duncan has five exams in his AP US history course. He has taken four and his grades have been a 93, 82, 91, and 89. What will Duncan need to make on his fifth exam to have a 90 average in the course?

    This is the most common format for mean questions.

    A. 90
    B. 92
    C. 93
    D. 95
    E. 100

Solve

This problem is a lot more intimidating than it is difficult. The **key is setting up your average equation.**

Set up your average equation and plug-in what you know.

$$average = \frac{sum}{number} \quad \rightarrow \quad 90 = \frac{93+82+91+89+x}{5}$$

$$90 = \frac{355+x}{5} \quad \rightarrow \quad 450 = 355+x$$

$$x = 95$$

Answer Choice **D** is correct.

Multiply both sides by **5**

Rules of the Road: Weighted Average

Weighted averages tend to confuse students but it's a topic that shows up on about 75% of tests. The good news, it's not that tough. You can calculate weighted average in two ways.

$$weighted\ average = \frac{(value\ 1)(number\ of\ 1) + (value\ 2)(number\ of\ 2)....}{total\ number}$$

-OR-

$$weighted\ average = \frac{number\ of\ 1}{Total}(value\ 1) + \frac{number\ of\ 2}{Total}(value\ 2)$$

The first method treats a weighted average like a regular average. We multiply the number of occurrences of a value (because things can happen more than once) and all of those together.

The second method divides each number by the total to get the weight of each individual category. Let's look at an example.

ACT Example: Weighted Average

1. Thirty students took a survey as part of a study on the use of social media. The time students use social media per week is shown below.

Time	Number of Students
3 hours	1
7 hours	9
11 hours	13
13 hours	7

There's a video on weighted average

Approximately, what is the average length of time students use social media per week?

This is the most common setup for weighted average

- **A.** 7.5 hours
- **B.** 8.0 hours
- **C.** 8.5 hours
- **D.** 9 hours
- **E.** 10 hours

Solve

First Method

$$\frac{(value\,1)(number\,of\,1)+(value\,2)(number\,of\,2)....}{total\,number} \rightarrow \frac{(3)(1)+(7)(9)+(11)(13)+(13)(7)}{30}$$

time • students

The question tells us there are 30 students total.

$$\frac{300}{30}=10\,hours\,on\,average$$

Second Method

$$\frac{number\,of\,1}{Total}(value\,1)+\frac{number\,of\,2}{Total}(value\,2) \rightarrow \frac{1}{30}(3)+\frac{9}{30}(7)+\frac{13}{30}(11)+\frac{7}{30}(13)$$

$$3.3\%(3)+30\%(7)+43.3\%(11)+23.3\%(13)$$

*We get the **percent weight** of each **value***

$10\,hours\,on\,average$

Answer Choice **E** is correct.

Rules of the Road: Median on the ACT

Median questions take a lot of forms, but you'll follow the same steps.

There's a video on Median

Steps to Solving

1. **Order your numbers from least to greatest** (or greatest to least)
2. **Find the middle number.** If your set has an even number of numbers, you'll average the two middle numbers together.
3. **Solve** if needed

Example: Median

1. What is the median of 9, 2, 3, 27, and 14?

Solve

$$2, 3, 9, 14, 27$$

2 numbers *less* than 9

2 numbers *greater* than 9

2. What is the median of 9, 2, 3, and 27?

Solve

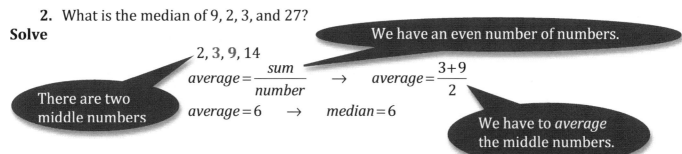

2, 3, **9**, 14

We have an even number of numbers.

$average = \dfrac{sum}{number}$ → $average = \dfrac{3+9}{2}$

There are two middle numbers

$average = 6$ → $median = 6$

We have to *average* the middle numbers.

ACT Example: Median

1. Four homes are for sale at \$130,000, \$90,000, \$210,000, and \$150,000. If a fifth house is added to the dataset, which price will result NOT in a median *less* than the median of the four houses?

    A. \$60,000
    B. \$100,000
    C. \$110,000
    D. \$130,000
    E. \$160,000

Solve

This is a "which" question, so we'll want to mark-off. Before we can do that, though, we'll need to find the median of the four houses.

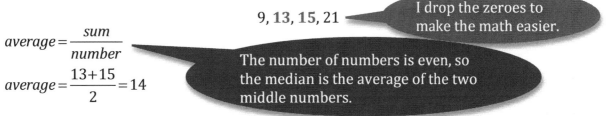

9, **13, 15**, 21

I drop the zeroes to make the math easier.

$average = \dfrac{sum}{number}$

$average = \dfrac{13+15}{2} = 14$

The number of numbers is even, so the median is the average of the two middle numbers.

Now we can mark-off, we're looking for whatever keeps the median the same (14) or makes it bigger.

    ~~A.~~ \$60,000 ← 6, 9, **13**, 15, 21
    ~~B.~~ \$100,000 ← 9, 10, **13**, 15, 21
    ~~C.~~ \$110,000 ← 9, 11, **13**, 15, 21
    ~~D.~~ \$130,000 ← 9, 13, **13**, 15, 21
    E. \$160,000 ← 9, 13, **15**, 16, 21

Numbers **smaller** than the median **make the median smaller.**

Numbers **larger** than the median **make the median larger**

Mode

In the tests I've reviewed there isn't a single mode question. It does, however, appear with other concepts, like median. That said, there's no rule against mode questions and you could see one on test day.

Definitions: Mode & Unique Mode

> **Mode** is the *value* that occurs most frequently.
> A **unique mode** stands alone. No other *value* has as many occurrences.

Example: Mode

1. What is the mode of 4, 8, 3, 9 ,2, 4, & 4?

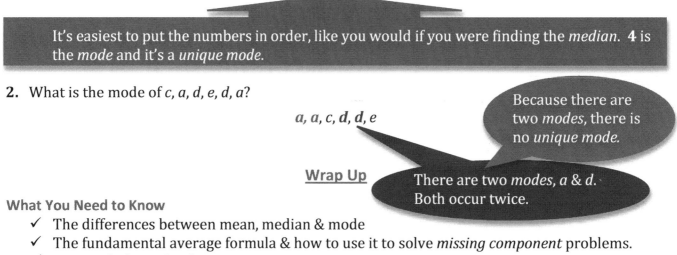

2, 3, **4, 4, 4,** 8, 9

It's easiest to put the numbers in order, like you would if you were finding the *median*. **4** is the *mode* and it's a *unique mode*.

2. What is the mode of *c, a, d, e, d, a*?

*a, a, c, **d, d,** e*

Because there are two *modes*, there is no *unique mode*.

Wrap Up

There are two *modes*, *a* & *d*. Both occur twice.

What You Need to Know
- ✓ The differences between mean, median & mode
- ✓ The fundamental average formula & how to use it to solve *missing component* problems.
- ✓ How to find weighted averages.
- ✓ How to find median for a dataset.
- ✓ How to find median for a frequency table.
- ✓ The definition of mode & unique mode.

Videos

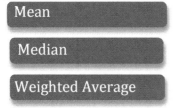

Mean

Median

Weighted Average

The Strategies
- ✓ Use the mean formula when average problems don't ask for the average.
- ✓ Make sure you order your data, write it down so you don't make a mistake. Take the point over a few seconds every time.
- ✓ On confusing word problems, start with setup. Find the first thing to do. You don't need an endgame to begin the problem.

Related Topics
- ✓ Data (there are several mean, median, mode problems here)

- ✓ Probability

Pre-Algebra: Mean, Median, & Mode

1. Company *A* and Company *B* both sell ACT math books in bulk. After 10 books there is a discount applied. Company *A* sells 18 books for a total of $144 dollars and Company *B* sells 23 books for 173 dollars, which is the better deal?

   A. Company *A* by 29 dollars per book
   B. Company *B* by 29 dollars per book
   C. Company *A* by 0.48 dollars per book
   D. Company *B* by 0.48 dollars per book
   E. Company *B* by 5.8 dollars per book

2. A set of five integers has a minimum of 1 and a maximum of 5. There is no mode. What *must* be the median?

   F. 1
   G. 2
   H. 3
   J. 4
   K. 5

3. In Jim's Ancient Greek course, he has scored 59, 93, 90, and 63 on four exams. What score must Jim receive on the fifth exam to have an 80 average?

   A. 61
   B. 78
   C. 84
   D. 90
   E. 95

4. The average of *a* and *b* is 22. The average of *a*, *b*, and *c* is 36. What is the value of *c*?

   F. 64
   G. 50
   H. 28
   J. 20
   K. 29

5. Detective Joe Friday is looking at his arrest statistics this week. He has arrested, 2, 4, 3, 6, 3, and 7 suspects in the last six days. For the seventh day of the week, which number of arrests of the week will result in a median arrests that is NOT three?

   A. 0
   B. 1
   C. 2
   D. 3
   E. 4

6. The fantastic Arithmetician is thinking of 5 numbers such that their mean is the same as their median. Four of the numbers are 80, 68, 92, and 80. What is the fifth number?

   F. 140
   G. 20
   H. 80
   J. 160
   K. 90

7. One hundred families were surveyed to determine the number of cars in the household. The results were:

0 cars	7 families
1 car	23 families
2 cars	50 families
3 cars	18 families
4 cars	2 families

   What is the average number of cars per household?

   A. 1 car
   B. 1.5 cars
   C. 1.85 cars
   D. 2 cars
   E. 2.4 cars

8. A data set contains 21 items and the median of that data set is 34. Eight items are added to the data set. Four are less than 34 and four are greater than 34. What *must* be true about the new median?

   F. median > 34
   G. median < 34
   H. median = 34
   J. median is an average of the new items.
   K. median is now equal to mean.

9. Jim has taken four exams in his Latin course. His average after the four exams is 83%. If he did not receive a score lower than 78% on any of the tests, what is the highest possible score Jim could have gotten on one test?

   A. 94
   B. 90
   C. 92
   D. 98
   E. 96

Pre-Algebra: Mean, Median, & Mode

1. Company A and Company B both sell ACT math books in bulk. After 10 books there is a discount applied. If Company A sells 18 books for a total of $144 dollars and Company B sells 23 books for 173 dollars, which is the better deal?

Correct Answer D

To find the better deal, we need to know what the average cost of each book is. The difference in total price doesn't matter, it's the price per book we're concerned with.

Company *A* sells 18 books for a total cost of $144.

$$Average = \frac{sum}{number} \rightarrow \frac{144}{18} = \$8 \, per \, book$$

Company *B* sells 23 books for a total cost of $173.

$$Average = \frac{sum}{number} \rightarrow \frac{173}{23} = \$7.52 \, per \, book$$

Company *B* sells the books cheaper than Company *A*

$8.00 – $7.52 = $0.48

Answer choice **D** is correct.

<u>What You May Have Done Wrong</u>
  A. You found the total difference in the cost of the books, but there are a different number of books sold. You also did it backwards, Company *B*'s books are cheaper.
  B. You found the total difference in the cost of the books, but there are a different number of books sold.
  C. You did everything right, but Company *B* has cheaper books.
  E. You found the difference in *total* cost of the books and then divided by the difference in the number of books sold.

2. A set of five integers has a minimum of 1 and a maximum of 5. There is no mode. What *must* be the median?

Correct Answer H

This is an interesting problem that includes both median and mode. It's a question needs to be unpacked in pieces. There are five integers with a minimum of 1 and a maximum of 5.

The second sentence tells us there is no unique mode. A *mode* is the most frequently occurring value (it's the number that shows up most often). Since there is no mode, every number appears the same number of times.

So, the integers *must be* 1, 2, 3, 4, and 5.

To find the median of any set, put the numbers in order.

$$1, 2, 3, 4, 5$$

The median is the *middle value* so,

$$1, 2, 3, 4, 5$$

Answer choice **H** is correct.

<u>What You May Have Done Wrong</u>
  All of the wrong answer choices are conceptual errors. Review your steps.

3. In Jim's Ancient Greek course, he has scored 59, 93, 90, and 63 on four exams. What score must Jim receive on the fifth exam to have an 80 average?

Correct Answer E

This is the classic setup for mean questions. We're given an average and we're missing one of the numbers. Like percent problems, we'll always be given two of the three components and have to solve for what's missing. Olug in what you know.

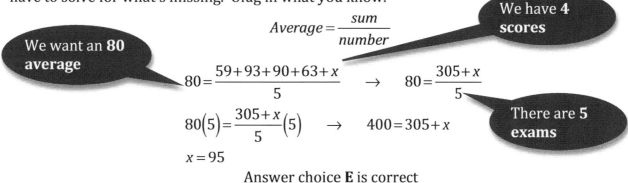

$$Average = \frac{sum}{number}$$

We want an **80** average

We have **4** scores

$$80 = \frac{59+93+90+63+x}{5} \quad \rightarrow \quad 80 = \frac{305+x}{5}$$

$$80(5) = \frac{305+x}{5}(5) \quad \rightarrow \quad 400 = 305+x$$

There are **5** exams

$$x = 95$$

Answer choice **E** is correct

What You May Have Done Wrong
  A. You averaged the four numbers as five *and* stopped there.
  B. You averaged the four numbers together, then averaged that answer (76.25) with 80.
  C. You averaged the four numbers together and then plugged that answer (76.25) into a new equation. That equation gives equal weight to all four of the known exams (combined) and the one missing exam.
  D. You may have guessed or made a calculation error.

4. The average of a and b is 22. The average of a, b, and c is 36. What is the value of c?

Correct Answer F

This is another common format for average questions. We're given an average but no values for a & b. Don't freak out, we actually **don't care what a and b are individually**.

$$Average = \frac{sum}{number} \quad \rightarrow \quad 22 = \frac{a+b}{2}$$

We can solve for what $a+b$ is and we won't need a or b individually.

$$22 = \frac{a+b}{2} \quad \rightarrow \quad a+b = (2)22 \quad \rightarrow \quad a+b = 44$$

You could write this as 22 + 22

We're given that the average of a, b, and c is 36. Let's set that up.

$$Average = \frac{sum}{number} \rightarrow 36 = \frac{a+b+c}{3}$$

Substitute 44 in for $a + b$ and solve.

$$36 = \frac{a+b+c}{3} \quad \rightarrow \quad 36 = \frac{44+c}{3}$$

$$(3)36 = 44+c \quad \rightarrow \quad 108 = 44+c \quad \rightarrow \quad c = 64$$

Answer choice **F** is correct.

What You May Have Done Wrong:
  G. You divided $22 + c$, instead of $44 + c$.
  H. You divided $44 + c$ by two instead of 3.
  J. You set the problem up as $44+ 44 + c$.
  K. You averaged 22 & 36.

H, J, & K are all *smaller* than 36. Since 22 is *smaller* than 36, c will need to be *larger than* 36.

5. **Detective Joe Friday is looking at his arrest statistics this week. He has arrested, 2, 4, 3, 6, 3, and 7 suspects in the last six days. For the seventh day of the week, which number of arrests of the week will result in a median arrests that is NOT three?**

Correct Answer E

This is a "which" question, so we're going to mark-off answer choices. The first step is putting our numbers in order.

$$2, 3, 3, 4, 6, 7$$

Before we add the seventh number, the median is 3.5

$$2, 3, 3, 4, 6, 7$$

> When we have an *even* number of numbers, we average the two middle values.

We need to pull the median *down* to three.

Let's look at a hypothetical where our missing number (we'll call it x) is less than 3.

$$\textit{x}, 2, 3, 3, 4, 6, 7$$

As you can see our median is three on the nose. If you go the other way, where x is greater than three, the *median* goes *up* to 4.

$$2, 3, 3, 4, 6, 7, \textit{x}$$

If the missing number is equal to 3, the median is three. So, the most the missing number could be is *3*. Answer choice 4 is larger and therefore is NOT the number.

$$2, 3, \textit{x}, 3, 4, 6, 7$$

Answer choice **E** is correct.

<u>What You May Have Done Wrong</u>

In all answer choices, you either missed the NOT or made a conceptual error.

6. **The fantastic Arithmetician is thinking of 5 numbers such that their mean is the same as their median. Four of the numbers are 80, 68, 92, and 80. What is the fifth number?**

Correct Answer H

This is a tricky question, but it's easier than it looks. You'll have to find either the mean or the median. We can't find the mean because we're missing *two components*: we don't have an average, and we're missing one of the numbers. We've got to work with the median, so let's order the numbers.

$$68, 80, 80, 92$$

Right now median = 80, the average of the middle numbers. The missing number can be in one of three places. It can be *below* 80, *at* 80, or *above* 80.

$$\textit{x}, 68, 80, 80, 92 \leftarrow \text{the median is still 80}$$
$$68, 80, 80, \textit{x}, 92 \leftarrow \text{the median is still 80}$$
$$68, 80, 80, 92, \textit{x}, \leftarrow \text{the median is still 80}$$

Because the median is 80, the mean must be 80. We can plug that *average* into the average formula and find the missing value.

$$Average = \frac{sum}{number} \rightarrow 80 = \frac{68+80+80+92+x}{5} \rightarrow 80 = \frac{320+x}{5} \rightarrow 400 = 320+x \rightarrow x = 80$$

Answer **H** is correct.

<u>What You May Have Done Wrong</u>

    F. You used 92 as the median.
    G. You used 68 as the median.
    J. You made a mistake calculating the mean, you probably left out an 80
    K. This is a calculation or conceptual error.

7. One hundred families were surveyed to determine the number of cars in the household. The results were:

> 0 cars 7 families
> 1 car   23 families
> 2 cars 50 families
> 3 cars 18 families
> 4 cars   2 families

What is the average number of cars per household?

Correct Answer C

This is a *weighted average* question.

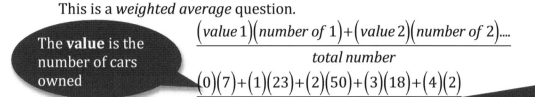

The **value** is the number of cars owned

$$\frac{(value\,1)(number\,of\,1)+(value\,2)(number\,of\,2)....}{total\,number}$$

The **number** is "how many families"

$$\frac{(0)(7)+(1)(23)+(2)(50)+(3)(18)+(4)(2)}{100\,families}$$

$$\frac{0+23+100+54+8}{100\,families} \rightarrow \frac{185\,cars}{100\,families} \rightarrow 1.85\,average$$

Answer **C** is correct.

<u>What You May Have Done Wrong</u>

A. You may have added the number of families and divided it by 100
B. This is a guess or a calculation error.
D. You may have picked the *mode* or made a calculation error.
E. This is a calculation or conceptual error.

8. A data set contains 21 items and the median of that data set is 34. Eight items are added to the data set. Four are less than 34 and four are greater than 34. What must be true about the new median?

Correct Answer H

This is a definition question and the data set is so large that it makes it hard to work with. There's also a number given for the median, which can be confusing.

Let's draw a diagram of this problem

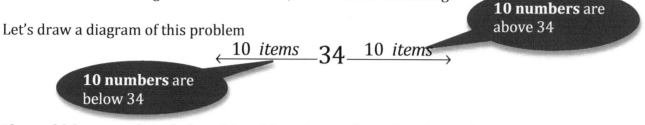

If we add four numbers below 34 and four items above 34, the median won't change.

$$\xleftarrow{\quad 10\ items\ +\ 4\ items\quad} 34 \xrightarrow{\quad 10\ items\ +\ 4\ items\quad}$$

Answer **H** is correct.

<u>What You May Have Done Wrong</u>
All of the other choices are the result of conceptual error. Review your steps.

9. Jim has taken four exams in his Latin course. His average after the four exams is 83%. If he did not receive a score lower than 78% on any of the tests, what is the highest possible score Jim could have gotten on one test?

Correct Answer D

This is an interesting problem. It's as much about maximums & minimums as it is about average.

For Jim to have received the highest possible score on a single exam his other exams must be the minimum possible score.

$$average = \frac{sum}{number}$$

$$83 = \frac{78+78+78+x}{4}$$

$$332 = 234 + x$$

$$x = 98$$

Answer choice **D** is correct.

<u>What You May Have Done Wrong</u>
Each of these answer choices represent a calculation error, or guess.

Introduction

I'm sorting tables, charts, and statistics questions in this section. There's a major overlap between this and the *mean, median, and mode* section. Most of the math in this section is *mean, weighted mean,* and *median,* but probability also shows up.

What You Need to Know

✓ How to find the proper fraction, or probability, from a table or chart
✓ How to use a frequency table to find *weighted average & median*
✓ How to use charts to find the *weighted average* or *median*
✓ Understand *correlation, line of best fit,* & *residuals*
✓ Understand random sampling

Review Pre-Algebra: Mean, Median...

The Formulas You Need

Weighted Average

$$\text{Weighted Average} = \frac{(value\,1)(number\,of\,1)+(value\,2)(number\,of\,2)....}{total\,number}$$

Median

Steps to Solving

1. **Order your numbers from least to greatest** (or greatest to least)
2. **Find the middle number.** If your set has an even number of numbers, you'll average the two middle numbers together.
3. **Solve** if needed

Probability

Review Pre-Algebra: Probability

$$probability = \frac{what\,you\,want}{everything}$$

ACT Example: Finding a Fraction from a Table

1. The Test Guy conducts a survey of 225 students to determine their college preferences. Students were asked whether they preferred small colleges or large universities. They were also asked whether they preferred in state or out of state schools. The results are shown on the table below. Based on the results, what is the likelihood that a randomly selected student wants to attend a small college given that they prefer in state schools?

A. $\dfrac{4}{11}$

B. $\dfrac{14}{27}$

C. $\dfrac{14}{45}$

D. $\dfrac{14}{45}$

E. $\dfrac{8}{45}$

	Small College	Large University	Total
In State	70	65	135
Out of State	40	50	90
Total	110	115	225

Solve

This is really a definition problem. You've got to figure out the numerator and denominator.

$$probability = \frac{\text{what you want}}{\text{everything}}$$

Likelihood means **probability**

Let's take a closer look at the question.

*What is the likelihood that a randomly selected student wants to attend a small college **given** that they prefer in-state schools?*

Given means they *have* to prefer in state schools. It's **everything** because it's *everyone* who prefers in-state. Or, "what are the odds that an in-state student wants to attend a small college.

Now we can find the values.

	Small College	Large University	Total
In State	70	65	135
Out of State	40	50	90
Total	110	115	225

Follow this method with similar problems based on charts.

$$probability = \frac{\text{what you want}}{\text{everything}} \rightarrow \frac{70}{135} = \frac{14}{27}$$

Answer choice **B** is correct.

There's a *video* on *Frequency Tables*

Definition: Frequency Table

A **frequency table** shows how many times a *value* occurs in a dataset.

ACT Example: Frequency Table

1. The class size of 30 courses in a college's political science department is shown by frequency below. Which class size interval is the median of the data?

   A. 10 - 30
   B. 30 - 50
   C. 50 - 100
   D. 100 - 150
   E. 150+

Class Size Interval	Frequency
under 10	3
10 - 30	6
30 - 50	4
50 - 100	5
100 - 150	9
150 +	3

Solve

We solve these frequency problems the same way as any median problem: order the data and find the middle value. The frequency is *how many times* (how many courses) have enrollments in those ranges. Starting at the lowest range, we count the frequencies (how many times something happens). The easiest way is to do this is using the table. Because there are 30 items, 30 classes, the median will be average of the 15th and 16th numbers.

Class Size Interval	Frequency	
under 10	3	3
10 - 30	6	3 + 6 = 9
30 - 50	4	3 + 6 + 4 = 13
50 - 100	5	3 + 6 + 4 + 5 = 18
100 - 150	9	
150 +	3	

The *median* is **between** 13 & 18, which is **a class size of 50 - 100**

Answer Choice **C** is correct.

Charts

On the ACT, bar charts are most common, but any type of chart is fair game. Questions about charts are very similar to questions about tables. The most frequent topics are *fractions* (probability), *median*, and *weighted average*.

ACT Example: Charts

1. A survey of 15 high school juniors asked the number of times the students had taken the ACT. Their responses are shown below. What, approximately, is the average number of attempts?

   A. 1
   B. 2.2
   C. 2.7
   D. 3.1
   E. 3.6

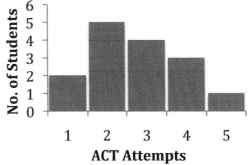

Solve

This is a *weighted average* question. We can't just average the number of attempts because each attempt has a different number of attempts. First, count the number of students per attempt.

1 attempt: 2 students	3 attempts: 4 students	5 attempts: 1 student
2 attempts: 5 students	4 attempts: 3 students	

Set up the weighted average formula.

$$Weighted\ Average = \frac{(value\ 1)(number\ of\ 1) + (value\ 2)(number\ of\ 2)....}{total\ number}$$

Plug-in the values & solve.

$$Weighted\ Average = \frac{(1)(2) + (2)(5) + (3)(4) + (4)(3) + (5)(1)}{15}$$

$$Weighted\ Average = \frac{41}{15} = 2.733 \approx 2.7\ attempts$$

Answer choice **C** is correct.

Sampling Topics

The ACT may ask you a definition question about random versus non-random sampling or the differences between a *census*, *survey*, and *experiment*.

Definitions: Random & Non-Random Sampling

Random Sampling selects a sample (a group of individuals) from a population. Everyone in the population has an equal chance of being selected for the sample. It's choosing the sample blindly.

Non-Random Sampling is sampling where not everyone has a chance of being chosen, or some individuals have a greater chance of being selected than others.

Examples: Random & Non-Random Sampling

1. The United States institutes a draft based on a lottery. The lottery randomly selects who will be drafted from the population of adults over 18 and under 45.

This is *random* sampling. There is no bias in the way the draftees are selected (it's a lottery) so everyone has an equal chance of being selected from the population of individuals between ages 18 and 45.

2. A researcher is trying to determine how popular college football is among the population of Michigan. On a Saturday afternoon in the fall, the researcher surveys the patrons at a sports bar in Ann Arbor Michigan.

This is *non-random* sampling. The researcher wants to determine how popular college football is in Michigan, but he only surveys in one place (not all Michigan residents have an equal chance of being selected). *There is also sample bias.* People at sports bars are *more likely* to like college football. People at sports bars in a college town*, during football season, are much more likely to like football. This kind of bias is called a
self-selecting sample.

   *The University of Michigan is in Ann Arbor Michigan

Definitions: Census, Surveys, & Experiments

A **census** includes **every** member of a population, *sample size = population size.* Censuses are great, but it may not be practial to perform a census if the population size is very big.

Surveys use a sample of individuals to draw conclusions about the population. Surveys can be questionnaires or interviews. Surveys can also be a review of records, like driving records, or hospital records.

Experiments are based on future events. Unlike surveys, where the results have already happened or the opinion is already formed, experiments haven't happened yet.

Examples: Census, Surveys, & Experiments

1. The United States holds a census every decade. The objective of that census is to count *every* individual in the United States and to collect statistics about them (age, sex, race, etc.)

This is a *census*; every individual in the population is counted.

2. Gallop conducts a public opinion poll of 1,000 adults. This sample is purported to represent the feeling of the nation as a whole.

This is a *survey*, a sample is chosen and the sample is supposed to reflect the population.

3. A medical researcher is conducting an experiment on a new asthma medication. A sample of patients is split into two groups. One group receives the new medication; the other group receives the placebo. After one month the researcher collects data on the medication's efficacy.

This is an *experiment*. We're using a sample to determine whether or not something *will work*. We're testing what the effects of the new medicine are, and comparing it to a control group. The researcher will draw conclusions about the population of asthma patients from this sample.

1. Erin is running for student government president and wants to do a poll to see what percent of the student body plans to vote for her. She surveys everyone in her homeroom. Which of the following describes Erin's poll?

   A. Randomized census
   B. Nonrandomized census
   C. Randomized experiment
   D. Randomized survey
   E. Nonrandomized survey.

> This is a "which" question, so **mark-off**

Solve

This is a mark-off *which* question. Go through each answer choice and mark-off as you go.

A. Randomized census
B. Nonrandomized census

Erin surveys everyone in her homeroom. This is a *sample* because the *whole* student body (population) votes on the student government president.

C. Randomized experiment

Erin isn't doing anything to the people she polls. There's nothing that happens to them in the future, Erin's poll is based on their present state (what they think of her *now*).

D. Randomized survey
E. Nonrandomized survey

Erin is *only* asking the people in her homeroom. Not all students have a chance to be chosen, so this isn't random sampling. Additionally, the people in Erin's homeroom are much more likely to have strong feelings (like or dislike) about Erin than other students.

Answer choice **E** is correct.

Bivariate Data & Correlation

Bivariate data is data from two variables. The variables are usually related.

Correlation is how the variables relate. Correlations can be *positive* or *negative*. In **positive correlation** as one variable increases, the other variable increases. In **negative correlation** as one variable increases, the other variable decreases.

Correlation also describes how closely the variables are related. Correlation can be *strong* or *weak* depending on how closely the variables are linked.

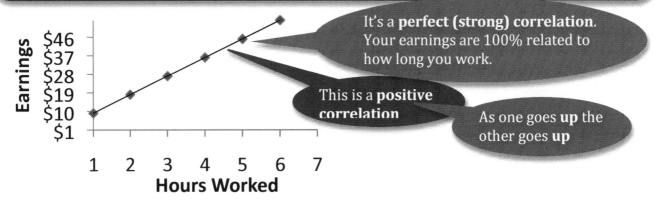

> It's a **perfect (strong) correlation**. Your earnings are 100% related to how long you work.

> This is a **positive correlation**

> As one goes **up** the other goes **up**

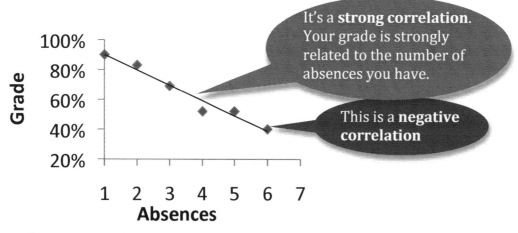

Line of Best Fit, Residuals, and Correlation Coefficients

Lines of best fit are lines that best represent the data on a scatter plot. The line may pass through all, some, or none of the points. It can be used to predict other values

Residuals are the *y* distance between a data point and it's corresponding point (same *x*-value) on the *line of best fit*.

Correlation coefficients measure how well the *line of best fit* corresponds with the dataset.

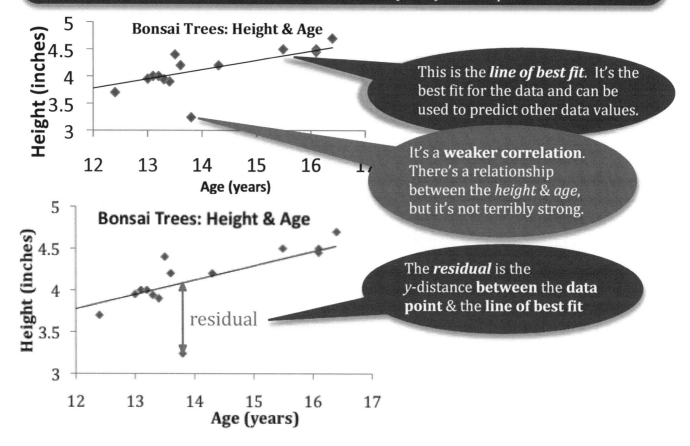

Correlation coefficients represent how well the *line of best fit* fits the dataset. It varies from -1 to 1. **-1** is a perfect *negative* correlation. **0** means **no correlation** at all. **1** is a perfect **positive** correlation.

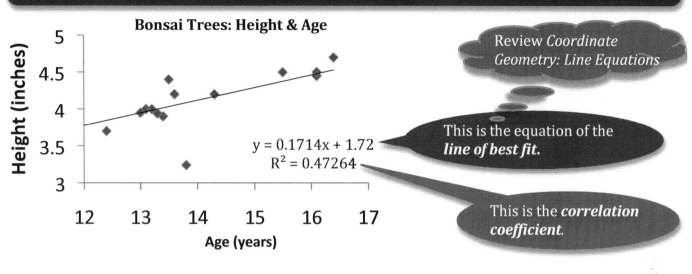

Review *Coordinate Geometry: Line Equations*

This is the equation of the *line of best fit*.

This is the *correlation coefficient.*

Wrap Up

What You Need to Know
- ✓ How to find the proper fraction, or probability, from a table or chart
- ✓ How to use a frequency table to find *weighted average & median*
- ✓ How to use charts to find the *weighted average* or *median*
- ✓ Understand *correlation*, *line of best fit*, & *residuals*
- ✓ Understand random sampling

Videos

Working with Data: Frequency Tables

Working with Data: Graphs

The Strategies
- ✓ Be careful, make sure you don't confuse value & frequency.
- ✓ Take the numbers from the exhibit and put them in a usable form.
- ✓ Don't be intimidated: the questions are easier than they look.

Related Topics
- ✓ Mean, Median, & Mode

- ✓ Probability

- ✓ Line Equations

Pre-Algebra: Data

Use the information below for questions 1 – 3.

2,000 high school juniors are asked how many times they expect to attempt the ACT. The results are shown in the bar chart below.

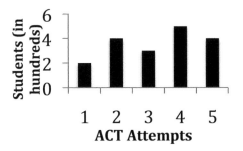

1. What percentage of students plan to take the ACT *less than* three times?

    A. 15%
    B. 30%
    C. 10%
    D. 0.3%
    E. 60%

2. What is the median number of times students plan to take the ACT?

    F. 1
    G. 2
    H. 3
    J. 4
    K. 5

3. What is the average number of planned ACT attempts?

    A. 3.00
    B. 3.20
    C. 2.95
    D. 2.75
    E. 3.40

4. Ania gives a survey to determine how well all customers like shopping at her store. She selects 200 customers randomly from all customers who had returned an item in the last six months. The survey is most susceptible to criticism on what grounds?

    F. The sample size is too small.
    G. The small size is too large.
    H. Not all customers were surveyed.
    J. The selection method of the sample is flawed.
    K. There is no valid criticism.

5. The correlation between the height, in inches, and the number of leaves in individuals in a certain species of plants. The *y*-values of each point are shown above the point.

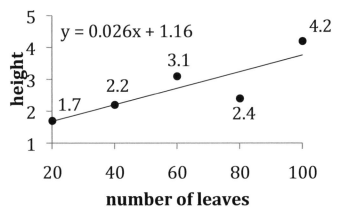

What is the absolute value of the largest residual?

    A. 2.4
    B. 3.24
    C. 0.84
    D. 1.3
    E. 1.45

Solutions: Data

1. What percentage of students plan to take the ACT *less than* three times?

Correct Answer B

This problem has a few wrinkles, you've got to find the part, you've got to find the whole, and you can't get mixed up by the "hundreds."

The whole is given to us; it usually will be, in the text before the chart.
"2,000 high school juniors" is our whole. You can, of course, add the height of each column to get the whole, but it takes time and introduces the possibility of error.

The part is the real trick, the question says "*less than* three times." That's the sum of one time & two times.

For one attempt, the y-value is 2 and for two attempts the y-value is because the y-axis is in hundreds, both one and two are worth three hundred each. So our percent calculation looks like this.

$$percent = \frac{part}{whole} \quad \rightarrow \quad percent = \frac{1\ time + 2\ times}{total}$$

$$percent = \frac{200 + 400}{2,000} \rightarrow \frac{6}{20} = 30\%$$

Answer choice B is correct.

<u>What You May Have Done Wrong</u>
    A. This is the percentage of students who expect to take the ACT 3 times.
    C. This is the percentage of students who expect to take the ACT once.
    D. You miscalculated your percent as 6/2,000. The y-values are in *hundreds*.
    E. This is either a math or conceptual error. Review your steps.

2. What is the median number of times students plan to take the ACT?

Correct Answer J

This is a median question that's tricky to set-up. Just like any median question we want to order the numbers and find the *middle value*. When we put these in order it's not 1, 2, 3, 4, 5. Those are *the values* for each data point. But we have *two hundred students* who plan to take the ACT one time, *four hundred students* who plan to take the ACT twice, and so on. There are 2,000 total students, so we'll need to find the average of the 1,000[th] and the 1,001[st] values. (We have to average them because 2,000 is an even number).

One Attempts   Two Attempts   Three Attempts
1 - 200   +   201 - 600   +   601 - 900

Once we go through all the students who plan one, two, and three attempts we're still not quite at the 1,000[th] or 1,001[st] value. Four attempts will get us there.

Four Attempts
900 – 1,401

The 1,000[th] and 1,001[st] students plan to take the ACT 4 times.

Answer choice J is correct.

<u>What You May Have Done Wrong</u>
    F. You may have guessed or made a conceptual error.
    G. You may have guessed or made a conceptual error.
    H. You probably took 3 attempts as the median because it's the middle *value*.
    K. You may have guessed or made a conceptual error.

3. What is the average number of planned ACT attempts?

Correct Answer C

This is a weighted average question. Fundamentally, weighted averages are no different than averages, but they certainly *feel* different.

$$average = \frac{sum}{number}$$

With weighted averages, we have a lot of occurrences of the same value.

In this case, we've got *two hundred* students who plan one attempt. It doesn't make a lot of sense to add 1+1+1+1+1+1+1+1+1.... So, multiply each value (1 attempt, 2 attempts) by the number of times (students).

$$average = \frac{(1)(200)+(2)(400)+(3)(300)+(4)(500)+(5)(400)}{2,000} \rightarrow average = \frac{5,900}{2,000} \rightarrow 2.95 \, attempts$$

Answer choice **C** is correct

What You May Have Done Wrong
  A. This is the average value of attempts, but not weighted for the amount of students.
  B. This is a calculation error. Review your steps.
  D. This is a calculation error. Review your steps.
  E. This is a calculation error. Review your steps.

4. Ania gives a survey to determine how well all customers like shopping at her store. She selects 200 customers randomly from all customers who had returned an item in the last six months. The survey is most susceptible to criticism on what grounds?

Correct Answer J

This is a wordy definition question. Let's put what Ania is trying to do in plainer language. This isn't something I would write down, but I would work through in my mind.

> *Ania wants to see how well people like shopping at her store. To do that, she's randomly surveying 200 people from the customers who have had to return something to her store.*

This is a mark-off question, so let's run through the answer choices.
  F. The sample size is too small.
     200 people is an adequate sample size for the shoppers of a single store.

  G. The small size is too large.
     *You can't really have too **big** a sample size.*

  H. Not all customers were surveyed.
     A survey is designed to use a sample that can represent the whole. A lot of the time it's tough to run a census (asking every single individual).

  J. The selection method of the sample is flawed.
     *The sample selection has **bias**. The people who are **returning items** to your store probably have a more negative view than the average customer. They can be included the sample, but they entire sample shouldn't be drawn from them.*

  K. There is no valid criticism.

5. The correlation between the height, in inches, and the number of leaves in individuals in a certain species of plants. The *y*-values of each point are shown above the point.

Correct Answer C

This is a confusing problem. We're looking for the biggest difference between a data point and the line of best fit. Let's look at the graph.

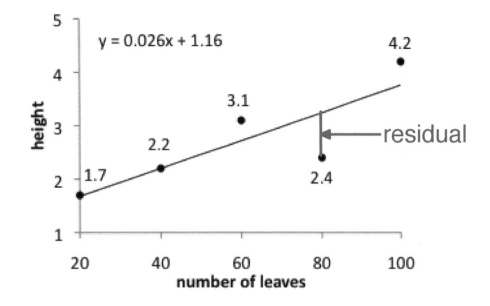

The *largest* residual is the biggest *y* gap between the data point and the line of best fit. By looking at the graph, the largest gap is between the point at (80, 2.4) and the line.

To find the residual, we'll need to find what the *y*-value of the line is when *x* is 80. The line equation is given to us at the top of the graph.

$$y = 0.026x + 1.16$$
$$y = 0.026(80) + 1.16$$
$$y = 2.08 + 1.16 = 3.24$$

Finally, find the difference between the line of best fit and the data point.
$$3.24 - 2.4 = 0.84$$

Answer choice **C** is correct.

<u>What You May Have Done Wrong</u>
A. This is the *y*-value of the point, which makes the largest residual, but it's not the largest residual.
B. You calculated the *y*-value of the line when *x* = 80, but you neglected to subtract 2.4 to find the size of the residual.
D. You subtracted 2.4 from 3.1, probably a guess calculation.
E. A guess or calculation error.

Elementary Algebra

The topics in the *Elementary Algebra* constitute 17 to 25 percent of the ACT Math section, or between 10 and 15 questions per test. Here's the question frequency and the corresponding ACT Score Report category or categories.

Operations[key skill]	1 – 3 questions	**PHM: Algebra**
Make an Equation[key skill]	2 – 4 questions	**MOD & PHM Algebra**
Plug-In	2 – 4 questions	**MOD & PHM Algebra**
Exponents[key skill]	0 – 2 questions	**MOD & PHM: Algebra**
Quadratics[key skill]	1 – 3 questions	**MOD & PHM: Algebra**
Inequalities	1 – 2 questions	**MOD & PHM: Algebra**
Absolute Value	0 – 2 questions	**PHM: Statistics**

IES: Integrating Essential Skills
PHM: Preparing for Higher Math
MOD: Modeling

A detailed explanation of the math score report is covered at the beginning of the book in the **Score Report**. There are four key skills in *Elementary Algebra*, so the importance of the topics is bigger than their question count.

Strategies

You've got to know your skills. There's no way around being comfortable with algebra operations and dealing with single variable equations. That said, you can make the ACT problems easier:

Break Questions Down

On **algebra operations**, write more not less. Don't be afraid go one step at a time.

One Statement at a Time

Just like *algebra operations*, break **make an equation** questions into single operation statements.

Don't Rearrange Until Necessary

Don't rearrange equations until you need to, plug-in variables first. Plugging in first is always the best policy on **plug-in** problems.

Deal with Exponents & Roots First

It's almost always easiest to deal with your roots & exponents right after you combine like terms.

Elementary Algebra: Pre-Test

1. For all real numbers x and y where $x = \dfrac{2y}{4} - 8$, $y = ?$

   A. ½x – 4
   B. 2x – 16
   C. 4x + 32
   D. 2x + 16
   E. 4x – 4

2. If $x = 7 + a$ and $y = 3 - 2a$, which expresses x in terms of y?

   A. $x = \dfrac{y-3}{2}$
   B. $x = 2y - 11$
   C. $x = 7 - \dfrac{y-3}{2}$
   D. $x = 7 + \dfrac{y-3}{2}$
   E. $x = 7 + \dfrac{y-3}{2}$

3. $\dfrac{x}{3} = \dfrac{x-2}{2}$?

   A. -6
   B. 6
   C. 3
   D. 2
   E. 4

4. What value of x makes the equation $\dfrac{2}{5}x - 3 = 9$ true?

   A. 30
   B. $4\dfrac{4}{5}$
   C. 15
   D. $2\dfrac{2}{5}$
   E. 12

5. For the equation $\dfrac{a}{k} = \dfrac{b}{10}$, if $a = 6$ when $b = 4$, when $a = 9$ what does b equal?

   A. 6
   B. 10
   C. 12
   D. 8
   E. 4

6. The formula for converting Celsius to Fahrenheit is $C = \dfrac{5}{9}(F - 32)$, what is the approximate temperature in Celsius if the temperature is $10°$ Fahrenheit?

   A. 12
   B. -12
   C. -39.6
   D. 39.6
   E. -22

7. The formula for finding the final velocity squared of an object is $v^2 = u^2 + 2ad$. Where final velocity (v) is 10 m/s, initial velocity (u) 4 m/s, distance (d) is 21 m, what is acceleration (a)?

   A. 2
   B. 4
   C. 8
   D. 10
   E. 13

8. An integer, x, is subtracted from ten, and the difference is multiplied by four. The result equals the same integer added to four and that sum multiplied by three. Which equation represents this relationship?

   A. 4(x – 10) = 3(x + 4)
   B. 4x -10 = 3x +4
   C. 4(x – 10) = 3x + 4
   D. x(10 – 4) = 3x
   E. 4(10 – x) = 3(x +4)

9. What number can you add to both the numerator and the denominator of $\dfrac{8}{11}$ to equal $\dfrac{2}{3}$?

   A. 4
   B. -2
   C. 2
   D. -3
   E. -6

10. You can find the number of ACT books in the Test Guy library by squaring the number of books and subtracting seventeen times the number of books. That difference is equal to 60. How many ACT books does the Test Guy own?

    A. 43
    B. 77
    C. 3
    D. 20
    E. 17

11. A new lawnmower cost 690 dollars. After an initial payment of 150 dollars, subsequent payments will be 60 dollars per month. How long until the lawnmower is paid off?

   A. 14 months
   B. 9 months
   C. 4.6 months
   D. 3.6 months
   E. 12 months

12. Annie opens a lemonade stand. She spends five dollars on markers and poster board to make her sign. Each glass of lemonade costs Annie $0.25 to make. What represents the total cost (*C*) of Annie's lemonade stand if she sells *x* glasses.

   A. $C = 0.25x + 5$
   B. $C = 5x + 0.25$
   C. $C = 5 - 0.25x$
   D. $C = 5.25x$
   E. $C = 0.25x - 5$

13. A taxi charges a $2.50 base charge for a ride and $0.40 for every third of a mile traveled. What represents the total cost of a taxi ride of *x* miles?

   A. $2.50 - 0.40x$
   B. $2.50 + 0.40x$
   C. $2.50x + 0.40x$
   D. $2.50x + 0.40$
   E. $2.50 + 1.20x$

14. Harper and Duke were both hired as circus dogs. Harper's salary starts at 25,000 dollars per year and each year she receives a 600-dollar raise. Duke starts out at 22,200 dollars per year and each year he receives a 1,000-dollar raise. What equation represents this relationship?

   A. $25,000 - 600x = 22,200 - 1,000x$
   B. $600x + 25,000 = 22,200 + 1,000x$
   C. $1,000x + 25,000 = 22,200 + 600x$
   D. $25,000x + 600 = 22,200x + 1,000$
   E. $25,000x + 1,000 = 22,200x + 600$

15. Plant A is seven centimeters tall and Plant B is eleven centimeters tall. They are both fertilized, and after fertilization Plant A grows at a rate of 1 cm. per week and Plant B grows at a rate of ½ cm. per week. After how many weeks will the two plants be equal in height?

   A. 4 weeks
   B. 5 weeks
   C. 6 weeks
   D. 8 weeks
   E. 9 weeks

16. What is the solution set of the equation $x^2 - 16x = 0$?

   A. 4 and 0
   B. 4 and -4
   C. 4 and 1
   D. 16 and 1
   E. 16 and 0

17. What values of *x* are the solutions for $(x - z)(x + y) = 0$?

   A. $-z$ and $-y$
   B. z and $-y$
   C. $-z$ and y
   D. z and y
   E. $-z(-y)$

18. Which is a factor of the equation $a^2 + 4ab + 3b^2 = 0$?

   A. $a^2 + 3b$
   B. $a^2 + b$
   C. $a - b$
   D. $a + b$
   E. $a + 4b$

19. $\left(2a + 4b\right)^2 = ?$

   A. $2a^2 + 4b^2$
   B. $4a^2 + 8b^2$
   C. $4a^2 + 16b^2$
   D. $4a^2 + 8ab + 16b^2$
   E. $4a^2 + 16ab + 16b^2$

20. What is the sum of the two solutions to the equation $x^2 + 3x - 18 = 0$?

   A. -3
   B. 3
   C. 9
   D. -9
   E. -18

21. Which statement is equal to $|x|$?

   A. x^2
   B. $x^2 - x$
   C. $\sqrt{2x}$
   D. $\sqrt{x^2}$
   E. $-|x|$

22. If $|x| = |y|$, which of the following *must* be true?

   A. $x = y$
   B. $x = -y$
   C. x & y are positive
   D. $x^2 = y^2$
   E. $x + y = 0$

23. If $x \neq y$, which CANNOT be true?

    A. $|x| = |y|$
    B. $|x| \neq |y|$
    C. $|x| + |y| = 0$
    D. $x + y = 0$
    E. $y < 0 < x$

24. Which of the following represents the inequality $|6x| \geq 6$?

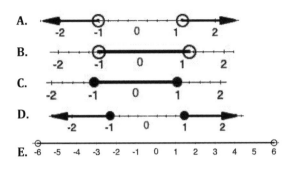

25. To override a presidential veto, a minimum of two-thirds of the Congress must vote to pass the bill. There are 100 voting members of the US Senate. Which inequality represents the number of votes (v) needed in the Senate.

    A. $v \geq 67$
    B. $v \leq 67$
    C. $v > 67$
    D. $v \geq 66$
    E. $v \leq 66$

26. Which inequality defines the solution set for the inequality $20 - 3x \leq 8$?

    A. $3 \leq x$
    B. $x \geq 4$
    C. $x \leq 4$
    D. $x \geq -4$
    E. $x \leq -4$

27. If four times a number n is added to negative 20, the result is positive. Which inequality gives the possible value(s) of n?

    A. $4n \geq -20$
    B. $n > -5$
    C. $n > 5$
    D. $n < -5$
    E. $n \geq 5$

28. If $0 > x > y > z$, which of the following expressions has the greatest value?

    A. $\dfrac{x}{y}$

    B. $\dfrac{y}{z}$

    C. $\dfrac{x}{z}$

    D. $\dfrac{z}{y}$

    E. $\dfrac{z}{x}$

29. $2\left(x^2 - 5x - 10\right) - \left(x^2 + x - 2\right) = ?$

    A. $2x^2 - 4x - 8$
    B. $x^2 - 11x - 18$
    C. $-3x^2 - 6x - 12$
    D. $-3x^2 - 4x - 8$
    E. $3x^2 - 4x - 12$

30. What is equivalent to $3x^3(x^2 + 4x + 2)$?

    A. $3x^6 + 12x^4 + 6x^3$
    B. $3x^5 + 7x^4 + 5x^3$
    C. $3x^6 + 12x^3 + 5x^3$
    D. $3x^5 + 12x^4 + 6x^3$
    E. $3x^6 + 12x^4 + 6x^3$

31. Given that $y = b^2c$, and $b = \frac{1}{2}$ and $y = 9$, what is c?

    A. 36
    B. 6 or -6
    C. 6
    D. -6
    E. 18

32. What is equivalent to $\left(-3x^2y\right)^3$?

    A. $-27x^5y^4$
    B. $-27x^6y^3$
    C. $27x^6y^3$
    D. $-9x^6y^3$
    E. $9x^6y^3$

33. If $x^3 - 4 = 4, x = ?$

    A. 2 or -2
    B. 0
    C. 2
    D. $\sqrt{8}$
    E. 512

34. What is the value of $x = \sqrt{a^2 + b^2}$, if $a = \sqrt{12}$, and $b = \sqrt{4}$ and $x > 0$?

    A. $\sqrt{200}$
    B. 40
    C. 4
    D. $\sqrt{160}$
    E. $\sqrt{180}$

35. What is equivalent to $\left(2\sqrt{x} - 4\sqrt{y}\right)^2$?

    A. $2x + 16y$
    B. $2x - 16y$
    C. $4x - 16y$
    D. $4x - 8\sqrt{xy} + 16y$
    E. $4x - 16\sqrt{xy} + 16y$

Pre-Test Answers

1.	D	Operations
2.	C	Operations
3.	B	Operations
4.	A	Operations
5.	A	Operations
6.	B	Operations
7.	A	Operations
8.	A	Make an Equation
9.	B	Make an Equation
10.	D	Make an Equation
11.	B	Make an Equation
12.	A	Make an Equation
13.	E	Make an Equation
14.	B	Make an Equation
15.	D	Make an Equation
16.	E	Factoring
17.	B	Factoring
18.	D	Factoring
19.	E	Factoring
20.	A	Factoring
21.	D	Absolute Value
22.	D	Absolute Value
23.	C	Absolute Value
24.	D	Absolute Value
25.	A	Inequalities
26.	B	Inequalities
27.	C	Inequalities
28.	E	Inequalities
29.	B	Exponents & Roots
30.	D	Exponents & Roots
31.	A	Exponents & Roots
32.	B	Exponents & Roots
33.	C	Exponents & Roots
34.	C	Exponents & Roots
35.	E	Exponents & Roots

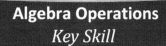
Algebra Operations
Key Skill

A linear equation has a highest power of "1" – an equation of the first degree.

The Background

While single variable linear equations make up a relatively small, if consistent, portion of the math section, the skills required are fundamentally important to many question types.

What You Need to Know

- ✓ Basic operations in equations
- ✓ How to deal with fractions in equations

There's a *video* on *Algebra Operations*

Rules of the Road: Equations

To solve equations, isolate the variable on one side of the equation and the numbers on the other. For example, $x = 2$.

To move numbers and variables from one side of an equation to the other, we must use the *opposite operation on both sides of the equation.*

Operation	Opposite	Operation	Opposite
Addition	Subtraction	Multiply	Divide
Subtraction	Addition	Divide	Multiply

Examples: Algebra Operations

1. $x + 4 = 7$, find x

$$x + 4 = 7$$
$$\underline{-4 = -4}$$
$$x = 3$$

isolate x

Since the 4 is added, we subtract.

2. $2x - 5 = 7$, find x

$$\underline{+5 = +5}$$
$$2x = 12$$

$$\frac{2x}{2} = \frac{12}{2} \rightarrow \frac{\cancel{2}x}{\cancel{2}} = 6$$

First, we want to isolate the term containing the x.

Since we are multiplying x by 2, we need to *divide* to remove the coefficient 2

1. For all real numbers x and y where $x = \dfrac{2y}{4} - 8$, $y = ?$

    A. ½x – 4
    B. $2x - 16$
    C. $4x + 32$
    D. $2x + 16$
    E. $4x - 4$

Solve

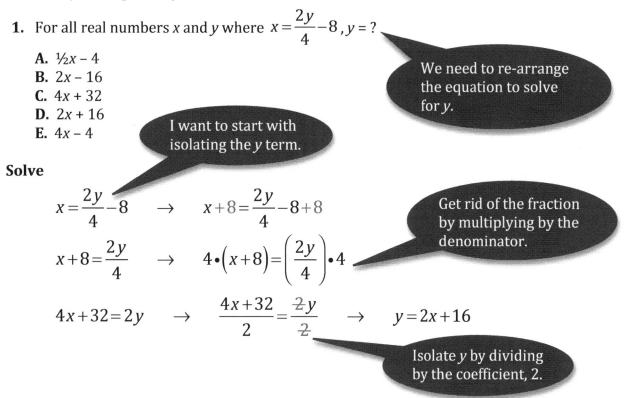

We need to re-arrange the equation to solve for y.

I want to start with isolating the y term.

$$x = \dfrac{2y}{4} - 8 \quad \rightarrow \quad x + 8 = \dfrac{2y}{4} - 8 + 8$$

$$x + 8 = \dfrac{2y}{4} \quad \rightarrow \quad 4 \cdot (x + 8) = \left(\dfrac{2y}{4}\right) \cdot 4$$

Get rid of the fraction by multiplying by the denominator.

$$4x + 32 = 2y \quad \rightarrow \quad \dfrac{4x + 32}{2} = \dfrac{2y}{2} \quad \rightarrow \quad y = 2x + 16$$

Isolate y by dividing by the coefficient, 2.

Answer choice **D** is correct.

2. If $x = 7 + a$ and $y = 3 - 2a$, which expresses x in terms of y?

    A. $x = \dfrac{y - 3}{2}$
    B. $x = 2y - 11$
    C. $x = 7 - \dfrac{y - 3}{2}$
    D. $x = 7 + \dfrac{y - 3}{2}$
    E. $x = 7 + \dfrac{y - 3}{2}$

Solve

This question has a complicated feel but it's more bark than bite. We need to get rid of a entirely, making an equation that looks like $x = \ldots$

Think of a as a bridge between x & y.

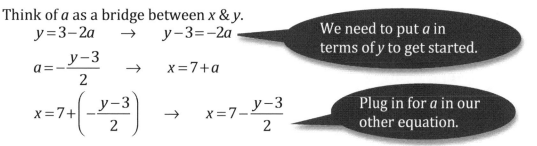

$$y = 3 - 2a \quad \rightarrow \quad y - 3 = -2a$$

We need to put a in terms of y to get started.

$$a = -\dfrac{y - 3}{2} \quad \rightarrow \quad x = 7 + a$$

$$x = 7 + \left(-\dfrac{y - 3}{2}\right) \quad \rightarrow \quad x = 7 - \dfrac{y - 3}{2}$$

Plug in for a in our other equation.

Answer choice **C** is correct.

3. $\dfrac{x}{3} = \dfrac{x-2}{2}$?

    A. -6
    B. 6
    C. 3
    D. 2
    E. 4

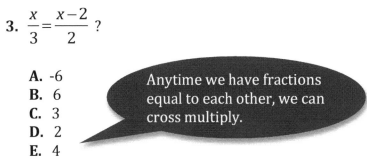

Anytime we have fractions equal to each other, we can cross multiply.

Solve

You can do this in pieces, or all at once. Whenever two fractions are equal to each other, cross-multiply.

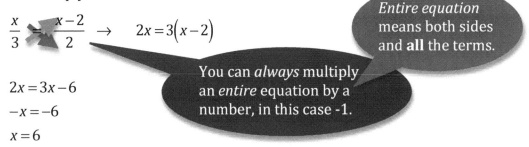

$$\dfrac{x}{3} = \dfrac{x-2}{2} \quad \rightarrow \quad 2x = 3(x-2)$$

$$2x = 3x - 6$$

$$-x = -6$$

$$x = 6$$

You can always multiply an entire equation by a number, in this case -1.

Entire equation means both sides and all the terms.

Answer choice **B** is correct.

4. What value of x makes the equation $\dfrac{2}{5}x - 3 = 9$ true?

    A. 30

    B. $4\dfrac{4}{5}$

    C. 15

    D. $2\dfrac{2}{5}$

    E. 12

Solve

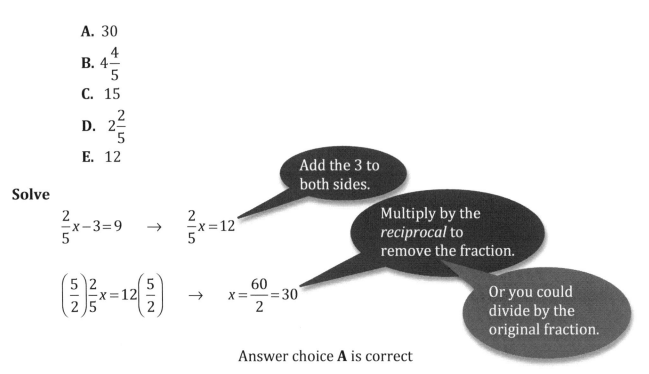

$$\dfrac{2}{5}x - 3 = 9 \quad \rightarrow \quad \dfrac{2}{5}x = 12$$

$$\left(\dfrac{5}{2}\right)\dfrac{2}{5}x = 12\left(\dfrac{5}{2}\right) \quad \rightarrow \quad x = \dfrac{60}{2} = 30$$

Add the 3 to both sides.

Multiply by the reciprocal to remove the fraction.

Or you could divide by the original fraction.

Answer choice **A** is correct

Plug-In Problems

Plug-in problems are *always* on ACT math sections. They show up as word problems, plug-in geometry problems, and straight algebra problems. The section *Intermediate Algebra: Algebraic Functions* covers some of the more advanced plug-in problems.

ACT Examples: Algebra Operations

5. For the equation $\dfrac{a}{k} = \dfrac{b}{10}$, if $a = 6$ when $b = 4$, when $a = 9$ what does b equal?

    A. 6
    B. 10
    C. 12
    D. 8
    E. 4

Solve

This is a confusing looking proportion problem. To start, plug in the givens and find k, and k is a constant (by the way the letter k is often used as a constant).

We're told that, "if $a = 6$ when $b = 4$."

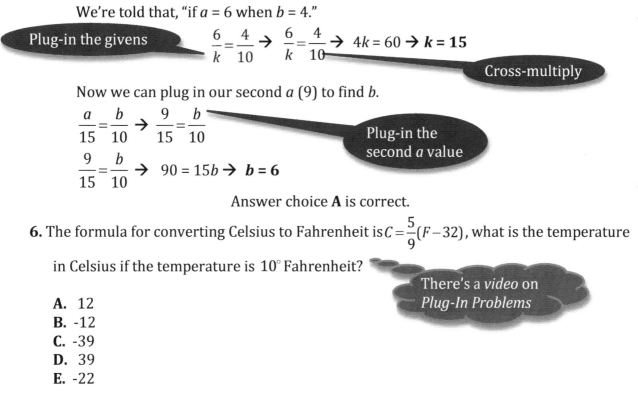

Plug-in the givens

$$\dfrac{6}{k} = \dfrac{4}{10} \rightarrow \dfrac{6}{k} = \dfrac{4}{10} \rightarrow 4k = 60 \rightarrow k = 15$$

Cross-multiply

Now we can plug in our second a (9) to find b.

$$\dfrac{a}{15} = \dfrac{b}{10} \rightarrow \dfrac{9}{15} = \dfrac{b}{10}$$

Plug-in the second a value

$$\dfrac{9}{15} = \dfrac{b}{10} \rightarrow 90 = 15b \rightarrow b = 6$$

Answer choice **A** is correct.

6. The formula for converting Celsius to Fahrenheit is $C = \dfrac{5}{9}(F - 32)$, what is the temperature in Celsius if the temperature is $10°$ Fahrenheit?

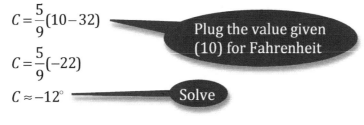

There's a *video* on *Plug-In Problems*

    A. 12
    B. -12
    C. -39
    D. 39
    E. -22

Solve

This is a plug-in problem, and they show up on every test. It's the same procedure, except we've got to plug in for a variable (or variables in some cases) first.

$$C = \dfrac{5}{9}(10 - 32)$$

Plug the value given (10) for Fahrenheit

$$C = \dfrac{5}{9}(-22)$$

$$C \approx -12°$$

Solve

Answer choice **B** is correct.

7. The formula for finding the final velocity squared of an object is $v^2 = u^2 + 2ad$. Where final velocity (v) is 10 m/s, initial velocity (u) 4 m/s, distance (d) is 21 m, what is acceleration (a)?

   A. 2
   B. 4
   C. 8
   D. 10
   E. 13

Solve

This plug-in problem has a bunch of variables. Be very careful plugging in, it's easy to switch one. I don't rearrange the equation before working these. I think it's faster and easier to plug the numbers in and solve as you go.

$$10^2 = 4^2 + 2a(21)$$
$$100 = 16 + 42a$$
$$84 = 42a$$
$$a = 2$$

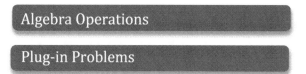
Be careful plugging in!

Answer choice **A** is correct.

Wrap Up

What You Need to Know
- ✓ The rules of exponents and roots.
- ✓ How to deal with fractions in equations

Videos

> Algebra Operations

> Plug-in Problems

The Strategies
- ✓ Don't mess these up. Write more, not less and you will avoid costly errors.
- ✓ Don't let re-arrange questions throw you off. Just find the first step and go from there.
- ✓ Be careful on plug-in problems. Make sure you plug in for the right variables.

Key Skill
Algebra operations are related to all algebra problems, many coordinate geometry problems, and some plane geometry & trig problems.

Elementary Algebra: Algebra Operations

1. What is x in terms of y in the equation
   $2x + 5y = 7x + 2$?

   A. $x = -y + 2$

   B. $x = -y + \dfrac{2}{5}$

   C. $x = y - \dfrac{2}{5}$

   D. $x = y - 2$

   E. $x = \dfrac{5}{9}y + \dfrac{2}{9}$

2. If all three of the algebraic expressions listed below are equivalent, what must be the value of g in terms of x?

   $$3x + 7x - g$$
   $$12x + 6x - 13x + \dfrac{2g}{3}$$
   $$6x + 10x - 3g$$

   F. $4x$

   G. x

   H. $2x$

   J. $3x$

   K. Cannot be determined.

3. What is y in terms of x if $x = \dfrac{3+x}{y-2}$?

   A. $y = 3x + 3$

   B. $y = -\dfrac{3}{2}$

   C. $y = \dfrac{3}{x} + 3$

   D. $y = \dfrac{2x}{3+x}$

   E. $y = \dfrac{x}{x+3} + 2$

4. Which is the expression $2\big[(xy - y) + (4a - y)\big]$ is equivalent to?

   F. $2xy - 3y + 4a$

   G. $2x - 2y + 8a$

   H. $2xy - 4y + 8a$

   J. $2xy + 8a$

   K. $2xy - 4a$

5. If $-a = 4b + 7$ and $7 - 2b = 3 + x$, then what is a in terms of x?

   A. $a = -2x + 15$

   B. $a = 2x + 17$

   C. $a = -2x - 1$

   D. $a = 4x - 15$

   E. $a = 2x - 15$

6. For what value of x is $8x + 4 = 5x - 4$ true?

   F. $-\dfrac{8}{3}$

   G. $-\dfrac{3}{8}$

   H. $\dfrac{8}{3}$

   J. -8

   K. $\dfrac{8}{13}$

7. If $3 - \dfrac{a}{3} = 8$, then $a = ?$

   A. 33

   B. 15

   C. -15

   D. $\dfrac{5}{3}$

   E. $\dfrac{11}{3}$

8. The formula for the volume of a right circular cone is $V = \dfrac{4}{3}\pi r^3$. What is approximately the radius of a cone that has a volume of 904 cm³?

   F. 5.8 cm

   G. 6 cm

   H. 14.6 cm

   J. 9.7 cm

   K. 2.3 cm

9. Molarity is a chemistry ratio describing moles (a fixed number of molecules) of solute per liter of solution. The formula for molarity is $M = \dfrac{moles}{liters}$. A solution is known to have a molarity of 0.6 M/l and a volume of 9 liters. How many moles are in the solution?

A. 0.067 moles
B. 15 moles
C. 5.4 moles
D. 9.6 moles
E. .67 moles

10. The function defined as

$y = 0.00003x^3 - 0.004x - 30$ is a curve.

Approximately, what will the y-coordinate be when the x-coordinate is 122?

F.   54
G. 5,417
H.   25
J.   24
K.   -30.00

11. Pipe diameter (d) is found by the formula

$d = \sqrt{\dfrac{4r}{\pi v}}$, where r is flow rate and v is velocity.

For a pipe with diameter of 18 cm, and a flow rate of 200 cm³/s, what is the velocity?

A. 14.14 m/s
B.   0.12 m/s
C. 60.00 m/s
D. 0.79 m/s
E.   6.84 m/s

12. If x = -2, then what is the value of $\dfrac{x^2 + 4x}{x^3 - x}$?

F. $\dfrac{2}{3}$

G. -$\dfrac{2}{3}$

H. $\dfrac{2}{5}$

J.   -$\dfrac{2}{5}$

K. 0

13. Let $c = 4a - 2b$. What happens to the value of c if the value of a decreases by 1 and the value of b increases by 1?

F. Decreases by 2
G. Decreases by 4
H. Decreases by 6
J. Increases by 6
K. Increases by 4

14. Function $f(x) = x^2 - 4x + 3$, what is $f(3)$?

A.   3
B.   1
C.   24
D. -15
E.   0

Algebra Operations: Solutions

1. What is *x* in terms of *y* in the equation $2x+5y=7x+2$?

Correct Answer C

If you're confused by what the question is asking, look at your answer choices. *Always look at your answer choices before you start working the problem.* We're looking for *x* = ..., and the answer choices tell you that. So, re-arrange, combine our like terms and leave a single *x* on one side of the equation.

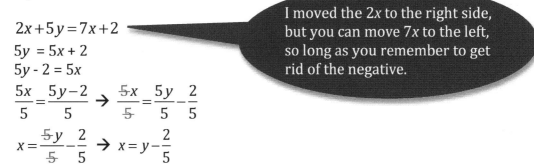

$$2x+5y=7x+2$$
$$5y = 5x + 2$$
$$5y - 2 = 5x$$

I moved the 2*x* to the right side, but you can move 7*x* to the left, so long as you remember to get rid of the negative.

$$\frac{5x}{5}=\frac{5y-2}{5} \rightarrow \frac{\cancel{5}x}{\cancel{5}}=\frac{5y}{5}-\frac{2}{5}$$

$$x=\frac{\cancel{5}y}{\cancel{5}}-\frac{2}{5} \rightarrow x=y-\frac{2}{5}$$

Answer choice **C** is correct.

What You May Have Done Wrong

A. This is a compound error. You forgot to divide 2 by 5 (or -5) and you had a sign error on the *y* (probably from failing to divide by a -5, when your particular setup required it).

B. You made a sign error. You probably moved the 7*x* to the right (which is fine to do) but forgot to divide by a negative 5.

D. You failed to divide -2 by 5.

E. You misunderstood the question or had setup problems.

2. If all three of the algebraic expressions listed below are equivalent, what must be the value of g in terms of x?

$$3x + 7x - g, \quad 12x + 6x - 13x + \frac{2g}{3}, \quad 6x + 10x - 3g$$

Correct Answer J

This is a problem written to scare you. Don't let it get to you: once you understand what's going on, the problem is not bad at all. Let's start with the text of the question itself.

"If all four of the algebraic expressions listed below are equivalent"

What they are saying is that each statement equals every other statement given. That means we can set the statements equal to each other. Even though we can use any of the three statements, I'm going to use the **first** and **last statement** to avoid the fraction in the second statement.

$$3x + 7x - g = 6x + 10x - 3g$$

Now, let's rearrange and find *g* in terms of *x*.

Set them equal.

$$3x + 7x - g = 6x + 10x - 3g \rightarrow 10x - g = 16x - 3g$$
$$2g = 6x \rightarrow g = 3x$$

Answer choice **J** is correct.

What You May Have Done Wrong

F. You made a calculation error in the second equation.

G. There are a few possible errors, depending on the expressions you used. Most likely you made a sign error.

H. You likely made a sign mistake.

K. You may not have understood the problem.

3. What is y in terms of x if $x = \dfrac{3+x}{y-2}$?

Correct Answer C

This is a tough rearrangement question that really requires us to be comfortable with fractions. Let's take a look.

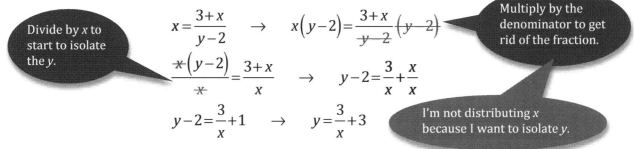

Divide by x to start to isolate the y.

Multiply by the denominator to get rid of the fraction.

$$x = \frac{3+x}{y-2} \quad \rightarrow \quad x(y-2) = \frac{3+x}{\cancel{y-2}}\cancel{(y-2)}$$

$$\frac{\cancel{x}(y-2)}{\cancel{x}} = \frac{3+x}{x} \quad \rightarrow \quad y-2 = \frac{3}{x} + \frac{x}{x}$$

$$y-2 = \frac{3}{x} + 1 \quad \rightarrow \quad y = \frac{3}{x} + 3$$

I'm not distributing x because I want to isolate y.

Answer choice **C** is correct

<u>What You May Have Done Wrong</u>
- **A.** You have a compound error here. Review your steps.
- **B.** You may have tried to divide the x on the left side, and incorrectly cancelled it.
- **D.** You have a compound error here. Review your steps.
- **E.** You have a compound error here. Review your steps.

4. Which is the expression $2\big[(xy - y) + (4a - y)\big]$ is equivalent to?

Correct Answer H

This problem asks us to remove the parentheses and brackets the expression. Essentially, we are expounding the expression.

There's nothing we can do in either set of parentheses. We can't subtract in either set.

$$2\big[(xy-y)+(4a-y)\big] \quad \rightarrow \quad 2\big[xy-y+4a-y\big]$$

$$2\big[xy+4a-2y\big] \quad \rightarrow \quad 2xy+8a-4y$$

Answer choice **H** is correct.

<u>What You May Have Done Wrong:</u>
- **F.** You distributed the 2 only to the first set of parentheses. You should have distributed it to everything within the bracket.
- **G.** You may have subtracted $xy - y$ and got x. You can't subtract terms that have different variables.
- **J.** You made a sign error causing your y terms to cancel.
- **K.** This is a compound error. You made a mistake distributing and a sign error.

5. If $-a = 4b + 7$ and $7 - 2b = 3 + x$, then what is a in terms of x?

Correct Answer E

This problem looks like a big headache. We have to do some re-arranging to find b in terms of x. That will allow us to plug-in and find a in terms of x. Let's start with our second equation, putting it in terms of $b=$

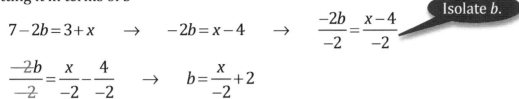

$$7 - 2b = 3 + x \quad \rightarrow \quad -2b = x - 4 \quad \rightarrow \quad \frac{-2b}{-2} = \frac{x-4}{-2}$$

Isolate b.

$$\frac{-2b}{-2} = \frac{x}{-2} - \frac{4}{-2} \quad \rightarrow \quad b = \frac{x}{-2} + 2$$

Now, plug-in for b in the second equation.

$$-a = 4b + 7 \quad \rightarrow \quad -a = 4\left(\frac{x}{-2} + 2\right) + 7$$

Multiply the entire equation by -1.

$$-a = \frac{4x}{-2} + 8 + 7 \quad \rightarrow \quad -a = -2x + 15$$

$$a = 2x - 15$$

Answer choice **E** is correct.

<u>What You May Have Done Wrong</u>
  A. You dropped (or forgot) the negative sign in front of a.
  B. You made a sign error in the first equation ($7 - 2b = 3 + x$).
  C. You've got a compound error. You didn't deal with the $-a$ and you had a sign problem.
  D. This is a compound error. Review your steps.

6. For what value of x is $8x + 4 = 5x - 4$ true?

Correct Answer F

This is a straightforward algebra problem. We'll need to put the x terms on one side and the constants on the other.

$$8x + 4 = 5x - 4 \quad \rightarrow \quad 3x = -8$$

$$x = -\frac{8}{3}$$

Answer choice **F** is correct.

<u>What You May Have Done Wrong</u>
  G. You inverted your fraction; you may have been trying to do the problem in your head.
  H. You dropped a negative sign.
  J. You didn't complete the problem. Review your steps.
  K. You miscalculated your denominator (adding $5x$ and $8x$ instead of finding their difference).

7. If $3 - \dfrac{a}{3} = 8$, then $a = ?$

Correct Answer C

This is a solve problem, and it's not that bad. Isolate the fraction first to make things easier on yourself.

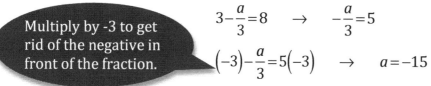

Multiply by -3 to get rid of the negative in front of the fraction.

$$3 - \frac{a}{3} = 8 \quad \rightarrow \quad -\frac{a}{3} = 5$$

$$(-3) - \frac{a}{3} = 5(-3) \quad \rightarrow \quad a = -15$$

Answer choice **C** is correct.

What You May Have Done Wrong

    A. You made an operation error adding 3 to 8 (instead of subtracting).
    B. You dropped a negative sign somewhere.
    D. You divided by 3 to remove the fraction; you should have multiplied by 3.
    E. This is a compound error. First, you added 3 to 8 (instead of subtracting). Second, you tried to remove the fraction by dividing by 1/3 when you should have multiplied.

8. The formula for the volume of a right circular cone is $V = \dfrac{4}{3}\pi r^3$. What is the radius of a cone that has a volume of 904 cm³?

Correct Answer G

This is a more sophisticated problem and you'll have to deal with exponents Let's plug in, isolate and solve.

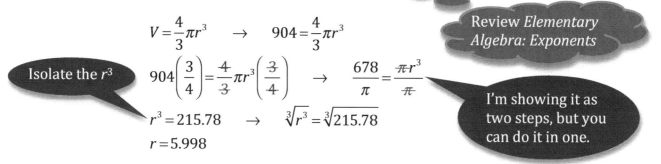

Review *Elementary Algebra: Exponents*

Isolate the r^3

I'm showing it as two steps, but you can do it in one.

$$V = \frac{4}{3}\pi r^3 \quad \rightarrow \quad 904 = \frac{4}{3}\pi r^3$$

$$904\left(\frac{3}{4}\right) = \frac{4}{3}\pi r^3 \left(\frac{3}{4}\right) \quad \rightarrow \quad \frac{678}{\pi} = \frac{\pi r^3}{\pi}$$

$$r^3 = 215.78 \quad \rightarrow \quad \sqrt[3]{r^3} = \sqrt[3]{215.78}$$

$$r = 5.998$$

Answer choice **G** is correct.

What You May Have Done Wrong

    F. You either made a math error or rounding error.
    H. You took the square root of the intermediate step (215.81) instead of the cube root.
    J. You took the cube root before you isolated the cube. You may want to review *algebra with exponents*. You also forgot to solve for the radius.
    K. You took the cube root before you isolated the cube. You may want to review *algebra with exponents*.

9. Molarity is a chemistry ratio describing moles (a fixed number of molecules) of solute per liter of solution. The formula for molarity is $M = \dfrac{moles}{liters}$. A solution is known to have a molarity of 0.6 M/l and a volume of 9 liters. How many moles are in the solution?

Correct Answer C

This is a relatively straightforward question, but it's long and the wordiness is confusing. The first sentence, for example, doesn't tell us anything we really need to know. All we really need is the formula and the two given components to find the third component.

Multiply by nine to remove the fraction.

$$M = \frac{moles}{liters} \quad \rightarrow \quad 0.6 = \frac{moles}{9}$$

$$9(0.6) = (9)\frac{moles}{9} \quad \rightarrow \quad moles = 5.4$$

Answer choice **C** is correct.

What You May Have Done Wrong
- **A.** You divided by nine instead of multiplying by nine. You may want to review fractions.
- **B.** Most likely you plugged-in incorrectly. You put .6 for liters and 9 for molarity.
- **D.** For some reason you added 9 and 0.6. You should review fractions and algebra.
- **E.** You made some math error, check through your calculations.

10. The function defined as $y = 0.00003x^3 - 0.004x - 30$ is a curve. Approximately, what will the y-coordinate be if the x-coordinate is 122?

Correct Answer J

This problem's function is in $y =$ form (remember $f(x)$ is the same as y). **In functions, x is our input and y is our output.** Let's plug-in and solve.

$$y = 0.00003x^3 - 0.004x - 30$$

$$y = 0.00003(122)^3 - 0.004(122) - 30$$

$$y = 0.00003(1,815,848)^3 - 0.004(122) - 30$$

$$y = 54.47544 - .488 - 30$$

$$y = 23.98744$$

Answer choice **J** is correct.

What You May Have Done Wrong:
- **F.** You may have only dealt with the first term and forgot to deal with the second and third terms, -0.004x and -30.
- **G.** You made an error entering the zeroes in the first term.
- **H.** You made a rounding error *or* you added the -.004x term.
- **K.** This is a compound error; walk through your steps.

11. Pipe diameter (d) is found by the formula $d = \sqrt{\dfrac{4r}{\pi v}}$, where r is flow rate and v is velocity. For a pipe with diameter of 18 cm, and a flow rate of 200 cm3/s, what is the velocity?

Correct Answer D

This is a plug in problem, and again we've got an exponent to deal with (the square root). Start by plugging in.

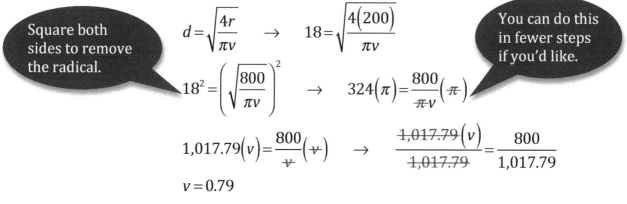

$$d = \sqrt{\dfrac{4r}{\pi v}} \quad \rightarrow \quad 18 = \sqrt{\dfrac{4(200)}{\pi v}}$$

Square both sides to remove the radical.

You can do this in fewer steps if you'd like.

$$18^2 = \left(\sqrt{\dfrac{800}{\pi v}}\right)^2 \quad \rightarrow \quad 324(\pi) = \dfrac{800}{\cancel{\pi} v}(\cancel{\pi})$$

$$1{,}017.79(v) = \dfrac{800}{\cancel{v}}(\cancel{v}) \quad \rightarrow \quad \dfrac{\cancel{1{,}017.79}(v)}{\cancel{1{,}017.79}} = \dfrac{800}{1{,}017.79}$$

$$v = 0.79$$

Answer choice **D** is correct.

<u>What You May Have Done Wrong</u>

   A. You solved incorrectly, putting in 324 (d^2) as the numerator.

   B. You plugged in incorrectly, putting the flow rate in for the diameter and vice versa.

   C. You tried to remove the square root by taking the square root of 18. This would not remove the root from the right hand side of the equation.

   E. This is a compound error; review your steps.

12. If x = -2, then what is the value of $\dfrac{x^2 + 4x}{x^3 - x}$?

Correct Answer F

This is a stripped down version of the standard *function style* plug-in problem.

$$\dfrac{x^2 + 4x}{x^3 - x} \quad \rightarrow \quad \dfrac{(-2)^2 + 4(-2)}{(-2)^3 - (-2)}$$

$$\dfrac{4 - 8}{-8 + 2} \quad \rightarrow \quad \dfrac{-4}{-6} = \dfrac{2}{3}$$

Answer choice **F** is correct.

<u>What You May Have Done Wrong</u>

   G. You had a sign problem. You forgot that a cube retains the original sign $-2^3 = -8$. You also may have not turned the $-x$ on the bottom into a +2.

   H. You had a sign problem. You forgot that a cube retains the original sign $-2^3 = -8$.

   J. You had a compound sign problem, review your steps.

   K. You incorrectly calculated your numerator. Remember, $x^2 = 4$, not -4. You also failed to multiply your second term (-2) by x.

13. Let $c = 4a - 2b$. What happens to the value of c if the value of a decreases by 1 and the value of b increases by 1?

Correct Answer H

This is a difficult problem, it can be solved algebraically, but it can be confusing to do so (although I will show it). It's better to pick numbers and plug in. Let's look at the algebra first.

<u>Algebra</u>

The original formula looks like this: $c = 4a - 2b$. The problem specifies that we change it in this way, $a - 1$ and $b + 1$. Let's plug the new a and b values in.

$$c = 4(a-1) - 2(b+1) \quad \rightarrow \quad c = 4a - 4 - 2b - 2$$
$$c = 4a - 2b - 6 \quad \rightarrow \quad c + 6 = 4a - 2b$$

Here's what the equation says. For c to equal $4a - 2b$ we need to add 6 to c. That means, c is six less than it was. **Therefore, c has decreased by six.**

<u>Picking Numbers</u>

Pick two easy to work with numbers for a and b and then plug them in to the equation to find an initial value of c. Let's say that $a = 1$ and $b = 2$.

$$c = 4(1) - 2(2) \quad \rightarrow \quad c = 4 - 4 \quad \rightarrow \quad c = 0$$

Now, we can change a and b according to the question and find a new c. First, let's find our new a and b.

$a - 1$	$b + 1$
$1 - 1 = 0$	$2 + 1 = 3$

Our new $a = 0$ and new $b = 3$. Let's plug in.

$$c = 4a - 2b \quad \rightarrow \quad c = 4(0) - 2(3)$$
$$c = 0 - 6 \quad \rightarrow \quad c = -6$$

Initially, c was 0 and now c is -6. So c has **decreased** by six.

Answer choice H is correct.

<u>What You May Have Done Wrong</u>

F. You may have eyeballed (guessed), or plugged in the changes, not values.
G. You may have eyeballed (guessed), or had some other problem.
J. You may have gotten the right answer but misunderstood it.
K. You may have eyeballed (guessed), or plugged in the changes, not values.

14. Function $f(x) = x^2 - 4x + 3$, what is $f(3)$?

Correct Answer E

This is a plug-in problem that requires you to know a little bit about functions. There's a section on problems like this, and you may want to check it out.

$$f(x) = x^2 - 4x + 3 \quad \rightarrow \quad f(3) = 3^2 - 4(3) + 3$$
$$f(3) = 9 - 12 + 3 \quad \rightarrow \quad f(3) = 0$$

You plug in 3 wherever x is in the equation.

Answer choice E is correct

<u>What You May Have Done Wrong</u>

A. You either made a mistake or you tried to factor the quadratic.
B. You either made a mistake or you tried to factor the quadratic.
C. You made an arithmetic error adding -12, instead of subtracting.
D. You probably made an order of operations error, adding three before you multiplied -4x.

Background

Make an equation problems aren't just elementary algebra problems (but that's what we'll cover in this section). Making an equation is a key skill, vital for ACT Math success.

What You Need to Know

✓ Making an algebraic expression from a word problem.
✓ Make a linear equation from a word problem.
✓ Find the solution to two linear systems by writing two equations and setting them equal.

> Review *Int. Alg.:*
> *Systems of Equations*

Making an Equation: Translating Text to Operations

Operation	Other Key Words
Addition	exceeds, plus, the sum of, more than, increased by
Subtraction	minus, less than, subtracted from, the difference of
Multiplication	times, twice, double, two-thirds*
Division	ratio, the quotient of, divided by
*any fraction would work here.	

I use *a number* below, but we could easily use any variable

Addition

three is added to a number	→ $n + 3$
eight plus a number	→ $n + 8$
the sum of six and a number	→ $n + 6$
five more than a number	→ $n + 5$

Subtraction

> Order matters in subtraction!

a number minus two	→ $n - 2$
two minus a number	→ $2 - n$
four less than a number	→ $n - 4$
x less than four	→ $x - 4$
six subtracted from a number	→ $n - 6$
a number subtracted from six	→ $6 - n$
the difference between six and a number	→ $n - 6$

> Order doesn't matter in multiplication

Multiplication

three times a number	→ $3n$
twice a number	→ $2n$
double a number	→ $2n$
two thirds a number	→ $\frac{2}{3}n$

Division

> Order matters in division!

the ratio of a number to 3	→ $\frac{n}{3}$
the ratio of 3 to a number	→ $\frac{3}{n}$
the quotient of a number & 2	→ $\frac{n}{2}$
the quotient of 2 & a number	→ $\frac{2}{n}$
a number divided by five	→ $\frac{n}{5}$

Making an Equation: Equality & Inequality

You'll also need to be able to convert text into equal signs & inequalities.

Equal/Inequality		Key Words
Equality	=	is, equals, the same as, equivalent to
Unequal	≠	Not the same as, not equal to
Greater Than	>	greater than, more, larger
Greater Than or Equal to	≥	greater than or equal to, at least, not less than
Less Than	<	less than, smaller
Less Than or Equal to	≤	less than or equal to, no more than, at most

Equal

a number is four	→ $n = 4$
a number equals six	→ $n = 6$
a number is the same as eight	→ $n = 8$
a number is equivalent to ten	→ $n = 10$

Inequality

a number is not the same as 3	→ $n \neq 3$
a number is not equal to five	→ $n \neq 5$

a number is greater than nine	→ $n > 9$
a number more than eleven	→ $n > 11$
a number is larger than one	→ $n > 1$

a number is at least sixteen	→ $n \geq 16$
a number is not less than 12	→ $n \geq 12$

a number is less than six	→ $n < 6$
a number is smaller than four	→ $n < 4$

a number is no more than two	→ $n \leq 2$
a number is at most twenty	→ $n \leq 20$

Rules of the Road: Take Small Bites

It is absolutely necessary to break questions down into single operation statements. Build your equation with these statements.

1. The sum of a number and six is multiplied by three

Let's break this into statements.

Statement 1: the sum of a number and six

$n + 6$

"a number" is the variable.

Statement 2: is multiplied by three.

$3(\text{sum}) \rightarrow 3(n + 6)$

This is tricky, the sum is multiplied by three.

2. Six is subtracted from two times a number.

Statement 1: six is subtracted from

$- 6$

It goes "backwards" because 6 is subtracted from.

Statement 2: two times a number

$2n$

$2n - 6$

3. Four times a number is equal to 20 minus that number.

Statement 1: four times a number
$$4n$$

> We can split the equation to the left & right of the "is equal to"

Statement 2: is equal to
$$4n =$$

Statement 3: 20 minus that number
$$20 - n \;\rightarrow\; 4n = 20 - n$$

4. One half of a number is larger than that number minus four.

Statement 1: one half of a number
$$\frac{1}{2}n \; or \; \frac{n}{2}$$

> Multiplying by ½ is the same as dividing by 2.

Statement 2: is larger than
$$>$$

Statement 3: that number minus four.
$$n - 4 \;\rightarrow\; \frac{1}{2}n > n - 4$$

5. The quotient of a number and four is three greater than another number minus three.

Statement 1: the quotient of a number and four
$$\frac{n}{4}$$

> Another number means another variable.

Statement 2: is three greater
$$+3 \;\rightarrow\; \frac{n}{4} + 3$$

> The equal sign is implied, and that makes it's tricky.

Statement 3: than another number minus three.
$$y - 3 \;\rightarrow\; = y - 3 \;\rightarrow\; \frac{n}{4} - 3 = y - 3$$

> By breaking questions into parts, you can quickly eliminate answer choices while avoiding errors.

Let's take a look at some ACT examples.

Video on *Text to Equation*

1. An integer, x, is subtracted from ten, and the difference is multiplied by four. The result equals the same integer added to four and that sum multiplied by three. Which equation represents this relationship?

> As you break down the statements mark off answer choices.

    A. $4(x - 10) = 3(x + 4)$
    B. $4x - 10 = 3x + 4$
    C. $4(x - 10) = 3x + 4$
    D. $x(10 - 4) = 3x$
    E. $4(10 - x) = 3(x + 4)$

Solve

Statement 1: x is subtracted from ten

$$10 - x$$

> Mark off what doesn't have $10 - x$

    A. ~~$4(x - 10) = 3(x + 4)$~~
    B. $4x - 10 = 3x + 4$
    C. ~~$4(x - 10) = 3x + 4$~~
    D. ~~$x(10 - 4) = 3x$~~
    E. $4(10 - x) = 3(x + 4)$

Statement 2: the difference is multiplied by four.

$$4(x - 10)$$

> "the difference" refers to Statement 1.

    A. ~~$4(x - 10) = 3(x + 4)$~~
    B. ~~$4x - 10 = 3x + 4$~~
    C. ~~$4(x - 10) = 3x + 4$~~
    D. ~~$x(10 - 4) = 3x$~~
    E. $4(10 - x) = 3(x + 4)$

Answer Choice **B** is correct.

2. What number can you add to both the numerator and the denominator of $\frac{8}{11}$ to equal $\frac{2}{3}$?

> It may be faster to test answers than to set up & solve the equation.

    A. 4
    B. -2
    C. 2
    D. -3
    E. -6

Solve

Statement 1: What number can you add to both the numerator and denominator... $\frac{+x}{+x}$

Statement 2: of $\frac{8}{11}$: $\frac{8+x}{11+x}$

> Our variable has to be in the same fraction as what we add.

Statement 3: to equal $\frac{2}{3}$: $\frac{8+x}{11+x} = \frac{2}{3}$

> Cross-multiply

Solving:

$$\frac{8+x}{11+x} = \frac{2}{3} \rightarrow \frac{8+x}{11+x} \bowtie \frac{2}{3}$$

$$3(x + 8) = 2(x + 11) \rightarrow 3x + 24 = 2x + 22 \rightarrow x = -2$$

Answer Choice **B** is correct.

3. You can find the number of ACT books in the Test Guy library by squaring the number of books and subtracting seventeen times the number of books. That difference is equal to 60. How many ACT books does the Test Guy own?

A. 43
B. 77
C. 3
D. 20
E. 17

Solve

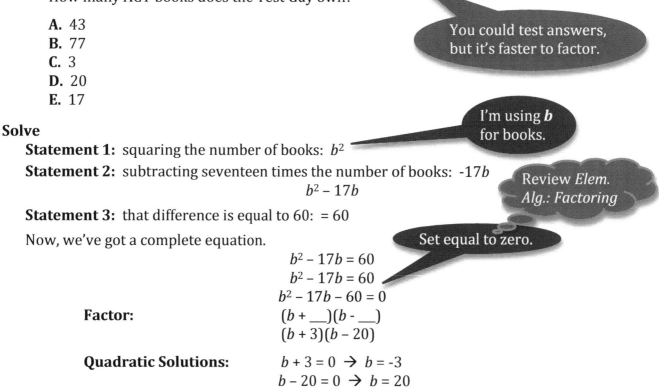

Statement 1: squaring the number of books: b^2

Statement 2: subtracting seventeen times the number of books: $-17b$
$$b^2 - 17b$$

Statement 3: that difference is equal to 60: $= 60$

Now, we've got a complete equation.

$$b^2 - 17b = 60$$
$$b^2 - 17b = 60$$
$$b^2 - 17b - 60 = 0$$

Factor:
$$(b + \underline{\quad})(b - \underline{\quad})$$
$$(b + 3)(b - 20)$$

Quadratic Solutions:
$$b + 3 = 0 \rightarrow b = -3$$
$$b - 20 = 0 \rightarrow b = 20$$

There can't be a *negative number of books*, so only 20 can be correct.

Answer choice **D** is correct

4. I offer a discount on Test Guy apparel to students. I produced a new t-shirt that I sell for $16 to students and $20 to non-students. I spent $3,000 dollars on the t-shirts and sold 80 to students, how many shirts do I need to sell to non-students to break even?

A. 88
B. 25
C. 86
D. 1,720
E. 92

Solve

There are two variables but we won't need to use both in the finished equation

Statement 1: Cost $16 for students: **16 for s**

Statement 2: Cost $20 for non-students: **20 for n**

Statement 3: I spent 3,000 dollars on the shirts: **= 3,000**

Statement 4: Sold 80 to students
$$80 = s \rightarrow 16s \rightarrow 80(16) \rightarrow 1,280$$

Solve: Because we want to break even, the *money in* has to equal the *money spent*.
money from students + money from non-students = 3,000
$$1,280 + 20n = 3,000$$

Rearrange and solve

$$20n = 1,780 \rightarrow n = \frac{1,720}{20} \rightarrow 86 \text{ shirts}$$

Answer **C** is correct.

Making an Equation: Linear Equations

Making a linear equation is the largest category of *make an equation* problems. Think of these problems as the *variable term* (slope) added to the *fixed term* (the *y*-intercept). The general form of a *variable & fixed* equation looks like this:

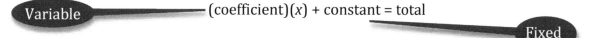

Variable ————— (coefficient)(x) + constant = total

Fixed

Rules of the Road: Fixed & Variable

The key to fixed & variable problems is to correctly identify the fixed component and the variable component.

Example: Fixed & Variable

1. When Harper & Duke go out for a walk, they spend 10 minutes putting their leashes on. The equation $w = 3b + 10$ models the time in *w* minutes a walk of *b* blocks takes. How long does it take to walk one block?

    Statement 1: ...they spend 10 minutes putting their leashes on.

    Use *logic* here. ————— +10

    They won't need to put on their leashes for *every block they walk*. Therefore, this is the *fixed* term.

    Statement 2: The equation $w = 3b + 10$ models the time in *w* minutes a walk of *b* blocks takes.

    $w = 3b + 10$

    We already know that the +10 is fixed. Now, we know that 3*b* is variable & *b* is the number of blocks.

    Therefore, the *variable* term 3*b* tells us that each block takes us three minutes to walk.

ACT Examples: Fixed & Variable

1. A new lawnmower cost 690 dollars. After an initial payment of 150 dollars, subsequent payments will be 60 dollars per month. How long until the lawnmower is paid off?

    A. 14 months
    B. 9 months
    C. 4.6 months
    D. 3.6 months
    E. 12 months

Solve

Let's look at the statements and come up with an equation.

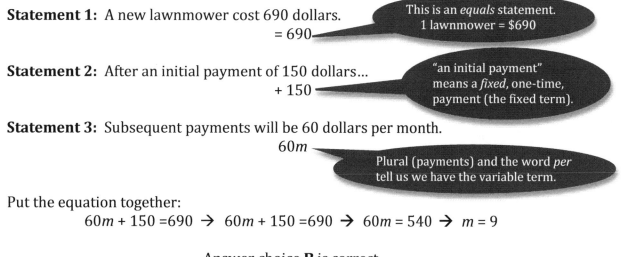

Statement 1: A new lawnmower cost 690 dollars.

= 690

This is an *equals* statement. 1 lawnmower = $690

Statement 2: After an initial payment of 150 dollars...

+ 150

"an initial payment" means a *fixed*, one-time, payment (the fixed term).

Statement 3: Subsequent payments will be 60 dollars per month.

60*m*

Plural (payments) and the word *per* tell us we have the variable term.

Put the equation together:

$60m + 150 = 690$ ➔ $60m + 150 = 690$ ➔ $60m = 540$ ➔ $m = 9$

Answer choice **B** is correct.

2. Annie opens a lemonade stand. She spends five dollars on markers and posterboard to make her sign. Each glass of lemonade costs Annie $0.25 to make. What represents the total cost (C) of Annie's lemonade stand if she sells x glasses.

    A. $C = 0.25x + 5$
    B. $C = 5x + 0.25$
    C. $C = 5 - 0.25x$
    D. $C = 5.25x$
    E. $C = 0.25x - 5$

Solve

    Statement 1: She spends five dollars on markers and posterboard to make her sign.

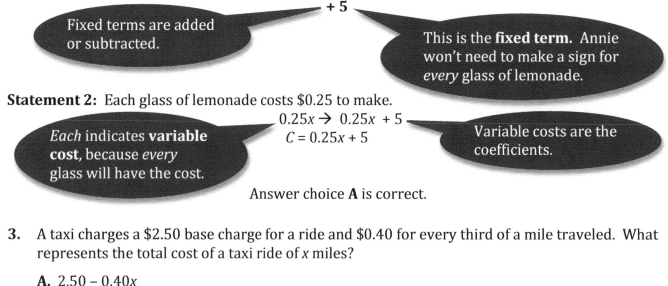

Statement 2: Each glass of lemonade costs $0.25 to make.

$0.25x \rightarrow 0.25x + 5$

$C = 0.25x + 5$

Answer choice **A** is correct.

3. A taxi charges a $2.50 base charge for a ride and $0.40 for every third of a mile traveled. What represents the total cost of a taxi ride of x miles?

    A. $2.50 - 0.40x$
    B. $2.50 + 0.40x$
    C. $2.50x + 0.40x$
    D. $2.50x + 0.40$
    E. $2.50 + 1.20x$

Solve

    This is a *variable + fixed* line equation.

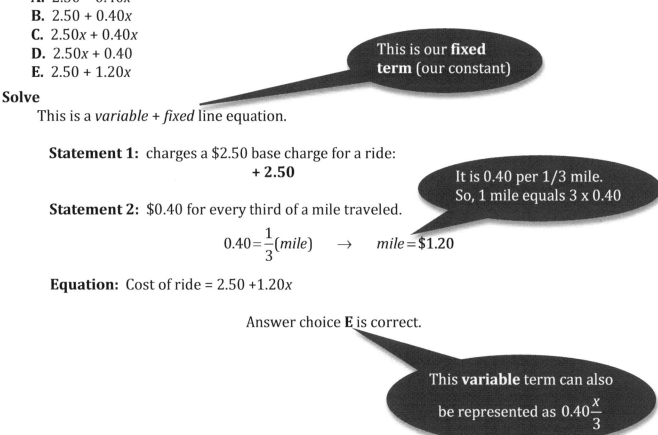

        Statement 1: charges a $2.50 base charge for a ride:

$$+ 2.50$$

        Statement 2: $0.40 for every third of a mile traveled.

$$0.40 = \frac{1}{3}(mile) \quad \rightarrow \quad mile = \$1.20$$

    Equation: Cost of ride $= 2.50 + 1.20x$

Answer choice **E** is correct.

Make Linear Equations: Setting Equal

One common type of *make an equation* question has you make two linear equations and set them equal. The question won't tell you explicitly to set the equations equal, you'll have to determine that from the wording of the question.

ACT Examples: Setting Equal

1. Harper and Duke were both hired as circus dogs. Harper's salary starts at 25,000 dollars per year and each year she receives a 600-dollar raise. Duke starts out at 22,200 dollars per year and each year he receives a 1,000-dollar raise. When solves, which equation represents how many years until Duke and Harper earn the same salary?

   A. $25,000 - 600x = 22,200 - 1,000x$
   B. $600x + 25,000 = 22,200 + 1,000x$
   C. $1,000x + 25,000 = 22,200 + 600x$
   D. $25,000x + 600 = 22,200x + 1,000$
   E. $25,000x + 1,000 = 22,200x + 600$

Solve

We need an equation for Harper and an equation for Duke. The variable will be *years* and we'll set the equations equal to find how many years it will take for Harper & Duke to earn the same amount.

Statements 1 & 2: Harper's salary starts at 25,000 dollars per year and each year she receives a 600-dollar raise.

Equation 1: Harper = $25,000 + 600x$ → Harper = $600x + 25,000$

~~A. 25,000 – 600x = 22,200 – 1,000x~~
B. $600x + 25,000 = 22,200 + 1,000x$
C. $600x + 25,000 = 22,000x + 1,000$
~~D. 25,000x + 600 = 22,200x + 1,000~~
~~E. 25,000x + 1,000 = 22,200x + 600~~

> Mark off after finding the first equation.

Statements 3 & 4: Duke starts out at 22,200 dollars per year and he receives an annual 1,000-dollar raise.

Equation 2: $22,200 + 1,000x$ → $1,000x + 22,200$

~~A. 25,000 – 600x = 22,200 – 1,000x~~
B. $600x + 25,000 = 22,200 + 1,000x$
~~C. 600x + 25,000 = 22,000x + 1,000~~
~~D. 25,000x + 600 = 22,200x + 1,000~~
~~E. 25,000x + 1,000 = 22,200x + 600~~

> I'm combining statements to show one half of the equation.

Answer choice **B** is correct.

2. Plant A is seven centimeters tall and Plant B is eleven centimeters tall. They are both fertilized, and after fertilization Plant A grows at a rate of 1 cm. per week and Plant B grows at a rate of ½ cm. per week. After how many weeks will the two plants be equal in height?

   A. 4 weeks
   B. 5 weeks
   C. 6 weeks
   D. 8 weeks
   E. 9 weeks

Solve

We're looking for when *Plant A = Plant B*. To do that, we'll need to find an equation for both plants *A & B*.

Statements 1 & 2: Plant A is seven centimeters tall and Plant B is eleven centimeters tall.

Statements 3 & 4: Plant A grows at a rate of 1 cm. per week and Plant B grows at a rate of ½ cm. per week.

Equations 1& 2:   *Plant A = 1x + 7*
                        Plant B = ½x + 11

> Remember, we are looking for when height *A = B*.

Solve: *Plant A = Plant B*

$$1x + 7 = \frac{1}{2}x + 11 \quad \rightarrow \quad \frac{1}{2}x = 4$$

$$x = 8$$

Answer choice **D** is correct

Wrap Up

What You Need to Know
   ✓ Making an algebraic expression from a word problem.
   ✓ Make a linear equation from a word problem.
   ✓ Find the solution to two linear systems by writing two equations and setting them equal.

Videos

> Text to Equation

> Making Linear Equations

The Strategies
   ✓ **Break word questions into single operation statements.** It is absolutely vital to *make an equation* problems.
   ✓ Most questions are line equations. Look for a *fixed term* (*y*-intercept) and a *variable term* (slope).

Key Skills
   Make an equation is a fundamental skill that crosses into almost all algebra and some plane geometry topics.

Elementary Algebra: Make an Equation

1. Jack Ketch cuts a 71-foot rope into two pieces. One piece is 19 feet longer than the other. What is the length of the longer piece?

   A. 26 feet
   B. 35.5 feet
   C. 90 feet
   D. 45 feet
   E. 22.5 feet

2. A moving van rental costs $40.00 per day plus $8.00 for every 100 miles, if Lucas rents a van to drive x miles over two days which equation represents his cost?

   F. $8.00x + 40.00$
   G. $0.08x + 80.00$
   H. $8.00x + 40.00$
   J. $0.80x + 80.00$
   K. $-0.08x + 40.00$

3. The electric company charges $11.00 per month for a meter. For every 10 kilowatt-hours the company charges $1.60. What equation represents the total cost for the use of k kilowatt-hours of electricity for a month?

   A. $11.00 - 0.16k$
   B. $0.16k + 11.00$
   C. $1.76k$
   D. $11.00 + 1.60k$
   E. $11.00 - 1.60k$

4. Two homes are purchased as investments. House A cost $100,000 and House B cost $50,000. If House A rises in value by $5,000 a year and House B rises in value by $10,000 per year, what equation determines the number of years (x) before the two houses are equal in value?

   F. 5 years
   G. 3.33 years
   H. 15 years
   J. 30 years
   K. 10 years

5. Parking in a parking garage costs $5.00 for the first hour and $3.00 for every hour after the first. What formula describes the total cost of parking in the garage for h hours?

   A. $3h + 2$
   B. $5h + 3$
   C. $3h + 5$
   D. $5h - 3$
   E. $3h - 2$

6. A lesson with the Test Guy's Android (RoboTutor) is billed at a different rate than the plain, boring, and terribly organic Test Guy. RoboTutor charges a fixed fee of $20.00 for any lesson plus a variable charge. The variable charge is the square of the number of ten-minute blocks. What is the cost of a forty-minute lesson?

   F. $22.00
   G. $1,620.00
   H. $36.00
   J. $180.00
   K. $1,820.00

7. A taxi ride in Test Guyville costs $5.00 plus a variable fee directly proportional to the square root of the number of miles traveled. If a 9-mile taxi ride costs $9.50, how much does a 36-mile ride cost?

   A. $18
   B. $23
   C. $14
   D. $11
   E. $113

8. Jason sells cars for Garrity motors. He earns a commission for each car sold plus a $500 weekly salary. Each car earns Jason the same commission. He sold 5 cars last week and his check was $1,400. This week he sold three cars, how much will his paycheck be?

   F. $800
   G. $540
   H. $1,040
   J. $1,540
   K. $1,640

9. The Test Guy is starting a t-shirt line. He borrowed $21,000 for machinery and a workshop. Each blank t-shirt costs $5.00 and printing costs $1.00 per shirt. Test Guy is selling each finished t-shirt for $13.00. Which equation best describes how many t-shirts the Test Guy needs to sell to pay off his loan?

    A. 3,000
    B. 2,625
    C. 3,500
    D. 1,616
    E. 2,100

10. The larger of two numbers exceeds twice the smaller number by 7. The sum of twice the larger number and five times the smaller number is 82. If s is the smaller number, which equation below determines the correct value of s?

    F. $2s + 2(5s + 7) = 82$
    G. $9s + 7 = 82$
    H. $2(2s + 7) + 5s = 82$
    J. $2s + 7 + 5s = 82$
    K. $2s + 14 + 5s = 82$

11. What number can you add to both the numerator and denominator of $\dfrac{3}{5}$ to equal $\dfrac{3}{4}$?

    A. 1
    B. -1
    C. -3
    D. 3
    E. 5

12. A jet takes off from an aircraft carrier by steam-powered catapult. Its initial velocity as it launches off the catapult is 165 miles per hour. The jet continues to accelerate at a rate related to the cube root of the number of seconds it has been in the air. After 27 seconds the jet is traveling at 300 miles per hour. Approximately, how fast will the jet be going after 64 seconds?

    F. 385 mph
    G. 373 mph
    H. 535 mph
    J. 462 mph
    K. 345 mph

Make an Equation: Solutions

1. Jack Ketch cuts a 71-foot rope into two pieces. One piece is 19 feet longer than the other. What is the length of the longer piece?

Correct Answer D

The key with making your own equation is to break the question into statements while not getting ahead of yourself. Many students try and drop variables and relationships in immediately, misunderstand something, and get stuck. I'm going to call the pieces *Piece A* & *Piece B*. Break the question into statements:

Statement 1: Jack Ketch cuts a 71-foot rope into two pieces.
$$Piece\ a + Piece\ b = 71\text{ feet}$$

Statement 2: One piece is 19 feet longer than the other.
$$Piece\ a = Piece\ b - 19\text{ feet*}$$

*It could be the other way around, *Piece b = Piece a* + 19 feet. If you do it this way, you'll find the length of the shorter piece and need to add 19 to it. This is a system of equations. We can substitute in for Piece 1 in the second equation.
$$Piece\ b - 19 + Piece\ b = 71\text{ feet} \rightarrow 2(Piece\ b) = 90\text{ feet} \rightarrow Piece\ b = 45\text{ feet}$$

Answer choice **D** is correct.

What You May Have Done Wrong

    A. You found the length of the shorter piece of rope.
    B. You divided the length of the rope (71 feet) in half, without adjusting for the differences in the lengths of the pieces.
    C. You misunderstood the question or had a setup problem.
    E. You misunderstood the question or had setup problems.

2. A moving van rental costs $40.00 per day plus $8.00 for every 100 miles, if Lucas rents a van to drive *x* miles over two days which represents his cost?

Correct Answer G

This is a common *make an equation* question format. Let's break down the statements.

Statement 1: A car rental costs $40.00 per day: $\text{cost per day} = 40.00\dfrac{\$}{day}$

Statement 2: $8.00 for every 100 miles: $\text{cost per distance} = \dfrac{\$8.00}{100\,\text{miles}} \rightarrow 0.08\dfrac{\$}{mile}$

This is similar to a *variable + fixed* (line equation) problem, but in this case *both* of our terms are *variable*. Let's start by calculating the cost of the van over two days.

$$2\,days \times \frac{\$40.00}{days} \rightarrow \$80.00$$

Putting the equation together: $\text{Van Rental} = 0.08x + 80.00$

Answer choice **G** is correct

What You May Have Done Wrong

    F. You have the van as a one-day rental (it's two) and the cost of 100 miles ($8.00) instead of the cost of one mile ($0.08).
    H. You have the van rental for one day (it's two) but the mileage term is correct.
    J. You miscalculated the mileage coefficient at $0.80 (it should be $0.08).
    K. You had a problem with setup. You may have originally set up the equation as $80 = 0.08x$.

3. The electric company charges $11.00 per month for a meter. For every 10 kilowatt-hours the company charges $1.60. What equation represents the total cost for the use of k kilowatt-hours of electricity for a month?

Correct Answer B

This is the most common format of *make an equation* problems. We're given a *fixed term* (y-intercept) and a *variable term* (slope) and we have to make a linear equation. Let's break down the statements.

Statement 1: The electric company charges $11.00 per month for a meter.
$$\text{meter cost} = 11.00 \text{ dollars}$$

Statement 2: For every 10 kilowatt-hours the company charges $1.60.
$$\text{cost per kilowatt hour} = \frac{\$1.60}{10 \text{ kW}} \quad \rightarrow \quad \$0.16 = 1 \text{ kW}$$

So, our equation will be the fixed cost of the meter *plus* the variable cost of each kilowatt-hour.
$$\text{Total Cost} = 0.16k + 11.00$$

Answer choice **B** is correct.

<u>What You May Have Done Wrong</u>
A. You need to add, not subtract, the k term.
C. You multiplied exponents. *Only* multiply exponents when you raise a power to a power.
D. You made a sign error in your first term.
E. You made a sign error in your first term. You also had an exponent error in your last term.

4. Two homes are purchased as investments. *House A* cost $100,000 and *House B* cost $50,000. If *House A* rises in value by $5,000 a year and *House B* rises in value by $10,000 per year, in how many years will the value of *House B* equal the value of *House A*?

Correct Answer K

This is a fairly common set up for a *set-equal* style problem. Essentially, we have an expensive home (House A) which increases in value slower than a cheaper home (House B). Eventually, House *B* will catch *A* and the prices will be equal.

House A = House B

Each house will have it's own equation that determines its value. If we set the equations equal and solve, we'll find how many years it takes for *B* to catch *A*.

$$House\ A = \text{variable} + \text{fixed} \qquad House\ B = \text{variable} + \text{fixed}$$
$$House\ A = 100,000 + 5,000x \qquad House\ B = 50,000 + 10,000x$$
$$House\ A = House\ B$$
$$5,000x + 100,000 = 10,000x + 50,000$$
$$50,000 = 5,000x$$
$$x = 10$$

Answer choice **K** is correct.

<u>What You May Have Done Wrong:</u>
F. You forgot to include *House A* yearly increases in price.
G. You correctly used the difference in house purchase prices but you *added* the annual value increase; you should have *subtracted*.
H. This is a compound error; review your steps.
J. You added the purchase prices (you should have taken the difference)

5. Parking in a parking garage costs $5.00 for the first hour and $3.00 for every hour after the first. What formula describes the total cost of parking in the garage for *h* hours?

Correct Answer A

Let's break the question down into statements. You've got to be careful because the rate changes. That changes the equation and it turns it into a *variable + fixed* linear equation

Statement 1: Parking in a parking garage costs $5.00 for the first hour....

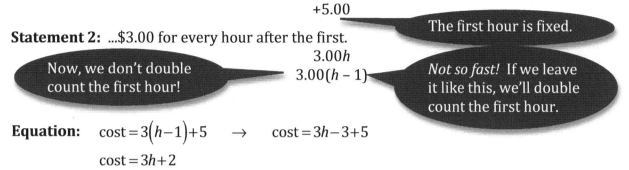

$$+5.00$$

The first hour is fixed.

Statement 2: ...$3.00 for every hour after the first.

$$3.00h$$

Now, we don't double count the first hour!

$$3.00(h-1)$$

Not so fast! If we leave it like this, we'll double count the first hour.

Equation: $\text{cost} = 3(h-1)+5 \quad \rightarrow \quad \text{cost} = 3h-3+5$

$$\text{cost} = 3h+2$$

Answer choice **A** is correct.

<u>What You May Have Done Wrong</u>
  B. You flipped the *fixed term* (5) and *variable term* (3) and you double counted the first hour.
  C. You double counted the first hour.
  D. This is a compound error, you probably made a mistake involving the first hour.
  E. You may have tried to get rid of double counting the first hour, or you may have made another mistake.

6. A lesson with the Test Guy's Android (RoboTutor) is billed at a different rate than the plain, boring, and terribly organic Test Guy. RoboTutor charges a fixed fee of $20.00 for any lesson plus a variable charge. The variable charge is the square of the number of ten-minute blocks. What is the cost of a forty-minute lesson?

Correct Answer H

This is a fairly involved question, you need to make an equation, deal with the exponent (square), and solve. While that combination is intimidating, **the key is being careful setting up your equation.**

Statement 1: RoboTutor charges a fixed fee of $20.00 for any lesson:

$$+20$$

Statement 2: The variable charge is the square of the number of ten-minute blocks.

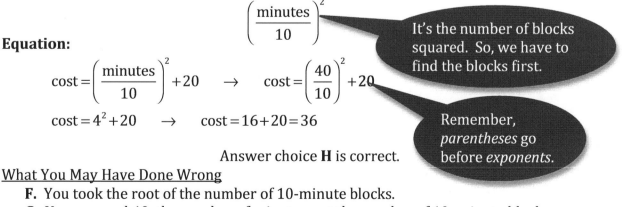

$$\left(\frac{\text{minutes}}{10}\right)^2$$

It's the number of blocks squared. So, we have to find the blocks first.

Equation:

$$\text{cost} = \left(\frac{\text{minutes}}{10}\right)^2 + 20 \quad \rightarrow \quad \text{cost} = \left(\frac{40}{10}\right)^2 + 20$$

$$\text{cost} = 4^2 + 20 \quad \rightarrow \quad \text{cost} = 16+20 = 36$$

Remember, *parentheses* go before *exponents*.

Answer choice **H** is correct.

<u>What You May Have Done Wrong</u>
  F. You took the root of the number of 10-minute blocks.
  G. You squared 40, the number of minutes not the number of 10- minute blocks.
  J. You may have squared first and then divided by 10.
  K. This is a compound error. Review your steps.

7. A taxi ride in Test Guyville costs $5.00 plus a variable fee based on the square root of the number of miles traveled. If a 9-mile taxi ride costs $9.50, how much does a 36-mile ride cost?

Correct Answer C

This problem has a different feel. They give us a "test case," the 9-mile ride and its cost. We'll use that to find the missing coefficient of the *variable* term. Let's break down the statements.

Statement 1: A taxi ride in Test Guyville costs $5.00 plus....

+5.00

Statement 2: A variable fee directly proportional to the square root of the number of miles traveled.

$$k\sqrt{m}$$

Directly proportional means *multiplication*

K is the coefficient of the *variable term.*

Statement 3: A 9-mile taxi ride costs $9.50.

9 miles = $9.50

Let's make the equation and plug-in the "test case" (9 miles = 9.50)

Equation: $\text{cost} = k\sqrt{m} + 5.00$

Plug-in: $9.50 = k\sqrt{9} + 5.00 \quad \rightarrow \quad 4.50 = 3k \quad \rightarrow \quad K = 1.50$

k is a constant and constants don't change. For any m, k will be the same. Now, we've got to plug in our value for k and our mileage (36) to solve for cost.

$$\text{cost} = k\sqrt{m} + 5.00 \quad \rightarrow \quad \text{cost} = 1.50\sqrt{36} + 5.00$$
$$\text{cost} = 9 + 5.00 \quad \rightarrow \quad \text{cost} = 14.00$$

Answer choice **C** is correct.

<u>What You May Have Done Wrong</u>

  A. You may have miscalculated the value of k as 3 and forgotten the fixed charge (5.00).
  B. You probably miscalculated the value of k as 3.
  D. You took the square root of 36 but did not multiply it by k.
  E. This is a compound error. You may have misunderstood "directly proportional."

8. Jason sells cars for Garrity motors. He earns a commission for each car sold plus a $500 weekly salary. Each car earns Jason the same commission. He sold 5 cars last week and his check was $1,400. This week he sold three cars, how much will his paycheck be?

Correct Answer H

This is a relatively straightforward *variable + fixed* (linear equation) problem with two steps. The first step is finding how much Jason earns *per* car, commission per car. Our second step is finding Jason's earnings if he sells three cars. Let's look at the statements.

Statement 1: He earns a commission for each car sold... *commission•cars*

Statement 2: ...plus a $500 salary: **+500**

Let's set up our equation and find the commission.

Jason's Paycheck = variable + fixed

Jason's Paycheck = (commission)(cars) + 500 → 1,400 = (commission)(5) + 500

900 = 5(*commission*) → 180 = *commission*

Now, find out how much Jason earns from selling three cars.

Jason's Paycheck = 500 + (commission)(cars) → Jason's Paycheck = 500 + (180)(3)

Jason's Paycheck = 1,040

Answer choice **H** is correct.

<u>What You May Have Done Wrong</u>
   F. You may have guessed or had a calculation problem.
   G. You may have guessed or had a calculation problem.
   J. You may have gotten the right answer but misunderstood it.
   K. You may have eyeballed (guessed), or plugged in the changes, not values.

9. The Test Guy is starting a t-shirt line. He borrowed $21,000 for machinery and a workshop. Each blank t-shirt costs $5.00 and printing costs $1.00 per shirt. Test Guy is selling each finished t-shirt for $13.00. Which equation best describes how many t-shirts the Test Guy needs to sell to pay off his loan?

Correct Answer A

This is a tricky problem. We're required to figure out the *breakeven* point of the business. That is, when the *money in = money out*. This is a set equal problem. Let's put the costs on one side and profit on the other.

$$\text{costs} = \text{profit}$$

Statement 1: He borrowed $21,000.... **+21,000**

Statement 2: Each blank t-shirt costs $5.00 and printing costs $1.00 per shirt:

$$\textbf{5.00}x + \textbf{1.00}x = \textbf{6}x$$

We now have the *fixed* and *variable* components for the cost half of the equation (remember, we're trying to make costs = profit).

Cost Equation: Cost = $6x + 21{,}000$

Statement 3: ...selling each finished t-shirt for $13.00

$$\textbf{13}x$$

That's all we need for our *money in* or *profit* side of the equation. The two sides equal each other, so our equation looks like.

$$\text{costs} = \text{profit} \quad \rightarrow \quad 6x + 21{,}000 = 13x$$
$$21{,}000 = 7x \quad \rightarrow \quad x = 3{,}000$$

In plain speak, it'll take 3,000 t-shirts, earning 7 dollars per shirt (13 – 6) to make back the $21,000 borrowed.

Another way to set up this problem is to set your equation equal to the amount of the loan.

$$13x - 6x = 21{,}000$$
$$7x = 21{,}000$$
$$\textbf{x = 3{,}000}$$

The 6x is negative because it is a cost.

Answer choice **A** is correct.

<u>What You May Have Done Wrong</u>

    B. You may have forgotten the 1-dollar printing cost and used $5 (instead of $6) as the *cost per shirt*.

    C. You either miscalculated the profit per shirt as $6, or divided the loan ($21,000) by the cost $6.

    D. You took the loan ($21,000) and divided it by the sale price of the shirts ($13) without dealing with the cost *per* shirt—the variable cost.

    E. This is a compound error. Review your steps.

10. **The larger of two numbers exceeds twice the smaller number by 7. The sum of twice the larger number and five times the smaller number is 82. If *s* is the smaller number, which equation determines the correct value of *s*?**

Correct Answer H

This is a really wordy question and because of it's wordy you have to be very careful with each statement.

Statement 1: The larger of two numbers exceeds twice the smaller number by 7.
$$L = 2s + 7$$

Statement 2: The sum of twice the larger and five times the smaller number is 82.

There are two variables — $2L + 5s = 82$

We've just got to write the second equation in terms of a single variable (*s*)
$$2L + 5s = 82$$
$$2(2s + 7) + 5s = 82$$

We could distribute and solve this equation, but the answer choices don't require it.

Answer choice H is correct.

<u>What You May Have Done Wrong</u>
 F. You flipped the terms, plugging in $2s + 7$ in the wrong place.
 G. You distributed the 2, but you failed to distribute it to the 7.
 J. You neglected to multiply the $2s + 7$ by 2.
 K. You distributed the 2 to the 7 but not the $2s$.

11. **What number can you add to the numerator and denominator of $\frac{3}{5}$ to equal $\frac{3}{4}$?**

Correct Answer D

This is a great problem to test answers on. The math is simple and there aren't many operations. It's just as fast to solve with algebra and I'm going to show that. There is only a single statement, which tells us we are adding the same unknown number to the numerator and the denominator. So, we add the same variable (*x*) to the top & bottom of the fraction.

Our equation looks like this: $\dfrac{3+x}{5+x} = \dfrac{3}{4}$

Cross-multiply.

Let's do the algebra.
$$\frac{3+x}{5+x} = \frac{3}{4} \quad \rightarrow \quad 4(3+x) = 3(5+x)$$
$$12 + 4x = 15 + 3x \quad \rightarrow \quad x = 3$$

Answer choice D is correct.

<u>What You May Have Done Wrong</u>
 A. This would make 4/6 or 2/3rds.
 B. You'd get 2/4 or 1/2
 C. Right number, wrong sign. You'll end up with zero.
 E. This is a compound error. Review your steps

12. A jet takes off from an aircraft carrier by steam-powered catapult. Its initial velocity as it launches off the catapult is 165 miles per hour. The jet continues to increase in speed at a rate related to the cube root of the number of seconds it has been in the air. After 27 seconds the jet is traveling at 300 miles per hour. Approximately, how fast will the jet be going after 64 seconds?

Correct Answer K

This is a really tough problem. It's long and it's got a weird exponent (cube root) part. Start with your statements

Statement 1: its initial velocity...is 165 miles per hour

$$165 \frac{miles}{hour} \text{ at time } 0$$

This is the fixed term.

Since time is important in the question, it's good to remember that this is the speed at time 0.

Statement 2: ...continues to increase in speed at a rate related to the cube root of the number of seconds...

$$rate \bullet \sqrt[3]{seconds}$$

Equation: $speed = x \bullet \sqrt[3]{time} + 165$

Statement 3: After 27 seconds the jet is traveling at 300 miles per hour.

$$300 \frac{miles}{hour} \text{ at time } 27$$

We've got to find the rate, and that rate isn't just the change in speed over time, it's the change in speed over the *cube root* of time.

To start, we'll plug in the "test case" 300 miles per hour at 27 seconds.

$$speed = x \bullet \sqrt[3]{time} + 165$$
$$300 = x \bullet \sqrt[3]{27} + 165$$
$$135 = x \bullet 3 \quad \rightarrow \quad x = 45$$

Now that we have x, we can plug back in and find the speed at 64 seconds.

$$speed = 45 \bullet \sqrt[3]{time} + 165$$
$$speed = 45 \bullet \sqrt[3]{64} + 165$$
$$speed = (45 \bullet 4) + 165 \quad \rightarrow \quad x = 345$$

Answer choice **K** is correct.

<u>What You May Have Done Wrong</u>
- **F.** You made a calculation error calculating your variable coefficient.
- **G.** You made a compound error; review your steps.
- **H.** You made a compound error; review your steps.
- **J.** You likely used a square root instead of a cube root.

Background

Algebra with exponents is an important topic on its own, averaging two questions per section. It's also a *key skill*, critical to many *intermediate algebra problems*.

What You Need to Know

✓ When you can combine terms in addition & subtraction
✓ How to combine terms in multiplication & division
✓ How to multiply & divide exponents
✓ How to take terms with exponents to powers.
✓ How and when to split or combine roots.
✓ How to deal with negative exponents.

Rules of the Road: Addition, Subtraction, & Combining Like Terms

In **addition & subtraction** we can **only combine like terms** *if* the terms have the **same variable** AND the variable is to the **same power**

Examples: Combining Like Terms in Addition & Subtraction

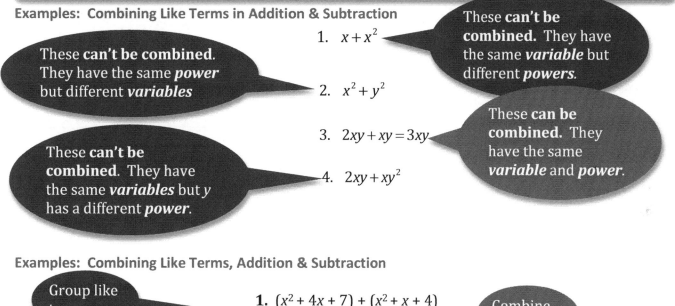

1. $x + x^2$

These **can't be combined.** They have the same *variable* but different *powers*.

These **can't be combined**. They have the same *power* but different *variables*

2. $x^2 + y^2$

3. $2xy + xy = 3xy$

These **can be combined.** They have the same *variable* and *power*.

These **can't be combined**. They have the same *variables* but y has a different *power*.

4. $2xy + xy^2$

Examples: Combining Like Terms, Addition & Subtraction

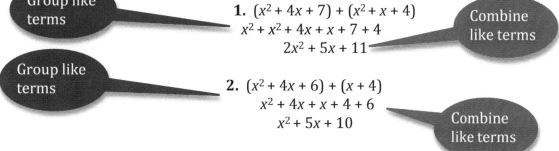

Group like terms

1. $(x^2 + 4x + 7) + (x^2 + x + 4)$
$x^2 + x^2 + 4x + x + 7 + 4$
$2x^2 + 5x + 11$

Combine like terms

Group like terms

2. $(x^2 + 4x + 6) + (x + 4)$
$x^2 + 4x + x + 4 + 6$
$x^2 + 5x + 10$

Combine like terms

ACT Example: Combining Like Terms, Addition & Subtraction

1. $2(x^2-5x-10)-(x^2+x-2)=?$

    A. $2x^2-4x-8$
    B. $x^2-11x-18$
    C. $-3x^2-6x-12$
    D. $-3x^2-4x-8$
    E. $3x^2-4x-12$

This is a common setup for like terms questions

Solve

We've got to combine like terms to find an equivalent expression. But first we've got to distribute the 2 into the first set of parentheses and the -1 into the second set of parentheses.

$$2(x^2-5x-10)-(x^2+x-2)$$

Distribute the 2

We distribute the negative sign as a -1.

$$2x^2-10x-20-x^2-x+2$$

$$2x^2-x^2-10x-x-20+2$$

Group like terms

$$x^2-11x-18$$

Combine like terms

Answer Choice **B** is correct.

Rules of the Road: Multiplication & Combining Like Terms

When **multiplying** variables, we can *always* combine them into a single term. Variables multiplied by themselves are *variable²*.

Examples: Combining Terms—Multiplication

1. $x \cdot y = xy$

Different variables can be written as a single term.

2. $x \cdot x = x^2$

3. $x \cdot yx = yx^2$

Rules of the Road: Operations with Exponents—Multiplying

When **multiplying** two terms with the **same variable** (base), **add** the **exponents**.

Let's look at an example where we have a number to plug in for a variable. It should make this clearer. Let's say that $x = 2$

$$x \cdot x^2 = x^{2+1} = x^3 \quad \rightarrow \quad 2^1 \cdot 2^2 = 2 \cdot 4 = 8$$
$$8 = 2^3$$

There's a video on Multiplying & Dividing Exponents

Take a look at the mechanics when x = 2

Examples: Multiplying Exponents

1. $x^2 \cdot x^2 = x^{2+2} = x^4$

> Both terms have the same base, x

2. $x^2 \cdot x = x^{2+1} = x^3$

> Even with different bases, we can still combine coefficients.

3. $2x^2 \cdot 4y^2 = 8x^2 y^2$

4. $(3x^2) \cdot (2x^3) = (3 \cdot 2)(x^{2+3}) = 6x^5$

> We distribute here, and still *add* exponents

5. $2x^2(x^4 + 1) = 2x^{4+2} + 2x^2 = 2x^6 + 2x^2$

Rules of the Road: Division & Combining Like Terms

When dividing, we can always combine into a single term. When we divide a variable by itself, the result is 1.

Examples: Combining Terms—Division

1. $x \div y = \dfrac{x}{y}$

> We can't simplify this any further.

> The x's cancel to 1

2. $x \div x = \dfrac{x}{x} = 1$

3. $2x \div x = \dfrac{2x}{x} = 2$

> The x's cancel to 1 but that doesn't affect the coefficient (2).

4. $x^2 \div x = \dfrac{x^2}{x} = x$

Rules of the Road: Dividing Exponents

When **dividing** terms with the **same variable (base), subtract the exponents.**

If x = 2:

$$x^2 \div x = \dfrac{x^2}{x^1} = x^{2-1} = x$$

> Take a look at the what happens when $x = 2$

$$2^2 \div 2 = \dfrac{4}{2} = 2$$

Examples: Dividing Exponents In and Out of Parentheses

1. $\dfrac{x^5}{x^2} = x^{5-2} = x^3$

> We have the same base here, so we *subtract* the exponents.

> We divide our coefficients just like any fraction.

2. $\dfrac{6x^3}{3x^2} = 2x^{3-2} = 2x^1$

> Make **negative** exponents **positive** by moving to the **denominator**.

3. $\dfrac{x^2}{x^4} = x^{2-4} = x^{-2} = \dfrac{1}{x^2}$

1. What is equivalent to $3x^3(x^2+4x+2)$?

    A. $3x^6+12x^4+6x^3$
    B. $3x^5+7x^4+5x^3$
    C. $3x^6+12x^3+5x^3$
    D. $3x^5+12x^4+6x^3$
    E. $3x^6+12x^4+6x^3$

Marking off works great on these questions. Find one term of the answer then mark off, and so on.

Solve

Marking off works great on this question type. Find the first term, mark-off, then move on to the next.

$$3x^3(x^2+4x+2) \quad \rightarrow \quad 3x^{3+2}+(3\bullet4)(x^{3+1})+(2\bullet3)(x^3)$$
$$3x^5+12x^4+6x^3$$

Answer choice **D** is correct.

Mark off as you go

2. Given that $y = b^2c$, and $b = ½$ and $y = 9$, what is c?

    A. 36
    B. 6 or -6
    C. 6
    D. -6
    E. 18

Solve

This is a plug in problem and it's fairly straightforward. Plug in for b, square b and solve for c.

Plug in for b

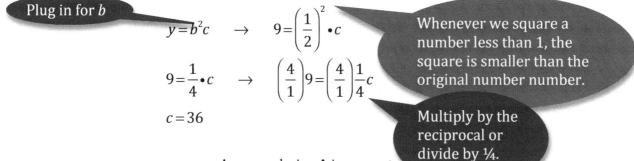

$$y=b^2c \quad \rightarrow \quad 9=\left(\frac{1}{2}\right)^2 \bullet c$$

$$9=\frac{1}{4}\bullet c \quad \rightarrow \quad \left(\frac{4}{1}\right)9=\left(\frac{4}{1}\right)\frac{1}{4}c$$

$$c=36$$

Whenever we square a number less than 1, the square is smaller than the original number number.

Multiply by the reciprocal or divide by ¼.

Answer choice **A** is correct.

When you take a term to a power, you multiply exponents.

Examples: Raising a Power to a Power

1. $(x^2)^4 = x^{2\bullet4} = x^8$

We are raising the *term* x^2 to the 4th power.

There's a *video* on *Multiplying & Dividing Exponents*

2. $(yx^2)^4 = y^{1\bullet4}x^{2\bullet4} = y^4x^8$

Everything inside the parentheses gets taken to the 4th power.

3. $(3x^2)^3(2x)^3 = (3^{1\bullet3}x^{2\bullet3})(2^{1\bullet3}x^{1\bullet3})$

$(27x^6)(8x^3)$

$216x^{6+3} = 216x^9$

Coefficients also get taken to the power.

Same base, so I *add* these exponents.

4. $\left(x^3\right)^{\frac{1}{2}} = x^{3\bullet\frac{1}{2}} = x^{\frac{3}{2}}$

The exponent ½ is another way to represent square root.

ACT Examples: Raising a Power to a Power

1. What is equivalent to $(-3x^2y)^3$?

A. $-27x^5y^4$

B. $-27x^6y^3$

C. $27x^6y^3$

D. $-9x^6y^3$

E. $9x^6y^3$

Each term in parentheses is being taken cubed (taken to the 3rd power).

Solve

$-3^3x^{2\bullet3}y^{1\bullet3}$

$-27x^6y^3$

Any negative number to an odd power (1,3,5...) will *remain negative*.

Answer choice **B** is correct.

Radicals: Square Roots & Cube Roots

Almost all the roots you find on the ACT are square or cube roots. I highly recommend that you memorize the perfect squares up to $12^2 = 144$.

Definitions

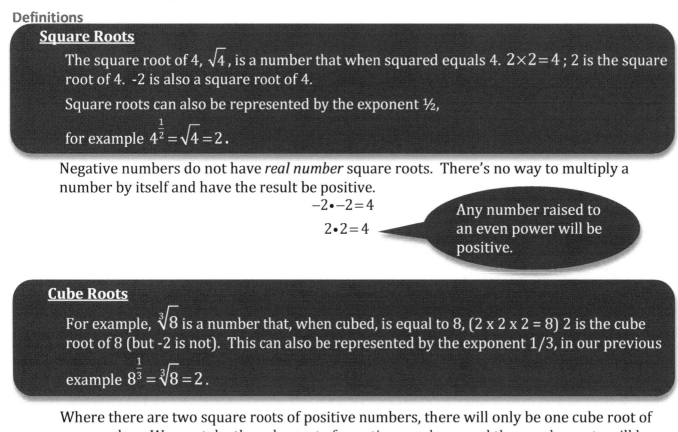

Square Roots

The square root of 4, $\sqrt{4}$, is a number that when squared equals 4. $2 \times 2 = 4$; 2 is the square root of 4. -2 is also a square root of 4.

Square roots can also be represented by the exponent ½,

for example $4^{\frac{1}{2}} = \sqrt{4} = 2$.

Negative numbers do not have *real number* square roots. There's no way to multiply a number by itself and have the result be positive.

$$-2 \bullet -2 = 4$$
$$2 \bullet 2 = 4$$

Any number raised to an even power will be positive.

Cube Roots

For example, $\sqrt[3]{8}$ is a number that, when cubed, is equal to 8, $(2 \times 2 \times 2 = 8)$ 2 is the cube root of 8 (but -2 is not). This can also be represented by the exponent 1/3, in our previous example $8^{\frac{1}{3}} = \sqrt[3]{8} = 2$.

Where there are two square roots of positive numbers, there will only be one cube root of *any* number. We can take the cube root of negative numbers, and those cube roots will be negative. Likewise, positive numbers will have positive cube roots.

Rules of the Road: Radicals

When we deal with variables under a radical we divide by that radical (or multiply by that radical's exponent).

If we need to take a root or use a power to solve an equation, we can only do it to *sides* of the equation, *not* terms.

Examples: Radicals

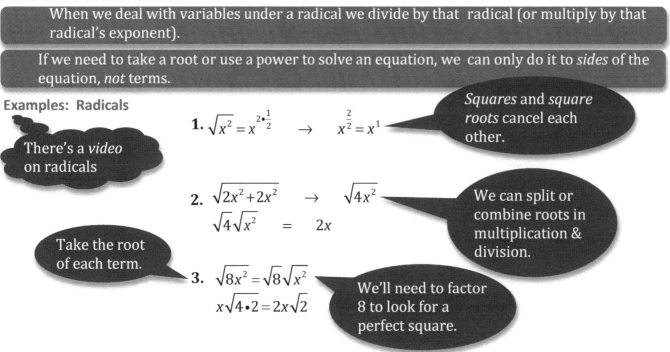

There's a *video* on radicals

1. $\sqrt{x^2} = x^{2 \bullet \frac{1}{2}} \quad \rightarrow \quad x^{\frac{2}{2}} = x^1$

Squares and *square roots* cancel each other.

2. $\sqrt{2x^2 + 2x^2} \quad \rightarrow \quad \sqrt{4x^2}$
   $\sqrt{4}\sqrt{x^2} \quad = \quad 2x$

We can split or combine roots in multiplication & division.

Take the root of each term.

3. $\sqrt{8x^2} = \sqrt{8}\sqrt{x^2}$
   $x\sqrt{4 \bullet 2} = 2x\sqrt{2}$

We'll need to factor 8 to look for a perfect square.

Examples (cont.): Radicals

4. $\sqrt{9x^2 - 4y^2}$

> Even though each term is a perfect square, we can't simplify. The terms can't be combined into a single term and I can't split roots if there's an addition or subtraction.

5. $\sqrt{\dfrac{x^4}{4}} = \dfrac{\sqrt{x^4}}{\sqrt{4}} = \dfrac{x^{4 \cdot \frac{1}{2}}}{2} = \dfrac{x^2}{2}$

ACT Examples: Radicals

1. If $x^3 - 4 = 4, x = ?$

    A. 2 or -2
    B. 0
    C. 2
    D. $\sqrt{8}$
    E. 512

> Remember, we can only take roots of *sides*! So we have to re-arrange first!

Solve

$x^3 - 4 = 4 \quad \rightarrow \quad x^3 = 8$

$\sqrt[3]{x^3} = \sqrt[3]{8} = 2$

Answer choice **C** is correct.

2. What is the value of $x = \sqrt{a^2 + b^2}$, if $a = \sqrt{12}$, and $b = \sqrt{4}$ and $x > 0$?

    A. $\sqrt{200}$
    B. 40
    C. 4
    D. $\sqrt{160}$
    E. $\sqrt{180}$

> We treat the radical like parentheses. Resolve each individual term then combine like terms.

Solve

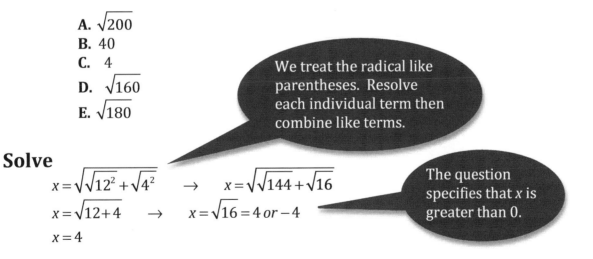

$x = \sqrt{\sqrt{12}^2 + \sqrt{4}^2} \quad \rightarrow \quad x = \sqrt{\sqrt{144} + \sqrt{16}}$

$x = \sqrt{12 + 4} \quad \rightarrow \quad x = \sqrt{16} = 4 \, or \, -4$

$x = 4$

> The question specifies that x is greater than 0.

Answer choice **C** is correct.

3. What is equivalent to $\left(2\sqrt{x}-4\sqrt{y}\right)^2$?

    A. $2x + 16y$
    B. $2x - 16y$
    C. $4x - 16y$

    D. $4x - 8\sqrt{xy} + 16y$

    E. $4x - 16\sqrt{xy} + 16y$

Solve

This is a tricky question, but it's really all about FOILing. We can't combine the terms in parentheses, so to square we'll have to multiply the binomial by itself and that means FOILing.

$$(2\sqrt{x}-4\sqrt{y})^2 \quad \rightarrow \quad (2\sqrt{x}-4\sqrt{y})(2\sqrt{x}-4\sqrt{y})$$

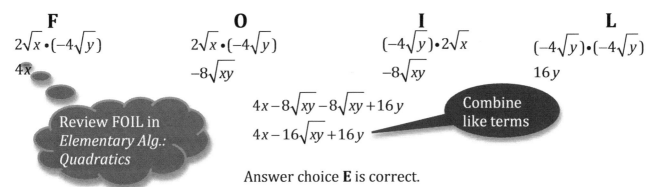

    F
$2\sqrt{x}\cdot(-4\sqrt{y})$
$4x$

    O
$2\sqrt{x}\cdot(-4\sqrt{y})$
$-8\sqrt{xy}$

    I
$(-4\sqrt{y})\cdot 2\sqrt{x}$
$-8\sqrt{xy}$

    L
$(-4\sqrt{y})\cdot(-4\sqrt{y})$
$16y$

Review FOIL in *Elementary Alg.: Quadratics*

$4x - 8\sqrt{xy} - 8\sqrt{xy} + 16y$

$4x - 16\sqrt{xy} + 16y$

Combine like terms

Answer choice **E** is correct.

Rules of the Road: Operations with Exponents—Negative Exponents

Negative exponents are a hallmark of *simplification* and *equivalence* questions. **You have to get rid of negative exponents; no answer is in its final form with a negative exponent.**

> A negative exponent is made positive by **moving the term with the negative exponent to the denominator.**

Examples: Negative Exponents

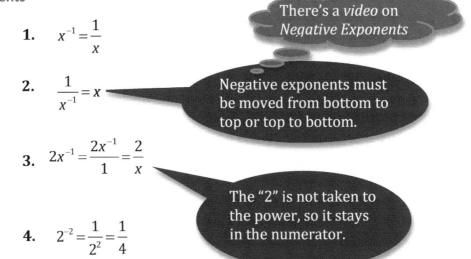

There's a *video* on *Negative Exponents*

1. $x^{-1} = \dfrac{1}{x}$

2. $\dfrac{1}{x^{-1}} = x$

Negative exponents must be moved from bottom to top or top to bottom.

3. $2x^{-1} = \dfrac{2x^{-1}}{1} = \dfrac{2}{x}$

The "2" is not taken to the power, so it stays in the numerator.

4. $2^{-2} = \dfrac{1}{2^2} = \dfrac{1}{4}$

Operations with negative exponents look tougher than they are. In reality, we don't do anything different from other exponent operations.

To multiply/divide with negative exponents we go follow the same addition/subtraction procedure.

Examples: Multiplication & Subtraction with Negative Exponents

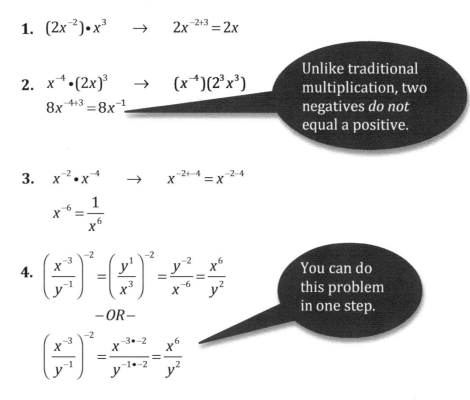

1. $(2x^{-2}) \bullet x^3 \quad \rightarrow \quad 2x^{-2+3} = 2x$

2. $x^{-4} \bullet (2x)^3 \quad \rightarrow \quad (x^{-4})(2^3 x^3)$
   $8x^{-4+3} = 8x^{-1}$

   Unlike traditional multiplication, two negatives *do not* equal a positive.

3. $x^{-2} \bullet x^{-4} \quad \rightarrow \quad x^{-2+-4} = x^{-2-4}$
   $x^{-6} = \dfrac{1}{x^6}$

4. $\left(\dfrac{x^{-3}}{y^{-1}}\right)^{-2} = \left(\dfrac{y^1}{x^3}\right)^{-2} = \dfrac{y^{-2}}{x^{-6}} = \dfrac{x^6}{y^2}$

   $-OR-$

   $\left(\dfrac{x^{-3}}{y^{-1}}\right)^{-2} = \dfrac{x^{-3 \bullet -2}}{y^{-1 \bullet -2}} = \dfrac{x^6}{y^2}$

   You can do this problem in one step.

Wrap Up

What You Need to Know
- ✓ When you can combine terms in addition & subtraction
- ✓ How to combine terms in multiplication & division
- ✓ How to multiply & divide exponents
- ✓ How to take terms with exponents to powers.
- ✓ How and when to split or combine roots.
- ✓ How to deal with negative exponents.

Videos

Multiplying & Dividing Exponents

Radicals

Negative Exponents

The Strategies
- ✓ *Marking off* works great on equivalence problems. Try it out.
- ✓ On confusing problems, see if *picking numbers* is a viable strategy.
- ✓ Remember that roots and exponents can cancel each other. You can only take a root (or increase to a power) the entire *sides* of equations.

Key Skill

Algebra with Exponents is a key skill. It's related to almost all *Intermediate Algebra* topics.

Elementary Algebra: Exponents

1. If $\dfrac{2x+y}{3} = x+2$, then what is $(x-y)^2$?

A. $\dfrac{36}{25}$

B. 36

C. 6

D. -6

E. 4

2. $(x^2+8x-3)-(2x^2+5x-3)$ is equivalent to:

F. $-3x^2+3x-6$

G. $-x^2+3x-6$

H. $-x^2+13x-6$

J. $-x^2+3x$

K. $3x^2+13x-6$

3. Which of the following expressions is equivalent to $-2x^2(5x^3y-2x^2)$?

A. $-10x^5y+4x^4$

B. $-10x^5y-4x^4$

C. $-10x^6y+4x^4$

D. $10x^6y+4x^4$

E. $10x^5y+4x^6$

4. Which of the following expresses z in terms of x for all real numbers x, y, z when $\sqrt{x} = y$ and $y^4 = z^2$?

F. $z=x^2$

G. $z=\sqrt{x}$

H. $z=\dfrac{x}{2}$

J. $z=2x$

K. $z=x$

5. If $x^2 = 25$ and $y^2 = 121$, then what is a possible value of $xy - y$?

F. 96

G. 2,904

H. 154

J. -454

K. -66

6. If a is a positive integer, which of the following expressions must be an even integer?

A. a^a

B. $\dfrac{a}{2}$

C. $a - 1$

D. 3^a

E. $a + a$

7. $4a^3 \cdot 9a^9 \cdot a^{-2}$ is equivalent to:

F. $36a^{12}$

G. $36a^{10}$

H. $-36a^{12}$

J. $36a^{56}$

K. $36a^{-56}$

8. Let $c = 4a - 2b$. What happens to the value of c if the value of a decreases by 1 and the value of b increases by 1?

A. Increases by 4

B. Decreases by 4

C. Decreases by 6

D. Increases by 6

E. Decreases by 2

Exponents: Solutions

1. If $\dfrac{2x+y}{3}=x+2$, then what is $(x-y)^2$?

Correct Answer B

This is a tricky question. We need to reorganize the equation to isolate what they are asking for—always use your answer choices for a guide. In this case, we want to re-arrange to isolate $x - y$ on one side. To start, let's get rid of the fraction.

$$3\left(\frac{2x+y}{3}\right)=3(x+2) \quad \rightarrow \quad 2x+y=3x+6$$

We've got to re-arrange, and we want to rearrange to make something that looks like "$x - y =$?"

$$2x+y=3x+6 \quad \rightarrow \quad y=x+6$$
$$0=x-y+6 \quad \rightarrow \quad x-y=-6$$

We want one side of the equation to have $x - y$

Which leaves us with,

$$x-y=-6$$

Now we can square both sides.

$$(x-y)^2=(-6)^2=36$$

Answer choice **B** is correct.

What You May Have Done Wrong
  A. This is a compound error, review your steps.
  C. You didn't square your answer and had a sign problem.
  D. This is a halfway answer, you forgot to square!
  E. You made some math error, check through your calculations.

2. $(x^2+8x-3)-(2x^2+5x-3)$ **is equivalent to:**

Correct Answer J

This is a common form for a combine like terms question. It's got an extra wrinkle; you'll have to distribute the negative sign into the second set of parentheses. Let's get rid of the parentheses (by distributing -1 into the second set) and combine like terms.

$$(x^2+8x-3)-(2x^2+5x-3)$$
$$x^2+8x-3-2x^2-5x+3$$

Distribute the -1 to *each* term.

Group like terms:

$$x^2-2x^2+8x-5x+3-3$$

Combine.

$$-x^2+3x$$

Answer choice **J** is correct.

As you combine terms mark off answer choices.

What You May Have Done Wrong
  F. You had a sign problem in your first and last terms.
  G. You messed up distributing your negative to your last term.
  H. You only distributed to the first term of the second set of parentheses but not all terms.
  K. You disregarded the negative sign entirely.

3. Which of the following expressions is equivalent to $-2x^2(5x^3y-2x^2)$?

Correct Answer A

This is a really standard format for an exponent problem. It's testing your ability to multiply exponents. **Whenever you're multiplying terms with the same base, you add the exponents.** Let's distribute.

$$-2x^2(5x^3y-2x^2) \quad \rightarrow \quad \big((5x^3y)(-2x^2)\big)-\big((2x^2)(-2x^2)\big)$$

$$(-10x^{3+2}y)-(-4x^{2+2}) \quad \rightarrow \quad -10x^5y+4x^4$$

> Do the problem in pieces and mark off as you

Answer choice **A** is correct

<u>What You May Have Done Wrong</u>
- **B.** You had a sign error with your second term. -2 x -2 = 4, not -4.
- **C.** You multiplied exponents. You *only* multiply exponents when you are raising a power to a new power.
- **D.** You made a sign error in your first term.
- **E.** You made a sign error in your first term. You also had an exponent error in your last term.

4. Which of the following expresses z in terms of x for all real numbers x, y, z when $\sqrt{x}=y$ and $y^4=z^2$?

Correct Answer K

This problem requires us to relate two variables (x and z) through a third variable (y). To do that, we're going to need the powers of y to be the same in both equations, allowing us to link both equations together. To start, get z to the 1st power and y to the second power.

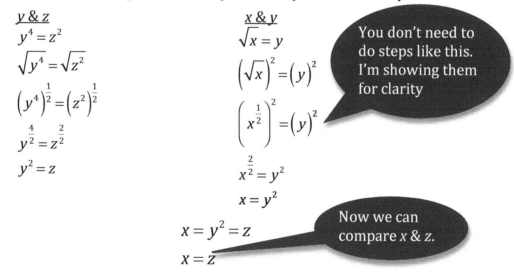

<u>y & z</u>
$$y^4=z^2$$
$$\sqrt{y^4}=\sqrt{z^2}$$
$$\left(y^4\right)^{\frac{1}{2}}=\left(z^2\right)^{\frac{1}{2}}$$
$$y^{\frac{4}{2}}=z^{\frac{2}{2}}$$
$$y^2=z$$

<u>x & y</u>
$$\sqrt{x}=y$$
$$\left(\sqrt{x}\right)^2=\left(y\right)^2$$
$$\left(x^{\frac{1}{2}}\right)^2=\left(y\right)^2$$
$$x^{\frac{2}{2}}=y^2$$
$$x=y^2$$

> You don't need to do steps like this. I'm showing them for clarity

$$x=y^2=z$$
$$x=z$$

> Now we can compare x & z.

Answer choice **K** is correct.

<u>What You May Have Done Wrong:</u>
- **F.** You most likely took the first equation to the 4th power and failed to take the root of the second equation.
- **G.** You may have just taken the root of the second equation
- **H.** You made a conceptual error.
- **J.** You made a conceptual error.

5. **Which If $x^2 = 25$ and $y^2 = 121$, then what is a possible value of $xy - y$?**

Correct Answer K

This is a problem that really tests whether you remember there is a positive & a negative root. If you do, the problem isn't so bad. The easiest way to solve this is probably to create a list of your possible solutions and find the one that matches. If you're clever, you may be able to knock at least one (and probably 2) answer(s) off as being too extreme.

x is either a positive or negative square root: $x^2 = 25$, so 5 or -5

y is either a positive or negative square root: $y^2 = 121$, so 11 or -11

x	y
+	+
+	-
-	+
-	-

> I'm showing this with tables to make it clearer, not as a suggestion for solving.

Which means we have four solutions.

x	y	xy – y	solution
+	+	(5)(11) - 11	44
+	-	(5)(-11) –(-11)	-44
-	+	(-5)(11)-11	-66
-	-	(-5)(-11)-(-11)	66

Answer choice **K** is correct.

6. **If a is a positive integer, which of the following expressions must be an even integer?**

Correct Answer E

This is a problem best solved by picking numbers and using those numbers to *test answer choices*. We know that a is a positive integer, so a is a whole number that is *greater than zero*. So, a could be odd or a could be even. I'm going to pick really easy numbers to work with, and test each answer choice with both the odd and even choice. **I'm using**

odd a value = 1
even a value = 2

Let's test answer choices, remember our correct choice will give us an even answer for both the *odd* and *even* plug-ins for a:

Even answers are shown in red.

Answer	Expression	Value when a =1	Value when a = 2
A	a^a	$1^1 = 1$	$2^2 = 4$
B	$\dfrac{a}{2}$	$\dfrac{1}{2} = \dfrac{1}{2}$	$\dfrac{2}{2} = 1$
C	$a - 1$	1-1 = 0	2 – 1 = 1
D	3^a	$3^1 = 3$	$3^2 = 9$
E	$a + a$	1 + 1 = 2	2 + 2 = 4

The only answer that results in only even values is **E**.

Answer choice **E** is correct.

7. $4a^3 \cdot 9a^9 \cdot a^{-2}$ is equivalent to:

Correct Answer G

This problem tests your ability to properly multiply exponents with the same base *and* deal with a negative exponent. Staring with the coefficients,

$$4a^3 \cdot 9a^9 \cdot a^{-2} \quad \rightarrow \quad 36a^3 \cdot a^9 \cdot a^{-2} \quad \rightarrow \quad 36a^{3+9+(-2)} \quad \rightarrow \quad 36a^{10}$$

Answer choice **G** is correct.

<u>What You May Have Done Wrong</u>

    F. You had a sign problem in your denominator (function *g*).

    H. You did everything correctly until you divided wrongly. You should have divided -6 by -12; you divided -12 by -6.

    J. You flipped your inputs. You plugged in -4 for *f* and -2 for *g*.

    K. You did everything correctly until you divided wrongly. You should have divided -6 by -12; you divided -12 by -6. You also had a sign problem.

8. Let $c = 4a - 2b$. What happens to the value of *c* if the value of *a* decreases by 1 and the value of *b* increases by 1?

Correct Answer C

This is a difficult problem, it can be solved algebraically, but it can be confusing to do so (although I will show it). It's probably easier to *pick numbers*. Let's look at the algebra first.

<u>Algebra</u>

    The problem says that we change it in this way, $a - 1$ and $b + $. Plug the new *a* and *b* values in.

$$c = 4(a-1) - 2(b+1) \quad \rightarrow \quad c = 4a - 4 - 2b - 2$$
$$c = 4a - 2b - 6 \quad \rightarrow \quad c + 6 = 4a - 2b$$

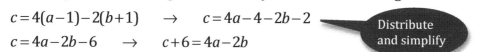
Distribute and simplify

    Originally, $c = 4a - 2b$. Now for *c* to equal $4a - 2b$ we have to add 6 to *c*. That means *c* is six less than it was. **Therefore, *c* has decreased by six.**

<u>Picking numbers</u>

    So, let's pick two easy to work with numbers for *a* and *b* and then plug them in to the equation to find an initial value of *c*. Let's say that $a = 1$ and $b = 2$.

$$c = 4(1) - 2(2) \quad \rightarrow \quad c = 4 - 4 = 0$$

    Now, we can change *a* and *b* according to the question and find a new *c*. First, we've got to change *a* & *b* according to the question.

$$\begin{array}{cc} \boldsymbol{a - 1} & \boldsymbol{b + 1} \\ 1 - 1 = 0 & 2 + 1 = 3 \end{array}$$

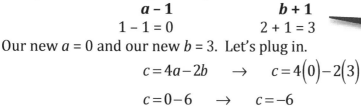
We subtract one from *a* & add one to *b* because the question says to.

Our new $a = 0$ and our new $b = 3$. Let's plug in.

$$c = 4a - 2b \quad \rightarrow \quad c = 4(0) - 2(3)$$
$$c = 0 - 6 \quad \rightarrow \quad c = -6$$

Initially, *c* was 0 and now *c* is -6. So *c* has **decreased** by six.

Answer choice **C** is correct.

<u>What You May Have Done Wrong</u>

    A. You may have eyeballed (guessed), or plugged in the changes, not values.

    B. You may have eyeballed (guessed), or had some other problem.

    D. You may have gotten the right answer but misunderstood it.

    E. You may have eyeballed (guessed), or plugged in the changes, not values. You also misunderstood the problem.

Background

Factoring equations is an important skill on the ACT. It shows up multiple times per test and can show up in *make an equation, systems of equations, rational expressions, radical expressions,* & *absolute value.*

What You Need to Know

- ✓ How to pull common factors out of expressions to create like terms or zeroes
- ✓ How to find the greatest common factor of numbers
- ✓ How to factor quadratics with positive, negative, and mixed signs
- ✓ How to find the solutions of factored quadratics
- ✓ How to factor expressions with powers greater than 2

Definitions: Factoring

Factoring is simplifying expressions by pulling out any common factors.

Factors are numbers you can multiply together to arrive at another number.

2 & 4 → Can be rewritten as $2 \cdot 1$ & $2 \cdot 2$. Both have a common factor of 2.

x^2 & $2x$ → Both have the common factor of x.

4 & 5 → Can be rewritten as $2 \cdot 2$ & $5 \cdot 1$ or $4 \cdot 1$ & $5 \cdot 1$. They do not share any factors other than one.

Mechanics: Factoring Expressions

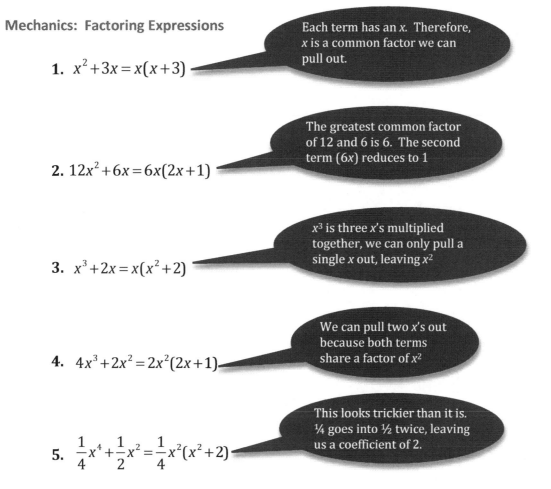

1. $x^2 + 3x = x(x+3)$

   Each term has an x. Therefore, x is a common factor we can pull out.

2. $12x^2 + 6x = 6x(2x+1)$

   The greatest common factor of 12 and 6 is 6. The second term ($6x$) reduces to 1

3. $x^3 + 2x = x(x^2+2)$

   x^3 is three x's multiplied together, we can only pull a single x out, leaving x^2

4. $4x^3 + 2x^2 = 2x^2(2x+1)$

   We can pull two x's out because both terms share a factor of x^2

5. $\frac{1}{4}x^4 + \frac{1}{2}x^2 = \frac{1}{4}x^2(x^2+2)$

   This looks trickier than it is. ¼ goes into ½ twice, leaving us a coefficient of 2.

Factoring Quadratic Equations

Factoring quadratic equations is a very significant portion of the ACT. In addition to direct factoring and solution questions, rational expressions, and some word problems depend on the ability to factor *and* a solid understanding of how factoring works.

Definitions

✓ **Quadratic Equations** are equations where the highest power is square and you set the equation equal to zero to solve. For example, $x^2+3x+2=0$ is ready to factor and solve.

✓ **The general form of a quadratic equation is** ax^2+bx+c**.** In the equation, a, b, c are coefficients.

✓ **Quadratic Equations have two solutions** because of the square, quadratic equations have two solutions. Very simply put, $x^2=4$ has two solutions $2\times2=4$ *AND* $-2\times-2=4$, so the solutions are 2 & -2.

✓ **Factors of Quadratics are used to find solutions.**
Let's look at our previous example $x^2=4$. By re-arranging the equation to equal zero, we have $x^2-4=0$. When factored, we get $(x + 2)(x - 2) = 0$. The two factors are $(x + 2)$ & $(x - 2)$.

> This is a *difference of squares.*

✓ **Solutions of Quadratics are found from their factors.** Again, let's look at our factors. Because $(x + 2)(x - 2) = 0$, we know that one of the two terms *must* be 0. The terms are multiplied together $(x+2)\bullet(x-2)=0$ and, therefore, one of the terms must be zero. So, either $x + 2 = 0$ or $x - 2 = 0$.

We set each term equal to zero and solve for x.

> These are the solutions for x. They are found by setting the factors = to zero.

$$x + 2 = 0 \quad or \quad x - 2 = 0$$
$$\underline{-2\ -2} \qquad \underline{+2\ +2}$$
$$x = -2 \qquad x = 2$$

Foiling: Expounding Parentheses to Check Answers

Let's take a bit of an aside from factoring to discuss FOIL. FOILing shows up in two ways on the ACT. We use FOIL to check factoring answers and to solve expounding problems.

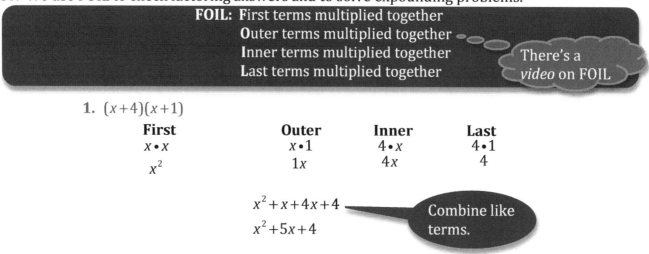

FOIL: First terms multiplied together
Outer terms multiplied together
Inner terms multiplied together
Last terms multiplied together

> There's a *video* on FOIL

1. $(x+4)(x+1)$

First	Outer	Inner	Last
$x \bullet x$	$x \bullet 1$	$4 \bullet x$	$4 \bullet 1$
x^2	$1x$	$4x$	4

$$x^2+x+4x+4$$
$$x^2+5x+4$$

> Combine like terms.

2. $(x-2)(x-3)$

First	Outer	Inner	Last
$x \cdot x$	$x \cdot -3$	$-2 \cdot x$	$-2 \cdot -3$
x^2	$-3x$	$-2x$	$+6$

$$x^2 - 3x - 2x + 6$$
$$x^2 - 5x + 6$$

> **Opposite signs** make a negative last term

3. $(x-3)(x+4)$

First	Outer	Inner	Last
$x \cdot x$	$x \cdot 4$	$-3 \cdot x$	$-3 \cdot 4$
x^2	$4x$	$-3x$	$-3 \cdot x$

$$x^2 + 4x - 3x - 12$$
$$x^2 + x - 12$$

6. $(x-1)^2$

First	Outer	Inner	Last
$x \cdot x$	$x \cdot -1$	$-1 \cdot x$	$-1 \cdot -1$
x^2	$-x$	$-x$	$+1$

> We don't "distribute" the square; we have to multiply the **quantity** $(x - 1)$ by itself.

$$x^2 - x - x + 1$$
$$x^2 - 2x + 1$$

> *Video* on Elementary Factoring

Rules of the Road: Before you Factor

1. Make sure your equation equals zero.

Rules of the Road: First Term

The first term determines what goes first in both of sets of parentheses.

The first term of a quadratic is split into the first terms in the parentheses, $x^2 + 3x + 2$ is **split among the parentheses like this $(\underline{x} \ldots)(\underline{x} \ldots) = x^2$**

The two first terms in parentheses *must* multiply together to equal the first term in the formula.

Rules of the Road: Last Term & Middle Terms

The last term partially determines what goes last in a set of parentheses but the middle term is necessary to completely determine it.

The last term in the parentheses must multiply together to equal **the last term of the equation**. In our previous example, $x^2 + 3x + 2$, our last terms *must* multiply together to equal 2.
$$(\ldots 2)(\ldots 1) = 2$$

> This could be $(\ldots1)(\ldots2)$ but order doesn't matter unless the first terms are different.

The coefficient of the middle term is the *sum* of the two last terms in parentheses. In our example, $x^2 + 3x + 2$, the last terms
$$(\ldots2)(\ldots1), 2+1 =3.$$
When we FOIL we'll get the terms $2x$ and $1x$, which adds to $3x$.

The factors of $x^2 + 3x + 2$ are $(x +2)(x+1)$.

Examples: Factoring with two Positive Signs

When both of the signs in our original equation are positive, *both* of our parentheses will have *addition* as the operation.

x^2 always breaks into x and x.

It doesn't matter where we put the second terms, because the signs and first terms are the same.

1. $x^2+6x+5=0$

$(x+\_\,)(x+\_\,)$

$(x+5)(x+1)$

Because the signs in front of the middle term ($6x$) is + and last term (5) is +, both of signs will be +

2. $x^2+9x+18=0$

$(x+\_\,)(x+\_\,)$

$(x+6)(x+3)$

The factors of 18: 18 x 1, 9 x 2, 6 x 3 Only 6 x 3 adds to 18!

We need two numbers that *multiply* to 18 and *add* to 9.

Examples: Factoring with a Positive End Sign and Negative Middle Sign

When the last sign is + and the middle sign is -, the parentheses will both have negative signs.

1. $x^2-2x+1=0$

$(x-\_\,)(x-\_\,)$

$(x-1)(x-1)$

Since the x and the negative sign are the same, the terms can go in any order.

The factors of 8: 8 x 1 and 4 x 2. Only -4 x -2 add up to -6

2. $x^2-6x+8=0$

$(x-\_\,)(x-\_\,)$

$(x-4)(x-2)$

Examples: Factoring with a Negative End Sign

The middle sign (here -) tells us that the larger number needs to be paired with the negative.

1. $x^2-2x-3=0$

$(x-\_\,)(x+\_\,)$

$(x-3)(x+1)$

Because the x's are identical we can place the + & - wherever

But it does matter where the last terms goes.

We need factors of 12 that have a difference of +4.

2. $x^2+4x-12=0$

$(x-\_\,)(x+\_\,)$

$(x-2)(x+6)$

Again, the middle sign (-) needs to be paired with the bigger number in the parentheses.

We need two numbers that multiply to - 18 and have a sum of -7. The only option is 2 and -9

3. $x^2-7x-18=0$

$(x-\_\,)(x+\_\,)$

$(x-9)(x+2)$

Definitions: The Solutions of Quadratic Equations

The factors equal zero when multiplied, so one of the two terms must be zero.

$$(factor\ A)(factor\ B)=0$$

To find the solutions, set both factors equal to zero, $factor\ A = 0$ and $factor\ B = 0$

Mechanics: The Solutions of Quadratic Equations

To find the solutions to a quadratic equation, set each factor equal to zero and solve for x (or whatever variable).

1. $(x-2)(x-1)=0$

    $x - 2 = 0$

    $x - 1 = 0$

    $x - 2 = 0 \rightarrow x = 2$

    $x - 1 = 0 \rightarrow x = 1$

    Set each term equal to zero.

    Solve for x.

2. $(x+4)(x+1)=0$

    $x + 4 = 0$

    $x + 1 = 0$

    $x + 4 = 0 \rightarrow x = -4$

    $x + 1 = 0 \rightarrow x = -1$

    Set each term equal to zero.

    Solve for x.

ACT Examples: Factoring Quadratics (Elementary Algebra)

1. What is the solution set of the equation $x^2 - 16x = 0$?

    A. 4 and 0
    B. 4 and -4
    C. 4 and 1
    D. 16 and 1
    E. 16 and 0

    Both terms share an x and we can factor that out of both terms.

    Solve

    $x^2 - 16x = 0$

    $x(x - 16) = 0$

    Set each factor equal to zero.

    $x = 0$ & $x - 16 = 0 \rightarrow x = 16$

    Solutions: x = 0, 16

    Answer choice **E** is correct.

2. What values of x are the solutions for $(x - z)(x + y) = 0$?

    A. $-z$ and $-y$
    B. z and $-y$
    C. $-z$ and y
    D. z and y
    E. $-z(-y)$

    Solve

    $$(x - z)(x + y) = 0$$

    $x - z = 0 \rightarrow x = z$ & $x + z = 0 \rightarrow x = -z$

    Set each term equal to zero.

    Answer choice **B** is correct.

2. Which is a factor of the equation $a^2 + 4ab + 3b^2 = 0$?

    A. $a^2 + 3b$
    B. $a^2 + b$
    C. $a - b$
    D. $a + b$
    E. $a + 4b$

Solve

This is a factoring problem, and you'll have to match up the answer choices with one of the factors. The equation is set equal to zero, so we can go ahead and factor.

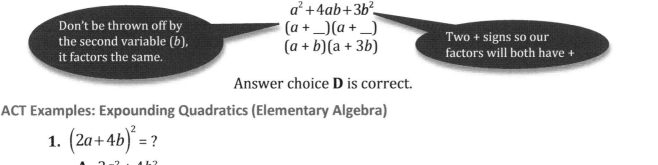

$$a^2 + 4ab + 3b^2$$
$$(a + \_)(a + \_)$$
$$(a + b)(a + 3b)$$

Don't be thrown off by the second variable (b), it factors the same.

Two + signs so our factors will both have +

Answer choice **D** is correct.

ACT Examples: Expounding Quadratics (Elementary Algebra)

1. $\left(2a + 4b\right)^2 = ?$

    A. $2a^2 + 4b^2$
    B. $4a^2 + 8b^2$
    C. $4a^2 + 16b^2$
    D. $4a^2 + 8ab + 16b^2$
    E. $4a^2 + 16ab + 16b^2$

Solve

When a binomial is squared you'll have to FOIL the binomial with itself.

We can *never* distribute a power into a binomial!

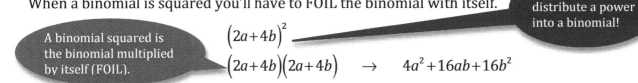

A binomial squared is the binomial multiplied by itself (FOIL).

$$\left(2a + 4b\right)^2$$
$$\left(2a + 4b\right)\left(2a + 4b\right) \quad \rightarrow \quad 4a^2 + 16ab + 16b^2$$

Answer **E** is correct.

1. What is the sum of the two solutions to the equation $x^2 + 3x - 18 = 0$?

    A. -3
    B. 3
    C. 9
    D. -9
    E. -18

There's a video on intermediate factoring.

Solve

This is a common setup for an intermediate factoring problem. You've just got one additional step. It's easy to miss, so be careful.

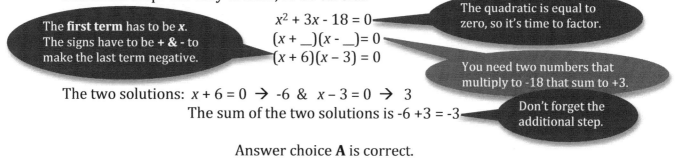

The **first term** has to be **x**. The signs have to be **+ & -** to make the last term negative.

The quadratic is equal to zero, so it's time to factor.

$$x^2 + 3x - 18 = 0$$
$$(x + \_)(x - \_) = 0$$
$$(x + 6)(x - 3) = 0$$

You need two numbers that multiply to -18 that sum to +3.

The two solutions: $x + 6 = 0 \rightarrow$ -6 & $x - 3 = 0 \rightarrow$ 3

The sum of the two solutions is -6 +3 = -3

Don't forget the additional step.

Answer choice **A** is correct.

2. If $(x + 6)$ is a factor of $4x^2 + 21x - 18$, what is the other factor of the equation?

    A. $x + 3$
    B. $4x - 3$
    C. $4x + 3$
    D. $4x - 18$
    E. $4x - 1$

Solve

This is a tough looking problem, but it's not that bad. You can factor the quadratic blindly (which would take awhile), but you don't have to. Use the factor given, $(x + 6)$ and use it to find the second factor. You'll use FOIL to help you factor.

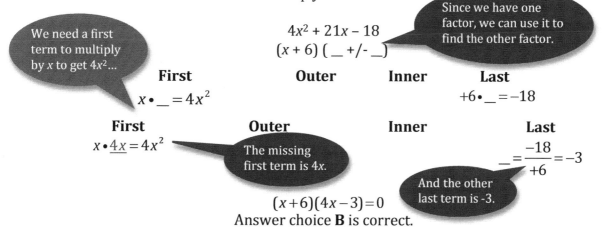

We need a first term to multiply by x to get $4x^2$...

Since we have one factor, we can use it to find the other factor.

$$4x^2 + 21x - 18$$
$$(x + 6) (\_ +/- \_)$$

First	Outer	Inner	Last
$x \cdot \_ = 4x^2$			$+6 \cdot \_ = -18$

First	Outer	Inner	Last
$x \cdot \underline{4x} = 4x^2$			$\dfrac{\_}{} = \dfrac{-18}{+6} = -3$

The missing first term is 4x.

And the other last term is -3.

$$(x+6)(4x-3)=0$$

Answer choice **B** is correct.

3. If $(x - 4)$ is a factor of $3x^2 - 7x + c = 0$, when what is c?

    A. 20
    B. 16
    C. -24
    D. -20
    E. -16

Solve

We've got to find the missing factor and then FOIL to find the missing c term.

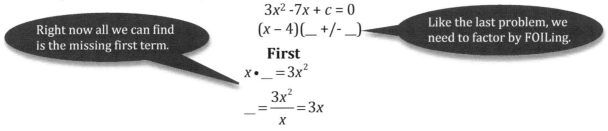

$$3x^2 - 7x + c = 0$$
$$(x - 4)(\_ \, +/- \, \_)$$

Right now all we can find is the missing first term.

Like the last problem, we need to factor by FOILing.

First
$$x \bullet \_ = 3x^2$$
$$\_ = \frac{3x^2}{x} = 3x$$

Now, we can figure out part of our middle term. Let's look at what we've got:
$$(x - 4)(3x +/- \_)$$

First	Outer	Inner	Last
$3x^2$	—	$-4 \bullet 3x = -12x$	c

The middle term has to equal $-7x$.

The inner & outer terms add to $-7x$

$$3x^2 - 7x + c = 0$$
$$-12x + \_ = -7x$$
$$\_ = -7x - (-12x)$$
$$\_ = 5x$$

The only way to do that is with a $+5x$.

First	Outer	Inner	Last
$3x^2$	$5x$	$-7x$	c

We have all of our other terms, now we can FOIL and find the last term.

$$(x - 4)(3x + 5)$$

First	Outer	Inner	Last
$3x^2$	$5x$	$-7x$	-20

Difference of Squares

There are quadratics with no middle term. They often aren't directly asked about but they commonly show up as parts of other problems.

Difference of squares have the format *perfect square – perfect square*.

The **factors** are $\left(\sqrt{\text{perfect square}} + \sqrt{\text{perfect square}}\right)\left(\sqrt{\text{perfect square}} - \sqrt{\text{perfect square}}\right)$

Example: Difference of Squares

$$x^2 - 4$$
$$(x + 2)(x - 2)$$
$$x^2 - 2x + 2x - 4$$
$$x^2 - 4$$

The middle terms cancel.

Wrap Up

What You Need to Know
- ✓ How to pull common factors out of expressions to create like terms or zeroes
- ✓ How to find the greatest common factor of numbers
- ✓ How to factor quadratics with positive, negative, and mixed signs
- ✓ How to find the solutions of factored quadratics
- ✓ How to factor expressions with powers greater than 2

Videos

> Elementary Factoring

> Expounding

> Intermediate Factoring

The Strategies
- ✓ Think about factoring whenever a variable is squared. You won't always factor, but it's always worth checking.
- ✓ You can factor (into two sets of parentheses) any quadratic with even powers.
- ✓ If you have a factor of a tough quadratic, factor back from FOIL.
- ✓ Don't forget about difference of squares

Key Skill

Factoring is related to:

- ✓ Pre-Algebra Factors
- ✓ Exponents
- ✓ Rational Expressions
- ✓ Systems of Equations
- ✓ Coordinate Geometry: Functions

Elementary/Intermediate Algebra: Quadratics

1. What is the sum of the solutions to the equation $x^2 - 25 = 0$?

   A. 10
   B. -5
   C. 5
   D. 0
   E. 25

2. For all real numbers, $(2x + 1)^2 = ?$

   F. $2x^2 + 1$
   G. $4x^2 + 1$
   H. $4x^2 + 2$
   J. $4x^2 + 4x + 1$
   K. $2x^2 + 4x + 1$

3. What values of x are solutions of the equation $(x - b)(x + a) = 0$?

   A. $-b$ and a
   B. b and $-a$
   C. $-b$ and $-a$
   D. b and a
   E. x and $-x$

4. If $x^2 - 6 = 30$, then $|x| - 2 = ?$

   F. 4
   G. -8
   H. $2\sqrt{2} - 2$
   J. 34
   K. 6

5. The expression $x^2 - 6x + 9$ is equivalent to?

   A. $(x - 3)(x - 6)$
   B. $(x - 3)(x + 3)$
   C. $(x - 3)^2$
   D. $(x + 3)^2$
   E. $(x - 1)(x - 9)$

6. Which is a factor of the equation $a^4 + 6a^2b^2 + 5b^4 = 0$?

   F. $a^2 + 5b$
   G. $a + 5b^2$
   H. $a^2 + \sqrt{5}b^2$
   J. $a + b^2$
   K. $a^2 + b^2$

7. If $f(x) = x^2 + 7x$ and $g(x) = 3x - 3$, for what value does $f(x) = g(x)$?

   A. 1
   B. 3
   C. -3
   D. -6
   E. -4

8. If $\left(x - 3\right)$ is a factor of $2x^2 + x + c$, what is the value of c?

   F. -7
   G. -21
   H. 4
   J. 2
   K. 7

Quadratics: Solutions

1. **What is the sum of the solutions to the equation $x^2 - 25 = 0$?**

Correct Answer D

You can solve this problem by using the definition of the *difference of squares* or by solving.

<u>Definition: Difference of Squares</u>

All difference of squares have factors: $\left(\sqrt{Square\ A} - \sqrt{Square\ B}\right)\left(\sqrt{Square\ A} + \sqrt{Square\ B}\right)$

$\sqrt{x^2} - \sqrt{25} = 0$ will have factors $(x-5)\ \&\ (x+5)$.

$$x - 5 = 0 \rightarrow x = 5$$
$$x + 5 = 0 \rightarrow x = -5$$

<u>Solving</u>

You can solve this problem without factoring. Instead of factoring into two sets of parentheses, isolate the x^2 term on one side of the equation.

$$x^2 - 25 = 0 \quad \rightarrow \quad x^2 = 25$$
$$\sqrt{x^2} = \sqrt{25} \quad \rightarrow \quad x = 5\ or -5$$

> There are two square roots.

Add the solutions to find the answer

$$5 + (-5) = 0$$

Answer choice **D** is correct.

<u>What You May Have Done Wrong</u>

    A. You didn't find the negative solution.

    B. This is one solution, not the sum of the solutions.

    C. This is one solution, not the sum of the solutions.

    E. 25 is the value of x^2 and not a solution the equation.

2. **For all real numbers, $(2x + 1)^2 = ?$**

Correct Answer J

Following the order of operations, we have to deal with Parentheses first. Since we can't make the binomial any simpler, we move on to exponents. To square a binomial, we have to multiply it by itself, we have to FOIL.

$(2x + 1)(2x + 1)$

First	**Outer**	**Inner**	**Last**
$2x \bullet 2x = 4x^2$	$1 \bullet 2x = 2x$	$1 \bullet 2x = 2x$	$1 \bullet 1 = 1$

$4x^2 + 4x + 1$

Answer choice **J** is correct.

<u>What You May Have Done Wrong</u>

    F. You tried to distribute the square.

    G. You distributed the square.

    H. You tried to distribute the square.

    K. You made an error in your first term when FOILING.

3. What values of *x* are solutions of the equation $(x - b)(x + a) = 0$?

Correct Answer B

This is a definition question. You have to remember that quadratic factoring (and solutions) work based on the principle that one of the two factors must equal zero. Because of the variables, the problem can look much tougher than it is.

$$(x - b)(x + a) = 0$$
$$x - b = 0$$
$$x + a = 0$$

Now solve for *x* in both equations to find the solutions.

$$x - b = 0 \rightarrow x = b$$
$$x + a = 0 \rightarrow x = -a$$

Answer choice **B** is correct.

<u>What You May Have Done Wrong</u>
- **A.** You didn't set equal to zero to find the solutions.
- **C.** You found the correct solution for *a* but got the sign wrong on *b*.
- **D.** You found the correct solution for *b* but got the wrong sign on *a*.
- **E.** You misunderstood the nature of solutions, review <u>here</u>.

4. If $x^2 - 6 = 30$, then $|x| - 2 = ?$

Correct Answer F

For some of you, there will be no need to factor, as once you re-arrange the question you'll see the solutions of x^2 without factoring. For the rest of us, this problem is easily factored as a difference of squares.

$$x^2 - 6 = 30 \quad \rightarrow \quad x^2 - 36 = 0$$
$$(x + 6)(x - 6) = 0$$

The solutions are 6 and -6

The second part of the question asks for the absolute value of *x*. Absolute value is always positive and therefore….

$$|6| = |-6| = 6.$$
$$|6| - 2 = 4$$
$$|-6| - 2 = 4$$

Answer choice **F** is correct.

<u>What You May Have Done Wrong</u>
- **G.** You forgot to use, or misunderstand absolute value.
- **H.** You made an algebra error involving the -6 in the original equation. This resulted in an equation like $x^2 = 24$.
- **J.** You did not factor, or find the roots of x^2
- **K.** This is the halfway answer. You found a solution for *x* but did not do the absolute value calculation.

5. **The expression $x^2 - 6x + 9$ is equivalent to?**

Correct Answer C

This factoring problem has a tiny wrinkle which shows up at the end. To begin with, let's factor the quadratic.

$$x^2 - 6x + 9$$
$$(x - \underline{\quad})(x - \underline{\quad})$$
$$(x - 3)(x - 3)$$

In the form above, the answer is not among our choices. We have to recall that a binomial squared is that term multiplied by itself (via FOIL).

$$(x - 3)(x - 3) = (x - 3)^2$$

Answer choice **C** is correct.

<u>What You May Have Done Wrong</u>
   A. You made a FOIL error.
   B. This would result in a negative end term, and no middle term, a difference of squares.
   D. This would result in a positive middle term.
   E. This would result in a middle term of -10x.

6. **Which is a factor of the equation $a^4 + 6a^2b^2 + 5b^4 = 0$?**

Correct Answer K

Although it doesn't look like it, this is just like factoring a quadratic because the leading (a^4) and tailing (b^4) powers are even. The fact that the five is not a perfect square (or perfect fourth power) does not matter; let's see why:

$$a^4 + 6a^2b^2 + 5b^4$$
$$(a^2 + \underline{\quad})(a^2 + \underline{\quad})$$
$$(a^2 + b^2)(a^2 + 5b^2)$$

$$a^2 \cdot a^2 = a^{2+2} = a^4$$

Of the two factors, only $a^2 + b^2$ is present, and that makes the correct answer choice.

Answer choice **K** is correct.

<u>What You May Have Done Wrong</u>
   F. You neglected that the b term must be squared.
   G. You neglected that the a term must be squared.
   H. You tried to take the square root of the entire problem, to reduce everything to squares.
   J. You neglected that the a term must be squared.

7. If $f(x)=x^2+7x$ and $g(x)=3x-3$, for what value does $f(x)=g(x)$?

Correct Answer C

This is a muddled sort of question. It involves function plug-in, and can be fairly intimidating. Once you handle the setup, though, we can factor and solve, or we can *test answers*. If you don't see the factoring immediately, then *testing answers* is the way to go. If you do spot the factoring; it will be a little quicker to factor.

Setup: If *f(x)* and *g(x)* equal each other, then the equations equal each other.

$$f(x)=g(x)$$
$$x^2+7x=3x-3$$

Set Equal to Zero: $x^2+7x=3x-3 \quad \rightarrow \quad x^2+4x+3=0$

Factoring: $\qquad\qquad x^2+4x+3=0 \quad \rightarrow \quad (x+3)(x+1)$

The solutions are *x* = -3 & -1. Both are solutions, but each answer choice has only one solution. We just pick the answer choice that either has -3 or -1.

Answer choice **C** is correct.

What You May Have Done Wrong

    A. You may have miscalculated 1 as a solution for *x*.
    B. You may have miscalculated 1 as a solution for *x*.
    D. Likely you made an algebra error, or you didn't get how to solve the problem.
    E. You may have added both solutions, or made another algebra error.

8. If $(x-3)$ is a factor of $2x^2 + x + c$, what is the value of c?

Correct Answer G

This question is a hard problem and requires some clever thinking.

$$2x^2 + x + c$$

$$(x-3)(\_ +/- \_)$$

We don't know if the operation will be **+ or -**

At this point, we know what our first term has to be $(2x^2)$ and one of the factors of that first term is x. Let's look at FOIL to illustrate this.

First	**Outer**	**Inner**	**Last**
$x \cdot \_ = 2x^2$	$x \cdot \_ = ?$	$-3 \cdot \_ = ?$	$-3 \cdot \_ = ?$

We can solve for the missing factor of the first term (the first spot in the second set of parentheses).

$$x \cdot \_ = 2x^2 \rightarrow \_ = \frac{2x^2}{x} \rightarrow \_ = 2x$$

$$(x-3)(\underline{2x} +/- \_)$$

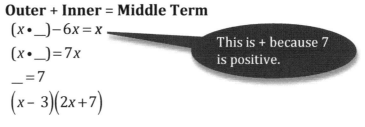

You don't need to do this algebra; I'm showing it to be thorough.

First	**Outer**	**Inner**	**Last**
$x \cdot \underline{2x} = 2x^2$	$x \cdot \_ = ?$	$-3 \cdot \underline{2x} = -6x$	$-3 \cdot \_ = ?$

Because we have the *inner value*, we can solve for our *middle term*.

Outer + Inner = Middle Term

$$(x \cdot \_) - 6x = x$$

$$(x \cdot \_) = 7x$$

$$\_ = 7$$

$$(x-3)(2x+7)$$

This is + because 7 is positive.

Now, we can calculate c (the product of our last terms) by FOIL.

$$(x-3)(2x+7)$$

First	**Outer**	**Inner**	**Last**
$x \cdot \underline{2x} = 2x^2$	$x \cdot \underline{7} = 7x$	$-3 \cdot \underline{2x} = -6x$	$-3 \cdot \underline{7} = -21$

$$c = -21$$

Answer choice **G** is correct.

Algebraic Inequalities
Key Skill

Background

Linear inequalities aren't often tested directly, but they are of fundamental importance for more complicated inequalities, absolute value problems, and coordinate geometry problems.

What You Need to Know

✓ How to convert text to an inequality
✓ How to solve algebraic inequalities

Definitions: Inequalities

Inequalities let us relate two quantities that aren't equal. We can say that one quality is less than or greater than the other. We can also say that they may equal each other.

Inequality		Key Words	Example	Meaning
Greater Than	>	greater than, more, larger, over	$x > 1$	x is larger than one
Greater Than/Equal to	≥	greater than or equal to, at least, not less than	$x \geq 1$	x is one or larger
Less Than	<	less than, smaller, beneath	$x < 1$	x is smaller than one
Less Than/Equal to	≤	less than or equal to, no more than, at most	$x \leq 1$	x is one or smaller

Rules of the Road: Solving Inequalities

Treat inequalities just like equations, with the inequality acting like an equal sign.
Except when you divide by a negative number. When you divide by a negative number, you *flip the inequality symbol*.

Examples: Solving Inequalities

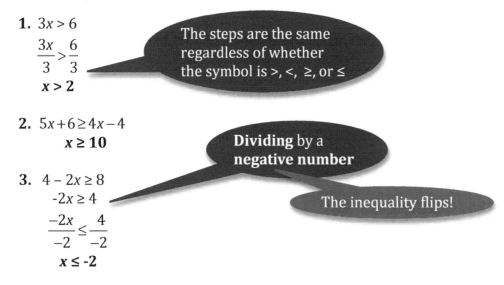

1. $3x > 6$

$$\frac{3x}{3} > \frac{6}{3}$$

$$x > 2$$

The steps are the same regardless of whether the symbol is >, <, ≥, or ≤

2. $5x + 6 \geq 4x - 4$

$$x \geq 10$$

Dividing by a **negative number**

3. $4 - 2x \geq 8$

$$-2x \geq 4$$

$$\frac{-2x}{-2} \leq \frac{4}{-2}$$

$$x \leq -2$$

The inequality flips!

ACT Example: Make an Inequality

1. To override a presidential veto, a minimum of two-thirds of the Congress must vote to pass the bill. There are 100 voting members of the US Senate. Which inequality represents the number of votes (v) needed in the Senate.

    A. $v \geq 67$
    B. $v \leq 67$
    C. $v > 67$
    D. $v \geq 66$
    E. $v \leq 66$

Solve

The question says that the "minimum" has to be two-thirds. That means that we'll be dealing with a v that has to be *greater than or equal to* two-thirds of 100. First, let's calculate how many votes two-thirds represents. This is a *which* question, so we'll mark-off.

$$100 \cdot \frac{2}{3} = 66.\overline{66}$$

Because we can't have partial votes, we round up and the minimum number of votes is 67. Even if the decimal worked out differently, for example 66.1.

We'd round up **any** decimal

Even though the question is written as a *greater than or equal to*, there are two possible inequalities:

$$v > 66 \ \textbf{OR} \ v \geq 67$$

Answer Choice **A** is correct.

ACT Example: Solving Inequalities

1. Which inequality defines the solution set for the inequality $20 - 3x \leq 8$?

    A. $3 \leq x$
    B. $x \geq 4$
    C. $x \leq 4$
    D. $x \geq -4$
    E. $x \leq -4$

Solve

This problem requires us to simplify the inequality. Remember, except for dividing by a negative number, we treat inequalities the same as equations.

$$20 - 3x \leq 8 \ \rightarrow \ 3x \leq -12$$
$$\frac{-3x}{-3} \geq \frac{-12}{-3}$$
$$x \geq 4$$

Flip the inequality symbol when dividing by a negative.

Answer Choice **B** is correct.

Definitions: Infinite or No Solutions

Algebraic inequalities can have **no solutions** or **infinite solutions** (works for every real number). When there are **no solutions** you can say that the inequality is true only for the empty set.

Examples: Infinite or No Solutions

1. What is the set of all real numbers x such that $2x - 5 < 2x - 3$?

$$2x - 5 < 2x - 3$$
$$-2x \qquad -2x$$
$$-5 < -3$$

The x's cancel

Move the x's to one side.

-5 is *always less than* -3, so the inequality is true for all real numbers.

2. What is the set of all real number x such that $4x + 4 \geq 4x + 6$?

$$4x + 4 \geq 4x + 6$$
$$-4x \qquad -4x$$
$$4 \geq 6$$

4 is *never greater* than 6, so for real numbers, the inequality will always be false. Or you can say, the inequality is true *only* for the *empty set*.

ACT Examples: Intermediate Inequalities

1. If four times a number n is added to negative 20, the result is positive. Which inequality gives the possible value(s) of n?

    A. $4n \geq -20$
    B. $n > -5$
    C. $n > 5$
    D. $n < -5$
    E. $n \geq 5$

Solve

This question is very similar to "make an equation" problems. Like make an equation, the easiest way to work this problem is to break it into bite sized pieces.

Statement 1: If four times a number...

$$4n$$

Let's break down the statements.

Statement 2: is added to -20

$$-4n - 20$$

Statement 3: ...is positive

$$>0 \rightarrow 4n - 20 > 0$$

The definition of positive is greater than zero.

Now, we can solve the inequality.

$$4n - 20 > 0$$
$$4n > 20$$
$$n > 5$$

Answer Choice **C** is correct.

2. If $0 > x > y > z$, which of the following expressions has the greatest value?

A. $\dfrac{x}{y}$

B. $\dfrac{y}{z}$

C. $\dfrac{x}{z}$

D. $\dfrac{z}{y}$

E. $\dfrac{z}{x}$

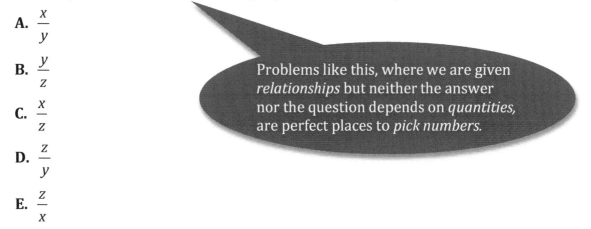

Problems like this, where we are given *relationships* but neither the answer nor the question depends on *quantities,* are perfect places to *pick numbers.*

Solve

This is a *mark-off* question that's much easier if you pick numbers (otherwise it's a real pain). Because 0 is the greatest number, x, y, & z will all be negative. **I'm going to say that $x = -1$, $y = -2$, & $z = -3$.**

$$0 > x\ > y\ > z$$
$$0 > -1 > -2 > -3$$

A. $\dfrac{x}{y} \rightarrow \dfrac{-1}{-2} = \dfrac{1}{2}$

B. $\dfrac{y}{z} \rightarrow \dfrac{-2}{-3} = \dfrac{2}{3}$

C. $\dfrac{x}{z} \rightarrow \dfrac{-1}{-3} = \dfrac{1}{3}$

D. $\dfrac{z}{y} \rightarrow \dfrac{-3}{-2} = \dfrac{3}{2}$

E. $\dfrac{z}{x} \rightarrow \dfrac{-3}{-1} = 3$

Because the negatives cancel, the right answer has the biggest numerator and smallest denominator.

Wrap Up

What You Need to Know
- ✓ How to convert text to an inequality
- ✓ How to solve algebraic inequalities

Videos

Inequalities

The Strategies
- ✓ Make sure you are careful with your operations. When you divide by a negative number, remember to flip your inequality symbol.
- ✓ On word problems, you may end up with a decimal in the answer. Use the inequality sign to help you round up or down.

Related Skills
- ✓ Make an Equation

- ✓ Absolute Value

Elementary/Intermediate Algebra: Inequalities

1. What is the solution set for the inequality $7-3x \leq 2x+5$?

   A. $x \leq \dfrac{2}{5}$

   B. $x \geq \dfrac{2}{5}$

   C. $x \geq -\dfrac{2}{5}$

   D. $x \leq 2$

   E. $x \geq -\dfrac{5}{2}$

2. What is the set of real numbers such that $3x+6 \leq 3x+1$?

   F. The set containing all real numbers
   G. The set containing all negative numbers & 0
   H. The set containing all negative numbers
   J. The set containing all nonnegative numbers
   K. The empty set

3. 575 students apply for a medical school. At most, the medical school can accept one-seventh of the applicants. Which of the following expressions is true about the number of students accepted (a)?

   A. $a = 82$
   B. $a < 82$
   C. $a < 83$
   D. $a \leq 83$
   E. $a > 82$

4. Taylar runs 5 days a week and in a month (consisting of exactly four weeks) she runs a maximum of 200 miles. The length of her runs varies from day-to-day. If d is the average distance of Taylar's runs, which of the inequalities below represents d?

   F. $d \geq 10$
   G. $d < 10$
   H. $d \leq 200$
   J. $d \leq 10$
   K. $d \leq 50$

5. If $x, y,$ and z are nonzero integers such that $x > y$ and $yz > xz$ what *must be true*?

   A. y is negative
   B. x is positive
   C. x and y are negative
   D. y is positive
   E. z is negative

1. What is the solution set for the inequality $7-3x\leq 2x+5$?

Correct Answer B

This is a *solve* question. There's no special tricks here, just re-arrange the inequality to isolate x on one side. If you found the term "solution set" confusing, don't forget to look at your answer choices for clues on how your final answer should look.

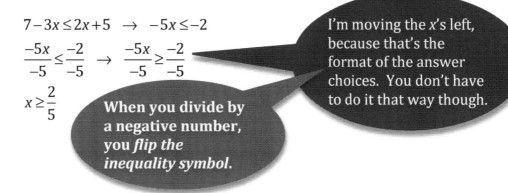

Answer choice **B** is correct.

What You May Have Done Wrong

    B. You forgot to *flip the inequality symbol.*

    C. You made an algebra error or an arithmetic error when you divided the negative numbers.

    D. You made an algebra error, adding $2x$ when you should have subtracted $2x$ (or vice versa with $3x$).

    E. You made a couple of algebra errors, review your steps.

2. What is the set of real numbers such that $3x+6\leq 3x+1$?

Correct Answer K

This is really a definition question, although you have to simplify the inequality.

$$3x+6\leq 3x+1$$
$$\underline{-3x\qquad -3x}$$
$$6\leq 1$$

Our inequality simplifies to $6 \leq 1$. Six is *never less than* 1, so the inequality is never true for real numbers. The empty set contains no real numbers (it's empty). So, the solution set for the inequality $3x+6\leq 3x+1$, is the *empty set*.

Answer choice **K** is correct.

What You May Have Done Wrong

    F. This would be correct if the inequality was always true, for example $1 \leq 2$.

    G. This is correct if the inequality is true for zero and all negative numbers. For example $2x \leq x$ would be true for 0 and all of the negative numbers.

    H. This is correct if the inequality is true for all negative numbers. For example $2x < x$ is true for all negative numbers.

    J. This is correct if the inequality is true for zero and all positive numbers. For example $2x \geq x$ is true for all positive numbers & 0.

3. 575 students apply for a medical school. At most, the medical school can accept one-seventh of the applicants. Which of the following expressions is true about the number of students accepted (a)?

Correct Answer C

This is a *make an inequality* question. Let's break it down into statements.

Statement 1: 600 students apply for a medical school
$$applicants = 575$$

Statement 2: At most, the medical medical school can accept 1/7 of the applicants.

$$accepted \leq \frac{1}{7}applicants$$

The most sets the **maximum**, so the acceptances will be less than or equal to.

So, we can plug-in applicants into our inequality to solve.

We can't accept 0.14 of a student. Since the inequality is *less than or equal* to, round down.

$$accepted \leq \frac{1}{7}(575) \quad \rightarrow \quad accepted \leq 82.14$$

$$accepted \leq 82$$

We can also put the inequality as a *less than*: $accepted < 83$

Answer choice **C** is correct

What You May Have Done Wrong
- **A.** This is the maximum number of admitted students, but the medical school can accept fewer students.
- **B.** You can have 82 students admitted, that's the maximum.
- **D.** You can't have 83 students; it would be slightly more than 1/7th of the applicants.
- **E.** Your inequality is backwards.

4. Taylar runs 5 days a week and in a month (consisting of exactly four weeks) she runs a maximum of 200 miles. The length of her runs varies from day-to-day. If d is the average distance of Taylar's runs, which of the inequalities below represents d?

Correct Answer J

This *make an inequality* problem has a unit conversion component to it. *At most* she runs 200 miles in four weeks. We can do this using dimensional analysis (or however you like to do your unit conversion problems).

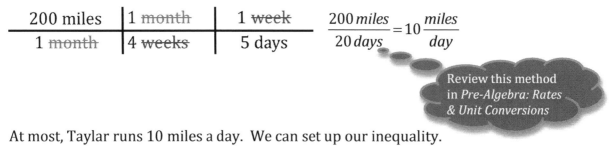

Review this method in *Pre-Algebra: Rates & Unit Conversions*

At most, Taylar runs 10 miles a day. We can set up our inequality.
$$d \leq 10$$

Answer choice **J** is correct.

What You May Have Done Wrong:
- **F.** Your inequality symbol is flipped.
- **G.** This is Taylar running *less than* 10 miles a day. She *can* run 10 miles a day.
- **H.** This is the distance Taylar runs in a month, d represents the distance run in a day.
- **K.** This is the distance Taylar runs in a month, d represents the distance run in a day.

5. If x, y, and z are nonzero integers such that $x > y$ and $yz > xz$ what *must be true*?

Correct Answer E

This is a tricky problem to setup, and you're going to have to rely on picking numbers and testing answer choices. Since you're looking for *must be true*, you want to try and prove that answer choices can be false.

We know that $x > y$, and that neither can equal zero. Let's pick a couple of sets of numbers for x & y. We can say that

$x = 2$ & $y = 1$
$x = -1$ & $y = -2$

> We also have a third possibility, a **positive** x & a **negative** y.

Let's also use $z = 3$ & $z = -3$

Let's start testing answer choices.

A. y is negative
   To test, show that y **can** be positive.
   $x = 2$, $y = 1$, & $z = -3$
   $$yz > xz$$
   $$1 \cdot (-3) > 2 \cdot (-3)$$
   $$-3 > -6$$

> I'm just going to show the tests that work. You may have to try a few before you hit the right one.

B. x is positive
   To test, show that x **can** be negative.
   $x = -1$, $y = 2$, & $z = -3$
   $$yz > xz$$
   $$-1 \cdot (-3) > 2 \cdot (-3)$$
   $$-3 > -6$$

C. x and y are negative
   To test, show that **either x or y can** be positive. (We already did this test with **A**).
   $x = 1$ & $y = -2$ & $z = -3$
   $$yz > xz$$
   $$(-2)(-3) > (-1)(-3)$$
   $$6 > -3$$

> With the *either* I only have to show that x or y can be positive.

D. y is positive
   To test, show that y **can** be negative. (We already did this with **C**).
   $x = 1$ & $y = -2$ & $z = -3$
   $$yz > xz$$
   $$(-2)(-3) > (-1)(-3)$$
   $$6 > -3$$

E. z is negative
   We've already seen that **A, B, C, & D** could be true. When you eliminate what's not correct, you're left with what is. That's the beauty of marking off. It's really difficult to prove something *must be true*, but it's easy to prove that something *could be false*.

Background

Absolute value stretches from pre-algebra through intermediate algebra. The majority of absolute value questions are about algebraic inequalities

What You Need to Know

- ✓ How to do operations with absolute value
- ✓ How to set up absolute value equations to find both solutions
- ✓ How to solve absolute value inequalities and graph on a number line.

Definitions: Absolute Value

Absolute Value is the how far away from 0 a number is on the number line.

The absolute value of 2 is 2.

The distance between 2 and 0 is two.

The absolute value of -2 is 2.

Absolute value is *always positive or zero*
$$|x| \geq 0$$

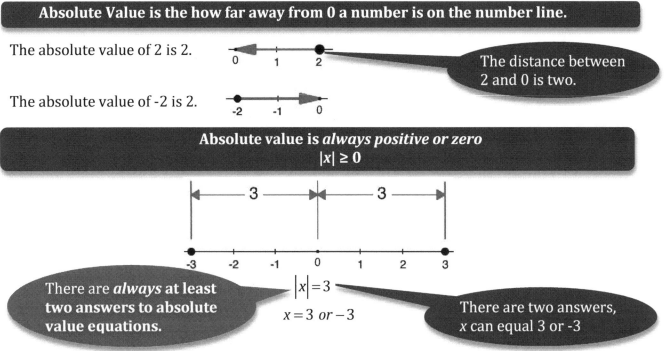

There are *always* at least two answers to absolute value equations.

$$|x| = 3$$
$$x = 3 \ or -3$$

There are two answers, *x* can equal 3 or -3

Absolute Value Operations

Treat absolute value bars like parentheses. Resolve the inside of the bars before applying the absolute value.

Rules of the Road: Absolute Value Operations

1. Resolve what's in the absolute value bars.
2. Take that answer and make it positive.
3. Continue to the other operations

Example: Absolute Value Operations

1. $|3-6| = ?$

$|-3| = 3$

2. $|3-6| + 7 = ?$

$|-3| + 7 = ?$

$3 + 7 = 10$

3. $2|3-6| + 7 = ?$

$2|-3| + 7 = ?$

$2(3) + 7 = ?$

$6 + 7 = 13$

1. Rearrange your equation to isolate the *absolute value.*
2. Always split the equation into negative & positive results.

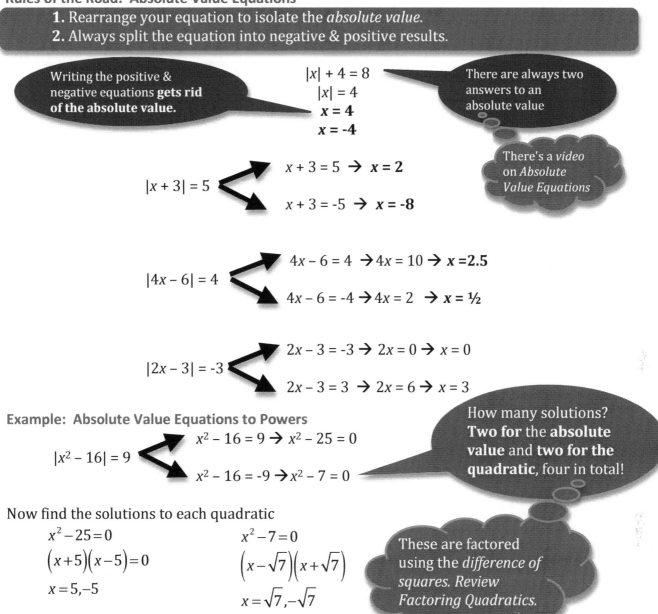

Writing the positive & negative equations **gets rid of the absolute value.**

$$|x| + 4 = 8$$
$$|x| = 4$$
$$x = 4$$
$$x = -4$$

There are always two answers to an absolute value

There's a *video* on *Absolute Value Equations*

$|x + 3| = 5$

$x + 3 = 5 \rightarrow x = 2$

$x + 3 = -5 \rightarrow x = -8$

$|4x - 6| = 4$

$4x - 6 = 4 \rightarrow 4x = 10 \rightarrow x = 2.5$

$4x - 6 = -4 \rightarrow 4x = 2 \rightarrow x = \frac{1}{2}$

$|2x - 3| = -3$

$2x - 3 = -3 \rightarrow 2x = 0 \rightarrow x = 0$

$2x - 3 = 3 \rightarrow 2x = 6 \rightarrow x = 3$

Example: Absolute Value Equations to Powers

$|x^2 - 16| = 9$

$x^2 - 16 = 9 \rightarrow x^2 - 25 = 0$

$x^2 - 16 = -9 \rightarrow x^2 - 7 = 0$

How many solutions?
Two for the **absolute value** and **two for the quadratic,** four in total!

Now find the solutions to each quadratic

$$x^2 - 25 = 0$$
$$(x+5)(x-5) = 0$$
$$x = 5, -5$$

$$x^2 - 7 = 0$$
$$(x - \sqrt{7})(x + \sqrt{7})$$
$$x = \sqrt{7}, -\sqrt{7}$$

These are factored using the *difference of squares. Review Factoring Quadratics.*

Solutions: $-5, 5, \sqrt{7}, -\sqrt{7}$

Absolute value inequalities work the same way as absolute value equations (we have two results). *Except, when you set up your two inequalities you flip the inequality sign of the negative answer.*

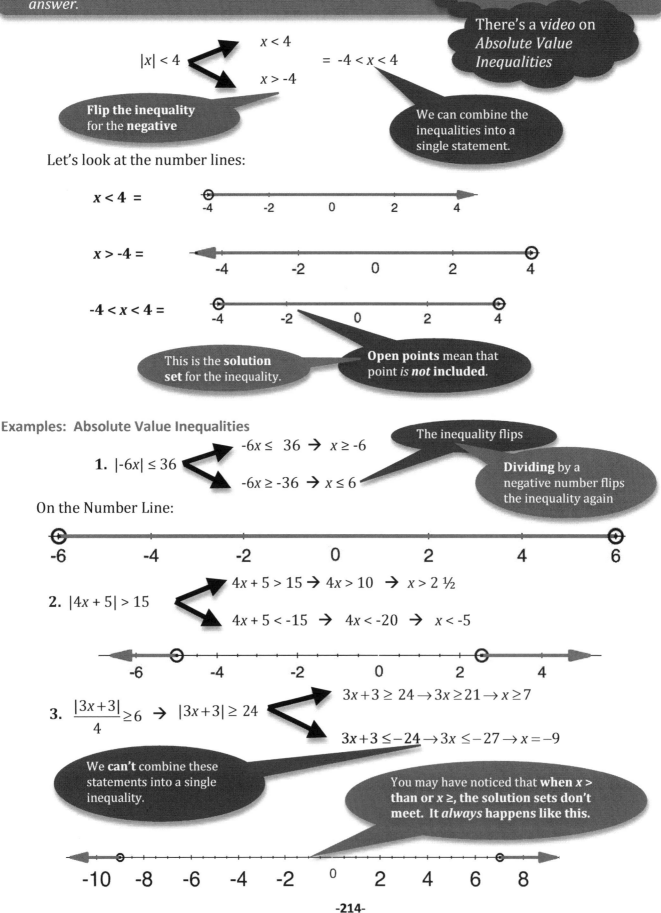

There's a *video* on *Absolute Value Inequalities*

$|x| < 4$

$x < 4$

$x > -4$

$= -4 < x < 4$

Flip the inequality for the **negative**

We can combine the inequalities into a single statement.

Let's look at the number lines:

$x < 4 =$

$x > -4 =$

$-4 < x < 4 =$

This is the **solution set** for the inequality.

Open points mean that point *is not* **included**.

Examples: Absolute Value Inequalities

1. $|-6x| \leq 36$

$-6x \leq 36 \rightarrow x \geq -6$

$-6x \geq -36 \rightarrow x \leq 6$

The inequality flips

Dividing by a negative number flips the inequality again

On the Number Line:

2. $|4x + 5| > 15$

$4x + 5 > 15 \rightarrow 4x > 10 \rightarrow x > 2\frac{1}{2}$

$4x + 5 < -15 \rightarrow 4x < -20 \rightarrow x < -5$

3. $\dfrac{|3x+3|}{4} \geq 6 \rightarrow |3x+3| \geq 24$

$3x+3 \geq 24 \rightarrow 3x \geq 21 \rightarrow x \geq 7$

$3x+3 \leq -24 \rightarrow 3x \leq -27 \rightarrow x = -9$

We **can't** combine these statements into a single inequality.

You may have noticed that **when x > than or x ≥, the solution sets don't meet.** It *always* happens like this.

1. Which statement is equal to $|x|$?

    A. x^2
    B. $x^2 - x$
    C. $\sqrt{2x}$
    D. $\sqrt{x^2}$
    E. $-|x|$

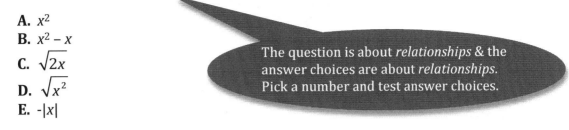

The question is about *relationships* & the answer choices are about *relationships*. Pick a number and test answer choices.

Solve

This is a "which" question, so we'll need to mark-off. It's also a great question to pick numbers on. We'll need to test a positive & a negative number because it's absolute value. I'm going to use 2 and -2.

    A. $x^2 \rightarrow 2^2 = 4 \rightarrow 4 \neq 2$

    B. $x^2 - x \rightarrow 2^2 - 2 \rightarrow 2 = 2$

    C. $\sqrt{2x} \rightarrow \sqrt{2 \cdot 2} \rightarrow \sqrt{4} = 2$

    D. $\sqrt{2^2} \rightarrow \sqrt{4} \rightarrow 2 = 2$

    E. $-|x| \rightarrow -|2| \rightarrow -2 \neq 2$

Because $|2| = 2$, the answers will need to equal 2.

Let's try answer choices B, C, & D with -2.

    B. $x^2 - x \rightarrow -2^2 - (-2) = 4 \rightarrow 6 \neq 2$

    C. $\sqrt{2x} \rightarrow \sqrt{2 \cdot (-2)} \rightarrow \sqrt{-4} \rightarrow 2i \neq 2$

    D. $\sqrt{x^2} \rightarrow \sqrt{2^2} \rightarrow 2 = 2$

2. If $|x| = |y|$, which of the following *must* be true?

    A. $x = y$
    B. $x = -y$
    C. x & y are positive
    D. $x^2 = y^2$
    E. $x + y = 0$

This is another good time to *pick numbers*.

Solve

I'm going to pick a number (1) that the absolute value of $|x|$ and $|y|$ equal. In a *must be true* question, all the answers *can* be true, but only one *has to* be true.

$$|x| = |y| = 1$$

I use 1 because it's easy.

$|x| = 1$, so $x = \mathbf{1}$ or $\mathbf{-1}$
$|y| = 1$, so $y = \mathbf{1}$ or $\mathbf{-1}$

A. $x = y$	This works if $x = 1$ & $y = 1$ or $x = -1$ & $y = -1$. But, it doesn't *have to* be true. If $x = 1$ and $y = -1$ or $x = -1$ and $y = 1$.
B. $x = -y$	This only works when x & y have opposite signs.
C. x & y are positive	The *absolute value* of x & y have to be positive, but both x and y can be negative.
D. $x^2 = y^2$	This *must be true*. Whenever we square a negative, the result is a positive. The same is true for a positive.
E. $x + y = 0$	This is only true when x and y have opposite signs.

3. If $x \neq y$, which CANNOT be true?

A. $|x| = |y|$

B. $|x| \neq |y|$

C. $|x| + |y| = 0$

D. $x + y = 0$

E. $y < 0 < x$

For a "CANNOT be true," mark-off answer choices that *could work.*

I'm *picking numbers.*

Solve

This is another "which" question, so we'll mark off. For "CANNOT be true" we want to eliminate answers by showing that they good be true. To do that, let's pick some numbers. **Let's say that $x = 1$ and $y = -1$. If I need to, I can also say that $x = -1$ and $y = 1$.**

We can also use numbers that have a different absolute value.

A. $|x| = |y|$

That *can* be true because $|1| = |-1|$.

B. $|x| \neq |y|$

Using 1 & -1, that isn't true, but your gut may tell you should test another set of numbers.

C. $|x| + |y| = 0$

Because x & y both can't equal zero, and a number's absolute value can't be negative, this *can never be true.*

D. $x + y = 0$

This can be true because $1 + (-1) = 0$

E. $y < 0 < x$

This can be true, with $y = -1$ and $x = 1$.

Let's look at **B** again. While $|x| \neq |y|$ when $x = 1$ and $y = -1$, we can change the numbers (for example $x = 1$ & $y = 2$) and it won't work.

Answer choice C is correct

4. Which of the following represents the inequality $|6x| \geq 6$?

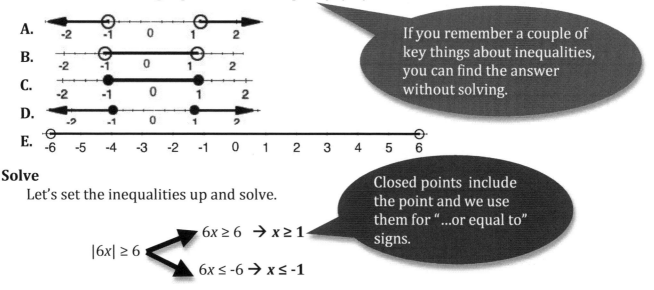

If you remember a couple of key things about inequalities, you can find the answer without solving.

Solve

Let's set the inequalities up and solve.

Closed points include the point and we use them for "...or equal to" signs.

$$|6x| \geq 6$$

$$6x \geq 6 \;\rightarrow\; x \geq 1$$

$$6x \leq -6 \;\rightarrow\; x \leq -1$$

The only possible choices are **A** and **D**, but only **D** has closed points. To solve the problem without any math, remember that , in absolute value, when x is less than (>) or less than or equal to (≥) we'll have a solution set that's a single line segment. Choices **B**, **C**, and **E** all represent inequalities where x is less than or less than or equal to. Since x is *greater than or equal to* it will be disconnected. Because it can be *equal to*, the end points will be closed.

When x is > or ≥, there won't be a connected solution set.

Answer choice **D** is correct.

Wrap Up

What You Need to Know
- ✓ How to do operations with absolute value
- ✓ How to set up absolute value equations to find both solutions
- ✓ How to solve absolute value inequalities and graph on a number line.

Videos

> Absolute Value

> Absolute Value Equations & Inequalities

The Strategies
- ✓ Treat absolute value bars like parentheses.
- ✓ There will always be at least two solutions for absolute value equations.
- ✓ Use a number line for help on inequalities problems.
- ✓ Write more, not less. These problems catch carelessness.

Related Skills
- ✓ Elementary Algebra: Inequalities
- ✓ Coorginate Geometry: Inequalities
- ✓ Elementary Algebra: Make an Equation

Elementary Algebra: Absolute Value

1. If x & y are nonzero integers, which of the following *must* be negative?

   A. $\left(|x|\right)\left(|y|\right) - 2x$

   B. $-x - y$

   C. $|x| - |y|$

   D. $\dfrac{|x|}{-|y|}$

   E. $-|x| + |y|$

2. $|6(-2) + 7| + |-4|$?

   F. 23
   G. -9
   H. 1
   J. 9
   K. 1

3. For optimal results, a barbecue smoker's temperature (in Fahrenheit) must satisfy the inequality $|x - 200| \leq 25$. All of the following temperatures are in this range *except*?

   A. 175
   B. 200
   C. 210
   D. 225
   E. 250

4. Which of the following expressions are equal to $|a|$ for all real numbers a?

   F. $-|a|$

   G. a^2

   H. a

   J. $\dfrac{a^2}{a}$

   K. $\sqrt{a^2}$

5. Which of the following graphs shows the solution set of the inequality $|2x| > 4$?

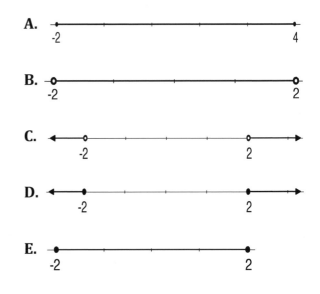

   A.
   B.
   C.
   D.
   E.

6. Which of the following *cannot be true* if $|a| \neq |b|$?

   F. $a \neq b$
   G. $a > b$
   H. $a < b$
   J. $a = b$
   K. $a > b > 0$

7. Which of the following are the rational solutions to the equation $|x^2 + 8| = 9$?

   A. 1
   B. 1, -1
   C. $\sqrt{17}$
   D. $\sqrt{17}$, $-\sqrt{17}$
   E. 1, -1, $\sqrt{17}$, $-\sqrt{17}$

Absolute Value: Solutions

1. If x & y are nonzero integers, which of the following must be negative?

Correct Answer D

This is a "which" question, so you'll want to mark-off. It's also a question where it's easiest to *pick numbers*. Because they're easy numbers, I'll say that $x = 1$ and $y = -1$.

A. $\left(|x|\right)\left(|y|\right) - 2x$ → $\left(|1|\right)\left(|-1|\right) - 2(1)$ → $-1 - 2 = -3$

B. $-x - y$ → $-1 - 1 = -2$

C. $|x| - |y|$ → $|1| - |-1|$ → $1 - 1 = 0$

D. $\dfrac{|x|}{-|y|}$ → $\dfrac{|1|}{-|-1|}$ → $\dfrac{1}{-1} = -1$

E. $-|x| + |y|$ → $-|1| + |-1|$ → $-1 + 1 = 0$

> In general pick numbers with **different signs & absolute values** works best.

1 & -1 marked off two answers (not so great). So, let's pick a different set of numbers that will have different signs *and* different absolute values. Let's try our remaining answer choices (**A**, **B**, & **D**) with $x = -2$ and $y = 1$.

> I'm also making x negative & y positive, to really shake things up.

A. $\left(|x|\right)\left(|y|\right) - 2x$ → $\left(|-2|\right)\left(|1|\right) - 2(-2)$ → $-2 + 4 = 2$

B. $-x - y$ → $-(-2) - 1 = 2 - 1 = 1$

D. $\dfrac{|x|}{-|y|}$ → $\dfrac{|-2|}{-|1|}$ → $\dfrac{2}{-1} = -2$

> Dividing a positive number by a negative (or vice versa) *always* gives a negative answer

Answer choice **D** is correct.

2. $\left|6(-2) + 7\right| + \left|-4\right|$?

Correct Answer J

This absolute value question has a bit of order of operations. First, we've got to simplify the inside of the absolute value bars.

$$\left|6(-2) + 7\right| + \left|-4\right| \quad \rightarrow \quad \left|-12 + 7\right| + \left|-4\right|$$
$$\left|-5\right| + \left|-4\right|$$

Now we can take the absolute value of each term.

$$\left|-5\right| + \left|-4\right|$$
$$5 + 4 = 9$$

Answer choice **J** is correct.

<u>What You May Have Done Wrong</u>

F. You "distributed" the absolute value, turning everything within the first absolute value bar positive before doing the operations in the bars.

G. You didn't take the absolute value of either set of bars.

H. You forgot to take the absolute value of the second set of bars.

K. You didn't take the absolute value of the first set of bars.

3. **For optimal results, a barbecue smoker's temperature (in Fahrenheit) must satisfy the inequality $|x-200| \leq 25$. All of the following temperatures are in this range *except*?**

Correct Answer E

This is a mark-off question, because of the *except*, and you can either *plug-in* the answer choices and look for the one that is not true (a number greater than 25), or you can solve the inequality. To get rid of the absolute value, write two inequalities with a positive and a negative solution.

$$x - 200 \leq 25$$
$$x - 200 \geq -25$$

> We have to *flip the inequality* for the **negative** solution

Now we can solve each inequality.

$$x - 200 \leq 25 \qquad\qquad x - 200 \geq -25$$
$$x \leq 225 \qquad\qquad\qquad x \geq 175$$

So, x has to be at least 175 and at most 225. If you have trouble visualizing this, draw a number line.

For absolute value inequalities, when x (or whatever variable) is *less than* or *less than or equal to*, our solution set will be one line segment (meet in the middle). Because we have less than or equal to, our points on our number line are closed & x *can* equal 175 or 225.

Answer choice E is correct

<u>What You May Have Done Wrong</u>
All of the wrong answer choices are within the range; review the steps.

4. **Which of the following expressions are equal to $|a|$ for all real numbers a?**

Correct Answer K

This is a *which* question, so we'll mark-off. Also, it's a great question for picking numbers. I'm going to pick two numbers for a, positive and negative and test them that way. I'll use 2 & -2. The absolute value of both 2 & -2 is +2; the correct answer will equal +2.

~~F.~~ $-|a|$ when I plug in both 2 and -2 the answer is -2.

~~G.~~ a^2 when I plug in 2 and -2 the answer is 4.

~~H.~~ a works for +2 but does not work for -2.

~~J.~~ $\dfrac{a^2}{a}$ works for +2 but does not work for -2

K. $\sqrt{a^2}$ works for both +2 and -2.

Let's take a look at the math

Positive 2: $\sqrt{a^2} \rightarrow \sqrt{2^2} \rightarrow \sqrt{4} = 2$

Negative 2: $\sqrt{a^2} \rightarrow \sqrt{-2^2} \rightarrow \sqrt{4} = 2$

Answer choice K is correct.

<u>What You May Have Done Wrong:</u>
F. This will never equal the absolute value of a, except when $a = 0$.
G. This only works when $a = 1$ or $a = -1$.
H. This works for positive numbers only.
J. This works for positive numbers only.

5. **Which of the following graphs shows the solution set of the inequality $|2x| > 4$?**

Correct Answer C

This is another mark-off problem, but you're likely going to have to solve. Let's talk about marking off first.

Because the symbol is *greater than* (>) the points on the graph will be open, because those points are not included in the solution set. *That lets us get rid of A, D, & E.* Now you've got to decide whether the solution set "meets in the middle" as one line segment, or goes to the positive & negative extremes. There's a trick for that, but let's solve.

$$|2x| > 4 \qquad\qquad |2x| > 4$$
$$2x > 4 \qquad\qquad 2x < -4$$
$$x > 2 \qquad\qquad x < -2$$

On the number line, it looks like this:

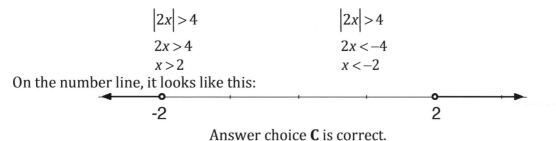

Answer choice **C** is correct.

<u>What You May Have Done Wrong</u>
  A. This is $-2 \le x \le 4$. It's got the wrong upper value (4), and the solution set is a line segment, but it needs to be two rays. Also, there need to be open points, not closed points.
  B. This is $-2 < x < 2$. The solution set is a line segment "meets in the middle." It needs to be two rays going to the extremes (negative & positive infinity).
  D. This is the right inequality, but it has closed points (only for inequalities that are *equal to*).
  E. This is $-2 \le x \le 2$, the solution set needs to go to the extremes, and have open points.

6. **Which of the following cannot be true if $|a| \ne |b|$?**

Correct Answer J

This, again, is a mark-off question. To find the right answer in a *cannot be true* question, try to prove that each answer choice *could* be true. It's also a great question to pick numbers on.

I'm going to say $a = 1$ & $b = -2$. I can flip these to $a = -2$ and $b = 1$, if I feel like I need to. As long as the absolute value of a doesn't equal the absolute value of b, I can make the numbers anything I want to. Remember, we're looking for the answer that *can't be true*.

  F. $a \ne b$
      This answer choice *must be true*. If the absolute values aren't equal, then the numbers can't be equal.
  G. $a > b$
      This *can* be true, using our values $a = 1$ & $b = -2$, $1 > -2$
  H. $a < b$
      This isn't true with our values $a = 1$ & $b = -2$, because 1 is not less than -2. But, a doesn't have to be greater than b. We can say that $a = -2$ & $b = 1$ and the inequality becomes true.
  J. $a = b$
      This **can't be true**. If the numbers have different absolute values, they will *always* have a different value. Even if numbers have the same absolute value, they can have different values.
  K. $a > b > 0$
      Although we picked a negative as one of our numbers, you can see how this *could be true*. We could easily say that $a = 2$ & $b = 1$, which would satisfy the inequality.

Answer **J** is correct.

7. **Which of the following are the rational solutions to the equation $|x^2+8|=9$?**

Correct Answer B

This is a tougher question. We're going to have two solutions for the absolute value (like always) and two additional solutions for the quadratic. To make things trickier, you need to know about rational numbers. Start by getting rid of the absolute value. To do that, rewrite the equation twice, once equaling 8 and once equaling -8.

$$x^2+8=9 \quad \& \quad x^2+8=-9$$

Now that you've got your two quadratic equations, solve each to find the four total solutions.

$$x^2+8=9$$
$$x^2-1=0$$
$$(x+1)(x-1)=0$$

 This is a *difference of squares.*

I think it's easier to skip the factoring and isolate the x^2.

$$x^2=1$$
$$\sqrt{x^2}=\sqrt{1}$$
$$x=1,-1$$

Let's deal with the second equation.

$$x^2+8=-9$$
$$x^2=-17$$
$$x=\sqrt{17},-\sqrt{17}$$

So, our four solutions are,

$$x = \text{-1, 1, } \sqrt{17}, -\sqrt{17}$$

The square root of any prime number is irrational. Also, the square root of any negative number is imaginary (not rational). Our real number solutions are 1 & -1.

If you had trouble getting through all of that, or you had difficulty remembering rational numbers, you can do some clever marking off.

You know that 1 & -1 are rational numbers, so you can mark-off answers not containing 1 &/or -1 (**C** & **D**). If you remember that you can't have a real square root of a negative number, you can mark off **E**.

Answer choice **B** is correct.

<u>What You May Have Done Wrong:</u>
   A. This is *a rational solution* but not all of the rational solutions.
   C. This is a solution, but it isn't rational.
   D. These are both solutions, but they aren't rational.
   E. You've got both of your rational solutions, but also your irrational solutions.

Intermediate Algebra

The topics in the *Intermediate Algebra* section constitute 15 to 25 percent of the ACT Math section, or between 10 and 15 questions per test. Here's the question frequency and the corresponding ACT Score Report category or categories.

Functions	1 – 2 questions	**PHM: Algebra**
Systems of Equations[key skill]	1 – 3 questions	**MOD & PHM Algebra**
Rational Expressions	0 – 2 questions	**MOD & PHM Algebra**
Radical Expressions	0 – 2 questions	**MOD & PHM: Algebra**
Series & Sequences	1 – 2 questions	**MOD & PHM: Algebra**
Complex Numbers	1 – 2 questions	**MOD & PHM: Numbers**
Matrices	0 – 2 questions	**PHM: Numbers**
Logs	0 – 2 questions	**PHM: Algebra**

IES: Integrating Essential Skills
PHM: Preparing for Higher Math
MOD: Modeling

A detailed explanation of the math score report is at the beginning of the book in the **Score Report.**

There's only one key skill in *Intermediate Algebra*. Systems of Equations is a very important topic, so you'll need to be comfortable solving them *and* setting them up in word problems.

Strategies

You've got to know your algebra. The good news is that there are very few new skills to pick up

Step-by-Step
> Don't be intimidated by complicated algebra questions. Find the first thing to do, whether it's grouping like terms, isolating a radical, factoring a quadratic, or removing a fraction. **You don't have to know how to finish the problem to start the problem**

60 Seconds Per Question—It can't be that Bad
> You only have 60 seconds per question; they can't put too much in (most) questions. If you find a place to start, you'll be most of the way home.

Function Questions are Plug-In Problems
> Don't let the notation confuse you.

Factor Quadratics
> If a question has a quadratic equation, you're probably going to factor it. Lean on that, particularly if you don't know how to start.

Know how to Solve Systems of Equations
> This is one skill I'd like you to have. It shows up multiple times per test, and on questions that are counted in other sections (mainly plane geometry).

Intermediate Algebra: Pre-Test

1. If $f(x)=x^2$, then what is $f(y+z)$?

    A. $y+z$

    B. $y+z^2$

    C. y^2+z^2

    D. $y^2+2yz+z^2$

    E. yx^2+zx^2

2. If $f(x)=x^2-4$, then what is $f(y^2+2)$?

    A. y^4

    B. y^4-2

    C. y^4-14

    D. y^2-2

    E. y^4+4y^2

3. Let function $f(x,y)$ be defined as

    $f(x,y)=x-y^2$ what is $f\left((a^2+b^2),(a-b)\right)$?

    A. 0

    B. $2a^2+4ab+2b^2$

    C. a^2+b^2

    D. $2ab$

    E. $a^2+2ab+b^2$

4. For functions f and g defined by

    $f(x)=2x^2-2$ and $g(x)=\sqrt{x+3}$, what is

    $g\circ f(-2)$?

    A. $\sqrt{-7}$

    B. 1

    C. 3

    D. 0

    E. 6

5. The functions $f(x)=4x+b$ and $g(x)=2x+6$ are such that $f\left(g(x)\right)=g\left(f(x)\right)$ and b is a real number. What does b equal?

    A. 0

    B. 18

    C. 2

    D. 8

    E. All real numbers.

6. What is $\dfrac{4x^2-5x}{20x^2}$ equivalent to (if $x\neq 0$)?

    A. $\dfrac{x-1}{5x}$

    B. $\dfrac{4x}{5x}$

    C. $-\dfrac{1}{20}$

    D. $\dfrac{1}{5x}$

    E. $\dfrac{1}{5}-\dfrac{1}{4x}$

7. Which of the following is equivalent to $\dfrac{x+3}{x+2}$?

    A. $\dfrac{2x+4}{2x+6}$

    B. $\dfrac{x+6}{x+4}$

    C. $\dfrac{4x+12}{4x+6}$

    D. $\dfrac{2x^2+6x}{2x^2+8x}$ ✓

    E. $\dfrac{2x+6}{2x+4}$

8. Assuming $x^2-y^2\neq 0$, which is equivalent to $\dfrac{(x^2+4xy+3y^2)(x-y)}{x^2-y^2}$?

    A. $\dfrac{x+3y}{x-y}$

    B. $\dfrac{4(x+y)}{x-y}$

    C. $x+3y$

    D. $\dfrac{x^2+4xy+3y^2}{x-y}$

    E. 3

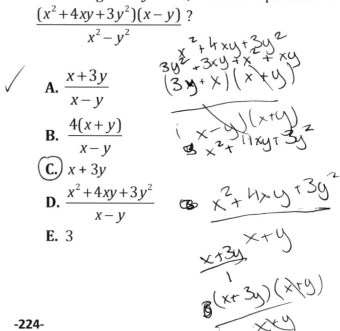

-224-

9. Given that $x > 3$, which of the following expressions is equivalent to

$$\frac{(2x^2+4x-6)(x+1)}{(2x^2-3x-5)(2x-2)}?$$

A. 1

B. $\dfrac{1}{2x-5}$

C. $x+3$

D. $\dfrac{x+3}{2x-5}$

E. $\dfrac{x+3}{x+1}$

(handwritten work)
$\dfrac{2(x^2+2x-3)(x+1)}{(2x^2-3x-5)\ \& \ (x-1)}$
$(2x-5)(x+1)$
$\dfrac{x^2+2x-3}{2x-5(x-1)}$
$2x^2+2x-5x-5 \quad (x+3)(x-1)$
$2x(x+1)-5(x+1) \quad \dfrac{(x+3)(x-1)}{2x-5(x+1)}$
$\dfrac{x+3}{2x-5}$

10. Given that $\sqrt{4x+9}=17$ what is x?

A. $\dfrac{9}{2}$

B. 8

C. 64

D. 2

E. 16

(handwritten) $\sqrt{4x}=8$

11. If $x^5 = 32$, then $x^2 + 3x$?

A. 12

B. 8

C. 10

D. -2

E. 4

(handwritten) $4+6$

12. If $\dfrac{x\sqrt{5}}{\sqrt{5}}=\dfrac{10}{2\sqrt{5}}$ is valid, then $x = ?$

A. $2\sqrt{5}$

B. $\sqrt{5}$

C. $10\sqrt{5}$

D. 5

E. 10

(handwritten)
$10\sqrt{5} = x\sqrt{5}(2\sqrt{5})$
$10\sqrt{5} = 2x \cdot 5$
$10\sqrt{5} = 10x$

13. The flow rate of two special pumps it determined by the impeller speed and the equation $r = \sqrt{\dfrac{2s}{15}}$. If Pump A has a flow rate that is four times Pump B's flow rate, the speed of Pump A's impeller is how many times the speed of Pump B's impeller?

A. 32

B. 16

C. 8

D. 4

E. 2

14. If $i=\sqrt{-1}$ and $i^2 + i^x = 0$, which could be a value for x?

(handwritten) $-1 + x = 0$

A. 1

B. 2

C. 3

D. 4

E. 5

15. If $i=\sqrt{-1}$, which is equivalent to $(3 - i)(4 + i)$?

A. $12 - i + i^2$

B. $13 - i$

C. $11 + i$

D. $11 - i$

E. 7

(handwritten)
$(3-i)(4+i)$
12
$12+3i-4i-i^2$
$12-i-i^2$
$13-i$

16. If $i^2 = -1$, which is equivalent to $\dfrac{i}{i-1}\cdot\dfrac{i^3}{i+1}?$

A. ½

B. 2

C. ½

D. -2

E. 1

(handwritten)
$\dfrac{i^4}{i^2+i-i-1}$
$\dfrac{1}{-1-1-2}$... $\dfrac{1}{-1-1}$

17. What is the matrix product of:

$$\begin{bmatrix} x \\ 1 \\ 2 \end{bmatrix} \times \begin{bmatrix} 2 & 0 & z \end{bmatrix}?$$

A. $\begin{bmatrix} 2x & 0 & 2z \end{bmatrix}$

B. $\begin{bmatrix} 2x & 2 & 4 \\ 0 & 0 & 0 \\ 4 & 0 & 2z \end{bmatrix}$

C. $\begin{bmatrix} 2x & 0 & xz \\ 2 & 0 & z \\ 4 & 0 & 2z \end{bmatrix}$

D. $2x + 2z$

E. The matrices cannot be multiplied

18. The determinant of a 2-by-2 matrix is defined as $ad - bc$ where $\begin{bmatrix} a & b \\ c & d \end{bmatrix}$, what is the determinant of the matrix $\begin{bmatrix} 2y & -y \\ 3x & -x \end{bmatrix}$, when $x = 4$ and $y = 2$?

A. 8
B. -8
C. -16
D. 16
E. -32

19. What is the value of x in following matrix equation?

$$4\begin{bmatrix} x & -2 \\ 3 & 5 \end{bmatrix} + \begin{bmatrix} 1 & 3 \\ 0 & 5 \end{bmatrix} = \begin{bmatrix} -3 & -5 \\ 12 & 25 \end{bmatrix}$$

A. -1
B. -4
C. -12
D. -6
E. 1

20. Which of the matrix products are defined?

I. $\begin{bmatrix} 0 & 2 & 3 \\ 7 & 5 & 1 \end{bmatrix} \times \begin{bmatrix} 1 & 3 \\ 0 & 2 \\ 2 & 5 \end{bmatrix}$

II. $\begin{bmatrix} 0 & 2 & 3 \\ 2 & x & a \\ y & 3 & 1 \end{bmatrix} \times \begin{bmatrix} 2 & 1 & 1 \\ w & 2 & 4 \end{bmatrix}$

III. $\begin{bmatrix} x & b \\ c & y^2 \\ a & b \end{bmatrix} \times \begin{bmatrix} x & y^3 & a \\ w & x^2 & y \end{bmatrix}$

A. I only
B. II only
C. III only
D. I & III only
E. I, II, & III only

21. If $\log_4 64 = x$, what is x?

A. 2
B. 8
C. 4
D. 3
E. 6

22. Which of the following is a value of x that satisfies $\log_x 27 = 3$?

A. 3
B. 4
C. -3
D. 1
E. 9

23. Which of the following expressions is equivalent to $\log(3y)$?

A. $\log 3y + \log$
B. $\log y - \log 3$
C. $\log 3 + \log y$
D. $3\log y$
E. $\log 3 - \log y$

24. Which of the following expressions is equivalent to $\log(xy)^2$?

   A. $2\log x + \log y$
   B. $\log x^2 + 2\log y^2$
   C. $2\log x + 2\log y$
   D. $2\log x^2 + 2\log y^2$
   E. $2\log - 2\log y$

25. The price of a medium popcorn and a large drink is $7.50 and the price of two medium popcorns and one large drink is $11.50. What is the price of a large drink?

   A. $3.50
   B. $8.00
   C. $4.00
   D. $5.50
   E. $4.50

26. If $3x - 2y = 15$ and $-2x + 6y = 4$, what is $3x + 5y$?

   A. 7
   B. 44
   C. 36
   D. 3
   E. 24

27. If $xy = 54$, $x + y = 15$, and $x < y$ what is $y - x$?

   A. 9
   B. 6
   C. -3
   D. 3
   E. 15

28. Nate has $3.49 in change. He has 6 more pennies than nickels, 4 more pennies than dimes, and two less pennies than quarters. How many dimes does Nate have?

   A. 3
   B. 5
   C. 7
   D. 9
   E. 11

29. The value of n is such that the difference between consecutive numbers in the list is the same. What is the value of n?

$$3, n, 31$$

   A. 15
   B. 13
   C. 21
   D. 23
   E. 17

30. As part of a pushup challenge, Nate does 5 pushups on day one and adds 5 pushups per day until day 14. How many pushups does Nate do in the challenge?

   A. 480
   B. 525
   C. 360
   D. 600
   E. 420

31. A finite arithmetic sequence has a last term of -3. There are 11 terms in the sequence. What is the mean divided by the median?

   A. 1
   B. 0
   C. -62
   D. 325
   E. 102

32. What is the fourth term of the geometric sequence below?

$$24a^8b^5c^2, \ 12a^6b^4c, \ 6a^4b^3, \ ...$$

   A. $2a^3b^2$
   B. $\dfrac{3a^3b}{c}$
   C. $2a^2b^2$
   D. $3a^2b^2$
   E. $\dfrac{3a^2b^2}{c}$

Pre-Test Answers

1.	D	Functions
2.	E	Functions
3.	D	Functions
4.	C	Functions
5.	B	Functions
6.	E	Rational Expressions
7.	E	Rational Expressions
8.	C	Rational Expressions
9.	D	Rational Expressions
10.	E	Radical Expressions
11.	C	Radical Expressions
12.	B	Radical Expressions
13.	B	Radical Expressions
14.	D	Complex Numbers
15.	B	Complex Numbers
16.	C	Complex Numbers
17.	C	Matrices
18.	A	Matrices
19.	A	Matrices
20.	D	Matrices
21.	D	Logarithms
22.	A	Logarithms
23.	C	Logarithms
24.	C	Logarithms

25.	A	Systems of Equations
26.	C	Systems of Equations
27.	D	Systems of Equations
28.	B	Systems of Equations
29.	E	Sequences & Series
30.	B	Sequences & Series
31.	A	Sequences & Series
32.	E	Sequences & Series

Background

The bulk of equation based function problems on the ACT are *plug-in* style *Elementary Algebra* problems (covered in *Elementary Algebra: Operations*). Functions and their graphs are robustly covered in graphing (covered in *Coordinate Geometry: The Graphs of Functions*).

What You Need to Know

✓ How to plug-in into function problems
✓ Where to start on composition of functions

> There's a *video* on *Algebraic Functions*

Definitions

$f(x)$ means the *function of x* that is; it is the output—the y value of a given x

> This is the **output (y)**. It's the function name (f) and the placeholder input. We don't do anything with them.

> This is the **relationship** between the **input** (x) and the **output** (y)

$$f(x) = x + 1$$

> x is a placeholder for what we will plug-in (**the input**) for x.

Let's look at some of the values.

Input	Relationship	Output: $f(x)$
x	$x + 1$	y
-2	-2+1	-1
-1	-1+1	0
0	0+1	1
1	1+1	2
2	2+1	3

Rules of the Road: Functions

We plug *whatever* is in the parentheses for x.

1. If $f(x) = 2x + 3$, what is $f(a^2)$?

> Plug in a^2 for x. We can't simplify any more.

$$f(x) = 2x + 3 \rightarrow f(x) = 2a^2 + 3$$

> Review *Elementary Algebra: Quadratics*

2. If $f(x) = x^2$, what is $f(a - b)$?

$$f(x) = x^2 \rightarrow f(x) = (a-b)^2 \rightarrow f(x) = (a-b)(a-b) \rightarrow \boldsymbol{f(x) = a^2 - 2ab - b^2}$$

Composition of functions requires us to evaluate two functions in order, using the result (output) from the first as the plug-in (input) of the second.

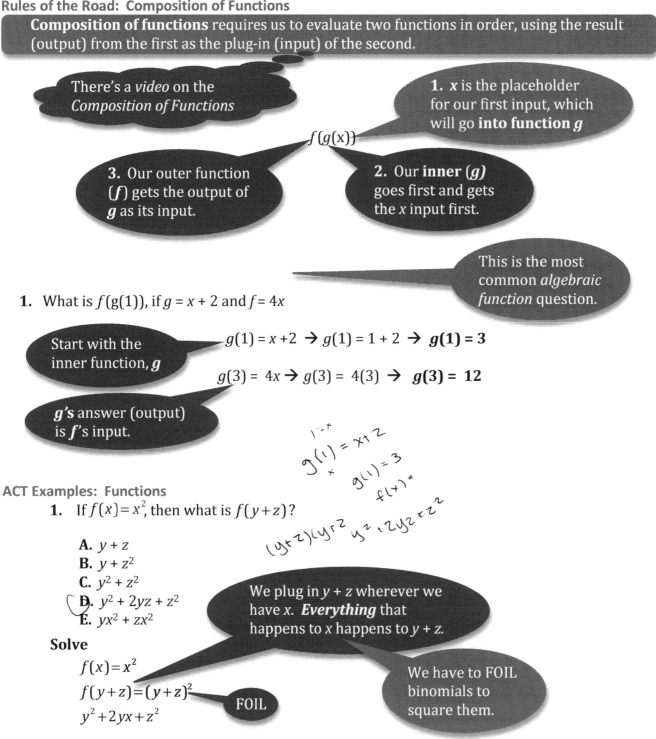

There's a *video* on the *Composition of Functions*

1. x is the placeholder for our first input, which will go **into function g**

$$f(g(x))$$

3. Our outer function (f) gets the output of g as its input.

2. Our **inner (g)** goes first and gets the x input first.

This is the most common *algebraic function* question.

1. What is $f(g(1))$, if $g = x + 2$ and $f = 4x$

Start with the inner function, g

$g(1) = x + 2$ → $g(1) = 1 + 2$ → $\mathbf{g(1) = 3}$

$g(3) = 4x$ → $g(3) = 4(3)$ → $\mathbf{g(3) = 12}$

g's answer (output) is f's input.

ACT Examples: Functions

1. If $f(x) = x^2$, then what is $f(y+z)$?

   A. $y + z$
   B. $y + z^2$
   C. $y^2 + z^2$
   D. $y^2 + 2yz + z^2$
   E. $yx^2 + zx^2$

Solve

$$f(x) = x^2$$
$$f(y+z) = (y+z)^2$$
$$y^2 + 2yx + z^2$$

FOIL

We plug in $y + z$ wherever we have x. **Everything** that happens to x happens to $y + z$.

We have to FOIL binomials to square them.

Answer choice **D** is correct.

2. If $f(x) = x^2 - 4$, then what is $f(y^2 + 2)$?

$= y^2 + 2$

A. y^4
B. $y^4 - 2$
C. $y^4 - 14$
D. $y^2 - 2$
(E.) $y^4 + 4y^2$

$(y^2 + 2)(y^2 + 2) - 4$

$y^4 + 4y^2$

Solve

> I skipped writing the other side of the equation to make things easier to read.

$f(x) = x^2 - 4$

$f(y^2 + 2) = (y^2 + 2)^2 - 4$

> FOIL

$= (y^2 + 2)(y^2 + 2) - 4$

$= y^4 + 4y^2 + 4 - 4$

$f(y^2 + 2) = y^4 + 4y^2$

Answer choice **E** is correct.

3. Let function $f(x, y)$ be defined as $f(x, y) = x - y^2$ what is $f\big((a^2 + b^2), (a - b)\big)$?

$x \quad y$

A. 0
B. $2a^2 + 4ab + 2b^2$
C. $a^2 + b^2$
(D.) $2ab$
E. $a^2 + 2ab + b^2$

> This is intimidating, but isn't really different than the other problems.
> $x = (a^2 - b^2) \ \& \ y = (a - b)$

Solve

$f(x, y) = x^2 - y^2$

$f\big((a^2 + b^2), (a - b)\big) = (a^2 + b^2) - (a - b)^2$

> Plug-in $(a^2 - b^2)$ for x and $(a - b)$ for y

$= (a^2 + b^2) - \big((a - b)(a - b)\big)$

> FOIL $(a - b)^2$

$= (a^2 + b^2) - (a^2 - 2ab + b^2)$

$= a^2 + b^2 - a^2 + 2ab - b^2$

> We still need the parentheses because of the -1.

$f\big((a^2 + b^2), (a - b)\big) = 2ab$

The solution is $2ab$.

Answer choice **D** is correct

$a^2 + b^2 - \big((a - b)(a - b)\big)$

$a^2 + b^2 - (a^2 - 2ab + b^2)$

$a^2 + b^2 - a^2 + 2ab - b^2$

$2ab$

4. For functions f and g defined by $f = 2x^2 - 2$ and $g = \sqrt{x+3}$, what is $g \circ f(-2)$?

A. $\sqrt{-7}$
B. 1
C. 3
D. 0
E. 6

(handwritten: $2(4) - 2$ $8 - 2 = 6$)

> This is composition of functions written in a different way. It's the same as $g(f(x))$

> Don't forget the order of operations— exponents first

Solve

(handwritten: $g(f(-2))$ $f = 6$ $g(6)$ $x = -2$ $g = 1$)

> Start with the inner parentheses, **plugging -2** in for function f.

$g(f(-2))$

$f(-2) = 2x^2 - 2 \quad \rightarrow \quad 2(-2)^2 - 2$

$= 2(4) - 2 = 6$

$g(6) = \sqrt{x+3} \quad \rightarrow \quad \sqrt{6+3}$

$g(6) = \sqrt{9} = 3$

$g(f(-2)) = 3$

Answer **C** is correct.

(handwritten: $g = 3$ $g(x) \sqrt{x+3}$ $g(6)\sqrt{6+3}$ $g(6) = \sqrt{9}$)

> We take the *output* from f and plug it in for g.

5. The functions $f(x) = 4x + b$ and $g(x) = 2x + 6$ are such that $f(g(x)) = g(f(x))$ and b is a real number. What does b equal?

A. 0
B. 18
C. 2
D. 8
E. All real numbers.

> With no number to plug-in the inner function, we will have to do some algebra.

(handwritten: $f(2x + b) = g(4x + b)$)

Solve

$f(g(x)) = g(f(x))$

$f(g(x)) = 2(4x + b) + 6 \qquad g(f(x)) = 4(2x + 6) + b$

> Distribute

> **Substitute** the inner function for the variable x in the outer function.

$2(4x + b) + 6 = 4(2x + 6) + b$

$8x + 2b + 6 = 8x + 24 + b$

> Now, we have an algebra problem; one variable will cancel.

$2b - b = 8x - 8x + 24 - 6$

$b = 0x + 18$

$b = 18$

> Re-arrange and combine like

Answer choice **B** is correct

Wrap Up

What You Need to Know
- ✓ How to plug-in into function problems
- ✓ Where to start on composition of functions

Videos

> Intermediate Functions

> Composition of Functions

The Strategies
- ✓ These are plug-in problems; plug everything in the parentheses in for *x*.

Related Skills
- ✓ Elementary plug-in problems.
- ✓ Coordinate Geometry Functions.

$$f(x) = 4x + 5$$
$$g(x) = 2x + 6$$

Intermediate Algebra: Functions

1. What is $f(g(-1))$ for functions defined as $g = \frac{x^2-x}{4}$ and $f = \frac{x}{x^2}$?

A. -1
B. ½
C. 2
D. -2
E. 1

(handwritten work)
$f(2)$
$g = (-1)^2 - (-1)$ over 4
$\frac{1}{2}$
$\cdot \frac{1}{4}$ $g(-1) = \frac{2}{4}$
$g(-1) = \frac{1}{2}$

2. Function s is defined as $s(x) = x^2 - 4x$, what is $s(2-a)$?

A. $a^2 - 4$
B. $a^2 - 4a - 4$
C. $a^2 - a - 12$
D. $a^2 - 5a - 4$
E. $-6a - 4$

(handwritten work)
$s(2-a) =$
$(2-a)(2-a) + 4(2-a)$
$4 - 4a + a^2 - 8 + 4a$
$a^2 - 4$

3. For the functions $f(x) = \frac{\sqrt[3]{3x}}{x+6}$ and $g(x) = 2x - 11$, what is $f(g(1))$?

A. 1
B. -1
C. $\frac{\sqrt[6]{12}}{10} - 11$
D. $\frac{1}{5}$
E. $-\frac{1}{5}$

(handwritten work)
$g(1) = 2 - 11$
$g(1) = -9$
$f(-9) = \frac{\sqrt[3]{-27}}{-9+6}$
$\frac{-3}{-3}$

4. What is the value of $\frac{f(10)}{g(-2)} - g(5)$ if $f(x) = x^2 - \frac{x}{2}$ and $g(x) = -3x - 1$?

A. 3
B. 90
C. 19
D. 35
E. -3

(handwritten work)
$\frac{10^2 - \frac{10}{2}}{-3(-2)-1} - (-15-1)$
$\frac{100-5}{5}$ $\frac{95}{5}$ $-(-16)$
$19 + 16$

5. What is $g(f(x))$ if $g(x) = x^2 - 4$ and $f(x) = 2x - 3$?

A. $4x^2 + 5$
B. $4x^2 - 12x + 5$
C. $2x^2 - 11$
D. $4x^2 - 9x + 5$
E. $2x^2 - 12x + 5$

(handwritten work)
$y = 2x - 3$
$x = f(x)$
$x = 2x - 3$
$(2x-3)(2x-3) x^2 - 4 = 2x - 3$
$4x^2 - 12x + 5$ $x^2 - 6x - 1$

6. A particular function is defined as $f(x,y) = \frac{3x^2 - 2y}{x}$ what is $f(-1, 2)$?

A. 7
B. -1
C. ½
D. -5
E. 1

(handwritten work)
$\frac{3(-1)^2 - 4}{-1}$
$\frac{3-4}{-1}$ $\frac{-1}{-1}$

7. The function defined as $f(a,b) = \frac{b^2 - a^2}{-3b}$ when $b = (x-y)$ and $a = (2x+y)$?

A. $\frac{-3x^2 + 2xy + 2y^2}{-3x + 3y}$
B. $\frac{x^2 + 2xy}{2x + y}$
C. $\frac{x^2 - 6xy}{x - y}$
D. $\frac{x^2 + 2xy}{x - y}$
E. $\frac{x^2}{x - y}$

Intermediate Functions: Solutions

1. What is $f(g(-1))$ for functions defined as $g = \dfrac{x^2 - x}{4}$ and $f = \dfrac{x}{x^2}$?

Correct Answer C

This is a composition of functions question. It is requires you to handle some fraction multiplication/division.

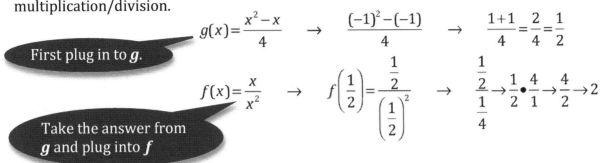

First plug in to **g**.

$$g(x) = \frac{x^2 - x}{4} \quad \rightarrow \quad \frac{(-1)^2 - (-1)}{4} \quad \rightarrow \quad \frac{1+1}{4} = \frac{2}{4} = \frac{1}{2}$$

Take the answer from **g** and plug into **f**

$$f(x) = \frac{x}{x^2} \quad \rightarrow \quad f\left(\frac{1}{2}\right) = \frac{\frac{1}{2}}{\left(\frac{1}{2}\right)^2} \quad \rightarrow \quad \frac{\frac{1}{2}}{\frac{1}{4}} \rightarrow \frac{1}{2} \cdot \frac{4}{1} \rightarrow \frac{4}{2} \rightarrow 2$$

What You May Have Done Wrong
A. This may be a halfway answer *and* you incorrectly started by solving for f first. You may have also guessed.
B. This is the halfway answer. You only calculated the answer go function g.
D. Most likely you made a sign mistake in function g's numerator.
E. You most likely made a mistake in your fraction operations. You may want to review fractions.

2. Function s is defined as $s(x) = x^2 - 4x$, what is $s(2 - a)$?

Correct Answer A

Almost every function problem is a plug-in problem. This one is no different.

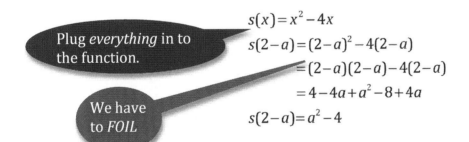

Plug *everything* in to the function.

We have to *FOIL*

$$s(x) = x^2 - 4x$$
$$s(2-a) = (2-a)^2 - 4(2-a)$$
$$= (2-a)(2-a) - 4(2-a)$$
$$= 4 - 4a + a^2 - 8 + 4a$$
$$s(2-a) = a^2 - 4$$

What You May Have Done Wrong
B. Most likely, you didn't FOIL your squared term.
C. You made a mistake in distributing your second x. The negative 4 needs to be applied to both terms.
D. You didn't distribute the -4. You distributed the 4.
E. Most likely you multiplied by 2 instead of squaring. You may want to review expounding.

3. For the function $f(x) = \dfrac{\sqrt[3]{3x}}{x+6}$ and $g(x) = 2x - 11$ what is $f(g(1))$?

Correct Answer A

This problem requires some handling of signs as well as radicals, but the process is the same, plug-in the inner function, g, and then plug in to the outer function, f.

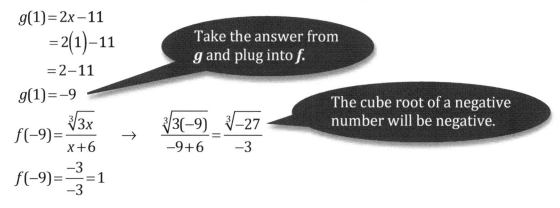

$g(1) = 2x - 11$

$\quad = 2(1) - 11$

$\quad = 2 - 11$

$g(1) = -9$

Take the answer from g and plug into f.

$f(-9) = \dfrac{\sqrt[3]{3x}}{x+6} \quad \rightarrow \quad \dfrac{\sqrt[3]{3(-9)}}{-9+6} = \dfrac{\sqrt[3]{-27}}{-3}$

The cube root of a negative number will be negative.

$f(-9) = \dfrac{-3}{-3} = 1$

Answer choice **A** is correct.

<u>What You May Have Done Wrong</u>

B. You most likely did the entire problem correctly but messed up your sign on the final answer. Remember, signs can make or break you.

C. You flipped your functions; you plugged 1 in for f instead of g.

D. There are a few problems here. You correctly solved the first function, f, but you had sign and operations problems plugging in to function g.

E. There are a few problems here. You correctly solved the first function, g, but you had sign and operations problems plugging in to function f.

4. What is the value of $\dfrac{f(10)}{g(-2)} - g(5)$ if $f(x) = x^2 - \dfrac{x}{2}$ and $g(x) = -3x - 1$?

Correct Answer D

This is a problem that rewards careful execution. You can write out all the equations (subbing in for) the function names, but I would solve each individually to save myself space, time, and possible confusion.

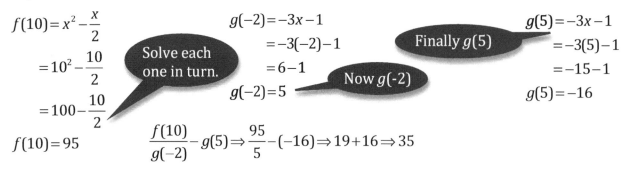

$f(10) = x^2 - \dfrac{x}{2}$

$\quad = 10^2 - \dfrac{10}{2}$

$\quad = 100 - \dfrac{10}{2}$

$f(10) = 95$

Solve each one in turn.

$g(-2) = -3x - 1$

$\quad = -3(-2) - 1$

$\quad = 6 - 1$

$g(-2) = 5$

Now $g(-2)$

Finally $g(5)$

$g(5) = -3x - 1$

$\quad = -3(5) - 1$

$\quad = -15 - 1$

$g(5) = -16$

$\dfrac{f(10)}{g(-2)} - g(5) \Rightarrow \dfrac{95}{5} - (-16) \Rightarrow 19 + 16 \Rightarrow 35$

Answer choice **D** is correct.

<u>What You May Have Done Wrong</u>

A. You probably messed up your operation on the result of $g(5)$, subtracting 16 instead of adding it.

B. You didn't plug in the right value for $g(5)$. You plugged in (-2) again.

C. This is the halfway answer. You forgot about subtracting the result of $g(5)$.

E. You most likely messed up the sign of $\dfrac{f(10)}{g(-2)}$ resulting in -19 instead of 19.

5. **What is $g(f(x))$ if $g(x) = x^2 - 4$ and $f(x) = 2x - 3$?**

Correct Answer B

In this case, you'll have to plug in the inner function f into the outer function g. We don't have any values so we just plug in the expression itself.

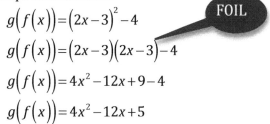

$$g(f(x)) = (2x-3)^2 - 4$$
$$g(f(x)) = (2x-3)(2x-3) - 4$$
$$g(f(x)) = 4x^2 - 12x + 9 - 4$$
$$g(f(x)) = 4x^2 - 12x + 5$$

Answer choice **B** is correct.

<u>What You May Have Done Wrong</u>
   A. You tried to distribute the square instead of FOILing. You may want to review <u>expounding</u>.
   C. You plugged g in for f; you need to plug f in to g.
   D. You made a mistake FOILing. You may want to review expounding.
   E. You made a mistake expounding, failing to square your 2, in front of the $2x$.

6. **A particular function is defined as $f(x,y) = \dfrac{3x^2 - 2y}{x}$ what is $f(-1, 2)$?**

Correct Answer E

This is a plug-in problem, but it's intimidating. You've got to realize that you plug in -1 for x and 2 for y. You follow the way the function is set up.

$$f(x,y) = \frac{3x^2 - 2y}{x} \quad \rightarrow \quad f(-1,2) = \frac{3x^2 - 2y}{x}$$

$$f(-1,2) = \frac{3(-1)^2 - 2(2)}{-1} \quad \rightarrow \quad f(-1,2) = \frac{3-4}{-1}$$

$$f(-1,2) = 1$$

Answer choice **E** is correct.

<u>What You May Have Done Wrong</u>
   A. You made a sign error, -1^2 equals 1, not -1.
   B. You flipped a sign somewhere along the way. Remember, signs will make you or break you.
   C. You plugged 2 in for the denominator and also dropped a sign.
   D. You simply plugged in x (-1) without using y (2).

7. The function defined as $f(a,b) = \dfrac{b^2 - a^2}{-3b}$ when $b = (x - y)$ and $a = (2x + y)$?

Correct Answer D

This is another plug in problem. It's really algebra heavy, and there's a lot to do. If, after plugging in, you have a hard time you may want to review *Intermediate Algebra: Rational Expressions*.

I'm going to show the calculations for the numerator and denominator separately because it will be easier to follow. For many students, this is the easiest way to do these problems on paper, but you have to remember to put the pieces back together!

<u>Numerator</u>

$b^2 - a^2 \quad \rightarrow \quad (x - y)^2 - (2x + y)^2$

$(x - y)(x - y) - (2x + y)^2$

$x^2 - 2xy + y^2 - \left((2x + y)(2x + y) \right)$

$x^2 - 2xy + y^2 - \left(4x^2 + 4xy + y^2 \right)$

$x^2 - 2xy + y^2 - 4x^2 - 4xy - y^2$

$Numerator = -3x^2 - 6xy$

FOIL one at a time to make your life easier.

<u>Denominator</u>

$-3b$

$-3(x - y)$

$Denominator = -3x + 3y$

Put both parts together.

$$f\left((2x + y)(x - y) \right) = \frac{-3x^2 - 6xy}{-3x + 3y}$$

None of the answer choices match, so we needed to do some factoring. We still leave the numerator incompletely factored. We could factor the numerator further (pulling out an x) but the answer choices aren't written that way.

$$\frac{-3x^2 - 6xy}{-3x + 3y} \Rightarrow \frac{x^2 + 2xy}{x - y}$$

Answer choice **D** is correct.

<u>What You May Have Done Wrong</u>

A. You didn't distribute the negative 1 in the numerator to *all* the terms in the parentheses (You only distributed it to the first term).

B. You did a great job with the problem—except you plugged *a* for the denominator instead of *b*.

C. You didn't factor your numerator completely. You may want to review factoring fractions.

E. You tried to distribute the squares in both numerator terms. You can't do that with binomial. You may want to review expounding.

Background

Systems of equations show up on every ACT math section at least once. Typically there are two (or even three) questio0.ns, but the *concepts* also appear in *make and equation* problems, *coordinate geometry*, & *plane geometry*.

What You Need to Know
- ✓ How to solve systems of linear equations by elimination (*adding equations*)
- ✓ How to solve systems of equations by *substitution*
- ✓ How to *make an equation*

Mechanics: Solving by Elimination (Adding/Subtracting Equations)

I personally prefer this method of solving *systems of equations*. I feel like it's faster, but—again—it's more of a personal preference.

> You can add or subtract equations, but **you must do it to *every term* on *both* sides of the equation.**

Example: Solving by Adding Equations

1. If $2x + y = 4$ and $3x - y = 3$, what is the value of y?

First, write the equations vertically.

The y's have opposite signs and the same coefficient, they cancel.

The goal is to cancel one of the variables, in this case y.

$$2x + y = 7$$
$$+\ 3x - y = 3$$
$$5x + 0y = 10$$

Now, we can solve for x

$$5x = 10 \rightarrow x = 2$$

Since we have the value of x, we'll plug that value back into either equation to solve for y.

$$2x + y = 7 \rightarrow 2(2) + y = 7$$
$$4 + y = 7 \rightarrow y = 3$$

2. If $x + 3y = 10$ and $3x + 3y = 18$, what is the value of x?

$$x + 3y = 10$$
$$+\ 3x + 3y = 18$$

We can't add yet. We don't have anything that will cancel.

Plug the x value into either equation to solve for y.

We can multiply one equation by -1, which will allows us to cancel the y terms when we add the equations.

$$x + 3y = 10$$
$$-1(3x + 3y = 18)$$
$$\rightarrow$$
$$x + 3y = 10$$
$$-3x - 3y = -18$$
$$-2x = -8$$
$$x = 4$$

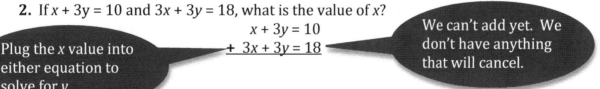

There's a video on Systems of Equations

-239-

Mechanics: Solving by Substitution

In substitution, we re-arrange the equation to isolate one variable and plug-in to the other equation.

1. If $2x + y = 4$ and $3x + y = 5$, what is the value of y?

We have two equations and we can rearrange for either variable. **Let's rearrange the first equation for y.**

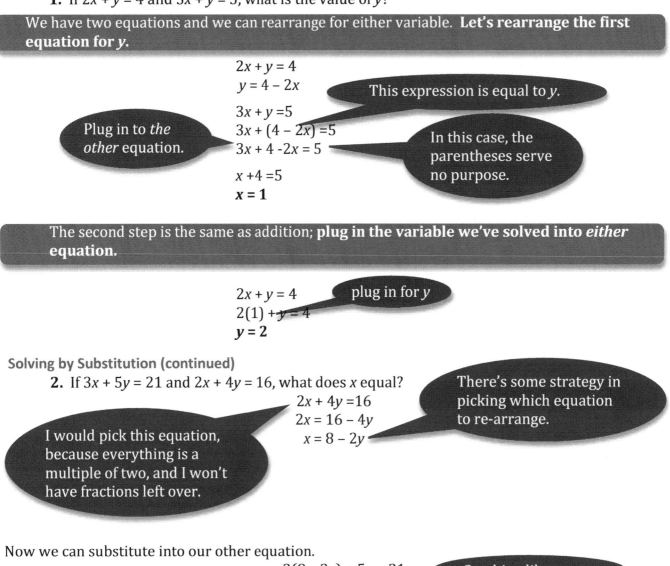

$$2x + y = 4$$
$$y = 4 - 2x$$

This expression is equal to y.

$$3x + y = 5$$
$$3x + (4 - 2x) = 5$$

Plug in to *the other* equation.

$$3x + 4 - 2x = 5$$

In this case, the parentheses serve no purpose.

$$x + 4 = 5$$
$$x = 1$$

The second step is the same as addition; **plug in the variable we've solved into *either* equation.**

$$2x + y = 4$$
$$2(1) + y = 4$$

plug in for y

$$y = 2$$

Solving by Substitution (continued)

2. If $3x + 5y = 21$ and $2x + 4y = 16$, what does x equal?

There's some strategy in picking which equation to re-arrange.

$$2x + 4y = 16$$
$$2x = 16 - 4y$$
$$x = 8 - 2y$$

I would pick this equation, because everything is a multiple of two, and I won't have fractions left over.

Now we can substitute into our other equation.

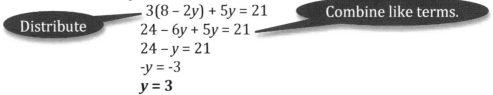

$$3(8 - 2y) + 5y = 21$$

Distribute

$$24 - 6y + 5y = 21$$

Combine like terms.

$$24 - y = 21$$
$$-y = -3$$
$$y = 3$$

Take the y value and plug it into *either* equation.

$$2x + 4y = 16$$
$$2x + 4(3) = 16$$
$$2x = 4$$
$$x = 2$$

1. The price of a medium popcorn and a large drink is $7.50 and the price of two medium popcorns and one large drink is $11.50. What is the price of a large drink?

A. $3.50
B. $8.00
C. $4.00
D. $5.50
E. $4.50

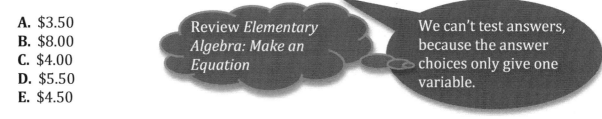

Review *Elementary Algebra: Make an Equation*

We can't test answers, because the answer choices only give one variable.

Statement 1: The price of a medium popcorn and a large drink is $7.50

$$1p + 1d = 7.50$$

Pick variables that represent the problem, so you won't get confused

Statement 2: the price of two medium popcorns & a large drink is $11.50.

$$2p + 1d = 11.50$$

Solving by Elimination

$$2p + 1d = 11.50$$
$$\underline{1p + 1d = 7.50}$$

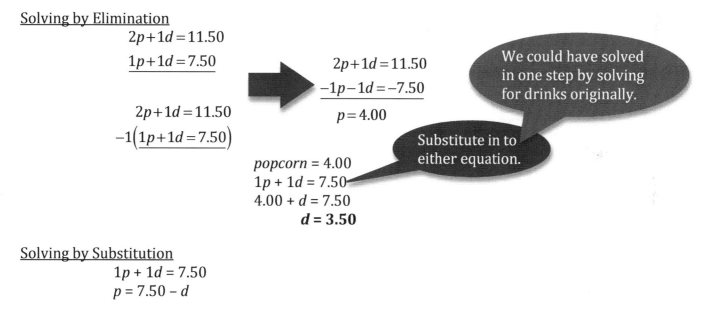

$$2p + 1d = 11.50$$
$$\underline{-1p - 1d = -7.50}$$
$$p = 4.00$$

We could have solved in one step by solving for drinks originally.

$$2p + 1d = 11.50$$
$$-1\left(1p + 1d = 7.50\right)$$

$$popcorn = 4.00$$
$$1p + 1d = 7.50$$
$$4.00 + d = 7.50$$
$$d = 3.50$$

Substitute in to either equation.

Solving by Substitution

$$1p + 1d = 7.50$$
$$p = 7.50 - d$$

$$2p + 1d = 11.50$$
$$2(7.50 - d) + d = 11.50$$
$$15 - 2d + d = 11.50$$

$$-d = -3.50$$
$$d = 3.50$$

Answer choice **A** is correct.

2. If $3x - 2y = 15$ and $-2x + 6y = 4$, what is $3x + 5y$?

      A. 7
      B. 44
      C. 36
      D. 3
      E. 24

Solving by Elimination

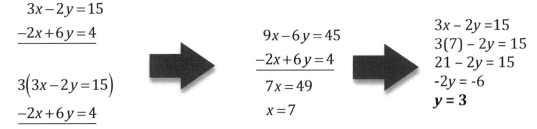

$$3x - 2y = 15$$
$$-2x + 6y = 4$$

$$3(3x - 2y = 15)$$
$$-2x + 6y = 4$$

$$9x - 6y = 45$$
$$-2x + 6y = 4$$
$$7x = 49$$
$$x = 7$$

$$3x - 2y = 15$$
$$3(7) - 2y = 15$$
$$21 - 2y = 15$$
$$-2y = -6$$
$$\boldsymbol{y = 3}$$

Now that we have our solution set, we can plug in to the final expression, "what is $3x + 5y$."
$$3x + 5y = ? \;\rightarrow\; 3(7) + 5(3) = 36$$

Solving by Substitution

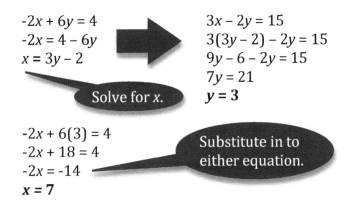

$$-2x + 6y = 4$$
$$-2x = 4 - 6y$$
$$x = 3y - 2$$

Solve for x.

$$3x - 2y = 15$$
$$3(3y - 2) - 2y = 15$$
$$9y - 6 - 2y = 15$$
$$7y = 21$$
$$\boldsymbol{y = 3}$$

$$-2x + 6(3) = 4$$
$$-2x + 18 = 4$$
$$-2x = -14$$
$$\boldsymbol{x = 7}$$

Substitute in to either equation.

Now that we have our solution set, we can plug in to the final expression, "what is $3x + 5y$."
$$3x + 5y = ?$$
$$3(7) + 5(3) = 36$$

Answer choice **C** is correct.

3. If $xy = 54$, $x + y = 15$, and $x < y$ what is $y - x$?

    A. 9
    B. 6
    C. -3
    D. 3
    E. 15

Solving by Substitution

You can't use *elimination* on this problem because one equation has x times y. There's no way to eliminate either x or y.

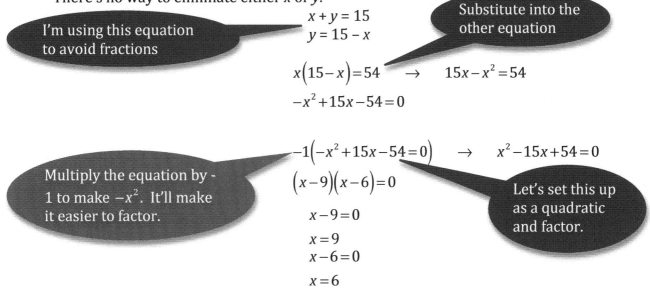

Solutions: 9 & 6
The problem tells us that $x < y$, we know that $x = 6$ and $y = 9$. Therefore, $y - x = 3$
Answer choice **D** is correct.

Systems of Equations With More Than Two Variables

Very occasionally, the ACT asks a word question with more than two variables. These usually involve change (pennies, nickels, dimes, & quarters) but they don't have to. These problems can't be solved by elimination; you'll have to use substitution.

ACT Example: Systems of Equations With More Than Two Variables

1. Nate has $3.49 in change. He has 6 more pennies than nickels, 4 more pennies than dimes, and two less pennies than quarters. How many dimes does Nate have?

A. 3
B. 5
C. 7
D. 9
E. 11

This problem is in a *video* on *Systems of Equations with more than 2 variables*

Solve

You can test answers on this problem. If you plug in for dimes, you can work backwards and number of other coins. Then you'd have to multiply the coins by their value and add them together to see if they equal $3.49. You can do it, but it can be very time consuming.

<u>Solving by Substitution</u>

Start by writing your equations. To do that, break the problem down into statements.

Statement 1: He has 6 more pennies than nickels: $n = p - 6$

Be careful with your equations.

Statement 2: 4 more pennies than dimes: $d = p - 4$

Statement 3: two less pennies than quarters: $q = p + 2$

So, we've got four variables *pennies, nickels, dimes, & quarters*. Right now we have three equations. **The number of equations has to equal the number of variables.** Also, you can probably figure out that we've got no way to solve without a final equation. Our last equation will be set equal to the amount of money Nate has. To make the math easier, multiply everything by 100 to get rid of the decimals.

$$0.01p = 0.05n = 0.10d = 0.25q = 3.49$$
$$100\left(0.01p = 0.05n = 0.10d = 0.25q = 3.49\right)$$
$$1p + 5n + 10d + 25q = 349$$

Multiply by 100 to get rid of the decimals.

Now substitute

$$1p + 5n + 10d + 25q = 349$$
$$1p + 5\left(p - 6\right) + 10\left(p - 4\right) + 25\left(p + 2\right) = 349$$
$$1p + 5p - 30 + 10p - 40 + 25p + 50 = 349$$
$$41p - 20 = 349$$
$$41p = 369$$
$$p = 9$$

We're looking for *dimes*, so plug into the dime equation.

$$d = 9 - 4$$
$$d = 5$$

Answer choice **B** is correct.

-244-

Wrap Up

What You Need to Know
- ✓ How to solve systems of linear equations by elimination (*adding equations*)
- ✓ How to solve systems of equations by *substitution*
- ✓ How to *make an equation*

Videos

> Systems of Equations

> Systems with more than 2 Variables

The Strategies
- ✓ Try elimination, but it won't work on all problems.
- ✓ On word problems, use variables that represent the items you're solving for
- ✓ The number of equations needs to equal the number of variables

Key Skill

Systems of equations are a key skill. Understanding how they work is necessary for many problem types including:

- ✓ Coordinate Geometry: Line Equations

- ✓ Plane Geometry: Four Sided Shapes

- ✓ Make an Equation

Intermediate Algebra: Systems of Equations

1. $2x + 3y = 13$ and $5x + 6y = 28$, what is the value of $3x + 5y$?

   A. 3
   B. 2
   C. 21
   D. 23
   E. 5

2. The cost of a soda and a candy bar is $6.00. The cost of two sodas and a candy bar is $10.75. How much is a candy bar?

   F. $4.75
   G. $1.25
   H. $2.25
   J. $3.25
   K. $1.00

3. If $xy = 36$ and $x + y = 15$ and $y > x$ then what is $x - y$?

   A. 3
   B. -9
   C. 12
   D. 9
   E. 15

4. If $3x + 4y = 6$ and $x - 2y = 12$ then what is the value of x?

   F. 3
   G. 18
   H. -3
   J. 6
   K. -18

5. If $2x - y = 1$ and $4x + 2y = 38$ then what is the value of y?

   A. 11
   B. 18
   C. 9
   D. 5
   E. 10

6. What is the sum of x and y if $3x + \dfrac{1}{2}y = -1$ and $x - 2y = 30$?

   F. 12
   G. -12
   H. -14
   J. -16
   K. -9

7. Isabella found $5.78 in loose change. She has two less quarters than dimes, one more nickel than dimes, and eight more pennies than dimes. How many quarters did Isabella find?

   A. 11
   B. 13
   C. 15
   D. 16
   E. 23

Systems of Equations: Solutions

1. $2x + 3y = 13$ and $5x + 6y = 28$, what is the value of $3x + 5y$?

Correct Answer C

This is a standard system of equations question with an additional step. I much prefer to solve systems by elimination. To do that, we'll need to be able to cancel one of the variables. The easiest way to get a variable to cancel is to use the y's. If we multiply the top equation by -2, we can get the y's to cancel.

$$-2(2x+3y=13)$$
$$5x+6y=28$$
$$\rightarrow$$
$$\begin{aligned} -4x-6y&=-26 \\ +\ \ 5x+6y&=28 \\ \hline x&=2 \end{aligned}$$

The y's cancel.

Now that we have x, we can plug in either equation to find y.

$$2x+3y=13 \quad \rightarrow \quad 2(2)+3y=13$$
$$4+3y=13 \quad \rightarrow \quad 3y=9 \quad \rightarrow \quad y=3$$

Now, plug in the expression: $3x+5y \quad \rightarrow \quad 3(2)+5(3) \quad \rightarrow \quad 6+15=21$

Answer choice **C** is correct.

<u>What You May Have Done Wrong</u>
- **A.** This is the value of y.
- **B.** This is the value of x.
- **D.** This is a calculation or conceptual error.
- **E.** This is a calculation or conceptual error.

2. **The cost of a soda and a candy bar is $6.00. The cost of two sodas and a candy bar is $10.75. How much is a candy bar?**

Correct Answer G

This problem first involves setting up your equations. We will break this down into statements. Remember we are solving for *candy bar*.

Statement 1: The cost of a soda and a candy bar is $6.00
Equation 1:   **1s + 1c = 6.00**

Statement 2: The cost of two sodas and a candy bar is $10.75
Equation 2:   **2s + 1c = 10.75**

Now, we're ready to solve. This problem lends itself well to either the elimination method or the substitution method. I will demonstrate the addition method.

$$\begin{aligned} 1s+1c&=\ \ 6.00 \\ +2s+1c&=10.75 \\ \hline \end{aligned} \quad \rightarrow \quad \begin{aligned} -1(1s+1c&=\ \ 6.00) \\ +\ \ 2s+1c&=10.75 \\ \hline \end{aligned} \quad \rightarrow \quad \begin{aligned} -1s-1c&=-6.00 \\ +2s+1c&=10.75 \\ \hline 1s\ \ \ \ &=\ \ 4.75 \end{aligned}$$

Let's substitute in the price of one soda ($4.75) and solve.

$$1s + 1c = 6.00 \rightarrow 4.75 + 1c = 6.00 \rightarrow c = 1.25$$

Answer choice **G** is correct.

<u>What You May Have Done Wrong</u>
- **F.** $4.75 is the cost of the soda, not the candy bar.
- **H.** You probably made an arithmetic error.
- **J.** You probably made an arithmetic error, or guessed.
- **K.** You probably made an arithmetic error, or guessed.

3. If $xy = 36$ and $x + y = 15$ and $y > x$ then what is $x - y$?

Correct Answer B

This equation *cannot* be solved by *adding the equations*, because the first equation has x and y joined by multiplication. I'm using *substitution*, and I'm going to rearrange our second equation to solve for x (we could use y just as easily). From a strategy standpoint, you may recognize this as a factoring problem. I need two numbers (factors of 36) that multiply to 36 and add to 15. If you realize this, you can skip the algebra and solve this problem very easily. I'll show both ways, starting with factoring.

<u>Factoring</u>

Factors of 36: ~~36 x 1 → 36 + 1 = 37~~
~~18 x 2 → 18 + 2 = 20~~
12 x 3 → 12 + 3 = 15

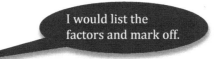

I would list the factors and mark off.

If $y > x$, then $y = 12$ & $x = 3$. Therefore, $x - y = -9$

<u>Substitution</u>

Rearrange: $x + y = 15$ → $x = 15 - y$

Substitute: $xy = 36$ → $y(15 - y) = 36$ → $15y - y^2 = 36$

Re-arrange the quadratic to solve by factoring.
$$y^2 - 15y + 36 = 0 \rightarrow (y - 3)(y - 12) = 0$$

The solutions to the quadratic equation are
$$y - 3 = 0 \rightarrow y = 3 \qquad y - 12 = 0 \rightarrow y = 12$$

We can try both factors in the equations, and remember that $y > x$, so the only way the equations work is if $y = 12$ and $x = 3$.

Therefore, $x - y = -9$

Answer choice **B** is correct

<u>What You May Have Done Wrong</u>
  A. This is a halfway answer; you got the value of x
  C. This is a halfway answer; you got the value of y
  D. You reversed the final calculation and subtracted $y - x$ instead of $y - x$.
  E. You likely added 3 and 12, or you incorrectly determined y to be -9.

4. If $3x + 4y = 6$ and $x - 2y = 12$ then what is the value of x?

Correct Answer J

This problem is equally straightforward to solve by *elimination* or by *substitution*. Although I have a personal preference for addition, I'm going to use substitution here—it works nicely on this problem. Remember, we are solving for x.

Rearrange: $x - 2y = 12$ → $x = 12 + 2y$

You could solve for x right away, but it's a little easier to solve for y first.

Substitute: $3(12 + 2y) + 4y = 6$

Solve: $36 + 6y + 4y = 6$ → $10y = -30$ → $y = -3$

Now, we can substitute the value of y (-3) into either equation. I'll use the first.
$$x - 2y = 12 \rightarrow x - 2(-3) = 12 \rightarrow x + 6 = 12 \rightarrow x = 6$$

Answer choice **J** is correct.

<u>What You May Have Done Wrong:</u>
  F. You probably miscalculated y as +3 and used that value (instead of solving for x).
  G. You miscalculated x, probably you dropped your – sign when plugging in -3 for y.
  H. This is the halfway answer. You never solved for x.
  K. You likely miscalculated y as -15.

5. If $2x - y = 1$ and $4x + 2y = 38$ then what is the value of y?

Correct Answer C

This problem can be solved by *elimination* or by *substitution*. I'm going to use addition on this problem. Remember, we are solving for y.

$$\begin{array}{l} 2x - y = 1 \\ 4x + 2y = 38 \end{array} \rightarrow \begin{array}{l} 2(2x - y = 1) \\ 4x + 2y = 38 \end{array} \rightarrow \begin{array}{l} 4x - 2y = 2 \\ 4x + 2y = 38 \\ \hline 8x \quad\quad = 40 \end{array} \rightarrow x = 5$$

Substitute and solve

$$2x - y = 1 \rightarrow 2(5) - y = 1 \rightarrow -y = -9 \rightarrow y = 9$$

Answer choice **C** is correct.

<u>What You May Have Done Wrong</u>
A. You likely found the correct value for x, but made a sign error when plugging in to the second equation.
B. You probably found the correct value for x but plugging in to the second equation forgot the coefficient 2 in front of the y.
D. This is the value for x; likely it is a halfway answer.
E. You probably found the correct value for x but somehow made an arithmetic error.

6. **What is the sum of x and y if** $3x + \dfrac{1}{2}y = -1$ **and** $x - 2y = 30$?

Correct Answer G

This problem can be solved by *substitution* or *addition*. Either works fine here, but I'll illustrate substitution. I'm going to re-arrange the second equation for x, to prevent fractions.

Rearrange: $x - 2y = 30 \rightarrow x = 30 + 2y$

Substitute: $3(30 + 2y) + \dfrac{1}{2}y = 1$

Solve: $90 + 6y + \dfrac{1}{2}y = -1 \rightarrow 6.5y = -91 \rightarrow y = -14$

Let's substitute our y value (-14) in for x in either equation.

$$x - 2y = 30 \rightarrow x - 2(-14) = 30$$
$$x + 28 = 30 \rightarrow x = 2$$

Now, add the x and y values. $-14 + 2 = -12$.

Answer **G** is correct.

<u>What You May Have Done Wrong:</u>
F. You probably miscalculated y as +3 and used that value (instead of solving for x).
H. You miscalculated x, probably you dropped your – sign when plugging in -3 for y.
J. This is the halfway answer. You never solved for x.
K. You likely miscalculated y as -15.

7. Isabella found \$5.78 in loose change. She has two less quarters than dimes, one more nickel than dimes, and eight more pennies than dimes. How many quarters did Isabella find?

Correct Answer B

This is a system of equations with more than two variables. It actually has four variables, *pennies, nickels, dimes,* & *quarters.* We need an equation for *each* variable.

We can't really use elimination, so we'll be substituting. Start with the equations that compare the number of two types of coins.

Statement 1: two less quarters than dimes

$$d = q + 2$$
$$q = d - 2$$

> We want everything in terms of one variable so we can substitute in. In this case we want to use *dimes.*

Statement 2: one more nickel than dimes

$$d = n - 1$$
$$n = d + 1$$

Statement 3: eight more pennies than dimes

$$d = p - 8$$
$$p = d + 8$$

We need one more equation that involves *all* of the variables. It will have to equal the value of the change, \$5.78. To make things easier, multiply everything (on both sides of the equation) by 100 to get rid of the decimals.

$$25q + 10d + 5n + 1p = 578$$
$$25(q-2) + 10(d) + 5(d+1) + 1(d+8) = 578$$
$$25q - 50 + 10d + 5d + 5 + d + 8 = 578$$
$$41d - 37 = 578$$
$$41d = 615$$
$$d = 15$$

> We have to multiply the number of coins times the value of each coin.

> Everything is in terms of dimes.

Don't fall for the halfway answer. We have the number of *dimes*, but we want the number of *quarters*.

$$q = d - 2$$
$$q = 15 - 2$$
$$q = 13$$

Answer choice B is correct.

<u>What You May Have Done Wrong</u>
A. You've made a calculation error. Review your steps.
C. This is the halfway answer, the number of dimes.
D. This is the number of nickels.
E. This is the number of pennies.

Background

Rational expressions are a small topic on the ACT and combine simplification with factoring (often factoring quadratics). **Rational Expressions questions are all about simplification by factoring**.

What You Need to Know

- ✓ How to cancel the common factors of a fraction
- ✓ How to factor quadratics
- ✓ The denominator of a rational expression cannot equal zero, or the expression is undefined

Definitions

Rational Numbers are numbers that can be expressed as a ratio of two integers (the denominator can't be equal to zero).

Expressions are operations with variables, like $2x$ or $x + 1$.

Terms are separated by addition and subtraction.

Factors are separated by multiplication or division.

Rules of the Road: Simplifying Fractions

Rational expressions are fractions and fractions are ratios. Let's look at a few examples of simplifying numeric fractions.

> The *only* way to simplify a fraction are common factors.

Let's look at a couple of examples to make this clearer.

1. $\dfrac{2}{4} \rightarrow \dfrac{1 \cdot 2}{2 \cdot 2} \rightarrow \dfrac{1 \cdot \cancel{2}}{2 \cdot \cancel{2}} \rightarrow \dfrac{1}{2}$

> We can factor a 2 out of both the numerator and denominator; we can then cancel the 2's.

You could also look at it this way:

$$\dfrac{2}{4} \rightarrow \dfrac{1 \cdot 2}{2 \cdot 2} \rightarrow \dfrac{1}{2} \cdot \dfrac{\cancel{2}}{\cancel{2}} \rightarrow \dfrac{1}{2} \cdot 1 = \dfrac{1}{2}$$

Simplifying Fractions

2. $\dfrac{2+1}{4+1} = \dfrac{3}{5}$ **But**, if I try to cancel the 1's → $\dfrac{2+\cancel{1}}{4+\cancel{1}} = \dfrac{2}{4}$

> **Not** equal to 3/5

Or, if I tried to cancel factors $\dfrac{(2 \cdot 1)+1}{(2 \cdot 2)+1} = \dfrac{2}{3}$

> **Not** equal to 3/5

Rules of the Road: Variables in Rational Expressions

> **Variables work the same as numbers. We can *only cancel factors*.**

Examples

1. $\dfrac{2x}{4x} \rightarrow \dfrac{1 \cdot 2 \cdot x}{2 \cdot 2 \cdot x} \rightarrow \dfrac{1 \cdot \cancel{2} \cdot \cancel{x}}{2 \cdot \cancel{2} \cdot \cancel{x}} \rightarrow \dfrac{1}{2}$

> We can cancel the variables because we aren't adding or subtracting them.

2. $\dfrac{2x^3}{x} = \dfrac{2 \cdot x^3}{x} = \dfrac{2 \cdot x \cdot x \cdot \cancel{x}}{\cancel{x}} = \dfrac{2x^2}{1} = 2x^2$

> To divide, subtract exponents.

3. $\dfrac{x}{x^2} = \dfrac{x}{x \cdot x} = \dfrac{\cancel{x}}{\cancel{x} \cdot x} = \dfrac{1}{x}$ **OR** $\dfrac{x}{x^2} = x - x^2 = x^{-1} = \dfrac{1}{x}$

4. $\dfrac{(x+2)}{2(x+2)} = \dfrac{\cancel{(x+2)}}{2\cancel{(x+2)}} = \dfrac{1}{2}$

> This binomial is a *factor*.

> The **numerator** & **denominator** are **factorable quadratics**

Usually, we see something a little more like this on the ACT.

5. $\dfrac{x^2+2x+1}{x^2+3x+2} \rightarrow \dfrac{(x+1)(x+1)}{(x+1)(x+2)} \rightarrow \dfrac{(x+1)\cancel{(x+1)}}{\cancel{(x+1)}(x+2)} \rightarrow \dfrac{(x+1)}{(x+2)}$

Rational Expressions & Zeroes

Recall that we can't have a zero in the denominator of a fraction. Dividing by zero is *undefined* (you can't split something into zero parts). When we have a rational expression question on the ACT, it will usually specify a condition that will prevent x from being 0. For example $x > 3$, just tells us that x won't be undefined for any value greater than three.

> Whenever **rational expressions** are **undefined**, there's a **vertical asymptote** on the graph.

Examples

1. $\dfrac{3x}{x}$ If $x = 0$, this rational expression is undefined.

2. $\dfrac{x^2-4}{x+3}$ If $x = -3$, this rational expression is undefined.

> *Vertical Asymptotes* are covered in *Coordinate Geometry: Graphing Functions*

Rational Expressions: ACT Examples

1. What is $\dfrac{4x^2-5x}{20x^2}$ equivalent to (assuming $x \neq 0$)?

   A. $\dfrac{x-1}{5x}$

   B. $\dfrac{4x}{5x}$

   C. $-\dfrac{1}{20}$

   D. $\dfrac{1}{5x}$

   E. $\dfrac{1}{5} - \dfrac{1}{4x}$

> Most *rational expression* questions require us to actually simplify the expression.

Solve

In this case, we'll want to factor our original rational expression: $\dfrac{4x^2-5x}{20x^2}$

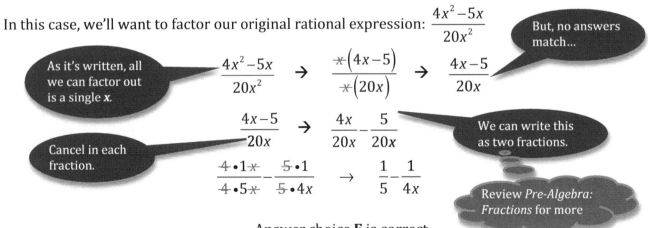

> But, no answers match...

> As it's written, all we can factor out is a single x.

$$\dfrac{4x^2-5x}{20x^2} \rightarrow \dfrac{\cancel{x}(4x-5)}{\cancel{x}(20x)} \rightarrow \dfrac{4x-5}{20x}$$

> Cancel in each fraction.

> We can write this as two fractions.

$$\dfrac{4x-5}{20x} \rightarrow \dfrac{4x}{20x} - \dfrac{5}{20x}$$

$$\dfrac{\cancel{4}\cdot 1\cancel{x}}{\cancel{4}\cdot 5\cancel{x}} - \dfrac{\cancel{5}\cdot 1}{\cancel{5}\cdot 4x} \rightarrow \dfrac{1}{5} - \dfrac{1}{4x}$$

> Review *Pre-Algebra: Fractions* for more

Answer choice **E** is correct.

Rational Expressions: ACT Examples

2. Which of the following is equivalent to $\dfrac{x+3}{x+2}$?

A. $\dfrac{2x+4}{2x+6}$

B. $\dfrac{x+6}{x+4}$

C. $\dfrac{4x+12}{4x+6}$

D. $\dfrac{2x^2+6x}{2x^2+8x}$

E. $\dfrac{2x+6}{2x+4}$

This problem works a little backwards. We're given the *simplified* form and we find the *un-simplified* form.

The only way to answer this question is *simplifying* the answer choices— marking off as we go.

Solve

A. $\dfrac{2x+4}{2x+6} \to \dfrac{2(x+2)}{2(x+3)} \to \dfrac{\cancel{2}(x+2)}{\cancel{2}(x+3)} \neq \dfrac{x+3}{x+2}$

There is nothing that we can factor.

B. $\dfrac{x+6}{x+4} \to \dfrac{x+6}{x+4} \neq \dfrac{x+3}{x+2}$

C. $\dfrac{4x+12}{4x+6} \to \dfrac{4(x+3)}{2(2x+3)} \to \dfrac{\cancel{4}(x+3)}{\cancel{2}(2x+3)} \to \dfrac{2(x+3)}{2x+3} \neq \dfrac{x+3}{x+2}$

D. $\dfrac{2x^2+6x}{2x^2+8x} \to \dfrac{2x(x+3)}{2x(x+4)} \to \dfrac{\cancel{2x}(x+3)}{\cancel{2x}(x+4)} \to \dfrac{x+3}{x+4} \neq \dfrac{x+3}{x+2}$

E. $\dfrac{2x+6}{2x+4} \to \dfrac{2(x+3)}{2(x+2)} \to \dfrac{\cancel{2}(x+3)}{\cancel{2}(x+2)} \to \dfrac{x+3}{x+2}$

3. Assuming $x^2 - y^2 \neq 0$, which is equivalent to $\dfrac{(x^2+4xy+3y^2)(x-y)}{x^2-y^2}$?

A. $\dfrac{x+3y}{x-y}$

B. $\dfrac{4(x+y)}{x-y}$

C. $x+3y$

D. $\dfrac{x^2+4xy+3y^2}{x-y}$

E. 3

This problem is covered in the *video* on *Rational Expressions*

Solve

$$\dfrac{(x^2+4xy+3y^2)(x-y)}{x^2-y^2} \to \dfrac{(x^2+4xy+3y^2)(x-y)}{(x+y)(x-y)} \to \dfrac{\cancel{(x+y)}(x+3y)\cancel{(x-y)}}{\cancel{(x+y)}\cancel{(x-y)}} \to \dfrac{(x+3y)}{1} = x+3y$$

It's a *Difference of Squares*

Answer choice **C** is correct.

4. Given that $x > 3$, which of the following expressions is equivalent to $\dfrac{(2x^2+4x-6)(x+1)}{(2x^2-3x-5)(2x-2)}$?

    A. 1

    B. $\dfrac{1}{2x-5}$

    C. $x+3$

    D. $\dfrac{x+3}{2x-5}$

    E. $\dfrac{x+3}{x+1}$

Solve

> For complicated rational expressions, check if the opposite binomial is a factor

$$\frac{(2x^2+4x-6)(x+1)}{(2x^2-3x-5)(2x-2)} \quad \rightarrow \quad \frac{\left(2x^2+4x-6\right)\left(x+1\right)}{\left(2x^2-3x-5\right)\left(2x-2\right)}$$

$$\frac{(2x-2)(x+3)(x+1)}{(x+1)(2x-5)(2x-2)} \quad \rightarrow \quad \frac{\cancel{(2x-2)}(x+3)\cancel{(x+1)}}{\cancel{(x+1)}(2x-5)\cancel{(2x-2)}}$$

$$\frac{x+3}{2x-5}$$

Answer choice **D** is correct.

Wrap Up

What You Need to Know
- ✓ How to cancel the common factors of a fraction
- ✓ How to factor quadratics
- ✓ The denominator of a rational expression cannot equal zero, or the expression is undefined

Videos

> Rational Expressions

The Strategies
- ✓ Look for common numeric and variable factors.
- ✓ Factor any quadratic you come across.
- ✓ On complicated quadratics, use opposing binomials as a guide to help you factor.

Related Skills
- ✓ Fractions

- ✓ Quadratic Equations

Intermediate Algebra: Rational Expressions

1. Which of the following is equivalent to
$$\frac{2x^2}{4x-8x^2}=?$$

A. $-\dfrac{1}{2}$

B. $\dfrac{2x}{4-4x}$

C. $\dfrac{2x}{1-8x}$

D. $\dfrac{x^2}{2x-4x^2}$

(E.) $\dfrac{x}{2-4x}$

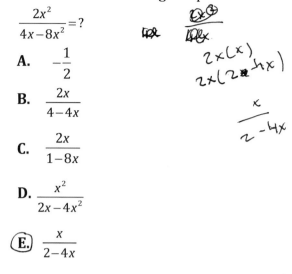

2. Which of the following is equivalent to $\dfrac{x^2}{y}=?$

F. $\dfrac{x^2+a}{y+a}$

G. $\dfrac{x^2-a}{y+a-4}$

H. $\dfrac{x^2y}{yx}$

J. $\dfrac{a^2x^2}{a^2y}$

K. $\dfrac{a^2+x^2}{a^2+y}$

$4x^4(6x^{\#}-2)$

3. For all nonzero values of x, $\dfrac{24x^8-8x^4}{4x^4}=?$

A. $6x^2-2$

B. $6x^4-2x$

C. $6x^4$

D. $6x^4-2$

E. $6x^4-2x$

$4x^2=0$

4. For all nonzero values of a and b $\dfrac{(9a^3)(4a^5b^2)}{14a^9b}=?$

F. $18ab$

G. $\dfrac{18ab}{7}$

H. $\dfrac{18a^6b}{7}$

J. $\dfrac{18b}{7a}$

K. $\dfrac{18b}{7ab}$

$\dfrac{36a^8b^2}{14a^9b}$ $\dfrac{2a^8b(18b^{\ell})}{2a^8b(7a)}$

5. For all values $x \neq -5$, which is equivalent to
$$\frac{2x^2+7x-15}{x+5}?$$
-30 $2x^2+10x-3x-15$

A. $2x-3$ $(8\cdot10)(x-3)$ $2x(x+5)-3(x+5)$

B. $x-3$

C. $\dfrac{2x-3}{x+5}$ $\dfrac{(2x-3)(x+5)}{x+5}$

D. $\dfrac{2x+3}{x+5}$

E. $2x+3$

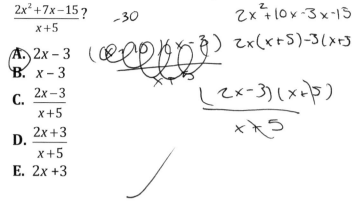

6. Simplify the following expression $\dfrac{x^2-4}{x-2} \div \dfrac{x+2}{2}?$

A. $\dfrac{(x+2)(x+2)}{x-2}$

B. $\dfrac{1}{2}$

C. 2

D. $\dfrac{2(x-2)}{x+2}$

E. $x-2$

$\dfrac{(x+2)(x-2)}{x-2}$

$x+2$ $\dfrac{x+2(x-2)}{x+2} \div \dfrac{x+2}{2}$

7. When the denominator is not zero, which is equivalent to the following expression $\dfrac{(x^2-11x+30)(x+4)}{(x^2-x-20)(x-6)}?$

A. $\dfrac{(x+5)}{(x+4)}$

B. $\dfrac{(x-5)}{(x-4)}$

C. $\dfrac{(x+5)}{x^2-4}$

D. 1

E. 0

$\dfrac{(x-5)(x-6)(x+4)}{(x+5)(x-4)(x-6)}$

1. **Which of the following is equivalent to** $\dfrac{2x^2}{4x-8x^2}=?$

Correct Answer E

This is a relatively straightforward factoring problem. At a glance, we can see that the coefficients are all multiples of two and we only have one variable (x). Let's take a look.

$$\frac{2x^2}{4x-8x^2} \rightarrow \frac{2\bullet x \bullet x}{(2\bullet 2\bullet x)-(2\bullet 2\bullet 2\bullet x\bullet x)} \rightarrow \frac{\cancel{2}\bullet \cancel{x}\bullet x}{(\cancel{2}\bullet 2\bullet \cancel{x})-(\cancel{2}\bullet 2\bullet 2\bullet \cancel{x}\bullet \cancel{x})}$$

$$\frac{x}{2-4x}$$

Answer choice **E** is correct.

<u>What You May Have Done Wrong</u>

A. You probably misread the first term in the denominator ($4x$) as $4x^2$.
B. This is a halfway answer, you factored out the x but not the 2.
C. There are a few things wrong here, you may want to review *Pre-Algebra: Fractions*
D. This is a halfway answer, you factored out the 2 but not the x.

2. **Which of the following is equivalent to** $\dfrac{x^2}{y}=?$

Correct Answer J

We're looking for an expression that simplifies to $\dfrac{x^2}{y}$. This is also a "which" question, so we'll mark off. This is a definition question, but you could pick numbers. If you need to pick numbers, I'd use $x=1$ and $y=2$, because they are easy to work with, it also gives me an easy fraction. I'm also going to say that a equals three. Our correct answer will equal ½ when we plug in our values.

$$\frac{x^2}{y} \rightarrow \frac{1^2}{2} \rightarrow \frac{1}{2} \ \& \ a=3$$

F. We can't factor out terms that are added or subtracted. Plugging in numbers
$$\frac{x^2+a}{y+a} \rightarrow \frac{1+3}{2+3} \rightarrow \frac{4}{5} \neq \frac{1}{2}$$

G. We can't factor out terms that are added or subtracted. Plugging in numbers
$$\frac{x^2-a}{y-a} \rightarrow \frac{1-3}{2-3} \rightarrow \frac{-2}{-1} \neq \frac{1}{2}$$

H. We can only simplify by cancelling out factors shared by *all the terms* in the fraction. Plugging in numbers $\dfrac{x^2 y}{yx^2} \rightarrow \dfrac{1^2\bullet 2}{2\bullet 1^2} \rightarrow \dfrac{2}{2} \neq \dfrac{1}{2}$

J. We are multiplying the top and bottom (all terms) by the same number—by the same factor (the square does not matter). Plugging in numbers $\dfrac{a^2 x^2}{a^2 y} \rightarrow \dfrac{3^2\bullet 1^2}{3^2\bullet 2} \rightarrow \dfrac{9}{18} = \dfrac{1}{2}$

K. We can't factor our terms that are only added or subtracted (the square on the a does not matter) $\dfrac{a^2+x^2}{a^2+y} \rightarrow \dfrac{3^2+1^2}{3^2+2} \rightarrow \dfrac{10}{11} \neq \dfrac{1}{2}$

Answer choice **J** is correct.

3. For all nonzero values of x, $\dfrac{24x^8 - 8x^4}{4x^4} = ?$

Correct Answer D

Let's pull out the common factors.

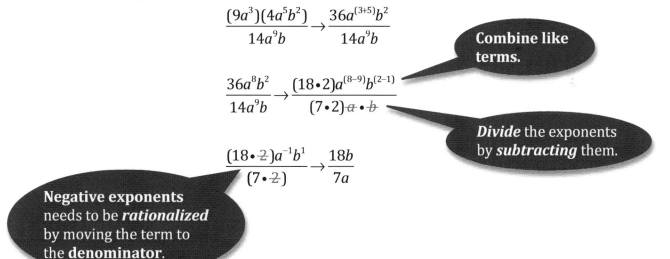

Cancel common factors.

$$\frac{24x^8 - 8x^4}{4x^4} \rightarrow \frac{(4\bullet 6\bullet x^4 \bullet x^4)-(4\bullet 2\bullet x^4)}{4\bullet x^4}$$

$$\frac{\cancel{4}\bullet \cancel{x^4}(6\bullet x^4 - 2)}{\cancel{4}\bullet \cancel{x^4}} \rightarrow \frac{6x^4 - 2}{1} \rightarrow 6x^4 - 2$$

Answer choice **D** is correct.

<u>What You May Have Done Wrong</u>
- **A.** You divided the exponents instead of subtracting.
- **B.** You incorrectly divided the first term; you divided the exponents instead of subtracting. You also incorrectly divided the $-8x^4$. The variable should become $x^0 = 1$.
- **C.** You incorrectly thought that $x^0 = 0$. Any number to the zero power equals 1.
- **E.** You incorrectly calculated the second term, $x^4 \div x^4 = x^{4-4} = x^0 = 1$

4. For all nonzero values of a and b, $\dfrac{(9a^3)(4a^5b^2)}{14a^9b} = ?$

Correct Answer J

We have a second step in this problem. We need to multiply the numerator before we can divide (simplify) the fraction.

$$\frac{(9a^3)(4a^5b^2)}{14a^9b} \rightarrow \frac{36a^{(3+5)}b^2}{14a^9b}$$

Combine like terms.

$$\frac{36a^8b^2}{14a^9b} \rightarrow \frac{(18\bullet 2)a^{(8-9)}b^{(2-1)}}{(7\bullet 2)\cancel{a}\bullet \cancel{b}}$$

Divide the exponents by *subtracting* them.

$$\frac{(18\bullet\cancel{2})a^{-1}b^1}{(7\bullet\cancel{2})} \rightarrow \frac{18b}{7a}$$

Negative exponents needs to be *rationalized* by moving the term to the **denominator**.

Answer choice **J** is correct.

<u>What You May Have Done Wrong</u>
- **F.** You either miscalculated, or forgot that a negative exponent means that a must be flipped to the denominator. You also incorrectly reduced the coefficients.
- **G.** You either miscalculated, or forgot that a negative exponent means that a must be flipped to the denominator.
- **H.** You multiplied the exponents in the numerator (you should have added).
- **K.** You either forgot, or incorrectly dealt with variable b.

5. **For all values** $x \neq -5$, **which is equivalent to** $\dfrac{2x^2+7x-15}{x+5}$ **?**

Correct Answer A

This expression can be simplified *only* if the denominator is a factor of the numerator. The numerator looks tricky to factor, with a coefficient in front of x^2, and mixed signs. But, **I can assume $x + 5$ is a factor**.

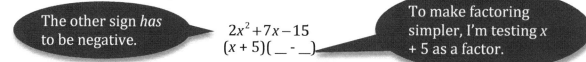

The other sign *has* to be negative.

$2x^2+7x-15$
$(x + 5)(\_ - \_)$

To make factoring simpler, I'm testing $x + 5$ as a factor.

The first terms must multiply to $2x^2 \rightarrow x \bullet \_ = 2x^2$, so our other first term must be $2x$.

$$(x + 5)(2x - \_)$$

Our last terms must multiply to -15. We already have +5, so our other last term is -3.

Our fully factored quadratic is $(x + 5)(2x - 3)$

Back to our rational expression...
$$\dfrac{(x+5)(2x-3)}{x+5} \rightarrow \dfrac{\cancel{(x+5)}(2x-3)}{\cancel{x+5}} \rightarrow \dfrac{2x-3}{1} \rightarrow 2x-3$$

Answer choice **A** is correct.

<u>What You May Have Done Wrong</u>
- **B.** You incorrectly factored the numerator. Review your steps.
- **C.** You didn't cancel your factors correctly.
- **D.** You had a sign problem when you factored (is should be $2x - 3$) *and* you failed to cancel properly.
- **E.** You had a sign problem when factoring.

6. **Simplify the following expression** $\dfrac{x^2-4}{x-2} \div \dfrac{x+2}{2}$ **?**

Correct Answer C

Anytime you have an operation involving rational expressions (an uncommon ACT problem) you'll want to simplify the fraction(s) as much as possible. If you don't recognize the numerator as a *difference of squares*, you may want to review that topic. Let's look at our left fraction first:

$$\dfrac{x^2-4}{x-2} \rightarrow \dfrac{(x+2)(x-2)}{(x-2)} \rightarrow \dfrac{(x+2)\cancel{(x-2)}}{\cancel{(x-2)}} \rightarrow x+2$$

You don't have to simplify the fraction first.

Now, our problem looks like this $(x+2) \div \dfrac{x+2}{2}$

We can't do anything to simplify our right fraction. So we're on to division. Remember, when we divide by a fraction, *we flip that fraction and then multiply.*

Like so, $\dfrac{x+2}{2} \rightarrow \dfrac{2}{x+2}$

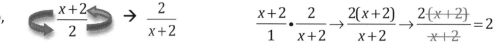

$$\dfrac{x+2}{1} \bullet \dfrac{2}{x+2} \rightarrow \dfrac{2(x+2)}{x+2} \rightarrow \dfrac{2\cancel{(x+2)}}{\cancel{x+2}} = 2$$

Answer choice **C** is correct.

<u>What You May Have Done Wrong</u>
- **A.** There are a few problems here. You probably did not flip your second fraction. In addition, you may have believed that $2(x - 2)$ meant you had two $x - 2$ terms (which would only be true in the case of $(x - 2)^2$..
- **B.** You may have flipped the first fraction (instead of the second).
- **D.** You may have incorrectly simplified the left fraction numerator to $x - 2$.
- **E.** This is a compound error. I suggest you take another look at <u>fractions</u>.

7. When the denominator is not zero, which is equivalent to the following expression $\dfrac{(x^2-11x+30)(x+4)}{(x^2-x-20)(x-6)}$?

Correct Answer D

Whenever we have quadratics in a fraction, we'll need to factor before we can simplify. Although neither the quadratic in the numerator nor denominator is too tough to factor, you can save time by testing the binomial in the denominator as a factor of the quadratic in the numerator and vice versa. Let's take a look:

$$\frac{(x^2-11x+30)(x+4)}{(x^2-x-20)(x-6)}$$

Let's start with the quadratic in the numerator (the red quadratic)

$$(x^2-11x+30)$$

> The second parentheses' sign has to be negative to give us a + last term.

$$(x-6)(\_\ -\_\ )$$

The first terms must multiply together to arrive at x^2, so our missing first term must be x. Our last terms must multiply to equal positive 30, and the only way to get there is with a -5. Remember, we can always check the middle term by FOIL. So, our factors are…

$$(x^2-11x+30)$$
$$(x-6)(x-5)$$

Let's put that back into our rational expression.

$$\frac{(x^2-11x+30)(x+4)}{(x^2-x-20)(x-6)} \rightarrow \frac{(x-6)(x-5)(x+4)}{(x^2-x-20)(x-6)}$$

$$\frac{\cancel{(x-6)}(x-5)(x+4)}{(x^2-x-20)\cancel{(x-6)}} \rightarrow \frac{(x-5)(x+4)}{(x^2-x-20)}$$

You may already see that the factors of our bottom quadratic are our numerator, but we can factor and check. Again, I'm going to check and see if our blue binomial (numerator) is a factor of our blue quadratic (denominator).

$$(x^2-x-20)$$
$$(x+4)(\_\ -\_\ )$$

Our first terms must multiply to x^2 and our last terms must multiply to -20. This gives us terms…

$$(x^2-x-20)$$
$$(x+4)(x-5)$$

Let's put that back into our partially simplified rational expression

$$\frac{(x-5)(x+4)}{(x+4)(x-5)} \rightarrow \frac{\cancel{(x-5)}\ \cancel{(x+4)}}{\cancel{(x+4)}\ \cancel{(x-5)}} = 1$$

Answer choice **D** is correct.

<u>What You May Have Done Wrong</u>
   A. You factored the top incorrectly and you also had trouble cancelling terms.
   B. You factored the top incorrectly and you also had trouble cancelling terms.
   C. This is a compound error. Review your steps.
   E. You probably factored both terms correctly but made a mistake in cancelling.

Background
Radical expressions, expressions & equations with radicals, are a relatively minor topic on the ACT, and can be tested directly or as part of another question type.

What You Need to Know
✓ The rules of exponents and roots.
✓ How to deal with fractions in equations

Definitions

A root can be written as an exponent $\sqrt{x} = x^{\frac{1}{2}}$, $\sqrt[3]{x} = x^{\frac{1}{3}}$

Squares and square roots cancel each other* $\sqrt{x^2} = x$

Multiplied roots can be combined/split $\sqrt{x} \cdot \sqrt{y} = \sqrt{xy} = \sqrt{x} \cdot \sqrt{y}$

Divided roots can be combined/split $\sqrt{\dfrac{x}{y}} = \dfrac{\sqrt{x}}{\sqrt{y}} = \sqrt{\dfrac{x}{y}}$

> Review *Elementary Algebra: Exponents* for more

*The math behind this is $\sqrt{x^2} = (x^2)^{\frac{1}{2}} = x^{2 \cdot \frac{1}{2}} = x^{\frac{2}{2}} = x$

Rules of the Road: Algebra Involving Radicals

To remove an exponent from a variable, we use the inverse power (the root).
To remove a root, we use the inverse power (the exponent).
Just like any operation, **what is done to one side of the equation *must* be done to the other.**

To Solve: Isolate the radical (and its contents) on one side and then remove the radical (by squaring, cubing, etc. both sides).

ACT Examples: Radicals Algebra

1. Given that $\sqrt{4x} + 9 = 17$ what is x?

> There's a *video* on *Radical Expressions*

    A. $\dfrac{9}{2}$

    B. 8
    C. 64
    D. 2
    E. 16

Solve

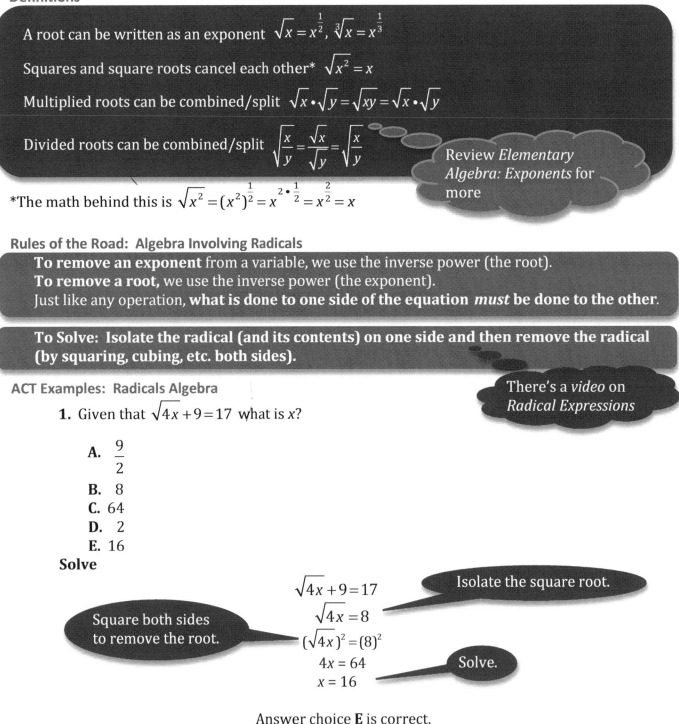

$$\sqrt{4x} + 9 = 17$$

> Isolate the square root.

$$\sqrt{4x} = 8$$

> Square both sides to remove the root.

$$(\sqrt{4x})^2 = (8)^2$$

$$4x = 64$$

> Solve.

$$x = 16$$

Answer choice **E** is correct.

2. If $x^5 = 32$, then $x^2 + 3x$?

    A. 12
    B. 8
    C. 10
    D. -2
    E. 4

Solve

$$x^5 = 32$$
$$\sqrt[5]{x^5} = \sqrt[5]{32}$$
$$x = 2$$

We need to find x first. Because the power is odd, there will only be one value for x.

Now we have a plug-in problem

$$x^2 + 3x$$
$$(2)^2 + 3(2) = 10$$

Answer choice C is correct.

Review Pre-Algebra: Fractions for more

Fractions with Radicals

Essentially, you'll follow the same steps as you would any radical equation.

We want to isolate the radical and solve. That can mean removing the fraction first, or removing the radical first.

Removing the fraction or removing the root first is a matter of preference. You can do either. Sometimes, it may be simpler remove the radical first, and sometimes it may be simpler to remove the fraction first.

Mechanics: Radical Expressions

1. $\sqrt{\dfrac{x}{2}} = 4 \quad \rightarrow \quad \left(\sqrt{\dfrac{x}{2}}\right)^2 = 4^2$

When the radical covers the entire fraction It's usually easier to remove the radical first.

$\dfrac{x}{2} = 4 \quad \rightarrow \quad 2\left(\dfrac{x}{2}\right) = 4 \cdot 2$

$x = 8$

2. $\dfrac{3}{\sqrt{2}} = \dfrac{x\sqrt{2}}{4} \quad \rightarrow \quad \dfrac{3}{\sqrt{2}} \quad \dfrac{x\sqrt{2}}{4}$

Cross-Multiply.

Whenever two fractions are equal, cross-multiply.

$x \cdot \sqrt{2} \cdot \sqrt{2} = 3 \cdot 4$

$2x = 12 \rightarrow x = 6$

ACT Examples: Radical Expressions

1. If $\dfrac{x\sqrt{5}}{\sqrt{5}} = \dfrac{10}{2\sqrt{5}}$ is valid, then $x = ?$

    A. $2\sqrt{5}$

    B. $\sqrt{5}$

    C. $10\sqrt{5}$

    D. 5

    E. 10

If the radical is only in the numerator or the denominator, it's often easier to get rid of the fraction first.

Solve

There are three ways to solve this problem:

1. Simplify the fractions
2. Remove the fractions first
3. Remove the radicals first

You can combine these, But I'll show you the "distinct" approach to each.

<u>Simplify the Fractions</u>

Cancel the $\sqrt{5}$'s

$$\frac{x\sqrt{5}}{\sqrt{5}} = \frac{10}{2\sqrt{5}} \quad \rightarrow \quad \frac{x\sqrt{5}}{\sqrt{5}} = \frac{2\cdot 5}{2\sqrt{5}}$$

5 can be factored as $\sqrt{5} \times \sqrt{5}$

$$x = \frac{\sqrt{5}\cdot\sqrt{5}}{\sqrt{5}} \quad \rightarrow \quad x = \sqrt{5}$$

<u>Remove the Fractions First</u>

Cross-multiply

$$\frac{x\sqrt{5}}{\sqrt{5}} = \frac{10}{2\sqrt{5}} \quad \rightarrow \quad \frac{x\sqrt{5}}{\sqrt{5}} \diagup\hspace{-0.6em}\diagdown \frac{10}{2\sqrt{5}}$$

$$x\sqrt{5}\cdot 2\sqrt{5} = 10\sqrt{5} \quad \rightarrow \quad x\cdot 2\sqrt{5}\cdot\sqrt{5} = 10\sqrt{5}$$

$$10x = 10\sqrt{5} \quad \rightarrow \quad x = \sqrt{5}$$

$\sqrt{5}\cdot\sqrt{5} = 5$

<u>Remove the Radicals First</u>

$$\frac{x\sqrt{5}}{\sqrt{5}} = \frac{10}{2\sqrt{5}} \quad \rightarrow \quad \left(\frac{x\sqrt{5}}{\sqrt{5}}\right)^2 = \left(\frac{10}{2\sqrt{5}}\right)^2$$

$$\frac{5x^2}{5} = \frac{100}{4\cdot 5} \quad \rightarrow \quad \frac{5x^2}{5} = 5$$

$$x^2 = 5 \quad \rightarrow \quad x = \sqrt{5}$$

Answer choice B is correct.

2. The flow rate of two pumps it determined by the impeller speed and the equation $r = \sqrt{\dfrac{2s}{15}}$. If Pump A has a flow rate that is four times Pump B's flow rate, the speed of Pump A's impeller is how many times the speed of Pump B's impeller?

    A. 32
    B. 16
    C. 8
    D. 4
    E. 2

Solve

We can rid ourselves of the radical first, or we can remove the fraction first. We have an extra wrinkle in this problem, we're given two variables and while we can make two equations (one for *Pump A* & one for *Pump B*) those equations won't be equal. **We'll either have to do some tricky algebra or pick numbers.**

<u>Picking Numbers</u>

We can say that $Pump\ A = \sqrt{\dfrac{2s}{15}}$ and $Pump\ B = \sqrt{\dfrac{2s}{15}}$ where *Pump A* and *Pump B* represent the flow rates of the pumps. We are told that **Pump A has a flow rate of four times Pump B.** I'm going to go ahead and pick numbers and say that **Pump A = 4 and Pump B = 1.** Now that we've got 4 for *Pump A* & 1 for *Pump B*, I can solve the equations either by getting rid of the radical first or fraction first.

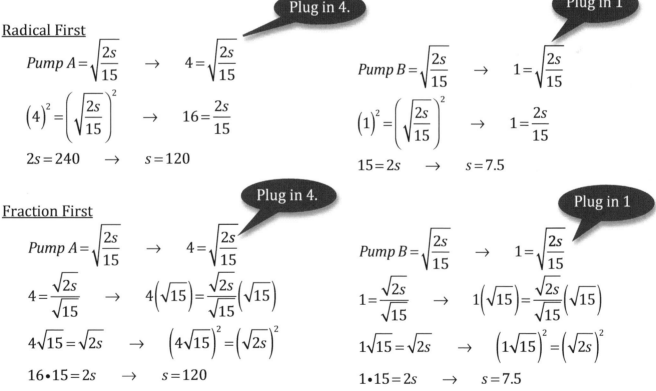

<u>Radical First</u>

Plug in 4.
$$Pump\ A = \sqrt{\frac{2s}{15}} \quad \rightarrow \quad 4 = \sqrt{\frac{2s}{15}}$$
$$(4)^2 = \left(\sqrt{\frac{2s}{15}}\right)^2 \quad \rightarrow \quad 16 = \frac{2s}{15}$$
$$2s = 240 \quad \rightarrow \quad s = 120$$

Plug in 1.
$$Pump\ B = \sqrt{\frac{2s}{15}} \quad \rightarrow \quad 1 = \sqrt{\frac{2s}{15}}$$
$$(1)^2 = \left(\sqrt{\frac{2s}{15}}\right)^2 \quad \rightarrow \quad 1 = \frac{2s}{15}$$
$$15 = 2s \quad \rightarrow \quad s = 7.5$$

<u>Fraction First</u>

Plug in 4.
$$Pump\ A = \sqrt{\frac{2s}{15}} \quad \rightarrow \quad 4 = \sqrt{\frac{2s}{15}}$$
$$4 = \frac{\sqrt{2s}}{\sqrt{15}} \quad \rightarrow \quad 4(\sqrt{15}) = \frac{\sqrt{2s}}{\sqrt{15}}(\sqrt{15})$$
$$4\sqrt{15} = \sqrt{2s} \quad \rightarrow \quad (4\sqrt{15})^2 = (\sqrt{2s})^2$$
$$16 \cdot 15 = 2s \quad \rightarrow \quad s = 120$$

Plug in 1.
$$Pump\ B = \sqrt{\frac{2s}{15}} \quad \rightarrow \quad 1 = \sqrt{\frac{2s}{15}}$$
$$1 = \frac{\sqrt{2s}}{\sqrt{15}} \quad \rightarrow \quad 1(\sqrt{15}) = \frac{\sqrt{2s}}{\sqrt{15}}(\sqrt{15})$$
$$1\sqrt{15} = \sqrt{2s} \quad \rightarrow \quad (1\sqrt{15})^2 = (\sqrt{2s})^2$$
$$1 \cdot 15 = 2s \quad \rightarrow \quad s = 7.5$$

To finish the problem, we'll need to find, "Pump A's impeller is how many times the speed of Pump B's impeller." That's a ratio, division gives us how many "times" a number goes into another number.

$$\frac{Pump\ A}{Pump\ B} = \frac{120}{7.5} = 16$$

Algebra

To solve this problem algebraically, we've got to set the equations equal. To do that, we'll need to multiply *Pump B* by 4 to make it equal to *Pump A*.

$$Pump\ A = 4\left(Pump\ B\right)$$

Now we can solve. In this case, it'll be easier to get rid of the radicals first and I'm just going to show that way.

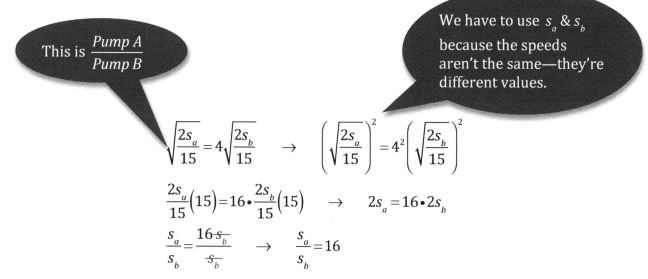

This is $\dfrac{Pump\ A}{Pump\ B}$

We have to use s_a & s_b because the speeds aren't the same—they're different values.

$$\sqrt{\frac{2s_a}{15}} = 4\sqrt{\frac{2s_b}{15}} \quad \rightarrow \quad \left(\sqrt{\frac{2s_a}{15}}\right)^2 = 4^2\left(\sqrt{\frac{2s_b}{15}}\right)^2$$

$$\frac{2s_a}{15}(15) = 16 \cdot \frac{2s_b}{15}(15) \quad \rightarrow \quad 2s_a = 16 \cdot 2s_b$$

$$\frac{s_a}{s_b} = \frac{16s_b}{s_b} \quad \rightarrow \quad \frac{s_a}{s_b} = 16$$

Answer choice **B** is correct.

Wrap Up

What You Need to Know
- ✓ The rules of exponents and roots.
- ✓ How to deal with fractions in equations

Videos

Radical Expressions

The Strategies
- ✓ Some questions work better by removing the radical first, some the fraction. Use whatever works for you.
- ✓ Remember that roots and exponents can cancel each other.

Related Skills
- ✓ Fractions

- ✓ Exponents

- ✓ Rational Expressions

Intermediate Algebra: Radical Expressions

1. If x is a real number such that $x^2 = 16$ then which of the following is/are the solution(s) to $x + x^2 - 2x$?

~~A.~~ 12
B. 20
C. 4
D. 4, 12
E. 12, 20

$x^2 = 16$
$x = \pm 4$

$4 * 16 - 8$

$4 + 8$
$-4 + 16 + 8$
$4 + 16$

2. If the expression $\sqrt{x-7} + 5 = 10$, then $x = ?$

A. 232
B. 32
C. 18
D. 82
E. 102

$\sqrt{x-7} + 5 = 10$
$(\sqrt{x-7}) = (5)$
$x - 7 = 25$
$x = 32$

3. What is the value of $\sqrt[3]{x^3 - y^3}$ when $x = \sqrt[3]{18}$ and $y = \sqrt[3]{-6}$?

A. $3\sqrt[3]{2}$
B. $\sqrt[3]{12}$
C. $\sqrt[3]{19}$
D. $2\sqrt[3]{3}$
E. 4

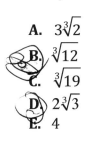

$3\overline{)24}$

$3\sqrt{8}\ \sqrt[3]{3}$

$2\sqrt[3]{3}$

4. What is a value of the expression $\sqrt{\dfrac{x}{2a}}$ if $x = 1$ and $a = 2$?

A. $\dfrac{1}{2}$
B. $\dfrac{1}{16}$
C. $\sqrt{2}$
D. $\dfrac{\sqrt{2}}{2}$
E. $\dfrac{1}{8}$

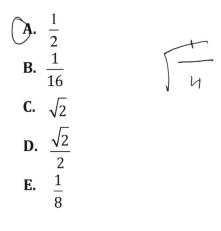

5. Given that $\sqrt{3x} + 6 = 15$, $x = ?$

A. 147
B. 9
C. 49
D. 63
E. 27

$(\sqrt{3x})^2 = (9)^{81}$

$3x =$

6. The solution set of $\sqrt{x+5} \leq 4$ is the set of real numbers x such that:

A. $x \leq -1$
B. $x \geq -1$
C. $x \geq 11$
D. $x \leq 11$
E. $x \leq 21$

$x + 5 \leq 6$

$x \leq 11$

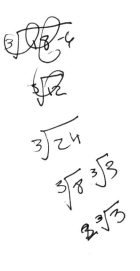

-265-

Radical Expressions: Solutions

1. If x is a real number such that $x^2 = 16$ then which of the following is/are the solution(s) to $x^2 - x$

Correct Answer E

The trick on remembering that all numbers have two square roots: 16 has square roots, 4 and -4. You can find the two values for x by rewriting as a difference of squares or by taking the root of both sides.

Difference of Squares: $x^2 = 16$ → $x^2 - 16 = 0$ → $(x+4)(x-4) = 0$
So, the factors are $x + 4 = 0$ and $x - 4 = 0$
The solutions are 4 & -4.

Square Root: $x^2 = 16$ → $\sqrt{x^2} = \sqrt{16}$ → $x = 4$ & -4

Now plug both 4 & -4 in the second expression.

Positive 4	Negative 4
$x^2 - x = ?$	$x^2 - x = ?$
$4^2 - 4 = ?$	$-4^2 - (-4) = ?$
$16 - 4 = 12$	$16 + 4 = 20$

> While we tend to focus on positive roots, remember each positive number has both a positive and a negative root.

Answer choice **E** is correct.

What You May Have Done Wrong

A. This is a halfway answer. You only found the solutions to $x^2 = 16$, you forgot to plug them in the second equation.
B. You got the solution for -4, but didn't get the +4 solution.
C. This is the hasty answer, and a halfway answer.
D. You may have made an operations error, incorrectly calculating the -4 answer.

2. If the expression $\sqrt{x-7} + 5 = 10$, then $x = ?$

Correct Answer B

First, group the like terms by moving the +5 to the other side of the equation and then square both sides

$$\sqrt{x-7} + 5 = 10 \quad \rightarrow \quad \sqrt{x-7} = 5$$
$$\left(\sqrt{x-7}\right)^2 = 5^2 \quad \rightarrow \quad x - 7 = 25$$
$$x = 32$$

Answer choice **B** is correct.

What You May Have Done Wrong

A. You made an algebra error when combining like terms, adding 5.
C. You made an algebra error. You subtracted 7 when you should add.
D. You didn't combine your like terms first. *We can only square sides, not individual terms.*
E. You didn't combine your like terms first. *We can only square sides, not individual terms.*

3. What is the value of $\sqrt[3]{x^3 - y^3}$ when $x = \sqrt[3]{18}$ and $y = \sqrt[3]{-6}$?

Correct Answer D

This problem tests your understanding of cancelling radicals with exponents. It also has a simplification component at the end.

Let's plug in and solve.

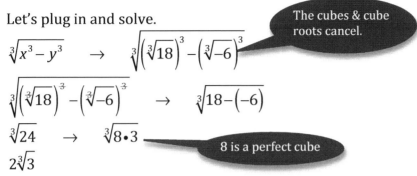

The cubes & cube roots cancel.

$$\sqrt[3]{x^3 - y^3} \quad \rightarrow \quad \sqrt[3]{\left(\sqrt[3]{18}\right)^3 - \left(\sqrt[3]{-6}\right)^3}$$

$$\sqrt[3]{\left(\sqrt[3]{18}\right)^3 - \left(\sqrt[3]{-6}\right)^3} \quad \rightarrow \quad \sqrt[3]{18 - (-6)}$$

$$\sqrt[3]{24} \quad \rightarrow \quad \sqrt[3]{8 \cdot 3}$$

8 is a perfect cube

$$2\sqrt[3]{3}$$

Answer choice **D** is correct.

What You May Have Done Wrong

A. You probably arrived at the right answer, but chose hastily.
B. You made an algebra error subtracting 6 instead of adding.
C. You may misunderstand the nature of cubes and cube roots.
E. You may misunderstand the nature of cubes and cube roots.

4. What is a value of the expression $\sqrt{\dfrac{x}{2a}}$ if $x = 1$ and $a = 2$?

Correct Answer A

This is a relatively straightforward plug-in problem. Let's plug in and solve:

$$\sqrt{\frac{x}{2a}} \quad \rightarrow \quad \sqrt{\frac{1}{2(2)}} \quad \rightarrow \quad \sqrt{\frac{1}{4}} = \frac{1}{2}$$

The square root of any fraction less than one will be *greater* than the number you took the root of. The square root of ¼ is actually ½.

Review *Elementary Algebra: Exponents* for more

Answer choice **A** is correct.

What You May Have Done Wrong

B. You either miscalculated, or forgot that a negative exponent means that *a* must be flipped to the denominator you also incorrectly reduced the coefficients.
C. You either miscalculated, or forgot that a negative exponent means that *a* must be flipped to the denominator
D. You multiplied the exponents in the numerator (you should have added.
E. You either forgot, or incorrectly dealt with variable *a*.

5. Given that $\sqrt{3x} + 6 = 15$, $x = ?$

Correct Answer E

This is another equation that can be solved by isolating the radical, squaring, and solving.

$$\sqrt{3x} + 6 = 15 \quad \rightarrow \quad \sqrt{3x} = 9$$

$$\left(\sqrt{3x}\right)^2 = 9^2 \quad \rightarrow \quad 3x = 81$$

$$x = 27$$

Answer choice **E** is correct.

<u>What You May Have Done Wrong</u>
- **A.** You made an algebra error. You added 6 instead of subtracting.
- **B.** You made an operations error (most likely). You squared the three inside the square root. Remember, that is the square root of three; its square is 3, not 9.
- **C.** You may have made an algebra error (adding 6) and compounded it by squaring the 3 (to 9) under the radical.
- **D.** You did not isolate the radical before squaring. You can only square sides, not terms.

6. The solution set of $\sqrt{x+5} \leq 4$ **is the set of real numbers x such that:**

Correct Answer D

Solving a radical inequality follows the same steps as following a radical equation. You isolate the radical, square both sides of the equation, and solve. In this case, the radical is already isolated.

$$\sqrt{x+5} \leq 4 \quad \rightarrow \quad \left(\sqrt{x+5}\right)^2 \leq 4^2$$

$$x + 5 \leq 16 \quad \rightarrow \quad x \leq 11$$

Answer choice **D** is correct.

<u>What You May Have Done Wrong</u>
- **A.** Most likely you only squared the side with the radical, and you did not square the other side. You may have ignored the radical altogether.
- **B.** Most likely you only squared the side with the radical, and you did not square the other side. You also flipped the inequality side, which you should *only* do if you divide by a negative number (not the case here).
- **C.** You also flipped the inequality side, which you should *only* do if you divide by a negative number (not the case here).
- **E.** This is an algebra error. You added 5 to 16 instead of subtracting. error.

Background

You're probably most familiar with *i* from the quadratic equation and imaginary zeroes. Quadratic equation questions are exceedingly rare, and usually we deal with complex numbers in terms of operations and *not* imaginary zeroes. On the ACT, *complex numbers* questions are definition based.

What You Need to Know

- ✓ The definition of *i*
- ✓ Treat *i* like a variable except when it's to a power other than 1
- ✓ You can't leave *i* in the denominator of a fraction.

Definitions: Imaginary & Complex Numbers

i **is the square root of -1.** Because we can't have a real root of a negative number, *i* **is imaginary.** $i = \sqrt{-1}$ & $i^2 = -1$

There's a *video* on *complex numbers*

Why can't we have a negative square root?

Any number multiplied by itself will result in a positive number (or zero). For example, -1 x -1 = 1.

Imaginary numbers include, $\sqrt{-4} = 2i, \sqrt{-9} = 3i$

In fact, the graph of the function $y = \sqrt{x}$ starts at 0, it's never negative.

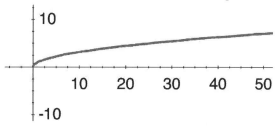

Definitions: Imaginary & Complex Numbers

Technically, all numbers are complex numbers. But we think of complex numbers as ***a real number + coefficient times I*** (for example 2*i* or *i*) is a complex number.

$$2 + i$$

The real part   The imaginary part

Rules of the Road: Imaginary & Complex Numbers

Treat *i* like a variable *but* remember that i^2 is equal to -1. Whenever *i* is to a power greater than 1, you'll have to factor -1's out.

ACT Examples: Imaginary & Complex Numbers

1. If $i = \sqrt{-1}$ and $i^2 + i^x = 0$, which could be a value for x?

A. 1
B. 2

This is a great mark-off question.

C. 3
D. 4
E. 5

Solve

If you're really comfortable with i, you may not need to do anything at all. Otherwise, just test the answer choices and mark-off as you go.

$$i^2 + i^x = 0$$
$$-1 + i^x = 0$$
$$i^x = 1$$

Get the term containing x by itself.

Check each answer choice to see what power will make i equal positive 1.

A. $1 \rightarrow i^1 \rightarrow i$
B. $2 \rightarrow i^2 \rightarrow -1$
C. $3 \rightarrow i^3 \rightarrow -1 + i$
D. $4 \rightarrow i^4 \rightarrow +1$
E. $5 \rightarrow i^5 \rightarrow +1 + i$

2. If $i = \sqrt{-1}$, which is equivalent to $(3 - i)(4 + i)$?

A. $12 - i + i^2$
B. $13 - i$
C. $11 + i$
D. $11 - i$
E. 7

Treat i like a variable

Solve

This is a straightforward FOIL problem:

First	Outer	Inner	Last
$3 \cdot 4 = 12$	$3 \cdot i = 3i$	$-i \cdot 4 = -4i$	$-i \cdot i = -i^2 = -(-1) = +1$

$$12 + 3i - 4i + 1 = \mathbf{13 - i}$$
Answer **B** is correct.

Signs and i can be tricky. Be careful!

3. If $i = \sqrt{-1}$, which is equivalent to $\dfrac{i}{i-1} \cdot \dfrac{i^3}{i+1}$?

    A. ½
    B. 2
    C. -½
    D. -2
    E. 1

Review Intermediate Algebra: Rational Expressions

Solve

Essentially this is a *rational expression* question. You've got to multiply the fractions and deal with *i*.

You can't leave *i* in the denominator of a fraction. Just like the square root of a prime number, we can't have irrational numbers in the denominator of a fraction. I talk about this somewhat more in the video.

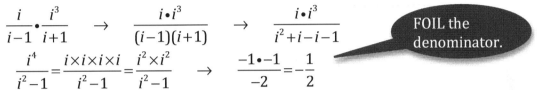

$$\frac{i}{i-1} \cdot \frac{i^3}{i+1} \rightarrow \frac{i \cdot i^3}{(i-1)(i+1)} \rightarrow \frac{i \cdot i^3}{i^2 + i - i - 1}$$

FOIL the denominator.

$$\frac{i^4}{i^2 - 1} = \frac{i \times i \times i \times i}{i^2 - 1} = \frac{i^2 \times i^2}{i^2 - 1} \rightarrow \frac{-1 \cdot -1}{-2} = -\frac{1}{2}$$

Answer **C** is correct.

Wrap Up

What You Need to Know
- ✓ The definition of *i*
- ✓ Treat *i* like a variable except when it's to a power other than 1
- ✓ You can't leave *i* in the denominator of a fraction.

Videos

    Complex Numbers

The Strategies
- ✓ Treat *i* like a variable except when it's to a power greater than 1.
- ✓ Complex numbers with the form *number + coefficient* x *i* have to be FOILed to get rid of the *i*.
- ✓ *i* is irrational and can't be in the denominator of a fraction.

Related Skills
- ✓ Fractions
- ✓ Rational Expressions
- ✓ Quadratics

1. If $i = \sqrt{-1}$ and $6i^x$ is a negative integer, what could be the value of x?

A. 1
B. 3
C. 4
D. 5
E. 6

2

2. If $i = \sqrt{-1}$ which of the following is equivalent to $(1-i)(3+4i)$?

F. $7 + i$
G. $3 - 4i$
H. $-1 + i$
J. $7 + 7i$
K. $3 + 4i$

$3 + 4i - 3i - 4i^2$

$3 + i - 4(-1)$

$3 + 4 + 1$

$7 + i$

3. The product of two complex numbers is 13. If one of the numbers is $3 + 2i$, what is the other number?

A. $3 + 2i$
B. i
C. $3 - 2i$
D. $9 + i$
E. $3 - i$

$(3+2i)(3-i)$

$9 - 3i + 6i + 2$

$3 + 2i(3+2i)$

$9 + 12i - 4i^2$

$3 + 2i(3-2i$

$9 - 6i + 6i + 4i^2$

$3i$ $9 - 4$

5

$(3-2i)(3+2i)$

$9 - 4(-1)$

$9 + 4$

$3 + 2i(9+i)$

$27 + 3i + 18i + 2i^2$

$27 + 21i - 2$

4. If $i = \sqrt{-1}$, which is equivalent to $\dfrac{i+4}{i^2} \cdot \dfrac{(i-4)}{2i}$?

F. $\dfrac{15i}{2}$
G. $\dfrac{-15i}{2}$
H. $6 - i$
J. $\dfrac{17i}{2}$
K. $8i$

$i^2 \to -16$

$\dfrac{i^2 - 16}{2i^3}$

$\dfrac{-1 - 16}{2(-1)}$

$\dfrac{-17}{2i} \left(\dfrac{1}{i}\right)$ $\dfrac{-17(\sqrt{-1})}{2i}$

$\dfrac{-17(\sqrt{-1})}{2}$ $\dfrac{-17}{2(-1)}$

5. If $i = \sqrt{-1}$, $\dfrac{6}{5+i}$ is equivalent to?

A. $\dfrac{3i}{2}$
B. $\dfrac{1i}{4}$
C. $\dfrac{15-3i}{13}$
D. $\dfrac{3i}{13}$
E. $\dfrac{9+3i}{13}$

$\dfrac{6}{5+\sqrt{-1}}$

Complex Numbers: Solutions

1. If $i = \sqrt{-1}$ and $6i^x$ is a negative integer, what could be the value of x?

Correct Answer E

This is a mark off question. Let's look at each answer choice.

A. $6i^1 \rightarrow 6i^1 = 6i$

   $6i = $ not an integer

B. $6i^3 \rightarrow 6i^3 = 6(-1)i$

   $-6i \rightarrow$ not an integer

C. $6i^4 \rightarrow 6i^2i^2 = 6(-1)(-1)$

   $6 = $ not a negative integer

D. $6i^5 \rightarrow 6i^2i^2i = 6(-1)(-1)i$

   $6i = $ not an integer

E. $6i^6 \rightarrow 6i^2i^2i^2$

   $6(-1)(-1)(-1)$

   $-6 = $ a negative integer!

Answer Choice **E** is correct.

2. If $i = \sqrt{-1}$, which of the following is equivalent to $(1-i)(3+4i)$?

Correct Answer F

This is a FOIL question. We treat i like a variable except when i is to a power other than 1.

First	Outer	Inner	Last
$1 \cdot 3 = 3$	$1 \cdot 4i = 4i$	$-i \cdot 3 = -3i$	$-i \cdot 4i = -4(i^2) = 4$

Let's combine like terms:

$3 + 4i - 3i + 4$

$3 + 4 + 4i - 3i$

$7 + i$

This problem is faster to solve using a graphing calculator, use the i button above the decimal (second → decimal on TI calculators).

Answer choice **F** is correct.

<u>What You May Have Done Wrong</u>

  G. You may not have FOILED, and you also neglected that $i \times i$ is i^2.
  H. You failed to remember the $(-)$ in front of $-4i^2$.
  J. You got your middle terms incorrect. Most likely you dropped the (-) from i when you multiplied your inner terms.
  K. You may not have FOILED; you may have tried to add the terms.

3. The product of two complex numbers is 13. If one of the numbers is 3 + 2*i*, what is the other number?

Correct Answer C

We know that $(3 + 2i)$(some number) = 13. Because the equation is equal to 15, we'll need to multiply $(3+2i)$ by a complex number that allows the *i*'s to cancel. *We know we have to multiply binomials, and we know they cannot have a middle term.* To cancel out that middle term, we've got to use a difference of squares.

$$(3 + 2i)(3 - 2i)$$

Let's FOIL to check...

First	**Outer**	**Inner**	**Last**
$3 \cdot 3 = 9$	$3 \cdot -2i = -6i$	$2i \cdot 3 = 6i$	$2i \cdot -2i = -4(i^2) = 4$

$$9 - 6i + 6i + 4 = 13$$

If you didn't pick up the difference of squares trick; this problem works great in a graphing calculator. The equation looks like this $(3 + 2i)$(some number) = 13. So we can divide 13 by $(3+2i)$ to find the answer. **Either way you'll get 3 – 2*i*.**

Answer choice **C** is correct.

<u>What You May Have Done Wrong</u>
   A. You may have guessed or missed a sign.
   B. We need to distribute the *i*, so multiplying by *i* wouldn't get rid of the *I*; it would just transfer *i* to the 3.
   D. This is a calculation or conceptual error.
   E. You incorrectly calculated the second term,

4. If $i = \sqrt{-1}$, which is equivalent to $\dfrac{i+4}{i^2} \cdot \dfrac{i-4}{2i}$?

Correct Answer J

This is an interesting fraction/complex number question. You can simplify the left fraction, but it would be a little more complicated. I'll multiply the fractions first.

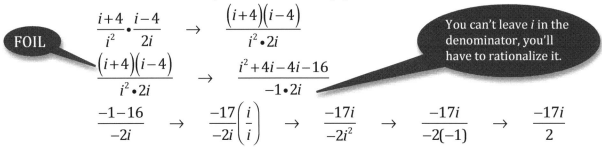

This problem is most quickly solved by using a graphing calculator, use the *i* button above the decimal (second → decimal on TI calculators). You'll have to translate the decimal coefficient to fraction form. Please learn how to do this by hand, but you can use [Math] [Enter] [Enter] it is worthwhile, however, to look at the math.

Answer choice **J** is correct.

<u>What You May Have Done Wrong</u>
   F. You incorrectly calculated your numerator as 15, probably by miscalculating 4 x -4 as 16 (instead of -16). You also made a sign mistake with the fraction itself.
   G. You incorrectly calculated your numerator as 15, probably by miscalculating 4 x -4 as 16 (instead of -16). You may have made a mistake converting from decimal form.
   H. You cross-multiplied, and you may want to review fractions.
   K. You probably cancelled incorrectly (cancelling i^2 from top and bottom and not combining the like terms in the numerator.

5. If $i = \sqrt{-1}$, $\dfrac{7}{5+i}$ is equivalent to?

Correct Answer C

We've got to rationalize the denominator, because i is an irrational number and we can't have irrational numbers in the denominator of a fraction. We treat $5 + i$ as a binomial, so we'll have to multiply (FOIL) by another binomial to get the middle terms to cancel. To do that, you'll use a *conjugate* to make a *difference of squares*.

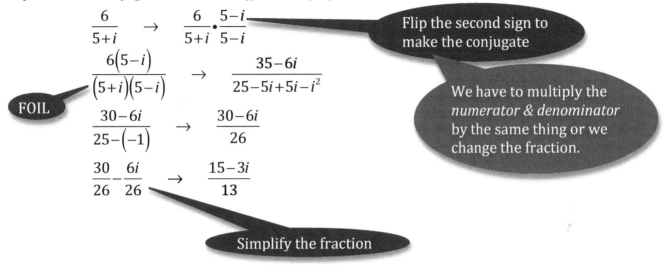

$$\frac{6}{5+i} \quad \rightarrow \quad \frac{6}{5+i} \cdot \frac{5-i}{5-i}$$

Flip the second sign to make the conjugate

$$\frac{6(5-i)}{(5+i)(5-i)} \quad \rightarrow \quad \frac{35-6i}{25-5i+5i-i^2}$$

FOIL

We have to multiply the *numerator & denominator* by the same thing or we change the fraction.

$$\frac{30-6i}{25-(-1)} \quad \rightarrow \quad \frac{30-6i}{26}$$

$$\frac{30}{26} - \frac{6i}{26} \quad \rightarrow \quad \frac{15-3i}{13}$$

Simplify the fraction

Answer choice **C** is correct.

What You May Have Done Wrong

A. You probably tried to multiply by $\dfrac{i}{i}$ which would just shift the i in the denominator.

B. You made an arithmetic error in the denominator and you failed to multiply the numerator by the conjugate.

D. You probably multiplied the numerator incorrectly.

E. This is a compound error; review your steps.

Background

Like many of the smaller topics on Intermediate Algebra, logs don't relate many other topics. Fortunately, there's not much to remember.

What You Need to Know
- ✓ Most log questions are based on the definition of logs. Put the logs in exponent form.
- ✓ The majority of questions can be solved using a graphing calculator. But some questions can't be solved on your calculator, and all log questions are easier and faster to solve by hand.

Definitions: Logarithms

> **Logarithms** tell us the exponent that will make a number to equal different number. **Logs are re-arranged exponents.**

$$y = b^x \text{ is the same as } \log_b(y) = x$$

Example: The Definition of Logs

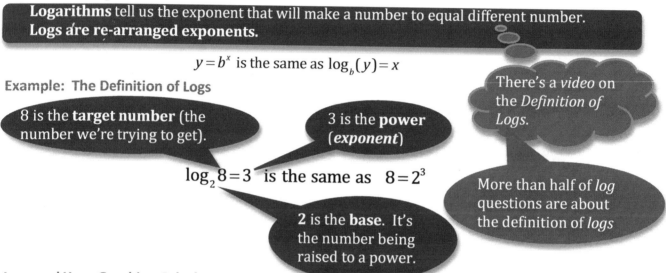

8 is the **target number** (the number we're trying to get).

3 is the **power** (*exponent*)

$$\log_2 8 = 3 \text{ is the same as } 8 = 2^3$$

There's a *video* on the *Definition of Logs.*

More than half of *log* questions are about the definition of *logs*

2 is the **base**. It's the number being raised to a power.

Logs and Your Graphing Calculator

This is one of the few times when you *can* solve quite a few problems with your graphing calculator. That said, the ACT can (and does) write problems to make your graphing calculator useless. **It's often easier and faster to skip the calculator and know the definition of logs.**

How to Use the "logBASE" on a TI Graphing Calculator
1. Go to the MATH menu
2. Either hit the A button, or scroll up/down until you get to A: logBASE(

```
NORMAL FLOAT AUTO REAL RADIAN MP
MATH NUM CMPLX PROB FRAC
4↑ ³√(
5: ˣ√
6: fMin(
7: fMax(
8: nDeriv(
9: fnInt(
0: summation Σ(
A: logBASE(
B: Solver…
```

3. You'll have this on your screen; enter your **base** and your **target number**. Hit ENTER to solve.

```
NORMAL FLOAT AUTO REAL RADIAN MP
log■(▦)
```

1. If $\log_4 64 = x$, what is x?

    A. 2
    B. 8
    C. 4
    D. 3
    E. 6

Solve

You can use your graphing calculator as discussed on the previous page and get your answer. **But, your graphing calculator won't be able to solve every log problem you run into, so learn the definition of logs!**

You can also re-write this as an exponential equation and solve.

$$\log_4 64 = x$$
$$4^x = 64$$

Now determine (if you don't know) what power of 4 equals 64.

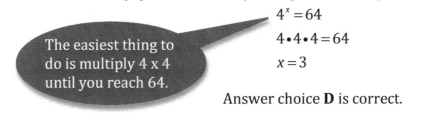

$$4^x = 64$$
$$4 \cdot 4 \cdot 4 = 64$$
$$x = 3$$

The easiest thing to do is multiply 4 x 4 until you reach 64.

Answer choice **D** is correct.

2. Which of the following is a value of x that satisfies $\log_x 27 = 3$?

    A. 3
    B. 4
    C. -3
    D. 1
    E. 9

You *can't* do this problem in your calculator.

Solve

This is a good example of a problem that you *can't* solve using your graphing calculator. We'll need to convert the log into exponent form and then we'll be able to solve for x.

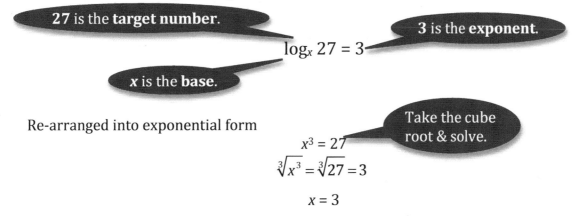

27 is the **target number**.

3 is the **exponent**.

$$\log_x 27 = 3$$

x is the **base**.

Re-arranged into exponential form

Take the cube root & solve.

$$x^3 = 27$$
$$\sqrt[3]{x^3} = \sqrt[3]{27} = 3$$
$$x = 3$$

Answer choice **A** is correct

$$x^3 = 27$$
$$x = 5$$

Two logarithm properties show up on the ACT: the power property and the product/quotient property. **Unlike problems about the definition of logs, properties problems are best left in logs and solved by applying the properties.**

Power Property: exponents in a log can be written as a coefficient in front of the log.

$$\log_{10} x^y = y\log_{10} x$$

$$\log_{10} x^3 = 3\log_{10} x$$

The **exponent** can be rewritten as a **coefficient**.

Product/Quotient Properties allows us to split or combine logs.

Product Power: $\log_{10} xy = \log_{10} x + \log_{10} y$

Quotient Power: $\log_{10} \dfrac{x}{y} = \log_{10} x - \log_{10} y$

Remind you of *multiplying/dividing* exponents?

Review in *Elementary Algebra: Exponents*

ACT Examples: Logarithm Properties

1. Which of the following expressions is equivalent to $\log(3y)$?

    A. $\log 3y + \log$
    B. $\log y - \log 3$
    C. $\log 3 + \log y$
    D. $3\log y$
    E. $\log 3 - \log y$

    There is no calculation required. This is a straight reading of log properties.

    Solve

    This is a log properties problem. You've have to know how the *product property* works. If, however, you were confused you could do a decent job of marking off answers that just wouldn't make sense (the subtraction in **B** & **E** doesn't make sense, for example).

    $$\log 3y$$
    $$\log 3 + \log y$$

    There's a *video* on *Log Properties*

    Answer choice **C** is correct

2. Which of the following expressions is equivalent to $\log(xy)^2$?

A. $2\log x + \log y$
B. $\log x^2 + 2\log y^2$
C. $2\log x + 2\log y$
D. $2\log x^2 + 2\log y^2$
E. $2\log - 2\log y$

This question requires us to apply the *power property* and the *product property*.

Solve

This problem involves *both power property* & the *product property*. Start by removing the parentheses using the power property.

Remove the *power* first

$\log(xy)^2$
$2\log(xy)$
$2\log x + 2\log y$

Now deal with the *product property*

Answer choice **C** is correct

Wrap Up

What You Need to Know
- ✓ The definition of logs and how to work with that definition
- ✓ The power property, product property, and quotient property of logs

Videos

Log Definitions

Log Properties

The Strategies
- ✓ Most log questions are based on the definition of logs. Put the logs in exponent form.
- ✓ The majority of questions can be solved using a graphing calculator. But some questions can't be solved on your calculator, and all log questions are easier and faster to solve by hand.

Related Skills
- ✓ Exponents

Intermediate Algebra: Logarithms

1. What values satisfies the equation

$\log_x 8 = 3$?

    A. 2.33
    B. 2
    C. 24
    D. 0.52
    E. 1.89

4. If a is an integer and $a > 1$, $\log_a \left(a^3\right)^2 = $?

    F. 5
    G. 1
    H. $\dfrac{3}{2}$
    J. 6
    K. $\dfrac{2}{3}$

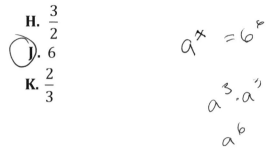

2. The value of $\log_{12}\left(12^4\right) = $?

    F. 4
    G. 12
    H. 8
    J. 2
    K. 6

5. If $\log_b x = a$ and $\log_b y = z$, then

$\log_b\left(\sqrt{xy}\right) = $?

    A. $a + z$
    B. $2(a + z)$
    C. $\dfrac{1}{2}(a+z)$
    D. az
    E. $2az$

3. For all values where $x > 1$ and

$\log_x\left(\dfrac{x^y}{x^5}\right) = -3$, what is the value of y?

    A. 2
    B. 8
    C. -15
    D. 15
    E. -8

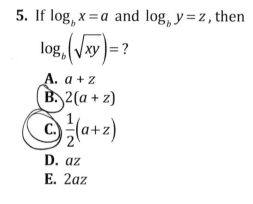

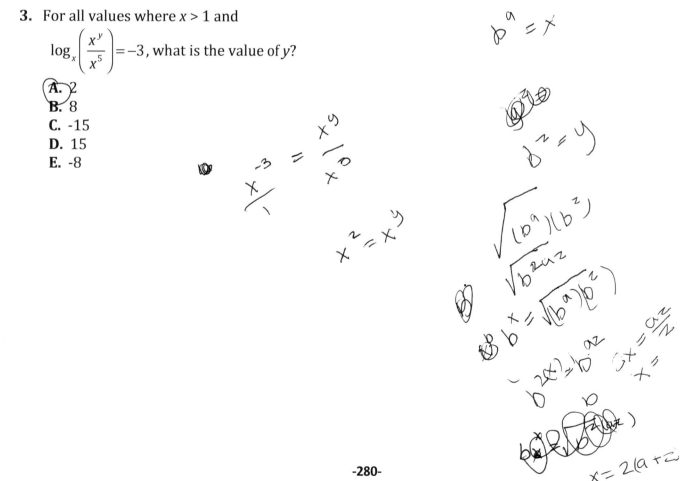

Logarithms: Solutions

1. What values satisfies the equation $\log_x 8 = 3$?

Correct Answer B

This is a really common format for log problems. Turning the log into exponential notation is the best way to solve these problems.

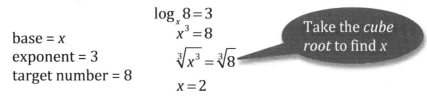

base = x
exponent = 3
target number = 8

$$\log_x 8 = 3$$
$$x^3 = 8$$
$$\sqrt[3]{x^3} = \sqrt[3]{8}$$
$$x = 2$$

Take the *cube root* to find x

Answer choice **B** is correct.

What You May Have Done Wrong
    A. You divided 8 by 3. Review logs.
    C. You multiplied 8 by 3. Review logs.
    D. This is $\log_8 3$. Remember that the ACT doesn't require you to use a calculator, and this would

        be a really tough calculation to do without one.
    E. This is $\log_3 8$. Remember that the ACT doesn't require you to use a calculator, and this would

        be a really tough calculation to do without one.

2. The value of $\log_{12}\left(12^4\right) = ?$

Correct Answer F

This is a great question to do in your calculator (although I swear it's faster if you're comfortable with the definition of logs).

On a TI Graphing Calculator
    Hit the MATH menu and scroll down/up to logBASE(
    Put 12 and (12^4) in the appropriate spots.
    Hit ENTER

Using the Definition of Logs
    base = 12
    target number = 4
    exponent = x

$$\log_{12}\left(12^4\right)$$
$$12^x = 12^4$$

Because the numbers are equal and the bases are the same, we can say that the **exponents are equal**.

$$x = 4$$

Answer choice **F** is correct.

What You May Have Done Wrong
    All of the wrong answer choices are conceptual errors. Review your steps.

3. For all values where $x > 1$ and $\log_x\left(\dfrac{x^y}{x^5}\right) = -3$, what is the value of y?

Correct Answer A

This is a log definition question that's requires you to know your exponent operations. Let's convert the log into exponential form.

base = x

exponent = -3

$$\log_x\left(\frac{x^y}{x^5}\right) = -3 \quad \rightarrow \quad x^{-3} = \frac{x^y}{x^5}$$

target number = $\left(\dfrac{x^y}{x^5}\right)$

To solve, let's get rid of the fraction and get x^y by itself.

$$x^{-3}\left(x^5\right) = \frac{x^y}{x^5}\left(x^5\right) \quad \rightarrow \quad x^2 = x^y$$

Because the bases are both x we can equate the exponents.

$$y = 2$$

Answer choice A is correct

<u>What You May Have Done Wrong</u>

B. You dealt with your exponents incorrectly, and this would result in a log of 3, not -3.

C. You *divided* the exponents when you should have subtracted.

D. You *divided* the exponents when you should have subtracted & made a sign mistake.

E. You had a sign problem.

4. If a is an integer and $a > 1$, $\log_a\left(a^3\right)^2 = ?$

Correct Answer J

This is a log definition question that also tests your skills with exponent operations. Let's look at the log.

base = a

target number = $\left(a^3\right)^2$ $\quad \log_a\left(a^3\right)^2$

exponent = x

Changing the log into exponential form: $a^x = \left(a^3\right)^2$

Because the *bases* are the same (they are both a), we can say that x (the answer to the log) is equal to the exponent of a on the right side of the equation.

$$a^x = \left(a^3\right)^2 \quad \rightarrow \quad a^x = a^{3 \cdot 2} = a^6$$

$$x = 6$$

$$\log_a\left(a^3\right)^2 = 6$$

> When we take a *power* to a *power*, **multiply the exponents.**

Answer choice J is correct.

<u>What You May Have Done Wrong:</u>

F. You *added* the exponents, instead of multiplying them.

G. You *subtracted* the exponents, instead of multiplying them.

H. You *divided* the exponents, instead of multiplying them.

K. You *divided* the exponents, instead of multiplying them.

5. If $\log_b x = a$ and $\log_b y = z$, then $\log_b\left(\sqrt{xy}\right) = ?$

Correct Answer C

This is a log properties problem. Log properties problems are best left in logs and the property applied.

First, xy is taken to a power (the square root), so using the **power property** we can get rid of the root. Square roots are the exponent 1/2.

$$\log_b\left(\sqrt{xy}\right) = \frac{1}{2}\log_b\left(xy\right)$$

The **power property** lets us move the exponent to a coefficient.

The **product property** let's us split the xy into two logs.

$$\frac{1}{2}\log_b\left(xy\right) = \frac{1}{2}\log_b x + \frac{1}{2}\log_b x$$

The **product property** lets us rewrite this as $\log x + \log y$.

Because $\log_b x = a$ and $\log_b y = z$, we can substitute a & z in for the two logs.

$$\frac{1}{2}\log_b\left(xy\right) = \frac{1}{2}a + \frac{1}{2}z$$

$$\frac{1}{2}\left(a+z\right)$$

Answer choice **C** is correct.

<u>What You May Have Done Wrong</u>
    A. You forgot to apply the *power property*
    B. You applied the *power property* incorrectly. Square roots are the exponent ½.
    D. You didn't correctly apply the *product property*.
    E. You applied neither property correctly. Review your steps.

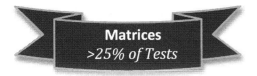

Background
Matrices problems are relatively simple on the ACT. Don't worry about some of the fancier applications (like expansions, or solving three variable systems of equations).

What You Need to Know
- ✓ When you can multiply matrices & how to do basic matrix multiplication
- ✓ How to solve one variable equations in matrices
- ✓ How to deal with plug-in determinant problems

Definitions: Matrices

A matrix is a rectangular array of numbers and/or variables arranged in rows and columns. A three by two matrix has three rows and two columns.

Rows $\longrightarrow$ $\begin{bmatrix} 1 & 2 \\ y & 1 \\ 0 & x \end{bmatrix}$ $\begin{bmatrix} 1 & 2 \\ y & 1 \\ 0 & x \end{bmatrix}$ **Columns** are *vertical*, **rows** are *horizontal*

Rules of the Road: Adding & Subtracting Matrices

To add or subtract matrices, the matrices must be the same size. Each term is added or subtracted to/by the term in the same spot on the other matrix.

$\begin{bmatrix} 1 & x \\ y & 2 \end{bmatrix}$ *and* $\begin{bmatrix} 1 \\ x \\ 2 \end{bmatrix}$ cannot be added because they have different dimensions.

Adding Matrices

$\begin{bmatrix} 1 & 0 \\ 1 & 2 \end{bmatrix} + \begin{bmatrix} 3 & 5 \\ 4 & 6 \end{bmatrix}$

$\begin{bmatrix} 1+3 & 0+5 \\ 1+2 & 4+6 \end{bmatrix} = \begin{bmatrix} 4 & 5 \\ 3 & 10 \end{bmatrix}$

Subtracting Matrices

$\begin{bmatrix} 1 & 0 \\ 1 & 2 \end{bmatrix} - \begin{bmatrix} 3 & 5 \\ 4 & 6 \end{bmatrix}$

$\begin{bmatrix} 1-3 & 0-5 \\ 1-2 & 4-6 \end{bmatrix} = \begin{bmatrix} -2 & -5 \\ -1 & -2 \end{bmatrix}$

ACT Examples: Matrix Operations

1. What is the value of x in following matrix equation?

$$4\begin{bmatrix} x & -2 \\ 3 & 5 \end{bmatrix} + \begin{bmatrix} 1 & 3 \\ 0 & 5 \end{bmatrix} = \begin{bmatrix} -3 & 1 \\ 3 & 10 \end{bmatrix}$$

A. -1
B. -4
C. -12
D. -6
E. 1

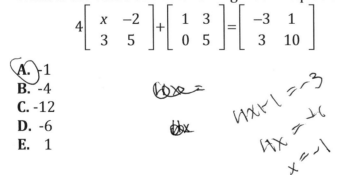

Solve

This is a multistep problem. You've got to do the scalar multiplication, "distributing" the 4 into the first matrix.

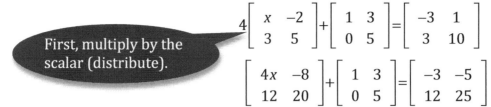

First, multiply by the scalar (distribute).

$$4\begin{bmatrix} x & -2 \\ 3 & 5 \end{bmatrix} + \begin{bmatrix} 1 & 3 \\ 0 & 5 \end{bmatrix} = \begin{bmatrix} -3 & 1 \\ 3 & 10 \end{bmatrix}$$

$$\begin{bmatrix} 4x & -8 \\ 12 & 20 \end{bmatrix} + \begin{bmatrix} 1 & 3 \\ 0 & 5 \end{bmatrix} = \begin{bmatrix} -3 & -5 \\ 12 & 25 \end{bmatrix}$$

Now that we've got the matrices simplified, we can work on the equation. We actually don't need much of the matrices; we're just interested in the x term. We can make an equation that looks like this:

We are only interested in the top left term in the matrices.

$$4x + 1 = -3$$
$$4x = -4$$
$$x = -1$$

We can boil the matrices into a single linear equation.

Answer choice **A** is correct.

Rules of the Road: Scalar Multiplication

Scalar multiplication is the simplest form of matrix multiplication. **Distribute the term outside the matrix to all spots in the matrix.**

$$x\begin{bmatrix} 1 & 0 \\ 3 & 2 \end{bmatrix} = \begin{bmatrix} 1x & 0x \\ 3x & 2x \end{bmatrix}$$

Rules of the Road: Matrix Multiplication

Matrix *multiplication* doesn't require matrices of the same size.
But, the *columns* of the *first* matrix must = the *rows* of the *second*.

columns of the first matrix = rows of the second matrix

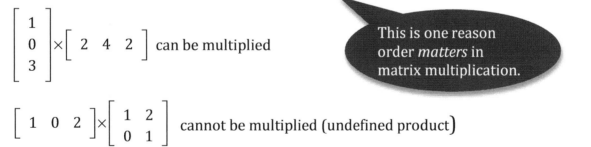

$$\begin{bmatrix} 1 \\ 0 \\ 3 \end{bmatrix} \times \begin{bmatrix} 2 & 4 & 2 \end{bmatrix} \text{ can be multiplied}$$

This is one reason order *matters* in matrix multiplication.

$$\begin{bmatrix} 1 & 0 & 2 \end{bmatrix} \times \begin{bmatrix} 1 & 2 \\ 0 & 1 \end{bmatrix} \text{ cannot be multiplied (undefined product)}$$

Rules of the Road: Matrix Multiplication (continued)

Steps to Solving

1. Make sure **the number of *columns* in the first matrix will equal the number of *rows* in the second ($c = r$).**
2. Find the size of the product. **The size of the product is the number or *rows* in the first matrix and the number of *columns* in the second matrix.**
3. Multiply the elements of each row in the first matrix by the elements of the columns in the second
4. Add those products together. That will give you your entries.

Don't fret: matrix multiplication on the ACT is very simple.

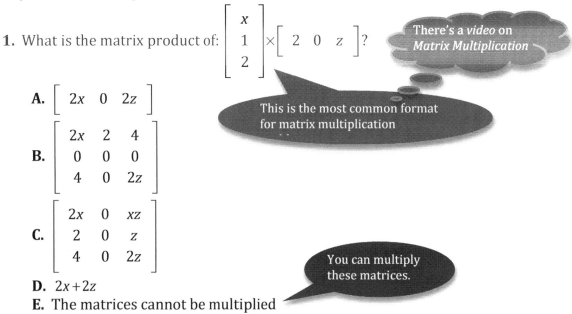

1. What is the matrix product of: $\begin{bmatrix} x \\ 1 \\ 2 \end{bmatrix} \times \begin{bmatrix} 2 & 0 & z \end{bmatrix}$?

There's a *video* on *Matrix Multiplication*

This is the most common format for matrix multiplication

A. $\begin{bmatrix} 2x & 0 & 2z \end{bmatrix}$

B. $\begin{bmatrix} 2x & 2 & 4 \\ 0 & 0 & 0 \\ 4 & 0 & 2z \end{bmatrix}$

C. $\begin{bmatrix} 2x & 0 & xz \\ 2 & 0 & z \\ 4 & 0 & 2z \end{bmatrix}$

You can multiply these matrices.

D. $2x + 2z$

E. The matrices cannot be multiplied

Solve

First, determine if you can multiply the matrix.

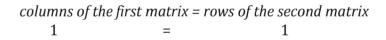

columns of the first matrix = rows of the second matrix
$$1 \quad = \quad 1$$

You can, if you want, determine the product size. The product size is the number of rows in the first matrix (3) and the number of columns in the second matrix (3). The resulting matrix is 3 x 3. You can mark off **A, D, & E**. Let's do the math:

$$\begin{bmatrix} x \\ 1 \\ 2 \end{bmatrix} \times \begin{bmatrix} 2 & 0 & z \end{bmatrix} = \begin{bmatrix} x \cdot 2 & x \cdot 0 & x \cdot z \\ 1 \cdot 2 & 1 \cdot 0 & 1 \cdot z \\ 2 \cdot 2 & 2 \cdot 0 & 2 \cdot z \end{bmatrix} = \begin{bmatrix} 2x & 0 & xz \\ 2 & 0 & z \\ 4 & 0 & 2z \end{bmatrix}$$

Answer choice **C** is correct.

2. Which of the matrix products are defined?

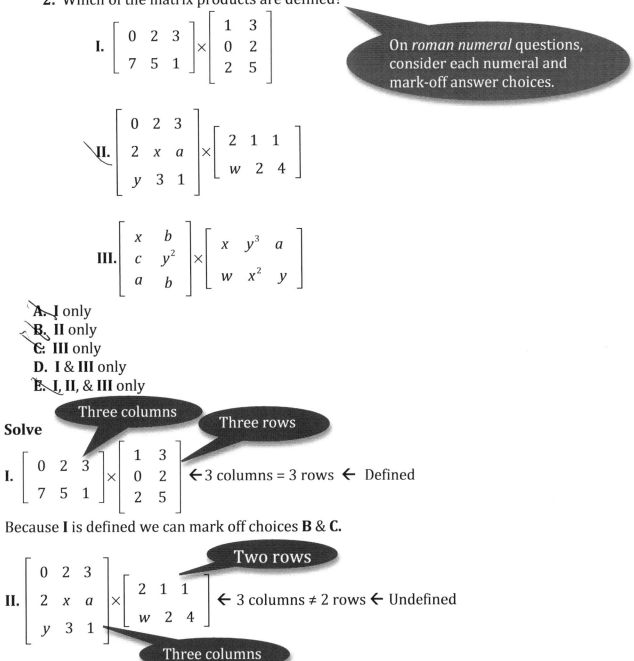

I. $\begin{bmatrix} 0 & 2 & 3 \\ 7 & 5 & 1 \end{bmatrix} \times \begin{bmatrix} 1 & 3 \\ 0 & 2 \\ 2 & 5 \end{bmatrix}$

On roman numeral questions, consider each numeral and mark-off answer choices.

II. $\begin{bmatrix} 0 & 2 & 3 \\ 2 & x & a \\ y & 3 & 1 \end{bmatrix} \times \begin{bmatrix} 2 & 1 & 1 \\ w & 2 & 4 \end{bmatrix}$

III. $\begin{bmatrix} x & b \\ c & y^2 \\ a & b \end{bmatrix} \times \begin{bmatrix} x & y^3 & a \\ w & x^2 & y \end{bmatrix}$

A. I only
B. II only
C. III only
D. I & III only
E. I, II, & III only

Solve

I. *Three columns* *Three rows*

$\begin{bmatrix} 0 & 2 & 3 \\ 7 & 5 & 1 \end{bmatrix} \times \begin{bmatrix} 1 & 3 \\ 0 & 2 \\ 2 & 5 \end{bmatrix}$ ← 3 columns = 3 rows ← Defined

Because **I** is defined we can mark off choices **B** & **C**.

II. $\begin{bmatrix} 0 & 2 & 3 \\ 2 & x & a \\ y & 3 & 1 \end{bmatrix} \times \begin{bmatrix} 2 & 1 & 1 \\ w & 2 & 4 \end{bmatrix}$ *Two rows* ← 3 columns ≠ 2 rows ← Undefined

Three columns

Because **II** is undefined we can mark off choice **E**.

III. $\begin{bmatrix} x & b \\ c & y^2 \\ a & b \end{bmatrix} \times \begin{bmatrix} x & y^3 & a \\ w & x^2 & y \end{bmatrix}$ *Two rows* ← 2 columns ≠ 2 rows ← Defined

Two columns

Because **III** is defined we can mark off choice **A**.

Answer choice **D** is correct.

Definition: Determinants

The *determinant* of a matrix is a number calculated from a square matrix. It is used for finding inverses & systems of equations.

The way we calculate the determinant of a 2 x 2 matrix is $ad - bc$, and a, b, c, d is defined as,

$$\begin{bmatrix} a & b \\ c & d \end{bmatrix}$$

There's a *video* on *determinants*.

The determinant of the matrix $\begin{bmatrix} 1 & 2 \\ 3 & 4 \end{bmatrix} = (1)(4) - (3)(2) = -2$

ACT Example: Determinants

1. The determinant of a 2-by-2 matrix is defined as $ad - bc$ where $\begin{bmatrix} a & b \\ c & d \end{bmatrix}$, what is

the determinant of the matrix $\begin{bmatrix} 2y & -y \\ 3x & -x \end{bmatrix}$, when $x = 4$ and $y = 2$?

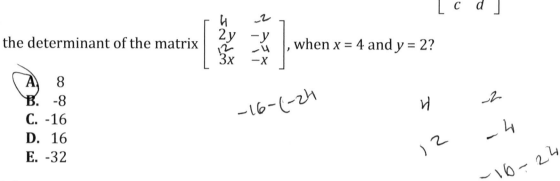

- **A.** 8
- **B.** -8
- **C.** -16
- **D.** 16
- **E.** -32

$-16 - (-24)$

$\begin{matrix} 4 & -2 \\ 12 & -4 \end{matrix}$

$-16 - 24$

Solve

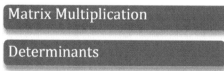

You could substitute 4 and 2 in first.

$ad - bc \quad \rightarrow \quad (2y)(-x) - (3x)(-y)$

$-2xy - (-3xy) \quad \rightarrow \quad -2 \cdot 4 \cdot 2 - (-3 \cdot 4 \cdot 2)$

$-16 + 24 = 8$

Answer choice **A** is correct.

Wrap Up

What You Need to Know
- ✓ When you can multiply matrices & how to do basic matrix multiplication
- ✓ How to solve one variable equations in matrices
- ✓ How to deal with plug-in determinant problems

Videos

Matrix Multiplication

Determinants

The Strategies
- ✓ For the most part, matrix operations questions are simple. Learn how to do them and leave the calculator out of it.
- ✓ Determinant questions are plug in problems.

Related Skills
- ✓ Algebra Operations

1. What is the matrix product of

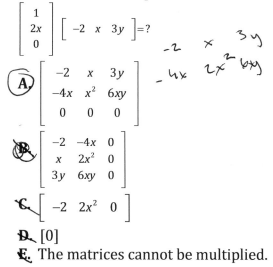

$$\begin{bmatrix} 1 \\ 2x \\ 0 \end{bmatrix} \begin{bmatrix} -2 & x & 3y \end{bmatrix} = ?$$

(handwritten) $-2 \quad x \quad 3y$
$-4x \quad 2x^2 \quad 6xy$

A. $\begin{bmatrix} -2 & x & 3y \\ -4x & x^2 & 6xy \\ 0 & 0 & 0 \end{bmatrix}$

B. $\begin{bmatrix} -2 & -4x & 0 \\ x & 2x^2 & 0 \\ 3y & 6xy & 0 \end{bmatrix}$

C. $\begin{bmatrix} -2 & 2x^2 & 0 \end{bmatrix}$

D. $[0]$

E. The matrices cannot be multiplied.

2. The determinant of a 2 by 2 matrix defined

as $\begin{bmatrix} a & b \\ c & d \end{bmatrix}$ is $ad - bc$. What is the

determinant of $\begin{bmatrix} 2 & x \\ -3x^2 & 3 \end{bmatrix}$?

F. $6 - 3x^3$
G. $6 + 3x^3$
H. $-9x^2 + 2x$
J. $-3x^3 - 6$
K. $-9x^2 + 2x$

(handwritten) $6 - (-3x^3$
$6 + 3x^3$

3. Solve the matrix equation for *x*.

$$\begin{bmatrix} 4 & 0 & 2 \\ 5 & 2 & 1 \\ 0 & 1 & 2x \end{bmatrix} - \begin{bmatrix} -3 & 2 & 0 \\ 0 & 6 & 2 \\ 1 & 2 & 3x \end{bmatrix} = \begin{bmatrix} 7 & 2 & 2 \\ 5 & 8 & 3 \\ 1 & 3 & 2 \end{bmatrix}$$

A. $\dfrac{2}{5}$

B. -3
C. 2
D. -2

E. $-\dfrac{2}{5}$

(handwritten) $2x - 3x = 2$
$-x = 2$
$x = -2$

4. The determinant of any 2 x 2 matrix

$\begin{bmatrix} a & b \\ c & d \end{bmatrix}$ is $ad - bc$. The determinant of

the $\begin{bmatrix} x+1 & 5 \\ 1 & x-3 \end{bmatrix}$ is equal to 0. What are

all possible values of *x*?

F. 2
G. 4
H. -1
J. 3
K. 4 & -2

(handwritten) $x^2 - 3x + x - 3 - 5 = 0$
$x^2 - 2x - 8 = 0$
$(x-4)(x+2) = 0$
$x - 4 = 0 \quad x + 2 = 0$
$x = 4 \qquad x = -2$

5. The number of rows in matrix A equals *c*. The number of columns in matrix B equals *r*. For which statement is the matrix product of AB defined?

A. $c \geq r$
B. $c > r$
C. $c = r$
D. $c \leq r$
E. $c < r$

(handwritten) $\begin{bmatrix} c \end{bmatrix} \begin{bmatrix} r \end{bmatrix}$

1. What is the matrix product of $\begin{bmatrix} 1 \\ 2x \\ 0 \end{bmatrix}$ $\begin{bmatrix} -2 & x & 3y \end{bmatrix}$ $=?$

Correct Answer A

First, we need to check if we can multiply these matrices. You can only multiply matrices if the number of **columns** in the **first matrix** equals the number of **rows** in the **second matrix**.

$$\begin{bmatrix} 1 \\ 2x \\ 0 \end{bmatrix} = one\ column \text{ and } \begin{bmatrix} -2 & x & 3y \end{bmatrix} = one\ row$$

Ok, we can go ahead with the multiplication. You can do this on your TI graphing calculator, but you have to enter both matrices and press a ton of buttons. It really is easier to multiply the matrices by hand.

$$\begin{bmatrix} 1 \\ 2x \\ 0 \end{bmatrix} \bullet \begin{bmatrix} -2 & x & 3y \end{bmatrix} \rightarrow \begin{bmatrix} 1\bullet(-2) & 1\bullet x & 1\bullet 3y \\ 2x\bullet(1) & 2x\bullet x & 2x\bullet 3y \\ 0\bullet(-2) & 0\bullet x & 0\bullet 3y \end{bmatrix} \rightarrow \begin{bmatrix} -2 & x & 3y \\ -4x & 2x^2 & 6xy \\ 0 & 0 & 0 \end{bmatrix}$$

Answer choice **A** is correct.

<u>What You May Have Done Wrong</u>
    B. You only multiplied the first row of the first matrix; all entries of both matrices are multiplied together.
    C. You multiplied your matrices incorrectly.
    D. You have a conceptual error, review matrix multiplication.
    E. You have a conceptual error, review matrix multiplication.

2. The determinant of a 2 by 2 matrix defined as $\begin{bmatrix} a & b \\ c & d \end{bmatrix}$ is $ad - bc$. What is the determinant of $\begin{bmatrix} 2 & x \\ -3x^2 & 3 \end{bmatrix}$?

Correct Answer G

This is a matrix based plug in problem. We're given the definition of the determinant and the matrix, so we need to set the problem up, plugging in the right values for a, b, c, & d.

$$a = 2 \quad b = x \quad c = -3x^2 \quad d = 3$$

Now solve:

$$ad - bc \quad \rightarrow \quad 2(3) - (x)(-3x^2)$$
$$6 - (-3x^3) \quad \rightarrow \quad 6 + 3x^3 \quad \rightarrow \quad 3x^3 + 6$$

Answer choice **G** is correct.

<u>What You May Have Done Wrong</u>
    F. You dropped a sign on the second term.
    H. You incorrectly found the determinant as $ab - cd$
    J. You flipped the terms of your determinant finding $bc - ad$
    K. You incorrectly calculated the second term.

3. Solve the matrix equation for x.

$$\begin{bmatrix} 4 & 0 & 2 \\ 5 & 2 & 1 \\ 0 & 1 & 2x \end{bmatrix} - \begin{bmatrix} -3 & 2 & 0 \\ 0 & 6 & 2 \\ 1 & 2 & 3x \end{bmatrix} = \begin{bmatrix} 7 & 2 & 2 \\ 5 & 8 & 3 \\ 1 & 3 & 2 \end{bmatrix}$$

Correct Answer D

This looks like a really complicated question, but it's actually pretty straightforward. All you'll need to do is solve for x and it's actually a straightforward linear equation. Every part of the matrix is solved (all the numbers) except for the very bottom right corner. Because we have numeric answers for everything, all we'll need to do is find x. So, re-write that part of the matrix as an equation.

$$2x - 3x = 2 \quad \rightarrow \quad -x = 2 \quad \rightarrow \quad x = -2$$

<u>What You May Have Done Wrong</u>
   - **A.** You added $2x$ & $3x$.
   - **B.** You misread your matrix and set your equation equal to the wrong number.
   - **C.** You dropped a sign or made another mistake.
   - **E.** You added $2x$ & $3x$ and made a sign error.

4. The determinant of any 2 x 2 matrix $\begin{bmatrix} a & b \\ c & d \end{bmatrix}$ is $ad - bc$. The determinant of $\begin{bmatrix} x+1 & 5 \\ 1 & x-3 \end{bmatrix}$ is equal to 0. What are all possible values of x?

Correct Answer K

This is a more complicated determinant question. We'll have to find the determinant, set it equal to 0, and then solve for x.

$$a = x+1, \quad b = 5, \quad c = 1, \quad d = x-3$$

$$ad - bc = 0 \quad \rightarrow \quad (x+1)(x-3) - (5)(1) = 0$$

$$x^2 - 3x + 1x - 3 - 5 = 0 \quad \rightarrow \quad x^2 - 2x - 8 = 0$$

Now we'll need to factor the quadratic.

$$x^2 - 2x - 8 = 0 \quad \rightarrow \quad (x-4)(x+2) = 0$$

$$x - 4 = 0 \rightarrow x = 4 \quad \& \quad x + 2 = 0 \rightarrow x = -2$$

x can equal 4 or -2.

Answer choice **K** is correct.

<u>What You May Have Done Wrong</u>
   - **F.** This is a possible value of x, but not *all* possible values of x.
   - **G.** This is a possible value of x, but not *all* possible values of x.
   - **H.** This is a solution to the original quadratic, not the equation.
   - **J.** This is a solution to the original quadratic, not the equation.

5. The number of rows in matrix A equals c. The number of columns in matrix B equals r. For which statement is the matrix product of AB defined?

Correct Answer C

This is a definition question. You've got to know when we can multiply matrices. Conceivably you could pick numbers and test answers, but it's impractical. You really need to remember that

$$C = R$$

Columns of first matrix = Rows of the second matrix.

Answer choice **C** is correct.

<u>What You May Have Done Wrong</u>
Each answer choice is a conceptual error. Make sure you know *when* you can multiply matrices.

Introduction

This is a fairly common topic. It shows up on more than 75% of tests and it's not uncommon to see it more than once a test. While I'm calling this section *sequences & series*, we're mostly interested in sequences. In fact, most questions are about arithmetic sequences.

What You Need to Know
- ✓ How to find missing terms in an arithmetic sequence
- ✓ How to find the sum (series) of an arithmetic sequence
- ✓ How to find the next term of a geometric sequence
- ✓ How to solve direct and inverse proportionality problems.

Definitions: Sequences & Series

> **Sequences** are a list of numbers related in some way. The relationship between consecutive terms is the same throughout the sequence.
>
> **Series** are the sum of a *sequence* of numbers.

Sequence: 1, 2, 3, 4, 5

This is an arithmetic sequence.

Series: 1 + 2 + 3 + 4 + 5

Definitions: Arithmetic & Geometric Sequences

> **Arithmetic Sequences** have a *common difference*. When you subtract consecutive terms (numbers next to each other), the difference is always the same.
>
> **Geometric Sequences** have a *common ratio*. When you **divide** consecutive terms, the ratio (fraction) is always the same.

Arithmetic Sequence: 1, 2, 3, 4, 5

Geometric Sequence: 1, 2, 4, 8, 16

$$2 - 1 = 1$$
$$3 - 2 = 1$$
$$4 - 3 = 1$$

The *ratio* is always the same.

The *difference* is always the same.

Rules of the Road: Finding Terms in an Arithmetic Sequences

> To find the **number** of **jumps** (changes).
> 1. **Find the range.**
> 2. **Divide the range by the number of *jumps***
> 3. **Work from the last term before/after the missing term, adding or subtracting to find the missing term(s)**

1. The value of n is such that the difference between consecutive numbers in the list is the same. What is the value of n?

$$3, n, 31$$

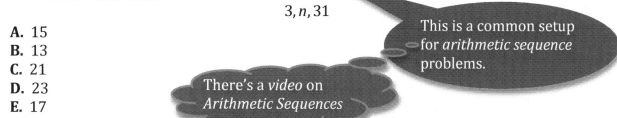

This is a common setup for *arithmetic sequence* problems.

There's a *video* on *Arithmetic Sequences*

A. 15
B. 13
C. 21
D. 23
E. 17

Solve

This is a common format for arithmetic sequence problems. You'll notice that the question doesn't say "arithmetic sequence" and that's pretty common. The word "consecutive" & "difference" are clues.

Find how many *jumps*. Jumps are the number of increases or decreases in the list we're given.

$$3, n, 31$$

There are two jumps: 3 to n & n to 31.

Find the range. Subtract the top & bottom terms.

$$31 - 3 = 28$$

Divide the range by the number of *jumps*.

$$\frac{28}{2} = 14$$

Add to find the missing term.

$$3 + 14 = 17 \quad \rightarrow \quad n = 17$$

Answer choice **E** is correct.

Rules of the Road: Finding the Sum (the series) of an Arithmetic Sequence

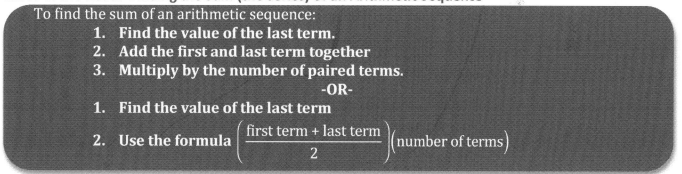

To find the sum of an arithmetic sequence:
1. **Find the value of the last term.**
2. **Add the first and last term together**
3. **Multiply by the number of paired terms.**

-OR-

1. **Find the value of the last term**
2. **Use the formula** $\left(\dfrac{\text{first term} + \text{last term}}{2} \right) \left(\text{number of terms} \right)$

Whichever way you choose to solve these questions is fine. I think remembering the *relationship* is easier (no formula) but it's up to you.

Example: Finding the Sum (the series) of an Arithmetic Sequence

1. What is the sum of the first 10 terms of the arithmetic sequence below?

$$2, 4, 6, ...$$

Solve

The first step, regardless of how you want to solve the problem, is finding the last term. The *common difference* between the terms is 2, so we multiply the common difference by the number of *jumps* (how many increases). *In these problems there will always be one less jump than the number of terms.*

increase = common difference × number of jumps   →   increase = 2 × 9 = 18

To find the last term, add the *first term* to the *increase*.

last term = first term + increase   →   last term = 2 + 18 = 20

This is a simple sequence, so we can easily show the sequence.

$$2, 4, 6, 8, 10, 12, 14, 16, 18, 20$$

Pair off the terms.

$$2, 4, 6, 8, 10, 12, 14, 16, 18, 20$$

$$2+20=22$$

$$4+18=22$$

Each pair adds to 22.

There are 5 pairs of terms, $22 \times 5 = 110$

Or we can use the formula.

$$\left(\frac{\text{first term + last term}}{2}\right)(\text{number of term}) \quad \rightarrow \quad \left(\frac{2+20}{2}\right)(10)=11\times10=110$$

ACT Example: Finding the Sum (the series) of an Arithmetic Sequence

1. As part of a pushup challenge, Nate does 5 pushups on day one and adds 5 pushups per day until day 14. How many pushups does Nate do in the challenge?

A. 480
B. 525
C. 360
D. 600
E. 420

Solve

Which way you do these problems depends on what you like. I think it's easier to remember the first method—the *pairs* method—but it's really whatever you're most comfortable with.

Find the last term.

increase = common difference × number of jumps   →   increase = 5 × 13 = 65

last term = first term + increase   →   last term = 5 + 65 = 70

Add the first and last term.

$$5+70=75$$

There are 14 terms, so

Multiply by the number of pairs.

$$75\times7=525$$

Or, use the equation:

$$\left(\frac{\text{first term + last term}}{2}\right)(\text{number of term}) \quad \rightarrow \quad \left(\frac{5+70}{2}\right)(14)=37.5\times14=525$$

Answer choice **B** is correct.

2. A finite arithmetic sequence has a last term of -3. There are 11 terms in the sequence. What is the mean divided by the median?

   A. 1
   B. 0
   C. -62
   D. 325
   E. 102

Solve

This is a weird definition question. You don't have enough information to solve this mathematically (though you could pick numbers). Arithmetic sequences all have the same distance between terms (common difference).

Let's pick some numbers so we can see how the problem works. It doesn't matter what the common difference is (the question is about relationships and the answer choices are in terms of a relationship). Let's make the common difference 1. Remember that -3 is our last term, so the sequence looks like this:

$$-13, -12, -11, -10, -9, -8, -7, -6, -5, -4, -3$$

The median number, the middle number, is -8.

$$-13, -12, -11, -10, -9, -8, -7, -6, -5, -4, -3$$

The mean, the average is -8.

$$average = \frac{-13 + -12 + -11 + -10 + -9 + -8 + -7 + -6 + -5 + -4 + -3}{11} \quad \rightarrow \quad \frac{-88}{11} = -8$$

So, the mean is equal to the median. And $\dfrac{mean}{median} = \dfrac{-8}{-8} = 1$

The math isn't too hard, but it's pretty time consuming. There's a trick, though. **The mean will always equal the median in an arithmetic sequence. That will always be the case.**

Answer choice **A** is correct.

Geometric Series

Geometric series aren't heavily tested on the ACT. In fact, most questions can be solved using common sense. They're definition questions, so know the terms below.

Definitions: Geometric Sequences, Common Ratio, & Proportionality

Geometric Sequences have a *common ratio*. When you **divide** consecutive terms, the ratio (fraction) is always the same.

The **common ratio** is what each term is *multiplied by* to get the next term. You can find the common ratio by *dividing* consecutive terms.

Constant of Proportionality (k) is the number that is multiplied or divided (and doesn't change). It's like the *common ratio*.

Directly proportional means as one *variable* **increases** as the other *variable* **increases**. It has the relationship $y = kx$.

Inversely proportional means as one *variable* **decreases** as the other *variable* **increases**. It has the relationship $y = \dfrac{k}{x}$.

ACT Example: Geometric Sequences

1. What is the fourth term of the geometric sequence below?

$$24a^8b^5c^2, \ 12a^6b^4c, \ 6a^4b^3, \ ...$$

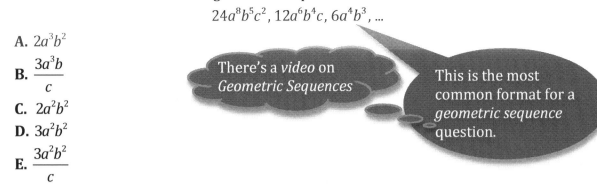

A. $2a^3b^2$

B. $\dfrac{3a^3b}{c}$

C. $2a^2b^2$

D. $3a^2b^2$

E. $\dfrac{3a^2b^2}{c}$

Solve

There are two ways to solve this. You can divide consecutive terms to find the *common ratio*. You can also work this problem in pieces and mark-off. It's much easier to mark-off. Let's look at finding the *common ratio* first.

Common Ratio

To find the common ratio, divide two consecutive terms. You'll need to know your exponent operations.

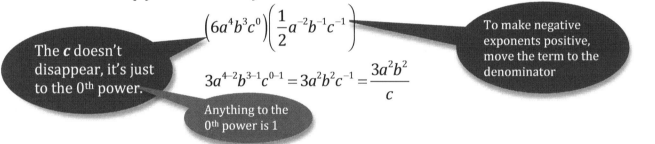

$$\frac{12a^6b^4c}{24a^8b^5c^2} = \frac{1}{2}a^{6-8}b^{4-5}c^{1-2} \qquad \rightarrow \qquad \frac{1}{2}a^{-2}b^{-1}c^{-1}$$

Subtract exponents to divide.

Now multiply the last term by the common ratio to find the fourth term.

$$\left(6a^4b^3c^0\right)\left(\frac{1}{2}a^{-2}b^{-1}c^{-1}\right)$$

The *c* doesn't disappear, it's just to the 0th power.

Anything to the 0th power is 1

To make negative exponents positive, move the term to the denominator

$$3a^{4-2}b^{3-1}c^{0-1} = 3a^2b^2c^{-1} = \frac{3a^2b^2}{c}$$

But, there's an easier way...

Marking Off

This is the simplest way to do this problem. Start with the coefficient and "eyeball" the change. After you're done with the coefficient, mark-off.

The Coefficient, by "eyeballing" you can see that the coefficient is halved each time, going from 24 to 12 to 6. So the 4th term should have a coefficient of 3. We can mark-off **A & C**.

The variable *a*, by "eyeballing" you can see that the *a* variable decreases in power by 2 each term. The third term is a^4, so the fourth term is a^2. You can mark off **B** (**A** is also out).

The variable *b*, by "eyeballing" you can see that the *b* variable decreases in power by 1 each term. The third term is b^3, so the fourth term is b^2. You can't mark-off anything new.

The variable *c*, by "eyeballing" you can see that the *c* variable decreases in power by 1 each time. The tricky part is the *c* term seems to disappear. It actually doesn't, remember that $c^0 = 1$ (any number to the 0th power is 1). The third term is c^0, so the fourth term is c^{-1}. When there's a negative exponent, you've got to make it positive. To make an exponent positive, we move it to the denominator. This lets us mark-off **D**.

Answer choice **E** is correct.

2. The value of x is directly proportional the value of y. When $x = 14$, $y = 2$. What is the value of x when $y = 7$?

A. 1
B. 8
C. 21
D. 49
E. 63

This is the most common format for a *proportionality* question.

Solve

This is a classic setup. On the surface, there's three variables x, y, and what y is multiplied by (k). The wording can be a little confusing, "x is directly proportional" means x equals.

So, y multiplied by a number equals x.

$$x = k \bullet y$$
$$14 = k \bullet 2$$
$$k = 7$$

We can find k by using the given "set" of x & y.

Remember, *verbs* are usually equal signs.

Now, we can plug in k and the second value for y to find x.

$$x = k \bullet y$$
$$x = 7 \bullet 7$$
$$x = 49$$

Review *Elementary Algebra: Make an Equation*

Answer choice **D** is correct.

Wrap Up

What You Need to Know
- ✓ How to find missing terms in an arithmetic sequence
- ✓ How to find the sum of an arithmetic sequence
- ✓ How to find the next term of a geometric sequence
- ✓ How to solve direct and inverse proportionality problems.

Videos

Arithmetic Sequences

Geometric Sequences

The Strategies
- ✓ In arithmetic sequences it's the *jumps* that are important.
- ✓ If you're drawing a blank, you can usually test answers.
- ✓ Mark off on geometric series questions
- ✓ You'll have to solve twice on proportionality questions, once to find the constant and once to find the answer.

Related Skills
- ✓ Make an equation
- ✓ Ratios & Proportions

Intermediate Algebra: Series & Sequences

1. What values of x & y make the difference between consecutive numbers the same?
$$13, x, y, 34$$

- **A.** $x = 20$ & $y = 27$ (circled)
- **B.** $x = 23.5$ & $y = 33.5$
- **C.** $x = 18$ & $y = 25$
- **D.** $x = 19$ & $y = 25$
- **E.** $x = 22$ & $y = 28$

✓

2. Which of the following is true about the arithmetic sequence below?
$$63, 51, 39, 27, 15, \ldots\ 3\ \text{-9}\ \text{-21}\ \text{-33}$$

- **F.** The sixth term in the sequence is 2.
- **G.** The ninth term in the sequence is -33. ⁻ (circled)
- **H.** The common ratio of terms is 12.
- **J.** The common ratio of terms is -12.
- **K.** The sum of the first six terms is 195.

✓

3. What is the sum of the first 14 terms of the arithmetic sequence shown below?
$$1, 5, 9, \ldots \qquad 57$$

- **A.** 307
- **B.** 329
- **C.** 378 (circled)
- **D.** 435
- **E.** 441

✓

4. What is the fourth term of the geometric sequence shown below?
$$-2xy^2,\ 4xy^4z,\ -8xy^6z^2,\ \ldots$$

- **F.** $16x^2y^8z^2$
- **G.** $16xy^8z$ $-2y^2z$
- **H.** $-16xy^8z^2$ $16xy^8z^3$
- **J.** $16xy^8z^3$ (circled)
- **K.** $-16x^2y^6z^2$

5. An arithmetic sequence of four terms has a common difference of 6, and the terms sum to 48. What is the last term of the sequence?

- **A.** 24
- **B.** 16
- **C.** 21 (circled)
- **D.** 42
- **E.** 3

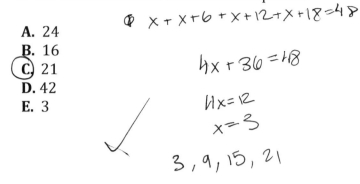

$$x + x+6 + x+12 + x+18 = 48$$
$$4x + 36 = 48$$
$$4x = 12$$
$$x = 3$$
$$3, 9, 15, 21$$

✓

6. The sum of three consecutive even integers is 114. What is the smallest integer?

- **F.** 34
- **G.** 36 (circled)
- **H.** 38
- **J.** 40
- **K.** 42

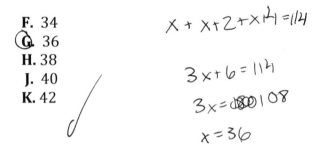

$$x + x+2 + x+4 = 114$$
$$3x + 6 = 114$$
$$3x = 108$$
$$x = 36$$

✓

Series & Sequences: Solutions

1. What values of x & y make the difference between consecutive numbers the same?

$$13, x, y, 34$$

Correct Answer A

Don't let the wording of the problem confuse you, this is just an *arithmetic sequence* problem. Remember, arithmetic sequences have the same difference between consecutive terms. You can *test answers* on these problems, but it's a little time consuming. **There are two numbers (x & y), so there are three *jumps*.**

We jump from 13 to x, x to y, & y to 34.

$$13, \underbrace{x}_{1}, \underbrace{y}_{2}, \underbrace{34}_{3}$$

Find the range of the series: **34 – 13 = 21**

Divide by the number of jumps.

$$\frac{range}{jumps} = \frac{21}{3} = 7$$

Starting with 13, add 7 to get x & then y

$$13 + 7 = 20 \rightarrow x = 20$$
$$20 + 7 = 27 \rightarrow y = 27$$

Answer choice **A** is correct.

What You May Have Done Wrong
 B. You calculated for two *jumps*, not three.
 C. This is a guess or conceptual error.
 D. This is a guess or conceptual error.
 E. This is a guess or conceptual error.

2. Which of the following is true about the arithmetic sequence below?

$$63, 51, 39, 27, 15, ...$$

Correct Answer G

This is a *which* question, so you'll need to mark off. I'd probably start with the "definition" answer choices (**H**, & **J**), to see if I can skip any calculations.

~~H.~~ The common ratio of consecutive terms is 12.
 ~~J.~~ The common ratio of consecutive terms is -12.

Neither **H** or **J** are true. A common ratio is a multiplier and is a term we use for *geometric sequences*. *Arithmetic sequences* have a common difference. To evaluate the remaining answer choices, we'll need the common difference. To find the common difference, subtract any two consecutive terms.

$$51 – 63 = -12$$

It seems like we'll have to do a lot of calculations to check the last three answers. In reality, you'll only need to check two of the three. **F** is fairly straightforward to calculate, and then you can choose between **G** & **K** to check.

 ~~F.~~ *The sixth term in the sequence is 2.* The fifth term in the sequence is 15, and 15 – 12 = 3,
 G. *The ninth term in the sequence is -33.* This works, 15, 3, -9, -21, -33.
 ~~K.~~ *The sum of the first six terms is 195.* This is the sum of the first five terms.

Answer choice **G** is correct.

3. What is the sum of the first 14 terms of the arithmetic sequence shown below?

$$1, 5, 9, ...$$

Correct Answer C

You can pound this question out on your calculator 1 + 5 + 9 + 13 + 17... (the common difference is 4). There's an easier way and you're less likely to make an error.

First, calculate your 14th term. The common difference is +4 and there are thirteen terms after the first term.

$$13 \times 4 = 52$$

$$52 + 1 = 53$$

$$Fourteenth\, Term = 53$$

Because the difference is the same between each term, the first term plus the fourteen term will be the same as the second term plus the thirteenth term. Take a look:

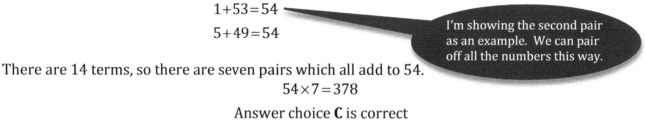

$$1 + 53 = 54$$

$$5 + 49 = 54$$

I'm showing the second pair as an example. We can pair off all the numbers this way.

There are 14 terms, so there are seven pairs which all add to 54.

$$54 \times 7 = 378$$

Answer choice **C** is correct

<u>What You May Have Done Wrong</u>
  A. You made a calculation error.
  B. You only found the sum of the first 13 terms
  D. You found the sum of the first 15 terms.
  E. You made a calculation error.

4. What is the fourth term of the geometric sequence shown below?

$$-2xy^2, 4xy^4z, -8xy^6z, ...$$

Correct Answer J

The consecutive terms in a geometric series have a common *multiple* called a *common ratio*. The easiest way to solve the problem is marking off. Start with the coefficient or one of the variables and mark-off all the answer choices that don't match.

Coefficient: The common multiple of the coefficient is -2 (or you could say that -2 is taken to a power). The coefficient of the third term is -8, so the fourth term is +16. We can mark off answer choices **H & K**.

x: The x doesn't change from term to term, so it will stay the same in the fourth term. We can mark off answer choice **F**.

y: The y term feels a little trickier than it is. The power goes up by 2 each term, so the fourth term will be y^8. We can't mark off new answer choice (but we could mark off **K** if you hadn't already).

z: The z term is also tricky. There's no z in the first term, but z shows up in the second & third term. So z's exponent goes up one each time and the fourth term will have z^3. The first term has z^0, and any number to the 0 power is equal to 1. We can mark off answer choice **G**.

Answer choice **J** is correct.

5. An arithmetic sequence of four terms has a common difference of 6, and the terms sum to 48. What is the last term of the sequence?

Correct Answer C

This is a pretty tough problem if you're not really sure what to do. It seems like a four variable system of equations, but it's not really. There's two ways to solve it, and there are very similar.

$$\text{first term + second term + third term + fourth term} = 48$$

We can put everything in terms of one term (one variable) because we know the *relationship* between the variables. Since we're solving for the fourth term, we'll put everything in terms of the fourth variable.

$$\text{fourth variable } = x$$
$$\text{third variable } = x - 6$$
$$\text{second variable} = x - 12$$
$$\text{first variable } = x - 18$$

Now, plug in and put everything in terms of x.

$$\text{first term + second term + third term + fourth term} = 48$$
$$x - 18 + x - 12 + x - 6 + x = 48$$
$$4x - 36 = 48$$
$$4x = 84$$
$$x = 21$$

We can solve this using pairs. There are four numbers, so there are two pairs.

$$\frac{48}{2} = 24 \ per \ pair$$

So first term + fourth term $= 24$. There is a difference of 18 between the first and last term. So, you can say:

$$\text{fourth variable} = x$$
$$\text{first variable } = x - 18$$

$$\text{first term + fourth term} = 24$$
$$x - 18 + x = 24$$
$$2x = 42$$
$$x = 21$$

Answer choice **C** is correct.

<u>What You May Have Done Wrong</u>
   A. You may have just divided 48 by 2 or guessed.
   B. You made a conceptual error, review your steps.
   D. You subtracted 6 from 48.
   E. This is the first term, not the last term.

6. The sum of three consecutive even integers is 114. What is the smallest integer?

Correct Answer G

This is a slightly different take on an arithmetic sequence question. They tell you that the integers are consecutive even integers (2 & 4 are examples) but they don't use the word sequence, so it can be tricky to see that's what you're working with. You can solve this problem a couple of ways (but it's really the same way).

One way to set the problem up is like the previous problem. The sum of the terms is 114, so you can make an equation.

$$\text{first term} + \text{second term} + \text{third term} = 114$$

We know how the terms relate to each other, so we can use a single variable for all three.

$$\text{first term} = x$$
$$\text{second term} = x + 2$$
$$\text{third term} = x + 4$$

$$\text{first term} + \text{second term} + \text{third term} = 114$$
$$x + x + 2 + x + 4 = 114$$
$$3x + 6 = 114$$
$$3x = 108$$
$$x = 36$$

You can also solve this problem by using averages. This method only works for arithmetic sequences with an odd number of terms. You can do it for sequences with an even number of terms, but it gets tricky.

$$average = \frac{sum}{number}$$
$$average = \frac{114}{3} = 38$$

38 will be our middle term (because everything is equally far apart, mean is equal to median). This only works with an odd number of terms though, if it's an even number there's no middle term. We know that all of the terms are two apart, so the smallest term is 38 – 2 = 36.

Answer G is correct.

<u>What You May Have Done Wrong</u>
   F. You made a calculation error or guessed.
   H. This is the middle term.
   J. This is the last term.
   K. You made a calculation error or guessed.

Coordinate Geometry

The topics in the *Intermediate Algebra* section constitute 15 to 20 percent of the ACT Math section, or between 9 and 12 questions per test. Here's the question frequency and the corresponding ACT Score Report category or categories

Lines^{key skill}	3 – 4 questions	**PHM: Algebra**
Distance & Midpoint	1 – 2 questions	**MOD & PHM Algebra**
Shapes	1 – 2 questions	**PHM Geometry**
Functions	1 – 3 questions	**PHM: Algebra**
Word Functions key skill	2 – 3 questions	**MOD & PHM: Functions**
Inequalities	0 – 2 questions	**MOD & PHM: Algebra**
Quadrants/Reflections	0 – 2 questions	**PHM: Functions**

IES: Integrating Essential Skills
PHM: Preparing for Higher Math
MOD: Modeling

A detailed explanation of the math score report is at the beginning of the book in **The Score Report**. There are two key skills in *Coordinate Geometry*. Both *Lines & Word Problem Functions* are related to multiple topics.

Strategies

It boils down to translating equations to graphs, graphs to equations, and understanding some key concepts of functions.

Know the Basic Equations
You've got to know the line equation, what equations make parabolas, how to find distance & midpoint, and the circle formula (covered in plane geometry)

Recognize When/If Functions have Zeroes
It's really helpful if you can quickly figure out where or if functions have zeroes. It's best if you know your *shifts*, but, if you don't, you can just plug-in 0 for y.

Use & Draw Diagrams
While the ACT Math diagrams aren't "drawn to scale," they really are useful (and are usually drawn to scale). Don't be afraid to eyeball things to mark-off. Drawing a sketch can help you mark-off and frame up the problem.

Mark-Off
Line equations, parabolas, zeroes, and other answer types have multiple parts. Whenever you have multiple parts to answer choices, you should mark-off.

Be Hands On
Manipulate the diagrams. Sketch out changes on given diagrams. Rotate the page for rotation questions (literally).

Coordinate Geometry: Pre-Test

1. What is the slope of a line that corresponds to the equation $4x + 3y = 21$?

A. 7

B. $\dfrac{3}{4}$

C. $\dfrac{4}{3}$

D. $-\dfrac{3}{4}$

E. $-\dfrac{4}{3}$

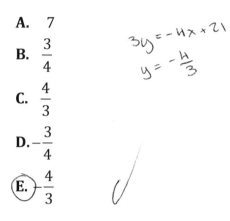

$3y = -4x + 21$

$y = -\dfrac{4}{3}$

2. A line passes through points (3,1) and (5,3). What is the equation of the line?

A. $y = 2x$

B. $y = x + 2$

C. $y = -x$

D. $y = x - 2$

E. $y = -2x$

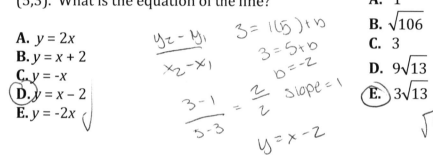

$\dfrac{y_2 - y_1}{x_2 - x_1}$

$3 = 1(5) + b$

$3 = 5 + b$

$b = -2$

$\dfrac{3-1}{5-3} = \dfrac{2}{2}$ slope = 1

$y = x - 2$

3. In the standard (x, y) coordinate plane, which of the following equations is perpendicular to the line $y = -\dfrac{4}{3}x + 8$?

A. $y = \dfrac{3}{4}x + 5$

B. $y = \dfrac{4}{3}x + 8$

C. $y = -\dfrac{3}{4}x + 8$

D. $y = -\dfrac{4}{3}x + \dfrac{1}{8}$

E. $y = -\dfrac{3}{4}x + \dfrac{1}{8}$

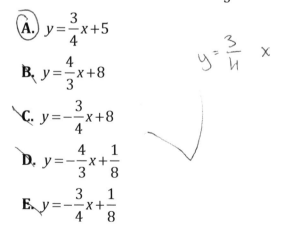

$y = \dfrac{3}{4} x$

4. What is the y-coordinate of the point, in the standard (x, y) coordinate plane, where $y = 5x + 1$ and $y = 2x + 4$ intersect?

A. 1

B. 6

C. 4

D. -3

E. -2

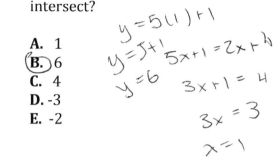

$y = 5(1) + 1$

$y = 5 + 1$

$y = 6$

$5x + 1 = 2x + 4$

$3x + 1 = 4$

$3x = 3$

$x = 1$

5. In the standard (x, y) coordinate plane, what is the distance, in units, between points (4, 3) and (-5, -3)?

A. 1

B. $\sqrt{106}$

C. 3

D. $9\sqrt{13}$

E. $3\sqrt{13}$

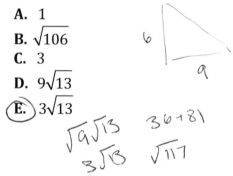

$\sqrt{9\sqrt{13}}$ $36 + 81$

$3\sqrt{13}$ $\sqrt{117}$

6. What is the sum of the x and y coordinates of the midpoint in a line segment that has endpoints of (7,2) and (-1, -3)?

A. 3.5

B. 2.5

C. 3.0

D. 2.0

E. 4.0

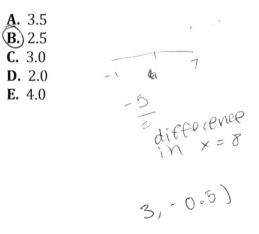

difference in $x = 8$

$3, -0.5)$

7. The graph is in the standard (x, y) coordinate plane. Which of the following systems of inequalities represents the solution set below?

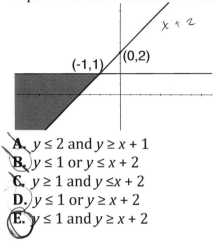

A. $y \le 2$ and $y \ge x + 1$
B. $y \le 1$ or $y \le x + 2$
C. $y \ge 1$ and $y \le x + 2$
D. $y \le 1$ or $y \ge x + 2$
E. $y \le 1$ and $y \ge x + 2$

8. The graph below is in the standard (x, y) coordinate plane and represents the graph of $y < ax + b$. What will be the signs of a and b?

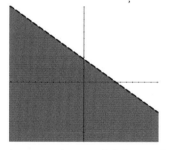

A. a is negative and b is positive
B. a is negative and b is negative
C. a is positive and b is negative
D. a is positive and b is positive
E. cannot be determined

9. A rectangle is in the standard (x, y) coordinate plane it has vertices of $(2,3)$, $(6,3)$, and $(2,-1)$. Which is the coordinate point of the fourth vertex?

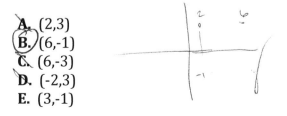

A. $(2,3)$
B. $(6,-1)$
C. $(6,-3)$
D. $(-2,3)$
E. $(3,-1)$

10. A rectangle with vertices of $(3,3)$, $(3, -2)$, $(-1,3)$ and $(-1,-2)$ is in the standard (x, y) coordinate plane. What percentage of the total area lies in quadrant II?

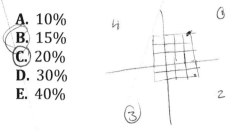

A. 10%
B. 15%
C. 20%
D. 30%
E. 40%

11. Triangle ABC is in the standard coordinate plane with vertex A at $(0,2)$ vertex B at $(-3,-4)$ and vertex C at $(3,-4)$. Triangle ABC also has x-intercepts of -1 and 1. $\overline{BC}$ is perpendicular to the x-axis. Approximately what percentage of the area of the triangle are in quadrants I & II?

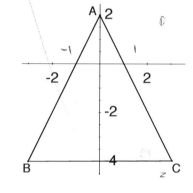

A. 25%
B. 50%
C. 18%
D. 11%
E. 40%

12. In the figure below, triangle *ABC* is in the standard (*x*, *y*) coordinate plane and has vertices of (-1,1), (2,4), and (5,1). What is the area of triangle *ABC*?

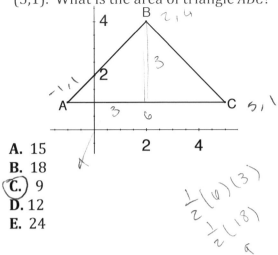

A. 15
B. 18
C. 9
D. 12
E. 24

$\frac{1}{2}(6)(3)$

$\frac{1}{2}(18)$

9

13. In which of the following quadrants will the product of the *x*-coordinate and *y*-coordinate of every point be negative?

A. I and II only
B. II only
C. IV only
D. II and III only
E. II and IV only

14. The graph shown below is in the standard (*x*, *y*) coordinate plane and is to be rotated 180° about the origin. Which quadrant will point *A* be in?

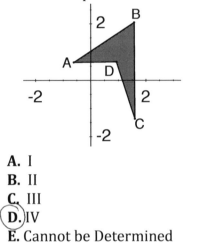

A. I
B. II
C. III
D. IV
E. Cannot be Determined

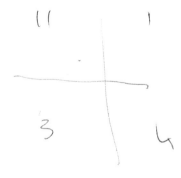

15. Which of the following reflects the
graph below across the *x*-axis?

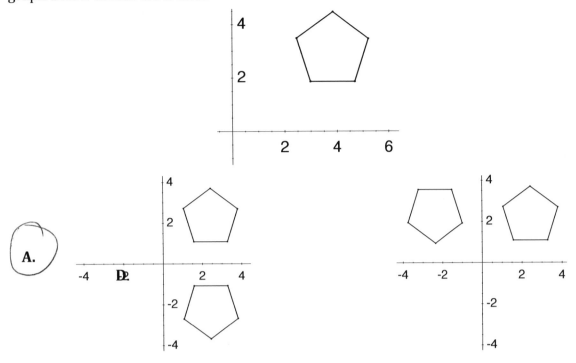

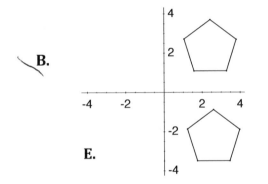

A.

D.

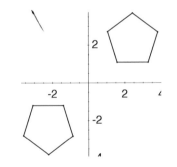

B.

E.

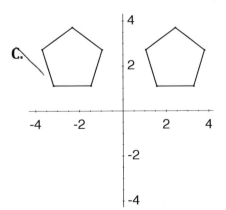

C.

16. Which of the following functions will have no real zeroes?

    A. $y = x^2 - 1$

    B. $y = x - 1$

    C. $y = x^2 + 1$

    D. $y = x^3$

    E. $y = \sqrt{x}$

17. The graph shown below is in the standard (x, y) coordinate plane. Which of the following equation is the function of the graph?

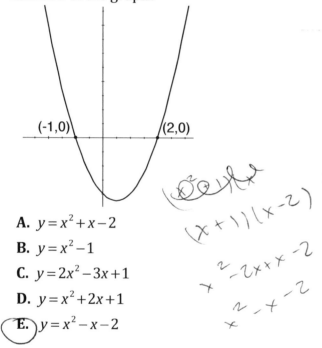

(-1,0)   (2,0)

    A. $y = x^2 + x - 2$

    B. $y = x^2 - 1$

    C. $y = 2x^2 - 3x + 1$

    D. $y = x^2 + 2x + 1$

    E. $y = x^2 - x - 2$

(handwritten) $(x+1)(x-2)$
$x^2 - 2x + x - 2$
$x^2 - x - 2$

18. The equation $y = \dfrac{x}{x^3 - 8}$ is graphed in the standard (x, y) coordinate plane. Where will the function have *no x coordinate?*

    A. 0

    B. 2

    C. -1

    D. 1

    E. -3

19. Which of the following is the equation of the graph below?

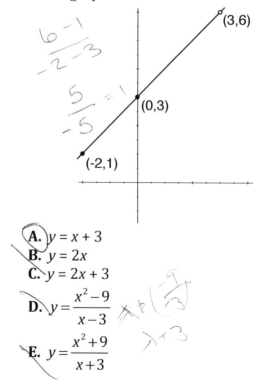

(3,6)

(0,3)

(-2,1)

(handwritten) $\dfrac{6-1}{-2-3}$, $\dfrac{5}{-5} = 1$

    A. $y = x + 3$

    B. $y = 2x$

    C. $y = 2x + 3$

    D. $y = \dfrac{x^2 - 9}{x - 3}$

    E. $y = \dfrac{x^2 + 9}{x + 3}$

20. The function $y=(x+3)^2+2$ is graphed in the standard (x,y) coordinate plane below.

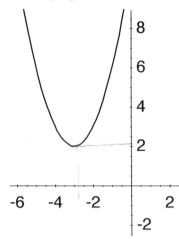

If the graph is shifted down three units, which of the following graphs will be the result?

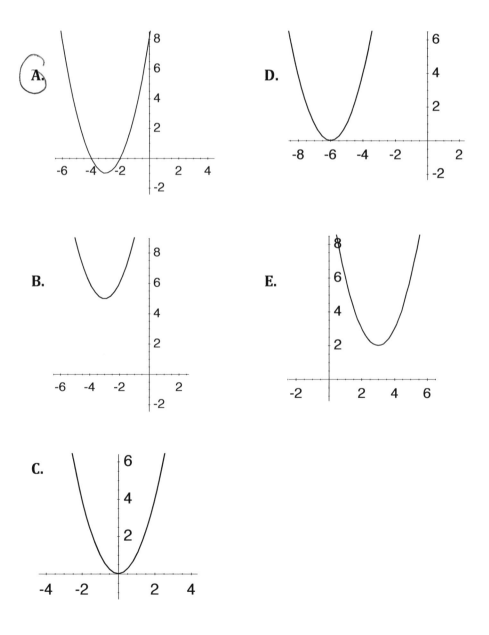

21. A bathtub is filling from the faucet and the drain is closed. The graph below shows the depth of the tube as a function of time since the faucet was turned on. At time 1 exactly *one* of the following events occurred, which of the following could it be?

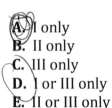

I. The faucet was turned off.
II. The rate of flow into the bathtub increased.
III. The drain was opened.

A. I only
B. II only
C. III only
D. I or III only
E. II or III only

22. The graph below shows Maria's distance from her home in miles. Three of the following five actions below describe Maria's movements in relation to her distance from home. In the correct order, which three is it?

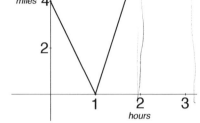

I. Maria walked home at a rate of four miles per hour.
II. Maria rode her bike at a rate of 12 miles per hour to the gym, six miles from home.
III. Maria worked out at the gym, which is six miles from her home for two hours.
IV. Maria jogged to the gym, six miles from her home, at a rate of 10 minutes per mile.
V. Maria rides her bike home at a rate of one mile per hour.

A. I, IV, & III
B. I, II, & V
C. I, II, V
D. II, IV, V
E. III, IV, III

23. The table below gives coordinate points for a line in the standard (x, y) coordinate plane. What does c equal?

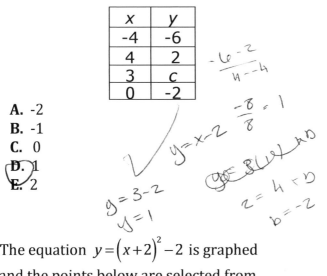

x	y
-4	-6
4	2
3	c
0	-2

   A. -2
   B. -1
   C. 0
   D. 1
   E. 2

24. The equation $y = (x+2)^2 - 2$ is graphed and the points below are selected from that graph. For the equation above, which value of x will give the least value of y?

x	y
-5	7
-3	-1
-1	-1
1	7
3	23
5	47

   A. 0
   B. 1
   C. 3
   D. -1
   E. -2

25. The table below gives the values of 2 functions f and g for selected values of x? One of the functions is linear and the other represents and exponential growth function. What is the value of the linear function when $x = -3$.

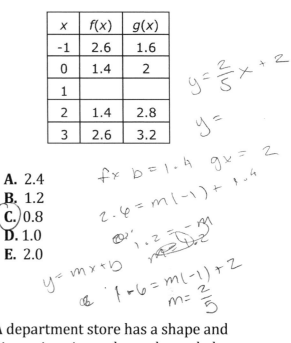

x	f(x)	g(x)
-1	2.6	1.6
0	1.4	2
1		
2	1.4	2.8
3	2.6	3.2

   A. 2.4
   B. 1.2
   C. 0.8
   D. 1.0
   E. 2.0

26. A department store has a shape and dimensions in yards, as shown below. Every wall in the department store is either parallel or perpendicular. The customer service counter if located exactly between point F and point D. If Jim enters the store at point B, How does he get to the customer service counter?

   A. 25-yards north and 30-yards west
   B. 35-yards south and 45-yards west
   C. 35-yards south and 40-yards west
   D. 20-yards south and 25-yards east
   E. 20-yards south and 15-yards east

1.	E	Line Equation		25.	C	Word Functions
2.	D	Line Equation		26.	B	Word Functions
3.	A	Line Equation				
4.	B	Line Equation				
5.	E	Midpoint & Distance				
6.	B	Midpoint & Distance				
7.	E	Inequalities				
8.	A	Inequalities				
9.	B	Shapes				
10.	B	Shapes				
11.	D	Shapes				
12.	C	Shapes				
13.	E	Quadrants				
14.	D	Quadrants				
15.	A	Quadrants				
16.	C	Functions				
17.	E	Functions				
18.	B	Functions				
19.	D	Functions				
20.	A	Functions				
21.	D	Word Functions				
22.	A	Word Functions				
23.	D	Word Functions				
24.	E	Word Functions				

Introduction

The slope-intercept form of line equations shows up *multiple* times per ACT. It is a key skill showing up in *make an equation* problems and many geometry sections.

What You Need to Know

- ✓ The *slope intercept* form of line equations
- ✓ How to find the *slope & y-intercept* of a line
- ✓ *Horizontal & vertical* lines
- ✓ *Parallel & perpendicular* lines
- ✓ The solution for a linear system of equations is when the lines intersect.

Definitions: Slope Intercept Form

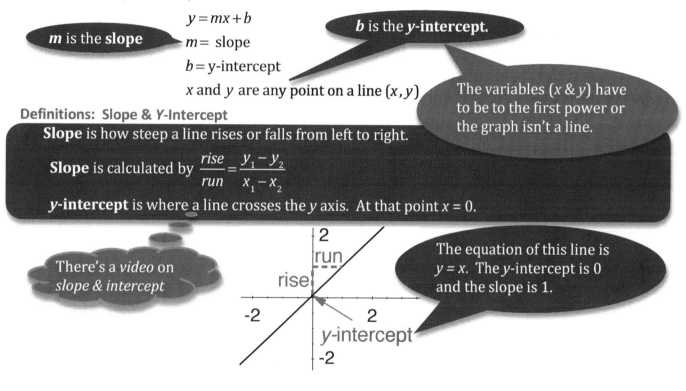

$$y = mx + b$$

m is the **slope**

$m = $ slope

$b = $ y-intercept

x and *y* are any point on a line (x, y)

b is the **y-intercept.**

The variables $(x \& y)$ have to be to the first power or the graph isn't a line.

Definitions: Slope & Y-Intercept

Slope is how steep a line rises or falls from left to right.

Slope is calculated by $\dfrac{rise}{run} = \dfrac{y_1 - y_2}{x_1 - x_2}$

y-intercept is where a line crosses the *y* axis. At that point $x = 0$.

There's a *video* on *slope & intercept*

The equation of this line is $y = x$. The y-intercept is 0 and the slope is 1.

Rules of the Road: Slope-Intercept Form

We can re-arrange any equation into $y = $ form. If both *x* and *y* are to the first power, the graph is a line.

1. What is the slope of a line that corresponds with the equation $4x + 3y = 21$?

A. 7

B. $\dfrac{3}{4}$

C. $\dfrac{4}{3}$

D. $-\dfrac{3}{4}$

E. $-\dfrac{4}{3}$

Solve

To solve, we'll rearrange the equation into $y=mx + b$ form.

$$4x+3y=21 \quad \rightarrow \quad 3y=21-4x$$

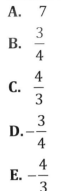

Rearrange the equation to $y = mx + b$

$$3y=-4x+21 \quad \rightarrow \quad \frac{3y}{3}=\frac{-4x+21}{3}$$

$$y=-\frac{4}{3}x+7$$

Answer Choice **E** is correct.

2. A line passes through points $(3,1)$ and $(5,3)$. What is the equation of the line?

A. $y = 2x$
B. $y = x + 2$
C. $y = -x$
D. $y = x - 2$
E. $y = -2x$

Video on this problem.

Solve

To solve, we'll need to find both the slope and the y-intercept. First, sketch a graph to get a feel for the line.

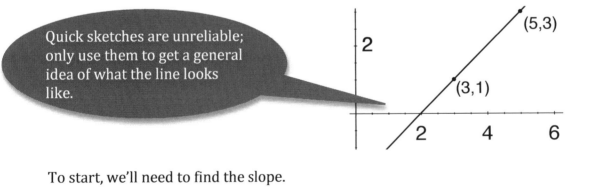

Quick sketches are unreliable; only use them to get a general idea of what the line looks like.

To start, we'll need to find the slope.

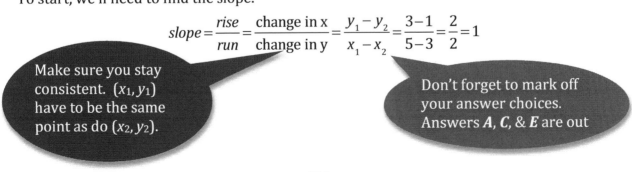

$$slope = \frac{rise}{run} = \frac{\text{change in x}}{\text{change in y}} = \frac{y_1 - y_2}{x_1 - x_2} = \frac{3-1}{5-3} = \frac{2}{2} = 1$$

Make sure you stay consistent. (x_1, y_1) have to be the same point as do (x_2, y_2).

Don't forget to mark off your answer choices. Answers **A**, **C**, & **E** are out

So, our equation looks like: $y = 1x + b$

Now, we can find the y-intercept. There are two ways to find the y-intercept. The first is to use the slope and count back to where x is zero.

The other way to find the y intercept is to plug in a point and solve.

Right now, our equation is $y = 1x + b$.
We can plug in one of our given points for x and y to reduce the number of variables in the equation to one—b. Let's use the point (3,1).

$$y = 1x + b \quad \rightarrow \quad 1 = 1(3) + b$$
$$1 = 3 + b \quad \rightarrow \quad b = -2$$

We've got our complete equation: $y = x - 2$.

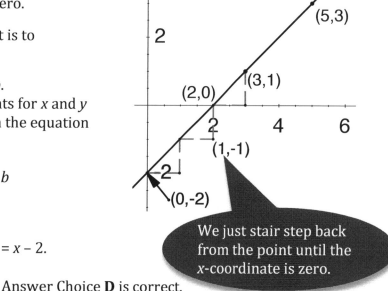

We just stair step back from the point until the x-coordinate is zero.

Answer Choice **D** is correct.

Definitions: Parallel & Perpendicular

Parallel Lines have the same slope. They have different y-intercepts (otherwise they'd be the same line). **Parallel lines never intersect.**

Perpindicular Lines have the **negative inverse slope** of each other.

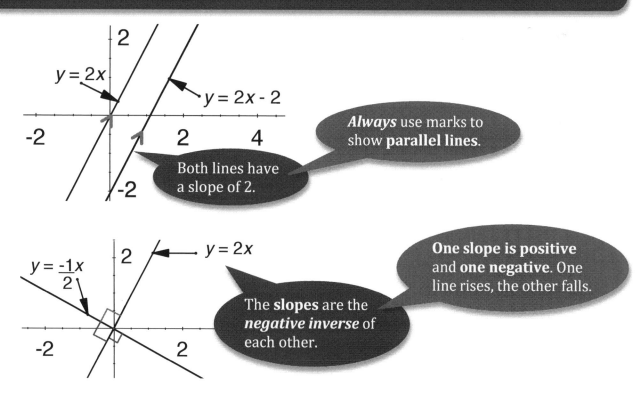

-315-

Rules of the Road: Parallel & Perpendicular Slopes

> Don't worry about the intercept when deciding whether lines are parallel or perpendicular. Only slope matters, not the intercepts.

ACT Examples: Parallel & Perpendicular Lines

1. In the standard (x, y) coordinate plane, which of the following equations is perpendicular to the line $y = -\frac{4}{3}x + 8$?

A. $y = \frac{3}{4}x + 5$

B. $y = \frac{4}{3}x + 8$

C. $y = -\frac{3}{4}x + 8$

D. $y = -\frac{4}{3}x + \frac{1}{8}$

E. $y = -\frac{3}{4}x + \frac{1}{8}$

Solve

This is really a definition question. The slope is the only thing that needs changed, and we have to remember that perpendicular lines have *negative inverse slopes*.

$$-\frac{4}{3} \rightarrow -\frac{3}{4} \quad \text{Flip the slope.}$$

$$-\frac{3}{4} \rightarrow \frac{3}{4} \quad \text{Now flip the sign.}$$

We don't need to change our intercepts; perpendicular/parallel lines can have any intercepts.

The slope of the perpendicular line will be $\frac{3}{4}$

Answer Choice **A** is correct.

Rules of the Road: Intersections

> **Two lines can intersect zero times, once, or an infinite numbers of times.** If they intersect zero times (never intersect), the lines are parallel. If the lines intersect infinite times, they are the same line.

> When two lines intersect, they share an (x, y) point.

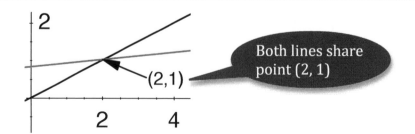

Both lines share point (2, 1)

(2,1)

Definitions: Slopes of Horizontal & Vertical Lines

Horizontal Lines have a **slope of zero**.
Vertical Lines have an **undefined slope**.

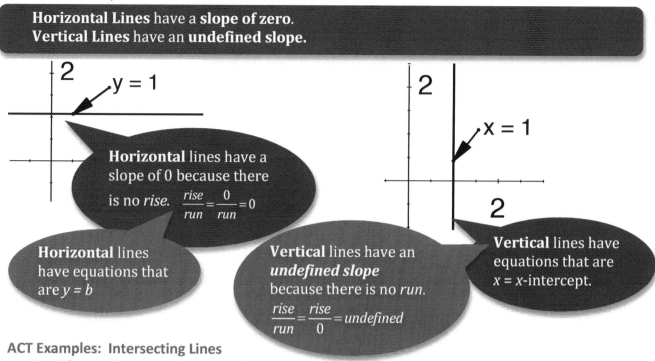

Horizontal lines have a slope of 0 because there is no *rise*. $\dfrac{rise}{run} = \dfrac{0}{run} = 0$

Horizontal lines have equations that are $y = b$

Vertical lines have an **undefined slope** because there is no *run*. $\dfrac{rise}{run} = \dfrac{rise}{0} = undefined$

Vertical lines have equations that are $x = x$-intercept.

ACT Examples: Intersecting Lines

1. What is the y-coordinate of the point, in the standard (x, y) coordinate plane, where $y = 5x + 1$ and $y = 2x + 4$ intersect?

   A. 1
   B. 6
   C. 4
   D. -3
   E. -2

Solve

This is a tough question to see what to do. One way to solve would be to plot both equations in your graphing calculator and find the intercept. I think it's faster to solve this algebraically and I encourage you to do so.

The lines will intersect when the (x, y) coordinates are equal. To find the x-coordinate, set the equations equal and solve for x.

$$y = 5x + 1 \text{ and } y = 2x + 4$$
$$5x + 1 = 2x + 4$$
$$3x = 3$$
$$x = 1$$

We have the value of x, let's plug-in to either equation to find the value of y.

$$y = 5(x) + 1$$
$$y = 5(1) + 1$$
$$y = 6$$

Answer choice **B** is correct.

<u>Wrap Up</u>

- ✓ The *slope intercept* form of line equations
- ✓ How to find the *slope & y-intercept* of a line
- ✓ *Horizontal & vertical* lines
- ✓ *Parallel & perpendicular* lines
- ✓ The solution for a linear system of equations is when the lines intersect.

Videos

The Strategies
- ✓ There are only two components to any line: slopw & *y*-intercept. Make sure you can recognize them and work with equations.
- ✓ Remember how horizontal, vertical, and perpendicular lines work.

Key Skill
The ability to recognize and use line equations is critical for ACT success. You'll need line equation skills in topics including:

- ✓ Make an Equation
- ✓ Angles
- ✓ Triangles

Coordinate Geometry: The Line Equation

1. What is the y-intercept of a line that passes through points (-2,-6) and (2, 4)?

   A.   0
   B.   -1
   C.   -2
   D.   1
   E.   3

$$\frac{10}{4} = \frac{5}{2}$$

$$4 = \frac{5}{2}(2) + b$$
$$4 = 5 + b \quad b = -1$$

2. What is the slope of a line parallel to the line $4x - 9y = 27$?

   F. $-\dfrac{1}{3}$

   G. $\dfrac{4}{9}$

   H.   -3

   J. $-\dfrac{4}{9}$

   K.   3

$$-9y = -4x + 27$$

3. What is the equation of the line shown below?

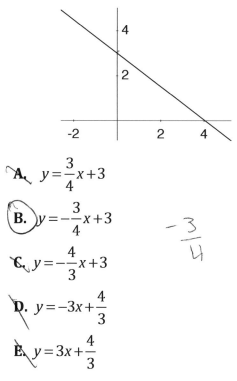

   A. $y = \dfrac{3}{4}x + 3$

   B. $y = -\dfrac{3}{4}x + 3$

   C. $y = -\dfrac{4}{3}x + 3$

   D. $y = -3x + \dfrac{4}{3}$

   E. $y = 3x + \dfrac{4}{3}$

$$\frac{-3}{4}$$

4. The table below gives ordered (x, y) pairs from a line. What is the value of $a + b$?

   F.   1
   G.   2
   H.   3
   J.   4
   K.   -2

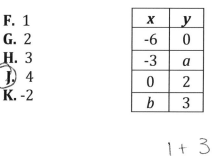

x	y
-6	0
-3	a
0	2
b	3

$$1 + 3$$

5. Brad makes a fixed amount per shift at his workplace. He also makes an hourly amount based on his productivity. Brad's pay is modeled by the equation $12x + 60 = 2y$, where x is the number of hours Brad works. If the model is correct, how much does Brad make in a five hour shift?

   A. $312.00
   B. $90.00
   C. $60.00
   D. $61.20
   E. $36.00

$$60 + 60 = 2y$$
$$120 = 2y$$
$$y = 60$$

6. What is the equation of the line shown below in the standard (x, y) coordinate plane?

   F. $y = -\dfrac{5}{2}x + 5$

   G. $y = -\dfrac{2}{5}x + 5$

   H. $y = -5x + 5$

   J. $y = 5x + 5$

   K. $y = -5x + \dfrac{5}{2}$

$$\frac{-5}{2}$$

The Line Equation: Solutions

1. **What is the y-intercept of a line that passes through points (-2,-6) and (2,4)?**

Correct Answer B

This is an intercept problem. You can't actually solve this by writing a line equation. If you do,

you'll get $y = \frac{5}{2}x + b \rightarrow y = \frac{5}{2}0 + b \rightarrow y = b$. We can't solve for both variables. (x is 0 because x is

always 0 when the line crosses the y-axis). You're going to have to use the slope and the given points to count up. You've got two points, so you can find the slope of the line. You'll use the slope to find the y-intercept.

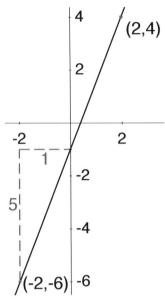

The slope is $\dfrac{rise}{run} = \dfrac{y_2 - y_1}{x_2 - x_1} \rightarrow \dfrac{4 - (-6)}{2 - (-2)} = \dfrac{10}{5} = \dfrac{5}{2}$

Starting from the bottom point, we go *up* 5 and *over* (right) 2. That takes us from x = -2 to x = 0. And the y-coordinate is the y-intercept -6 + 5 = -1.

Answer choice **B** is correct.

<u>What You May Have Done Wrong</u>

    A. This is the x value of the y-intercept.

    C. You made an arithmetic or conceptual error.

    D. You made an arithmetic or conceptual error.

    E. You made an arithmetic or conceptual error.

2. **What is the slope of a line parallel to the line 4x – 9y = 27?**

Correct Answer G

There's two components to this question: parallel lines have the same slope & you have to re-arrange the given equation to y = mx + b. This is a *which* question, so you'll mark-off. But it's not much of a mark-off question. There's really no way around finding the slope.

$$4x - 9y = 27 \quad \rightarrow \quad -9y = 27 - 4x$$

$$y = -3 + \frac{4}{9}x \quad \rightarrow \quad y = \frac{4}{9}x - 3$$

Answer choice **G** is correct.

<u>What You May Have Done Wrong</u>

    F. You made a calculation error or guessed.

    H. This is the middle term.

    J. This is the last term.

    K. You made a calculation error or guessed

3. What is the equation of the line shown below?

Correct Answer B

This is a great mark-off question. We've got to find the *y*-intercept & slope and mark-off as we go. Because it's easier to find the *y*-intercept, start there. The *y*-intercept looks like it's between 2 and 4, so we'll say it's three. We don't know *exactly* what it is, but none of the other *y*-intercepts are close. We can get rid of **D** & **E**. The slops is a little trickier, because the line falls from left to right, the slope is negative. We can get rid of **A**.

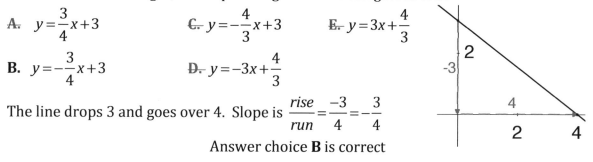

A. ~~$y = \dfrac{3}{4}x + 3$~~

C. ~~$y = -\dfrac{4}{3}x + 3$~~

E. ~~$y = 3x + \dfrac{4}{3}$~~

B. $y = -\dfrac{3}{4}x + 3$

D. ~~$y = -3x + \dfrac{4}{3}$~~

The line drops 3 and goes over 4. Slope is $\dfrac{rise}{run} = \dfrac{-3}{4} = -\dfrac{3}{4}$

Answer choice **B** is correct

4. The table below gives ordered (x, y) pairs from a line. What is the value of $a + b$?

Correct Answer J

This is a harder question. You've got to reconstruct the line from the given points. You can do that by making the line equation or just use the slope.

<u>Find the Equation</u>

The table gives you the *y*-intercept—remember, the *y*-intercept is when $x = 0$. So the *y*-intercept is 2. So far, the equation is $y = mx + 2$. Now we need to find the slope. We only have two complete points (-6,0) and (0,2), so we'll have to use those to find the slope.

$$slope = \dfrac{rise}{run} = \dfrac{y_2 - y_1}{x_2 - x_1} \quad \rightarrow \quad slope = \dfrac{2 - 0}{0 - (-6)} = \dfrac{2}{6} = \dfrac{1}{3}$$

The complete equation is $y = \dfrac{1}{3}x + 2$. We can plug-in and solve to find *a* & *b*.

x	y
-6	0
-3	a
0	2
b	3

$(-3, a) \rightarrow \quad y = \dfrac{1}{3}(-3) + 2 \quad \rightarrow \quad y = -1 + 2 \quad \rightarrow \quad y = 1$

$(b, 3) \rightarrow \quad y = \dfrac{1}{3}(3) + 2 \quad \rightarrow \quad y = 1 + 2 \quad \rightarrow \quad y = 3$

<u>Find & Use the Slope</u>

You can use the slope and "count up" to find *a* & *b*. First, find the slope:

$$slope = \dfrac{rise}{run} = \dfrac{y_2 - y_1}{x_2 - x_1} \quad \rightarrow \quad slope = \dfrac{2 - 0}{0 - (-6)} = \dfrac{2}{6} = \dfrac{1}{3}$$

Now use the slope to count up. Start with point (-6,0) and add 3 to the *x* and 1 to the *y*.

$$\begin{array}{cc} -6, & 0 \\ +3 & +1 \\ \hline -3 & 1 \end{array}$$

a is the *y*-value, so $a = 1$. To find *b* follow the same procedure but start with point (0,2), $b = 3$.

$$\begin{array}{cc} 0, & 2 \\ +3 & +1 \\ \hline 3 & 3 \end{array}$$

$a + b = 4 \rightarrow 1 + 3 = 4$

Answer choice **J** is correct.

<u>What You May Have Done Wrong</u>

F. That's the value of *a*.

G. You may have subtracted $b - a$ or made a mistake when finding *a*.

H. This is the value of *b*.

K. You may have subtracted $a - b$, or made a mistake with *a* and/or *b*.

5. **Brad makes a fixed amount per shift at his workplace. He also makes an hourly amount based on his productivity. Brad's pay is modeled by the equation $12x + 60 = 2y$, where x is the number of hours Brad works. If the model is correct, how much does Brad make in a five hour shift?**

Correct Answer C

In the equation, Brad's earnings are represented by the variable y. So, we'll want to set the equation up in slope intercept form.

$$12x + 60 = 2y \quad \rightarrow \quad 6x + 30 = y$$
$$y = 6x + 30$$

Now, plug in 5 for x.

$$y = 6x + 30 \quad \rightarrow \quad y = 6(5) + 30$$
$$y = 30 + 30 \quad \rightarrow \quad y = 60$$

Brad makes \$60 in a five hour shift.

Answer choice **C** is correct.

<u>What You May Have Done Wrong</u>
   A. You multiplied 60 by 5.
   B. You forgot to divide 60 by 2.
   D. You plugged in 5 for y.
   E. This is how much Brad makes for a 1 hour shift.

6. **What is the equation of the line shown below in the standard (x, y) coordinate plane?**

Correct Answer F

This is a two-part problem. First, find the y-intercept and mark-off.

The y-intercept is between 4 & 6, so it's got to be 5. You can be sure of this because it's the only answer between 4 & 6. We can mark-off **K**.

The slope is clearly negative, and that wil allow us to mark-off letter **J**. We can calculate slope to finish the question. The only pointswe have are the y-intercept (0,5) and the x-intercept (2,0).

$$slope = \frac{rise}{run} = \frac{y_2 - y_1}{x_2 - x_1} \quad \rightarrow \quad slope = \frac{5-0}{0-2} = \frac{5}{-2} = -\frac{5}{2}$$

Answer **F** is correct.

<u>What You May Have Done Wrong</u>
   G. You inverted the slope, putting *run* over *rise*.
   H. You miscalculated or misunderstood the slope.
   J. You miscalculated or misunderstood the slope.
   K. You miscalculated or misunderstood the slope, and you made a mistake with your y-intercept.

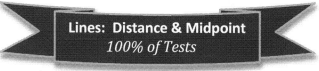
Introduction

The distance formula shows up on nearly every ACT, and midpoint is a little less common. Both formulas are worth remembering and are easy to remember with a few tricks.

What You Need to Know

✓ The distance formula (or use the Pythagorean Theorem)
✓ How to find the midpoint (average x, average y)
✓ How to find the function of an angle on a co-ordinate axis, which sides are opposite, adjacent, and hypotenuse.

Definitions: The Distance Formula

The Distance Formula finds the straight line distance between two points.

$$distance = \sqrt{\left(x_1 - x_2\right)^2 + \left(y_1 - y_2\right)^2}$$

There's a *video* on the *Distance Formula*

Rules of the Road: The Distance Formula

The distance formula is really the *Pythagorean Theorem*—use that, it is easier to remember.

Distance has two components: the change in x and the change in y.

The distance formula is the Pythagorean Theorem, except we have to find how long the legs of the triangle are.

The Distance Formula

$$distance = \sqrt{\left(x_1 - x_2\right)^2 + \left(y_1 - y_2\right)^2}$$

$$distance = \sqrt{\left(3 - 0\right)^2 + \left(3 - 1\right)^2}$$

$$distance = \sqrt{\left(3\right)^2 + \left(2\right)^2}$$

$$distance = \sqrt{9 + 4}$$

$$distance = \sqrt{13}$$

The Pythagorean Theorem

$$a^2 + b^2 = c^2$$

$$3^2 + 2^2 = c^2$$

$$9 + 4 = c^2$$

$$c^2 = 13$$

$$c = \sqrt{13}$$

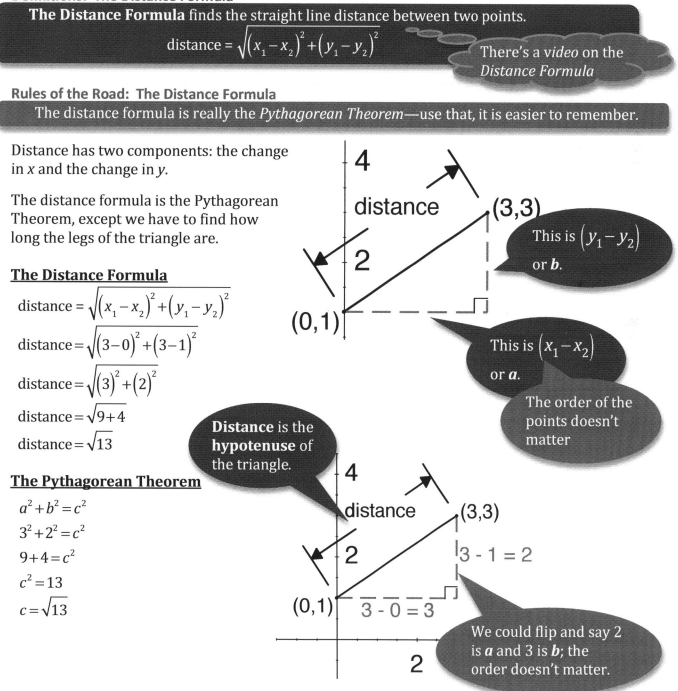

This is $\left(y_1 - y_2\right)$ or **b**.

This is $\left(x_1 - x_2\right)$ or **a**.

The order of the points doesn't matter

Distance is the **hypotenuse** of the triangle.

We could flip and say 2 is **a** and 3 is **b**; the order doesn't matter.

1. In the standard (x, y) coordinate plane, what is the distance, in units, between points $(4, 3)$ and $(-5, -3)$?

  A. 1
  B. $\sqrt{106}$
  C. 3
  D. $9\sqrt{13}$
  E. $3\sqrt{13}$

Solve

Let's start by sketching a graph.

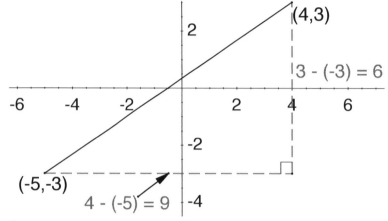

Now plug into the Pythagorean Theorem:

$$a^2 + b^2 = c^2 \quad \rightarrow \quad 9^2 + 6^2 = c^2$$

$$81 + 36 = c^2 \quad \rightarrow \quad c^2 = 117$$

$$c = \sqrt{117} \rightarrow \sqrt{3 \cdot 3 \cdot 13} \rightarrow 3\sqrt{13}$$

Simplify the radical.

Answer Choice **E** is correct.

Definitions: The Distance Formula

The Midpoint Formula finds the middle point of a line segment by taking the average of the x and y endpoints.

$$\text{midpoint} = \left(\frac{x_1 + x_2}{2}, \frac{y_1 + y_2}{2} \right)$$

$$\text{midpoint} = \left(\frac{x_1 + x_2}{2}, \frac{y_1 + y_2}{2} \right)$$

$$\text{midpoint} = \left(\frac{1+5}{2}, \frac{1+5}{2} \right)$$

$$\text{midpoint} = (3,3)$$

There's a *video* on *Midpoint*.

Rules of the Road: Midpoint

> To find the midpoint, **take the average of the x and y endpoints.**
> $$\text{midpoint} = \left(average\ x, average\ y\right)$$

Recall that average is calculated by $average = \dfrac{\text{sum of all terms}}{\text{number of terms}}$

ACT Examples: Midpoint

1. What is the sum of the x and y coordinates of the midpoint in a line segment that has endpoints of (7,2) and (-1, -3)?

   A. 3.5
   B. 2.5
   C. 3.0
   D. 2.0
   E. 4.0

Solve

Let's sketch a graph. The graph will give us a good idea of the signs in our midpoint. Let's do the math.

$$\text{midpoint} = \left(average\ x, average\ y\right)$$

$$\text{midpoint} = \left(\frac{7+(-1)}{2}, \frac{2+(-3)}{2}\right)$$

$$\text{midpoint} = \left(3, -\frac{1}{2}\right)$$

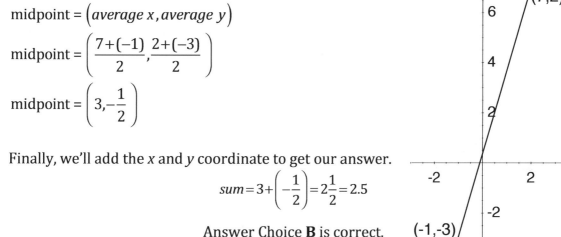

Finally, we'll add the x and y coordinate to get our answer.

$$sum = 3 + \left(-\frac{1}{2}\right) = 2\frac{1}{2} = 2.5$$

Answer Choice **B** is correct.

Wrap Up

What You Need to Know
✓ The distance formula (or use the Pythagorean Theorem)
✓ How to find the midpoint (average x, average y)
✓ How to find the function of an angle on a co-ordinate axis, which sides are opposite, adjacent, and hypotenuse.

Videos

> The Distance Formula

> The Midpoint Formula

The Strategies
✓ Draw sketches on both midpoint & distance questions if a diagram isn't provided.
✓ Use the Pythagorean Theorem for the distance formula, it's easy to remember

Related Skills
✓ The Pythagorean Theorem (Right Triangles)
✓ Trig: Find the Side

Distance & Midpoint: Problems

1. $\overline{AB}$ has endpoints of $(3,-1)$ and $(5, 9)$.
What is the midpoint of $\overline{AB}$?

  A. $(6,2)$
  B. $(4,5)$
  C. $(4,4)$
  D. $(8,8)$
  E. $(2,6)$

2. In the standard (x, y) coordinate plane, what is the distance, in coordinate units, between $(-1, 3)$ and $(4, 6)$?

  F. 8
  G. 34
  H. $\sqrt{34}$
  J. 17
  K. $3\sqrt{2}$

3. In the standard (x, y) coordinate plane, a line segment has an endpoint on the origin. The other endpoint is at $(-30, 25)$. What is the midpoint of the line segment?

  A. $(15, 12.5)$
  B. $(12.5, -15)$
  C. $(12.5, 15)$
  D. $(0, 0)$
  E. $(-15, 12.5)$

4. What is the distance in the standard (x, y) coordinate plane, for a line segment with endpoints $(-4, 6)$ and $(0, 14)$?

  F. $4\sqrt{26}$
  G. $4\sqrt{5}$
  H. 20
  J. 8
  K. $4\sqrt{3}$

5. In the standard (x, y) coordinate plane, a line segment $\overline{AB}$ has an endpoint A of $(10,4)$ and midpoint of $(6,0)$. What are the coordinates of point B?

  A. $(14,8)$
  B. $(8,2)$
  C. $(5,5)$
  D. $(8,-2)$
  E. $(2,-4)$

6. The triangle below is in the standard (x, y) coordinate plane with vertices as marked. What is the area of the triangle?

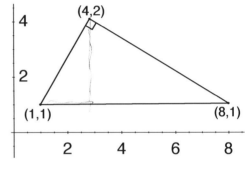

  F. 21
  G. 20
  H. 10.5
  J. 28
  K. 14

1. $\overline{AB}$ has endpoints of (3,-1) and (5, 9). What is the midpoint of $\overline{AB}$?

Correct Answer C

This is a *midpoint* question. To find the midpoint, we find the average of the endpoints of both the *x* and *y*.

$$\text{midpoint} = (\textit{average x, average y}) \quad \rightarrow \quad \text{midpoint} = \left(\left(\frac{x_1+x_2}{2}\right),\left(\frac{y_1+y_2}{2}\right)\right)$$

$$\text{midpoint} = \left(\left(\frac{3+5}{2}\right),\left(\frac{-1+9}{2}\right)\right) \quad \rightarrow \quad \text{midpoint} = \left(\left(\frac{8}{2}\right),\left(\frac{8}{2}\right)\right)$$

$$\text{midpoint} = (4,4)$$

Answer choice **C** is correct.

<u>What You May Have Done Wrong</u>
  A. You made an arithmetic error, averaging the *x* of the first with the *y* of the second.
  B. You dropped the sign on the -1, which caused you to miscalculate *y* in the midpoint.
  D. This is a halfway answer. You added the points but forgot to divide to find the average.
  E. You made an arithmetic error, averaging the *x* of the first with the *y* of the second.

2. In the standard (x, y) coordinate plane, what is the distance, in coordinate units, between (-1, 3) and (4, 6)?

Correct Answer H

This is a *distance* question. We can either have the distance formula memorized or use the Pythagorean Theorem.

First, let's sketch a graph. Now that we have the leg lengths of the right triangle, we can find the hypotenuse.

$$a^2+b^2=c^2 \quad \rightarrow \quad 5^2+3^2=c^2$$
$$c^2=25+9 \quad \rightarrow \quad c=\sqrt{34}$$

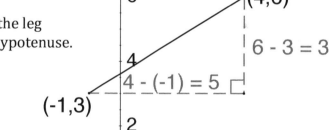

Or, we could use the distance formula (which is just the Pythagorean Theorem without calculating the sides first).

$$d=\sqrt{(x_1-x_2)^2+(y_1-y_2)^2} \quad \rightarrow \quad d=\sqrt{(4-(-1))^2+(6-3)^2} \quad \rightarrow \quad d=\sqrt{(5)^2+(3)^2} \rightarrow \sqrt{34}$$

This can't be simplified.

Answer choice **H** is correct.

<u>What You May Have Done Wrong</u>
  F. You may have taken the square root of each individual side, you have to take the square root of the sum.
  G. This is the value of the distance squared, or hypotenuse squared.
  J. You may have divided 34 by 2. Make sure you understand square roots.
  K. You made an error calculating the base, check your steps.

3. In the standard (x, y) coordinate plane, a line segment has an endpoint on the origin. The other endpoint is at (-30, 25). What is the midpoint of the line segment?

Correct Answer E

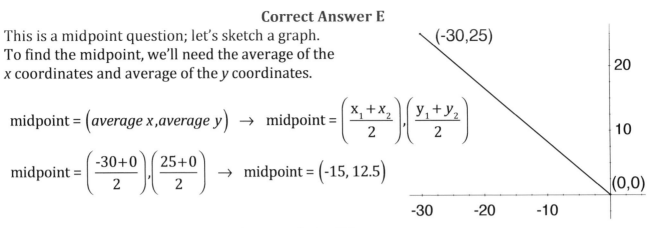

This is a midpoint question; let's sketch a graph.
To find the midpoint, we'll need the average of the
x coordinates and average of the y coordinates.

$$\text{midpoint} = \left(average\ x, average\ y\right) \rightarrow \text{midpoint} = \left(\frac{x_1 + x_2}{2}\right)\left(\frac{y_1 + y_2}{2}\right)$$

$$\text{midpoint} = \left(\frac{-30+0}{2}\right)\left(\frac{25+0}{2}\right) \rightarrow \text{midpoint} = \left(-15, 12.5\right)$$

Answer choice **E** is correct

What You May Have Done Wrong
    A. You dropped your sign on your x-coordinate.
    B. You flipped the order of the points.
    C. You flipped the order of your points *and* you dropped the sign on your x-coordinate.
    D. This is the origin, one of the endpoints.

4. What is the distance in the standard (x, y) coordinate plane, for a line segment with endpoints $(-4, 6)$ and $(0, 14)$?

Correct Answer G

This is a *distance formula* question. We can either have the distance formula memorized or use the Pythagorean Theorem. We can either use the Pythagorean Theorem or the distance formula.

$$a^2 + b^2 = c^2$$
$$4^2 + 8^2 = c^2$$
$$16 + 64 = 80 = c^2$$
$$c = \sqrt{80}$$
$$c = \sqrt{4 \cdot 20} \rightarrow 2\sqrt{4 \cdot 5} \rightarrow 4\sqrt{5}$$

We can also use the distance formula.

$$\text{distance} = \sqrt{\left(x_1 - x_2\right)^2 + \left(y_1 - y_2\right)^2} \quad \rightarrow \quad \text{distance} = \sqrt{\left(0-(-4)\right)^2 + \left(14-6\right)^2}$$

$$\text{distance} = \sqrt{\left(4\right)^2 + \left(8\right)^2} \rightarrow \sqrt{16+64} \quad \rightarrow \quad \text{distance} = \sqrt{80} \rightarrow \sqrt{4 \cdot 20} = 4\sqrt{5}$$

Answer choice **G** is correct.

What You May Have Done Wrong:
    F. You miscalculated the length of one leg of the triangle as 20.
    H. Most likely, you had a problem factoring the square root.
    J. You had an arithmetic error, probably sign related.
    K. You had an arithmetic error, probably sign related.

5. In the standard (x, y) coordinate plane, a line segment $\overline{AB}$ has an endpoint A of (10,4) and midpoint of (6,0). What are the coordinates of point B?

Correct Answer E

This midpoint question has a twist. We've got a midpoint and an endpoint and we'll need to find the other midpoint. The easiest way to do this is to find the direction from the given endpoint to the midpoint and then replicate the change in x and y from that midpoint to our missing endpoint.

It's important to draw a good sketch and keep your points clear. From the endpoint to the midpoint, we go left (negative) four and down (negative) four.

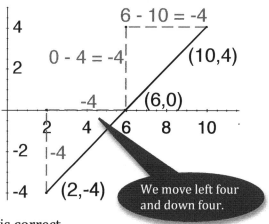

Subtract 4 from both the x & y to find the endpoint.

$$\big((6-4),(0-4)\big)$$
$$\big(2,-4\big)$$

Answer choice **E** is correct.

__What You May Have Done Wrong__
A. You used (6,0) as an endpoint and (10,4) as a midpoint.
B. You found the midpoint of (10,4) and (6,0).
C. You made an arithmetic error, flipping your points.
D. You've made a compound error, review your steps.

6. The triangle below is in the standard (x, y) coordinate plane with vertices as marked. What is the area of the triangle?

Correct Answer H

This is a triangle area question with a distance component. The question tries to trick you into using the distance formula (or Pythagorean Theorem) to find the length of the base and the perpendicular height. But, we can use the coordinate plane to give us a base and perpendicular height *without* using the distance formula.

Because one line is parallel to the x-axis, we subtract the y values to find the length. We draw a line straight up (perpendicular to the x axis) to find our *height*.

Now we can find the area of the triangle.

$$area = \frac{1}{2}base \bullet height$$

$$area = \frac{1}{2} 7 \bullet 3 = 10.5$$

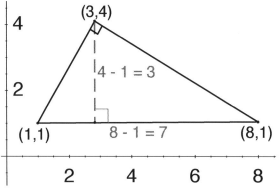

Answer **H** is correct.

__What You May Have Done Wrong__
F. You forgot the divide the area by 2 (or multiply by ½).
G. This is a compound error. Check your steps.
J. This is a compound error. Review your steps.
K. This is a compound error. Review your steps.

Introduction
Questions involving the definition and manipulation of the coordinate plane show up on every test. For the most part, these questions are based on definitions and are conceptual.

What You Need to Know
- ✓ Which quadrants are which
- ✓ How to reflect a point across the *x* or *y* axis
- ✓ How figures are rotated

There's a *video* on Quadrants, Reflections, & Rotation

Definitions: Quadrants
Quadrants are labeled counterclockwise starting in the top right.

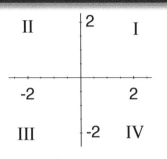

Definitions: Reflections
Reflections across the x-axis keep the same x-coordinate and the y-coordinate's sign flips.
Reflections across the y-axis keep the same y-coordinate and the x-coordinate's sign flips.
Reflections make *mirror images*.

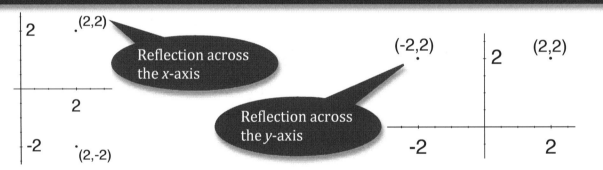

Reflection across the x-axis

Reflection across the y-axis

Definitions: Rotations
Rotations spins figures around the origin

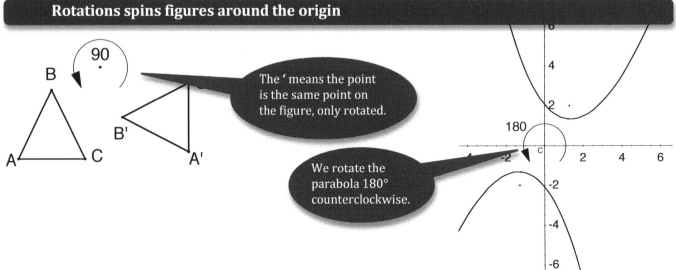

The ' means the point is the same point on the figure, only rotated.

We rotate the parabola 180° counterclockwise.

ACT Examples: Quadrants, Reflections, and Rotations

1. In which of the following quadrants will the product of the *x* coordinate and *y* coordinate of every point be negative?

    A. I and II only
    B. II only
    C. IV only
    D. II and III only
    E. II and IV only

Solve

To solve, sketch a coordinate axis and label the signs of points in those quadrants. The product of any point will be...

$$x \text{ coordinate} \cdot y \text{ coordinate} = product$$

So, for any product to be negative, the *x* and *y* coordinates must be different signs. This only occurs in quadrant II and quadrant IV.

Answer choice **E** is correct.

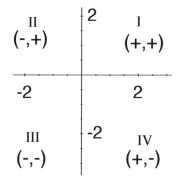

2. Which of the following reflects the graph below across the *x*-axis?

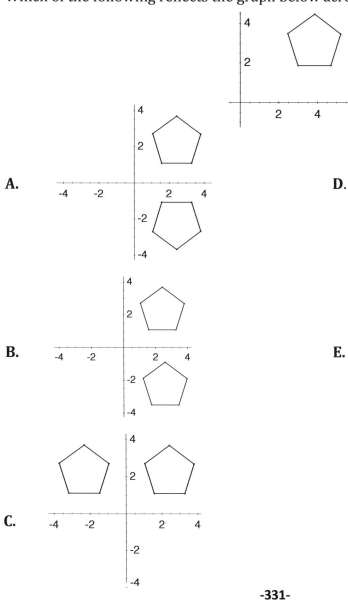

Solve

This is a definition question. A reflection about the *x*-axis, we're folding the coordinate plane in half horizontally.

Answer choice **A** is correct.

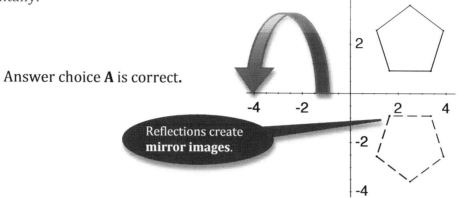

Reflections create **mirror images**.

3. The graph shown below is in the standard (x, y) coordinate plane and is to be rotated 180° about the origin. Which quadrant will point *A* be in?

A. I
B. II
C. III
D. IV
E. Cannot be Determined

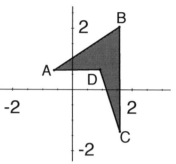

Solve

The key is remembering you rotate the graph from the origin not from a point on the shape. When we rotate the graph 180° the quadrants move diagonally. What's in quadrant I goes to quadrant III & what's in quadrant II goes to quadrant IV. Point *A* is in quadrant II and when it is rotated, it ends up in quadrant IV.

Answer choice **D** is correct.

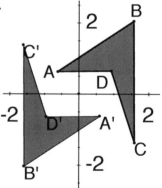

<u>Wrap Up</u>

What You Need to Know
- ✓ Which quadrants are which
- ✓ How to reflect a point across the *x* or *y* axis
- ✓ How figures are rotated

Videos

Quadrants, Rotations, & Reflections

The Strategies
- ✓ Use the diagram; remember reflections make mirror images and rotations go around the origin.

Related Skills
- ✓ Coordinate Geometry Shapes

Coordinate Geometry: Quadrants, Reflections, & Rotations

1. Point *P* is in the standard coordinate plane shown below, and point *P* does not rest on an axis. For the *x* and *y* coordinates to have the same sign, what quadrant(s) could point *P* be in?

    A. I only
    B. IV only
    C. III only
    D. II & IV only
    E. I & III only

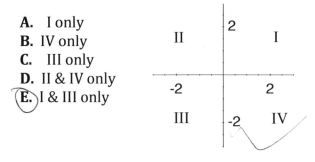

4. Point *D* is in the standard (x, y) coordinate plane and is not on an axis. If the product of point *D*'s *x* and *y*-coordinates is positive, which quadrants could point *D* be in?

    F. Quadrant I only
    G. Quadrants I and II only
    H. Quadrants I and III only
    J. Quadrants II and IV only
    K. Quadrant I and II only

2. The graph shown below is in the standard (x, y) coordinate plane and will be rotated 180° about the origin. What quadrant will point *C* be in?

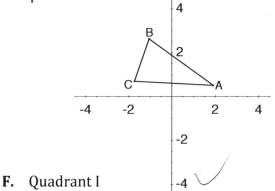

    F. Quadrant I
    G. Quadrant II
    H. Quadrant III
    J. Quadrant IV
    K. Cannot be Determined

5. Point *B* has coordinates of (2,-2) in the standard (x, y) coordinate plane. Point *B* is rotated 90° clockwise around the origin. What quadrant will the rotated point, point *B'*, be in?

    A. Quadrant I
    B. Quadrant II
    C. Quadrant III
    D. Quadrant IV
    E. Cannot be Determined

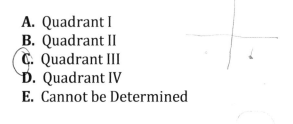

3. Point *A* has the coordinates (1,1) in the standard (x, y) coordinate plane. Point *B* is point *A* reflected across the *x*-axis. What is the sum of the *y*-coordinates of point *A* and point *B*?

    A. 0
    B. 1
    C. 2
    D. 3
    E. -2

6. Line segment *AB* is in the standard (x, y) coordinate plane with endpoints as marked. $\overline{AB}$ is reflected across the *x*-axis. What is the slope of the resulting line segment $\overline{A'B'}$?

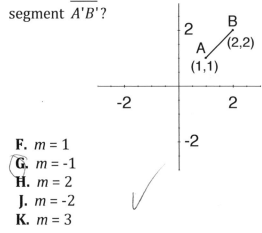

    F. $m = 1$
    G. $m = -1$
    H. $m = 2$
    J. $m = -2$
    K. $m = 3$

1. Point P is in the standard coordinate plane shown below, and point *P* does not rest on an axis. For the x and y coordinates to have the same sign, what quadrant(s) could point P be in?

Correct Answer E

This is a *quadrant question*. To solve this problem, mark up your diagram with the signs the *x*, and *y*-coordinates will have in each quadrant.

The only quadrants that have the same sign for both the *x* and the *y* coordinates are quadrants I and quadrants III.

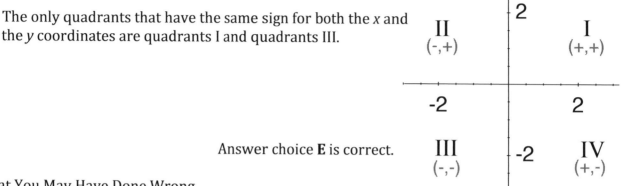

Answer choice **E** is correct.

<u>What You May Have Done Wrong</u>
> **For all wrong answer choices, you most likely misunderstood the question. Review your steps.**

2. The graph shown below is in the standard (x, y) coordinate plane and will be rotated 180° about the origin. What quadrant will point C be in?

Correct Answer J

This is a *rotation question*. We're going to "spin" the triangle in the coordinate axis 180°. As we spin it, the points move diagonally across coordinates. Meaning, the point in quadrant I moves to quadrant III and the points in quadrant II moves to quadrant IV.

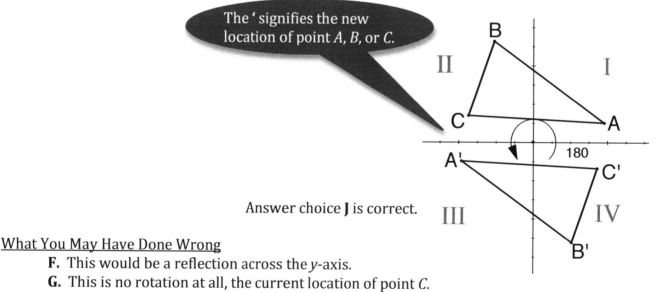

The ' signifies the new location of point *A*, *B*, or *C*.

Answer choice **J** is correct.

<u>What You May Have Done Wrong</u>
> **F.** This would be a reflection across the *y*-axis.
> **G.** This is no rotation at all, the current location of point *C*.
> **H.** This would be a 90° counterclockwise rotation.
> **K.** You may have misunderstood the problem, or guessed.

3. **Point _A_ has the coordinates (1,1) in the standard (x, y) coordinate plane. Point _B_ is point _A_ reflected across the x-axis. What is the sum of the y-coordinates of point _A_ and point _B_?**

Correct Answer A

This is a _reflection question_. Let's sketch a quick diagram:

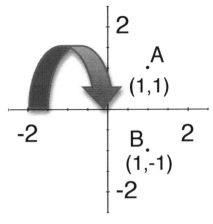

Essentially, we are "folding" the coordinate plane across the x-axis (like a piece of paper). This causes point _A_ to flip down and point _B_ will keep the same x-coordinate coordinate. The y-coordinate will have the same _absolute value_ but will have a the opposite sign.

Our coordinate points are _A_ = (1,1) and _B_ = (1,-1)

The sum of the y-coordinates will be 1 + (-1) = 0

Answer choice **A** is correct

<u>What You May Have Done Wrong</u>
    B. You may have misunderstood the question. Review your steps.
    C. You found the sum of the x-coordinates.
    D. You may have misunderstood the question. Review your steps.
    E. You may have misunderstood the question. Review your steps.

4. **Point D is in the standard (x, y) coordinate plane and is not on an axis. If the product of point D's x and y-coordinates is positive, which quadrants could point D be in?**

Correct Answer H

This is a _quadrant question_. To solve, sketch & label the quadrants and label the signs of the (x, y) coordinates in each quadrant.

Quadrant I: $+ \bullet + = +$

~~Quadrant II:~~ $- \bullet + = -$

Quadrant III: $- \bullet - = +$

~~Quadrant IV:~~ $- \bullet + = -$

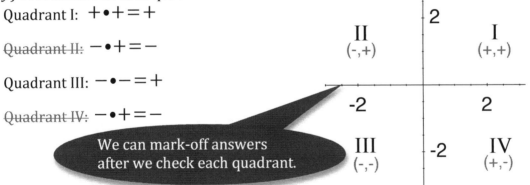

We can mark-off answers after we check each quadrant.

Answer choice **H** is correct.

<u>What You May Have Done Wrong:</u>
    F. This is a halfway answer, quadrant I's product is positive, but it won't be the only quadrant.
    G. Quadrant II will be negative, you may have gotten hung up on the fact that it has a positive y-coordinate.
    J. The products of these quadrants are both negative. You may have misread your question.
    K. Quadrant II will be negative, you may have gotten hung up on the fact that it has a positive y-coordinate.

5. Point B has coordinates of (2,-2) in the standard (x, y) coordinate plane. Point B is rotated 90° clockwise around the origin. What quadrant will the rotated point, point B', be in?

Correct Answer A

This is a *rotation question*. We need to spin the graph counterclockwise by 1/4th circle (90°).

This moves point *B* **up** into quadrant I.

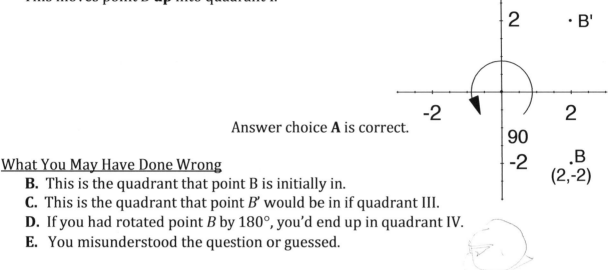

Answer choice **A** is correct.

<u>What You May Have Done Wrong</u>
    B. This is the quadrant that point B is initially in.
    C. This is the quadrant that point *B'* would be in if quadrant III.
    D. If you had rotated point *B* by 180°, you'd end up in quadrant IV.
    E. You misunderstood the question or guessed.

6. Line segment $\overline{AB}$ is in the standard (x, y) coordinate plane with endpoints as marked. $\overline{AB}$ is reflected across the x-axis. What is the slope of the resulting line segment $\overline{A'B'}$?

Correct Answer G

This is a *reflection question* that also requires you to understand *slope*. We're reflecting across the *x*-axis, so let's start by marking up our diagram.

When we reflect across the *x*-axis, the *x*-coordinates remain the same, and the *y*-coordinates flip signs. We can also think of it as the bottommost point becoming the topmost, and vice versa.

We can now calculate our new slope.

$$slope = \frac{rise}{run} = \frac{y_2 - y_1}{x_2 - x_1} = \frac{-2-(-1)}{2-1} = -\frac{1}{1} = -1$$

Answer **G** is correct.

<u>What You May Have Done Wrong</u>
    F. This is the original slope.
    H. You either miscalculated the slope or had an error in finding the reflected points.
    J. You either miscalculated the slope or had an error in finding the reflected points.
    K. You either miscalculated the slope or had an error in finding the reflected points.

Introduction

On the ACT, graphing inequalities usually means finding the solution of a system of liner inequalities. Often, we don't need to do many (or even any) calculations—you'll just need to understand the inequality and properly read the graph.

What You Need to Know

✓ Graphing lines (covered in *Coord Geo: The Line Equation*)
✓ How to interpret linear inequalities (covered in *Elem. Algebra: Inequalities*)
✓ Graphing linear inequalities

Definitions: The Graphs of Linear Inequalities

Linear inequalities are graphed as a line with shading above or below to include the other answers of the inequality.

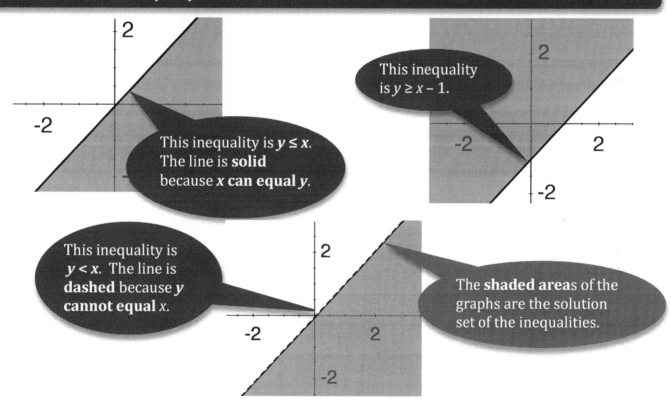

This inequality is $y \leq x$. The line is **solid** because *x can equal y*.

This inequality is $y \geq x - 1$.

This inequality is $y < x$. The line is **dashed** because *y cannot equal* x.

The **shaded areas** of the graphs are the solution set of the inequalities.

Rules of the Road: Graphing Linear Inequalities

> **There are two steps to graphing inequalities:**
> 1. Graph the line using the slope and *y*-intercept.
> 2. If **y is greater** than the *x* expression shade **above (towards the positive)** of the line.
>   If **y is less** than the *x* expression shade **below (towards the negative)** of the line.

Mechanics: Graphing Linear Inequalities

1. Graph the function $y \leq 2x - 2$.

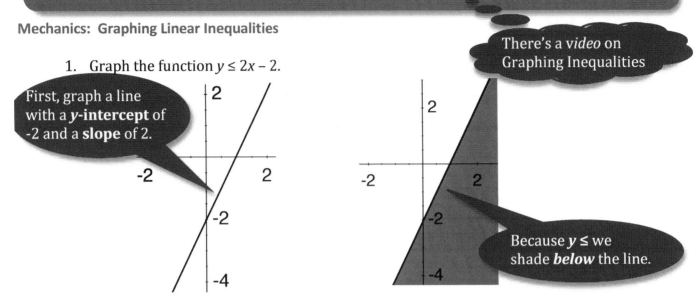

First, graph a line with a **y-intercept** of -2 and a **slope** of 2.

There's a *video* on Graphing Inequalities

Because $y \leq$ we shade **below** the line.

Rules of the Road: Graphing Systems of Inequalities

> The steps are the same in graphing systems of inequalities but we only shade the area that *both* inequalities share.

1. Graph the system of inequalities: $y < -2x + 1$ and $y \leq 3x - 1$?

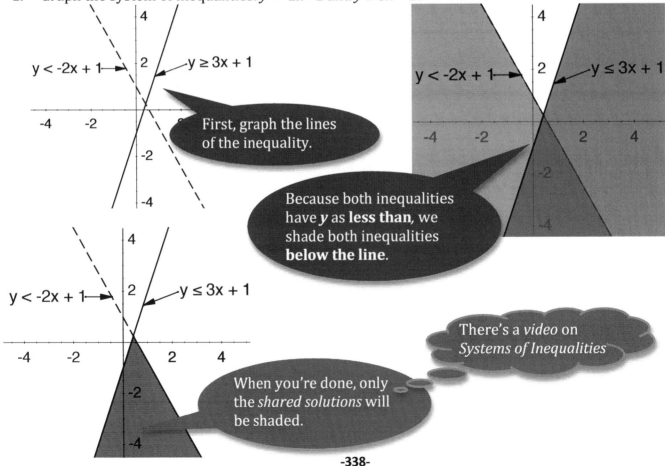

First, graph the lines of the inequality.

Because both inequalities have **y** as **less than**, we shade both inequalities **below the line**.

When you're done, only the *shared solutions* will be shaded.

There's a *video* on *Systems of Inequalities*

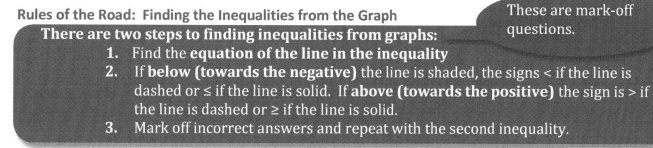

These are mark-off questions.

There are two steps to finding inequalities from graphs:
1. Find the **equation of the line in the inequality**
2. If **below (towards the negative)** the line is shaded, the signs < if the line is dashed or ≤ if the line is solid. If **above (towards the positive)** the sign is > if the line is dashed or ≥ if the line is solid.
3. Mark off incorrect answers and repeat with the second inequality.

ACT Examples: Graphing Systems of Inequalities

1. The graph is in the standard (x, y) coordinate plane. Which of the following systems of inequalities represents the solution set below?

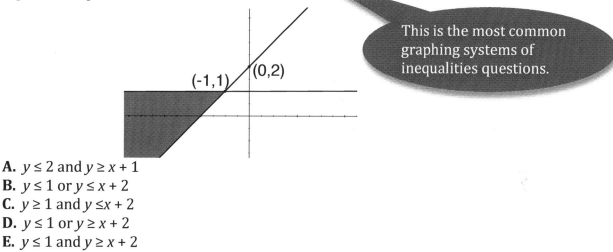

This is the most common graphing systems of inequalities questions.

   A. $y \leq 2$ and $y \geq x + 1$
   B. $y \leq 1$ or $y \leq x + 2$
   C. $y \geq 1$ and $y \leq x + 2$
   D. $y \leq 1$ or $y \geq x + 2$
   E. $y \leq 1$ and $y \geq x + 2$

Solve

Typically, on the ACT, we work from the graph *to* find the inequalities. Let's look at the horizontal line.

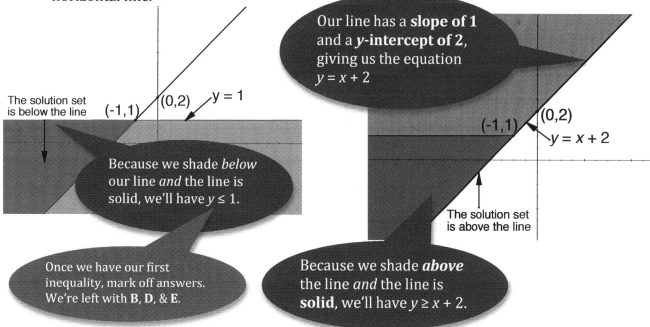

Our line has a **slope of 1** and a **y-intercept of 2**, giving us the equation $y = x + 2$

The solution set is below the line

Because we shade *below* our line *and* the line is solid, we'll have $y \leq 1$.

The solution set is above the line

Once we have our first inequality, mark off answers. We're left with **B**, **D**, & **E**.

Because we shade *above* the line *and* the line is solid, we'll have $y \geq x + 2$.

The last trick is to know that the answer has to have "and." For our segment to be the only segment shaded, it has to be the overlap of $y \leq 1$ *and* $y \geq x + 2$.

Answer choice **E** is correct.

2. The graph below is in the standard (x, y) coordinate plane and represents the graph of $y < ax + b$. What will be the signs of a and b?

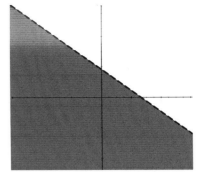

   A. a is negative and b is positive
   B. a is negative and b is negative
   C. a is positive and b is negative
   D. a is positive and b is positive
   E. cannot be determined

$y = mx + b$

Solve

While this is an inequality question, it's really about line equations. In the problem a is the slope and b is the y-intercept. The line falls from left-to-right, so the slope is negative. The y-intercept is *above* the x-axis, and is positive.

Answer choice **A** is correct.

Wrap Up

What You Need to Know
   ✓ Graphing lines
   ✓ How to interpret linear inequalities
   ✓ Graphing linear inequalities

Videos

   Graphing Inequalities

   Systems of Inequalities

The Strategies
   ✓ Break these questions into pieces, use the answer choices as guides. Don't view the problem as a complicated whole, turn it into small, easily determined pieces.
   ✓ These are almost always mark-off questions.

Related Skills

Graphing inequalities is related to:

   ✓ Graphing lines

   ✓ Inequalities

Coordinate Geometry: Inequalities

1. Which of the following systems of inequalities is represented by the shaded region of the graph below?

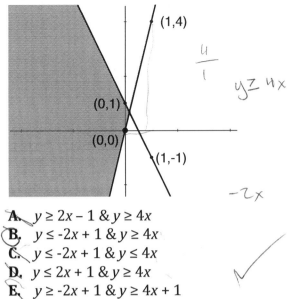

A. $y \geq 2x - 1$ & $y \geq 4x$
B. $y \leq -2x + 1$ & $y \geq 4x$
C. $y \leq -2x + 1$ & $y \leq 4x$
D. $y \leq 2x + 1$ & $y \geq 4x$
E. $y \geq -2x + 1$ & $y \geq 4x + 1$

2. The inequality $y \leq ax + b$ is graphed below and a and b are constants. What are the signs of a and b?

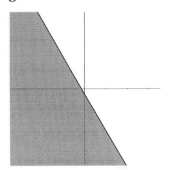

F. $a = -$ & $b = +$
G. $a = +$ & $b = -$
H. $a = -$ & $b = -$
J. $a = +$ & $b = +$
K. Cannot be Determined

3. At a bake sale lemon bars are sold for $3 and cookies are sold for $2. The bake sale's goal is to raise $900. Which of the following graphs represents all possible combinations of sales that raise at least 900 dollars?

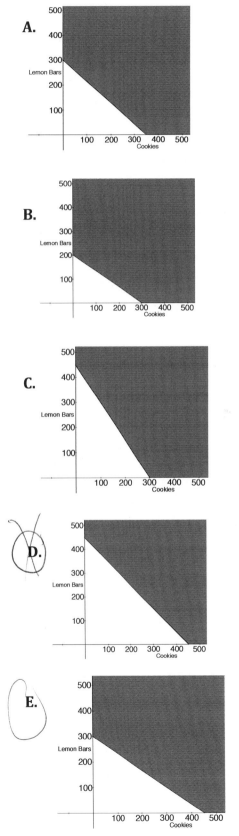

4. The graph below is in the standard (x, y) coordinate plane and the shaded area represents the solution of a system of linear inequalities. Which set of inequalities gives the solution graphed below?

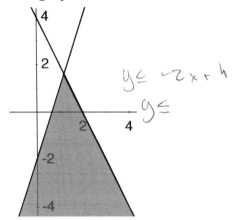

$y \le -2x + 4$
$y \le$

F. $y \le 3x - 2$ and $y \le -2x + 4$
G. $y \ge 3x - 2$ and $y \ge -2x + 4$
H. $y \le 3x + 4$ and $y \le -2x - 4$
J. $y \ge 3x + 4$ and $y \le -2x - 4$
K. $y \le 3x - 2$ and $y \ge -2x + 4$

5. The shaded region of the graph shown below is the solution set for which of the following systems of inequalities?

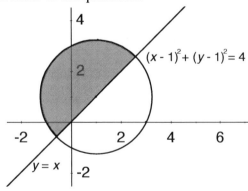

A. $y > x$ and $(x - 1)^2 + (y - 1)^2 \le 4$
B. $y \ge x$ and $(x - 1)^2 + (y - 1)^2 \le 4$
C. $y < x$ and $(x - 1)^2 + (y - 1)^2 \ge 4$
D. $y \ge x$ and $(x - 1)^2 + (y - 1)^2 \ge 4$
E. $y \ge x$ and $(x - 1)^2 + (y - 1)^2 < 4$

6. Which of the following equations best represents the system of inequalities below?

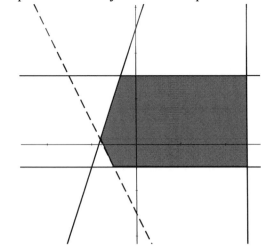

F. $-1 \le y \le 3, x \ge 5, y \le 3x + 5, y > -2x - 3$
G. $-1 \le y \le 3, x \le 5, y \ge 3x + 5, y > -2x - 3$
H. $-1 \le y \le 3, x \le 5, y \le 3x + 5, y > -2x - 3$
J. $-1 \ge y \ge 3, x \le 5, y \le 3x + 5, y > -2x - 3$
K. $-1 \ge y \ge 3, x \ge 5, y \le 3x + 5, y > -2x - 3$

$y \le 3$
$y \le$

Systems of Inequalities: Solutions

1. **Which of the following systems of inequalities is represented by the shaded region of the graph below?**

Correct Answer B

This is a great mark-off question. I would solve this question in pieces; find one inequality, mark-off, and then find the second inequality. You can start with either inequality.

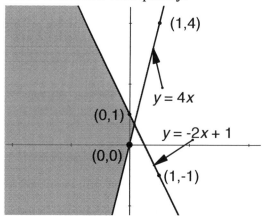

The first line has a positive slope of 4 and a y-intercept of zero. So the equation of the line is $y = 4x$.
Because the *uphill* side of the line is shaded we've got the inequality of $y \geq 4x$.

We can mark off **C & E**.

The second line has a slope of -2 and a y-intercept of +1. The equation of the line is $y = -2x +1$.
Because *below* the line is shaded, we have the inequality $y \leq -2x +1$.

Answer choice **B** is correct.

<u>What You May Have Done Wrong</u>

    A. The y-intercept of the first inequality is wrong (should be +1, not -1). The slope of that inequality is also wrong.

    C. The second inequality is $\geq$, not $\leq$. Remember the uphill side is shaded.

    D. The slope of the first inequality is wrong. It should be -2.

    E. The second inequality has a y-intercept of 0, not 1.

2. **The inequality $y \leq ax + b$ is graphed below and a and b are constants. What are the signs of a and b?**

Correct Answer H

This is another mark-off question. It's much easier to decide a or b and then mark-off. You're also much less likely to make a simple mistake.

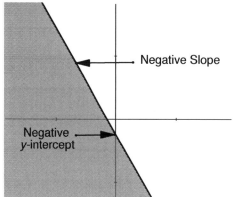

First, determine the slope (a). Since the graph falls from left to right, the slope is negative. This allows us to mark-off **G & J**.

Second, look at the y-intercept. The line intercepts the y-axis *below* the x-axis, making the value of b negative. This allows us to mark-off **F**.

Because we have the graph, and the line is visible we can determine the signs of constants a and b. Remember, we don't have to have a *value* for a and b, just the sign. This rules out **K**

Answer choice **H** is correct.

<u>What You May Have Done Wrong</u>

    F. The sign of b is negative.

    G. The sign of a is negative.

    J. The sign of a and b are negative.

    K. The answer can be determined.

3. At a bake sale lemon bars are sold for $3 and cookies are sold for $2. The bake sale's goal is to raise $900. Which of the following graphs represents all possible combinations of sales that raise at least 900 dollars?

Correct Answer E

This is a mark-off question that requires a unique approach. Any point on the line *must equal exactly 900 dollars*. The only way to really do tackle this problem is to look at the two points we know. We know that the *x*-intercept is when only cookies are sold (*x*-axis) and no lemon bars are sold (*y*-axis).

The same is true the other way around. The *y*-intercept will be when the bake sale sells *only* lemon bars and no cookies. We can calculate what those intercepts need to be. Remember, lemon bars cost $3 and cookies cost $2.

All lemon bars: $\dfrac{\$900}{\$3} = 300 \ lemon \ bars$

> If we sell 0 of one item, this is how much we need of the other to hit a minimum of 900.

All cookies: $\dfrac{\$900}{\$2} = 450 \ cookies$

So, the *y*-intercept (lemon bars) needs to be 300. The *x*-intercept (cookies) needs to be 450.

Answer choice **E** is correct

What You May Have Done Wrong

    A. At the *x*-intercept (only cookies sold) we don't reach $900.
    B. We don't reach $900 on either the *x* or *y*-axis.
    C. We go too high on lemon bars and too low on cookies.
    D. You go too high on lemon bars.

4. The graph below is in the standard (x, y) coordinate plane and the shaded area represents the solution of a system of linear inequalities. Which set of inequalities gives the solution graphed below?

Correct Answer F

This inequality question has a line equation component to it. First, let's see if we can determine the equations of the lines. The negative sloping line can be determined. It's got a slope of -2 and a *y*-intercept of +4.

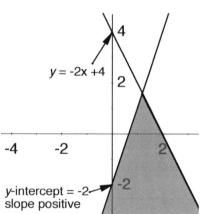

The positive sloping line *can't* be determined. We just know it's got a *y*-intercept of -2 and a positive slope.

But, we actually don't need the slopes. If you glanced at your answer choices at the outset, all the answer choices have matching slopes (-2 and 3).

We can mark off answer choices with incorrect *y*-intercepts, getting rid of **H** and **J**. So, all we need to do is determine whether the shading is *above* or *below* each line. Both functions are shaded below the lines, which gives us inequalities of $y \le -2x + 4$ and $y \le 3x - 2$.

Answer choice **F** is correct.

What You May Have Done Wrong:

    For a complete discussion of answer choices, see the explanation above.

5. The shaded region of the graph shown below is the solution set for which of the following systems of inequalities?

Correct Answer B

This is a weird inequality question because of the circle equation. We still want to mark off, but we may need to add a trick to get the answer.

First, mark off the line to get rid of a few answers.

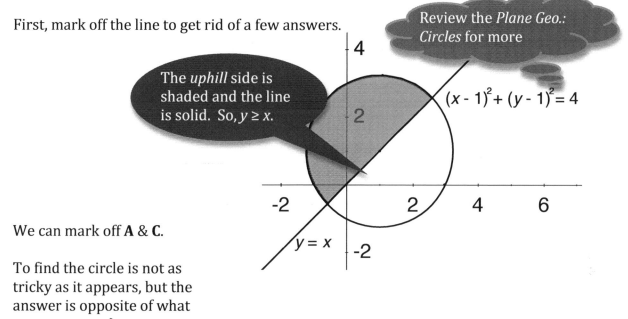

The *uphill* side is shaded and the line is solid. So, $y \geq x$.

Review the *Plane Geo.: Circles* for more

$(x - 1)^2 + (y - 1)^2 = 4$

$y = x$

We can mark off **A** & **C**.

To find the circle is not as tricky as it appears, but the answer is opposite of what you may guess).

First, you can know how circle inequalities work (great if you do, but don't worry about it). **If the circle is a < or ≤ the inside of a circle is shade. If it's > or ≥ the *outside* (all the outside) of the circle is shaded.**

The other way to handle the circle is to pick a shaded point, plug it into the inequality and see if the answer is less or greater than 4. I'm going to pick (0,1).

$$(x-1)^2 + (y-1)^2 = 4$$
$$(0-1)^2 + (1-1)^2 = 4$$
$$1+0=4$$
$$1 \leq 4$$

So the circle inequality is $(x-1)^2 + (y-1)^2 \leq 4$. We know it has to be ≤ and not < because the line of the circle is solid.

Answer choice **B** is correct.

What You May Have Done Wrong

    A. The linear inequality should be ≥ because the line is solid.
    C. The linear inequality should be ≥. The line is solid *and* the shading (solution) is *uphill* (above) the line.
    D. The circle inequality needs to be ≤. If it's greater than, the entire outside of the circle would be shaded, plug-in a point to see for yourself.
    E. The circle inequality needs to be ≤ because the line of the circle is solid.

6. Which of the following equations best represents the system of inequalities graphed below?

Correct Answer H

This question is, frankly, a pain in the neck. A couple of things make it more manageable. First, you'll notice that the answer choices are in the same order. That's generally the case for complicated part based questions and you should always glance at your answer choices before starting. Second, it's a mark-off question and you can take it one piece at a time. For simplicity, look at each inequality in order. .

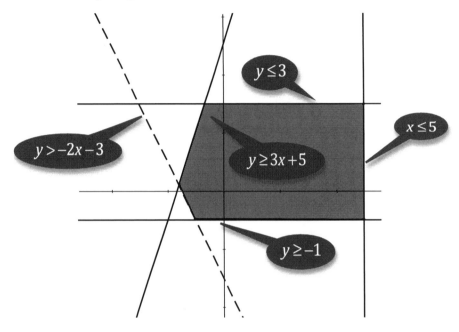

The first inequality in all the answer choices describes two horizontal lines. The shaded region shows the area *between* the horizontal lines is shaded. That means y is *between* the values. The shading is *below* the top line and *above* of the bottom line. The values are all the same (-1 & 3). So, we have $-1 \le y \le 3$. This lets us mark-off **J** & **K**.
(By the way, the graphs of **J** & **K** would be shaded above and below those lines, not in the middle).

The second inequality is the vertical line. Again, all the values are five, so we don't need to worry about that. Since we've got a vertical line, *below* is to the negative and *above* is to the positive. Since the negative side is shaded, we know that $x \le 5$. We can mark off **F** (and **K** if you haven't already).

The third inequality is the positively sloping line. It's shaded on the *downhill* side so we've got $y \le 3x + 5$. That allows us to mark off **G**.

At this point, we've marked off **F**, **G**, **J**, and **K**. So we know the answer has to be **H**. Let's take a look at the last inequality anyway.

The last inequality is a negatively sloping line which is dotted. This means it is not an "equal to" inequality, it's either < or >. It's shaded on the *uphill* side making our inequality $y > -2x - 3$.

Answer **H** is correct.

<u>What You May Have Done Wrong</u>
Review the steps above for a complete discussion of every answer choice.

Introduction
The ACT likes to ask about shapes (squares, circles, and triangles) on the coordinate plane. These questions show up *every* test and can take many forms, but let's take a look at some of the most common questions.

What You Need to Know
- ✓ How to find the area of triangles, rectangles, & parallelograms
- ✓ How to label quadrants

Rules of the Road: Triangle Area & Altitude

> We **always use perpendicular altitude (height) to calculate area.** Perpendicular means perpendicular from the base of the triangle.

ACT Examples: Triangle Area & Altitude
1. In the figure below, triangle *ABC* is in the standard (x, y) coordinate plane and has vertices of $(-1,1)$, $(2,4)$, and $(5,1)$. What is the area of triangle *ABC*?

    A. 15
    B. 18
    C. 9
    D. 12
    E. 24

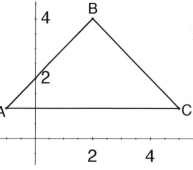

Solve

Start by marking up your vertices and finding your height and base (altitude).

Now we can find the area.

$$area = \frac{1}{2} base \cdot height$$

$$area = \frac{1}{2} 6 \cdot 3 = 9$$

base & height are *always* perpendicular

Answer choice **C** is correct.

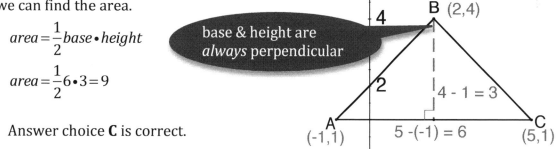

Rules of the Road: Area by Quadrant

To find the area of a shape in a particular quadrant, you'll use similar shapes (and proportions).

ACT Examples: Area by Quadrant

1. A rectangle with vertices of (3,3), (3, -2), (-1,3) and (-1,-2) is in the standard (x, y) coordinate plane. What percentage of the total area lies in quadrant II?

    A. 10%
    B. 15%
    C. 20%
    D. 30%
    E. 40%

There's a video on Area by Quadrant

Solve

Start by sketching out our diagram and marking the quadrants and the length of the sides. Also mark up the small rectangle with its sides as the borders of quadrant 2.

Using the sides, find the area of the whole rectangle and the quadrant II rectangle.

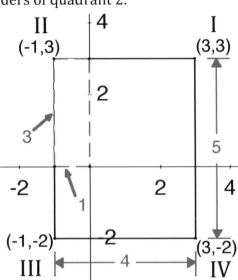

Large Rectangle

$area = length \cdot width$

$area = 5 \cdot 4 = 20$

Small Rectangle

$area = length \cdot width$

$area = 3 \cdot 1 = 3$

Now find the percentage.

$percent = \dfrac{part}{whole} = \dfrac{3}{20} = 15\%$

Answer choice **B** is correct.

2. Triangle *ABC* is in the standard coordinate plane with vertex *A* at (0,2) vertex *B* at (-3,-4) and vertex *C* at (3,-4). Triangle *ABC* also has *x*-intercepts of -1 and 1. $\overline{BC}$ is perpendicular to the *x*-axis. Approximately what percentage of the area of the triangle are in quadrants I & II?

A. 25%
B. 50%
C. 18%
D. 11%
E. 40%

Solve

These are similar triangles; they share angle *A* and $\overline{BC}$ is parallel to the *x*-axis, so the triangles are similar.

Let's find the bases and the heights (remember we only care about the height perpendicular to the base).

Let's find the area of our triangles:

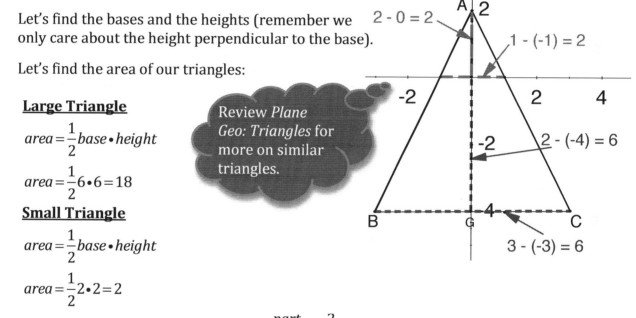

Large Triangle

$area = \dfrac{1}{2}base \bullet height$

$area = \dfrac{1}{2}6 \bullet 6 = 18$

Review *Plane Geo: Triangles* for more on similar triangles.

Small Triangle

$area = \dfrac{1}{2}base \bullet height$

$area = \dfrac{1}{2}2 \bullet 2 = 2$

$$percent = \dfrac{part}{whole} = \dfrac{2}{18} = 11.1\%$$

Answer choice **D** is correct.

Rules of the Road: Find the Vertex

To find the missing vertex (corner) of rectangles/squares use matching sides and 90° angles.

1. A rectangle is in the standard (x, y) coordinate plane it has vertices of (2,3), (6,3), and (2,-1). Which is the coordinate point of the fourth vertex?

A. (2,3)
B. (6,-1)
C. (6,-3)
D. (-2,3)
E. (3,-1)

Solve

Start by sketching out our rectangle with our known vertices.

We know that each point will have another point with the same y-coordinate. Every point is either exactly left/right or up/down of two other points.

We can move down four from point (6,3) or four right of (2,-1).

Either way we'll get point (6, -1).

Answer Choice **B** is correct.

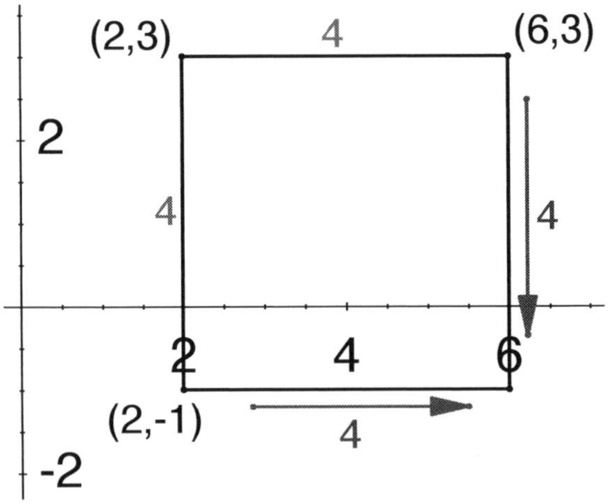

Wrap Up

What You Need to Know

- ✓ How to find the area of triangles, rectangles, & parallelograms
- ✓ How to label quadrants

Videos

Area by Quadrant

The Strategies

- ✓ Use or draw the diagram, everytime.
- ✓ These problems have a weird feel to them; just find the first thing to do.

Related Skills

Trig Identities is related to:

- ✓ Triangles
- ✓ Four Sided Shapes
- ✓ Quadrants

Coordinate Geometry: Shapes

1. A county has the shape shown below and it's borders run east-west and north-south. Abingdon is marked as point A and Bakersfield is marked at point B. Tom's restaurant is halfway between Abingdon and Bakersfield. If you're leaving from Abingdon, how many miles is it to Tom's restaurant?

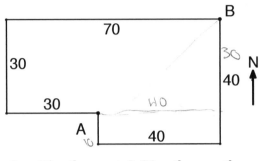

A. 15 miles east & 20 miles north
B. 20 miles east & 15 miles north
C. 40 miles east & 30 miles north
D. 20 miles west & 15 miles north
E. 40 miles west & 30 miles North

2. The vertices of a rectangle are (3,4), (-2,-2), (-2,4), & (3,-2). Approximately, what percent of the rectangle's area lies in quadrant II?

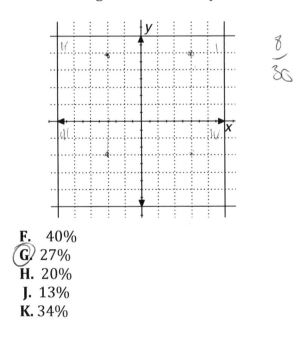

F. 40%
G. 27%
H. 20%
J. 13%
K. 34%

3. What is the altitude of the triangle below?

A. 3
B. 4
C. 5
D. 6
E. 7

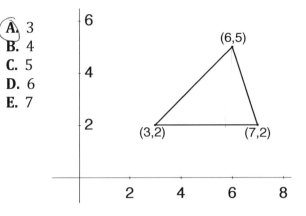

4. If the figure below is placed in the standard (x, y) coordinate plane such that point A is at the origin and $\overline{FE}$ is perpendicular to the y-axis, which could be the coordinate point of E?

Note: all sides are parallel or perpendicular.

F. (4,2)
G. (4,1)
H. (4,-2)
J. (1,4)
K. (5,6)

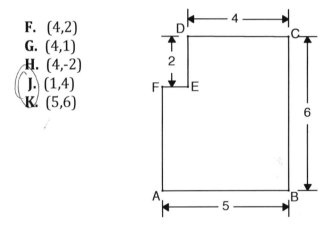

5. The triangle below has vertices as marked. Point D can be moved along a line while points E & F remain stationary. If the area of the triangle does not change when point D is moved, what is the slope of the line point D can move down?

A. 3
B. $\frac{1}{2}$
C. -1
D. -2
E. -3

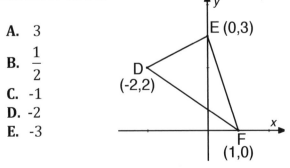

Coordinate Geometry Shapes: Solutions

1. A county has the shape shown below and it's borders run east-west and north-south. Abingdon is marked as point A and Bakersfield is marked at point B. Tom's restaurant is halfway between Abingdon and Bakersfield. If you're leaving from Abingdon, how many miles is it to Tom's restaurant?

Correct Answer B

This is a midpoint question, but it doesn't really feel like one. Let's start marking up the diagram.

If you weren't clear on what the question is asking, the answer choices help. (Remember, *always* look at your answer choices before you get started on a question). What we're looking for is the *x* distance and the *y* distance from point *A* & *B*.

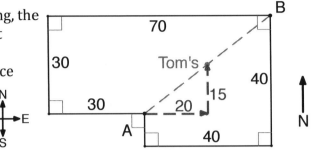

Leaving from point *A*, you have to go 20 miles *east* and 15 miles *north*.

Answer choice **B** is correct.

<u>What You May Have Done Wrong</u>
  - **A.** You flipped your east & north distances.
  - **C.** This is the distance from point *A* to point *B*. You need half the distance.
  - **D.** You flipped your east and west. When north is up, east is right and west is left.
  - **E.** This is the distance from point *A* to point *B*. You need half the distance. You also flipped your east and west. When north is up, east is right and west is left.

2. The vertices of a rectangle are (3,4), (-2,-2), (-2,4), & (3,-2). What percent of the rectangle's area lies in quadrant II?

Correct Answer G

This problem isn't too bad. You need to know the quadrants. There are a couple of calculations, but they're both straightforward. Start by marking the vertices and drawing the rectangle.

The area of the rectangle can be found by counting the number of small squares, but it's easier to find the side lengths and multiply to find the area.

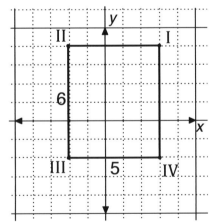

$$area = length \cdot width \quad \rightarrow \quad area = 6 \cdot 5$$
$$area = 30$$

You can either count the number of squares in quadrant II or find the area of that smaller rectangle. Either way you should get 8 squares in quadrant II. Let's find the percent.

$$percent = \frac{part}{whole}$$

$$percent = \frac{8}{30} \rightarrow 26.\overline{66}\% \approx 27\%$$

Answer choice **G** is correct.

<u>What You May Have Done Wrong</u>
  - **F.** This is the area in quadrant I.
  - **H.** This is the area in quadrant IV.
  - **J.** This is the area in quadrant III
  - **K.** This is problem with your setup; review your steps.

3. **What is the altitude of the triangle below?**

Correct Answer A

This is really a definition question asking if you know what an altitude is and how to find it.

In slanted side shapes (triangles, parallelograms, trapezoids, etc.) we're really concerned with the up & down perpendicular height. It's going to be the line that goes to the top of the figure and will be perpendicular to the base. We use that altitude (height) to find the area.

First, mark-up your figure. The altitude will be the difference in the *y*-coordinate of the top point (6,5) and the *y*-coordinate of the base.

$$5 - 2 = 3$$

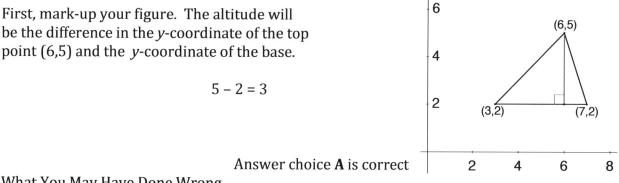

Answer choice **A** is correct

<u>What You May Have Done Wrong</u>
    B. You either found the base or you may have swapped your *x* & *y* in the top point.
    C. You may have just taken the *y*-value of the top point or made an arithmetic error.
    D. You may have just taken the *y*-value of the top point or made an arithmetic error.
    E. You may have taken the *x*-value of the rightmost point or guessed.

4. If the figure below is placed in the standard (x, y) coordinate plane such that point A is at the origin and $\overline{FE}$ is perpendicular to the y-axis, what could be the coordinate point of E? Note: all sides are parallel or perpendicular.

Correct Answer J

This question is a lot more confusing than it is difficult. Let's break it down into statements.
Statement 1: *$\overline{A}$ is at the origin.* We know that point A will be at (0,0)

Statement 2: *$\overline{FE}$ is perpendicular to the y-axis.* We know that line segment FE will be parallel to the *x*-axis.

Statement 3: *all sides are parallel or perpendicular.*
    We know that every side will be parallel or perpendicular to the *x* & *y* axes. We also know that $\overline{AF}$ sits on the *y*-axis because it goes straight up from point A.

Let's mark up the diagram. We need to do a little subtraction to find the length of $\overline{AF}$ & $\overline{FE}$. Because every side is parallel or perpendicular:

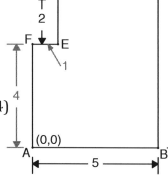

$$\overline{AF} + \overline{DE} = \overline{BC} = 6$$
The side we want, $\overline{AF}$, is 6 – 2 = 4
$$\overline{FE} + \overline{DC} = \overline{AB} = 5$$
The side we want , $\overline{FE}$, is 5 – 4 = 1.
So, from point A, go *up* 4 and *right* 1 to get to point E. *E* is at point (1,4)

Answer choice **J** is correct.

<u>What You May Have Done Wrong:</u>
    F. You may have just read off the distances near point *E*.
    G. You flipped your *x* & *y* coordinates.
    H. You put point *C* at (0,0).
    K. Those are the coordinates of point *C*.

5. **The triangle below has vertices as marked. Point *D* can be moved along a line while points *E* & *F* remain stationary. If the area of the triangle does not change when point *D* is moved, what is the slope of the line point *D* can move down?**

Correct Answer E

This problem is really intimidating and it's fairly tricky. Recall that the area of a triangle is found by $area = \frac{1}{2} base \bullet height$. Because we read left to right, most people automatically think of $\overline{DF}$ is our base. It could be, except we can move *D*, and when we move *D* the base changes. We couldn't keep the area the same for all the positions we can move *D*.

E & *F* don't move, so they have to be the base. The height is the perpendicular line from $\overline{EF}$ to point *D*.

To keep the area the same, the *base* has to stay the same, so the base is $\overline{EF}$.

The *height* also has to stay the same. To do that, *D* can't get any closer or any farther away from the base, $\overline{EF}$.

The only way for *D* to stay the same distance from $\overline{EF}$ is for the added line to have the **same slope** as $\overline{EF}$.

Let's find the slope of $\overline{EF}$.

$$slope = \frac{rise}{run} = \frac{y_1 - y_2}{x_1 - x_2}$$

$$slope = \frac{3-0}{0-1} = -3$$

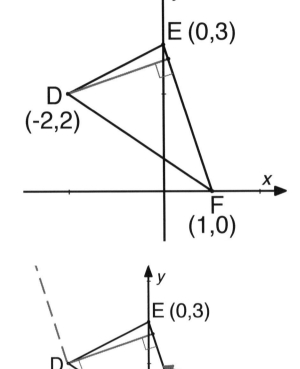

Answer choice **E** is correct.

<u>What You May Have Done Wrong</u>
- **A.** You probably did everything right, except you dropped a sign.
- **B.** You calculated the slope of $\overline{DE}$.
- **C.** You probably calculated the slope of $\overline{DE}$, and thought that it should be the inverse (which would make it perpendicular).
- **D.** You may have guessed or miscalculated the slope of $\overline{EF}$.

Introduction

Every ACT asks about the graphs of functions. Linear functions are covered in depth in the *Coordinate Geo: Line Equation.* Aside from lines, the ACT asks about *parabolas* and *absolute value* functions, with only occasional coverage of root functions, cubic functions, and functions of other powers.

What You Need to Know

- ✓ The definition of functions & the vertical line test
- ✓ What the zeroes of a function are and how to find them
- ✓ How vertical asymptotes work
- ✓ The shifts, translations, & transformations of a parabola

> Remember *f(x)* means *y*.
> Review *Intermediate Algebra: Functions*

Definitions: Functions

Functions are defined as equations with any *input* of x resulting in one and *only one* output of y.

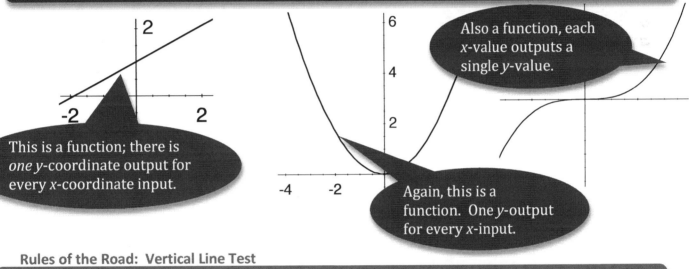

Also a function, each *x*-value outputs a single *y*-value.

This is a function; there is *one y*-coordinate output for every *x*-coordinate input.

Again, this is a function. One *y*-output for every *x*-input.

Rules of the Road: Vertical Line Test

You can test whether a graph is a function by drawing vertical lines and seeing if any *x*-coordinate has two *y*-coordinates.

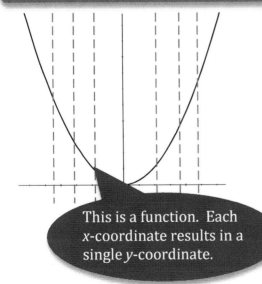

This is a function. Each *x*-coordinate results in a single *y*-coordinate.

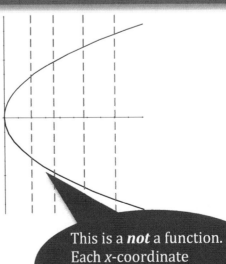

This is a **not** a function. Each *x*-coordinate results in more than one *y*-coordinate.

Definitions: Zeroes of a Function

The zero of a function is where the graph of a function crosses the x-axis—y is zero. Not all functions have real number zeros. The maximum number of zeros is equal to the power of the function.

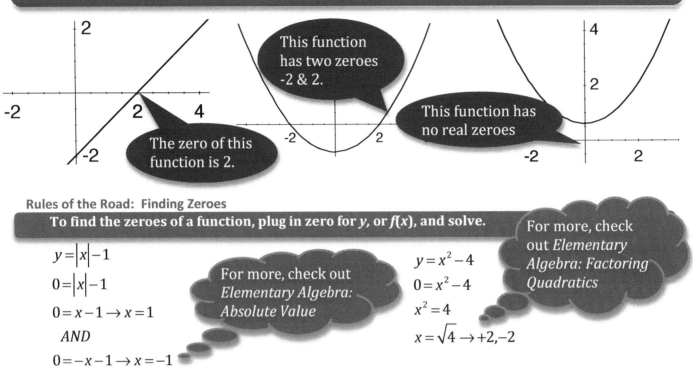

This function has two zeroes -2 & 2.

The zero of this function is 2.

This function has no real zeroes

Rules of the Road: Finding Zeroes

To find the zeroes of a function, plug in zero for y, or $f(x)$, and solve.

For more, check out *Elementary Algebra: Factoring Quadratics*

$y = |x| - 1$

$0 = |x| - 1$

$0 = x - 1 \rightarrow x = 1$

$\quad AND$

$0 = -x - 1 \rightarrow x = -1$

For more, check out *Elementary Algebra: Absolute Value*

$y = x^2 - 4$

$0 = x^2 - 4$

$x^2 = 4$

$x = \sqrt{4} \rightarrow +2, -2$

ACT Examples: Finding Zeroes

1. Which of the following functions will have no real zeroes?

A. $y = x^2 - 1$

B. $y = x - 1$

C. $y = x^2 + 1$

D. $y = x^3$

E. $y = \sqrt{x}$

Remember, questions using the word *which* are great mark-off questions!

Solve

To solve, we plug in zero for y and solve for x. As long as we can get a *real number answer*, we've got a zero for the function.

A. $y = x^2 - 1$ Plug-in zero and you'll get $0 = x^2 - 1 \rightarrow 1 = x^2 \quad \rightarrow$ **$x = 1, -1$**

B. $y = x - 1$ Plug-in zero and you'll get $0 = x - 1 \rightarrow$ **$x = 1$**

C. $y = x^2 + 1$ Plug-in zero and you'll get $0 = x^2 + 1 \rightarrow -1 = x^2 \rightarrow$ **$x = \sqrt{-1}$**

D. $y = x^3$ Plug-in zero and you'll get $0 = x^3 \rightarrow \sqrt[3]{0} = \sqrt[3]{x^3} \rightarrow$ **$x = 0$**

E. $y = \sqrt{x}$ Plug-in zero and you'll get $0 = \sqrt{x} \rightarrow 0^2 = \left(\sqrt{x}\right)^2 \rightarrow$ **$x = 0$**

C is the answer because there is no real number square root of a negative number. It's much easier to solve the problem if you know your translations. You can "see" by looking at the equation that $y = x^2 + 1$ never crosses an axis.

Answer choice **C** is correct.

2. The graph shown below is in the standard (x, y) coordinate plane. Which of the following equation is the function of the graph?

A. $y = x^2 + x - 2$

B. $y = x^2 - 1$

C. $y = 2x^2 - 3x + 1$

D. $y = x^2 + 2x + 1$

E. $y = x^2 - x - 2$

(-1,0)   (2,0)

Solve

This is as much about *factoring* and quadratic equations as it is about the definition of zeroes. To find the zeroes, set the equation equal to zero and factor. Or, you could plug-in the zeroes to the answer choices. I think it's faster to factor, but there's not much of a difference. The solutions are -1 & 2; so let's find the factors.

$x = -1 \rightarrow x + 1 = 0 \rightarrow (x + 1)$
$x = 2 \rightarrow x - 2 = 0 \rightarrow (x - 2)$

Remember, this is a *which* question, so we can run through each and factor them quickly. We'll be looking for *solutions* of -1 and 2.

A. $y = x^2 + x - 2 \rightarrow y = (x + 2)(x - 1) \rightarrow x = 1, -2$

B. $y = x^2 - 1 \rightarrow y = (x + 1)(x - 1) \rightarrow x = 1, -1$

C. $y = 2x^2 - 3x + 1 \rightarrow y = (2x - 1)(x - 1) \rightarrow x = 1, \tfrac{1}{2}$

D. $y = x^2 + 2x + 1 \rightarrow y = (x + 1)(x + 1) \rightarrow x = 1$

E. $y = x^2 - x - 2 \rightarrow y = (x + 1)(x - 2) \rightarrow x = 2, -1$

Answer choice **E** is correct.

Definitions: Vertical Asymptotes

A **vertical asymptote** is a line the graph of a function approaches, but never touches or crosses.

The graphed function has the equation $y = \dfrac{x^2}{x - 1}$. Set the denominator equal to zero to find the asymptote.

$$x - 1 = 0 \rightarrow x = 1$$

We can't divide something into zero parts, that operation is always *undefined*. So, the function can *never* have a value where the denominator is zero..

But a numerator that's zero works perfectly fine. Here's an example using a simple fraction.

$$\frac{0}{2} = 0 \ but \ \frac{2}{0} = undefined$$

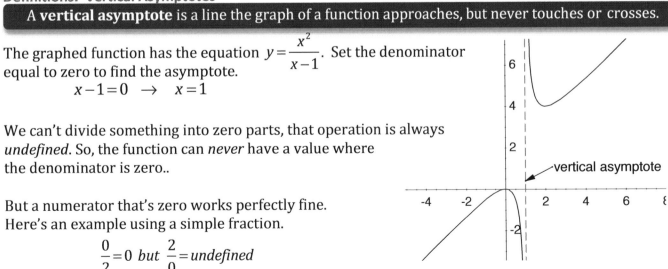

vertical asymptote

1. The equation $y = \dfrac{x}{x^3 - 8}$ is graphed in the standard (x, y) coordinate plane. Where will the

function have *no x* coordinate?

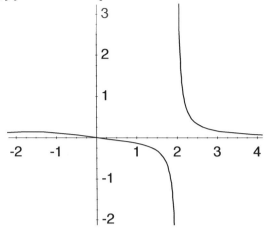

A. 0
B. 2
C. -1
D. 1
E. -3

Solve

This is a vertical asymptote question. You can either use the graph (the vertical asymptote is visible) or you can use algebra. By looking at the graph, we see that that both parts of the function approach $x = 2$, but they never intersect it.

Alternatively, we can set the denominator equal to zero and solve. Remember, a vertical asymptote occurs when we have a denominator set equal to zero.

$$y = \dfrac{x}{x^3 - 8}$$

Set the denominator equal to zero.

$$x^3 - 8 = 0 \quad \rightarrow \quad x^3 = 8$$
$$\sqrt[3]{x^3} = \sqrt[3]{8} \quad \rightarrow \quad x = 2$$

Answer choice **B** is correct.

2. Which of the following is the equation of the graph below?
    A. $y = x + 3$
    B. $y = 2x$
    C. $y = 2x + 3$
    D. $y = \dfrac{x^2 - 9}{x - 3}$
    E. $y = \dfrac{x^2 + 9}{x + 3}$

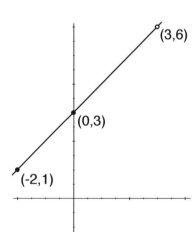

Solve

This is a very rarely tested concept, the holes of a graph. The line has an open point (a hole). So, for the *x* value $x = 3$, we have no point on the line. This isn't an asymptote, because the function (the line) doesn't curve up or down to approach it. It just "jumps" it.
That's called a slant asymptote, but we don't need to worry about that.

When we have holes, we have a *rational expression*. The hole will occur wherever the denominator of the rational expression equals zero. This, automatically, gives you the answer (choice **D**) because when $x = 3$, $\dfrac{3^2 - 9}{3 - 3} = undefined$.

You may be confused about why our graph is a straight line. It's because our numerator is divisible by the denominator.

$$\frac{x^2 - 9}{x - 3} = \frac{(x+3)(x-3)}{x-3} = \frac{(x+3)\cancel{(x-3)}}{\cancel{x-3}} = x + 3$$

Review *Intermediate Algebra: Rational Expressions*

Answer Choice **D** is correct.

Parabolas

Parabolas are on every test, but they aren't always asked about directly. The key thing to remember is that parabolas are the graphs of a quadratic equations. **If parabolas open up or down (like cups or umbrellas) they are functions. If they open left or right, they are *not* functions.**

There's a *video* on *Parabolas*

Definitions: Parabolas

Parabolas are the graph of quadratics. They are defined by the general equation $y = ax^2 + bx + c$. They look like a U or an upside down and are symmetric about their vertex.

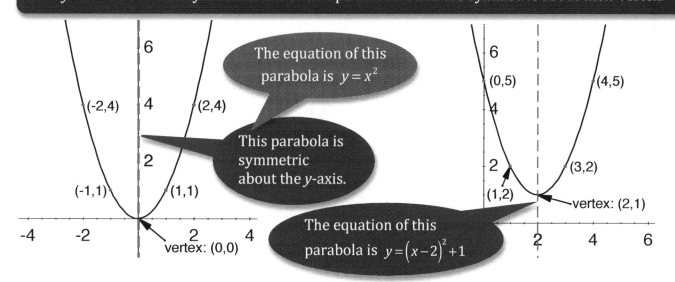

The equation of this parabola is $y = x^2$

This parabola is symmetric about the *y*-axis.

The equation of this parabola is $y = (x-2)^2 + 1$

Let's plug some inputs in to the *x* in $y = x^2$ and look at the *y* outputs.

Input	Equation	Output
0	$y = 0^2 = 0$	0
1	$y = 1^2 = 1$	1
-1	$y = -1^2 = 1$	1
2	$y = 2^2 = 4$	4
-2	$y = -2^2 = 4$	4

Because we square all of our inputs (our *x* values) our outputs (our *y* values) will all be positive. That's why parabolas are U-shaped curves.

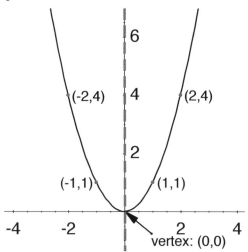

> **The zeroes of a quadratic function are where the parabola crosses the x-axis.** We can use these points to find the *factors* of the quadratic *and* the equation of the quadratic.

The parabola to the right crosses the x-axis at -1 and 3.
By definition, y is equal to zero at those points. Any quadratic equation in its factored form will be:

(factor)(factor) = 0

Since our solutions for $y = 0$ are -1 and 3, we can say

$x = -1$
$x = 3$

We can rearrange our solutions for zero to get our factors.

$x - 1 = 0$
$x - 3 = 0$

Our factors are $(x - 1)$ and $(x - 3)$. We can write our equation as

$0 = (x + 1)(x - 3)$

If we needed to, we could FOIL and get our equation in standard form.

$x^2 - 2x - 3 = 0$

Review *Elementary Algebra: Factoring Quadratics*

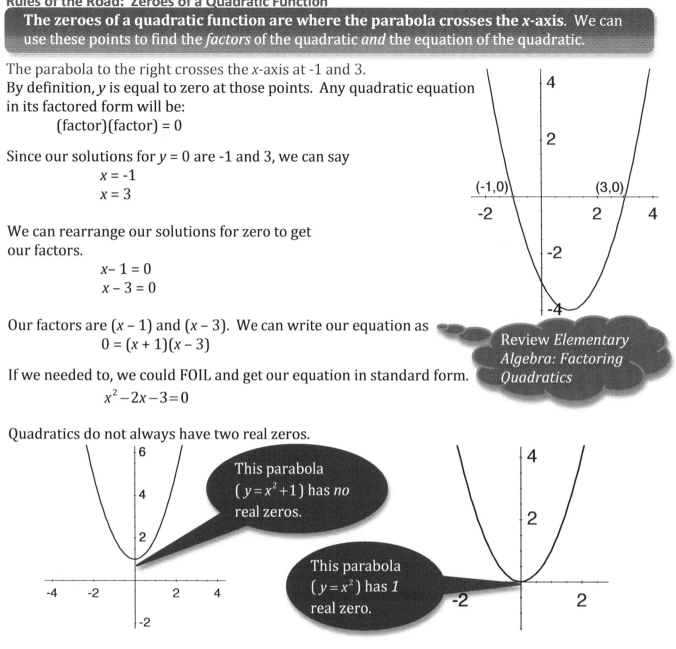

Quadratics do not always have two real zeros.

This parabola $(y = x^2 + 1)$ has *no* real zeros.

This parabola $(y = x^2)$ has *1* real zero.

Definitions: Shifts & Translations

> When we deal with functions, adding or subtracting a constant (a number) causes the graph to shift up or down.

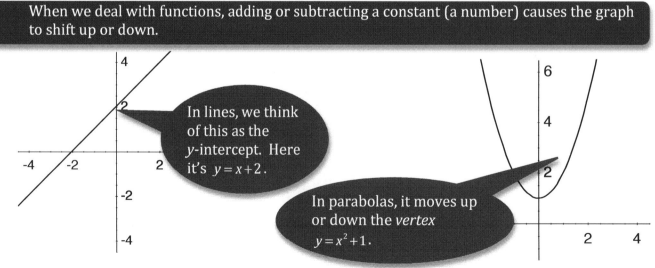

In lines, we think of this as the y-intercept. Here it's $y = x + 2$.

In parabolas, it moves up or down the *vertex* $y = x^2 + 1$.

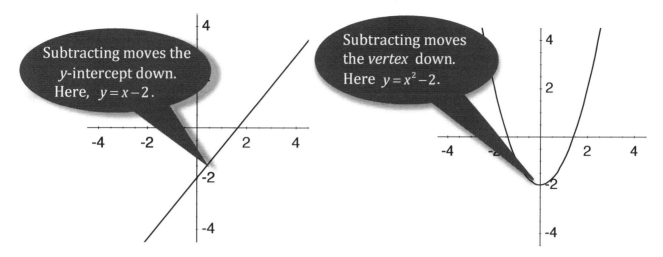

Why does it work this way? Take $y = x^2 + 1$, for example. Whenever we plug in our x value (input) our y value is automatically increased by 1. Because of the square (preventing negative numbers) the smallest x^2 can be is 0, making the smallest y value possible $y = 0^2 + 1 = 1$.

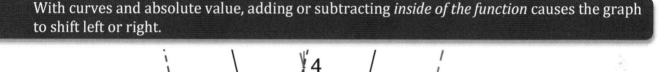

With curves and absolute value, adding or subtracting *inside of the function* causes the graph to shift left or right.

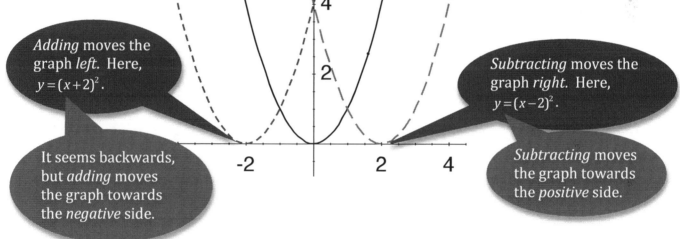

Inside the function means that the same operation happening to x happens to the number we are adding or subtracting. In the case of the parabolas above, we're squaring the number (+2 and -2) along with the x. Here are a few more examples:

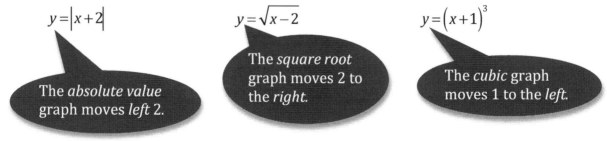

The translations of a parabola tell us where the *vertex* is.
The Vertex is the bottommost or topmost point in a parabola.

The equation for the parabola to the right is $y = x^2$. Its vertex is (0,0). That makes sense when you think about the *x*-input and the *y*-output. The input (*x*) is 0, our output *y* is zero. In this equation, it can never be less than 0.

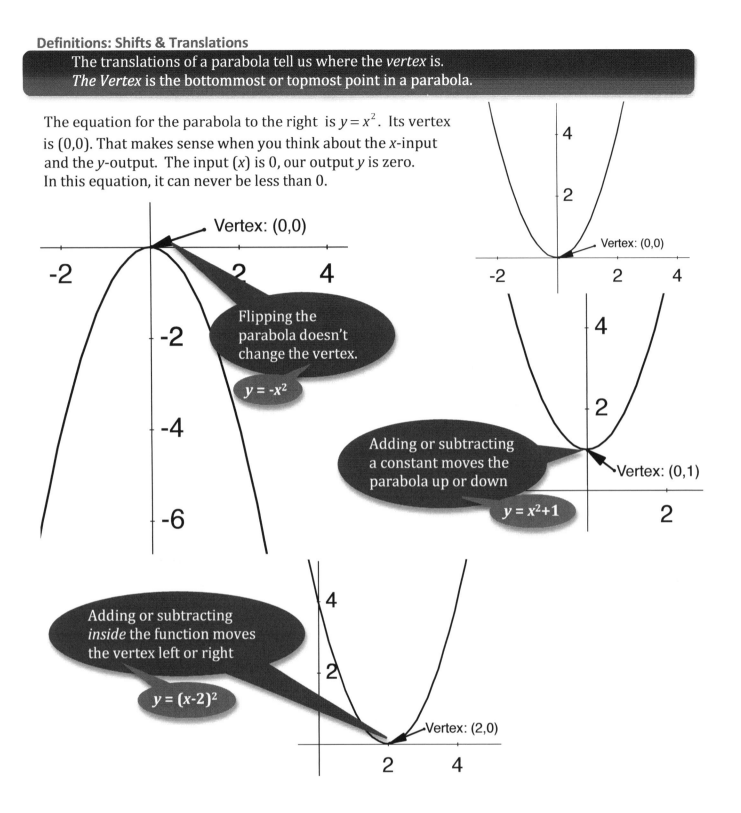

Vertex: (0,0)

Flipping the parabola doesn't change the vertex.

$y = -x^2$

Vertex: (0,0)

Adding or subtracting a constant moves the parabola up or down

Vertex: (0,1)

$y = x^2 + 1$

Adding or subtracting *inside* the function moves the vertex left or right

$y = (x-2)^2$

Vertex: (2,0)

> If the x^2 term has a *negative* coefficient, the parabola opens down (looks like an umbrella).

Let's look at the parabola $y = -x^2$. The parabola is identical to $y = -x^2$ except it opens down. Let's look at some values to see why.

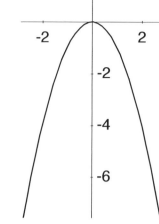

Input	Equation	Output
0	$y = (-1)0^2 = 0$	0
1	$y = (-1)1^2 = -1$	1
-1	$y = (-1)-1^2 = -1$	1
2	$y = (-1)2^2 = -4$	4
-2	$y = (-1)-2^2 = -4$	4

> With Parabolas a coefficient in front of x^2 (*a* in ax^2) changes the *width* of a parabola. A coefficient *less than 1* makes the parabola *wider*. A coefficient *greater than 1* makes the parabola *skinnier*.

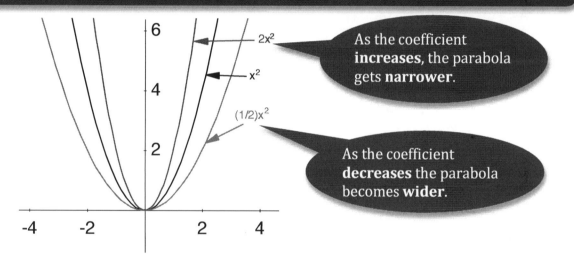

As the coefficient **increases**, the parabola gets **narrower**.

As the coefficient **decreases** the parabola becomes **wider**.

The fact that parabolas get narrower as the coefficient increases can be confusing. But, the parabola gets narrower because it the y-value increases *faster*. Check out the table below.

Input	$y = x^2$	$y = 2x^2$
0	0	0
1	1	2
2	4	8
3	9	18
4	16	32

The parabola goes *up* twice as fast.

1. The function $y=(x+3)^2+2$ is graphed in the standard (x,y) coordinate plane below.

If the graph is shifted down three units, which of the following graphs will be the result?

This is the most common format of shifts and translations questions.

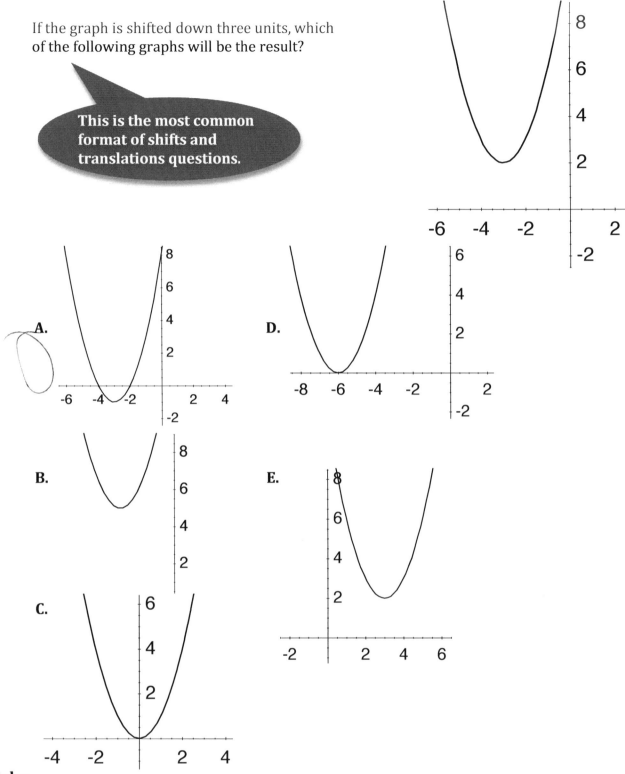

Solve

There are a couple of ways you can solve this problem. The first way is to know your translations, find the original <u>vertex</u> of the parabola and then move it *down* three units. The second (and probably easier) way is to look at the graph, and move it down three.

Finding the Vertex

First, let's find the point of the vertex. The original function has the equation $y = (x+3)^2 + 2$. The equation describes a <u>parabola</u> and it moves 3 *left* and 2 *down*. This will result in a parabola with a vertex of (-3,2). When we shift the parabola three units down we end up with (-3,-1). The only parabola that has a negative *y* coordinate for the vertex is letter **A**.

Eyeballing the Vertex

By looking at the original graph, we can tell that the vertex sits at a *y*-coordinate of 2. We can move it down 3 by paying attention to our graph.

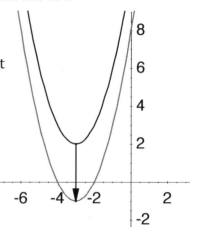

Now we can look at our graphs and the only answer that makes sense will be letter A.

Answer choice **A** is correct.

Wrap Up

What You Need to Know
- ✓ The definition of functions & the vertical line test
- ✓ What the zeroes of a function are and how to find them
- ✓ How vertical asymptotes work
- ✓ The shifts, translations, & transformations of a parabola

Videos

The Zeroes of Functions

Translations & Shifts

Parabolas

The Strategies
- ✓ These are usually mark-off questions; use your answer choices as leverage.
- ✓ Don't reach for the calculator right away; it's almost always the long way around.
- ✓ Know your translations, transformations, & shifts. It's well worth memorizing.

Related Skills

Coordinate Functions are related to:

- ✓ Algebraic functions

- ✓ Quadratics

- ✓ Lines

- ✓ Rational Expressions

- ✓ Absolute Value

Coordinate Geometry: Functions

1. Which of the following functions have exactly two real zeroes?

A. $y = x^2 + 1$

B. $y = -x^2 + 1$

C. $y = x^2$

D. $y = (x-1)^2 + 1$

E. $y = (x-1)^2$

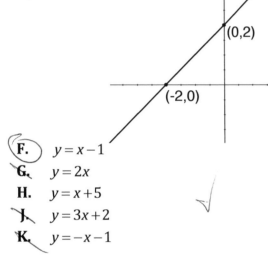

2. The graph below is in the standard (x, y) coordinate plane. If the graph is shifted down three units, what will be the equation of the function?

(0,2)

(-2,0)

F. $y = x - 1$

G. $y = 2x$

H. $y = x + 5$

J. $y = 3x + 2$

K. $y = -x - 1$

3. The function $y = \dfrac{3x+1}{x^3+1}$ is graphed below. What is the equation of the graph's vertical asymptote?

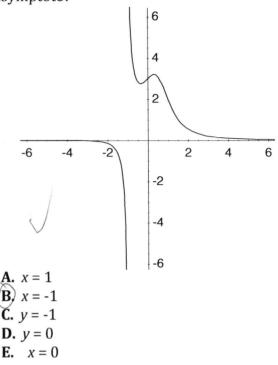

A. $x = 1$

B. $x = -1$

C. $y = -1$

D. $y = 0$

E. $x = 0$

4. What is the vertex of a parabola with the equation $y = (x-2)^2 + 1$?

F. (1,2)

G. (-2,1)

H. (2,1)

J. (-2,-1)

K. (4,1)

$y - 1 \qquad x - 2$

$(2, 1)$

5. The graph below shows a function in the (x, y) coordinate plane with a vertex as marked. What is the equation of that function?

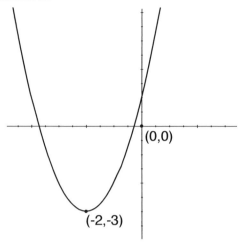

(0,0)

(-2,-3)

   A. $y=(x-2)(x-3)$
   B. $y=(x+2)(x-3)$
   C. $y=(x+2)(x-3)$
   D. $y=(x+2)^2-3$
   E. $y=(x-2)^2-3$

6. Which of the following functions has *no x*-value where $y = -1$?

   F. $y=x^2-2$
   G. $y=\sqrt{x}-4$
   H. $y=x$
   J. $y=-x$
   K. $y=|x|$

7. What are the *x*-intercepts for the parabola defined by the equation $y=x^2+5x+4$?

   A. (0,4) & (0, 1)
   B. (4,0) & (1,0)
   C. (-4,0) & (-1,0)
   D. (0,-4) & (0,-1)
   E. (5,0) & (4,0)

$(x+4)(x+1)$

$x=-4$

8. A Parabola is defined by the equation $(x-2)(x-2)=3$. What is the vertex of the parabola?

   A. (-2,-3)
   B. (2,-3)
   C. (-3,2)
   D. (2,2)
   E. (-2,-2)

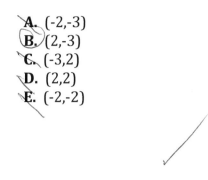

9. A parabola has *x*-intercepts of 4 & -2. What is its vertex?

   A. (1,-9)
   B. (3,-3)
   C. (-2,4)
   D. (2,1)
   E. (2,-7)

$(x-4)(x+2)=$

$x^2-2x-8=0$

1. **Which of the following functions have exactly two real zeroes?**

Correct Answer B

This is a definition question. We've got to remember that the zeroes of a function are the *x*-intercepts. Like any question with the word "which" in it is a great mark-off question. The best way to do this is to know your translations. Alternatively, you could factor and see which has two real zeroes, or use your graphing calculator.

A. $y = x^2 + 1$ This function will have no real zeroes, because the +1 shifts the vertex of the parabola up 1.

B. $y = -x^2 + 1$ This function *will have two real zeroes*. The +1 shifts the parabola up 1, and the $-x^2$ causes the parabola to open *down*. This means the vertex is at +1 and it opens down, crossing the *x*-axis twice.

C. $y = x^2$ This function has one real zero. The vertex of this parabola will be (0,0) and it will open upwards.

D. $y = (x-1)^2 + 1$ This function has no real zeroes; the -1 is a lateral shift (to the right) and won't affect the zeroes. The +1 is a vertical shift, shifting the parabola up 1, and the parabola will not have any real zeroes.

E. $y = (x-1)^2$ This function has one real zero. The -1 is a lateral shift (to the right) and only has one real zero.

2. **The graph below is in the standard (x, y) coordinate plane. If the graph is shifted down three units, what will be the equation of the function?**

Correct Answer F

This is a vertical shift question, combined with a *line equation* question. You'll need to shift the graph down three and find the line equation, but you can do those steps in either order.

The new *y*-intercept will be 2 – 3 = -1.

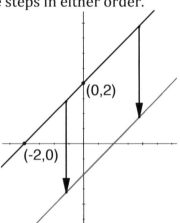

The slope stays the same, & we can use the two original points to calculate the slope.

$$slope = \frac{rise}{run} = \frac{2-0}{0-(-2)} = \frac{2}{2} = 1$$

Putting the equation together, we get

$$y = x - 1$$

Answer choice **F** is correct.

<u>What You May Have Done Wrong</u>

G. You've made a mistake calculating the slope *and* the *y*-intercept. You may want to review line equations.

H. You shifted the line *up* three (instead of down three).

J. You've made a mistake calculating the slope *and* the *y*-intercept. You may want to review line equations.

K. You may have misunderstood the question. You correctly changed the *y*-intercept, but you reversed the slope.

3. The function $y = \dfrac{3x+1}{x^3+1}$ is graphed below. What is the equation of the graph's vertical asymptote?

Correct Answer B

This *vertical asymptote* question is all about definitions. The vertical asymptote is where we'll see the graph approach, but never cross. It also splits the graph of the function into two pieces. If we look at our graph, you can see that it approaches, but never crosses when $x = -1$. You also need to know that the equation of vertical lines are $x = constant$. (Horizontal lines have the equation $y = constant$).

You can also solve the problem with algebra. Vertical asymptotes are when the equation is *undefined*—when the denominator is equal to zero.

$y = \dfrac{3x+1}{x^3+1}$ → $x^3+1=0$ → $x^3=-1$ →

$\sqrt[3]{x^3} = \sqrt[3]{-1}$ → **x = -1**

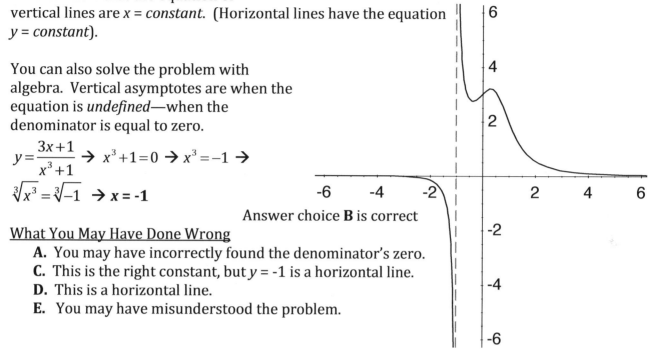

Answer choice **B** is correct

<u>What You May Have Done Wrong</u>
    A. You may have incorrectly found the denominator's zero.
    C. This is the right constant, but $y = -1$ is a horizontal line.
    D. This is a horizontal line.
    E. You may have misunderstood the problem.

4. What is the vertex of a parabola with the equation $y = (x-2)^2 + 1$?

Correct Answer H

This is a question about *translations*. You could plug it in your graphing calculator, or (and better) you could know your translations.

$$y = (x-2)^2 + 1$$

The -2 is undergoing the same operation as the x (both are squared), so the -2 is a lateral shift. Negative shifts move the graph *left* (positive direction). The +1 is a *vertical shift* and moves the graph up 1. A parabola with the equation $y = x^2$ has a vertex of (0,0). We shift that vertex *left two* and *up one*. So, our vertex is (2,1).

You can do this problem on your graphing calculator by entering the equation into **y=**, hitting **GRAPH** and then using **TRACE** to follow the parabola to its lowest point.

Answer choice **H** is correct.

<u>What You May Have Done Wrong:</u>
    F. You flipped your x and y points, and wrote your ordered pair (y, x), instead of (x, y).
    G. You incorrectly found the x-coordinate of your vertex.
    J. Your x & y coordinates are incorrect. You may want to review your translations.
    K. It's likely you expounding your quadratic, which is counterproductive.

5. **The graph below shows a function in the (x, y) coordinate plane with a vertex as marked. What is the equation of that function?**

Correct Answer D

This is translation question that works a bit backwards.

The vertex of the parabola is at (-2,-3), which means we've translated our vertex *left two* and *down three*. This is also a "which" question and, as such, a good question to *mark-off*.

A. The factored quadratic gives us the *x*-intercepts (zeroes) of the parabola, *not* the vertex.
B. The factored quadratic gives us the *x*-intercepts (zeroes) of the parabola, *not* the vertex.
C. The factored quadratic gives us the *x*-intercepts (zeroes) of the parabola, *not* the vertex.
D. This is the correct horizontal shift; it moves the graph left two and it's the correct vertical shift.
E. This is the correct vertical shift, but you're horizontal shift is *right*, when it should be left.

Answer choice **D** is correct.

6. **Which of the following functions has *no* x-value when *y* = -1?**

Correct Answer K

This is another mark-off question with several approaches.

Knowing Your Functions

The fastest way to deal with this question is to know the general graphs of functions and their translations.

Plug-In

Since *y* = -1 doesn't result in a real number, we can plug in -1 for *y* and solve for *x*. The correct answer is the choice that doesn't have a real number solution.

Graphing

The slowest way to work this problem is to plug these questions into your graphing calculator and eyeballing the graphs.

F. This is a parabola shifted down 2 from (0,0), meaning the vertex is at (0,-2). Since the parabola opens up, there is a value for *y* = -1. If we plug in -1 for *y*, we can solve for *x* and get an *x* value of 1.

G. This is a square root equation that has been shifted down 4. If we solve for *y* = -1, we'll get the *x* $= \sqrt{3}$

H. This is a linear function. If we plug in -1 for *y*, then *x* = 1.

J. This is a linear function. If we plug in -1 for *y*, then *x* = -1.

K. This is an absolute value function. Absolute value can't, by definition, be less than 0. The graph **isn't** shifted down so its lowest point will be 0.

Answer **K** is correct.

7. **What are the *x*-intercepts for the parabola defined by the equation** $y = x^2 + 5x + 4$ **?**

Correct Answer C

This is a definition and factoring question. You've got to remember that the *x*-intercepts of a quadratic (parabola) are the solutions to that equation when *y* = 0. To find the solutions, we have to factor.

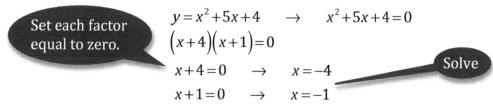

$$y = x^2 + 5x + 4 \quad \rightarrow \quad x^2 + 5x + 4 = 0$$

Set each factor equal to zero.

$$(x+4)(x+1) = 0$$

$$x + 4 = 0 \quad \rightarrow \quad x = -4$$

$$x + 1 = 0 \quad \rightarrow \quad x = -1$$

Solve

The *x*-intercept occurs when *y* = 0, so the points will be (-4, 0) & (-1, 0)

Answer **C** is correct.

<u>What You May Have Done Wrong:</u>

A. You've got a couple of problems here. First, your points are flipped. Remember that the *x*-intercepts occur when *y* = 0. Second, 4 and 1 are the factors, not the solutions.

B. 4 and 1 are the factors, not the solutions, you have to set each factor equal to zero to find the solutions (the *x*-intercepts).

D. You flipped the points. Remember that the *x*-intercepts occur when *y* = 0.

E. You probably just pulled the constants out of the equation. Review your steps.

8. **A Parabola is defined by the equation** $(x-2)(x-2) = 0$ **. What is the vertex of the parabola?**

Correct Answer B

This is a tricky version of a *translations* question. The simplest way to solve it is to rewrite the equation.

$$(x-2)(x-2) = 3 \quad \rightarrow \quad (x-2)^2 - 3 = 0$$

$$y = (x-2)^2 - 3$$

Now that we have the equation, we can use our knowledge of translations to solve.

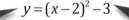

$$y = (x-2)^2 - 3$$

The -2 is *inside* the function, so it shifts the parabola two to the right.

The -3 is *outside* of the function, so it shifts the parabola three down.

So our vertex is shifted from (0,0) to (2,-3).

This is actually a good problem to plug into your graphing calculator. Plug in, graph, and then use TRACE to find your answer.

Answer **B** is correct.

<u>What You May Have Done Wrong:</u>

A. You've got your *x*-coordinate wrong. Negative number *inside* the function move the graph to the right.

C. You flipped your *x* and *y*-coordinates. Be careful!

D. You incorrectly solved for the zeros (not the vertex of the function).

E. You just pulled the factors out.

9. A parabola has *x*-intercepts of 4 and negative 2. What is its vertex?

Correct Answer A

This problem requires a bit of critical thinking. By the way, this problem is pretty common on the new SAT.

The easiest way to handle this problem is to use the *x*-intercepts to make factors.

$$\begin{array}{ccc} x=4 & & x-4=0 \\ & \rightarrow & \\ x=-2 & & x+2=0 \end{array}$$

Because you have the factors, you can write your equation.

$$0=(x-4)(x+2)$$
$$y=(x-4)(x+2)$$

You can plug this equation into your graphing calculator, graph it, and use the TRACE button to find your vertex.

The other way to do this problem is really worth talking about (and you ought to take a look at it). Recall that parabolas are symmetrical around their vertex. That means for any given height (*y*-value) the *x*-values will be the same distance from that line of symmetry. Look at the parabola below for an **example**.

-a + a = 0.

Average = $\dfrac{0}{2}=0$

So, we can say that the *x*-coordinate of the vertex is the average of any two points at the same height (*y*-value).

Because the *x*-intercepts are at the same height, we can average them together to get the *x*-coordinate of the vertex.

The *x*-intercepts are 4 and -2. $average=\dfrac{sum}{2}=\dfrac{4-2}{2}=1$

The *x*-coordinate of our vertex is 1. We plug in to the equation to find the *y*-coordinate.

$$\begin{array}{ccc} y=(x-4)(x+2) & \rightarrow & y=(1-4)(1+2) \\ y=3\bullet-3 & \rightarrow & y=-9 \end{array}$$

The vertex lies at point (1,-9).

You can actually stop here. There's only one answer choice with the right *x*-coordinate.

Answer **A** is correct.

What You May Have Done Wrong:
  B. You probably made an error in calculation. Review your steps.
  C. You used the *x*-intercepts as an ordered pair. They aren't, they are the *x* values of two *different points.*
  D. You may have averaged 4 and 2 together.
  E. You added your *x*-intercepts and then probably guessed on the *y*-value using the reasonable (and correct) deduction that the vertex needs to be well below zero.

Introduction

The ACT likes to give you "real world" word problems and have you translate them to graphs, or vice versa. I'm calling this section "Word Problem Functions," but it's a catchall for any function question type that has no equation or graph.

What You Need to Know

✓ Be able to translate text into operations
✓ Translate text into equations
✓ Graphically interpret pictures and relate them to text
✓ Understanding of parabolas

Rules of the Road: Function Word Problems

- **Break problems down into small pieces**
- **Pay attention to changes in slope and curves**

Generally, function word problems are about piecewise functions. Piecewise functions are functions that have more than one piece. They'll have changes in slope (for line segments) or changes in curve (for curves).

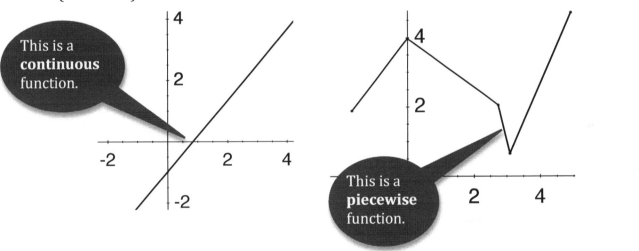

This is a **continuous** function.

This is a **piecewise** function.

1. A bathtub is filling from the faucet and the drain is closed. The graph below shows the depth of the tube as a function of time since the faucet was turned on. At time 1 exactly *one* of the following events occurred, which of the following could it be?

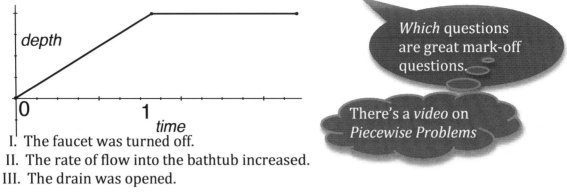

I. The faucet was turned off.
II. The rate of flow into the bathtub increased.
III. The drain was opened.

A. I only
B. II only
C. III only
D. I or III only
E. II or III only

Solve

Whenever we see a *Roman numeral question* evaluate each numeral and mark-off answer choices.

At time 1, the slope changed to zero, meaning the tub is no longer filling. Remember, only one of these events happens, so we consider each Roman numeral choice by itself, not in conjunction with other choices. Answers that have choices mean that either choice (but not both) can be true. Let's run through this.

I. **The faucet was turned off.**
This makes sense. If we turn off the faucet and the drain is closed, the level will stay the same. (The drain *has* to stay closed because only *one* event can happen at a time). So our right answer ***has* to have "I" in it**. That means we can mark off **B**, **C**, and **E**.

II. **The rate of flow to the bathtub increased.**
Even though we don't need to evaluate II (because our answer is either **A** or **D**), I'm going to discuss II just to be thorough. If we turn the faucet up (increase the flow) our flow would get steeper at time one. Instead our flow drops to zero. This means that II cannot be correct.

III. **The drain was opened.**
This is the more difficult answer choice to understand. If we open the drain and the faucet is still on (remember it has to be because only one change can happen). In that case, it's conceivable for the flow of the faucet into the tub to equal the flow out of the tub from the drain. This means that Roman numeral III has to be included and that answer choice **A** can't be correct because it does not include Roman numeral III. This leaves answer choice **D** as our only answer.

Answer choice **D** is correct.

2. The graph below shows Maria's distance from her home in miles. Three of the following five actions below describe Maria's movements in relation to her distance from home. In the correct order, which three is it?

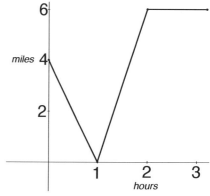

    I. Maria walked home at a rate of four miles per hour.
    II. Maria rode her bike at a rate of 12 miles per hour to the gym, six miles from home.
    III. Maria worked out at the gym, which is six miles from her home for two hours.
    IV. Maria jogged to the gym, six miles from her home, at a rate of 10 minutes per mile.
    V. Maria rides her bike home at a rate of one mile per hour.

    A. I, IV, & III
    B. I, II, & V
    C. I, II, V
    D. II, IV, V
    E. III, IV, V

Solve

This is a great problem to mark-off on. Remember, anytime we have a Roman numerals question, you'll want to mark-off the Roman numerals. In this question, however, we'll want to have a decent idea of what we are looking for before we evaluate the answer choices (we'll want to know what each piece of the function tells us). Let's look at the graph and discuss each piece.

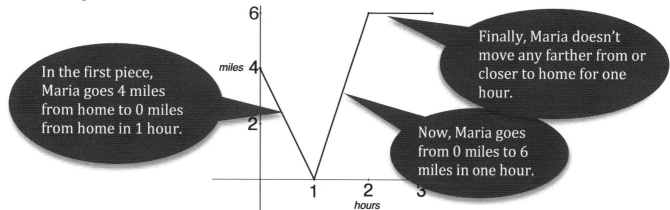

First Piece: 4 miles to home in one hour, matches Roman numeral **I** and lets us mark off **D** & **E**.

Second Piece: Six miles an hour away from home, matches Roman numeral **IV**. Roman numeral II would have her arriving at the gym in *half an hour*. You can mark-off **B** & **C**, leaving you with only answer choice **A**. If you aren't very comfortable, or you have a little time check the third piece to see if it makes sense.

Third Piece: She doesn't move anywhere for at least one hour, fits Roman numeral **III** because while working out at the gym, she doesn't get closer or farther away from home. Answer choice **A** is correct.

Point Based Questions

Point based questions involve a table of points that we've got to convert into a graph, or we've got to determine the nature of the graph—most frequently we'll have to tell line from curve.

Rules of the Road: Point Based Questions

- **Check from point to point for consistent slope.** Changes in slope from point-to-point mean you have a curve.
- **The slope of a line is always the same.** The change in y will always be the same for a change of one x.
- **Remember that parabolas are symmetrical around their vertex.**

Let's look at a couple of graphs:

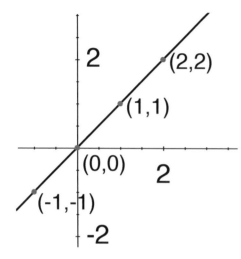

The y-difference between the $(0,0)$ and $(1,1)$ points is 1. The y-difference between $(2,2)$ and $(1,1)$ is 1. There is the same slope between the points $\dfrac{1-0}{1-0} = \dfrac{2-1}{2-1}$.

That makes sense, because the slope of a line never changes along its length.

There's a *video* on *Point-Based Questions*

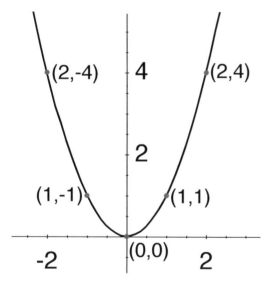

The y-difference between the $(0,0)$ and $(1,1)$ is 1. The difference between $(1,1)$ and $(2,4)$ is 3. The points don't have the same slope between them $\dfrac{4-1}{2-1} \neq \dfrac{1-0}{1-0}$. Because the slopes aren't the same, we've got a curve.

Review *slope* in *Coordinate Geo: The Line Equation*

ACT Examples: Point Based Questions

1. The table below gives coordinate points for a line in the standard (x, y) coordinate plane. What does c equal?

A. -2
B. -1
C. 0
D. 1
E. 2

x	y
-4	-6
4	2
3	c
0	-2

Solve

There are a couple of ways to do this, and let's take a look at both.

Find the Equation

To find the equation, we need the slope and the y-intercept. The y-intercept is given (remember, the y-intercept is when x equals 0). So, our y-intercept is -2.

To find the slope, we'll have to use two complete points (we can't use the point containing c). I'm using (-4,-6) and (0,-2)

$$slope = \frac{rise}{run} = \frac{-6-(-2)}{-4-0} = \frac{-4}{-4} = 1$$

Now we have our equation, $y = x - 2$, we plug in our value for x (3).

$$y = x - 2 \rightarrow y = 3 - 2 \rightarrow y = 1$$

Find the Slope

Another way to handle these problems is do just deal with the slope. First, let's find the slope.

$$slope = \frac{rise}{run} = \frac{-6-(-2)}{-4-0} = \frac{-4}{-4} = 1$$

You can "eyeball this" but *be careful*!

Now we can just count up (or back) from a point. Starting at $x = 0$ and $y = -2$. We count up to 3 from zero, and for every one x we go, we go up one y. So y will increase by 3, going from -2 to 1.

This is the method I prefer.

Answer choice **D** is correct.

2. The equation $y=(x+2)^2-2$ is graphed and the points below are selected from that graph.

For the equation above, which of the values of x will give the least value of y?

A. 0
B. 1
C. 3
D. -1
E. -2

x	y
-5	7
-3	-1
-1	-1
1	7
3	23
5	47

Notice that some of our answer choices aren't on the table above.

Parabolas are covered in Coord. Geo: Functions

Solve

Like the previous problem, we've got some options. Regardless of which method you choose, the first job is to recognize that the equation, and its points, will make a parabola. Parabolas are always symmetrical around their *vertex*. Let's go through our methods.

Plug Into the Equation

We can plug each of the answer choices into the equation for x and find which returns the smallest y-value. An x-value of -2 will return a y that is -2.

Know Your Translations

If you recall your translations from the function $y=x^2$, you'll see that the -2 shifts our vertex down two spots from (0,0). Since our parabola opens up (there's no negative sign in front of x^2), the vertex will be the lowest point on our graph, making y minimum -2.

I like this method

Graph Using Your Calculator

We could enter the equation in our *stat plot*, *graph* it and find the vertex using *trace*. For most of us, this takes a little too long.

Using Your Table

If you look at $x = -3$ and -1, you'll notice that they both have the same y-value, meaning that the parabola *turned* between them—meaning that the vertex is between them. We can always find the x-coordinate of the vertex by averaging two points that have the same y-height (although usually we use the zeros).

I like this method too!

I think that using the table and knowing your translations is the simplest way to solve this problem, but any of the above ways works.

Answer choice **E** is correct.

3. The table below gives the values of 2 functions f and g for selected values of x? One of the functions is linear. What is the value of the linear function when $x = -3$.

A. 2.4
B. 1.2
C. 0.8
D. 1.0
E. 2.0

x	$f(x)$	$g(x)$
-1	2.6	1.6
0	1.4	2
1		
2	1.4	2.8
3	2.6	3.2

Solve

This problem is a bit intimidating, but it's easily managed if you break it into parts. First, recall that a linear function is a line and that any exponential function is a curve.

We need to figure out which function is linear. Looking at function $f(x)$ we see that two different x values ($x = 0$ and $x = 2$) both have the same y value ($y = 2$). The only lines that can have the same y-values for two x-values are horizontal, and that's not the case here (because we have other y values for $f(x)$). *So, we know that $f(x)$ is the exponential function.* If you didn't notice the identical y-values, you could calculate the slope of each function twice. If the slope changes, you've got a curve.

x	$f(x)$	$g(x)$
-1	2.6	1.6
0	**1.4**	2
1		
2	**1.4**	2.8
3	2.6	3.2

Two identical y-values means $f(x)$ is a curve.

The missing values are a trick to keep you from seeing the curve. It may also trick you into calculating the answer for 1 (instead of -3).

Now that we know $g(x)$ is linear, we can either find the slope, or simply use the increase in $g(x)$ for every increase of one x.

Since y increases 0.4 for every 1 x, we can work backwards and say that y **decreases** by 0.4 for every 1 x we go **negative**. From our smallest point (-1, 1.6), we subtract (1, 0.4) twice to get to -3.

$$(-1, 1.6)$$
$$-(1, 0.4)$$
$$\underline{-(1, 0.4)}$$
$$(-3, 0.8)$$

Answer choice **C** is correct.

4. The table below gives the x and y coordinates of points in the linear function $f(x)$. What is the equation of $f(x)$?

x	-3	-1	1	3	5
y	12	4	-4	-12	-20

A. $f(x) = 4x + 3$
B. $f(x) = -4x + 4$
C. $f(x) = 2x$
D. $f(x) = 2x + 2$
E. $f(x) = -4x$

Review *Intermediate Algebra: Functions* for more

Solve

The question tells us that we need a linear function. Don't let the $f(x)$ or the use of the word "function" confuse you, we're looking for the line that goes through all these points in $y = mx + b$ form.

$y = mx + b$ has two components, the y-intercept and the slope. We can find either first, and let's start with the y-intercept.

Looking at the middle of the table, we have points $x = -1$ and $x = 1$. In the middle of those points (midpoint) we'll have $x = 0$, which is the x-coordinate of our y-intercept. We can average the two y-values to find the y-coordinate of our y-intercept.

You may be able to "eyeball" the y-intercept.

$$y - \text{intercept} = \frac{4+(-4)}{2} = \frac{0}{2} = 0$$

Because the y-intercept is 0, b is zero. We can mark off **A**, **B**, and **D**.

Now, we need to find the slope. We can use any two points to find the slope. I'll use the same points $(-1,4)$ and $(1,-4)$.

$$\text{slope} = \frac{rise}{run} = \frac{y_2 - y_1}{x_2 - x_1} = \frac{4-(-4)}{-1-1} = \frac{8}{-2} = -4$$

$$f(x) = -4x$$

Answer choice **E** is correct.

This is an odd question type, where we are given a shape on a coordinate axis and we've got to find a point *within* that shape.

ACT Examples: Finding the Point

1. A department store has a shape and dimensions in yards, as shown below. Every wall in the department store is either parallel or perpendicular. The customer service counter if located exactly between point *F* and point *D*. If Jim enters the store at point *B*, How does he get to the customer service counter?

   A. 25-yards north and 30-yards west
   B. 35-yards south and 45-yards west
   C. 35-yards south and 40-yards west
   D. 20-yards south and 25-yards east
   E. 20-yards south and 15-yards east

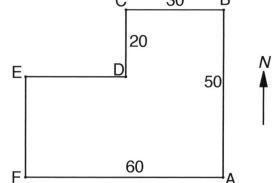

Solve

First, let's markup our diagram, with the location of the customer service counter, and the missing dimensions.

Because we've got our customer service marked, we see that from point *B*, we go South and West. These questions are great for marking off, and we can go ahead and get rid of answer choices **A** and **D**.

We'll need to break down the dimensions a little more to proceed.

Customer service is halfway between *F* and *D*, which means halfway in the *x*- direction and halfway in the *y*-direction.

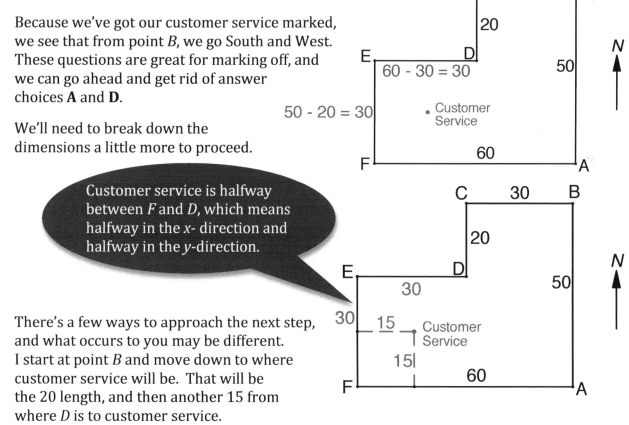

There's a few ways to approach the next step, and what occurs to you may be different. I start at point *B* and move down to where customer service will be. That will be the 20 length, and then another 15 from where *D* is to customer service.

$$20 + 15 = 35 \text{ yards south}$$

Now, moving from point *B* again (remember, before we found the *y* distance). We go west 30 to get to the point *D* and then we have another 15 to go to get to customer service.

$$30 + 15 = 45 \text{ yards west}$$

We can mark-off again at this point.

Answer choice **B** is correct.

Wrap Up

What You Need to Know
- ✓ Be able to translate text into operations
- ✓ Translate text into equations
- ✓ Graphically interpret pictures and relate them to text
- ✓ Understanding of parabolas

Videos

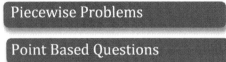

Piecewise Problems

Point Based Questions

The Strategies
- ✓ Break these into pieces. Whether they're word problems or table based problems.
- ✓ Look for changes in slope in piecewise and look for the vertex in parabolas.

Key Skill
This is a key skill, and it's related to:

- ✓ Make an Equation

- ✓ Coordinate Geometry Functions

- ✓ Algabraic Functions

1. John's landscaping service has a pricing model where he charges 5 dollars per visit plus 10 dollars an hour for work. He only charges for full hours. Which graph represents John's pricing model?

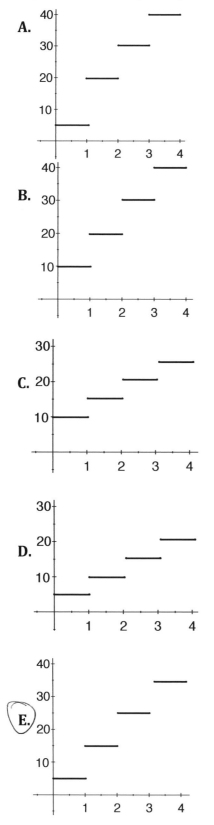

A.

B.

C.

D.

E.

2. A smart phone has a fixed amount of battery capacity. The graph of Sasha's phone's battery capacity along with time, in hours, is shown below. Three of the following five events occur, in order, which three is it?

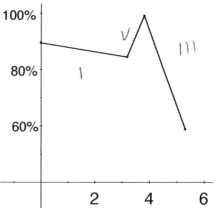

I. Sasha is at school, her phone is on but she's not using it. The phone doe not lose much battery when it is not being used.

II. Sasha is using an app while her phone is charging. The app requires as much energy as the phone receives from charging.

III. Sasha is using snapchat, an app that uses a lot of battery.

IV. Sasha has her phone turned off.

V. Sasha is charging her phone.

F. III, IV, II

G. I, IV, III

H. I, V, III

J. II, V, I

K. III, I, V

3. The table below gives coordinate points for a linear function in the standard Cartesian coordinate plane. What is the value of a?

x	y
-3	4
-1	1
1	a
3	-5
5	-8

A. -2
B. 2
C. -3
D. 3
E. 4

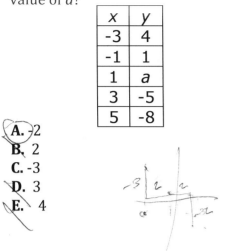

4. A quadratic equation is graphed and selected points from that graph are shown on the table below. What is the x-coordinate of the maximum point of the function?

x	-2	-3	2	3
y	0	-5	0	-5

F. 3
G. 0
H. 1
J. 2
K. -2

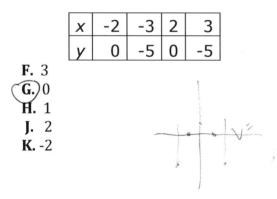

5. The function $f(x)=(x-2)^2-4$ is graphed and points from that graph are shown in the table below. What is the minimum point on the graph?

A. (-4,2)
B. (0,0)
C. (2,-4)
D. (1,-2)
E. (-2,-2)

6. The graph below shows Sasha's distance from home over time.

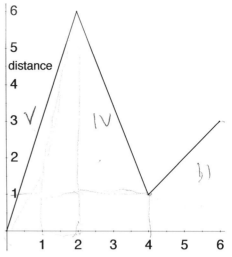

Three of the following events describe Sasha's movements over time. In order, which three is it?

  I.   Sasha leaves her friend's house (one mile from her home) and walks to the store at a rate of two miles an hour.
  II. Sasha leaves her friend's house (one mile from her home) and walks to the store at a rate of one mile an hour.
  III. Sasha leaves home and walks to the lake at six miles an hour.
  IV. Sasha leaves the lake and walks to her friend's house at 2.5 miles an hour.
  V.   Sasha leaves home and walks to the lake at three miles an hour.

F. V, IV, II
G. III, IV, I
H. V, IV, I
J. III, II, I
K. II, IV, V

1. John's landscaping service has a pricing model where he charges 5 dollars per visit plus 10 dollars an hour for work. He only charges for full hours. Which graph represents John's pricing model?

Correct Answer E

This is a definition question. We've got a fixed and a variable component. It's also a "which" question, which is a great *mark-off* question. Break the question into parts:

The Fixed Part (*y*-intercept)
John charges five dollars per visit.
This is the fixed component, which is always the *y*-intercept. We need a *y*-intercept of 5, which allows us to mark off **B** and **C**.

The Variable Part (the sort of slope)
...and 10 dollars an hour for work.
This is the variable component, the more John works, the more he makes. If John charged his time continuously (by the minute, or even second), we'd have a line with a slope. But because he charges by the hour (and doesn't count part of an hour), we have a "stair step" graph. Each step should be 10 higher than the previous step, so we can mark off **A** (which has an initial step of 15) and **D** (which has increases of 5).

Answer choice **E** is correct.

What You May Have Done Wrong

Check above for a discussion of the answer choices.

2. A smart phone has a fixed amount of battery capacity. The graph of Sasha's phone's battery capacity is shown along with time, in hours, is shown below. Three of the following five events occur, in order, which three is it?

Correct Answer H

Anytime there are roman numerals, it's a great mark-off question (we also have a "which"). Since we have to go in order, it's best to start at the beginning. In this problem, we aren't concerned about the *x*-axis because we aren't given any times in our Roman numeral choices.

Piece 1: A Gradual Decrease
Roman numeral I fits this part of the graph. II and V would have no slope (horizontal lines), IV would have a positive slope, and III should have a steeply negative slope. We can mark off **F**, **J**, and **K**.

Piece 2: A Sharp Increase
Roman numeral V fits this part of the graph. I and III have negative slopes, II and IV have no slopes (horizontal lines). We can mark-off **G**. We don't even need to look at the third piece.

Piece 3: A Sharp Decrease
Roman numeral III fits this part of the graph. I has a negative slope, but it's not steep enough. II and IV have no slope (horizontal lines), and V has a positive slope.

Answer choice **H** is correct.

3. The table below gives coordinate points for a linear function in the standard Cartesian coordinate plane. What is the value of a?

Correct Answer A

Don't let "linear function" fool you. All it's talking about is a line. In this case, all we really care about is the slope. We can solve this in either by finding the *slope* or by *counting*.

Slope Calculation

We can use any two points to calculate the slope. Let's use the first two.

$$slope = \frac{rise}{run} = \frac{y_1 - y_2}{x_1 - x_2} = \frac{4-1}{-3-(-1)} = \frac{3}{-2} = -\frac{3}{2}$$

Using the point (-1,1) we can count over two and down three, giving us (1,-2). Our answer is -2.

Counting

This is an informal way to solve this problem. I think it's actually easier. Looking at the difference in the first two points on our chart will allow us to "count" to our missing value.

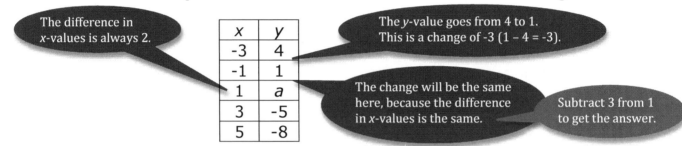

The difference in x-values is always 2.

The y-value goes from 4 to 1. This is a change of -3 (1 – 4 = -3).

x	y
-3	4
-1	1
1	a
3	-5
5	-8

The change will be the same here, because the difference in x-values is the same.

Subtract 3 from 1 to get the answer.

Answer choice **A** is correct

What You May Have Done Wrong

B. You added three. The line falls from left to right.
C. This is a halfway answer, it's the amount of change between y points.
D. This is an incorrect halfway answer.
E. This is a compound error. Review your steps.

4. A quadratic equation is graphed and selected points from that graph are shown on the table below. What is the maximum point of the function?

Correct Answer G

This is a question about the graphs of parabolas. On the ACT, we're concerned with parabolas that open up or open down. If they open up (like a cup) then they have a minimum point. If they open down, they have a maximum point. So, the question tells us which kind of parabola we're dealing with. Because the question acts for a maximum, *the parabola opens down.*

Parabolas are symmetrical around their vertex. We can take any two points with the same y-value and average them to find the x-coordinate. Average the two x-intercepts highlighted to the left.

x	-2	-3	2	3
y	0	-5	0	-5

$$average = \frac{sum}{number} = \frac{-2+2}{2} = 0$$

This parabola is symmetric about the v-axis.

Answer choice **G** is correct.

What You May Have Done Wrong:

F. This is the y-coordinate of the vertex (maximum).
H. You may have guessed, or made a compound error.
J. You may have guessed, or had an arithmetic error.
K. You may have just used the chart, assuming it had the maximum, or averaged points with different y-values

5. The function $f(x)=(x-2)^2-4$ is graphed and points from that graph are shown in the table below. What is the minimum point on the graph?

Correct Answer C

First, we've got to realize that we're dealing with a parabola. The *minimum* point is the same as the *vertex* of the parabola (the topmost or, in this case, bottommost point on the graph). There are several ways to handle this problem.

Knowing Your Translations

The -2 inside the parentheses is a horizontal shift. A negative shift moves the graph to the right, giving us a vertex with an
x-coordinate of +2. The -4 outside the parentheses is a vertical shift that moves the vertex *down* 4. This gives us a *y*-coordinate of -4. The vertex is (2,-4).

Using Your Calculator

You can plug the equation into your calculator and use the TRACE function to find the minimum.

Plugging in Points

You can plug in the answer choices. First, you plug in the *x*-value and see if it equals the *y*-value of the point. That allows you to mark-off **A**, **D**, and **E**. **C** is a lower point (on the *y*-coordinate) than **B**, so by elimination **C** is the vertex. This method works fine but it is very time consuming.

Answer choice **C** is correct.

What You May Have Done Wrong

A. These are the correct values, but you plugged *x* for *y* and vice versa.
B. This is a point on the parabola, but it's not its minimum
D. You may have guessed, or made a compound error.
E. You may have guessed, or made a compound error.

6. The graph below shows Sasha's distance from home over time. Three of the following events describe Sasha's movements over time. In order, which three is it?

Correct Answer F

We've got to match each piece of the graph with the right letter & there is also a rate component. This is a great mark-off question and it's most easily done piece by piece.

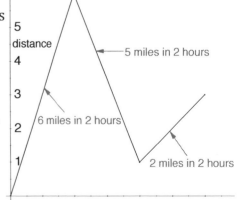

Piece 1: 0 to 6 miles in two hours. We know that Sasha has to leave from home because she starts at 0 miles (leaving us with **III** and **V**). The rate is calculated by

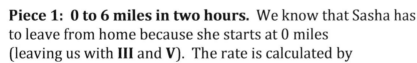

$$rate = \frac{distance}{time} = \frac{6}{2} = 3\,mph$$

This leaves us with **V**, and we can mark-off letters **G**, **J**, and **K**.

Piece 2: 6 to 1 miles in two hours. Sasha has to leave the lake, so the only choice that fits is **IV**. Unfortunately, that doesn't let us mark off any more answers.

Piece 3: 1 to 3 miles in two hours

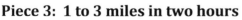

We know Sasha is leaving her friend's house (because it is one mile from home). That limits our options to **I** and **II**. We just need to calculate the rate, which is 1 mph. **II** fits the third piece. In sequence, our events are **V, IV, II**.

Answer **F** is correct.

Plane Geometry

The topics in the *Plane Geometry* section constitute 15 to 20 percent of the ACT Math section, or between 9 and 12 questions per test. Here's the question frequency and the corresponding ACT Score Report category or categories.

Triangles	3 – 4 questions	**IES & PHM: Geometry**
Right Triangleskey skill	1 – 2 questions	**IES, MOD, & PHM: Geo.**
4-Sided Shapes	1 – 2 questions	**IES & PHM: Geometry**
Combo Shapes	1 – 3 questions	**PHM: Geometry**
Other Polygons	2 – 3 questions	**IES & PHM: Geometry**
3D Geometry	0 – 2 questions	**MOD & PHM: Algebra**

IES: Integrating Essential Skills
PHM: Preparing for Higher Math
MOD: Modeling

A detailed explanation of the math score report is in the front of the book under the **score report**. There is only one key skill in *Plane Geometry*. *Right Triangles* is a really important topic. You'll see it in other *Plane Geometry* topics and, obviously, it it's the basis of *Trigonometry*.

Strategies

It's all about the right knowledge and the right application. You've got to know some concepts, but most importantly, you've got to apply them in an even controlled manner. Go step-by-step and mark-up your diagrams and you'll be rewarded on test day.

Know your Basics

> You've got to know your basic area, perimeter, and circumference formulas. Add the Pythagorean Theorem to that list along with how to find the volume of right cylinders and rectangular prisms.

Know your Special Right Triangles

> Know the 3, 4, 5 (and its multiples) and the 5, 12, 13. It's also really helpful to know the angle based special right triangles, 30°, 60°, 90° and 45°, 45°, 90°.

Use the Diagrams

> The ACT doesn't draw diagrams "to scale," but they are pretty accurate. Use them if you're stuck or to make sure your answer makes sense.

Mark-up Diagrams

> If a question describes a diagram, and one isn't provided, then draw the diagram. Again, do your best to move all the information from the question onto the diagram. Mark-up your diagrams. Your goal should be to completely dispense with the question and move all the relevant information onto the diagram.

When things get complicated, look for right triangles

> If you've got a combo shape question, or an ambiguous looking circle question (with a chord), look for right triangles. That will be the key to solving.

Go Step-by-step

> Almost all plane geo problems are multi-step. Go one step at a time—don't trip over your own feet!

1. The figure below shows a plan for a square room with measurements in square feet. The shaded area will be a square carpet and the un-shaded area will be tile. If the dimensions are as marked, how many square feet of tile will be needed?

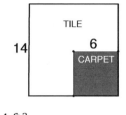

14   6

TILE

CARPET

A. 144 ft²
B. 160 ft²
C. 190 ft²
D. 108 ft²
E. 96 ft²

2. A rectangular television is hung on the middle of a rectangular wall so that the space to either side is equal and the space above and below is equal. What is the perimeter of the television?

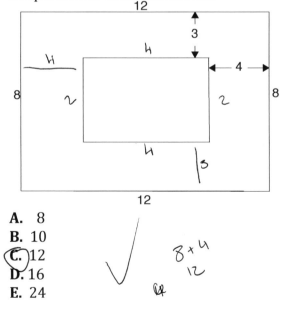

A. 8
B. 10
C. 12
D. 16
E. 24

$8 + 4$
12

3. The parallelogram below is on the standard x,y coordinate plane. What is its area?

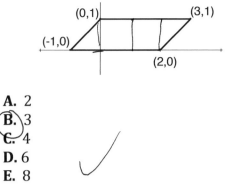

A. 2
B. 3
C. 4
D. 6
E. 8

4. In the figure below, ABCD is a trapezoid and has angles as marked. What is the measure of ∠ACB?

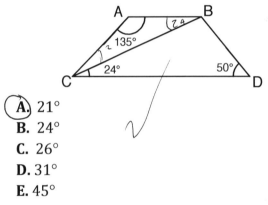

A. 21°
B. 24°
C. 26°
D. 31°
E. 45°

5. In the figure below, ABCD is a trapezoid and has sides with lengths as marked. What is the area of the trapezoid?

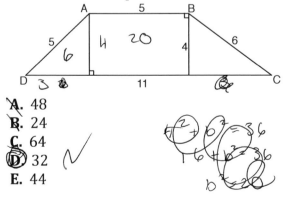

A. 48
B. 24
C. 64
D. 32
E. 44

6. If the two horizontal lines are parallel, what is the value of x in the diagram below?

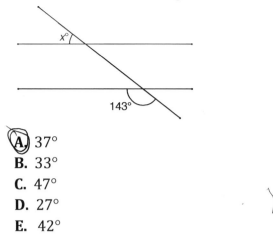

143°

(A.) 37°
B. 33°
C. 47°
D. 27°
E. 42°

7. Line segments AB and CD are parallel. What is the measure of the angle marked?

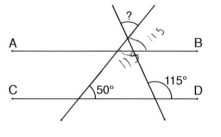

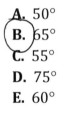

A. 50°
(B.) 65°
C. 55°
D. 75°
E. 60°

8. What is the value of x in the diagram below?

3x - 14   x + 6

(A.) 47
B. 180
C. 64
D. 38
E. 42

$x + 6 + 3x - 14 = 180$
$4x - 8 = 180$
$4x = 188$
$x = 47$

9. The triangle below has interior angles as marked. The exterior angles have measures of $a°, b°, c°$ as shown. What is the sum of a, b, and c?

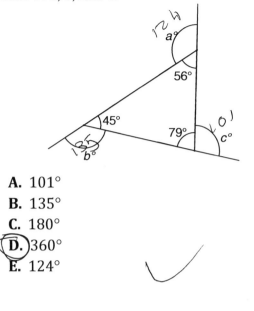

56°
45°
79°

A. 101°
B. 135°
C. 180°
(D.) 360°
E. 124°

10. The nonagon below is regular. What is the measure of angle x?

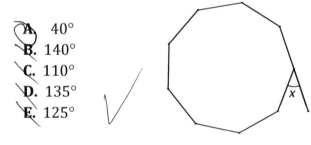

A. 40°
B. 140°
C. 110°
D. 135°
E. 125°

11. In the pentagon below, four of the five angles have measures as marked. What is the value of x?

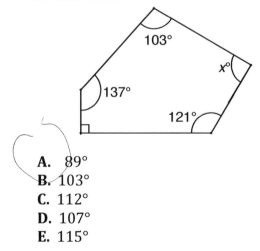

103°
137°
121°

A. 89°
B. 103°
C. 112°
D. 107°
E. 115°

12. The triangle below has a perimeter of 17. What is the length of its longest side?

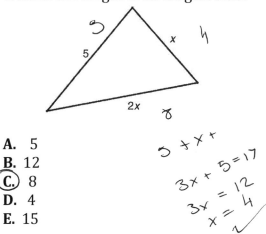

- **A.** 5
- **B.** 12
- **C.** 8
- **D.** 4
- **E.** 15

$5 + x +$

$3x + 5 = 17$

$3x = 12$

$3x = 4$

$x = 4$

13. The triangle below has an area has an area of 16. Its base is marked, what is its height?

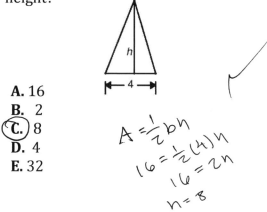

- **A.** 16
- **B.** 2
- **C.** 8
- **D.** 4
- **E.** 32

$A = \frac{1}{2}bh$

$16 = \frac{1}{2}(4)h$

$16 = 2h$

$h = 8$

14. What is the value of x in the given triangle?

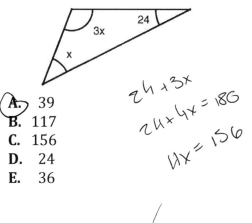

- **A.** 39
- **B.** 117
- **C.** 156
- **D.** 24
- **E.** 36

$24 + 3x$

$24 + 4x = 180$

$4x = 156$

15. In the figure below, line segments *AB* and *CD* are parallel. Line segments *EF* and *EG* are congruent. What is the measure of ∠FEG?

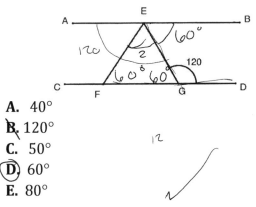

- **A.** 40°
- **B.** 120°
- **C.** 50°
- **D.** 60°
- **E.** 80°

12

16. Which of the following CANNOT be two angles of an isosceles triangle?

- **A.** 10° and 140°
- **B.** 30° and 120° 180 ✓
- **C.** 45° and 90° ✓
- **D.** 65° and 50° ✓
- **E.** 55° and 70° ✓

$140 + 20$

160

17. The triangles below have lengths given and *DE* is parallel to *BC*. What is the length of *AD*?

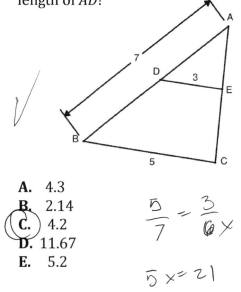

- **A.** 4.3
- **B.** 2.14
- **C.** 4.2
- **D.** 11.67
- **E.** 5.2

$\frac{5}{7} = \frac{3}{6} \times$

$5x = 21$

18. In the figure below, ΔABC and ΔDEF are similar. What is the perimeter of ΔDEF?

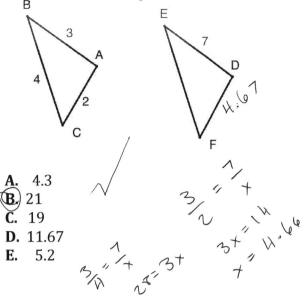

A. 4.3
B. 21
C. 19
D. 11.67
E. 5.2

$\frac{3}{2} = \frac{7}{x}$

$2\cdot7 = 3x$

$\frac{3}{2} = \frac{7}{x}$

$3x = 14$

$x = 4.66$

19. The diagram below shows a telephone pole that is perpendicular to the ground. A wire is attached to the pole ten feet from the ground. The wire is 14 feet long and runs from the pole, at an angle, to the ground x distance away. What is the length of x?

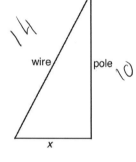

A. 9.8 feet
B. 17.2 feet
C. 4 feet
D. 16 feet
E. 8 feet

$10^2 + x^2 = 14^2$

$100 + x^2 = 196$

$x^2 = 96$

20. The square below has a diagonal with a length as marked. What is the area of the square?

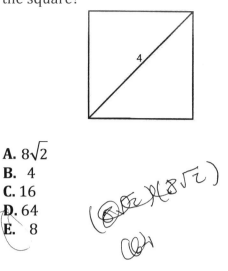

A. $8\sqrt{2}$
B. 4
C. 16
D. 64
E. 8

$(8\sqrt{2})(8\sqrt{2})$

64

21. A 20-foot ladder leaning against a building is hits the building at 16 feet above the ground. The ground and the building are perpendicular. How far from the building is the base of the ladder?

A. 22 feet
B. 16 feet
C. 12 feet
D. 10 feet
E. 14 feet

22. A 26-foot long ramp is built such that it makes a 30-degree angle with the ground, as shown below. The ramp ends at the door of a building, and the building is perpendicular with the ground. How high is the top of the ramp?

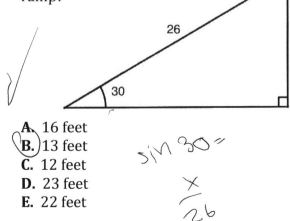

A. 16 feet
B. 13 feet
C. 12 feet
D. 23 feet
E. 22 feet

$\sin 30 =$

$\frac{x}{26}$

23. Points *B* and *C* lie on the circle below, where *A* is the center. What is the measure of angle *x*?

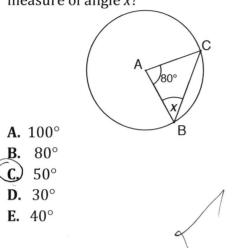

A. 100°
B. 80°
C. 50°
D. 30°
E. 40°

24. Point *A* is the center of the circle and the chord *CB* is 3 cm above the center. $\overline{AB}$ is a radius, what is the length of chord $\overline{CB}$?

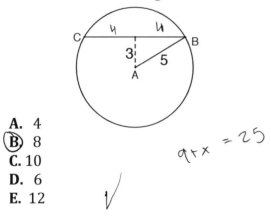

A. 4
B. 8
C. 10
D. 6
E. 12

$9+x = 25$

25. The square below has a side length of 4 and is inscribed into the circle, as shown. What is the area of the circle?

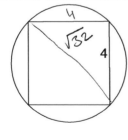

A. 4π
B. 16π
C. 8π
D. 32π
E. 64π

4^2

26. Square *ABCD* has an area of 16. Points *E, F, G, H* are the midpoints of their respective sides and *EGFH* is a square. What is the area of *EFGH*?

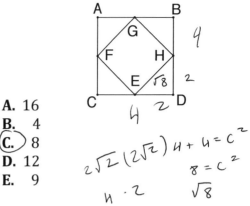

A. 16
B. 4
C. 8
D. 12
E. 9

$2\sqrt{2}(2\sqrt{2})4 + 4 = c^2$
$4 \cdot 2$ $8 = c^2$
                    $\sqrt{8}$

27. The circle below has a circumference of 25. What is its approximate radius?

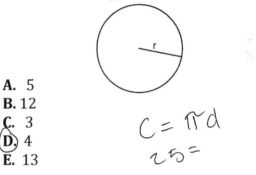

A. 5
B. 12
C. 3
D. 4
E. 13

$C = \pi d$
$25 =$

28. There are two circles, *Circle A & Circle B*. *Circle A* has a radius of 1 and *Circle B* has a radius of 2. What is the ratio of *Circle A*'s area to *Circle B*'s area?

A. 1:2
B. 2:3
C. 1:4
D. 3:8
E. 2:5

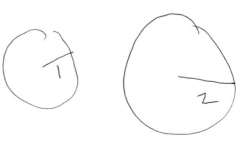

$A = \pi r^2$
$A_1 \pi$ $A = 4\pi$

29. What is the length of minor arc $\overset{\frown}{BC}$?

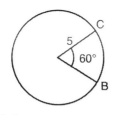

- **A.** 31.4
- **B.** 5.2
- **C.** 12.5
- **D.** 8.4
- **E.** 13.1

30. A circular dance floor has a diameter of 15 feet and is complete except for the missing 30° sector below. Approximately how many square feet of wood flooring is needed to complete the floor?

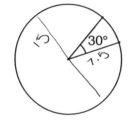

- **A.** 19 ft²
- **B.** 59 ft²
- **C.** 177 ft²
- **D.** 15 ft²
- **E.** 18 ft²

31. A circle in the standard (x,y) coordinate plane is tangent to the x-axis at 3 and the y-axis at -3. Which of the following is an equation of the circle.

- **A.** $(x-3)^2+(y+3)^2=3$
- **B.** $(x-3)^2+(y+3)^2=9$
- **C.** $(x-3)^2+(y-3)^2=3$
- **D.** $(x-3)^2+(y-3)^2=9$
- **E.** $(x+3)^2+(y-3)^2=9$

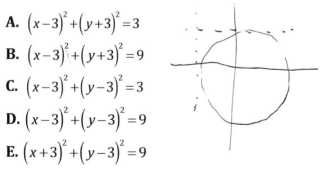

32. A circle is inscribed in a square, as shown below. The vertices of the square are as marked. What is the equation of the circle?

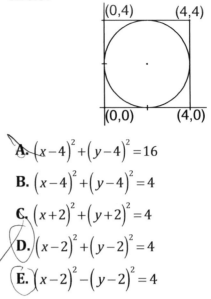

- **A.** $(x-4)^2+(y-4)^2=16$
- **B.** $(x-4)^2+(y-4)^2=4$
- **C.** $(x+2)^2+(y+2)^2=4$
- **D.** $(x-2)^2+(y-2)^2=4$
- **E.** $(x-2)^2-(y-2)^2=4$

33. The figure below is a water tanks that is a rectangular prism. It has dimensions marked in feet. If the tank is 90% full, how many cubic feet of water are in the tank?

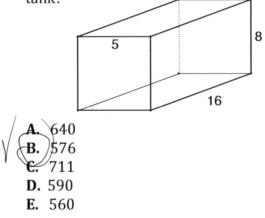

- **A.** 640
- **B.** 576
- **C.** 711
- **D.** 590
- **E.** 560

34. A salt canister is a right cylinder with a diameter of four inches and a height of seven inches. What is the volume of the cylinder?

- **A.** 28π
- **B.** 56π
- **C.** 14π
- **D.** 21π
- **E.** 25π

35. The rectangular prism below has sides in meters as marked, what is its surface area?

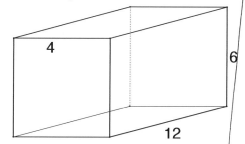

- **A.** 144 m²
- **B.** 214 m²
- **C.** 288 m²
- **D.** 196 m²
- **E.** 272 m²

36. An oatmeal container is a right cylinder with a height of 14 and a radius of 3. What is its **total** surface area?

(the lateral surface area of a right cylinder is found by the expression $2\pi r \cdot h$).

- **A.** 84π
- **B.** 18π
- **C.** 93π
- **D.** 91π
- **E.** 102π

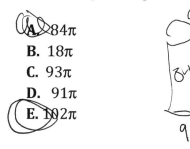

37. The figure below consists of a semicircle and a rectangle with dimensions marked. Approximately, what is the *outside* perimeter of the figure?

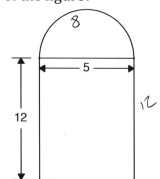

- **A.** 36
- **B.** 37
- **C.** 45
- **D.** 44
- **E.** 42

38. In the figure below all line segments intersect at 90° angles. What is the perimeter of the figure?

- **A.** 46
- **B.** 32
- **C.** 36
- **D.** 24
- **E.** 40

39. In the figure below, $\overline{AB}$ and $\overline{CD}$ are parallel and those line segments are perpendicular to $\overline{AF}, \overline{CE}, and \overline{DB}$. What is the area of polygon *AFECDB*?

- **A.** 15
- **B.** 19
- **C.** 20
- **D.** 22
- **E.** 23

40. How many diagonals are in the hexagon below?

- **A.** 24
- **B.** 9
- **C.** 18
- **D.** 12
- **E.** 6

	Answer	Section		Answer	Section
1.	B	Four Sided Shapes	26.	C	Combo Shapes
2.	C	Four Sided Shapes	27.	D	Circles
3.	B	Four Sided Shapes	28.	C	Circles
4.	A	Four Sided Shapes	(29.)	B	Circles
5.	D	Four Sided Shapes	30.	D	Circles
6.	A	Angles	(31.)	)B	Circles
7.	B	Angles	32.	D	Circles
8.	A	Angles	33.	B	3D Geometry
9.	D	Angles	34.	A	3D Geometry
10.	A	Angles	35.	C	3D Geometry
(11.)	A	Angles	36.	E	3D Geometry
12.	C	Triangles	37.	B	Other Polygons
13.	C	Triangles	38.	E	Other Polygons
14.	A	Triangles	39.	B	Other Polygons
15.	D	Triangles	40.	B	Other Polygons
16.	A	Triangles			
17.	C	Triangles			
18.	B	Triangles			
19.	A	Right Triangles			
(20.)	E	Right Triangles			
21.	C	Right Triangles			
22.	B	Right Triangles			
23.	C	Combo Shapes			
24.	B	Combo Shapes			
(25.)	C	Combo Shapes			

No shapes shown?

Angles
Key Skill

Introduction

Angle questions aren't on every test but the concepts are. Angles show up in almost every plane geometry topic, particularly triangles. The definition of parallel lines is especially important.

What You Need to Know

- ✓ The definition of *parallel* & *perpendicular lines*
- ✓ The definition of *complementary* & *supplementary* angles
- ✓ How to use *vertical* & *corresponding* angles
- ✓ How to find the measure of an interior angle & the sum of the interior angles of a polygon
- ✓ How to find an exterior angle of a polygon

Definitions: Perpendicular Lines

Perpendicular Lines intersect & make 90° angles.

These lines are **perpendicular**, making four 90° angles.

These line segments are **perpendicular**, making a 90° angle.

Complementary angles are either of a pair of angles that add to 90°.

Angles *x* and *y* are complementary.

Definitions: Other Angle Terms

Acute angles have measures less than 90°.
Right angles have measures of 90°.
Obtuse angles have measures greater than 90°.
Bisectors (to bisect) cut an angle in half with a line or line segment.

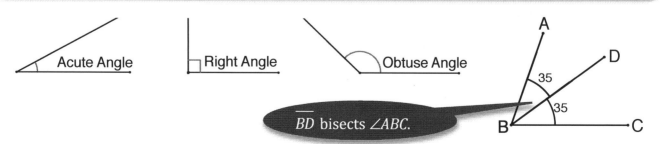

Acute Angle

Right Angle

Obtuse Angle

$\overline{BD}$ bisects ∠ABC.

Parallel Lines are lines that have the same slope, and they never intersect. The distance between parallel lines never changes.

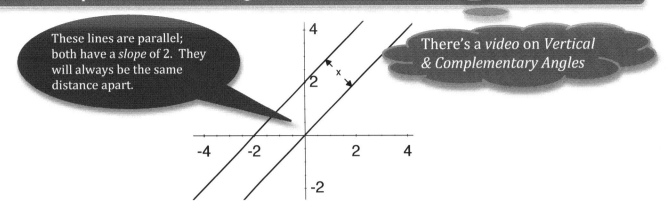

These lines are parallel; both have a *slope* of 2. They will always be the same distance apart.

There's a *video* on *Vertical & Complementary Angles*

When two parallel lines are intersected by another line, called a *transversal*, it makes pairs of identical angles called **corresponding angles**.

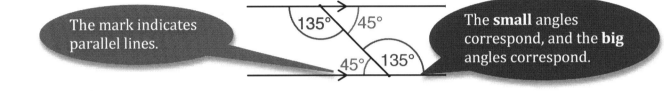

The mark indicates parallel lines.

The **small** angles correspond, and the **big** angles correspond.

Definitions: Vertical Angles

Vertical angles are the angles opposite each other when two lines intersect.

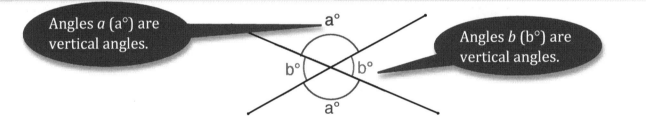

Angles *a* (a°) are vertical angles.

Angles *b* (b°) are vertical angles.

ACT Examples: Corresponding Angles, Vertical Angles, & Parallel Lines

1. What is the value of *x* in the diagram below?

A. 37°
B. 33°
C. 47°
D. 27°
E. 42°

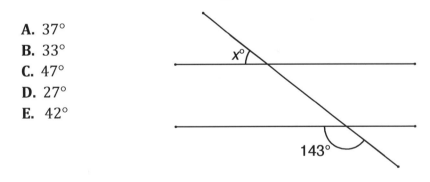

Solve

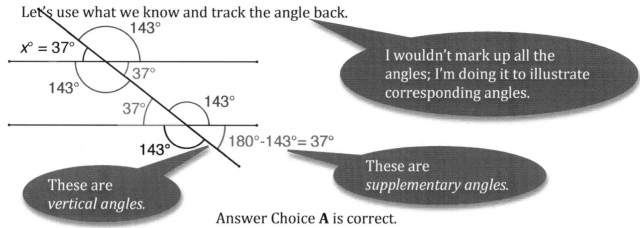

Let's use what we know and track the angle back.

$x° = 37°$

143°

143°

37°

37°

143°

37°

143°

143°

$180°-143°= 37°$

I wouldn't mark up all the angles; I'm doing it to illustrate corresponding angles.

These are *supplementary angles.*

These are *vertical angles.*

Answer Choice **A** is correct.

2. Line segments *AB* and *CD* are parallel. What is the measure of the angle marked?

A. 50°
B. 65°
C. 55°
D. 75°
E. 60°

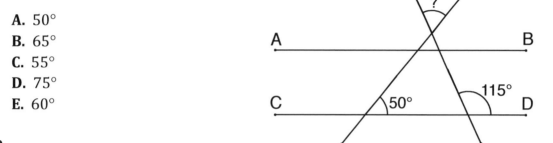

Solve

There are a couple of triangles made by the two diagonal lines and the parallel lines, and they are the key to solving the problem. Recall that the interior angles of triangles sum to 180°

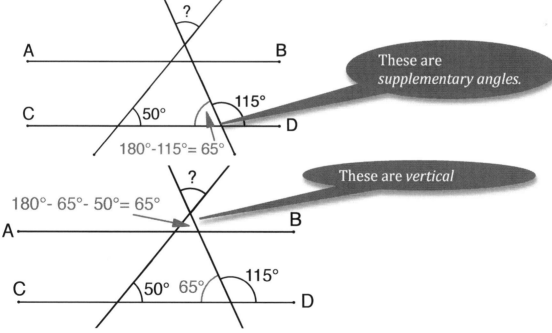

These are *supplementary angles.*

These are *vertical*

The missing angle of the triangle is 65°. That 65° angle is a vertical angle with the one we're looking for, therefore that angle is also 65°.

Answer choice **B** is correct.

Definitions: Supplementary Angles

A *straight line* is a 180° angle. Two angles that add up to 180° are called *supplementary angles*.

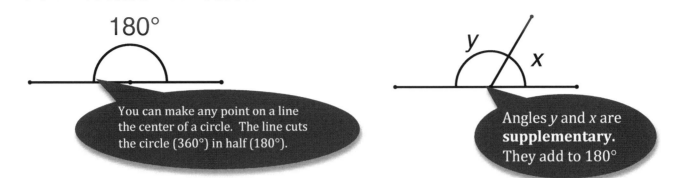

180°

You can make any point on a line the center of a circle. The line cuts the circle (360°) in half (180°).

y   *x*

Angles *y* and *x* are **supplementary**. They add to 180°

ACT Examples: Rectangles & Squares

1. What is the value of *x* in the diagram below?

A. 47°
B. 180°
C. 64°
D. 38°
E. 42°

3*x* - 14

x + 6

Solve

We know that the sum of the two expressions (3*x* – 14 and *x* + 4) is 180°.

$$3x - 14 + x + 6 = 180 \quad \rightarrow \quad 4x - 8 = 180$$

$$4x = 188 \quad \rightarrow \quad x = 47°$$

Answer Choice **A** is correct.

Exterior Angles

Exterior angles show up in triangles, but also in 5+ sided shapes.

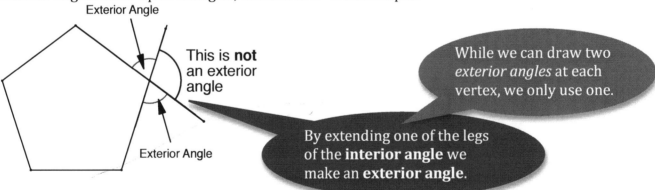

Exterior Angle

This is **not** an exterior angle

Exterior Angle

While we can draw two *exterior angles* at each vertex, we only use one.

By extending one of the legs of the **interior angle** we make an **exterior angle**.

Definition: Exterior Angles

Two exterior angles can be made at the vertex of each angle.
To make an exterior angle, you extend one side of the polygon (one leg of the interior angle).
An *interior* angle and *exterior* angle are supplementary, they sum to 180°.
The sum of the exterior angles in a polygon with *any* number of sides is 360°.

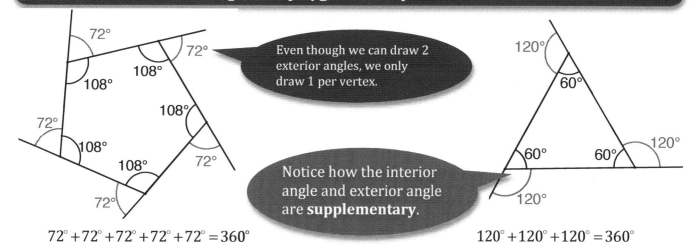

Even though we can draw 2 exterior angles, we only draw 1 per vertex.

Notice how the interior angle and exterior angle are **supplementary**.

$$72° + 72° + 72° + 72° + 72° = 360°$$

$$120° + 120° + 120° = 360°$$

Rules of the Road: Exterior Angles

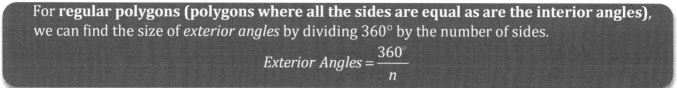

For **regular polygons (polygons where all the sides are equal as are the interior angles)**, we can find the size of *exterior angles* by dividing 360° by the number of sides.

$$Exterior\ Angles = \frac{360°}{n}$$

ACT Examples: Exterior Angles

1. The triangle below has interior angles as marked. The exterior angles have measures of $a°$, $b°$, $c°$ as shown. What is the sum of a, b, and c?

A. 101
B. 135
C. 180
D. 360
E. 124

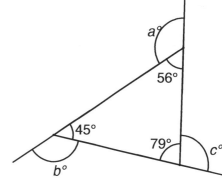

Solve

We can do this problem two ways. Exterior angles as are *supplementary* to interior angle. Find and then add the angles.

Subtract from 180° to find the size of the **exterior angle.**

The other way to handle this problem requires no calculation at all. The sum of the exterior angles is always 360°.

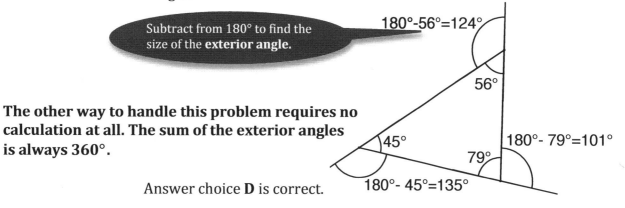

Answer choice **D** is correct.

2. The nonagon below is regular. What is the measure of angle *x*?

A. 40°
B. 140°
C. 110°
D. 135°
E. 125°

Solve

There are two ways to solve this problem. The first is to recall that our exterior angles sum to 360°. A nonagon has 9 sides (we can count if you don't know). So, we've got $\frac{360°}{9} = 40°$.

The other way to handle this question is to recall that exterior angles are supplementary to the interior angles. To find the interior angles, we'll need to either recall the formula, $(n-2) \cdot 180°$, or use the count-up method.

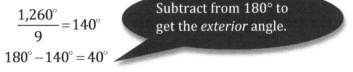

There's a *video* on *Exterior Angles*

Formula: $(n-2) \cdot 180°$ → $7 \cdot 180°$ → $1{,}260°$

Side Counting:

We add 180° for each side after the third (a triangle). I'm showing it all, but you don't need to write it out.

Triangles have a sum of 180°.
4-sided shapes have a sum of 360°.
5-sided shapes have a sum of 540°.
6-sided shapes have a sum of 720°.
7-sided shapes have a sum of 900°.
8-sided shapes have a sum of 1,080°.
9-sided shapes have a sum of 1,260°.

Now that we have the sum of the interior angles, we divide by the number of angles to get our interior angle.

$$\frac{1{,}260°}{9} = 140°$$

Subtract from 180° to get the *exterior* angle.

$$180° - 140° = 40°$$

Answer choice **A** is correct.

Interior Angles

Interior angles of polygons with more than 4-sides are the most frequently asked about question involving larger polygons. It's also a key component to a lot of other questions.

Definition: Interior Angles

The **interior angles** of a polygon make the corners of a shape.

There's a *video* on *Interior Angles*

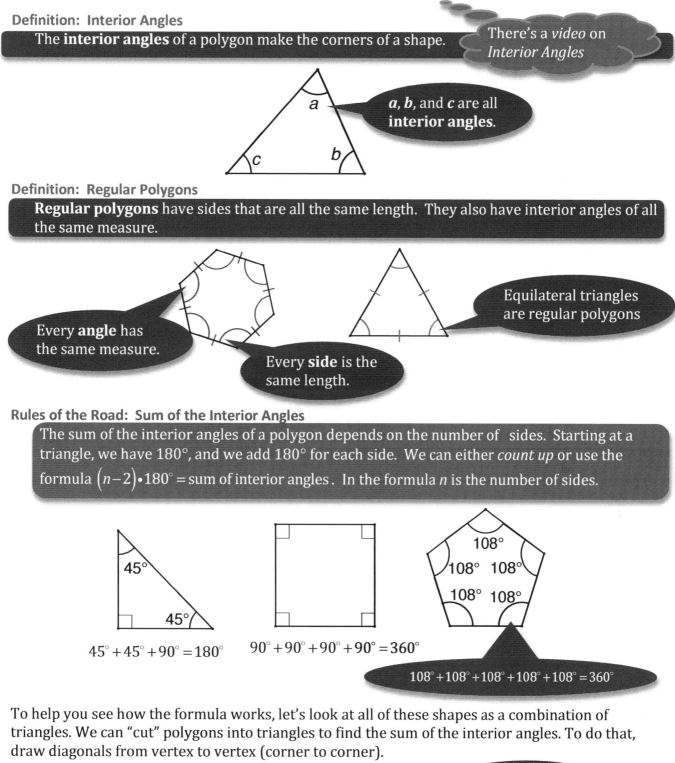

a, *b*, and *c* are all **interior angles**.

Definition: Regular Polygons

Regular polygons have sides that are all the same length. They also have interior angles of all the same measure.

Every **angle** has the same measure.

Every **side** is the same length.

Equilateral triangles are regular polygons

Rules of the Road: Sum of the Interior Angles

The sum of the interior angles of a polygon depends on the number of sides. Starting at a triangle, we have $180°$, and we add $180°$ for each side. We can either *count up* or use the formula $(n-2)\cdot180° = \text{sum of interior angles}$. In the formula n is the number of sides.

$$45° + 45° + 90° = 180°$$ $$90° + 90° + 90° + 90° = 360°$$

$$108° + 108° + 108° + 108° + 108° = 360°$$

To help you see how the formula works, let's look at all of these shapes as a combination of triangles. We can "cut" polygons into triangles to find the sum of the interior angles. To do that, draw diagonals from vertex to vertex (corner to corner).

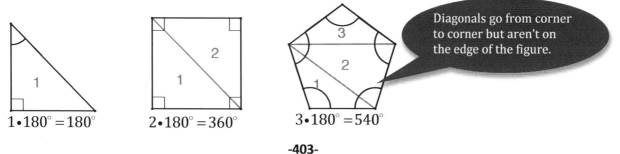

Diagonals go from corner to corner but aren't on the edge of the figure.

$$1\cdot180° = 180°$$ $$2\cdot180° = 360°$$ $$3\cdot180° = 540°$$

ACT Examples: Interior Angles

1. In the pentagon below, four of the five angles have measures as marked. What is the value of *x*?

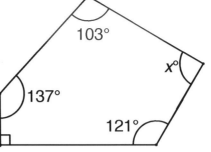

A. 89°
B. 103°
C. 112°
D. 107°
E. 115°

Solve

The first step in the problem is to figure out the sum of interior angles in a pentagon. Pentagons have five sides, two more than a triangle, so we add $180° + 180° + 180° = 540°$. We can also plug the number of sides in to the equation:

$$(n-2) \bullet 180° = \text{sum of interior angles}.$$

Doing it this way, the math looks like this:

$$(n-2) \bullet 180° = \text{sum of interior angles}$$

$$(5-2) \bullet 180° = \text{sum of interior angles}$$

$$3 \bullet 180° = 540°$$

Now that we've have the sum of the interior angles (540°), we can subtract to find *x*.

$$540° - 103° - 137° - 90° - 121° = x$$

$$x = 89°$$

Answer choice **A** is correct.

Wrap Up

What You Need to Know

✓ The definition of *parallel & perpendicular lines*
✓ The definition of *complementary & supplementary* angles
✓ How to use *vertical & corresponding* angles
✓ How to find the measure of an interior angle & the sum of the interior angles of a polygon
✓ How to find an exterior angle of a polygon.

Videos

> Vertical & Supplementary Angles

> Interior Angles

> Exterior Angles

The Strategies

✓ Look for supplementary angles. They show up frequently.
✓ Mark up parallel lines. Whenever you have parallel lines, they're usually key in solving the problem.

Related Skills

✓ All shapes sections in coordinate geometry
✓ All shapes questions in plane geometry

Plane Geometry Angles: Problems

1. In the figure below, lines *l* and *m* are parallel. What is the value of angle *a*?

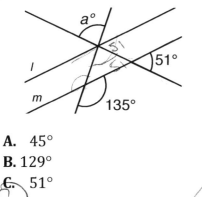

    A. 45°
    B. 129°
    C. 51°
    D. 84°
    E. 81°

2. In the figure below, ∠CAB has a measure of 74° and $\overline{AD}$ is a bisector. What is the measure of ∠DAE?

    F. 53°
    G. 16°
    H. 58°
    J. 37°
    K. 21°

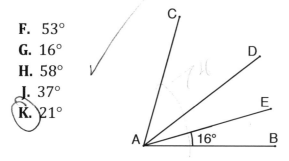

3. In the figure below, lines *a* and *b* are parallel, and line *c* is a transversal. What is the value of 2*x* – *y*?

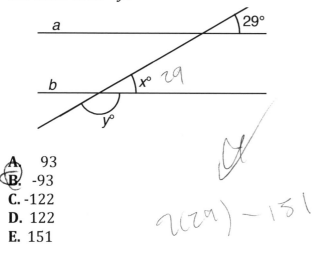

    A. 93
    B. -93
    C. -122
    D. 122
    E. 151

4. In the figure below lines *l* and *m* are parallel. What is the value of *x*?

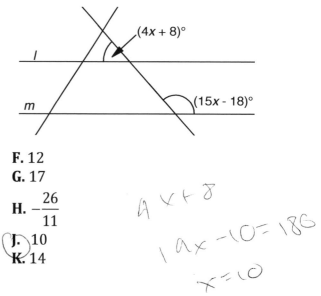

    F. 12
    G. 17
    H. $-\dfrac{26}{11}$
    J. 10
    K. 14

$4x + 8$

$14x - 10 = 186$

$x = 10$

5. In the figure below, point *G* is the intersection of $\overline{AB}, \overline{CD},$ and $\overline{EF}$. What is the measure of ∠CGF?

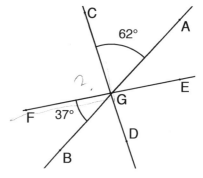
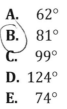

    A. 62°
    B. 81°
    C. 99°
    D. 124°
    E. 74°

6. In the figure below, *l* and *m* are parallel and *a* and *b* are transversals. How many angles formed by lines *l*, *m*, *a*, and *b* have a measure of 60°?

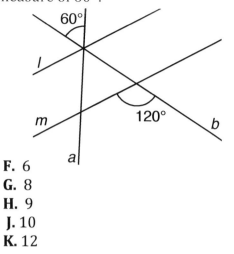

F. 6
G. 8
H. 9
J. 10
K. 12

7. In the figure below, *D*, *A*, *C* are collinear. What is the value of *x*?

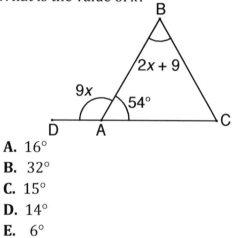

A. 16°
B. 32°
C. 15°
D. 14°
E. 6°

8. What is the measure of angle *a* in the figure below?

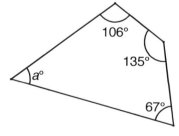

F. 119°
G. 158°
H. 52°
J. 62°
K. 102°

9. In the hexagon below, what is the measure of angle *b*?

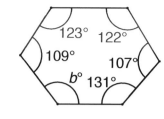

A. 128°
B. 52°
C. 309°
D. 163°
E. 142°

10. The polygon below is a regular hexagon. What is the value of *a + b + c*?

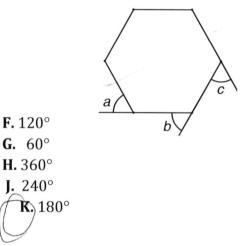

F. 120°
G. 60°
H. 360°
J. 240°
K. 180°

11. In the figure below, *A*, *B*, *C*, and *D* are collinear. What is the measure of ∠*BEC*?

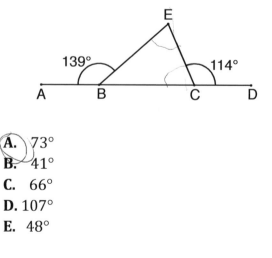

A. 73°
B. 41°
C. 66°
D. 107°
E. 48°

Angles: Solutions

1. In the figure below, lines *l* and *m* are parallel. What is the value of angle *a*?

Correct Answer D

We've got a triangle in two parallel lines. Let's mark up our figure; we'll use vertical and supplementary angles to find two of the three angles in the triangle.

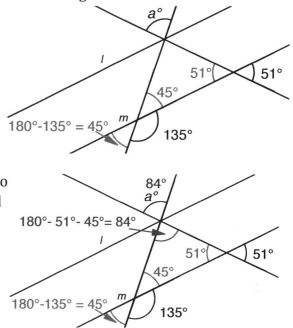

Now that we have those angles, subtract from 180° to find the middle angle. That middle angle is a vertical angle to angle *a*.

Answer choice **D** is correct.

<u>What You May Have Done Wrong</u>

    A. That's the supplementary angle for 135°.

    B. That is a supplementary angle to 51°.

    C. That's the bottom angle of the triangle.

    E. You probably made a calculation error.

2. In the figure below, $\angle CAB$ has a measure of 74° and $\overline{AD}$ is a bisector. What is the measure of $\angle DAE$?

Correct Answer K

This problem is testing whether you know the definition of *bisect*. Bisect, or a bisector splits an angle in half.

The question tells us the entire angle is 74°, so the bisector splits the large angle into two smaller angles, $\angle CAD$ and $\angle DAB$.

Those angles will measure $\dfrac{74°}{2} = 37°$.

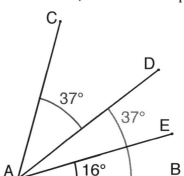

So, the measure of $\angle DAE$ will be $\angle DAB$ - $\angle EAB$

$$\angle DAB - \angle EAB = \angle DAE \quad \rightarrow \quad 37° - 16° = 21°$$

Answer choice **K** is correct.

<u>What You May Have Done Wrong</u>

    F. You *added* 57° and 16° instead of subtracting.

    G. You may have guessed, or misread the problem.

    H. You subtracted 16° from the entire measure (74°).

    J. This is the halfway answer. You found the size of $\angle DAB$.

3. **In the figure below, lines *a* and *b* are parallel, and line c is a transversal. What is the value of 2x − y?**

Correct Answer B

This is a fairly straightforward question based on parallel lines and their corresponding angles. Let's mark up our diagram.

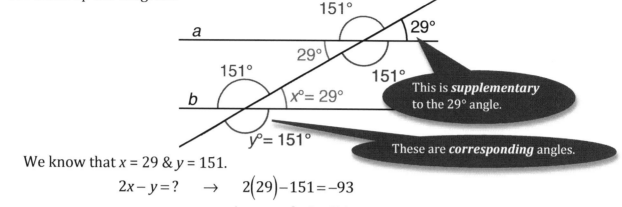

We know that x = 29 & y = 151.

$$2x - y = ? \quad \rightarrow \quad 2(29) - 151 = -93$$

Answer choice **B** is correct

<u>What You May Have Done Wrong</u>

    A. You inverted the order of subtraction.
    C. You subtracted *y* from a single *x* (it should be 2*x*).
    D. You inverted the order of subtraction *and* you forgot to multiply *x* by 2.
    E. This is a halfway answer (the value of *y*).

4. **In the figure below lines *l* and *m* are parallel. What is the value of *x*?**

Correct Answer J

This is a corresponding angles question with an algebra twist. We've got corresponding angles because lines *l* and *m* are parallel.

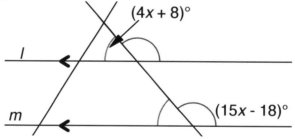

The **small** angle (4*x* + 8) and the **big** angle (15*x* – 18) are supplementary (they add to 180°).

$$(4x+8)+(15x-18)=180$$
$$19x-10=180$$
$$19x=190$$
$$x=10$$

Answer choice **J** is correct.

<u>What You May Have Done Wrong:</u>

    F. You probably made an algebra error.
    G. You made an algebra error, subtracting 10 when you should have added.
    H. You set the expressions equal to each other instead of 180°.
    K. You had an algebra error, subtracting 4*x* from 15*x*.

5. In the figure below, point G is the intersection of $\overline{AB}$, $\overline{CD}$, and $\overline{EF}$. What is the measure of $\angle CGF$?

Correct Answer B

This is a vertical angle question, let's markup what we know. Half of the headache in this question is the number of angles and letters. To make things simpler, mark up the angle you're looking for. The sum of all the angles in the diagram is 360°. We can subtract from 360° to find the angle we want.

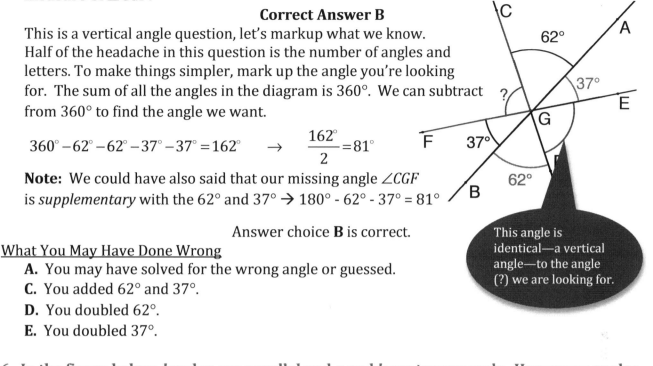

$$360° - 62° - 62° - 37° - 37° = 162° \qquad \rightarrow \qquad \frac{162°}{2} = 81°$$

Note: We could have also said that our missing angle $\angle CGF$ is *supplementary* with the 62° and 37° → 180° - 62° - 37° = 81°

Answer choice **B** is correct.

This angle is identical—a vertical angle—to the angle (?) we are looking for.

<u>What You May Have Done Wrong</u>

   A. You may have solved for the wrong angle or guessed.

   C. You added 62° and 37°.

   D. You doubled 62°.

   E. You doubled 37°.

6. In the figure below, *l* and *m* are parallel and *a* and *b* are transversals. How many angles formed by lines *l*, *m*, *a*, and *b* have a measure of 60°?

Correct Answer J

This question combines supplementary and vertical angles with parallel lines. The best way to solve this is to mark up each angle in our diagram.

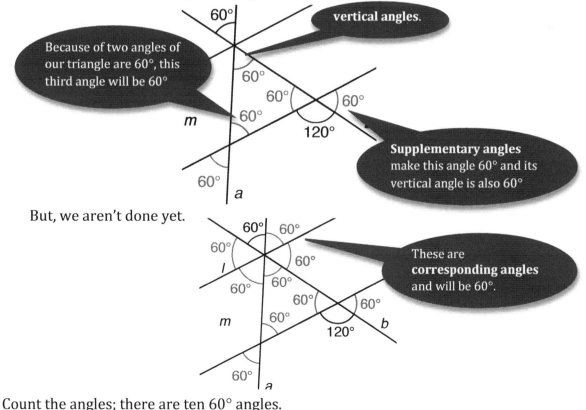

Because of two angles of our triangle are 60°, this third angle will be 60°

vertical angles.

Supplementary angles make this angle 60° and its vertical angle is also 60°

But, we aren't done yet.

These are **corresponding angles** and will be 60°.

Count the angles; there are ten 60° angles.

Answer **J** is correct.

7. In the figure below, *D, A, C* are collinear. What is the value of *x*?

Correct Answer D

We've got a triangle with an *exterior angle* included. The *only* way to do this is to use the fact that interior and exterior angles are *supplementary*. The problem wants to trick you into trying to use the triangle angles, but there's **not enough information**. We just don't have enough information because we don't have the other base angle ($\angle BCA$).

Any interior angle and its exterior angle are supplementary. We can set up an equation:

$$9x + 54 = 180°$$
$$9x = 126°$$
$$x = 14°$$

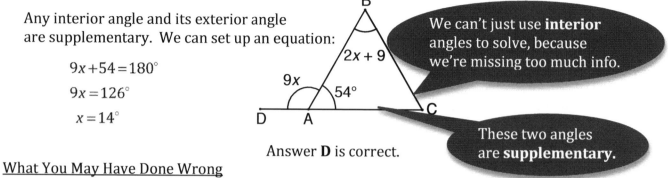

Answer **D** is correct.

What You May Have Done Wrong

A. You set $9x$ and $2x + 9$ equal to $180°$. We don't know these are supplementary angles, and, in fact, they are not.

B. You assumed that triangle *ABC* is isosceles, and $\angle BCA$ equaled $54°$. This is not the case, and we can't solve the problem just using the interior angles of the triangle.

C. You probably made a calculation error, or made a mistake similar to choice **1B**.

E. You set $9x$ equal to $54°$.

8. What is the measure of angle *a* in the figure below?

Correct Answer H

This is a four-sided shape, and like all four-sided shapes the interior angles sum to $360°$.

If you needed to, you could split it in triangles (2).
Or count up from three sides and add $180°$ for each side over three, or plug into the equation

$$(n-2) \cdot 180° = \text{sum of the interior angles}$$

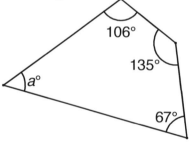

Because we know the shape sums to $360°$, we can subtract to find the missing angle.

$$360° - 106° - 135° - 67° = a° \quad \rightarrow \quad a° = 52°$$

Answer **H** is correct.

What You May Have Done Wrong

F. You forgot to subtract the $67°$ angle.

G. You forgot to subtract the $106°$ angle.

J. You probably made a calculation error.

K. This is a calculation error.

9. In the hexagon below, what is the measure of angle *b*?

Correct Answer A

This is an interior angles question. To solve this, you'll need to find the sum of the interior angles in a hexagon, and subtract the given angles from the sum. The difference will be the measure of angle *b*.

To get the sum of the interior angles, we can use the formula, count up the sides or split the hexagon into triangles. Let's look at each, briefly.

The Formula

n is the number of sides.

$$(n-2) \cdot 180° = \text{sum of the interior angles}$$

$$(6-2) \cdot 180° = \text{sum of the interior angles}$$

$$4 \cdot 180° = \text{sum of the interior angles}$$

$$\text{sum of the interior angles} = 720°$$

Counting Sides

We have six sides, three over a triangle. So, we start with 180° (for three sides) and add 180° for each side.

$$180° + 180° + 180° + 180° = 720°$$

Now subtract all the angles from 720° to get the answer.

720 – 131 – 107 – 122 – 123 – 109 = 128°

Answer **A** is correct.

What You May Have Done Wrong

B. You used 540°, the measure of a pentagon and disregarded the negative answer.

C. You used 900° instead of 720°.

D. This is a guess or a calculation error.

E. This is a guess or a calculation error.

10. The polygon below is a regular hexagon. What is the value of $a + b + c$?

Correct Answer K

This is an exterior angle question. Because we have a regular polygon, we know that the interior angles are equal to each other and the exterior angles are equal to each other. There are two ways to solve, using *exterior angles* or using *supplementary angles*

Using Exterior Angles

The easiest way to solve this is to remember that the sum of the *exterior angles* for **any polygon** is equal to 360°. Our exterior angles are equal, so dividing by six will give us their size.

$$\frac{360°}{6} = 60°$$

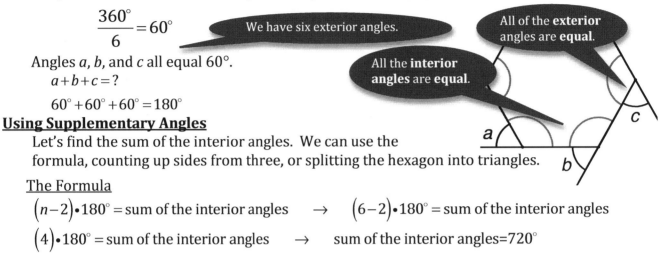

We have six exterior angles.

All of the **exterior** angles are **equal**.

All the **interior** angles are **equal**.

Angles a, b, and c all equal 60°.

$a + b + c = ?$

$60° + 60° + 60° = 180°$

Using Supplementary Angles

Let's find the sum of the interior angles. We can use the formula, counting up sides from three, or splitting the hexagon into triangles.

The Formula

$(n-2) \cdot 180° =$ sum of the interior angles $\rightarrow$ $(6-2) \cdot 180° =$ sum of the interior angles

$(4) \cdot 180° =$ sum of the interior angles $\rightarrow$ sum of the interior angles $= 720°$

Counting Sides

Counting up from the first three sides, we have three more (6 total). The first three sides give us 180° and *each* additional side gives us another 180°.

$$180° + 180° + 180° + 180° = 720°$$

Answer **K** is correct.

What You May Have Done Wrong

F. This is the measure of a single interior angle, or two of the angles.

G. This is the measure of a single exterior angle—a halfway answer.

H. This is the measure of three interior angles, or the measure of all of the exterior angles.

J. This is the measure of two interior angles or four exterior angles.

11. In the figure below, A, B, C, and D are collinear. What is the measure of $\angle BEC$?

Correct Answer A

This is an *internal/external angles* question that has a bit about triangles. We'll need to use the exterior angles and the fact that they are supplementary with interior angles to find our missing angle.

$180° - 139° = 41°$ $\rightarrow$ $180° - 114° = 66°$

The sum of the interior angles of a triangle is 180°, and we can subtract our known interior angles from 180° to get our missing angle.

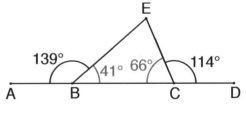

$$180° - 41° - 66° = 73°$$

Answer **A** is correct.

What You May Have Done Wrong

B. This is a halfway answer; you stopped early or found the wrong angle.

C. This is a halfway answer; you stopped early or found the wrong angle.

D. You summed the two known interior angles but didn't subtract them from 180°.

E. You used 66° for *both* of the interior angles at the base.

Background

Triangles are the most frequently tested shape on the ACT. Area, perimeter, side length, similar triangles, internal angles, and trig functions are all directly tested. Additionally, triangles are often key in the *find the missing angle* and *combination shape* questions.

What You Need to Know

- ✓ How to find the *perimeter* & *area* of a triangle.
- ✓ How to use *angles* to solve for an angle in a triangle
- ✓ The definition of *isosceles* & *equilateral* triangles
- ✓ How to solve *similar* triangles.

Definitions: Perimeter, Area, & Internal Angles

Perimeter is the sum of all a triangle's sides.

Area: The area of a triangle is found by the formula $\frac{1}{2}base \cdot height$.

Interior Angles: The sum of the interior angles of a triangle is $180°$.

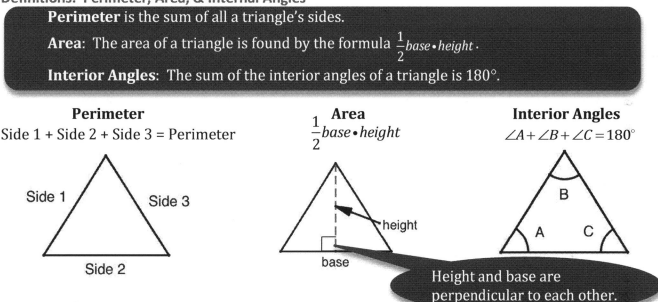

Perimeter	Area	Interior Angles
Side 1 + Side 2 + Side 3 = Perimeter	$\frac{1}{2}base \cdot height$	$\angle A + \angle B + \angle C = 180°$

Height and base are perpendicular to each other.

ACT Examples: Perimeter

2. The triangle below has a perimeter of 17. What is the length of its longest side?

A. 5
B. 12
C. 8
D. 4
E. 15

Solve

Because we understand perimeter, we can make an equation.

$$perimeter = side + side + side$$
$$17 = 5 + x + 2x$$
$$12 = 3x$$
$$x = 4$$

This is the length of the *shortest side*.

Plug in what we know.

We know two sides know, *x* (4) and 5. Let's find the last side.

$$longest = 2x = 2(4) = 8$$

8 is the longest side.

Answer choice **C** is correct.

Example: Area

1.

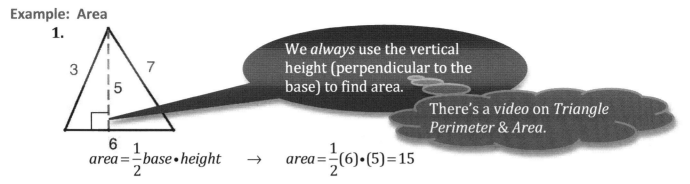

$$area = \frac{1}{2} base \cdot height \quad \rightarrow \quad area = \frac{1}{2}(6) \cdot (5) = 15$$

ACT Example: Area

2. Triangle *ABC* has an area of 16. Its base is marked, what is its height?

A. 16
B. 2
C. 8
D. 4
E. 32

Solve

We know the formula for the area of a triangle, so plug in the given information and solve for height.

$$area = \frac{1}{2} base \cdot height \quad \rightarrow \quad 16 = \frac{1}{2}(4) \cdot height$$

$$16 = 2 \cdot height \quad \rightarrow \quad height = 8$$

Solve for height

Answer choice **C** is correct.

Example: Angles

1.

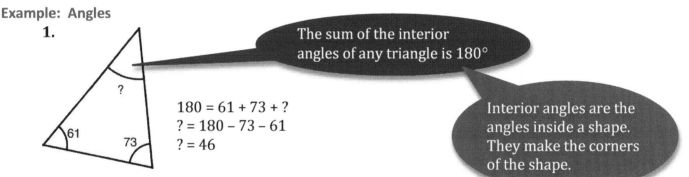

The sum of the interior angles of any triangle is 180°

$$180 = 61 + 73 + ?$$
$$? = 180 - 73 - 61$$
$$? = 46$$

Interior angles are the angles inside a shape. They make the corners of the shape.

ACT Example: Angles

2. What is the value of *x* in the given triangle?

A. 39
B. 117
C. 156
D. 24
E. 36

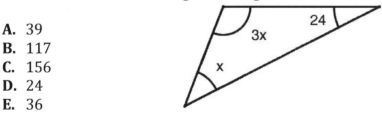

Solve

Because we know that the interior angles of all triangles add to 180°, we can write an equation.

$$x + 3x + 24 = 180 \quad \rightarrow \quad 4x = 156$$
$$x = 39$$

Combine like terms.

Answer choice **A** is correct.

Relationships & Triangles

The relationship between the interior angles and the sides of triangles is an important concept for a solid understanding of triangles.

Definitions

Sides are formed by the opposite angle.
The *larger* the angle the *larger the side*
The *smaller* the angle the *smaller the side*

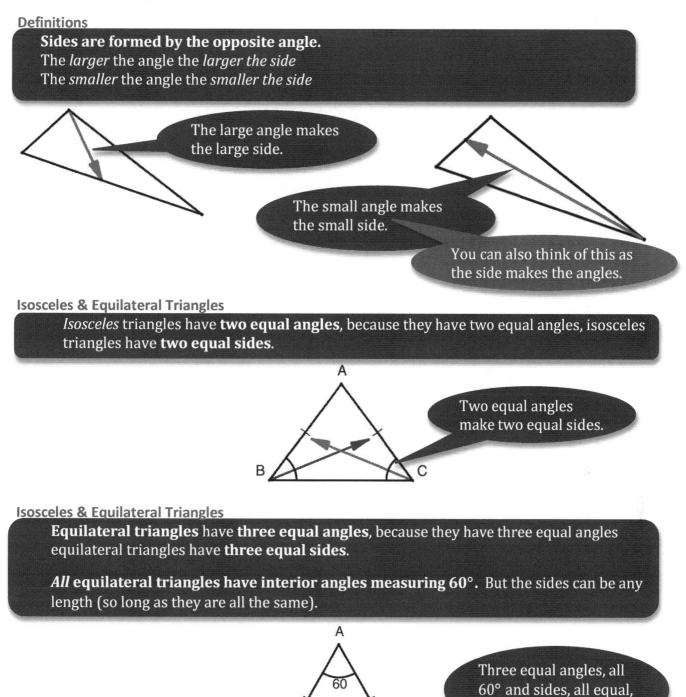

The large angle makes the large side.

The small angle makes the small side.

You can also think of this as the side makes the angles.

Isosceles & Equilateral Triangles

Isosceles triangles have **two equal angles**, because they have two equal angles, isosceles triangles have **two equal sides**.

Two equal angles make two equal sides.

Isosceles & Equilateral Triangles

Equilateral triangles have **three equal angles**, because they have three equal angles equilateral triangles have **three equal sides**.

All equilateral triangles have interior angles measuring 60°. But the sides can be any length (so long as they are all the same).

Three equal angles, all 60° and sides, all equal, of any length.

1. In the figure below, line segments *AB* and *CD* are parallel. Line segments *EF* and *EG* are congruent. What is the measure of ∠FEG?

A. 40°
B. 120°
C. 50°
D. 60°
E. 80°

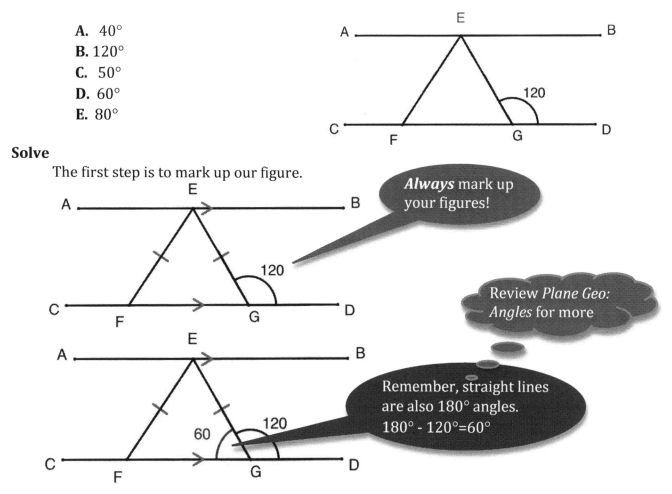

Solve

The first step is to mark up our figure.

Always mark up your figures!

Review *Plane Geo: Angles* for more

Remember, straight lines are also 180° angles.
180° - 120°=60°

Once we have two angles of a triangle, we can always find the third.

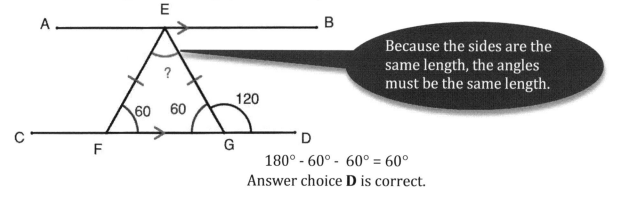

Because the sides are the same length, the angles must be the same length.

180° - 60° - 60° = 60°

Answer choice **D** is correct.

2. Which of the following CANNOT be two angles of an isosceles triangle?

    A. 10° and 140°
    B. 30° and 120°
    C. 45° and 90°
    D. 65° and 50°
    E. 55° and 75°

> The word *"which"* tells us we *have* to use the answer choices.

Solve

The only way to solve is to evaluate each answer choice.

    A. 10° and 160°   → 180° – 10° – 160° = 10°
    B. 30° and 120°   → 120° – 30° – 120° = 30°
    C. 45° and 90°   → 180° – 45° – 90° = 45°
    D. 65° and 50°   → 180° – 65° – 50° = 65°
    E. 55° and 75°   → 180° – 55° – 75° = 50°

> Find the third angle of the triangle by subtracting from 180, and see if it matches either of the other two angles.

Answer choice **E** is correct.

Similar Triangles

Similar triangles show up frequently on the ACT. These problems are really *proportion* problems. You may want to review *Pre-Algebra: Ratios & Proportions* for more on those skills.

Definition

> Similar triangles have **equal angles** but are **different sizes**. When you match up the sides (large to large, etc.) they will all have the same ratio.

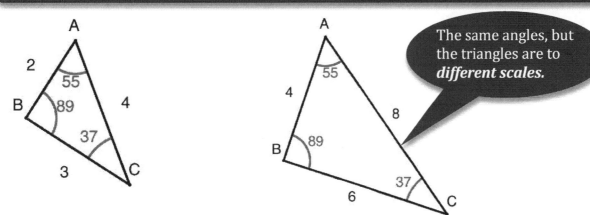

> The same angles, but the triangles are to *different scales.*

Let's take a look at the ratios.

Side	Large	Small	Large/Small
Small	4	2	2
Medium	6	3	2
Large	8	4	2
Perimeter	18	9	2

> The ratio $\dfrac{\text{large}}{\text{small}}$ is the same for each pair of sides

> The ratio also works when comparing the *perimeters*.

> It **does not** work for *area.*

1. The triangles below have lengths given and *DE* is parallel to *BC*. What is the length of *AD*?

A. 4.3
B. 2.14
C. 4.2
D. 11.67
E. 5.2

There's a *video* on *Similar Triangles*

Solve

First, let's mark up the figure, to show the parallel segments.

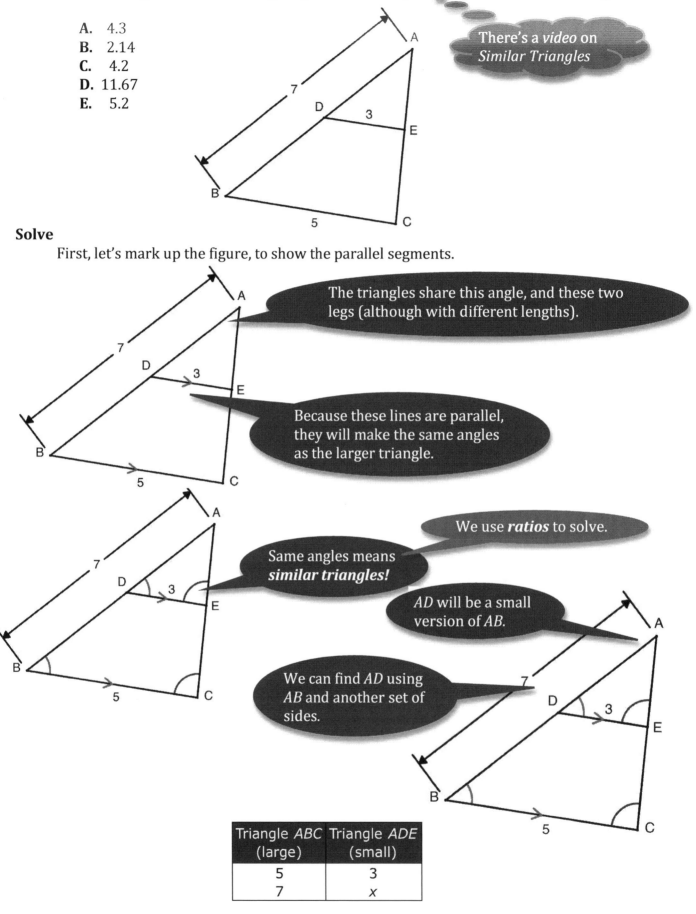

The triangles share this angle, and these two legs (although with different lengths).

Because these lines are parallel, they will make the same angles as the larger triangle.

We use *ratios* to solve.

Same angles means *similar triangles!*

AD will be a small version of *AB*.

We can find *AD* using *AB* and another set of sides.

Triangle *ABC* (large)	Triangle *ADE* (small)
5	3
7	*x*

Let's set up the ratios.

Large : Small
5 : 3
7 : x

We put the same sides on each line.

Remember, ratios are fractions. So, let's turn them into fractions!

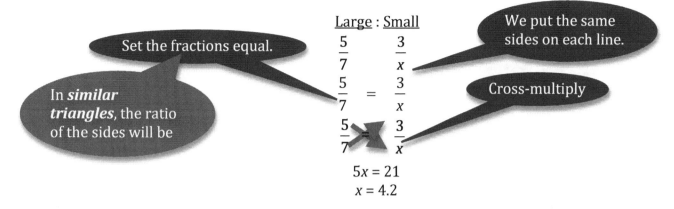

Set the fractions equal.

In **similar triangles**, the ratio of the sides will be

Large : Small

$$\frac{5}{7} \qquad \frac{3}{x}$$

We put the same sides on each line.

$$\frac{5}{7} = \frac{3}{x}$$

Cross-multiply

$$\frac{5}{7} \bowtie \frac{3}{x}$$

$$5x = 21$$
$$x = 4.2$$

Answer choice **C** is correct.

2. In the figure below, $\triangle ABC$ and $\triangle DEF$ are similar. What is the perimeter of $\triangle DEF$?

A. 18
B. 21
C. 16
D. 9
E. 27

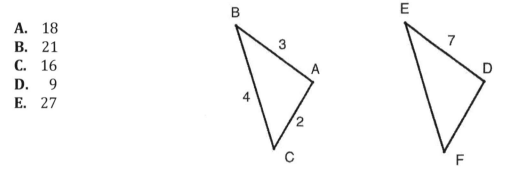

Solve

Remember, with perimeters the ratio of the corresponding sides will be the same as the ratio of the perimeters. The perimeter of the small triangle is $4 + 3 + 2 = 9$.

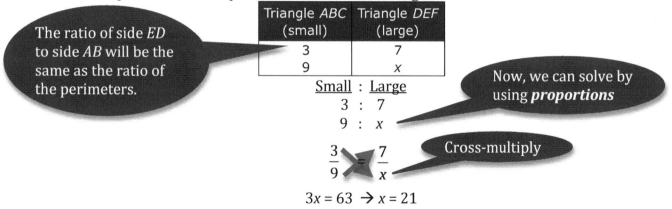

The ratio of side *ED* to side *AB* will be the same as the ratio of the perimeters.

Triangle *ABC* (small)	Triangle *DEF* (large)
3	7
9	x

Small : Large
3 : 7
9 : x

Now, we can solve by using **proportions**

$$\frac{3}{9} \bowtie \frac{7}{x}$$

Cross-multiply

$$3x = 63 \rightarrow x = 21$$

Answer choice **B** is correct.

Wrap Up

What You Need to Know

- ✓ How to find the *perimeter* & *area* of a triangle.
- ✓ How to use *angles* to solve for an angle in a triangle
- ✓ The definition of *isosceles* & *equilateral* triangles
- ✓ How to solve *similar* triangles.

Videos

Perimeter & Area of a Triangle

Similar Triangles

The Strategies

- ✓ Frequently, these problems will have a bit of algebra. Remember to use your givens or what is true of all triangles (the interior angles sum to 180 degrees).
- ✓ Set similar triangle questions up as proportions.
- ✓ Remember that the angles opposite equal sides are equal.
- ✓ Know how to use *supplementary*, *vertical*, and *corresponding* angles.

Related Skills

Triangles is very close to a key skill, and you'll find related skills all over the test.

- ✓ Proportion
- ✓ Angles
- ✓ Right Triangles
- ✓ Combo Shapes
- ✓ Trigonometry

Triangles: Problems

1. In the late afternoon, two buildings on level ground have shadows that end at the same place. The taller building is 60 feet tall and the shorter building is 45 feet tall. The shadow cast by the taller building is 100 feet long. How far are the buildings apart?

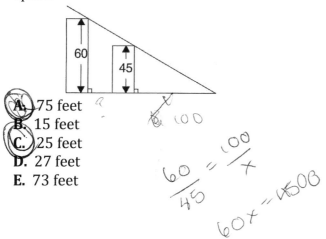

   A. 75 feet
   B. 15 feet
   C. 25 feet
   D. 27 feet
   E. 73 feet

2. A triangle similar to $\triangle ABC$ has a height of 4. What is its area?

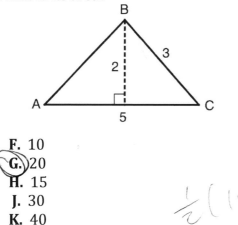

   F. 10
   G. 20
   H. 15
   J. 30
   K. 40

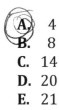

3. A triangle has sides of 8 inches and 14 inches. Which CANNOT be the length of the third side?

   A. 4
   B. 8
   C. 14
   D. 20
   E. 21

4. F is on line segment $\overline{AB}$; G and E are on $\overline{CD}$. Line segments AB and CD are parallel. $\overline{FG}$ and $\overline{FE}$ are congruent. What is the measure of $\angle GFE$?

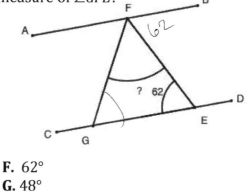

   F. 62°
   G. 48°
   H. 118°
   J. 56°
   K. 62°

5. Angle DEA measures 14°, what does $\angle EAB$ measure?

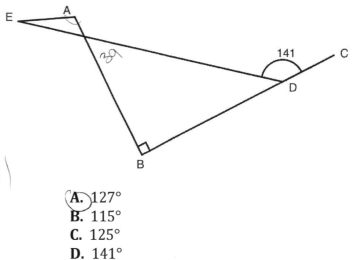

   A. 127°
   B. 115°
   C. 125°
   D. 141°
   E. 90°

6. Line segments *AB* and *BC* are perpendicular. What is the sum of angles ∠*BAF* and ∠*BCF*?

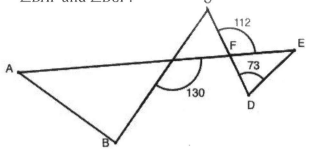

F. 82°

G. 102°

H. 62°

J. 40°

K. 108°

7. Point *A* is the center of the circle below. What is the measure of ∠*CBA*?

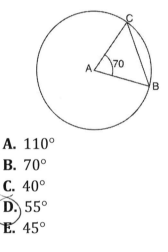

A. 110°

B. 70°

C. 40°

D. 55°

E. 45°

8. In the following diagram of Δ*ABC*, what is the value of *x*?

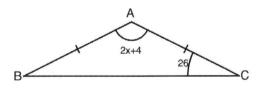

F. 128°

G. 11°

H. 62°

J. 124°

K. 75°

9. The line segments marked in the diagram below are congruent. Angle *ADB* is as marked, what is the value of *a*?

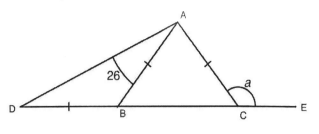

A. 76°

B. 52°

C. 128°

D. 154°

E. 120°

10. What is the measure, in degrees, of the largest internal angle in triangle *ABC*?

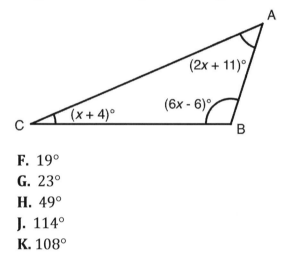

F. 19°

G. 23°

H. 49°

J. 114°

K. 108°

11. In Δ*DEF*, $a \leq 3b$. What is the maximum value of *a*?

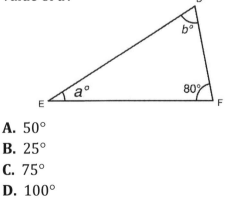

A. 50°

B. 25°

C. 75°

D. 100°

E. 67°

Triangles: Solutions

1. **In the late afternoon, two buildings on level ground have shadows that end at the same place. The taller building is 60 feet tall and the shorter building is 45 feet tall. The shadow cast by the taller building is 100 feet long. How far are the buildings apart?**

Correct Answer C

This is a *similar triangle* problem. We have a shared angle, the vertex where the shadows end. And we have two congruent angles (the 90° angles). Let's mark up our figure and see what we need. With similar triangles, we want to set up ratios that compare *corresponding sides*.

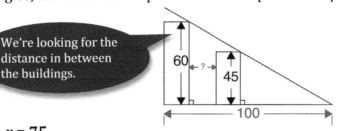

Large : Small
60 : 45
100 : x

Set up our fractions...

$$\frac{60}{100} = \frac{45}{x} \rightarrow 60x = 4,500 \rightarrow x = 75$$

By subtracting our two distances, we get the distance between the buildings.

$$100 - 75 = 25 \text{ feet}$$

<u>What You May Have Done Wrong</u>
- **A.** That is the length of the smaller building's shadow, not the distance between.
- **B.** You either have a compound error, or simply took the difference of the building heights. Review your steps.
- **D.** You miscalculated the shadow of the smaller building *and* you failed to subtract.
- **E.** You miscalculated the shadow of the smaller building.

2. **A triangle similar to △ABC has a height of 4. What is its area?**

Correct Answer G

It's tempting to find the area of triangle *ABC* and double it (our conversion factor). But that doesn't work, the *perimeter* of similar triangles *is proportional* the area is **not** proportional. Use the triangle given, *ABC*, to construct our other triangle.

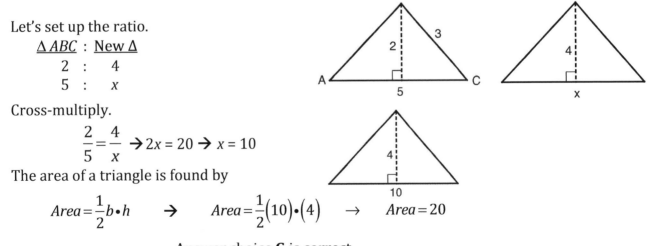

Let's set up the ratio.

△ ABC : New △
2 : 4
5 : x

Cross-multiply.

$$\frac{2}{5} = \frac{4}{x} \rightarrow 2x = 20 \rightarrow x = 10$$

The area of a triangle is found by

$$Area = \frac{1}{2}b \cdot h \quad \rightarrow \quad Area = \frac{1}{2}(10) \cdot (4) \quad \rightarrow \quad Area = 20$$

Answer choice **G** is correct.

<u>What You May Have Done Wrong</u>
- **F.** You may have calculated the area of the original triangle and doubled it.
- **H.** You probably miscalculated the area of the original triangle and tried to scale it.
- **J.** You may have scaled the triangle correctly *but* used the wrong side for height.
- **K.** You may have forgotten to take ½ the *b* x *h*.

3. A triangle has sides of 8 inches and 14 inches. Which CANNOT be the length of the third side?

Correct Answer A

This is a *triangle inequality theorem* question. All we have to do is calculate the range of potential sides and find the answer choice outside of that range. The triangle inequality theorem tells us that the third side of any triangle has to meet these inequalities.

$$larger\ side - smaller\ side < 3^{rd}\ side < larger\ side + smaller\ side$$
$$14 - 8 < 3^{rd}\ side < 14 + 8$$
$$4 < 3^{rd}\ side < 22$$

The only answer not within that range is 4, because the third side must be *greater* than 4!

Answer choice A is correct

<u>What You May Have Done Wrong</u>

For all wrong answer choices, review the steps above. All are valid side lengths except choice A.

4. F is on line segment $\overline{AB}$, G and E are on $\overline{CD}$. Line segments AB and CD are parallel. $\overline{FG}$ and $\overline{FE}$ are congruent. What is the measure of $\angle GFE$?

Correct Answer J

This is a question that seems to test your angle knowledge (and it does) but it's not the parallel lines that are the key. It's the *isosceles* triangles. First off, let's mark up our diagram.

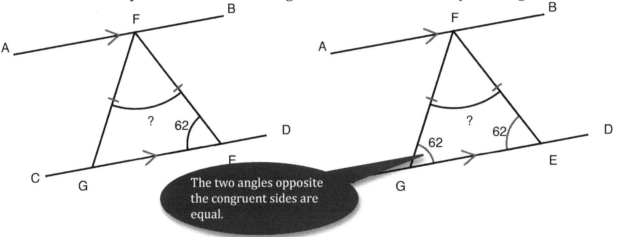

The two angles opposite the congruent sides are equal.

To find angle *GFE*, subtract: $180 - 62 - 62 = 56$

Answer choice J is correct.

<u>What You May Have Done Wrong:</u>
F. That is the size of the other base angle (*FGE*).
G. You made a calculation error or misunderstood the problem.
H. You forgot that 180° is split among *three* angles.
K. You made a calculation error or misunderstood the problem.

5. Angle *DEA* measures 14°, what does $\angle EAB$ measure?

Correct Answer B

This is an angle question. Let's markup our given angle, our *supplementary angle*, and run through our angles.

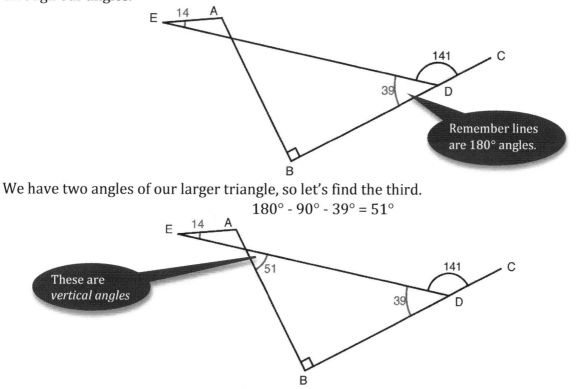

We have two angles of our larger triangle, so let's find the third.

$$180° - 90° - 39° = 51°$$

The small triangle has two angles of 14° & 51°, subtract from 180° to find the third angle $\angle EAB$.

$$180° - 14° - 51° = 115°.$$

Answer choice **B** is correct.

<u>What You May Have Done Wrong</u>

    A. You probably put 39° as the top angle (opposite to the small triangle).

    C. You probably made an arithmetic error.

    D. You may have guessed.

    E. You may have guessed or misunderstood the problem.

6. Line segments *AB* and *BC* are perpendicular. What is the sum of angles ∠*BAF* and
   ∠*BCF*?

Correct Answer G

Let's mark up our figure with our given information, our supplemental angles, and the angles
we are looking for.

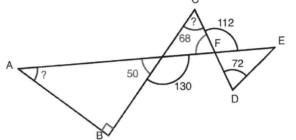

We already have enough information to find the leftmost angle, ∠*BAF*: 180° - 90° - 50° = 40°.
Now we can use opposite angles to help find the other angle.

So, our last angle will be 180° - 68° - 50° = 62°

The sum of our angles will be 40° + 62° = 102°

Answer G is correct.

This angle is
also a 50° angle.

<u>What You May Have Done Wrong</u>
  F. You made some sort of calculation error.
  H. You found at least one of the angles, but didn't add them.
  J. You found at least one of the angles, but didn't add them.
  K. You made some sort of calculation error.

7. Point *A* is the center of the circle below. What is the measure of ∠*CBA*?

Correct Answer D

This triangle problem masquerades as a circle problem, but we actually need some knowledge of
circles to solve. First, let's mark up our figure.

Because *A* is the center of the circle $\overline{AC}$ and $\overline{AB}$ both go from
the center to the edge. **Therefore, line segments *AC* and
AB are both *radiuses* of the circle.**

Let's mark up our diagram.

A is the center of
the circle.

We have an isosceles
triangle, and these
angles (*BAC* and *ACB*
are equal).

Because segments
AC and *AB* are both
radiuses, they are
equal.

Since those angles are equal, we can find them.

$$180° - 70° = 110° \rightarrow \frac{110}{2} = 55°$$

Answer D is correct.

<u>What You May Have Done Wrong</u>
  A. You found *both* missing angles but failed to divide.
  B. You may have misunderstood which angles were equal.
  C. You may have misunderstood which angles were equal.
  E. You likely made a calculation error.

8. In the following diagram of △ABC, what is the value of x?

Correct Answer H

This is an isosceles triangle question that has an algebra twist. To start, let's mark up the congruent angles, which are the angles opposite are congruent sides.

Let's find the measure of the third angle.
$$180° - 26° - 26° = 128°$$

Now, we can set the expression for the top angle equal to 128°.
$$2x + 4 = 128$$
$$2x = 124$$
$$x = 62°$$

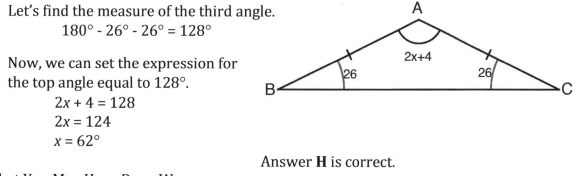

Answer **H** is correct.

<u>What You May Have Done Wrong</u>
    F. This is the halfway answer. Make sure you remember what the question is asking.
    G. You set the expression equal to 26°.
    J. You failed to divide by 2 to find x.
    K. You subtracted 26° from 180° and set that result (154°) equal to the expression. You neglected the other 26° angle.

9. The line segments marked in the diagram below are congruent. Angle *ADB* is as marked, what is the value of *a*?

Correct Answer C

We've got two isosceles triangles, and it is important to understand how they will work together. Let's start marking up our diagram.

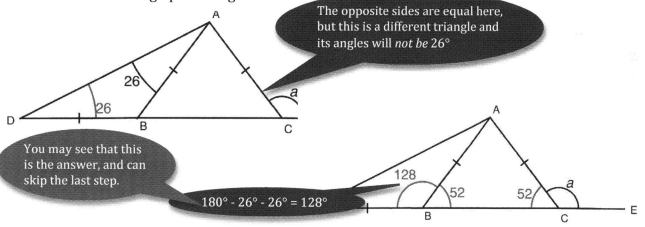

The opposite sides are equal here, but this is a different triangle and its angles will *not be 26°*

You may see that this is the answer, and can skip the last step.

$$180° - 26° - 26° = 128°$$

Now, we can find angle *a* because it's supplementary with the 52° angle ∠*ACB*)
$$180° - 52° = 128°$$

Answer **C** is correct.

<u>What You May Have Done Wrong</u>
    A. This is the top angle (∠*BAC*) in △*ABC*
    B. This is one of the internal angles for △*ABC*.
    D. You did not to subtract *both* of the 26° angles.
    E. You may have guessed or you assumed that the △*ABC* was an equilateral triangle. We don't have any information that line segment *BC* is equivalent to *AB* and *AC*.

10. What is the measure, in degrees, of the largest interior angle in triangle *ABC*?

Correct Answer K

This is more of an algebra problem. Recall that the sum of a triangle's interior angles is 180 degrees.

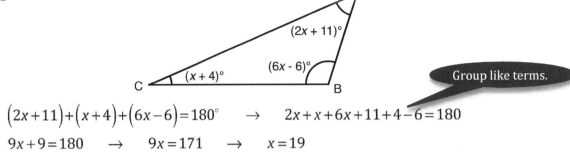

Group like terms.

$$(2x+11)+(x+4)+(6x-6)=180° \quad \rightarrow \quad 2x+x+6x+11+4-6=180$$

$$9x+9=180 \quad \rightarrow \quad 9x=171 \quad \rightarrow \quad x=19$$

Now, a look at the triangle shows that $\angle CBA$ is our biggest angle. Let's plug in 19 and find the measure of the angle.

$$6x-6=? \quad \rightarrow \quad 6(19)-6=?$$

$$114-6=108$$

Answer **K** is correct.

<u>What You May Have Done Wrong</u>
   F. This is the halfway answer. You forgot to *solve* after arriving at 19.
   G. You found the smallest interior angle.
   H. You found the medium sized interior angle.
   J. You made an algebra error, adding 6 where you should have subtracted it.

11. In $\triangle DEF$, $a \le 3b$. What is the maximum value of a?

Correct Answer C

This problem is much more about the *inequality* than the triangle. Really, we only need to know the sum of the interior angles of a triangle (180°).

$a° + b° + 80° = 180°$
$a° + b° = 100°$

Ok, we know that the sum of angles *a* and *b* is equal to 100°. We also know that $a \le 3b$.
Because *a* is less than or equal to 3*b*, the *maximum value* of *a* is when $a = 3b$. Like a system of equations we can substitute in.

$$a° + b° = 100° \rightarrow 3b + b = 100° \rightarrow 4b = 100° \rightarrow b = 25$$

Let's plug it back in and solve for *a*.
$$a° + b° = 100° \rightarrow a° + 25° = 100° \rightarrow a = 75°$$

Even though we are looking for *a*, it's easier to substitute in *b*.

Answer **C** is correct.

<u>What You May Have Done Wrong</u>
   A. This is probably a compound error. Review your steps.
   B. You found the minimum value of *b*.
   D. That's the value of *a* + *b*.
   E. This is some sort of algebra error. Check your steps.

Right Triangles
Key Skill

Background
Right triangles are a favorite of the ACT. They're tested directly and as a part of other problem types.

What You Need to Know
- ✓ The Pythagorean Theorem
- ✓ The side based special right triangles
- ✓ The angle based special right triangles.

Definitions: Right Triangles

> Right Triangles are triangles with a **right (90°) angle.**
> **Hypotenuse:** The side **opposite** the right angle.
> **Legs:** The sides of the right triangle that are **not the hypotenuse.**

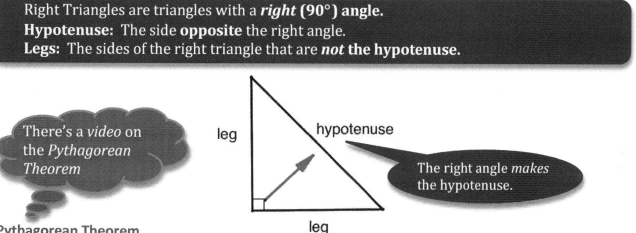

There's a *video* on the *Pythagorean Theorem*

leg

hypotenuse

The right angle *makes* the hypotenuse.

leg

Pythagorean Theorem
The *Pythagorean Theorem* is a multi-use tool on the ACT. It shows up frequently in triangles, combo shape questions, and is the heart of some tricky to remember formulas (the distance formula & the circle formula).

The Pythagorean Theorem defines the relationship between the sides of right triangles.

$$a^2 + b^2 = c^2$$

a and b are the legs, and they are interchangeable.

c is the hypotenuse.

Order doesn't matter in addition.

Example: Pythagorean Theorem
1. What is the length of the missing side?

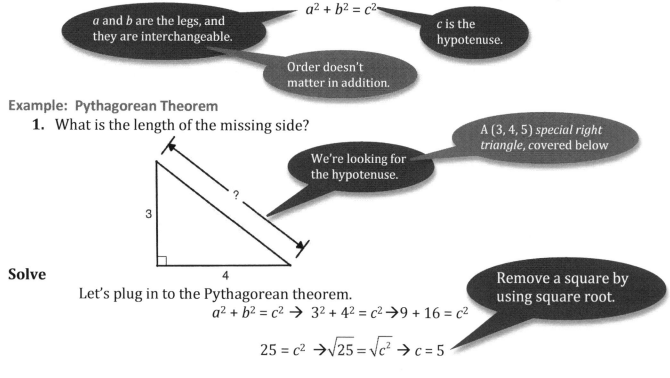

A $(3, 4, 5)$ *special right triangle,* covered below

We're looking for the hypotenuse.

3

?

4

Solve
Let's plug in to the Pythagorean theorem.

Remove a square by using square root.

$$a^2 + b^2 = c^2 \rightarrow 3^2 + 4^2 = c^2 \rightarrow 9 + 16 = c^2$$

$$25 = c^2 \rightarrow \sqrt{25} = \sqrt{c^2} \rightarrow c = 5$$

1. The diagram below shows a telephone pole that is perpendicular to the ground. A wire is attached to the pole ten feet from the ground. The wire is 14 feet long and runs from the pole, at an angle, to the ground *x* distance away. What is the length of *x*?

   A. 9.8 feet
   B. 17.2 feet
   C. 4 feet
   D. 16 feet
   E. 8 feet

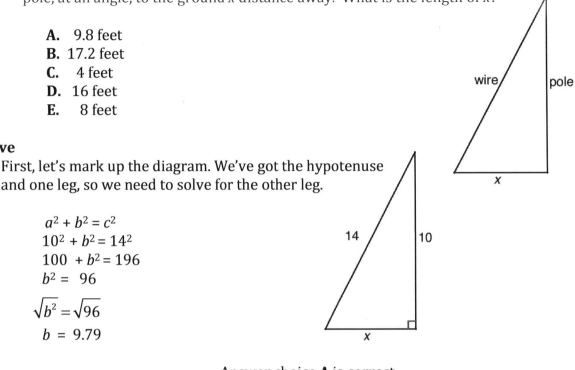

Solve

First, let's mark up the diagram. We've got the hypotenuse and one leg, so we need to solve for the other leg.

$$a^2 + b^2 = c^2$$
$$10^2 + b^2 = 14^2$$
$$100 + b^2 = 196$$
$$b^2 = 96$$
$$\sqrt{b^2} = \sqrt{96}$$
$$b = 9.79$$

Answer choice **A** is correct.

2. The square below has a diagonal, with length marked. What is the area of the square?

   A. $8\sqrt{2}$
   B. 4
   C. 16
   D. 64
   E. 8

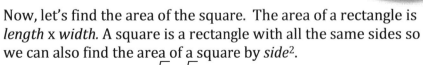

Solve

I marked up my square to remind myself that squares consist of two right triangles and that each side of a square is the same length (*x*).

We don't know the length of the legs, but they are the same length (because they are sides of a square). Since they are the same length, we can put them in terms of a single variable (*x*).

$$a^2 + b^2 = c^2 \rightarrow x^2 + x^2 = 4^2$$
$$2x^2 = 16 \rightarrow x^2 = 8$$
$$\sqrt{x^2} = \sqrt{8} \rightarrow x = \sqrt{8}$$

Another *special right triangle* (45°, 45°, 90°)

Now, let's find the area of the square. The area of a rectangle is *length* x *width*. A square is a rectangle with all the same sides so we can also find the area of a square by *side²*.

$$\sqrt{8} \cdot \sqrt{8} = area \rightarrow area = 8$$

Answer choice **E** is correct.

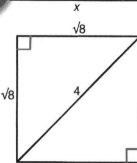

Special Right Triangles

There are some right triangles that are worth memorizing. They show up frequently on the ACT and knowing them can make you a faster, higher scoring test taker. Additionally, the angle based 45°-45°-90° and 30°-60°-90° are (occasionally) tested directly and are doubly worth knowing.

Angle Based: 45°, 45°, 90°

Let's start with the 45°, 45°, 90°. It's the *only* isosceles right triangle because after a 90° angle, there's only 90° more to split evenly into two 45° angles.

Using $1 = x$ and the Pythagorean Theorem:
$$a^2 + b^2 = c^2 \rightarrow 1^2 + 1^2 = c^2$$
$$c^2 = 2 \rightarrow c = \sqrt{2}$$

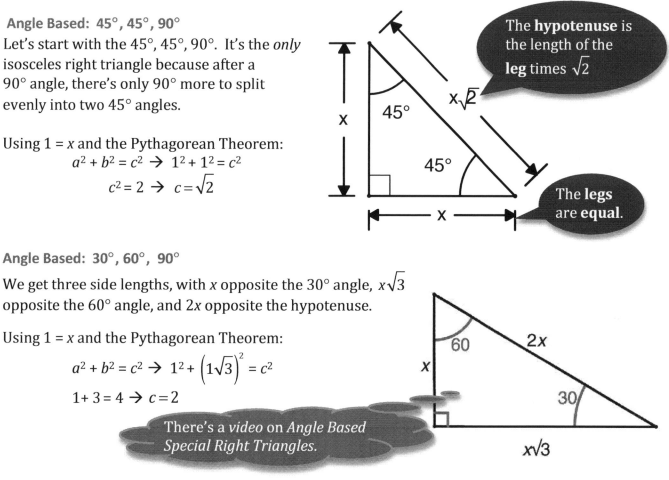

The **hypotenuse** is the length of the **leg** times $\sqrt{2}$

The **legs** are **equal**.

Angle Based: 30°, 60°, 90°

We get three side lengths, with x opposite the 30° angle, $x\sqrt{3}$ opposite the 60° angle, and $2x$ opposite the hypotenuse.

Using $1 = x$ and the Pythagorean Theorem:
$$a^2 + b^2 = c^2 \rightarrow 1^2 + \left(1\sqrt{3}\right)^2 = c^2$$
$$1 + 3 = 4 \rightarrow c = 2$$

There's a *video* on *Angle Based Special Right Triangles.*

Side Based Special Right Triangles

The side-based triangles are "special" because the sides are all *whole numbers*. While there are many triangles that have sides that are only whole numbers, we are really only interested in two (and their multiples).

Side Based: 3, 4, 5

The 3, 4, 5 is a **favorite of the ACT** and it works in multiples.

If we multiply all sides of a 3, 4, 5 by 2, we get 6, 8, 10, similar triangles.

$$a^2 + b^2 = c^2 \rightarrow 3^2 + 4^2 = c^2$$
$$9 + 16 = 25 \rightarrow c = 5$$

We can multiply the sides by any number (in this case 2) and have a larger version of the 3, 4, 5.

On the ACT you'll see the 3, 4, 5; the 6, 8, 10; and the 9, 12, 15 most frequently.

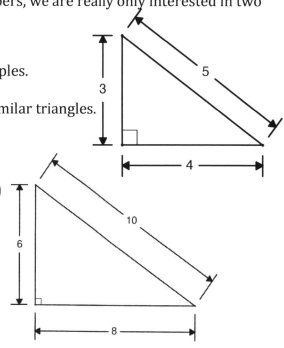

Side Based: 5, 12, 13

The 5, 12, 13 is common and worth knowing, it shows up almost as often as the 3, 4, 5. You'll also a multiple of the 5, 12, 13: the 10, 24, 26.

There's a *video* on *Side Based Special Right Triangles.*

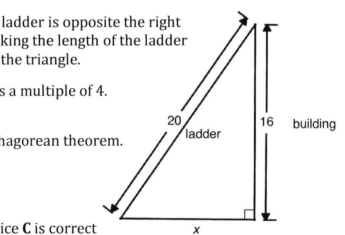

ACT Examples: Special Right Triangles

1. A 20-foot ladder leaning against a building is hits the building at 16 feet above the ground. The ground and the building are perpendicular. How far from the building is the base of the ladder?

   A. 22 feet
   B. 16 feet
   C. 12 feet
   D. 10 feet
   E. 14 feet

Solve

If the question describes a diagram, draw it. The ladder is opposite the right angle created by the ground and the building, making the length of the ladder the *hypotenuse.* The building is the vertical *leg* of the triangle.

You may recognize 20 as a multiple of 5 and 16 as a multiple of 4. It's a multiple of the 3, 4, 5, special right triangle

If you didn't see the 3, 4, 5, you could use the Pythagorean theorem.

$$a^2 + b^2 = c^2 \ \rightarrow \ 16^2 + b^2 = 20^2$$
$$256 + b^2 = 400 \ \rightarrow \ b^2 = 144 \ \rightarrow \ b = 12$$

Answer choice **C** is correct

2. A 26-foot long ramp is built such that it makes a 30-degree angle with the ground, as shown below. The ramp ends at the door of a building, and the building is perpendicular with the ground. How high is the top of the ramp?

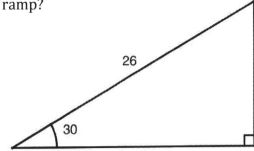

   A. 16 feet
   B. 13 feet
   C. 12 feet
   D. 23 feet
   E. 22 feet

Solve

You can use trig to solve this problem. You'd use the sin of 30° with the hypotenuse (26). **But, it's faster and easier if you recognize the triangle as a 30°, 60°, 90°.**

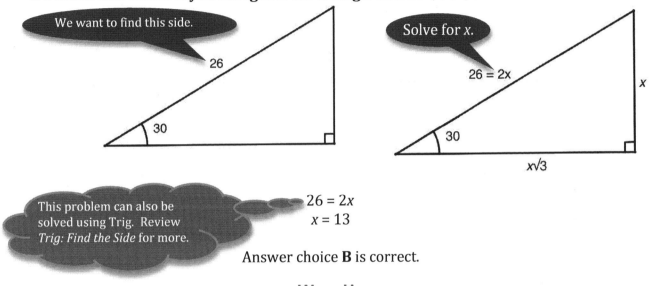

We want to find this side.

Solve for x.

This problem can also be solved using Trig. Review *Trig: Find the Side* for more.

$$26 = 2x$$
$$x = 13$$

Answer choice **B** is correct.

Wrap Up

What You Need to Know
   ✓ The Pythagorean Theorem
   ✓ The side based special right triangles
   ✓ The angle based special right triangles.

Videos

> The Pythagorean Theorem

> Angle Based Special Right Triangles

> Side Based Special Right Triangles

The Strategies
   ✓ Look for special right triangles. They're everywhere on the ACT.
   ✓ Use the Pythagorean theorem. Don't let sides in terms of variables throw you off.

Key Skill

Right triangles are a key skill, particularly the Pythagorean Theorem.
   ✓ Combination Shapes
   ✓ All of Trigonometry
   ✓ Pythagorean Theorem: the Distance Formula
   ✓ Pythagorean Theorem: The Circle Formula

Right Triangles: Problems

1. A ladder is leaned against a building. The wall of the building is perpendicular to the ground. The ladder is fifteen feet long and it reaches twelve feet up the wall. How many feet is the base of the ladder from the wall?

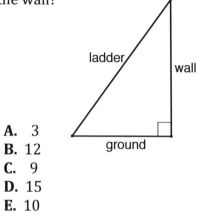

A. 3
B. 12
C. 9
D. 15
E. 10

2. A tree is perpendicular to the ground and is 36 feet tall. A flagpole is 24 feet tall and is also perpendicular to the ground. The sun strikes the tree and the flagpole at an angle such that the shadows of the tree and flagpole end at the same place. What is distance (d) between the tree and the flagpole?

A. 5
B. 10
C. 7.5
D. 9
E. 12

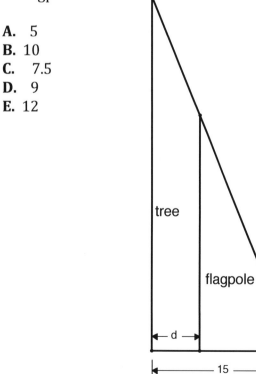

3. What is the perimeter of the figure below?

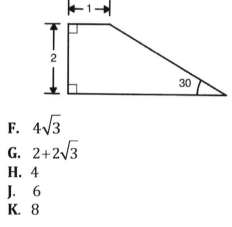

A. 22
B. 26
C. 29
D. 21
E. 23

4. What is the area of the shape below?

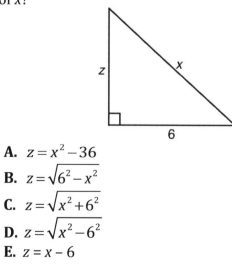

F. $4\sqrt{3}$
G. $2+2\sqrt{3}$
H. 4
J. 6
K. 8

5. What is the length of z in terms of in terms of x?

A. $z=x^2-36$
B. $z=\sqrt{6^2-x^2}$
C. $z=\sqrt{x^2+6^2}$
D. $z=\sqrt{x^2-6^2}$
E. $z=x-6$

6. For the triangles in the figure below, which of the following ratios must be equivalent to the ratio of the sides $\overline{CD}:\overline{AB}$?

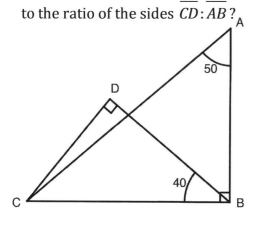

    F. $\angle BDC : \angle ABC$

    G. $\overline{AC}:\overline{BC}$

    H. $\overline{AB}:\overline{CD}$

    J. $\overline{CD}:\overline{BC}$

    K. perimeter $\triangle BCD$: perimeter $\triangle ABC$

7. The sides of square $ABCD$ are 6 inches. Points E, F, G, H are the midpoints of the respective sides of the square. What is the area of square $EFGH$?

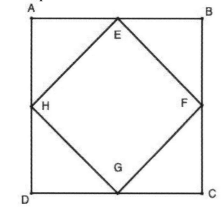

    A. 8

    B. 18

    C. 9

    D. 36

    E. $9\sqrt{2}$

8. $\overline{AE}$ bisects $\overline{BC}$. $\overline{DE}$ and $\overline{EF}$ are congruent. What is the measure of angle x?

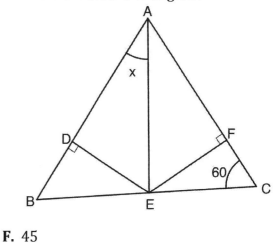

    F. 45

    G. 30

    H. 25

    J. 60

    K. Cannot be Determined.

1. **A ladder is leaned against a building. The wall of the building is perpendicular to the ground. The ladder is fifteen feet long and it reaches twelve feet up the wall. How many feet is the base of the ladder from the wall?**

Correct Answer C

This is a Pythagorean Theorem question. We've got two sides of a right triangle and we need the third. First, mark-up your sides. The Pythagorean theorem

$$a^2 + b^2 = c^2 \quad \rightarrow \quad 12^2 + b^2 = 15^2$$
$$144 + b^2 = 225 \quad \rightarrow \quad b^2 = 81$$
$$\sqrt{b^2} = \sqrt{81} \quad \rightarrow \quad b = 9$$

If you remember your *special right triangles* you may see that this is actually a 3,4,5 special right triangle. Remember, these triangles work in *multiples* so we can say:

$$3 \times 3 = 9 \quad \rightarrow \quad 4 \times 3 = 12 \quad \rightarrow \quad 5 \times 3 = 15$$

Answer choice C is correct.

<u>What You May Have Done Wrong</u>
   B. You may have recognized that this is a 3,4,5 triangle but didn't find the multiple.
   C. You may have assumed that the triangle was an isosceles right triangle; it's not.
   D. The hypotenuse is 15, and no leg can be as long as the hypotenuse.
   E. This could be a miscalculation or a guess.

2. A tree is perpendicular to the ground and is 36 feet tall. A flagpole is 24 feet tall and is also perpendicular to the ground. The sun strikes the tree and the flagpole at an angle such that the shadows of the tree and flagpole end at the same place. What is distance (*d*) between the tree and the flagpole?

Correct Answer A

This is a similar triangles question. Like most similar triangle questions, we solve using ratios. First, mark up your figure. The heights are corresponding sides (opposite the same angle) and so are the lengths of the shadows. The ratio looks like this:

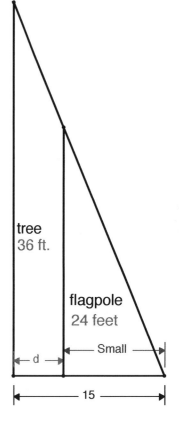

<u>**Small**</u> : <u>**Large**</u>
    24   :   36
small : 15

Cross-multiply to find the length of the small side

$$36(small) = 360 \quad \rightarrow \quad small = 10$$

But, we're not done yet. You have to subtract the *small* (10) from the large to find the length of *d*.
$$15 - 10 = d = 5$$

If you recognize special right triangles, you may notice this is the multiple of the 5,12,13 special right triangle. That makes the large triangle:

<u>**Small**</u>	:	<u>**Large**</u>
$5 \times 2 = 10$		$5 \times 3 = 15$
$12 \times 2 = 24$		$12 \times 3 = 36$
$13 \times 2 = 26$		$13 \times 3 = 39$

The difference between the two "5" sides will be the length of *D*.

Answer choice A is correct.

<u>What You May Have Done Wrong</u>
    B. This is the length of the flagpole's shadow, not the difference.
    C. You just halved the total shadow length. Review the steps.
    D. This may be a guess or you made a mistake with your ratios.
    E. You may have just subtracted the heights.

3. **What is the perimeter of the figure below?**

Correct Answer A

This is a perimeter question perimeter and to start we'll need to find the length of the missing side.

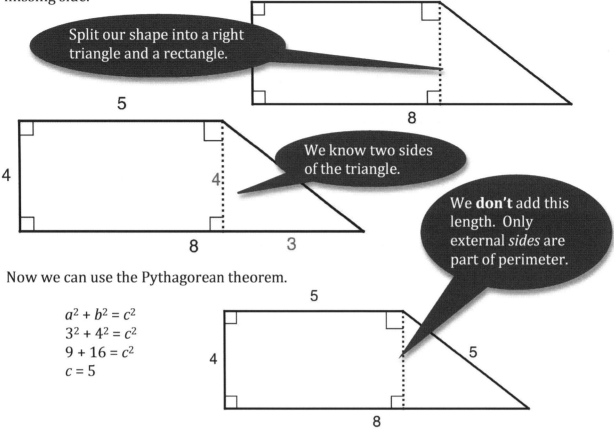

Now we can use the Pythagorean theorem.

$$a^2 + b^2 = c^2$$
$$3^2 + 4^2 = c^2$$
$$9 + 16 = c^2$$
$$c = 5$$

Let's calculate the perimeter: 4 + 5 + 8 + 5 = 22

Answer choice **A** is correct.

<u>What You May Have Done Wrong</u>

    B. You added the internal length of 4.

    C. You added the internal length of 4 *and* added the base of the triangle (3), double counting that side of the shape.

    D. You miscalculated the missing length.

    E. You miscalculated the missing length.

4. **What is the area of the shape below?**

Correct Answer G

This is a tougher question; one you'd most likely see this towards the end of the test. It's very manageable though, and don't let it intimidate you. The first job it to split our shape into a rectangle and a right triangle. The area of the rectangle is 2 x 1 = 2. Let's find the area of the triangle.

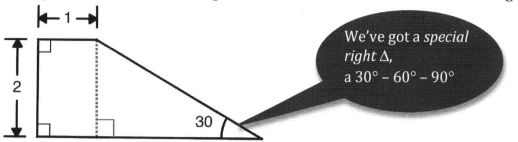

The height of the triangle is the same as the rectangle (2). You can solve this using trig, but it's faster if you remember the special right triangle.

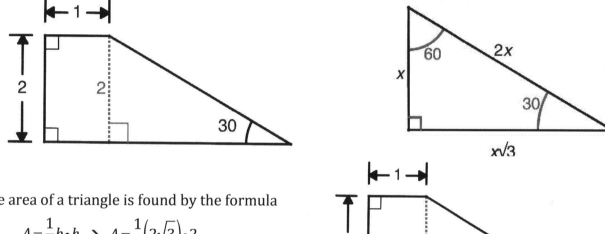

The area of a triangle is found by the formula

$$A = \frac{1}{2}b \cdot h \rightarrow A = \frac{1}{2}\left(2\sqrt{3}\right) \cdot 2$$

$$A = \frac{4\sqrt{3}}{2} \rightarrow A = 2\sqrt{3}$$

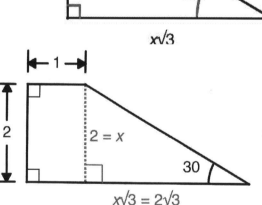

We add the area of the rectangle (2) to the area of the triangle

$$2 + 2\sqrt{3}$$

We can't combine these further.

Answer choice **G** is correct.

<u>What You May Have Done Wrong</u>

    F. You combined terms, you can't add unless without a shared root.

    H. This is a compound error, review your steps.

    J. You miscalculated the area of the triangle as 4.

    K. This is a compound error, review your steps.

5. **What is the length of z in terms of in terms of x?**

Correct Answer D

This is a Pythagorean theorem question that looks more difficult than it is. We'll need to re-arrange the Pythagorean theorem to solve for one of the legs (z). Let's plug in for a, b, c.

$$a^2 + b^2 = c^2 \rightarrow z^2 + 6^2 = x^2$$
$$z^2 = x^2 - 6^2 \rightarrow z = \sqrt{x^2 - 6^2}$$

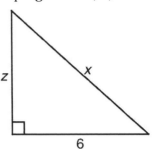

Answer choice **D** is correct

<u>What You May Have Done Wrong</u>
- **A.** This is a halfway answer. You forgot to take the square root of the right side.
- **B.** You solved with 6 as the hypotenuse.
- **C.** You have z set up as the hypotenuse, z is a leg.
- **E.** You can only split roots if you are multiplying or dividing. The result here would be different if you subtracted *before* the square root or *after* the root.

6. **For the triangles in the figure below, which of the following ratios must be equivalent to the ratio of the sides $\overline{CD} : \overline{AB}$?**

Correct Answer K

This problem can be a headache if you don't mark up your figure properly. Mark up the sides *and* the angles. It's also a *which* question, so you'll mark-off to find your answer. *ABC* & *BCD* are *similar triangles.*

Let's look at the given ratio.

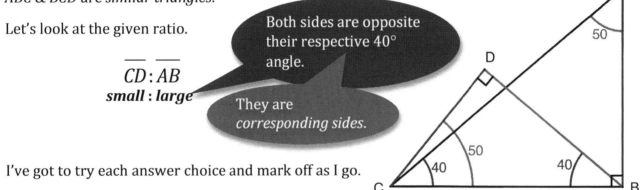

I've got to try each answer choice and mark off as I go.

- **F.** These are equal angles 40 : 40, and they **don't correspond to the ratios of the sides**.
- **G.** The sides correspond (both hypotenuses) but the **ratio is flipped**, you have *large : small* but it should be *small : large*.
- **H.** These are corresponding sides (both sides match up to the 40° angle in their respective triangles). But the **ratio is flipped**, you have *large : small* instead of *small : large*.
- **J.** **You aren't comparing corresponding sides**. The 40° angle corresponds to *CD* but side *BC* corresponds to either a 90° on the same triangle ($\triangle BCD$) *or* the 50° angle on $\triangle ABC$.

By elimination, we know that answer choice **K** is correct. Let's take a look at why **K** works.

small : *large*

perimeter $\triangle BCD$: perimeter $\triangle ABC$

Because the triangles are similar, the corresponding sides will have the same ratio of *small : large*. The perimeter will also have that ratio.

Answer choice **K** is correct.

7. The sides of square *ABCD* are 6 inches. Points *E, F, G, H* are the midpoints of the respective sides of the square. What is the area of square *EFGH*?

Correct Answer B

This problem seems to be about two squares, but in reality, to solve we'll use right triangles. To start, let's mark up our figure with the given information.

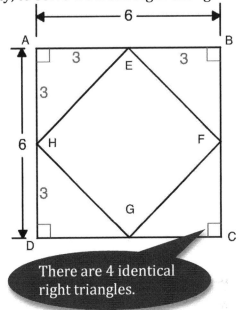

The sides of the small square are the hypotenuses of the four right triangles. Use the Pythagorean Theorem to find the side length.

$$a^2 + b^2 = c^2 \rightarrow 3^2 + 3^2 = c^2$$
$$c^2 = 18 \rightarrow c = \sqrt{18} = 3\sqrt{2}$$

Now, we can find the area by *length* x *width* or side².

$$\left(3\sqrt{2}\right)^2 = 18$$

Answer choice **B** is correct.

There are 4 identical right triangles.

<u>What You May Have Done Wrong</u>

   A. You made a calculation error.
   C. You used 3 as the side of square *EFGH*.
   D. That is the area of the large square *ABCD*. You should notice the area of *EFGH* should be *less* than the area *ABCD*.
   E. It looks like you had a calculation error. $\sqrt{2} \cdot \sqrt{2} = 2$

8. $\overline{AE}$ bisects $\overline{BC}$. $\overline{DE}$ and $\overline{EF}$ are congruent. What is the measure of angle *x*?

Correct Answer G

This is an intimidating problem. Start by marking up the figure.

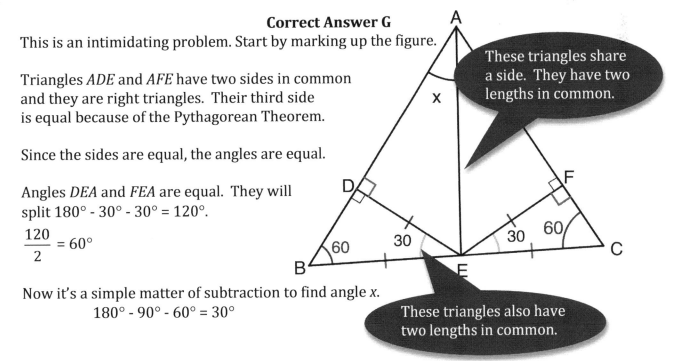

Triangles *ADE* and *AFE* have two sides in common and they are right triangles. Their third side is equal because of the Pythagorean Theorem.

Since the sides are equal, the angles are equal.

Angles *DEA* and *FEA* are equal. They will split 180° - 30° - 30° = 120°.

$$\frac{120}{2} = 60°$$

These triangles share a side. They have two lengths in common.

These triangles also have two lengths in common.

Now it's a simple matter of subtraction to find angle *x*.
$$180° - 90° - 60° = 30°$$

<u>What You May Have Done Wrong:</u>

   Each wrong answer is an error in understanding or in calculation. Check through the steps.

Introduction

There's a bunch of four-sided shapes and all of them are tested. Area, perimeter, combination shape questions, angle questions, and proportion questions are all fair game. We'll look at each category, and I've sorted each shape based on how often they show up.

What You Need to Know

- ✓ How to find the perimeter of four-sided shapes
- ✓ How to find the area of *squares* & *rectangles*
- ✓ How to find the area of a *parallelogram*
- ✓ How to find the area of a *trapezoid*
- ✓ How to find the missing angle of a *parallelogram* & a *trapezoid*

Definitions: Commonalities of Four-sided Shapes.

Quadrilaterals are four-sided shapes
All four-sided shapes have interior angles that sum to 360°

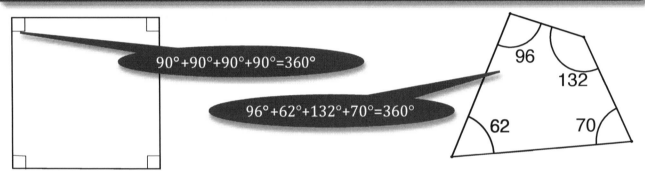

We can also see this by breaking the quadrilaterals into two triangles—the sum of a triangle's interior angles equals 180°.

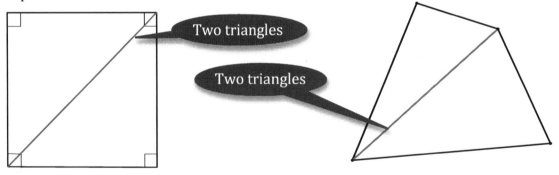

Squares & Rectangles

Squares and rectangles are the most common four-sided shapes on the ACT.

Definitions: Rectangles & Squares

Rectangles are four-sided shapes that have two sets of parallel sides. These sets meet at four 90°angles.

Squares are rectangles whose sides are all the same length.

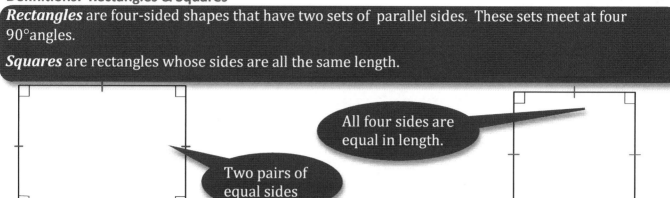

All four sides are equal in length.

Two pairs of equal sides

Area & Perimeter of Rectangles & Squares

Perimeter of a rectangle, square, or any shape, is the sum of the length of the sides.
Area of a rectangle or square is defined as *length* x *width*.

Let's say the length of the previous rectangle is 2 and width is 1 and the square has sides of 1.

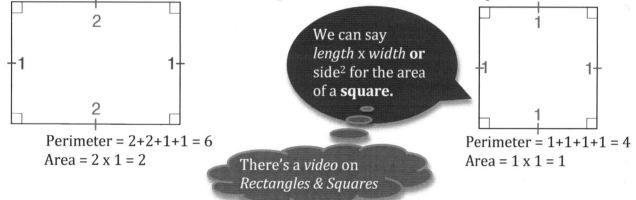

We can say *length* x *width* **or** side^2 for the area of a **square**.

There's a *video* on *Rectangles & Squares*

Perimeter = 2+2+1+1 = 6
Area = 2 x 1 = 2

Perimeter = 1+1+1+1 = 4
Area = 1 x 1 = 1

ACT Examples: Rectangles & Squares

1. In the figure shows a plan for a square room with measurements in square feet. The shaded area will be a square carpet and the un-shaded area will be tile. If the dimensions are as marked, how many square feet of tile will be needed?

A. 144 ft²
B. 160 ft²
C. 190 ft²
D. 108 ft²
E. 96ft²

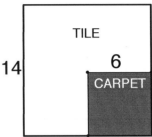

Solve

The easiest way to solve this is to find the area of the room (the entire diagram) and subtract the area of the shaded square. Since both shapes are squares we can use *area = side²* for both.

Room Area	Carpet Area	Tile Area
$Area = side^2$	$Area = side^2$	Tile Area = Room − Carpet
$Area = 14^2$	$Area = 6^2$	Tile Area = $196 \text{ ft}^2 - 36 \text{ ft}^2$
$Area = 196 \text{ ft}^2$	$Area = 36 \text{ ft}^2$	Tile Area = 160 ft^2

Answer Choice **B** is correct.

2. A rectangular television is hung on the middle of a rectangular wall so the space to either side is equal and the space above and below is the same. What is the perimeter of the television?

A. 8
B. 10
C. 12
D. 16
E. 24

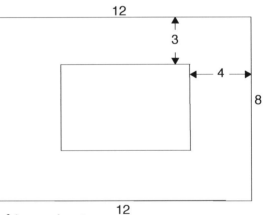

Solve

We need to find the sides of the television to find its perimeter.

$$length = 12 - 4 - 4 = 4$$
$$width = 8 - 3 - 3 = 2$$

The perimeter is the sum of the four sides.
$$4 + 4 + 2 + 2 = 12$$

Answer choice **C** is correct.

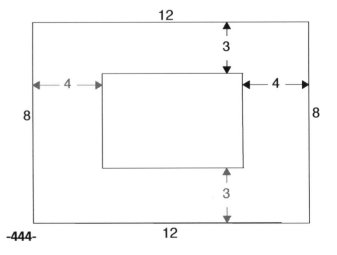

Definitions: Parallelogram

Parallelograms are four-sided shapes with **two pairs** of **parallel** sides, the corresponding sides are equal in length. There aren't restrictions as to angle interior measures of a parallelogram.

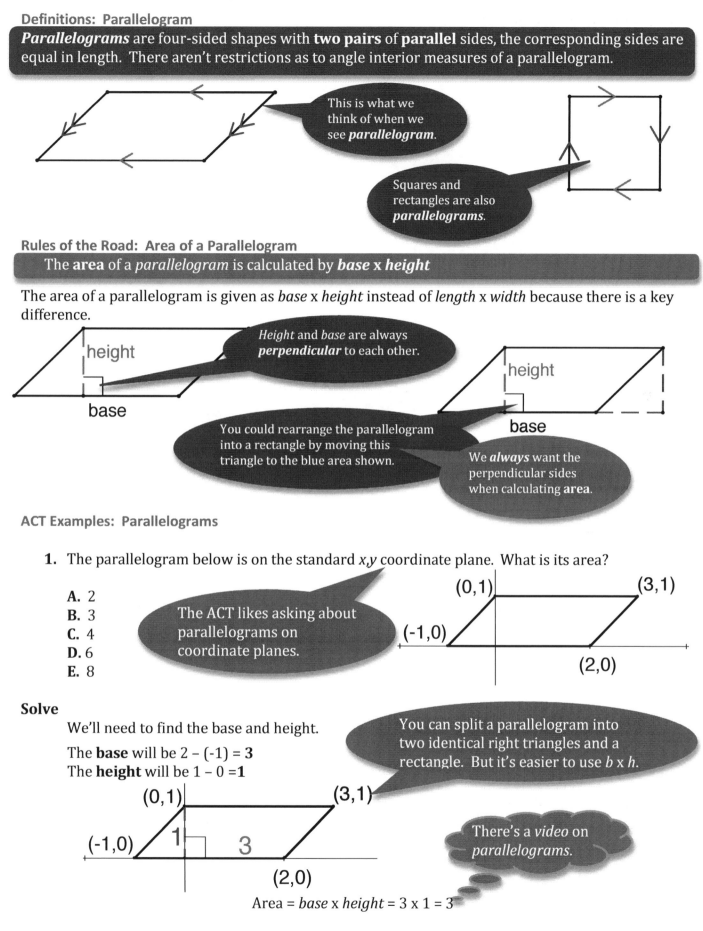

This is what we think of when we see *parallelogram*.

Squares and rectangles are also *parallelograms*.

Rules of the Road: Area of a Parallelogram

The **area** of a *parallelogram* is calculated by *base* x *height*

The area of a parallelogram is given as *base* x *height* instead of *length* x *width* because there is a key difference.

height

base

Height and *base* are always *perpendicular* to each other.

You could rearrange the parallelogram into a rectangle by moving this triangle to the blue area shown.

height

base

We *always* want the perpendicular sides when calculating **area**.

ACT Examples: Parallelograms

1. The parallelogram below is on the standard *x,y* coordinate plane. What is its area?

A. 2
B. 3
C. 4
D. 6
E. 8

The ACT likes asking about parallelograms on coordinate planes.

(0,1)　　　　(3,1)

(-1,0)

(2,0)

Solve

We'll need to find the base and height.

The **base** will be 2 – (-1) = **3**
The **height** will be 1 – 0 = **1**

You can split a parallelogram into two identical right triangles and a rectangle. But it's easier to use *b* x *h*.

(0,1)　　　　(3,1)

(-1,0)　　1　　3

(2,0)

There's a *video* on *parallelograms*.

Area = *base* x *height* = 3 x 1 = 3

Answer choice **B** is correct.

Trapezoids

Trapezoids have fewer restrictions, so the ACT has a broader range of questions they can ask. Most commonly, the ACT asks about trapezoid angles, with trapezoid area a less frequent topic.

Definitions: Trapezoids

Trapezoids are four-sided shapes that have *only* one pair of parallel sides.
Isosceles Trapezoids are trapezoids that have equal base angles.

Where rectangles and squares are parallelograms, rectangles, squares, and parallelograms are *not* trapezoids.

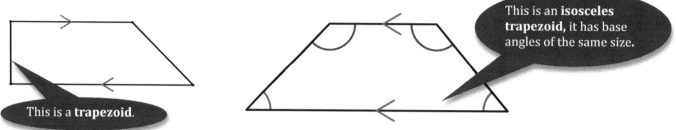

Trapezoids have two bases. Those bases are parallel, and they are of unequal lengths (they have to be unequal in length or we'd end up with a rectangle or parallelogram). The height of a trapezoid is perpendicular to the bases.

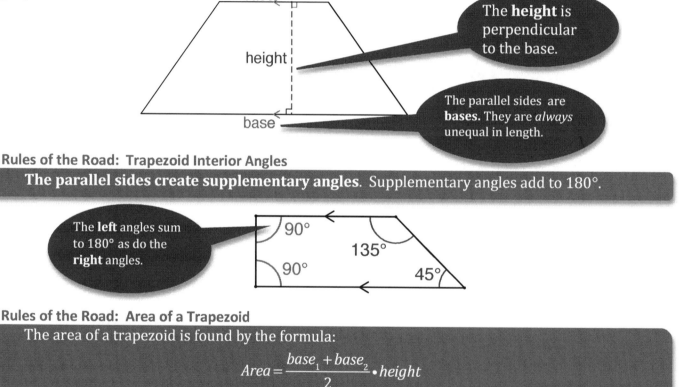

Rules of the Road: Trapezoid Interior Angles

The parallel sides create supplementary angles. Supplementary angles add to 180°.

The **left** angles sum to 180° as do the **right** angles.

Rules of the Road: Area of a Trapezoid

The area of a trapezoid is found by the formula:

$$Area = \frac{base_1 + base_2}{2} \cdot height$$

This is a tricky formula to remember, sometimes the ACT provides it and sometimes it doesn't. When it is not provided, however, the ACT usually gives you enough information to solve the problem. It's up to you whether to memorize the formula, as it is not a very frequent topic and the answer can often be found without the formula. If you'd like to remember it here's a hint:

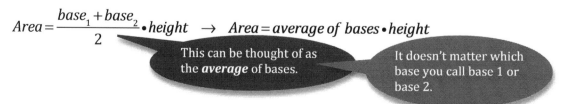

$$Area = \frac{base_1 + base_2}{2} \cdot height \quad \rightarrow \quad Area = average\ of\ bases \cdot height$$

This can be thought of as the *average* of bases.

It doesn't matter which base you call base 1 or base 2.

-446-

1. In the figure below, *ABCD* is a trapezoid and has angles as marked. What is the measure of ∠*ACB*?

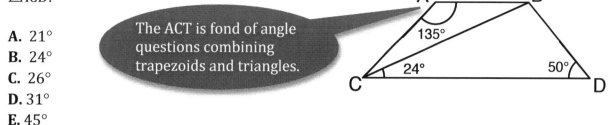

A. 21°

B. 24°

C. 26°

D. 31°

E. 45°

The ACT is fond of angle questions combining trapezoids and triangles.

Solve

There are several ways to solve this, let's take a look at a few. The simplest way to solve this question is to remember that the parallel lines in a trapezoid create supplementary angles on each side of the trapezoid.

We can say...

$$180° - ∠BAC - ∠BCD = ∠ACD$$
$$180° - 135° - 24° = 21°$$

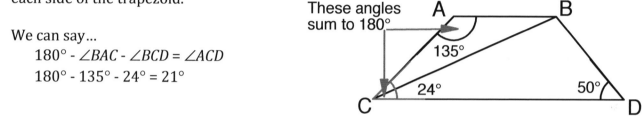

These angles sum to 180°

Another way to handle this problem is to make use of corresponding angles created by parallel lines.

We have two angles of Δ*ABC*, subtract to find the third.
$$180° - 135° - 24° = 21°$$

There's a *video* on *Trapezoids*.

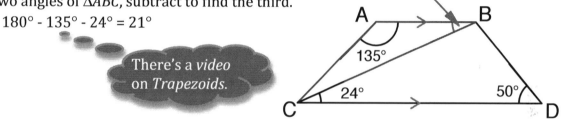

This angle corresponds (is the same as) the 24° ∠ABC

Answer choice **A** is correct.

2. In the figure below, *ABCD* is a trapezoid and has sides with lengths as marked. What is the area of the trapezoid?

A. 48
B. 24
C. 64
D. 32
E. 44

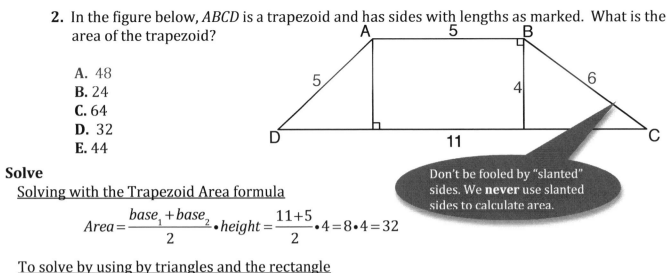

Don't be fooled by "slanted" sides. We **never** use slanted sides to calculate area.

Solve

Solving with the Trapezoid Area formula

$$Area = \frac{base_1 + base_2}{2} \cdot height = \frac{11+5}{2} \cdot 4 = 8 \cdot 4 = 32$$

To solve by using by triangles and the rectangle

First, calculate the area of the rectangle:

$$area = length \cdot width$$

$$area = 5 \cdot 4 = 20$$

Now, we've got to figure out the triangles. We don't know the base of each individual triangle, but we know their bases sum to 6 (11 − 5). We can make one big triangle out of our two triangles.

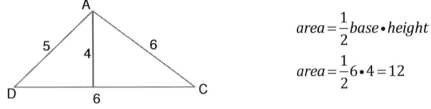

$$area = \frac{1}{2} base \cdot height$$

$$area = \frac{1}{2} 6 \cdot 4 = 12$$

Add the area of the rectangle and the area of the triangles:

20 + 12 = 32.

Answer choice **D** is correct.

Wrap Up

What You Need to Know
- ✓ How to find the perimeter of four-sided shapes
- ✓ How to find the area of *squares & rectangles*
- ✓ How to find the area of a *parallelogram*
- ✓ How to find the area of a *trapezoid*
- ✓ How to find the missing angle of a *parallelogram* & a *trapezoid*

Videos

> Squares & Rectangles

> Parallelograms

> Trapezoids

The Strategies
- ✓ Make sure you draw a diagram if one isn't provided.
- ✓ On "slanted side shapes" use the *height* not the slanted side.
- ✓ Remember *corresponding angles* on "find the angle" questions.

Related Skills
- ✓ Angles
- ✓ Triangles
- ✓ Right Triangles
- ✓ Combo Shapes

Four Sided Shapes: Problems

Use the following information for questions 1-3:

Frame

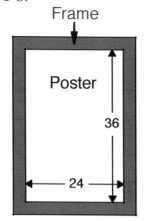

1. Steve runs a frame shop. He is framing a 24 by 36 inch poster and the glass he uses to cover the poster will cover the *only* the poster. How many square inches of glass does Steve need?

   A. 128 in²
   B. 860 in²
   C. 864 in²
   D. 576 in²
   E. 1,296 in²

2. The frame itself is one inch thick, and therefore one inch to every side of the poster. How much area does the poster cover when framed?

   F. 925 in²
   G. 962 in²
   H. 988 in²
   J. 912 in²
   K. 936 in²

3. What is the minimum length of frame board that Steve will need to make the frame?

   A. 124 inches
   B. 120 inches
   C. 122 inches
   D. 130 inches
   E. 144 inches

4. A rectangle with a perimeter of 64 centimeters has a length that is three times the width. What is the area of the rectangle?

   F. 240 cm²
   G. 192 cm²
   H. 208 cm²
   J. 214 cm²
   K. 147 cm²

5. Plywood is sold in rectangular sheets 4 ft by 8 ft. How many sheets are necessary to build a sub floor (wall to wall) in a room 14 by 18?

   A. 7
   B. 9
   C. 8
   D. 10
   E. 11

6. The parallelogram in the diagram below, *ABCD*, has dimensions marked in meters. What is the area of the parallelogram in square meters?

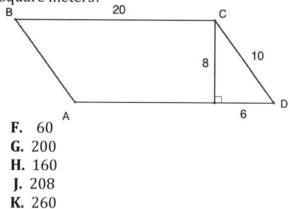

   F. 60
   G. 200
   H. 160
   J. 208
   K. 260

7. In trapezoid *ABCD* the angles are as marked and ∠*ADC* measures 65°. What is angle theta?

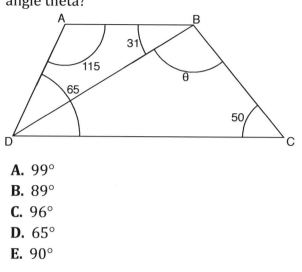

A. 99°
B. 89°
C. 96°
D. 65°
E. 90°

8. In the quadrilateral shown below, what is the measure of ∠*A*?

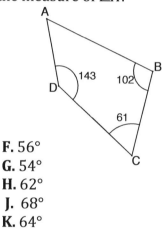

F. 56°
G. 54°
H. 62°
J. 68°
K. 64°

9. The figure below is a parallelogram. What is its area?

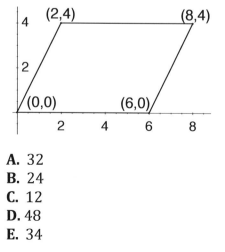

A. 32
B. 24
C. 12
D. 48
E. 34

10. For trapezoid *ABCD* shown below, $\overline{AB}$ & $\overline{CD}$ are parallel. In terms of $x°$, what is the measure of angle ∠*ABC*?

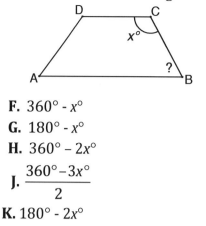

F. 360° - $x°$
G. 180° - $x°$
H. 360° − 2$x°$
J. $\dfrac{360° - 3x°}{2}$
K. 180° - 2$x°$

11. The isosceles trapezoid below has parallel sides of 25 and 35 inches. What is the area of the trapezoid?

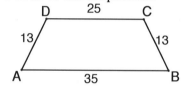

A. 60 inches²
B. 30 inches²
C. 390 inches²
D. 360 inches²
E. 455 inches²

12. For parallelogram *ABCD* shown below what is the sum of ∠*y* and ∠*x*?

F. 180°
G. 180°- $a°$
H. 180°- $a°$- $b°$
J. 360° - 2$a°$
K. 180°- 2$a°$

13. Mike is planning to paint a rectangular wall. He'll need *two* coats of paint. Each quart of paint covers 72 square feet. How many quarts of paint will Mike need to finish both coats?

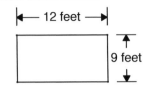

- **A.** 2 quarts
- **B.** 3 quarts
- **C.** 4 quarts
- **D.** 5 quarts
- **E.** 1 quart

14. *ABCD* is a trapezoid and has sides as marked. What is the height of the trapezoid?

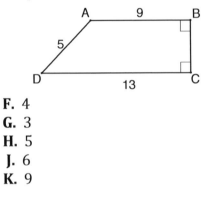

- **F.** 4
- **G.** 3
- **H.** 5
- **J.** 6
- **K.** 9

15. In the figure below, *ABCD* is a square with an area of 64. Rectangle *EFGH* has an area of 24 and a side as marked. What is the length of $x + y$?

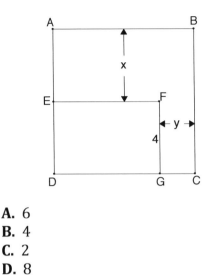

- **A.** 6
- **B.** 4
- **C.** 2
- **D.** 8
- **E.** 10

16. Mr. Grout is going to replace the tile in his Turkish bath. The bath is rectangular and measures 16ft by 20 ft. Mr. Grout has selected tile that are 6 inches square. How many tiles does he need to purchase?

- **F.** 320 tiles
- **G.** 640 tiles
- **H.** 80 tiles
- **J.** 1,280 tiles
- **K.** 1,600 tiles

Four Sided Shapes: Solutions

1. Steve runs a frame shop. He is framing a 24 by 36 inch poster and the glass he uses to cover the poster will cover the *only* the poster. How many square inches of glass does Steve need?

Correct Answer C

This is a question (a clue is square inches). We're given the dimensions of the poster 24 by 36.

$$Area = length \cdot width \quad \rightarrow \quad Area = 24\, inches \cdot 36\, inches$$

$$Area = 864\, inches^2$$

Answer choice **C** is correct.

<u>What You May Have Done Wrong</u>

    A. This is the perimeter; we need the area.
    B. Calculator error.
    D. You multiplied 24 x 24. The poster is not a square.
    E. You multiplied 26 x 26. The poster is not a square.

2. The frame itself is one inch thick, and therefore one inch to every side of the poster. How much area does the poster cover when framed?

Correct Answer H

We've got another rectangle area question. We'll need to figure out the new dimensions of the rectangle. The poster gets 1 inch added to *each* side. This turns our dimensions from 24 by 36 to 26 by 38.

$$Area = length \cdot width \quad \rightarrow \quad Area = 26\, inches \cdot 38\, inches$$

$$Area = 988\, inches^2$$

Answer choice **H** is correct.

<u>What You May Have Done Wrong</u>

    F. You only added one to each side and multiplied 25 by 37.
    G. You multiplied 25 by 38.
    J. You only added 2 to the length and multiplied 38 by 24
    K. You added two to the width and multiplied 26 by 36.

3. What is the minimum length of frame board that Steve will need to make the frame?

Correct Answer A

This is a tricky perimeter question, but you have to look at your diagram. If the frame board is only the length of the poster, we'll end up with gaps at the corners. The frame board has to overlap and at it's simplest would look something like this.

We add two inches to one set of sides to account for the overlap.

perimeter = sum of the sides

perimeter = (24 + 2)+(24 + 2) + 36 + 36

perimeter = 124 inches

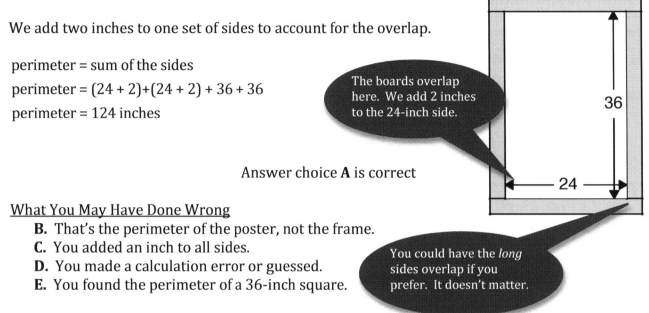

The boards overlap here. We add 2 inches to the 24-inch side.

Answer choice **A** is correct

You could have the *long* sides overlap if you prefer. It doesn't matter.

What You May Have Done Wrong
    B. That's the perimeter of the poster, not the frame.
    C. You added an inch to all sides.
    D. You made a calculation error or guessed.
    E. You found the perimeter of a 36-inch square.

4. A rectangle with a perimeter of 64 centimeters has a length that is three times the width. What is the area of the rectangle?

Correct Answer G

While the ACT lumps these problems in the plane geometry section, they are really more like *systems of equations* (review in *Intermediate Algebra: Systems of Equations*).

There are two variables (*width & length*), but only one equation given (perimeter).

$$length + length + width + width = 64$$

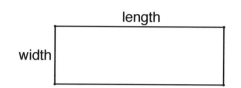

Because the length is 3 times the width, we can make this statement.

$$3 \bullet width = length$$

I can use that statement to re-write my lone equation (perimeter) with one variable.

Our equation can be written:

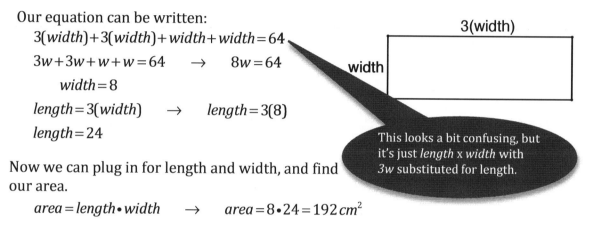

$3(width) + 3(width) + width + width = 64$

$3w + 3w + w + w = 64 \quad \rightarrow \quad 8w = 64$

$width = 8$

$length = 3(width) \quad \rightarrow \quad length = 3(8)$

$length = 24$

This looks a bit confusing, but it's just *length x width* with *3w* substituted for length.

Now we can plug in for length and width, and find our area.

$$area = length \bullet width \quad \rightarrow \quad area = 8 \bullet 24 = 192 \, cm^2$$

Answer choice **G** is correct.

<u>What You May Have Done Wrong</u>
- **F.** You may have miscalculated the length, or the width.
- **H.** You miscalculated your length, width, or both.
- **J.** You miscalculated your length, width, or both.
- **K.** You miscalculated your length, width, or both.

5. **Plywood is sold in rectangular sheets 4 feet by 8 feet. How many sheets are necessary to build a sub floor (wall to wall) in a room 14 feet by 18 feet?**

Correct Answer C

This is a rectangle area question with a *maximum/minimum* component.

Let's start by sketching the rectangles.

A sketch can make it easier to see that we need the areas of both the plywood & the room.

Drywall (small)
$area = length \cdot width$
$area = 8 \cdot 4$
$area = 32 \, \text{ft}^2$

Wall (large)
$area = length \cdot width$
$area = 18 \cdot 14$
$area = 252 \, \text{ft}^2$

Now we can find out how many of our drywall sheets will cover the entire room. We can do that by dividing the area of the wall (large rectangle) by the area of a sheet of drywall (small rectangle).

$$\frac{252}{32} = 7.875 \, \text{sheets}$$

We round up to 8 sheets.

Note: even if we had only 7.05 sheets (or some number we'd normally round down), we'd *still* round up. We'd need 8 sheets or we'd have a gap in the plywood, a hole in the floor.

Answer choice **C** is correct.

<u>What You May Have Done Wrong</u>

All of the wrong answer choices are miscalculations or misunderstandings of the problems. Check your steps.

6. **The parallelogram in the diagram below, *ABCD*, has dimensions marked in meters. What is the area of the parallelogram in square meters?**

Correct Answer H

This is a parallelogram area question and there are two ways to solve. You could split into two right triangles and a rectangle and find the respective areas. The much simpler way to do this is to remember that the area of a parallelogram is *base* x *height*. Recall that base and height are *always* perpendicular.

$area = base \cdot height$
$area = 20 \cdot 8$
$area = 160$

Answer **H** is correct.

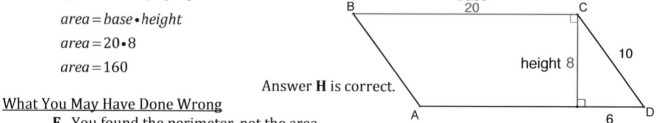

<u>What You May Have Done Wrong</u>

    F. You found the perimeter, not the area.

    G. You used the *slanted side* (10) to find the area. We **never** use the slanted side.

    J. You added six to the base, to get 26. You essentially double counted.

    K. You added six to the base, to get 26 *and* you multiplied by the slanted side (10).

7. **In trapezoid ABCD the angles are as marked and ∠ADC measures 65°. What is angle theta?**

Correct Answer A

This is a trapezoid angle problem. There's a few ways to solve, and let's look at the easiest first. Trapezoids, like all shapes with four sides, have interior angles that sum to 360°. Trapezoids have two sides (the bases) that are parallel. Only one angle is missing, so we can subtract our known from 360 and we'll get angle θ.

$$360 - 65 - 115 - 31 - 50 = \text{angle theta} = 99°$$

We can also use the parallel lines to find complementary angles.

So, we've got a 31° for ∠BDC. Using triangle BDC, angle theta is $180° - 50° - 31° = 99°$.

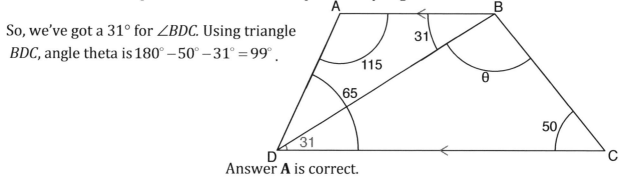

Answer **A** is correct.

<u>What You May Have Done Wrong</u>

   B. You made an arithmetic error.

   D. You misconstrued ∠BDC as 34°.

   C. You probably misunderstood how trapezoids work review your steps.

   E. You made a conceptual error or guessed.

8. **In the quadrilateral shown below, what is the measure of ∠A?**

Correct Answer G

Don't be thrown off by our weird quadrilateral. We know that *all* four sided shapes have interior angles that sum to 360°. We know three of the angles; we can subtract and find the fourth angle.

$$360 - 102 - 143 - 61 = 54°$$

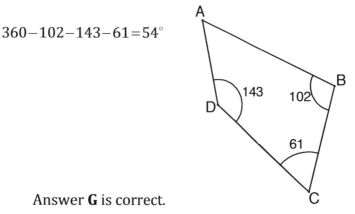

Answer **G** is correct.

<u>What You May Have Done Wrong</u>

   All of the answers are miscalculations. Check your numbers.

9. The figure below is a parallelogram. What is its area?

Correct Answer B

Let's mark up our diagram. We're going to have to find the base and height using the coordinate points.

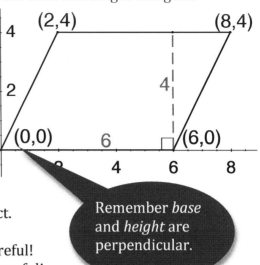

Height	**Base**
$y_1 - y_2$	$x_1 - x_2$
$4 - 0 = 4$	$6 - 0 = 6$

So, now we find the area by *base* x *height*.

$$area = base \cdot height$$
$$area = 6 \cdot 4$$
$$area = 24$$

Answer **B** is correct.

What You May Have Done Wrong

A. You probably miscalculated the base as 8. Be careful!

C. You probably miscalculated the height as 2. Be careful!

D. You made an error with your sides, review your steps.

E. This is a compound error; review your steps.

---

10. For trapezoid ABCD shown below, $\overline{AB}$ and $\overline{CD}$ are parallel. In terms of $x°$, what is the measure of angle $\angle ABC$?

Correct Answer G

This is a trapezoid angle problem with an algebra twist. You may end up marking off, if you don't see this question right away.

Recall that trapezoids create two sets of supplementary angles, a left set and a right set where the slanted sides intersect with the two parallel bases. All we know for sure is $x + ? = 180°$

We can rearrange to find $\angle ABC$
$$? = 180° - x°$$

Answer **G** is correct.

What You May Have Done Wrong

F. This is the measure of all the remaining angles in the trapezoid.

H. This is a trap! This sort of thinking would work with a parallelogram, but it would give you the value of two angle **?** marks. Remember, there doesn't have to be any relation between the angles on the left and on the right, except that each side will add up to 180°.

J. This would find the angle in question *if* this were a parallelogram. Remember, there doesn't have to be any correlation between the angles a trapezoid except that each side (right and left) will add up to 180°.

K. Review your steps.

11. The isosceles trapezoid below has parallel sides of 25 and 35 inches. What is the area of the trapezoid?

Correct Answer D

This is a tricky trapezoid question, but you can use the formula for trapezoid area or split into triangles and solve. Either way, you'll need to know isosceles trapezoids.

<u>Splitting into triangles</u>

Isosceles trapezoids have equal base angles. They also have equal non-parallel sides. When we make two right triangles, they'll be identical.

The difference between the bottom base and top base is

$35 - 25 = 10$. That 10 is evenly split, $\frac{10}{2}$, giving each

triangle a base of 5. We can now use the Pythagorean Theorem to find the missing side.

$$a^2 + b^2 = c^2 \quad \rightarrow \quad 5^2 + b^2 = 13^2$$
$$b^2 = 144 \quad \rightarrow \quad b = 12$$

The height is 12.

The two triangles are identical

It's a 5, 12, 13 Special Right Triangle

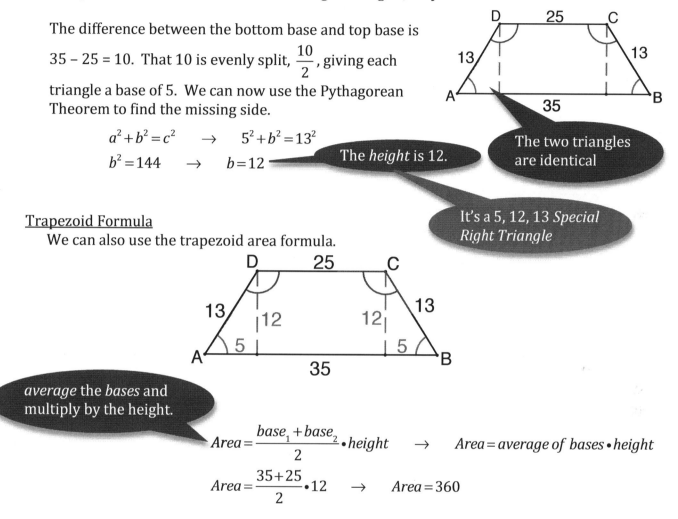

<u>Trapezoid Formula</u>

We can also use the trapezoid area formula.

average the bases and multiply by the height.

$$Area = \frac{base_1 + base_2}{2} \cdot height \quad \rightarrow \quad Area = average\ of\ bases \cdot height$$

$$Area = \frac{35 + 25}{2} \cdot 12 \quad \rightarrow \quad Area = 360$$

Answer **D** is correct.

<u>What You May Have Done Wrong</u>

    A. You incorrectly found the area of the triangles. Check your calculations.

    B. You probably used triangles, and only found the area of a single triangle.

    C. You multiplied 13 by the average of the bases. Remember, we *never use slanted sides* to find area.

    E. You multiplied 35 by the slanted side (13).

12. For parallelogram ABCD shown below what is the sum of ∠y and ∠x?

This parallelogram question is straightforward, but there is a bit of algebra. Recall that each side (left angles and right angles) of a parallelogram are supplementary angles (sum to 180°).

$$x° + b° = 180°$$
$$y° + a° = 180°$$

$$y° = x°$$
$$a° = b°$$

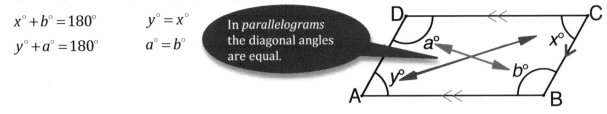

In *parallelograms* the diagonal angles are equal.

We also know that the diagonal angles of a parallelogram are always equal. So, we can run through our answer choices, by keeping in mind the statements we were able to make.

F. These angles are identical, and only add up to 180° with their supplement.
G. This is the measure of angle *y*. It would also be the measure of angle *x*, because those two angles are equal.
H. This would work if we subtracted *a* and *b* from 360°. As it is, we'd probably end up with a negative number (because *a* and *b* appear to be larger than 90°).
J. This works! 360° is the sum of all the interior angles and angle *a* and *b* are equal. By multiplying the value of *a* by two and subtracting it, we are—essentially—subtracting both *a* and *b* leaving only *x* and *y*.
K. This would result in a negative measure, *a* appears to be larger than 90 degrees.

Answer **J** is correct.

---

13. Mike is planning to paint a rectangular wall. He'll need two coats of paint. Each quart of paint covers 65 square feet. How many quarts of paint will Mike need to finish both coats?

This is a rectangle area question with a little kick at the end. We've got to remember to *double the area* because he's going to paint *two coats*).

Let's find the area:

$$area = length \cdot width \quad \rightarrow \quad area = 12 \cdot 9$$
$$area = 108 \, ft^2$$

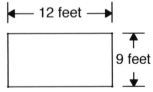

Now double the area to account for both coats: $108 \, ft^2 \cdot 2 = 216 \, ft^2$

To find the number of quarts, divide 216 by 70. $\dfrac{216}{65} = 3.32 \, quarts$

It's a trap! If we round down to 3 quarts, Mike won't have enough to finish the second coat. **So we have to round up to 4 quarts.**

Answer **C** is correct.

What You May Have Done Wrong
    A. You probably forgot to double the area.
    B. You rounded down, instead of up.
    D. You miscalculated the area, probably a calculator error.
    E. You may have used the perimeter instead of the area.

14. *ABCD* is a trapezoid and has sides as marked. What is the height of the trapezoid?

Correct Answer G

This is a trapezoid question, and it's really about being able to breakup the trapezoid into a triangle and a rectangle. Let's mark up the diagram. Because $\overline{BC}$ is perpendicular, the entire difference from the top base to the bottom base is on the left side.

By finding the difference 13 – 9 = 4, we've got the base of the triangle. Using the *Pythagorean Theorem*, we can find the height of the triangle, which is also the height of the trapezoid.

$$a^2 + b^2 = c^2 \quad \rightarrow \quad 4^2 + b^2 = 5^2$$
$$b^2 = 9 \quad \rightarrow \quad b = 3$$

Answer **G** is correct.

<u>What You May Have Done Wrong</u>
   F. You may have been overeager. Or made another error.
   H. You may have taken the hypotenuse (the slanted side) for the height.
   J. You either made a calculation error, or guessed.
   K. You forgot to take your square root, made a calculation error, or guessed.

15. In the figure below, *ABCD* is a square with an area of 64. Rectangle *EFGH* has an area of 24 and width as marked. What is the length of *x* + *y*?

Correct Answer A

This is a *rectangle area* question. Let's work with our givens, markup our diagram and go from there. We can use the area of square *ABCD* to find its side length (remember, all sides of a square are equal).

$$area = side^2 \rightarrow 64 = side^2$$
$$\sqrt{64} = \sqrt{side^2} \rightarrow side = 8$$

We can also work backwards to find the missing length of the rectangle.

$$area = length \cdot width \quad \rightarrow \quad 24 = length \cdot 4$$
$$length = 6$$

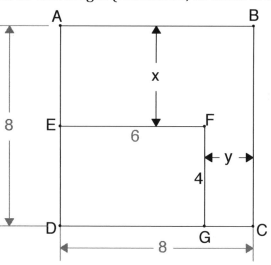

Now, we can find the length of *x* and *y* respectively.

$$x = 8 - 4 = 4$$
$$y = 8 - 6 = 2$$
$$x + y = 4 + 2 = 6$$

Answer **A** is correct.

<u>What You May Have Done Wrong</u>
   B. You got the value of *x*. This is a halfway answer.
   C. This is the value of *y*, a halfway answer.
   D. That's the length of the side of the square.
   E. This is a compound error. Check your steps.

16. Mr. Grout is going to replace the tile in his Turkish bath. The bath is rectangular and measures 16ft by 20 ft. Mr. Grout has selected tile that are 6 inches square. How many tiles does he need to purchase?

Correct Answer J

This is a rectangle area problem, but the tough part is the unit conversions. Let's draw a couple of diagrams. We'll need to either convert feet to inches or inches to feet. It doesn't matter which way we go. I'm going to convert inches to feet.

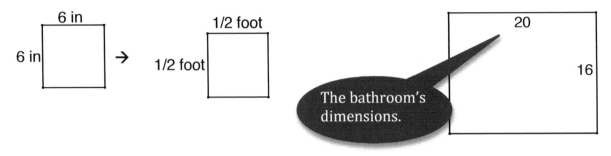

The easiest way to solve these problems is to find the areas of both the room and the tile (in the same units).

Room Area

$$area = length \cdot width$$
$$area = 16 \ feet \cdot 20 \ feet$$
$$area = 320 \ feet^2$$

Tile Area

$$area = length \cdot width$$
$$area = \frac{1}{2} \ foot \cdot \frac{1}{2} \ foot$$
$$area = \frac{1}{4} \ foot^2$$

To find how many tiles it will take to cover 320 square feet, divide the area of the room by the area of each tile.

$$\frac{320 \ ft^2}{\frac{1}{4} \ ft^2} = 1{,}280$$

Answer **J** is correct.

<u>What You May Have Done Wrong</u>

F. This would be correct if each tile was 1 ft square. You probably made a conversion error.

G. You made a mistake in finding the area of the tile.

H. This is a compound error. You either tried to count the tiles, or you made a conversion error.

K. This is a compound error. Check your steps.

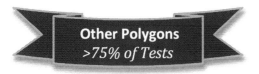

Introduction

This is a bit of a catchall category, including unusual shapes, and specific types of questions that aren't covered elsewhere. Many of these questions will require you to know the properties of other shapes.

What You Need to Know

✓ How to find the perimeter and area of unusual shapes
✓ How to find the number of diagonals in a polygon

Definitions: Perimeter & Area

Regardless of how many sides, or even curves in a shape, a shape's perimeter is the sum of the outside edges.

Remember, perimeter is like the length of the fence and area is like the size of the yard.

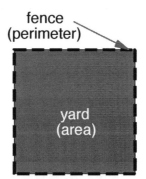

fence
(perimeter)

yard
(area)

Definitions: Area

Area is the size of the yard. Area is *always* in square units.

Rules of the Road: Area

Break unusual shapes into basic shapes to find the area.
We can also make a basic shape and subtract to find the area.

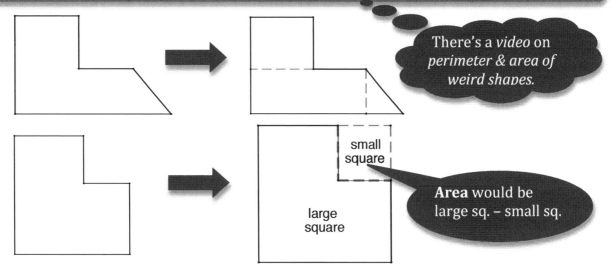

There's a *video* on *perimeter & area of weird shapes.*

small square

large square

Area would be large sq. – small sq.

1. The figure below consists of a semicircle and a rectangle with dimensions marked. Approximately, what is the outside perimeter of the figure?

A. 36
B. 37
C. 45
D. 44
E. 42

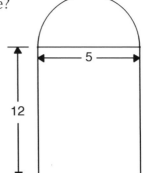

Solve

To solve, we have need the circumference of the semicircle and *part* rectangle's perimeter. The circumference of a circle is found by the formula:

$$circumference = 2\pi r$$

$$OR$$

$$circumference = \pi d$$

$$circumference = \pi d$$

$$circumference = (3.14)(5)$$

$$circumference = 15.70$$

Because this is a *semicircle* (a half-circle) we need to divide the circumference by two.

$$circumference = \frac{15.70}{2} = 7.85$$

Add the part of the rectangle that's on the *outside* of the shape.

Add up the rectangle lengths.
$$12 + 12 + 5 = 29$$

We don't use this length. It's not an outside boundary.

Now, let's add the semicircle.
$$29 + 7.85 = 36.85$$

$$perimeter \approx 37$$

Answer Choice **B** is correct.

2. In the figure below all line segments intersect at 90° angles. What is the perimeter of the figure?

    A. 46
    B. 32
    C. 36
    D. 24
    E. 40

This is a common question type.

Solve

The key to understanding this problem is to use the fact that *all* the sides are parallel or perpendicular because everything meets at 90° angles.

Because everything is perpendicular, or parallel, the shape gets no wider or narrow from top to bottom or from side to side.

Let's extend the outermost sides and take a look.

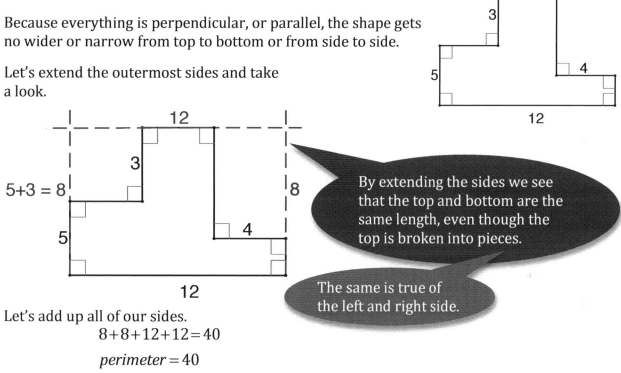

By extending the sides we see that the top and bottom are the same length, even though the top is broken into pieces.

The same is true of the left and right side.

Let's add up all of our sides.
$$8+8+12+12=40$$

$$perimeter = 40$$

Answer choice **E** is correct.

3. In the figure below, $\overline{AB}$ and $\overline{CD}$ are parallel and perpendicular to $\overline{AF}, \overline{CE}, and \overline{DB}$. What is the area of polygon *AFECDB*?

A. 15
B. 19
C. 20
D. 22
E. 23

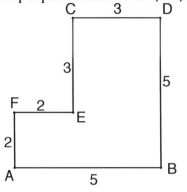

Solve

There are two ways to solve this problem. We can split the shape into rectangles, or make a large rectangle and subtract out the missing portion.

> Because every side is either parallel or perpendicular to each other, every angle will be a right angle.

<u>Solving by Splitting into Rectangles</u>

Let's split our diagram into two equal rectangles.

Sum the areas to find the area of the entire shape.

$$4 + 15 = 19$$

$$area = 19$$

> Be careful with your dimensions!

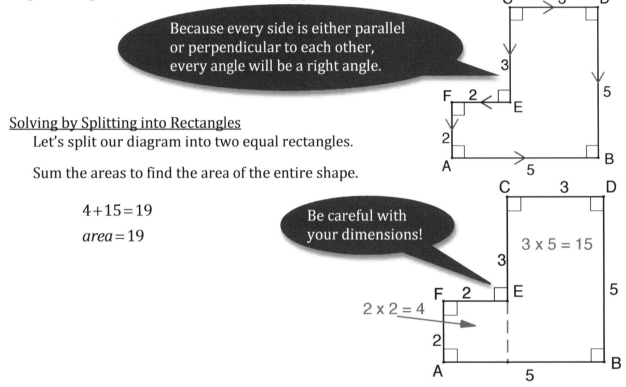

Solving by Using Negative Space

We start by making one large rectangle by extending sides.

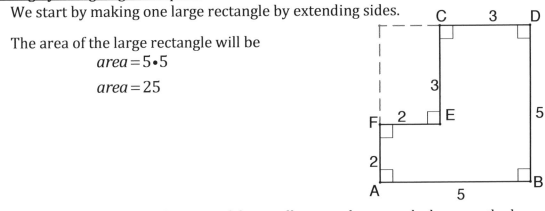

The area of the large rectangle will be
$$area = 5 \cdot 5$$
$$area = 25$$

We'll need to subtract the area of the small rectangle we made, because the large rectangle includes that area.
$$small\ area = 2 \cdot 3$$
$$small\ area = 6$$

To find the area of our polygon, we'll subtract the small area from the large area.
$$area = 25 - 6 = 19$$

Answer choice **B** is correct.

Definition: Diagonals

Diagonals are straight lines joining corners of a shape by passing through the inside of the shape. The corners connected aren't adjacent.

Diagonals are not part of the shape. They *do not* sit on the edge.

not diagonals

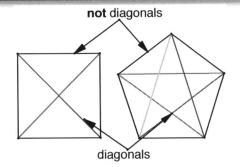

diagonals

Rules of the Road: Diagonals

The number of diagonals in a polygon with *n* sides can be found by the formula $\dfrac{n(n-3)}{2}$.

The number of diagonals can also be found by drawing the possible diagonals from one corner (vertex), multiplying those diagonals by the number of vertexes and then dividing that product by 2.

A square has one diagonal per corner and four corners.
$$\frac{1 \cdot 4}{2} = 2\ \text{diagonals}$$

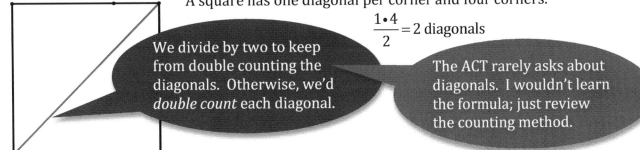

We divide by two to keep from double counting the diagonals. Otherwise, we'd *double count* each diagonal.

The ACT rarely asks about diagonals. I wouldn't learn the formula; just review the counting method.

ACT Examples: Diagonals

1. How many diagonals are in the hexagon below?

    A. 24
    B. 9
    C. 18
    D. 12
    E. 6

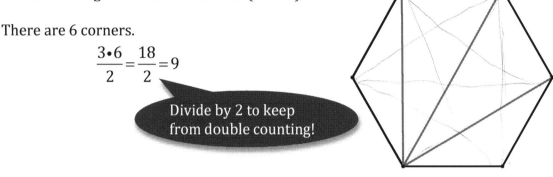

Solve

To solve, draw the number of diagonals from any corner (vertex).
We have 3 diagonals from the corner (vertex).

There are 6 corners.

$$\frac{3 \cdot 6}{2} = \frac{18}{2} = 9$$

Divide by 2 to keep from double counting!

Answer choice **B** is correct.

Wrap Up

What You Need to Know
- ✓ How to find the perimeter and area of unusual shapes
- ✓ How to find the number of diagonals in a polygon

Videos

Unusual Shapes: Perimeter & Area

The Strategies
- ✓ Break the shape down into shapes you recognize.
- ✓ Pay attention to parallel and perpendicular lines (on perimeter questions).

Related Skills
- ✓ Angles

- ✓ All Plane Geo shapes topics

Plane Geometry: Other Polygons

1. The figure below has an area of 32 square centimeters and is broken into eight equal squares. What is the perimeter of the figure?

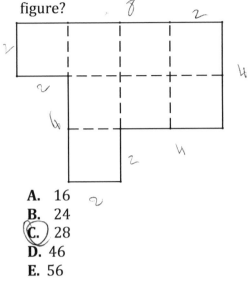

A. 16
B. 24
C. 28
D. 46
E. 56

2. How many diagonals are there in the regular nonagon below?

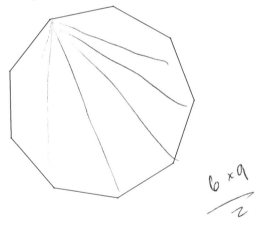

F. 9
G. 18
H. 27
J. 45
K. 54

Use the information below for questions 3 & 4.

3. Below is the map of a park with units in meters. All borders of the park run north/south or east/west. The park & recreations department is planning a fence around the entire park. How much fence is required?

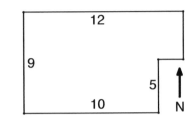

A. 36 meters
B. 40 meters
C. 42 meters
D. 48 meters
E. 108 meters

4. What is the area of the park?

F. 116 m²
G. 98 m²
H. 108 m²
J. 90 m²
K. 120 m²

5. The figure below consists of rectangle *ABCD* and arc *BC*. *BC* is a semicircle. What is the approximate area of the figure?

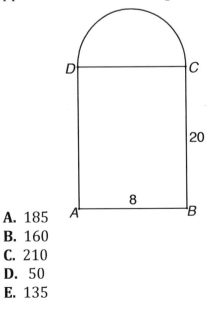

A. 185
B. 160
C. 210
D. 50
E. 135

-469-

1. **The figure below has an area of 32 square centimeters and is broken into eight equal squares. What is the perimeter of the figure?**

Correct Answer C

This is an interesting question. We've got to find the side lengths to find the perimeter, and since the shape is irregular, we'll have to use the smaller squares.

Because the squares are equal, they'll have an equal portion of the area. There are 8 squares and the total area is 32 square centimeters.

$$\frac{32\,area}{8\,squares} = 4\,area\,per\,square$$

We'll need to take the area and find the side lengths. Squares are rectangles with four equal sides. If the area of a rectangle is *length* x *width* the area of a square is $side^2$.

$area = side^2$

$4 = side^2$

$side = 2$

Here's the painful part to find the perimeter we'll have to count up the 2's.

$8 + 4 + 4 + 2 + 2 + 4 + 2 + 2 = 28$

-OR-

$14 \times 2 = 28$

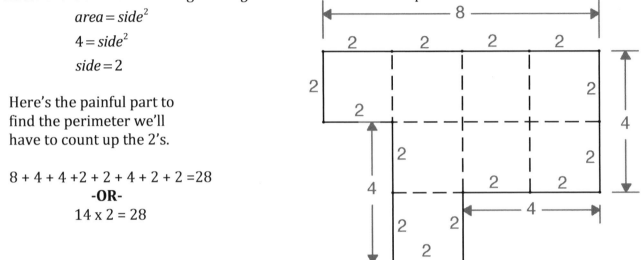

Answer choice **C** is correct.

<u>What You May Have Done Wrong</u>

    A. You treated each side of the shape as 2.

    B. You miscounted.

    D. You miscounted or made a conceptual error.

    E. You used the area of each square to find the perimeter.

2. How many diagonals are there in the regular nonagon below?

Correct Answer H

There's a formula for diagonals, but don't bother. The easiest way to find the number of diagonals is to pick a vertex (corner) and count the number of diagonals from that point.

A diagonal is a line that goes from vertex to vertex (corner to corner) that doesn't sit on the shape.

There are six diagonals from any point nonagon. Each corner will have six diagonals. And there are nine corners (nine sides) on a nonagon. If you didn't know how many sides, you could count them.

$$6 \times 9 = 54$$

But, there's a problem. If we multiply the number of diagonals and corners, we'll *double count* the diagonals.

For example, the first diagonal (diagonal 1) could also be drawn from what we're thinking of as the endpoint. So we'll need to divide the diagonals by 2.

$$\frac{diagonals \bullet sides}{2} \quad \rightarrow \quad \frac{6 \bullet 9}{2} = 27\ diagonals$$

Answer choice **H** is correct.

<u>What You May Have Done Wrong</u>
   F. That's the number of sides in a nonagon.
   G. That's double the number of sides in a nonagon.
   J. This is a calculation or conceptual error.
   K. You didn't divide your diagonals by 2. You double counted each diagonal.

3. **Below is the map of a park with units in meters. All borders of the park run north/south or east/west. The park & recreations department is planning a fence around the entire park. How much fence is required?**

Correct Answer C

This is a perimeter question. The length of the fence goes around all of the sides of the shape. The diagram is missing sides, and that's the real difficulty of the question.

All of the park's borders run either north/south or east/west. That means they all intersect at 90°angles. The length (12) is the same on the top & bottom. The width (9) is the same on the left and right .

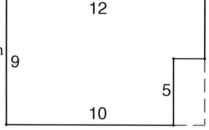

Even with the piece missing, the perimeter will be the same as a rectangle that's 12 by 9.

Perimeter = 12 + 12 + 9 + 9 = 42

Answer choice **C** is correct

<u>What You May Have Done Wrong</u>
   A. You added the sides given, but didn't find the missing sides.
   B. You correctly used 9 as the right side, but you forgot the piece missing from the bottom.
   D. You treated all sides as 12, or made a calculation error.
   E. This is the area of a 12 x 9 rectangle.

4. What is the area of the park?

Correct Answer G

While the perimeter of the park is the same as a rectangle of the same size (12 x 9), the area won't be. This problem has an extra step. We'll need the missing dimensions of two sides.

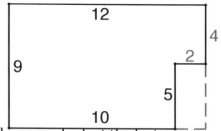

Because the top & bottom have to be the same length, the missing length will be
$$12 - 10 = 2 \text{ m}^2$$

The sides will both be 9, and
$$9 - 5 = 4 \text{ m}^2$$

For why the top & bottom and left & right sides have to be the same, look at the last problem.

We can solve this in two ways, by making two smaller rectangles or making a large rectangle and subtracting the "missing" rectangle. Neither way is faster; use the one you like.

Using Negative Space

Find the area of the large rectangle 12 x 9 and then subtract the area of the small, missing rectangle 2 x 5.

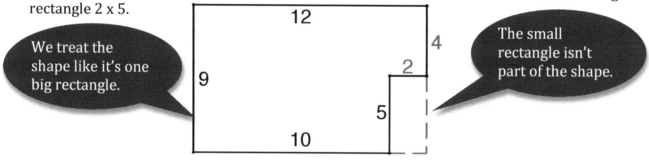

We treat the shape like it's one big rectangle.

The small rectangle isn't part of the shape.

Area Big Rectangle = 12 x 9 = 108 m²
Area Missing Rectangle = 2 x 5 = 10 m²
Area Shape = 108 – 10 = 98 m²

Splitting into Rectangles

You can split the shape up in a couple of ways, but I'm just going to show one.

Split off the little rectangle on the end and find the area of both rectangles.

Larger Rectangle: 9 x 10 = 90 m²
Smaller Rectangle: 4 x 2 = 8 m²

Area of the shape = 90 + 8 = 98 m²

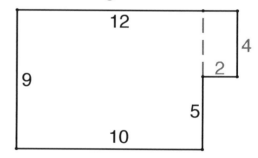

Answer choice **G** is correct.

What You May Have Done Wrong:

F. You made the large rectangle 12 x 9 instead of 12 x 9.
H. This is the area of the large rectangle, without subtracting the small rectangle.
J. This is the area of the 10 x 9 rectangle; you didn't add the rectangle on the end.
K. You made a conceptual error.

5. The figure below consists of rectangle *ABCD* and arc *BC*. *BC* is a semicircle. What is the approximate area of the figure?

Correct Answer A

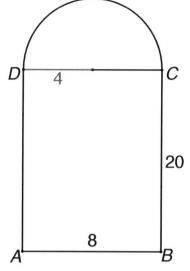

This problem looks harder than it is. All I've got to do is add the area of the semicircle with the area of a rectangle.

Let's start with the area of the rectangle:

$area = length \times width \quad \rightarrow \quad area = 8 \times 20$

$area = 160$

For the semicircle, we'll need the radius. The diameter of the circle equals the length of the rectangle, so the diameter is 8. The radius is half the diameter, 4.

Area of the semicircle:

$$area = \pi r^2 \quad \rightarrow \quad area = \pi 4^2$$
$$area = 16\pi \approx 50.27$$

A semicircle is only half of a circle, so we need to divide the area of the circle by 2.

$$area = \frac{50.27}{2} = 25.14$$

To find the area of the figure, add the area of the rectangle and the semicircle.

$$area = 160 + 25.14$$
$$area = 185.14 \approx 185$$

Answer choice **A** is correct.

<u>What You May Have Done Wrong</u>
    B. This is the area of the rectangle.
    C. This is the area of the rectangle & an *entire* circle.
    D. This is the area of the *entire* circle
    E. You subtracted the area of the semicircle from the rectangle.

Background
Circles are the second most tested shape (behind *triangles*). Circles are often combined with other shapes, and you'll find more on circles in *Plane Geo: Combination Shapes*.

What You Need to Know
- ✓ How to find the circumference & area of a circle.
- ✓ How to find arc length in terms of degrees & circumference.
- ✓ How to find sector area
- ✓ How to deal with inscribed angles.

Definitions: Circles

Circles are incredibly simple shapes. If you know the *radius* and the *center*, you can completely locate and describe a circle. In plane geometry, we usually don't care about the location of the circle.

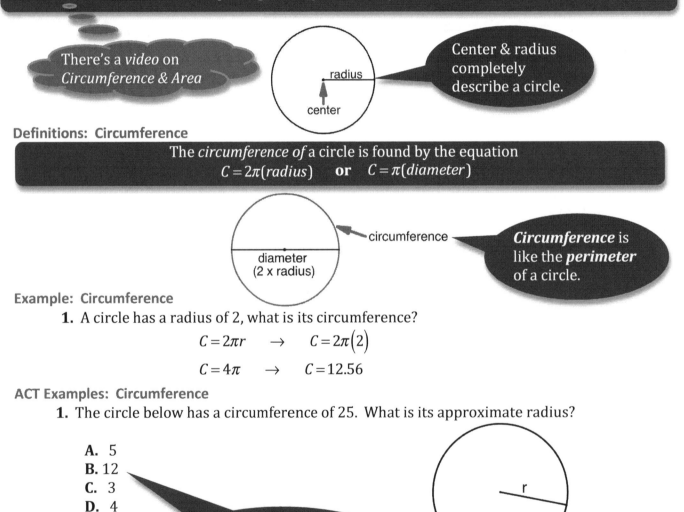

There's a *video* on *Circumference & Area*

radius
center

Center & radius completely describe a circle.

Definitions: Circumference

The *circumference of* a circle is found by the equation
$$C = 2\pi(radius) \quad \textbf{or} \quad C = \pi(diameter)$$

diameter
(2 x radius)

circumference

Circumference is like the *perimeter* of a circle.

Example: Circumference
   1. A circle has a radius of 2, what is its circumference?
$$C = 2\pi r \quad \rightarrow \quad C = 2\pi(2)$$
$$C = 4\pi \quad \rightarrow \quad C = 12.56$$

ACT Examples: Circumference
   1. The circle below has a circumference of 25. What is its approximate radius?

   A. 5
   B. 12
   C. 3
   D. 4
   E. 13

Sometimes we'll want to get an approximate value (so we use 3.14 for π).

r

$\pi r d$

Solve

This is a plug-in problem, plug in the *circumference* and solve for radius.

$$C = 2\pi r \quad \rightarrow \quad 25 = 2\pi r$$

$$\frac{25}{2\pi} = \frac{2\pi r}{2\pi} \quad \rightarrow \quad \frac{25}{2(3.14)} = \frac{2\pi r}{2(3.14)}$$

$$r = 3.98 \approx 4$$

I'm looking for an approximation here, so I'm using 3.14 for pi. You can use 3.14 or your pi

Answer choice **D** is correct

Definition: Area of a Circle

The area of a circle is found by the formula $A = \pi r^2$

The **area** is like the *grass in the yard*. The **circumference** is like the *length of the fence*.

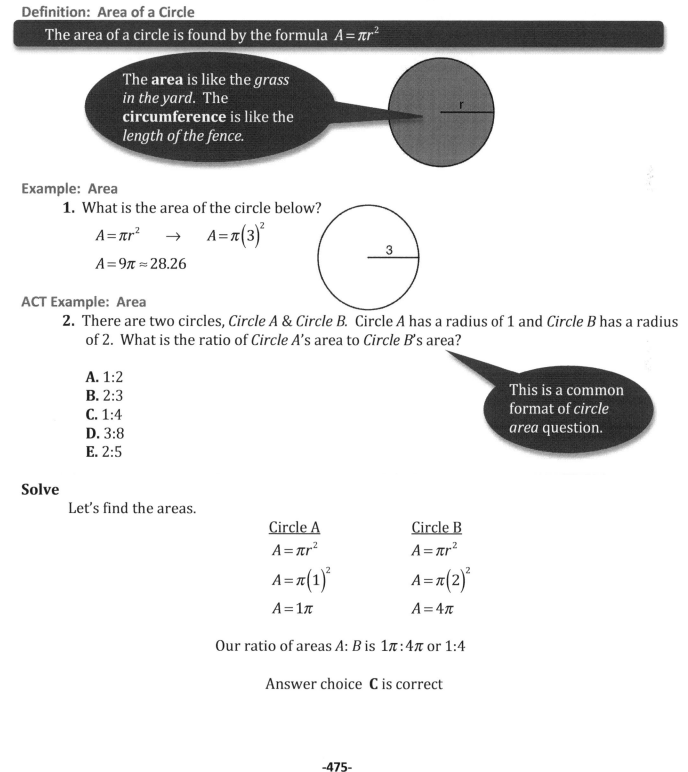

Example: Area

1. What is the area of the circle below?

$$A = \pi r^2 \quad \rightarrow \quad A = \pi (3)^2$$

$$A = 9\pi \approx 28.26$$

ACT Example: Area

2. There are two circles, *Circle A* & *Circle B*. Circle A has a radius of 1 and *Circle B* has a radius of 2. What is the ratio of *Circle A*'s area to *Circle B*'s area?

A. 1:2
B. 2:3
C. 1:4
D. 3:8
E. 2:5

This is a common format of *circle area* question.

Solve

Let's find the areas.

Circle A	Circle B
$A = \pi r^2$	$A = \pi r^2$
$A = \pi (1)^2$	$A = \pi (2)^2$
$A = 1\pi$	$A = 4\pi$

Our ratio of areas $A : B$ is $1\pi : 4\pi$ or 1:4

Answer choice **C** is correct

Definitions: Angles & Arcs

A *circle* has 360°. A *central angle's* vertex is the center of the circle.

The *vertex* of this angle is the center of the circle.

Each leg of a *central angle* is a *radius*.

45°

45°

This piece of the *circumference* is an *arc*. It can be measured as 45°

An inscribed angle has its **vertex on the edge of the circle.**
The arc created by the inscribed angle is twice the size of the angle.

The vertex is on the edge of the circle.

90°

45°

The **arc** measures *twice* the **angle**.

Example: Inscribed Angles

1. In the circle below *A* is the center, what is the measure of the arc created by ∠*CDB*?

The arc is a semi-circle (diameter)

C · A · B

D

A 90° angle inscribed on the circle

The length of the arc will be $2 \cdot 90° = 180°$

There's a *video* on *Sector Area & Arc Length*

Definitions: Arcs & Sectors

Arcs can be measured in degrees.
Arc length can also be measured as a piece (percentage) of the circumference of the circle—a piece of the fence.
Sector Area is a piece of the area—a piece of the yard or a piece of pizza.

Rules of the Road: Arc Length & Sector Area

Arc length is found by the formula
$$arc\ length = circumference \cdot percent$$
Sector area is found by the formula
$$sector\ area = area \cdot percent$$

Percent is how much of the circle (360°) the angle represents.

Review *Pre-Alg: Percents*

$$percent = \frac{part}{whole} = \frac{angle}{360}$$

Example: Arc Length

1. The circle below has a radius of 2 cm. What is the length of the minor arc shown below?

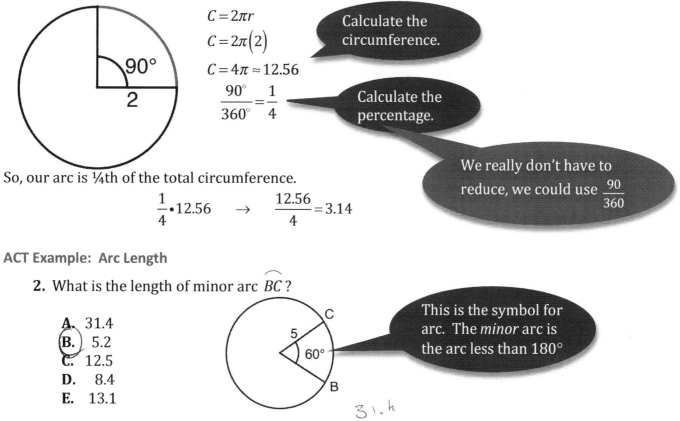

$C = 2\pi r$

$C = 2\pi(2)$

Calculate the circumference.

$C = 4\pi \approx 12.56$

$\dfrac{90°}{360°} = \dfrac{1}{4}$

Calculate the percentage.

We really don't have to reduce, we could use $\dfrac{90}{360}$

So, our arc is ¼th of the total circumference.

$$\dfrac{1}{4} \cdot 12.56 \quad \rightarrow \quad \dfrac{12.56}{4} = 3.14$$

ACT Example: Arc Length

2. What is the length of minor arc $\overparen{BC}$?

A. 31.4
B. 5.2
C. 12.5
D. 8.4
E. 13.1

This is the symbol for arc. The minor arc is the arc less than 180°

31.h

Solve

We're looking for the minor arc, which is defined by the central angle 60° (instead of the 300° angle that is also made by those two line segments).

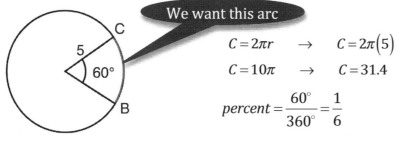

We want this arc

$C = 2\pi r \quad \rightarrow \quad C = 2\pi(5)$

$C = 10\pi \quad \rightarrow \quad C = 31.4$

$percent = \dfrac{60°}{360°} = \dfrac{1}{6}$

arc length = circumference • percent

arc length = $31.4 \cdot \dfrac{1}{6}$

arc length = 5.233

Answer choice **B** is correct.

Example: Sector Area

1. The circle below has a radius of 4 cm. What is the area of the sector below?

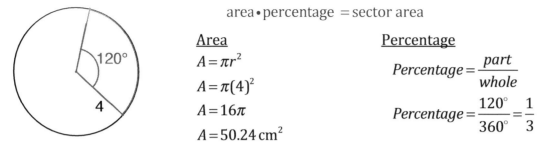

$$area \cdot percentage = sector\ area$$

<u>Area</u>

$A = \pi r^2$

$A = \pi (4)^2$

$A = 16\pi$

$A = 50.24\ cm^2$

<u>Percentage</u>

$Percentage = \dfrac{part}{whole}$

$Percentage = \dfrac{120°}{360°} = \dfrac{1}{3}$

Multiply the percentage by the area to find the *sector's area.*

$$area \cdot percentage = sector\ area$$

$$50.24 \cdot \dfrac{1}{3} = 16.75\ cm^2$$

ACT Example: Sector Area

2. A circular dance floor has a diameter of 15 feet and is complete except for the missing 30° sector below. Approximately how many square feet of wood flooring is needed to complete the floor?

A. 19 ft²
B. 59 ft²
C. 177 ft²
D. 15 ft²
E. 18 ft²

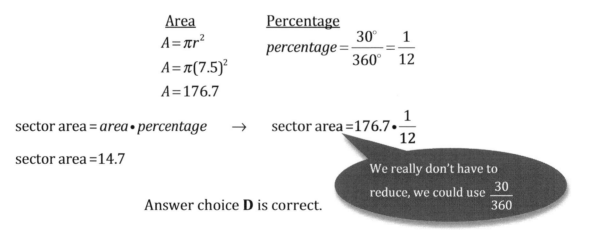

Solve

Let's find the radius from the diameter given in the question (15 feet).

$$radius = \dfrac{15}{2} = 7.5\ feet$$

$$sector\ area = area \cdot percentage$$

<u>Area</u>

$A = \pi r^2$

$A = \pi (7.5)^2$

$A = 176.7$

<u>Percentage</u>

$percentage = \dfrac{30°}{360°} = \dfrac{1}{12}$

sector area = *area • percentage* → sector area $= 176.7 \cdot \dfrac{1}{12}$

sector area $= 14.7$

We really don't have to reduce, we could use $\dfrac{30}{360}$

Answer choice **D** is correct.

The Circle Formula

The circle formula can be tough to remember. It's not really used in calculations but it does show us the radius and the center of the circle (the most important information about a circle).

Definition: The Circle Formula

The center-radius form (the one we use) of the circle equation is $(x-h)^2 + (y-k)^2 = r^2$, where (h, k) is the center of the circle.

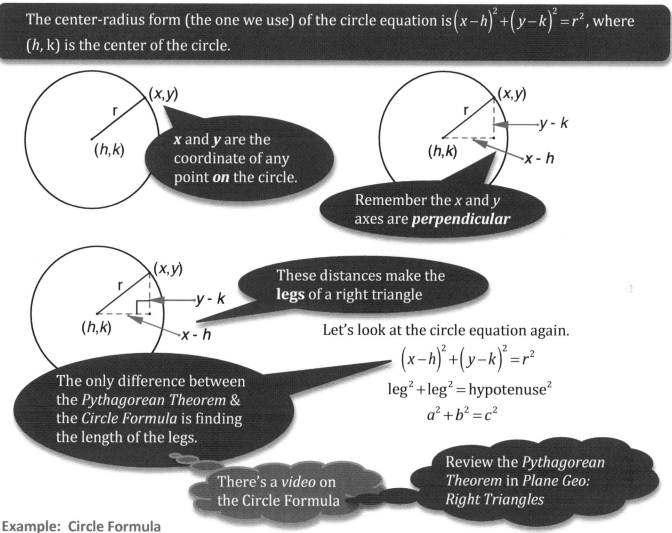

Let's look at the circle equation again.

$$(x-h)^2 + (y-k)^2 = r^2$$

$$\text{leg}^2 + \text{leg}^2 = \text{hypotenuse}^2$$

$$a^2 + b^2 = c^2$$

Example: Circle Formula

1. A circle has a radius of 4 and its center is at the origin. What is the formula of that circle?

Let's draw the circle, write the general formula and plug in.

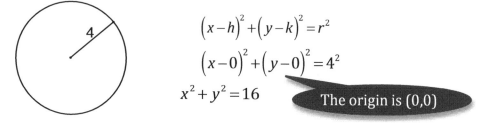

$$(x-h)^2 + (y-k)^2 = r^2$$

$$(x-0)^2 + (y-0)^2 = 4^2$$

$$x^2 + y^2 = 16$$

The origin is (0,0)

16

2. A circle in the standard (x,y) coordinate plane is tangent to the x-axis at 3 and the y-axis at -3. Which of the following is an equation of the circle.

A. $(x-3)^2+(y+3)^2=3$

B. $(x-3)^2+(y+3)^2=9$

C. $(x-3)^2+(y-3)^2=3$

D. $(x-3)^2+(y-3)^2=9$

E. $(x+3)^2+(y-3)^2=9$

> This is a common setup, and it's a great *mark-off* question

Solve

Anytime you have a word problem that describes a figure—draw the figure. To answer the question, we need both the *radius* and the *center* of the circle.

The circle is tangent at points (3,0) & (0,-3), the x & y axes are at those points, and any line tangent to a circle is perpendicular to the radius. We can draw straight lines down from (3,0) & right from (0,-3) until the lines cross at (3,-3).

You can think about it this way. The circle hits the axes at the x or y coordinate of its center. Basically, where it hits the x-axis is the x-coordinate of the center. The same is true with the y-coordinate.

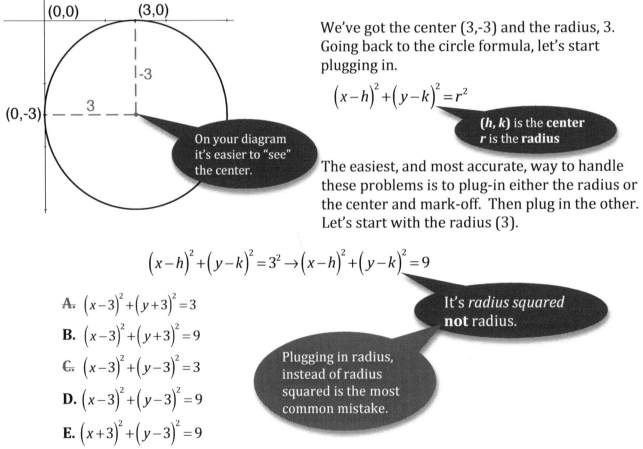

> On your diagram it's easier to "see" the center.

We've got the center (3,-3) and the radius, 3. Going back to the circle formula, let's start plugging in.

$$(x-h)^2+(y-k)^2=r^2$$

> (h, k) is the **center**
> r is the **radius**

The easiest, and most accurate, way to handle these problems is to plug-in either the radius or the center and mark-off. Then plug in the other. Let's start with the radius (3).

$$(x-h)^2+(y-k)^2=3^2 \rightarrow (x-h)^2+(y-k)^2=9$$

A. $(x-3)^2+(y+3)^2=3$

B. $(x-3)^2+(y+3)^2=9$

C. $(x-3)^2+(y-3)^2=3$

D. $(x-3)^2+(y-3)^2=9$

E. $(x+3)^2+(y-3)^2=9$

> It's *radius squared* **not** radius.

> Plugging in radius, instead of radius squared is the most common mistake.

Plug-in the center (3,-3).

$$\left(x-h\right)^2+\left(y-k\right)^2=9 \rightarrow \left(x-3\right)^2+\left(y+3\right)^2=9$$

A. $\left(x-3\right)^2+\left(y+3\right)^2=3$

B. $\left(x-3\right)^2+\left(y+3\right)^2=9$

C. $\left(x-3\right)^2+\left(y-3\right)^2=3$

D. $\left(x-3\right)^2+\left(y-3\right)^2=9$

E. $\left(x+3\right)^2+\left(y-3\right)^2=9$

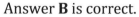

It's $(x-h)$ & $(y-k)$
not $(x+h)$ & $(y+k)$

Plugging in $(x+h)$ &
$(y+k)$ is the second
most common mistake.

Answer **B** is correct.

3. A circle is inscribed in a square, as shown below. The vertices of the square are as marked. What is the equation of the circle?

A. $\left(x-4\right)^2+\left(y-4\right)^2=16$

B. $\left(x-4\right)^2+\left(y-4\right)^2=4$

C. $\left(x+2\right)^2+\left(y+2\right)^2=4$

D. $\left(x-2\right)^2+\left(y-2\right)^2=4$

E. $\left(x-2\right)^2-\left(y-2\right)^2=4$

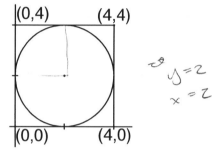

$y=2$

$x=2$

Solve

The square doesn't change anything. We find the center, the radius, and plug them in. In this case, you may not need to do much work. You can eyeball the center and the radius fairly easily. You'll still want to mark-off.

The radius (2): $\left(x-h\right)^2+\left(y-k\right)^2=r^2$

$$\left(x-h\right)^2+\left(y-k\right)^2=2^2$$

$$\left(x-h\right)^2+\left(y-k\right)^2=4$$

The center (2,2): $\left(x-h\right)^2+\left(y-k\right)^2=r^2$

$$\left(x-2\right)^2+\left(y-2\right)^2=r^2$$

A. $\left(x-4\right)^2+\left(y-4\right)^2=16$

B. $\left(x-4\right)^2+\left(y-4\right)^2=4$

C. $\left(x+2\right)^2+\left(y+2\right)^2=4$

D. $\left(x-2\right)^2+\left(y-2\right)^2=4$

E. $\left(x-2\right)^2-\left(y-2\right)^2=4$

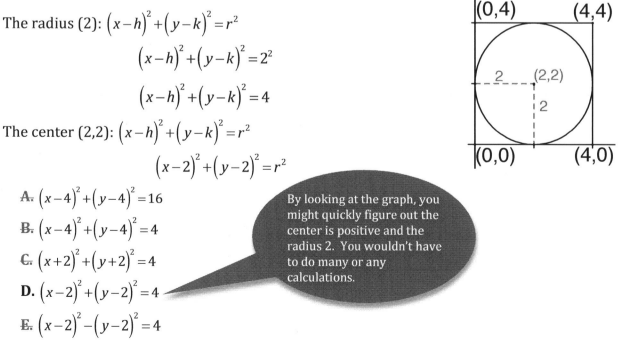

By looking at the graph, you might quickly figure out the center is positive and the radius 2. You wouldn't have to do many or any calculations.

Answer **D** is correct.

Wrap Up

What You Need to Know
- ✓ How to find the circumference & area of a circle.
- ✓ How to find arc length in terms of degrees & circumference.
- ✓ How to find sector area
- ✓ How to deal with inscribed angles.

Videos

> Circumference & Area

> Arc Length & Sector Area

> The Circle Formula

The Strategies
- ✓ You've got to know your formulas.
- ✓ Use the answer choices as guides. You'll mark-off on a lot of questions.
- ✓ The Circle Formula is on almost every test. It's best remembered by the Pythagorean Theorem.
- ✓ Draw diagrams when they aren't provided.

Key Skill
- ✓ Combination Shapes

- ✓ The Unit Circle

- ✓ 3D Geometry

- ✓ Coordinate Geo: Shapes

Circles: Problems

1. The equation of a circle in the standard (x,y) coordinate plane is $x^2 + (y-1)^2 = 4$.
At which points does the circle intercept the y-axis?

A. (0,-2) and (0,2)
B. (0,-1) and (0,3)
C. (0,-3) and (0,5)
D. (0,-5) and (0,3)
E. (0,-15) and (0,17)

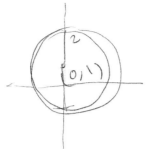

4. An ingenious way to cut grass is to tie a goat to a post. Brendan's goat eats all the grass that it can reach. If the goat is on a 9-yard rope, approximately how large an area can it clear?

F. 64 yd²
G. 28 yd²
H. 57 yd²
J. 81 yd²
K. 254 yd²

2. The responses to a survey about recreational preferences are recorded represented on a circle graph. 15% of respondents preferred hiking, 10% waterskiing, 25% swimming, and 10% mountain biking. The rest of the respondents prefer indoor activities. What is the degree measure of the indoor activities sector?

F. 40°
G. 180°
H. 216°
J. 144°
K. 200°

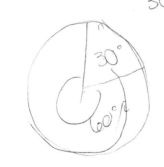

5. A triathlon consists of a 112 Mile bike ride, a marathon (26.2 mile run) and a 2.4 mile swim. The route planned by a triathlon's organizers is perfectly circular, with the start line also being the finish line. If you were to cut straight through the track, crossing the center, how far would you travel?

A. 22.4 miles
B. 35.7 miles
C. 140.6 miles
D. 44.8 miles
E. 40.4 miles

3. The two shaded circles are tangent at the center of the larger circle. The radius of both smaller circles is 2. What is the approximate area of the un-shaded area?

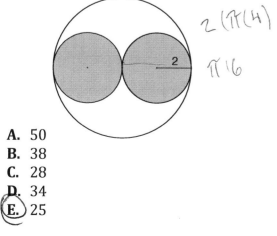

A. 50
B. 38
C. 28
D. 34
E. 25

6. A circle is tangent to the x-axis at -4 and tangent to the y-axis at 4. What is the equation of that circle?

F. $(x+2)^2 + (y-2)^2 = 4$
G. $(x+4)^2 + (y-4)^2 = 16$
H. $(x-4)^2 + (y+4)^2 = 16$
J. $(x+4)^2 + (y-4)^2 = 4$
K. $(x-4)^2 + (y-4)^2 = 16$

7. Two circles have radii of 5 and 11 inches, respectively. What is the ratio of their areas?

   A. 25:121
   B. 5:11
   C. 25π:121
   D. 10:22
   E. 25:121π

8. In the circle below, A is the center and $\overline{CB}$ is a diameter. Which of the following is the largest arc or angle?

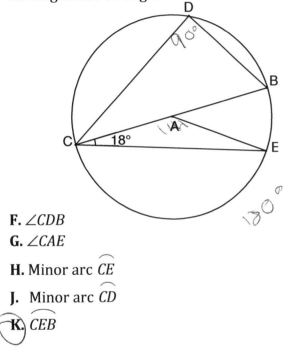

   F. $\angle CDB$
   G. $\angle CAE$
   H. Minor arc $\overarc{CE}$
   J. Minor arc $\overarc{CD}$
   K. $\overarc{CEB}$

9. A is the center of the circle below. What is the measure of minor arc $\overarc{DB}$ created by $\angle CBD$?

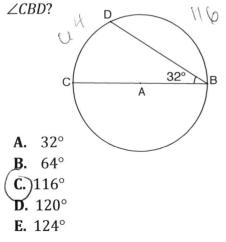

   A. 32°
   B. 64°
   C. 116°
   D. 120°
   E. 124°

10. What is the arc length of minor arc $\overarc{BC}$, if A is the center of the circle below?

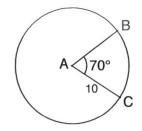

   F. 13.1
   G. 12.2
   H. 12.1
   J. 6.1
   K. 11.5

11. What is the approximate area of the sector created by $\angle BAC$?

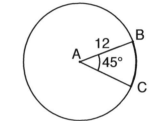

   A. 144π
   B. 36π
   C. 72π
   D. 3π
   E. 18π

Use the following information for questions 12 – 13

A special target is set up for an archery competition. The target is a set of concentric circles. The innermost circle has a radius of 3 inches and each of the other circle's radius increases by 3 inches over the next smaller circle. The point value of each circle is as marked.

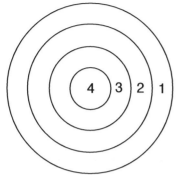

12. What is the area of the target worth two points?

    A. 6π
    B. 32π
    C. 45π
    D. 108π
    E. 144π

13. Darts can only be counted as having hit one ring (scored once). If a dart can be assumed to hit the target, what is the percent likelihood that it scores two or less?

    F. 25%
    G. 56%
    H. 44%
    J. 31%
    K. 50%

14. The circle below has a center of A. $\overline{EB}$ and $\overline{FD}$ are diameters, $\overset{\frown}{BC}$ and $\overset{\frown}{CD}$ are congruent. What is the measure of minor arc $\overset{\frown}{ED}$?

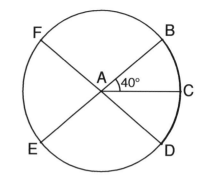

    A. 80°
    B. 140°
    C. 200°
    D. 100°
    E. 90°

Circles: Solutions

1. The equation of a circle in the standard (x,y) coordinate plane is $x^2 + (y-1)^2 = 4$. At which points does the circle intercept the y-axis?

Correct Answer B

We can do this two ways, by graphing or with algebra.

<u>Graphing</u>

First, pull the *center* & the *radius* out of the equation.

$$(x-h)^2 + (y-k)^2 = r^2 \qquad \textbf{So} \qquad r^2 = 4, r = 2$$

$$x^2 + (y-1)^2 = 4 \qquad\qquad h = 0 \text{ and } k = 1$$

Our radius is 2 and our center is (0,1). Let's sketch our circle.

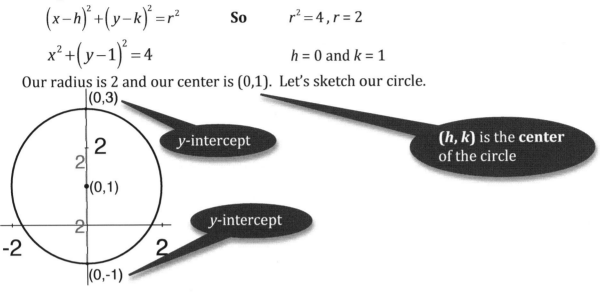

The *y*-intercepts are (0,-1) & (0,3)

<u>Algabraically</u>

We have *y*-intercepts whenever *x* is zero. Set *x* equal to zero.

$$x^2 + (y-1)^2 = 4 \qquad \rightarrow \qquad 0 + (y-1)^2 = 4$$

This is a quadratic, so we'll have two answers.

Take the root to get rid of the square. 4 has two roots, +2 & -2.

$$\sqrt{(y-1)^2} = \sqrt{4}$$

$$y - 1 = 2$$

$$y - 1 = -2$$

$$\begin{array}{cc} y-1=2 & y-1=-2 \\ y=3 & \text{and} \quad y=-1 \end{array}$$

Our *y*-intercepts are (0,-1) & (0,3)

Answer choice **B** is correct.

<u>What You May Have Done Wrong</u>

    A. You used (0,0) as the center. The center is (0,1).

    C. You have used 4 as the radius, when you should have used 2.

    D. You used 4 as the radius (2 is the radius) *and* you had the wrong center.

    E. You squared 4 to get a radius of 16. You should have taken the square root of 4 to get the radius (2).

2. The responses to a survey about recreational preferences are recorded represented on a circle graph. 15% of respondents preferred hiking, 10% waterskiing, 25% swimming, and 10% mountain biking. The rest of the respondents prefer indoor activities. What is the degree measure of the indoor activities sector?

Correct Answer J

This is an arc question that combines percentages and degrees. We'll find the percentage that prefer indoor degrees and then convert that percentage into degrees.

First let's add our given percentages.
$$15\% + 10\% + 25\% + 10\% = 60\%$$

Subtract from 100% to find what percentage of the circle are the "indoor activities".
$$100\% - 60\% = 40\%$$

So, the answer will be 40% of the entire measure of degrees in a circle (360°).
$$360° \cdot 0.40 = 144°$$

Answer choice **J** is correct.

<u>What You May Have Done Wrong</u>
   F. That is the percentage, not the degree measure, of the circle.
   G. You may have made an addition error when adding your percentages.
   H. This is the degree measure for 60% (the outdoor activities).
   K. Check your steps, this is a compound error.

3. The two shaded circles are tangent at the center of the larger circle. The radius of both smaller circles is 2. What is the approximate area of the un-shaded area?

Correct Answer E

This problem looks trickier than it is. We don't have a formula to find the area of those odd shapes left un-shaded. But, what we can do is find the area of the large, un-shaded circle and subtract from it the area of both of the smaller, shaded circles.

<u>Area of Large Circle</u>

$A = \pi r^2$

$A = \pi(4)^2$

$A = \pi 16$

$A = \pi(4)^2$

$A = 50.24$

<u>Area Small Circles</u>

$A = \pi r^2$

$A = \pi(2)^2$

$A = \pi 4$

$A = \pi 4$

$A = 12.56$

Unshaded Area = Large Circle - Small Circles

Unshaded Area = 50.24 - 25.12

Unshaded Area = 25.12

The radius of the large circle is the diameter of the smaller circles.

Answer choice **E** is correct

<u>What You May Have Done Wrong</u>
   A. This is the area of the large circle, a halfway answer.
   B. You only subtracted one small circle, not both.
   C. Review your steps. This is a compound error.
   D. Review your steps. This is a compound error.

4. An ingenious way to cut grass is to tie a goat to a post. The goat will eat down all the grass that it can reach. If the goat is on a 9-yard rope, approximately how large an area can it clear?

Correct Answer K

This is a *circle area* question. The rope allows the goat to move anywhere within a circle with a nine yard radius. The rope is the radius. A diagram isn't provided so draw it.

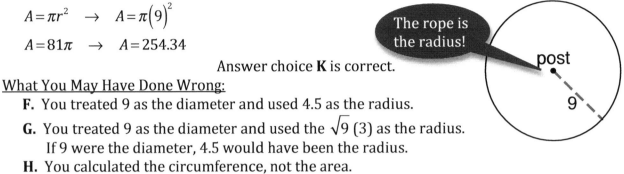

$$A = \pi r^2 \quad \rightarrow \quad A = \pi (9)^2$$

$$A = 81\pi \quad \rightarrow \quad A = 254.34$$

Answer choice **K** is correct.

<u>What You May Have Done Wrong:</u>
- **F.** You treated 9 as the diameter and used 4.5 as the radius.
- **G.** You treated 9 as the diameter and used the $\sqrt{9}$ (3) as the radius. If 9 were the diameter, 4.5 would have been the radius.
- **H.** You calculated the circumference, not the area.
- **J.** You squared the radius but forgot to multiply it by pi.

5. A triathlon consists of a 112 mile bike ride, a marathon (26.2 mile run) and a 2.4 mile swim. The route planned by the triathlon's organizers is perfectly circular, with the start line also being the finish line. If you were to cut straight through the track, crossing the center, how far would you travel?

Correct Answer D

This is a circumference problem, and the sum of the events is the circumference. From there, it works backwards. We'll have to find the diameter from the circumference.

Run + Swim + Bike = Circumference
26.2 + 2.4 + 112 = 140.6

We can work backwards to find the diameter.

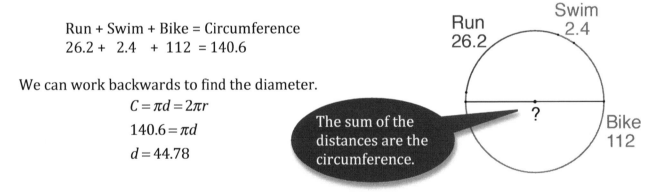

$$C = \pi d = 2\pi r$$

$$140.6 = \pi d$$

$$d = 44.78$$

Answer choice **D** is correct.

<u>What You May Have Done Wrong</u>
- **A.** You found the radius, not the diameter.
- **B.** You used 112 as the circumference.
- **C.** This is a halfway answer, the circumference. (You also may have misunderstood the question).
- **E.** This is a compound error. Review your steps.

6. A circle is tangent to the x-axis at -4 and tangent to the y-axis at 4. What is the equation of that circle?

Correct Answer G

Let's sketch our circle. To find the center, use the tangent points. A line that's perpendicular to each axis will cross through the center. We can draw up from $x = -4$, and over (left) from $y = 4$. The lines meet at (-4, 4)—the center of the circle.

We can plug that information into the general equation.

$r = 4$

$(h,k) = (-4,4)$

$$\left(x-h\right)^2 + \left(y-k\right)^2 = r^2 \quad \rightarrow \quad \left(x+4\right)^2 + \left(y-4\right)^2 = 4^2$$

$$\left(x+4\right)^2 + \left(y-4\right)^2 = 4^2$$

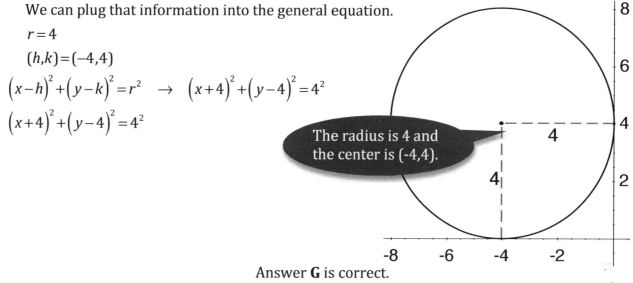

The radius is 4 and the center is (-4,4).

Answer **G** is correct.

<u>What You May Have Done Wrong</u>

 F. You misconstrued the radius as 2, and consequently your center as (-2,2)

 H. You reversed your center x,y coordinates using (4,-4) instead of (-4,4)

 J. You failed to square your radius.

 K. You have your center point as (4,4) instead of (-4,4).

7. Two circles have radii of 5 and 11 inches, respectively. What is the ratio of their respective areas?

Correct Answer A

This is a relatively straightforward problem. We'll need to find the areas of both circles, and compare them in a ratio. Although the sketch doesn't really do much for us, it's a good habit to *always sketch*.

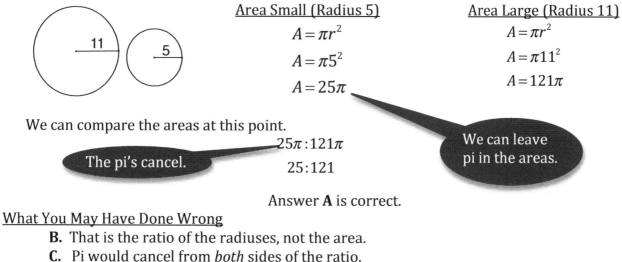

<u>Area Small (Radius 5)</u>	<u>Area Large (Radius 11)</u>
$A = \pi r^2$	$A = \pi r^2$
$A = \pi 5^2$	$A = \pi 11^2$
$A = 25\pi$	$A = 121\pi$

We can leave pi in the areas.

We can compare the areas at this point.

The pi's cancel.

$$25\pi : 121\pi$$

$$25 : 121$$

Answer **A** is correct.

<u>What You May Have Done Wrong</u>

 B. That is the ratio of the radiuses, not the area.

 C. Pi would cancel from *both* sides of the ratio.

 D. That is the ratio of the circumferences.

 E. Pi would cancel from *both* sides of the ratio.

8. In the circle below A is the center and *CB* is a diameter. Which of the following is the largest arc or angle?

Correct Answer K

The word "which" indicates that we will have to evaluate each answer choice. Let's mark up our diagram as we go to evaluate answer choices.

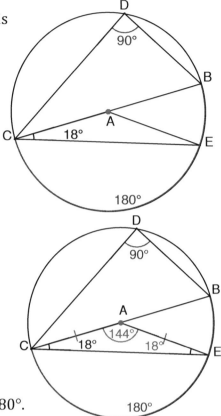

Answer **F** (∠*CDB*) makes a semi-circle arc, 180°. Since the arc is 180°, the inscribed angle is half of that arc, 90°.

Answer **G** is greater than 90° and less than 180° because *CB* is 180°.

Answer **H** this is the arc described by the angle in **G**. It will be between 90° and 180°. We can calculate the measure of the angle, but we won't need to. That calculation is shown on the second diagram.

A is the center, meaning that $\overline{CA}$ and $\overline{AE}$ are both radii and are the same length. That means ∠*ACE* and ∠*AEC* are equal (18°). 180° - 18° - 18° = 144°

Answer **J** is the minor arc described by the angle *DBC*. Just eyeballing the arc, we can see that it's more than 90° and less than 180°.

Answer **K** is a semicircle arc, because *CB* is a diameter and is 180°.

F. ∠*CDB* = 90°   J. ⌒*CD* = <180°

G. ∠*CAE* = 144°   **K.** ⌒*CEB* = 180°

H. ⌒*CE* = 144°

Answer **K** is correct.

9. *A* is the center of the circle below. What is the measure of minor arc $\overset{\frown}{DB}$ created by ∠CBD?

Correct Answer C

This is an *inscribed angle* question, and you've got to remember that **inscribed angles make an arc double the measure of the angle.**

The minor arc *CD* is 64°. Since *CB* is a diameter it splits the circle into two semicircles and the arc *CB* is 180°.

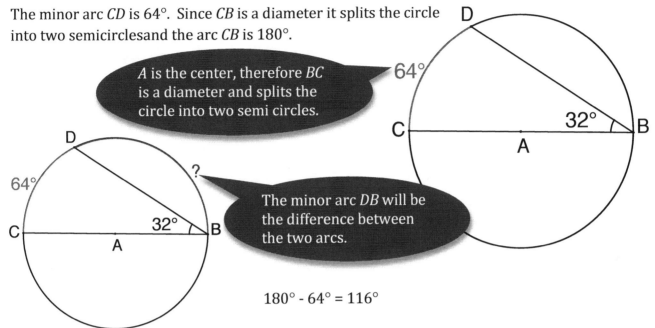

180° - 64° = 116°

Answer **C** is correct.

What You May Have Done Wrong

    A. This would be the measure of the arc created by angle *CBD* if *CBD* had a vertex at the center of the circle.

    B. This is the arc created by the angle *CBD* (arc *CD*). We aren't asked about that angle.

    D. You may have made a guess here, or some sort of compound error. Review your steps.

    E. This is most likely an arithmetic error.

10. What is the arc length of minor arc $\overset{\frown}{BC}$, if A is the center of the circle below?

Correct Answer G

Whenever we have two points on a circle the points create two different arcs, a **major arc** (greater than 180°)and a **minor arc** (less than 180°).

So, we're looking for the arc created by the 70°. Let's find the circumference and the portion of the circle that 70° represents.

arc length = circumference • portion

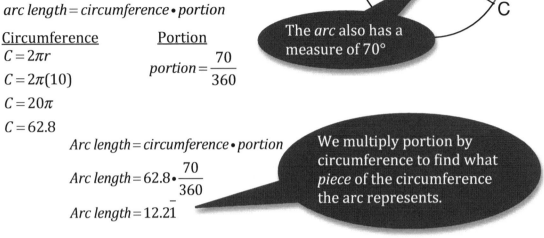

<u>Circumference</u>
$$C = 2\pi r$$
$$C = 2\pi(10)$$
$$C = 20\pi$$
$$C = 62.8$$

<u>Portion</u>
$$portion = \frac{70}{360}$$

The *arc* also has a measure of 70°

Arc length = circumference • portion
$$Arc\ length = 62.8 \bullet \frac{70}{360}$$
$$Arc\ length = 12.\overline{21}$$

We multiply portion by circumference to find what *piece* of the circumference the arc represents.

Answer G is correct.

<u>What You May Have Done Wrong</u>
- **F.** This is most likely a calculation error. Check your steps.
- **H.** This is a rounding error. Round up for 5 and over, down for under 5.
- **J.** You may have made a calculation error.
- **K.** You forgot to double the radius when finding circumference.

11. What is the approximate area of the sector created by ∠BAC?

Correct Answer E

There's not much for us to mark up on our figure. The key is to find the area of the entire circle and what portion is 45° of a circle.

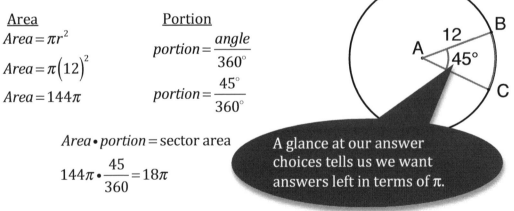

<u>Area</u>
$$Area = \pi r^2$$
$$Area = \pi(12)^2$$
$$Area = 144\pi$$

<u>Portion</u>
$$portion = \frac{angle}{360°}$$
$$portion = \frac{45°}{360°}$$

Area • portion = sector area
$$144\pi \bullet \frac{45}{360} = 18\pi$$

A glance at our answer choices tells us we want answers left in terms of π.

Answer E is correct.

<u>What You May Have Done Wrong</u>
- **A.** This is the halfway answer. You found the area of the *entire* circle.
- **B.** This is the area of ¼th of the circle.
- **C.** This is the area of ½ the circle.
- **D.** You found the arc length, not the sector area.

12. What is the area of the target worth two points?

Correct Answer C

We don't have a formula for finding the area of a ring, but there's a workaround.

The first step is to markup our figure with the radii of each concentric circle (we just add 3 to each).

Now, let's consider the 2-point ring. We can say that the two inch ring is the outside piece of a circle with a radius of 9. To find just the piece we want, subtract the circle that is not part of the ten ring, the 3 and 4-point areas.

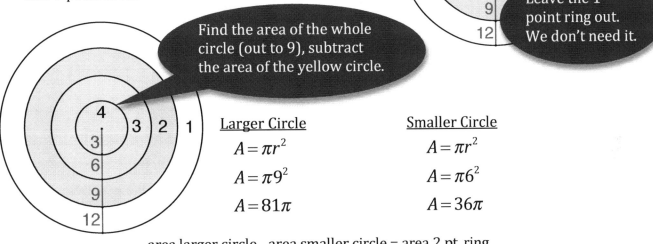

Find the area of the whole circle (out to 9), subtract the area of the yellow circle.

Leave the 1-point ring out. We don't need it.

Larger Circle	Smaller Circle
$A = \pi r^2$	$A = \pi r^2$
$A = \pi 9^2$	$A = \pi 6^2$
$A = 81\pi$	$A = 36\pi$

area larger circle - area smaller circle = area 2 pt. ring

$$81\pi - 36\pi = 45\pi$$

Answer **C** is correct.

What You May Have Done Wrong

- **A.** You may have used the circumferences.
- **B.** You used the point values for the radii instead of the measures.
- **D.** You included the 1-point ring in your calculation.
- **E.** That is the area of the *entire* target.

13. Darts can only be counted as having hit one ring. If a dart can be assumed to hit the target, what is the percent likelihood that it scores two or less?

Again, we're interested in area. The likelihood of scoring a particular score will be the area of that or those segments over the area of the whole.

Let's calculate the area of the *entire* target and the area of the portion we don't want the 3 and 4-point regions.

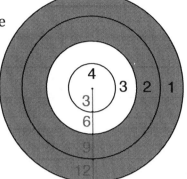

<u>Whole Target Area</u>

$$Area = \pi r^2$$

$$Area = \pi (12)^2$$

$$Area = 144\pi$$

<u>3 & 4 Point Region</u>

$$Area = \pi r^2$$

$$Area = \pi (6)^2$$

$$Area = 36\pi$$

$$probability = \frac{desired\ outcome}{all\ outcomes}$$

$$probability = \frac{36\pi}{144\pi} \rightarrow \frac{1}{4}$$

Answer **F** is correct.

<u>What You May Have Done Wrong</u>

    G. You found the likelihood of scoring greater than one.
    H. You found the likelihood of scoring one.
    J. You included the 1-point ring in your calculation.
    K. You made a calculation error or guessed.

14. The circle below has a center of A. $\overline{EB}$ and $\overline{FD}$ are diameters, $\overparen{BC}$ and $\overparen{CD}$ are congruent. What is the measure of minor arc $\overparen{ED}$?

Correct Answer D

This is a question that requires you to be comfortable with angles, arcs and the relationship between the two.

Because we know that arcs *BC* and *CD* are congruent, and that both arcs are made by central angles, we know angle *BAC* & angle *CAB* both equal 40°.

We also know that line segments *EB* and *FD* are diameters. That's important because they intersect at center *A*. **At the center, *EB* & *FD* create two pairs of vertical angles.**

These are equal arcs.

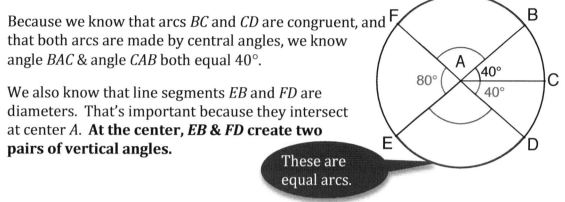

This means that angle *FAE* is equal to the sum of angles *BAC* and *CAD*. It also means that angles *FAB* and *EAD* are equal. So, we can subtract our known angles from the total degrees in a circle.

$$360° - 80° - 80° = 200°$$

That 200° is split equally among angles *FAB* and *EAD*.

$$\frac{200}{2} = 100°$$

Each angle, $\angle EAD$ and $\angle FAB$ equals 100°. These are both central angles, so their arcs will equal the angles.

$$\overparen{ED} = 100°$$

Answer **D** is correct.

<u>What You May Have Done Wrong</u>

    A. You calculated the wrong arc.

    B. You used 40° as the *entire* angle size for *BAD* and *FAE* (they are 80°).

    C. You either forgot to divide by 2 (giving the combined arc values) or you multiplied by 2 (which you *only* do with *inscribed angles*).

    E. You made a calculation error or you guessed.

Combo Shapes: Circles

Combo shapes involving circles are a common way to test your knowledge of circles, triangles, rectangles, and squares. Questions that would be relatively straightforward with a single shape *seem* much more complex when multiple shapes are in the diagram.

What You Need to Know

- ✓ A line perpendicular to a chord that passes through the center bisects the chord.
- ✓ A rectangle inscribed in a circle will have a diagonal that's the diameter of the circle.
- ✓ The *Pythagorean Theorem*, the area formulas for circles, triangles and rectangles, the definition of isosceles triangles

Definitions: Chords

Chords are line segments and both **ends lie on the circle.**
Diameters are the longest possible chords.

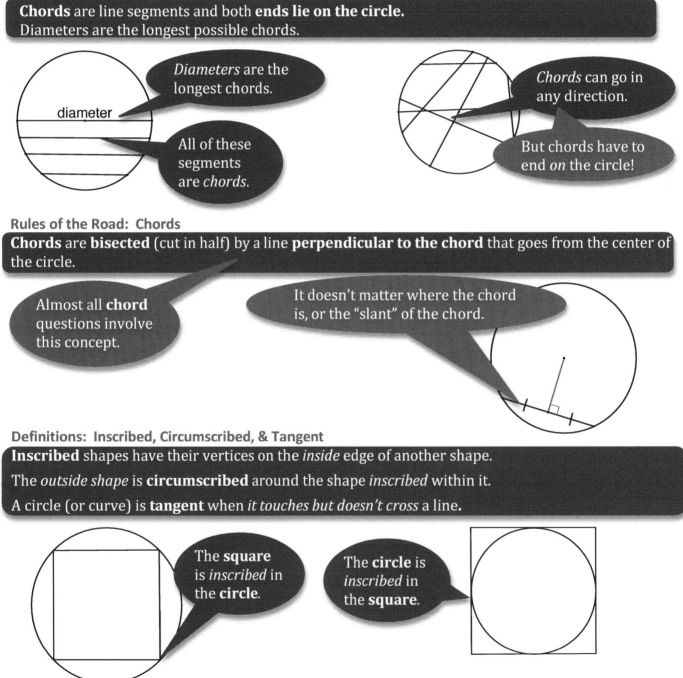

Rules of the Road: Chords

Chords are **bisected** (cut in half) by a line **perpendicular to the chord** that goes from the center of the circle.

Definitions: Inscribed, Circumscribed, & Tangent

Inscribed shapes have their vertices on the *inside* edge of another shape.

The *outside shape* is **circumscribed** around the shape *inscribed* within it.

A circle (or curve) is **tangent** when *it touches but doesn't cross* a line.

Triangles & Circles

This is the most common combo shape setup, and they tend require either the *Pythagorean Theorem* or the definition of *isosceles triangles*.

ACT Examples: Triangles & Circles

1. Points *B* and *C* lie on the circle below, where *A* is the center. What is the measure of angle *x*?

A. 100°
B. 80°
C. 50°
D. 30°
E. 40°

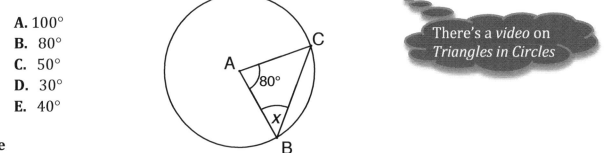

Solve

This is a definition question. Since *A* is the center of the circle, and *C* and *B* are both on the edge, we've got two radiuses.

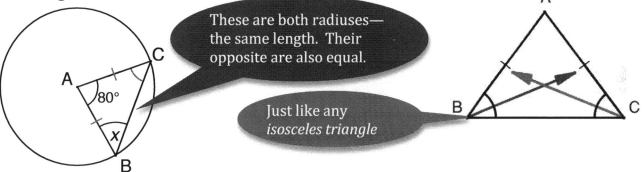

These are both radiuses— the same length. Their opposite are also equal.

Just like any *isosceles triangle*

The triangle, like all triangles, has interior angles that add to 180°. We know one angle is 80°; therefore our other two angles share 100°.

$$180° - 80° = 100°$$

$$\text{angle } x = \frac{100°}{2} = 50°$$

The angles split the remaining 100° equally.

Answer Choice **C** is correct.

2. Point *A* is the center of the circle and the chord *CB* is 3 cm above the center. $\overline{AB}$ is a radius, what is the length of chord $\overline{CB}$?

A. 4
B. 8
C. 10
D. 6
E. 12

Solve

We've got a point measured from a line. The shortest distance from any point to a line is a *perpendicular line*. A line that's perpendicular to a chord and hits the center of the circle *bisects the chord*.

We've got a right triangle, and remember the chord is split into halves.

> A point measured from a line makes a perpendicular line.

We have a right triangle with two sides, so use the Pythagorean Theorem.

$$a^2 + b^2 = c^2 \quad \rightarrow \quad 3^2 + b^2 = 5^2$$
$$9 + b^2 = 25 \quad \rightarrow \quad b^2 = 16$$
$$b = 4$$

> This is a 3, 4, 5 *special right triangle*

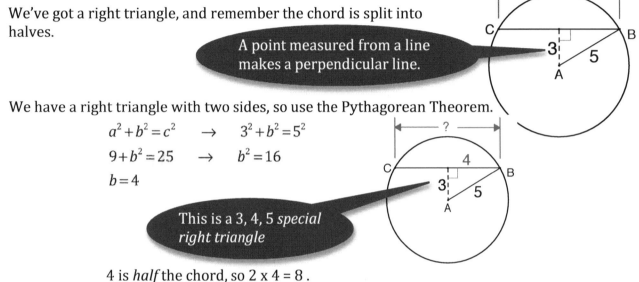

4 is *half* the chord, so 2 x 4 = 8.

Answer choice **B** is correct.

Squares/Rectangles & Circles

Squares and circles are tested in a few different ways: area, circumference, and/or perimeter. In these questions, you're tasked with understanding the relationship between radius and side length. You'll need to use *right triangles* & the *Pythagorean Theorem*.

Squares/Rectangles: Rules of the Road

> All **squares & rectangles inscribed in circles** have *diagonals* that are the **diameter of the circle.**

The 90° angle sits on the circle (it is inscribed). All inscribed angles create an arc that is double their measure.

A 90° angle will make a 180° arc, also known as a *semicircle*, half of a circle. Circles are split in half *only* through the center, only by diameters. **The hypotenuse of the right triangles created will be the diameter.**

> Review inscribed angles and arcs in *Plane Geo: Circles*

> Inscribed angles have an arc double their measure.

Squares/Rectangles & Circles

1. The square below has a side length of 4 and is inscribed into the circle, as shown. What is the area of the circle?

    A. 4π

    B. 16π

    C. 8π

    D. 32π

    E. 64π

Solve

First, we've got to find the radius of the circle. The diameter of the circle is also a diagonal of the square. That diagonal/diameter is the hypotenuse of the right triangles the diagonal makes.

Let's calculate the length of the hypotenuse.

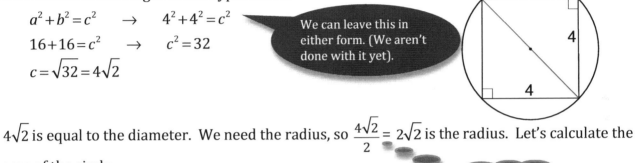

$$a^2 + b^2 = c^2 \quad \rightarrow \quad 4^2 + 4^2 = c^2$$

$$16 + 16 = c^2 \quad \rightarrow \quad c^2 = 32$$

$$c = \sqrt{32} = 4\sqrt{2}$$

> We can leave this in either form. (We aren't done with it yet).

$4\sqrt{2}$ is equal to the diameter. We need the radius, so $\dfrac{4\sqrt{2}}{2} = 2\sqrt{2}$ is the radius. Let's calculate the area of the circle.

> There's a *video* on *Circles in Squares*

$$A = \pi r^2 \quad \rightarrow \quad A = \pi\left(2\sqrt{2}\right)^2$$

$$A = \pi\left(4 \cdot 2\right) \quad \rightarrow \quad A = 8\pi$$

Answer choice **C** is correct.

Combo Shapes: Squares & Squares

Like circle combo questions square combo questions involve right triangles and the use of the *Pythagorean Theorem.*

ACT Examples: Squares & Squares

1. Square *ABCD* has an area of 16. Points *E*, *F*, *G*, *H* are the midpoints of their respective sides and *EGFH* is a square. What is the area of *EFGH*?

    A. 16
    B.   4
    C.   8
    D. 12
    E.   9

There's a video on Squares in Squares

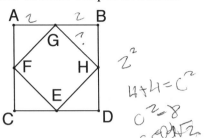

Solve

Let's markup our figure. Because we knew that the larger square has an area of 16, we can calculate the side length.

$$A = Side^2 \quad \rightarrow \quad 16 = Side^2$$
$$\sqrt{16} = Side \quad \rightarrow \quad Side = 4$$

The hypotenuse of our right triangle is equal to the sides of the square *EFGH.*

$$a^2 + b^2 = c^2 \quad \rightarrow \quad 2^2 + 2^2 = c^2$$
$$c^2 = 8 \quad \rightarrow \quad c = \sqrt{8} = 2\sqrt{2}$$

Plug in the side to find the area.

$$A = Side^2 \quad \rightarrow \quad A = \left(\sqrt{8}\right)^2 \quad \rightarrow \quad A = 8$$

Answer choice **C** is correct.

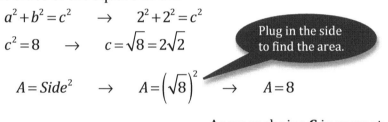

All of these sides are equal to each other, ½ the side.

Wrap Up

What You Need to Know
  ✓ A line perpendicular to a chord that passes through the center bisects the chord.
  ✓ A rectangle inscribed in a circle will have a diagonal that's the diameter of the circle.
  ✓ The *Pythagorean Theorem*, the area formulas for circles, triangles and rectangles, the definition of isosceles triangles.

Videos

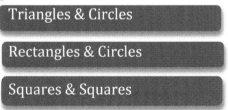

Triangles & Circles

Rectangles & Circles

Squares & Squares

The Strategies
  ✓ Look for *right triangles.* You'll use them on most of these problems, and be ready to pull out the *Pythagorean Theorem.*
  ✓ Don't be intimidated; look for shapes you know and a solid first step.

Related Skills
  ✓ Triangles
  ✓ Right Triangles
  ✓ Circles
  ✓ Squares/Rectangles

Combo Shapes: Problems

1. A circle is tangent to all sides of a square, as shown below. The radius of the square is marked in feet. What is the area of the square?

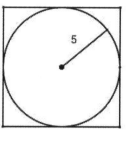

    A.   50
    B. 100
    C. 120
    D. 200
    E.   80

2. The rectangle below is inscribed in the circle. What is the approximate area of the circle?

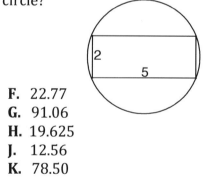

    F. 22.77
    G. 91.06
    H. 19.625
    J. 12.56
    K. 78.50

3. The graph below is in the standard x, y coordinate axis. What is the equation of the circle inscribed in the square?

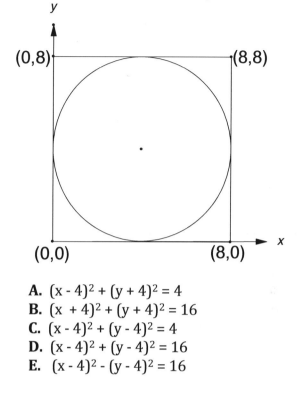

    A. $(x - 4)^2 + (y + 4)^2 = 4$
    B. $(x + 4)^2 + (y + 4)^2 = 16$
    C. $(x - 4)^2 + (y - 4)^2 = 4$
    D. $(x - 4)^2 + (y - 4)^2 = 16$
    E. $(x - 4)^2 - (y - 4)^2 = 16$

4. Figure *ABCD* below is a square with side lengths of 8 feet. Inscribed within *ABCD* is a figure whose vertices bisect the sides of *ABCD*. The figure has angles as marked. What is the area of that figure?

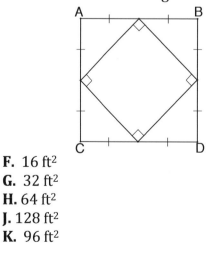

    F. 16 ft^2
    G. 32 ft^2
    H. 64 ft^2
    J. 128 ft^2
    K. 96 ft^2

5. *A* is the center of the circle below; *B* and *C* are points on that circle. What is the measure of ∠*CAB*?

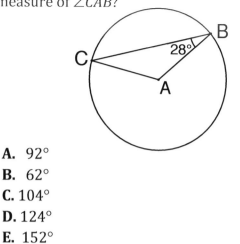

   A. 92°
   B. 62°
   C. 104°
   D. 124°
   E. 152°

6. In the diagram below, *A* is the center of a circle. The radius of the circle is 5. What is the length of the distance from the center of the circle to the chord?

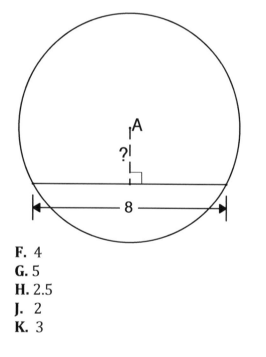

   F. 4
   G. 5
   H. 2.5
   J. 2
   K. 3

7. The figure below consists two squares; the shaded square is inscribed in square *IJKL*. The vertices of the inscribed square bisect the sides of *IJKL* and square *IJKL* has sides with the length in meters as marked. What is the area of the unshaded portion of the diagram?

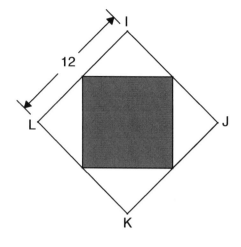

   A. 36 m²
   B. 72 m²
   C. 144 m²
   D. 108 m²
   E. 216 m²

8. The circle below has a center of *O*, with diameters of $\overline{DC}$ and $\overline{FE}$. Angle *OCE* is as marked. What is the measure of minor arc *FC*?

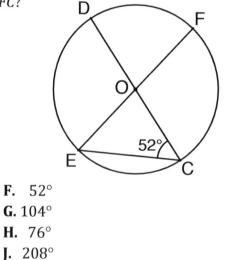

   F. 52°
   G. 104°
   H. 76°
   J. 208°
   K. 100°

Combo Shapes: Solutions

1. A circle is tangent to all sides of a square, as shown below. The radius of the square is marked in feet. What is the area of the square?

Correct Answer B

This is a circle inscribed in a square. Let's mark up our figure.

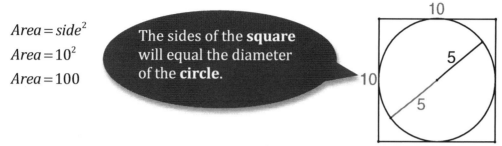

$Area = side^2$

$Area = 10^2$

$Area = 100$

The sides of the **square** will equal the diameter of the **circle**.

Answer choice **B** is correct.

<u>What You May Have Done Wrong</u>
- **A.** You may have misconstrued this as a rectangle with sides of 5 and 10.
- **C.** This is a compound error, check your steps.
- **D.** You probably got a big over eager here. Look through your steps.
- **E.** This is a compound error, check your steps.

2. The rectangle below is inscribed in the circle. What is the approximate area of the circle?

Correct Answer F

Whenever a rectangle (or square) is inscribed in a circle the arcs created by the angles are semicircles (180°). Semicircles are exactly ½ of the circle, and the line that creates a semicircle is a *diameter*.

The *diameter* is the *hypotenuse* of two right triangles. We can find the length by using the Pythagorean Theorem.

$a^2 + b^2 = c^2$ → $2^2 + 5^2 = c^2$

$c^2 = 29$ → $c = \sqrt{29}$

The length of the **diameter**

We need the length of the radius to find the area of the circle.

$radius = \dfrac{diameter}{2} = \dfrac{\sqrt{29}}{2}$

$Area = \pi r^2$ → $Area = \pi\left(\dfrac{\sqrt{29}}{2}\right)^2$ → $Area = 7.25\pi \approx 22.765$

This **hypotenuse** is a **diameter** of the circle.

Answer choice **F** is correct.

<u>What You May Have Done Wrong</u>
- **G.** You used $\sqrt{29}$ as the radius; it's the diameter.
- **H.** You used 5 as the diameter and 2.5 as the radius.
- **J.** You used 2 as the radius.
- **K.** You used 5 as the radius. Look at the steps.

3. What is the equation of the circle inscribed in the square?

Correct Answer D

This is a circle formula problem. Mark up the diagram; it will give us the information we need: the center, and the radius.

The center of the circle will be the center of the square. We can find the center of the circle by using the lengths of the sides. The center is (4,4) and the radius is 4.

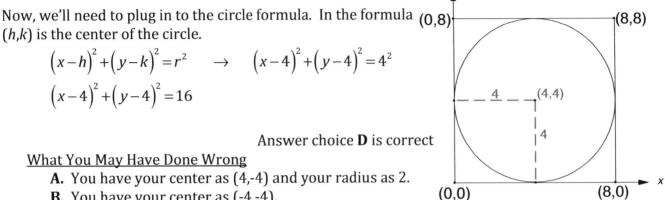

Now, we'll need to plug in to the circle formula. In the formula (h,k) is the center of the circle.

$$(x-h)^2+(y-k)^2=r^2 \quad \rightarrow \quad (x-4)^2+(y-4)^2=4^2$$

$$(x-4)^2+(y-4)^2=16$$

Answer choice **D** is correct

<u>What You May Have Done Wrong</u>
- **A.** You have your center as (4,-4) and your radius as 2.
- **B.** You have your center as (-4,-4).
- **C.** You have your radius as 2.
- **E.** This is picky, but in between your parentheses there is a *subtraction sign* (-) there needs to be an *addition sign* (+).

---

4. Figure *ABCD* is a square with side lengths of 8. Inscribed within *ABCD* is a figure whose vertices bisect the sides of *ABCD*. The figure has angles as marked. What is the area of that figure?

Correct Answer G

This problem has a lot of confusing, intimidating wording. Let's look at the figure, and mark up the diagram.

These are 45°- 45°- 90° triangles, so each side of the square equals $4\sqrt{2}$. But if you didn't recognize that you could always use the Pythagorean Theorem

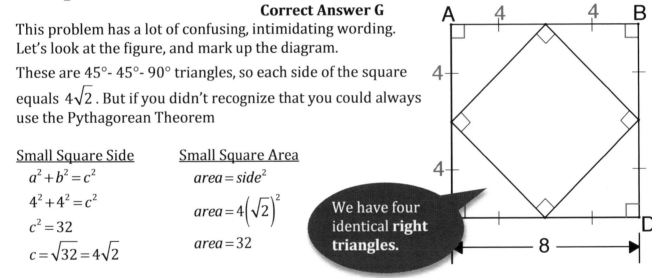

<u>Small Square Side</u>
$$a^2+b^2=c^2$$
$$4^2+4^2=c^2$$
$$c^2=32$$
$$c=\sqrt{32}=4\sqrt{2}$$

<u>Small Square Area</u>
$$area=side^2$$
$$area=4\left(\sqrt{2}\right)^2$$
$$area=32$$

We have four identical **right triangles.**

Answer choice **G** is correct.

<u>What You May Have Done Wrong:</u>
- **F.** You treated 4 as the side length of the inscribed square.
- **H.** You treated 8 as the side length of the inscribed square.
- **J.** This is a compound error review your steps.
- **K.** This is a compound error review your steps.

5. *A* is the center of the circle below; *B* and *C* are points on that circle. What is the measure of ∠*CAB*?

Correct Answer D

This is a triangle and circle questions, let's markup the diagram. Because *B* and *C* are on the circle and *A* is the center, $\overline{AC}$ and $\overline{AB}$ are both radii—which means they are the same length.

It also means that $\triangle ABC$ is an *isosceles triangle* and angles *CBA* and *ACB* are equal both 28°.

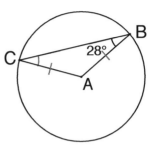

Angle *CAB* will be $180° - 28° - 28° = 124°$

Answer **D** is correct.

<u>What You May Have Done Wrong</u>
- **A.** This is a compound error. Review your steps.
- **B.** You subtracted 28° from 90°.
- **C.** You made an arithmetic error.
- **E.** You only subtracted a single 28° angle.

6. In the diagram below, A is the center of a circle. The radius of the circle is 5. What is the length of the distance from the center of the circle to the chord?

Correct Answer K

This is a circle triangle combo but that may not be easy to see. Our missing side, the hypotenuse of the triangle, is a radius—it goes from the center to the edge of the circle.

We know the hypotenuse is 5.

Any line that passes through the center of a circle and is perpendicular to a chord bisects the chord. *Basically, a line from the center* of a circle *to a chord splits the chord in half.*

The base of the triangle made by the chord will be ½ the length of the chord. We know that because we can solve by using the Pythagorean Theorem.

$$a^2 + b^2 = c^2 \quad \rightarrow \quad 4^2 + b^2 = 5^2$$
$$16 + b^2 = 25 \quad \rightarrow \quad b^2 = 9$$
$$b = 3$$

Answer **K** is correct.

<u>What You May Have Done Wrong</u>
- **F.** This is the chord cut in half. You may have misunderstood the question.
- **G.** This is the hypotenuse, or the radius of the circle.
- **H.** You may have just cut the hypotenuse in half, not a terrible guess, review the steps.
- **J.** You may have eyeballed—or guessed in some other fashion—review the steps

7. The figure below consists two squares; the shaded square is inscribed in square *IJKL*. The vertices of the inscribed square bisect the sides of *IJKL* and square *IJKL* has sides with the length in meters as marked. What is the area of the unshaded portion of the diagram?

Correct Answer B

This is a more complicated example of a square/square combo problem. But the mechanics are the same.

The un-shaded area is four equivalent right triangles. We can find the area of the triangles or we can find the area of the large square and subtract the area of the shaded square. Let's look at both ways:

Large Square Area – Shaded Square Area

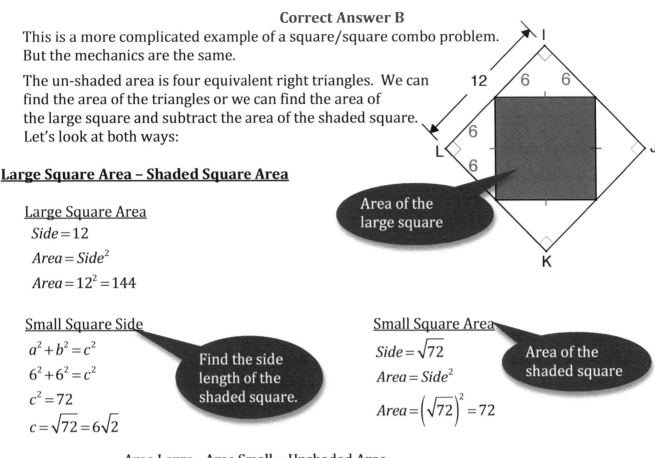

Large Square Area

$Side = 12$

$Area = Side^2$

$Area = 12^2 = 144$

Small Square Side

$a^2 + b^2 = c^2$

$6^2 + 6^2 = c^2$

$c^2 = 72$

$c = \sqrt{72} = 6\sqrt{2}$

Find the side length of the shaded square.

Small Square Area

$Side = \sqrt{72}$

$Area = Side^2$

$Area = \left(\sqrt{72}\right)^2 = 72$

Area of the shaded square

Area Large - Area Small = Unshaded Area

144 - 72 = 72

Triangle Area

Since we know that we have 4 identical right triangles, we can find the area of one and multiply it by 4 to get the un-shaded area.

$area = \frac{1}{2}\left(base \bullet height\right)$

$area = \frac{1}{2}\left(6 \bullet 6\right) = 18$

Unshaded Area = 4 • 18 = 72

Base & height are interchangeable.

*Base and height are **always** perpendicular to each other.*

The 4 right triangles are identical.

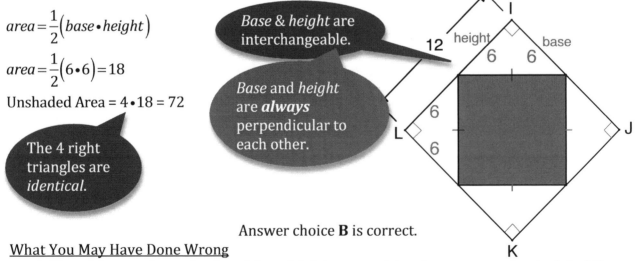

Answer choice **B** is correct.

What You May Have Done Wrong

A. You either made a mistake with multiplying your triangles, or you miscalculated the area of the shaded square. Review your steps.

C. You only calculated the area of the large square, a halfway answer.

D. You probably miscalculated the area of the shaded square as 36.

E. You added the areas. Review your steps.

8. The circle below has a center of O, with diameters of $\overline{DC}$ and $\overline{FE}$. Angle *OCE* is as marked. What is the measure of minor arc *FC*?

Correct Answer G

This is a circle triangle combo that requires knowledge of arcs. Mark up our figure. We've got an isosceles triangle. Our top angle, angle *O* will equal
$$180° - 52° - 52° = 76°$$

Our top angle will be opposite (vertical) angles with the top $\angle 76°$ angle.

$\overline{DC}$ is a diameter, and the arcs it creates are both semicircles (180° arcs). We can say that arc *DFC* is equal to 180°. Arc *DF* will equal the measure of its angle (because the angle has a vertex at the middle) so arc *DF* = 76°. The remaining part of the semicircle is the arc we are looking for $\overset{\frown}{FC}$.

$$\text{Semicircle} - \overset{\frown}{FD} = \overset{\frown}{FC}$$
$$180° - 76° = 104°$$

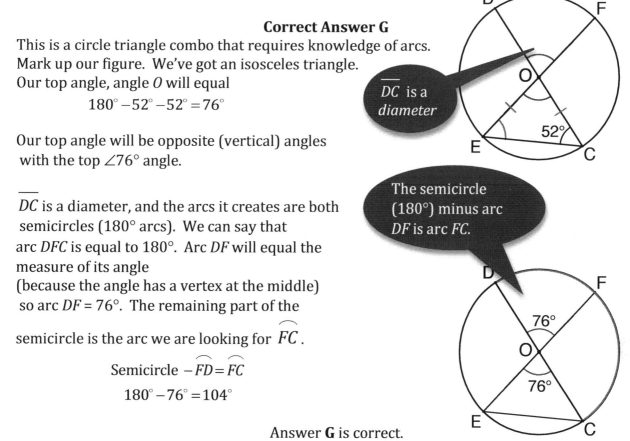

Answer **G** is correct.

<u>What You May Have Done Wrong</u>

    F. This is the measure of either bottom angle in the triangle.

    H. That's the measure of the top pair of vertical angles.

    J. That's double the measure of the arcs. You may have just taken the circle and subtracted 2 x 76°.

    K. You subtracted all of the angles you had found from 360°.

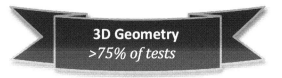

Introduction

3D Geometry is not a large topic, but it shows up fairly commonly. There's not a lot to learn. There are two big topics in 3D geometry: volume and surface area.

What You Need to Know

- ✓ How to find the volume of a *right cylinder* & a *rectangular prism*.
- ✓ How to find the surface area of a *rectangular prism*.
- ✓ How to find the surface area of a *right cylinder* including finding the *lateral surface area*.

Definitions: Volume & Surface Area

Volume is the amount of space (in three dimensions) an object takes up. You can think of the volume as how much water a drinking glass holds. **Volume is always given in units cubed.**

Surface area is the total area all the surfaces of a three dimensional object. You can think of it as how many of square inches of glass are in a drinking glass.

Definitions: Rectangular Prism & Right Cylinder

A **rectangular prism** is a six shided 3D shape where all of the corners are 90°. Six-sided dice, shoeboxes, and bricks are all examples. Cubes are rectangular prisms.

A **right cylinder** is a 3d shape with circular ends that are connected by a perpendicular height. Paper-towel rolls and coin rolls are examples.

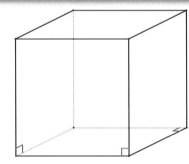

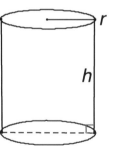

The ACT focuses on these two shapes

Rules of the Road: Volume

For **rectangular prisms** and **right cylinders** we find the area of one of the ends (top or bottom) and multiply by the height.

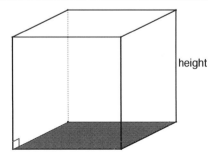

Volume = area • height

Volume = length • width • height

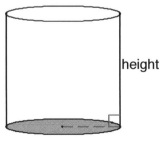

Volume = area • height

Volume = πr^2 • height

1. The figure below is a water tanks that is a rectangular prism. It has dimensions marked in feet. If the tank is 90% full, how many cubic feet of water are in the tank?

    A. 640
    B. 576
    C. 711
    D. 590
    E. 560

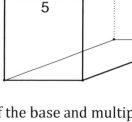

Solve

To find the area of a rectangular prism, find the area of the base and multiply by the height.

$$Volume = area \cdot height$$
$$Volume = length \cdot width \cdot height$$
$$Volume = 5\ feet \cdot 16\ feet \cdot 8\ feet = 640\ feet^3$$

Now, we have to multiply by 90% to find the amount of cubic water.

$$\left(640\ feet^3\right)\left(0.90\right) = 576\ feet^3$$

Answer Choice **B** is correct.

2. A salt canister is a right cylinder with a diameter of four inches and a height of seven inches. What is the volume of the cylinder?

    A. 28π
    B. 56π
    C. 14π
    D. 21π
    E. 25π

There's a *video* on *volume*.

You'll need to know how to find the volume of *right cylinders* & *rectangular prisms*.

Solve

First, sketch the figure.

To find the area of the circle, we'll need half the diameter (divide the diameter by 2). The diameter is 4 so, the radius is 2.

Now, we plug in to the area formula for a circle and then multiply by height.

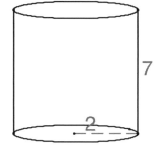

$$Volume = area \cdot height \quad \rightarrow \quad Volume = \pi 2^2 \cdot 7$$
$$Volume = 4\pi \cdot 7 \quad \rightarrow \quad Volume = 28\pi$$

Answer Choice **A** is correct.

Rules of the Road: Rectangular Prism Surface Area

The **surface area** of a 3d shape the **sum of the areas** of each side.

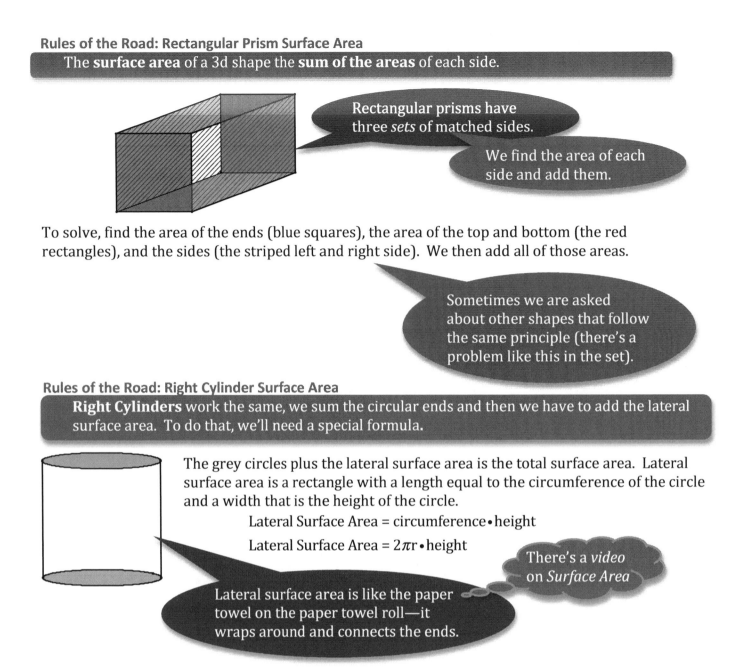

Rectangular prisms have three *sets* of matched sides.

We find the area of each side and add them.

To solve, find the area of the ends (blue squares), the area of the top and bottom (the red rectangles), and the sides (the striped left and right side). We then add all of those areas.

Sometimes we are asked about other shapes that follow the same principle (there's a problem like this in the set).

Rules of the Road: Right Cylinder Surface Area

Right Cylinders work the same, we sum the circular ends and then we have to add the lateral surface area. To do that, we'll need a special formula.

The grey circles plus the lateral surface area is the total surface area. Lateral surface area is a rectangle with a length equal to the circumference of the circle and a width that is the height of the circle.

Lateral Surface Area = circumference•height

Lateral Surface Area = $2\pi r$•height

There's a *video* on *Surface Area*

Lateral surface area is like the paper towel on the paper towel roll—it wraps around and connects the ends.

1. The rectangular prism below has sides in meters as marked, what is its surface area?

- **A.** 144 m^2
- **B.** 214 m^2
- **C.** 288 m^2
- **D.** 196 m^2
- **E.** 272 m^2

Solve

This problem is a bit of a pain, you've got three sets of sides to calculate and keep straight. I would use a formal setup to make sure that I don't either skip or double count a side or sides.

Here's how I'm considering the sides.

The Ends

$$End\ Area = 4 \bullet 6 = 24\ m^2$$

The Left/Right Sides

$$Side\ Area = 12 \bullet 6 = 72\ m^2$$

The Top/Bottom

$$Top\ /\ Bottom\ Area = 4 \bullet 12 = 48\ m^2$$

To make things simpler, I would ignore the unit when adding.

Sum all of the sides.

$$24\ m^2 + 24\ m^2 + 72\ m^2 + 72\ m^2 + 48\ m^2 + 48\ m^2 = 288\ m^2$$

Answer Choice **C** is correct.

2. An oatmeal container is a right cylinder with a height of 14 and a radius of 3. What is its **total** surface area?
(the lateral surface area of a right cylinder is found by the expression $2\pi r \bullet h$).

- **A.** 84π
- **B.** 18π
- **C.** 93π
- **D.** 91π
- **E.** 102π

If right cylinder surface area is on the test, the ACT will give you the formula for lateral surface area.

Solve

Sketch the right cylinder, it's a good habit and will keep you from mixing up your dimensions.

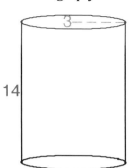

<u>Area of the Top or Bottom</u>

$area = \pi r^2 \quad \rightarrow \quad area = \pi 3^2$

$area = 9\pi \quad \rightarrow \quad area\ top\ \&\ bottom = 9\pi \times 2$

$area\ top\ \&\ bottom = 18\pi$

<u>Lateral Surface Area</u>

Lateral Surface Area = circumference•height

Lateral Surface Area = $2\pi r$•height

Lateral Surface Area = $2\pi(3)$•14

Lateral Surface Area = 6π•14

Lateral Surface Area = 84π

$Surface\ Area = area\ top\ \&\ bottom + lateral\ surface\ area$

$Surface\ Area = 18\pi + 84\pi = 102\pi$

Answer choice **E** is correct.

<u>Wrap Up</u>

What You Need to Know
- ✓ How to find the volume of a *right cylinder* & a *rectangular prism*.
- ✓ How to find the surface area of a *rectangular prism*.
- ✓ How to find the surface area of a *right cylinder* including finding the *lateral surface area*.

Videos

Volume of a Rectangular Prism & Right Cylinder

Surface Area of Prisms & Cylinders

The Strategies
- ✓ It's always area times height.
- ✓ Any shape you're unfamiliar with, like a pyramid, will have a given formula and it'll be a plug-in problem.

Related Skills

3D shapes are related to:

- ✓ Four Sided Shapes, Rectangles & Squares

- ✓ Circles

3D Geometry: Problems

1. A pup tent is shaped like the diagram below with measurements in feet. The pup tent is a right triangular prism but the tent has no floor. How much canvas is necessary to produce the tent?

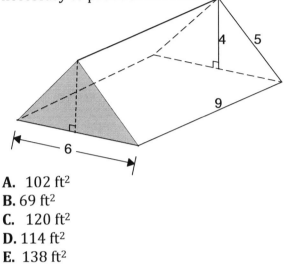

- **A.** 102 ft²
- **B.** 69 ft²
- **C.** 120 ft²
- **D.** 114 ft²
- **E.** 138 ft²

2. A section of open-ended pipe is 24 inches in diameter and three feet long. The ends of the pipe are perpendicular to the sides. What is the approximate volume of this section of pipe?

- **F.** 6.2 feet³
- **G.** 21.1 feet³
- **H.** 18.8 feet³
- **J.** 9.4 feet³
- **K.** 23.5 feet³

3. A rectangular prism has dimensions in inches as marked. What is the surface area of the prism?

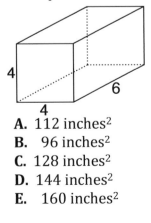

- **A.** 112 inches²
- **B.** 96 inches²
- **C.** 128 inches²
- **D.** 144 inches²
- **E.** 160 inches²

4. The figure below is a right pyramid with a square base. The length of each side of the base is 12 and the slant height is 15. What is the surface area of the pyramid?

Note: *slant height* is the height from the center of a base to the top (the point).

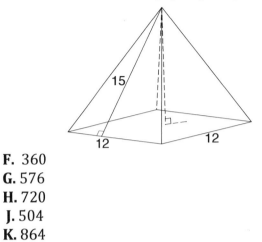

- **F.** 360
- **G.** 576
- **H.** 720
- **J.** 504
- **K.** 864

5. A pool is a rectangular prism with a length of 16 feet, a width if 8 feet and a depth of 10 feet. If 1,000 cubic feet of water are put into the pool, approximately how deep will the water be?

- **A.** 7.8 feet
- **B.** 0.8 feet
- **C.** 6.4 feet
- **D.** 12.5 feet
- **E.** 10.0 feet

6. In the diagram below, a sphere with a radius of 3 is inscribed in a cube so that the sphere is tangent to all six sides of the cube. What is the surface area of the cube?

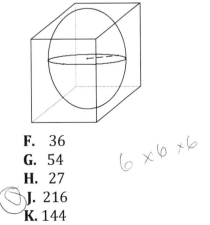

6 x 6 x 6

- **F.** 36
- **G.** 54
- **H.** 27
- **J.** 216
- **K.** 144

3D Geometry: Solutions

1. A pup tent is shaped like the diagram below with measurements in feet. The pup tent is a right triangular prism but the tent has no floor. How much canvas is necessary to produce the tent?

Correct Answer D

This is a *surface area* problem, and while we don't cover right triangular prisms in the material the process is the same. We find the area of each side of the shape (except the bottom in this case). Let's look at our figure. We have two rectangles and two triangles (remember, the bottom is not counted).

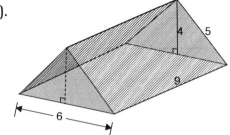

Area Rectangles

$Area = length \cdot width$

$Area = 9 \cdot 5 = 45$

Area Triangles

$Area = \frac{1}{2}(base \cdot height)$

$Area = \frac{1}{2}(6 \cdot 4) = 12$

Tent Surface Area = triangle + triangle + rectangle + rectangle

Tent Surface Area = 12 + 12 + 45 + 45 = 114

Answer choice **D** is correct.

<u>What You May Have Done Wrong</u>
- **A.** You forgot to include *both* triangles
- **B.** You forgot to include *both* rectangles
- **C.** You miscalculated the triangle area.
- **E.** You miscalculated the triangle area.

2. A section of open-ended pipe is 24 inches in diameter and three feet long. The ends of the pipe are perpendicular to the sides. What is the volume of this section of pipe?

Correct Answer J

This is a *right-cylinder volume* questions. We know the pipe is a right cylinder because the pipe is uniform in diameter (the sides are parallel) and the ends are perpendicular to the sides of the pipe. Let's draw a sketch.

We need to convert one of the measurements.
Because **the answer choices are in feet**, convert inches to feet, and halve 2 feet to find our radius (1 foot).

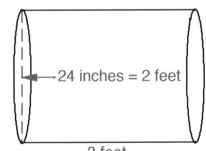

Let's find the area of the pipe ends:

$Area = \pi r^2 \quad \rightarrow \quad Area = \pi 1^2 \quad \rightarrow \quad Area = 3.14$

Now, multiply by the height (or length in this diagram).

$Volume = area \cdot height \quad \rightarrow \quad Volume = 3.14\ feet^2 \cdot 3\ feet$

$Volume = 9.42\ feet^3$

Answer choice **J** is correct.

<u>What You May Have Done Wrong</u>
- **F.** You, most likely, used two as the height (length).
- **G.** You flipped your dimensions, using 3 ft as the diameter and 2 ft as the length.
- **H.** You used the diameter to calculate the area of the circle.
- **K.** You made an arithmetic error.

3. A rectangular prism has dimensions as marked. What is the surface area of the prism?

Correct Answer C

This is a *surface area* question. To solve, find the area of all six sides. Because we have two square sides (our ends), the other sides, top/bottom and left/right, are equal.

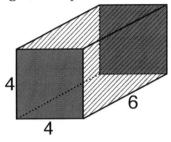

Ends (Front/Back)

$Area = 4\,inches \cdot 4\,inches = 16\,inches^2$

$Area\ both\ squares = 2 \cdot 16 = 32\,inches^2$

Top/Bottom

$Area = 6\,inches \cdot 4\,inches = 24\,inches^2$

$Area\ top\ \&\ bottom = 2 \cdot 24 = 48\,inches^2$

Left/Right

$Area = 6\,inches \cdot 4\,inches = 24\,inches^2$

$Area\ left\ \&\ right = 2 \cdot 24 = 48\,inches^2$

The square has four equal sides, so the four rectangular sides will be equal.

Surface Area = Ends + Top & Bottom + Left & Right

Surface Area = 32 + 48 + 48 = 128

Answer choice **C** is correct

What You May Have Done Wrong
   A. You only added the area of one square.
   B. You forgot to add the area of both squares.
   D. You miscalculated the area of the ends.
   E. You probably made an arithmetic error, and over counted the number of squares.

4. **The figure below is a right pyramid with a square base. The length of each side of the base is 12 and the slant height is 15. What is the surface area of the pyramid?**

Note: slant height is the height from the center of a base to the top (the point).

Correct Answer J

This is a *surface area* problem. As with any surface area problem, we've just got to find the area of all the sides and sum them up. We know the triangles are identical because they all have the same base, and the *slant height*.

The only trick is the *slant height* piece. While we don't use "slanted sides" to find area, **this is actually the perpendicular (up and down) height of each 2 dimensional triangle**. So, we can split the 3d shape into a bunch of 2d shapes (four identical triangles and a square).

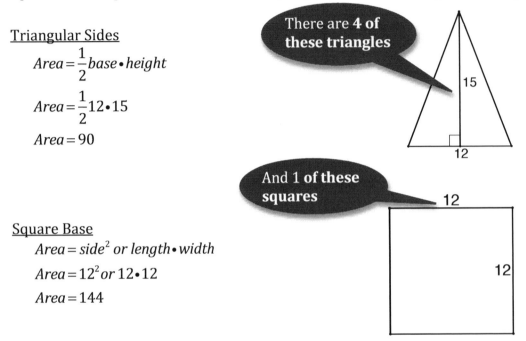

Triangular Sides

$$Area = \frac{1}{2} base \cdot height$$

$$Area = \frac{1}{2} 12 \cdot 15$$

$$Area = 90$$

Square Base

$$Area = side^2 \; or \; length \cdot width$$

$$Area = 12^2 \; or \; 12 \cdot 12$$

$$Area = 144$$

Surface Area = square base + triangle + triangle + triangle + triangle

Surface Area = 144 + 90 + 90 + 90 + 90 = 504

Answer choice **J** is correct.

What You May Have Done Wrong:

F. You neglected to add the square base.
G. You found four squares, review your steps.
H. You didn't take half the area for your triangles and did not add your base.
K. You didn't take half the area for your triangles.

5. A pool is a rectangular prism with a length of 16 feet, a width if 8 feet and a depth of 10 feet. If 1,000 cubic feet of water are put into the pool, approximately how deep will the water be?

Correct Answer A

This is a *volume* question with an extra twist. First, let's sketch and label a rectangular prism. We'll need to calculate the volume of our rectangular prism.

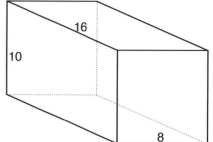

$Volume = area \cdot height$

$Volume = length \cdot width \cdot height$

$Volume = 16\ feet \cdot 8\ feet \cdot 10\ feet$

$Volume = 1,280\ feet^3$

Now, we can find out what portion (percent) of the total volume (1,280 ft³) the 1,000 ft³ represents.

$$percent = \frac{part}{whole} \rightarrow percent = \frac{1,000}{1,280} = 0.78 = 78\%$$

Finally, we can find out how high the water reaches.

$depth = percentage\ filled \cdot height \quad \rightarrow \quad depth = 78\% \cdot 10\ feet$

$depth = 7.8\ feet$

Answer choice **A** is correct.

What You May Have Done Wrong
B. This is a halfway answer; you didn't multiply by the depth.
C. You got the percentage correct, but you multiplied by 8 instead of 10.
D. You got the percentage correct, but you multiplied by 16 instead of 10 (or you divided by your percentage).
E. This is a halfway answer (the depth).

6. In the diagram below, a sphere with a radius of 3 is inscribed in a cube so that the sphere is tangent to all six sides of the cube. What is the surface area of the cube?

Correct Answer J

This is a *surface area* question, but it's really more about definitions. *Tangent* means that the sphere will touch, but not go through the sides of the cube. If the radius is 3, the sphere will have a diameter of 6. Because it is tangent tothe cube, the sides will be equal to the diameter (6 as well).

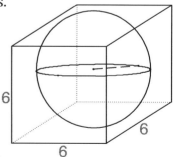

Since we have a cube, all of the faces (sides) will be equal. We merely have to find one side, and multiply by the number of sides (6)

$Side\ Area = length \cdot width \quad \rightarrow \quad Side\ Area = 6 \cdot 6 = 36$

$Surface\ Area = 6 \cdot Side\ Area \quad \rightarrow \quad Surface\ Area = 6 \cdot 36 = 216$

Answer **J** is correct.

What You May Have Done Wrong
F. This is a halfway answer. You found the surface area of a *single side*.
G. You used 3 as the side of each square.
H. You found the volume of a cube with 3 as the side.
K. You multiplied the area of a square by 4; cubes have six sides.

Trigonometry

The topics in the *Trigonometry* section constitute 7 to 10 percent of the ACT Math section, or between 4 and 6 questions per test. Here's the question frequency and the corresponding ACT Score Report category or categories.

Find the Side	1 – 2 questions	**PHM: Geometry**
Find the Function	0 – 2 questions	**PHM: Geometry**
Unit Circle	0 – 1 questions	**PHM: Geometry**
Trig Identities	0 – 1 questions	**PHM: Geometry**
Arc Functions	0 – 1 questions	**PHM: Geometry**
Graphs of Functions	0 – 1 questions	**PHM: Geometry**

IES: Integrating Essential Skills
PHM: Preparing for Higher Math
MOD: Modeling

A detailed explanation of the math score report is in the beginning of the book under the **Score Report**.

There aren't any key topics in *Trigonometry*. Focus on understanding the functions, that's the core of *Trigonometry* topics. If you're going for a 30+ score, spend time understanding Graphs, Identities, and the Unit Circle.

Strategies

There are a few things you have to know but not many. After that, it's all about right triangles and setup.

Know Sine, Cosine, & Tangent

There's no way around knowing those three functions. SOHCAHTOA is a great way to remember it.

Know the Axis Measures of the Unit Circle

The left-side of the *x*-axis is 0 and each 90 degrees goes up $\frac{\pi}{2}$ until you get back to the positive side of the *x*-axis. You don't need to know specific angles in radians, just the boundaries of the quadrants.

Setup Diagram Problems

If you've got a diagram problem, label your diagram (even the sides with O, A, & H, if it helps). Remember, unit circle problems are right triangle problems.

Setup Diagram Problems

If you've got a diagram problem, label your diagram (even the sides with O, A, & H, if it helps

Ratios & Proportions

Find the function, find the side, and find the angle are ratio & proportion problems. Treat them accordingly.

Crazy Identity Problems are Plug-in Problems

If you've got a diagram problem, label your diagram (even the sides with O, A, & H, if it helps

Trigonometry: Pre-Test

1. For right triangle △ *FEG* below, what is the tan *G*?

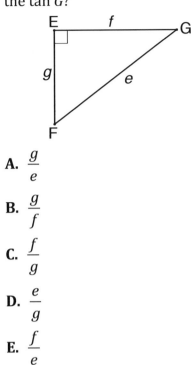

   A. $\dfrac{g}{e}$

   B. $\dfrac{g}{f}$

   C. $\dfrac{f}{g}$

   D. $\dfrac{e}{g}$

   E. $\dfrac{f}{e}$

2. In the right triangle shown below, which of the following statements is true about angle *C*?

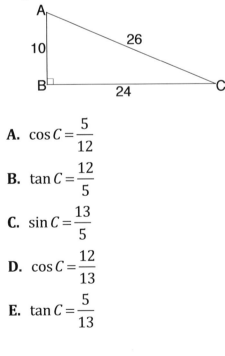

   A. $\cos C = \dfrac{5}{12}$

   B. $\tan C = \dfrac{12}{5}$

   C. $\sin C = \dfrac{13}{5}$

   D. $\cos C = \dfrac{12}{13}$

   E. $\tan C = \dfrac{5}{13}$

3. If the sine of ∠*ABC* is $\dfrac{3}{5}$. What is the cos of ∠*ABC*?

   A. $\dfrac{4}{5}$

   B. $\dfrac{5}{3}$

   C. $\dfrac{5}{4}$

   D. $\dfrac{4}{3}$

   E. $\dfrac{3}{4}$

4. In right triangle *ABC* the sin of ∠*A* = $\dfrac{a}{c}$, what is the cos of ∠*B*?

   A. $\dfrac{a}{c}$

   B. $\dfrac{b}{c}$

   C. $\dfrac{c}{a}$

   D. $\dfrac{b}{a}$

   E. $\dfrac{c}{b}$

5. The cosine of angle α is $\dfrac{12}{13}$ and the tan of angle α is $\dfrac{5}{12}$. What is the sine of angle α?

   A. $\dfrac{13}{12}$

   B. $\dfrac{12}{13}$

   C. $\dfrac{5}{13}$

   D. $\dfrac{5}{\sqrt{313}}$

   E. $\dfrac{12}{\sqrt{313}}$

6. The length of side $\overline{AB}$ of $\triangle ABC$ is 12. The tan of $\angle C$ is $\dfrac{5}{4}$. How long is side $\overline{CB}$?

C

$\frac{5}{4}$ 4 toa

5·4

10·8

12÷x

S

toa

10×12=12

8×1.2=9.4

$tan(\frac{5}{4})$ 12

adin

$tan(\frac{5}{4}) = \dfrac{12}{x}$

A

12

B

A. 15
B. 9.6
C. 9
D. 18
E. 13

7. Charlie is trying to calculate the height of a building. The angle of elevation from the ground is 42° and Charlie is 50 feet from the building. Which of the expressions gives the length, in feet, of the height of the building?

A. 50 sin 42°
B. 50 cos 42°
C. 50 tan 42°
D. 75 feet
E. 33 feet

8. Margo is planning a wheelchair ramp for a volunteer project. The ramp will rise 1.5 feet to a doorway and the ramp will extend 10.3 feet. What is the angle of elevation of the ramp?

1.5

10.3

A. $\cos^{-1}\left(\dfrac{-1.5}{10.3}\right)$

B. $\sin^{-1}\left(\dfrac{-1.5}{10.3}\right)$

C. $\tan^{-1}\left(\dfrac{1.5}{10.3}\right)$

D. $\tan^{-1}\left(\dfrac{10.3}{1.5}\right)$

E. $\sin^{-1}\left(\dfrac{10.3}{1.5}\right)$

9. A triangle has sides as marked and a hypotenuse of $\sqrt{185}$. Which of the following expressions will give the measure of angle x?

11

x

8

A. $\tan^{-1}\left(\dfrac{8}{11}\right)$

B. $\tan^{-1}\left(\dfrac{8}{\sqrt{185}}\right)$

C. $\sin^{-1}\left(\dfrac{8}{\sqrt{185}}\right)$

D. $\cos^{-1}\left(\dfrac{8}{\sqrt{185}}\right)$

E. $\cos^{-1}\left(\dfrac{8}{11}\right)$

10. Angle C measures $\dfrac{7\pi}{2}$ radians from its initial side to its terminal side. Angle D has the same initial side and same terminal side as Angle C. What could be the measure of Angle D?

A. 270°
B. 90°
C. 180°
D. 360°
E. 540°

11. For which angles between 0 and 2π is sine $= -\dfrac{1}{2}$?

A. $\dfrac{\pi}{4}$ and $\dfrac{3\pi}{4}$

B. $\dfrac{7\pi}{6}$ and $\dfrac{11\pi}{6}$

C. $\dfrac{\pi}{2}$ and $\dfrac{3\pi}{2}$

D. $\dfrac{3\pi}{4}$ and $\dfrac{5\pi}{6}$

E. $\dfrac{\pi}{3}$ and $\dfrac{2\pi}{3}$

12. When $\sin = 0.534$, which could be true of θ?

A. $\dfrac{\pi}{2} < \theta < \dfrac{5\pi}{6}$

B. $\dfrac{5\pi}{4} < \theta < \dfrac{3\pi}{2}$

C. $\dfrac{7\pi}{6} < \theta < \dfrac{3\pi}{2}$

D. $\dfrac{3\pi}{2} < \theta < \dfrac{5\pi}{3}$

E. $\dfrac{9\pi}{5} < \theta < \dfrac{11\pi}{6}$

13. Given that $\tan\theta = \dfrac{4}{3}$ and $0° \le \theta \le 360°$, what are all possible values of $\sin\theta$?

    A. $\dfrac{3}{4}$ only

    B. $\dfrac{3}{4}$ only $-\dfrac{3}{4}$

    C. $\dfrac{4}{5}$ only

    D. $-\dfrac{4}{5}$ only

    E. $\dfrac{4}{5}$ and $-\dfrac{4}{5}$

14. Which of the following trigonometric functions is equivalent to the expression $(\sin\theta)(\cot\theta)$?

Note: $\cot\theta = \dfrac{1}{\tan\theta}$

A. $\sin\theta$

B. $\cos\theta$

C. $\tan\theta$

D. $\csc\theta$

E. $\sec\theta$

15. Three ships the *Sophie*, the *Madee,* and the *Taylar* are on lake Michigan. The *Madee* is 7 miles from the *Taylar* and the *Sophie* is 5 miles from the *Madee* and the measure of angle T is 42°. What equation would give the measure of angle S?

(Note: For a triangle with sides of length a, b, and c that are opposite $\angle A, \angle B, \angle C$, respectively, $\dfrac{\sin A}{a} = \dfrac{\sin B}{b} = \dfrac{\sin C}{c}$.)

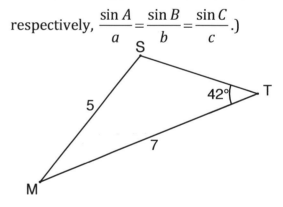

A. $\dfrac{\sin S}{7} = \dfrac{\sin 42°}{5}$

B. $\dfrac{\sin S}{5} = \dfrac{\sin 42°}{7}$

C. $\dfrac{\sin S}{\sin 42°} = \dfrac{5}{7}$

D. $\dfrac{\sin 42°}{\sin S} = \dfrac{7}{5}$

E. $\sin S = \dfrac{\sin 42°}{5} - 7$

16. Alexa is looking at two landmarks, a statue and a tree. The tree is 0.7 miles from Alexa and the statue is 1.8 miles from Alexa. The angle between the line of sight to the statue and the line of sight to the tree is 20°. The distance from the tree to the statue is given by which expression?

(Note: For a triangle with sides of length a, b, and c that are opposite $\angle A, \angle B, \angle C$, respectively, $c^2 = a^2 + b^2 - 2ab\cos C$.)

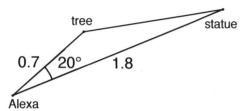

A. $\sqrt{0.7^2 + 1.8^2 - \cos 20°}$

B. $\sqrt{0.7^2 + 1.8^2 - 0.7 \cdot \cos 20°}$

C. $\sqrt{0.7^2 + 1.8^2 + 2 \cdot 0.7 \cdot 1.8 \cdot \cos 20°}$

D. $\sqrt{0.7^2 + 1.8^2 - 2 \cdot 0.7 \cdot 1.8 \cdot \cos 20°}$

E. $\sqrt{0.7^2 + 1.8^2}$

17. A trigonometric function with equation $y = a\cos(bx + c) + d$ has real numbers values for a, b, c, d. The function is graphed on the standard (x, y) plane below. The *period* of this function $f(x)$ is the smallest positive number p so that the value of $f(x)$ and $f(x + p)$ are the same for every real number value of x. What is the period of the function?

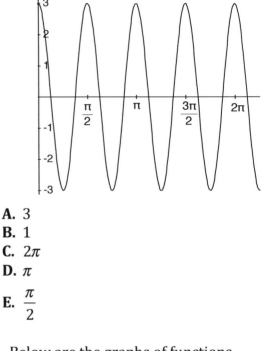

A. 3

B. 1

C. 2π

D. π

E. $\dfrac{\pi}{2}$

18. Below are the graphs of functions $y = \sin(x)$ and $y = a\sin(x) + b$, where a and b are real numbers. Which of the following statements about a and b is true?

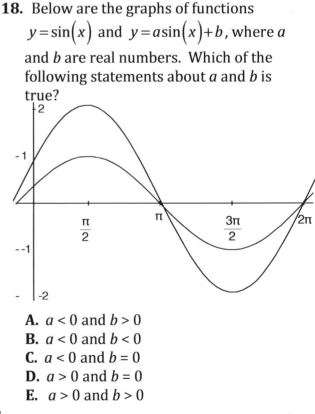

A. $a < 0$ and $b > 0$

B. $a < 0$ and $b < 0$

C. $a < 0$ and $b = 0$

D. $a > 0$ and $b = 0$

E. $a > 0$ and $b > 0$

	Answer	**Section with Solution**
1.	B	Trig Functions
2.	D	Trig Functions
3.	A	Trig Functions
4.	A	Trig Functions
5.	C	Trig Functions
6.	B	Find the Side
7.	C	Find the Side
8.	C	Find the Angle
9.	D	Find the Angle
10.	A	The Unit Circle
11.	B	The Unit Circle
12.	A	The Unit Circle
13.	E	The Unit Circle
14.	B	Identities
15.	A	Identities
16.	D	Identities
17.	E	Graphs of Functions
18.	D	Graphs of Functions

Introduction

I call these the *big three* functions. You'll need to know how they are defined and their properties.

What You Need to Know

✓ The definitions of sine, cosine, and tangent
✓ Trig functions are ratios.
✓ Use trig functions as ratios, find other functions *and* solve for a side.
✓ The same angle (identical measure) always has the same value for trig functions. The corresponding angles of similar right triangles have identical trig functions.

Definitions: Trig Functions

Trig functions are always the same for the same angle in a right triangle. It doesn't matter how big the triangle is, because trig functions are a ratio of the length of the sides.

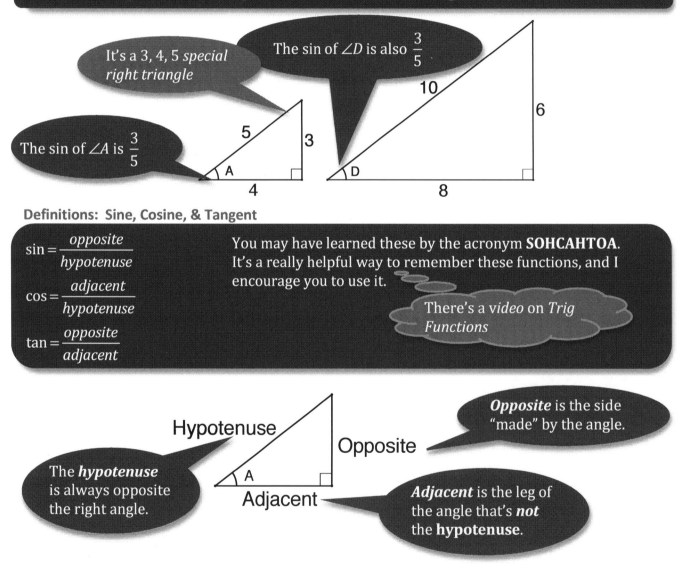

It's a 3, 4, 5 *special right triangle*

The sin of ∠D is also $\frac{3}{5}$

The sin of ∠A is $\frac{3}{5}$

Definitions: Sine, Cosine, & Tangent

$$\sin = \frac{opposite}{hypotenuse}$$

$$\cos = \frac{adjacent}{hypotenuse}$$

$$\tan = \frac{opposite}{adjacent}$$

You may have learned these by the acronym **SOHCAHTOA**. It's a really helpful way to remember these functions, and I encourage you to use it.

There's a *video* on *Trig Functions*

Opposite is the side "made" by the angle.

The **hypotenuse** is always opposite the right angle.

Adjacent is the leg of the angle that's *not* the **hypotenuse**.

Definitions (cont.): Sine, Cosine, & Tangent

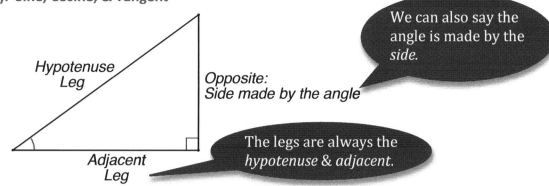

Hypotenuse Leg

Opposite: Side made by the angle

We can also say the angle is made by the side.

The legs are always the *hypotenuse & adjacent.*

Adjacent Leg

ACT Examples: Defining Functions

1. For right triangle △ *FEG* below, what is the tan *G*?

   A. $\dfrac{g}{e}$

   B. $\dfrac{g}{f}$

   C. $\dfrac{f}{g}$

   D. $\dfrac{e}{g}$

   E. $\dfrac{f}{e}$

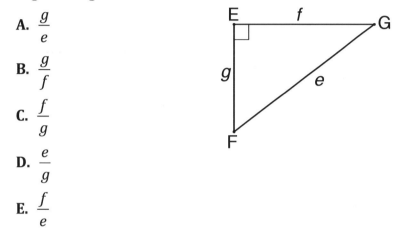

Solve

Mark up your diagram and identify your sides.
Tan is defined as *TOA.*

$$\tan = \frac{opposite}{adjacent} \rightarrow \frac{g}{f}$$

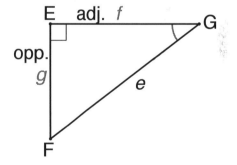

Answer Choice **B** is correct.

2. In the right triangle shown below, which of the statements is true about angle C?

A. $\cos C = \dfrac{5}{12}$

B. $\tan C = \dfrac{12}{5}$

C. $\sin C = \dfrac{13}{5}$

D. $\cos C = \dfrac{12}{13}$

E. $\tan C = \dfrac{5}{13}$

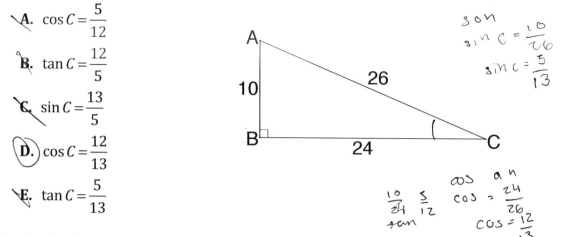

Solve

This is a "which" question, so it's a great mark-off question, markup the triangle.

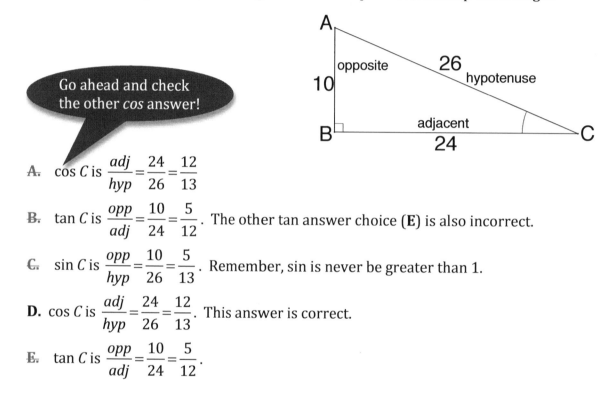

Go ahead and check the other *cos* answer!

A. $\cos C$ is $\dfrac{adj}{hyp} = \dfrac{24}{26} = \dfrac{12}{13}$

B. $\tan C$ is $\dfrac{opp}{adj} = \dfrac{10}{24} = \dfrac{5}{12}$. The other tan answer choice (**E**) is also incorrect.

C. $\sin C$ is $\dfrac{opp}{hyp} = \dfrac{10}{26} = \dfrac{5}{13}$. Remember, sin is never be greater than 1.

D. $\cos C$ is $\dfrac{adj}{hyp} = \dfrac{24}{26} = \dfrac{12}{13}$. This answer is correct.

E. $\tan C$ is $\dfrac{opp}{adj} = \dfrac{10}{24} = \dfrac{5}{12}$.

Rules of the Road: Finding Functions from Functions

Occasionally, we'll be asked to find a function from a function or functions. In these problems, the ACT won't provide a triangle.

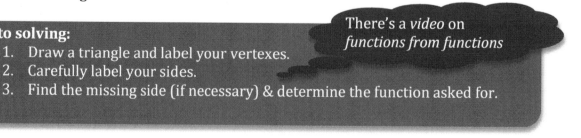

Steps to solving:
1. Draw a triangle and label your vertexes.
2. Carefully label your sides.
3. Find the missing side (if necessary) & determine the function asked for.

There's a *video* on *functions from functions*

1. If the sine of $\angle ABC$ is $\dfrac{3}{5}$. What is the cos of $\angle ABC$?

A. $\dfrac{4}{5}$

B. $\dfrac{5}{3}$

C. $\dfrac{5}{4}$

D. $\dfrac{4}{3}$

E. $\dfrac{3}{4}$

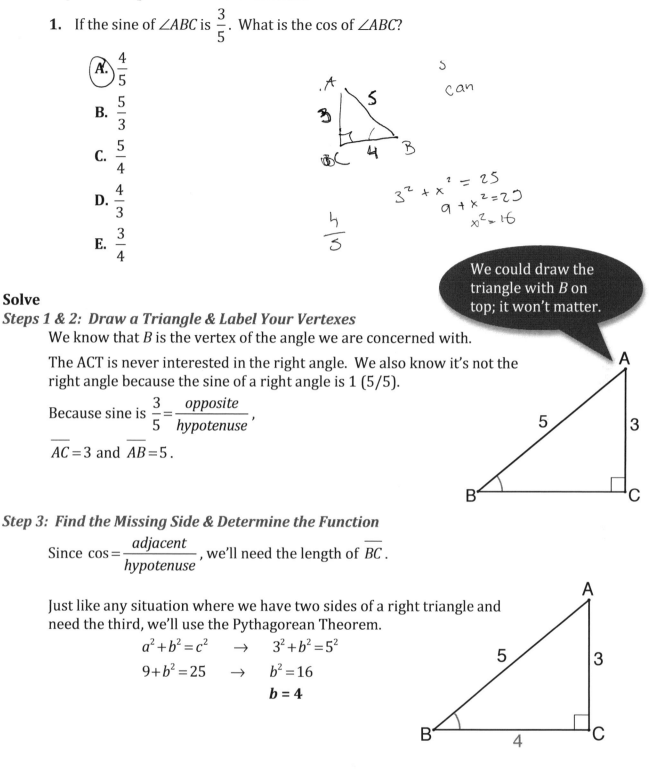

Solve

Steps 1 & 2: Draw a Triangle & Label Your Vertexes

We know that B is the vertex of the angle we are concerned with.

The ACT is never interested in the right angle. We also know it's not the right angle because the sine of a right angle is 1 (5/5).

Because sine is $\dfrac{3}{5} = \dfrac{opposite}{hypotenuse}$,

$\overline{AC} = 3$ and $\overline{AB} = 5$.

We could draw the triangle with B on top; it won't matter.

Step 3: Find the Missing Side & Determine the Function

Since $\cos = \dfrac{adjacent}{hypotenuse}$, we'll need the length of $\overline{BC}$.

Just like any situation where we have two sides of a right triangle and need the third, we'll use the Pythagorean Theorem.

$$a^2 + b^2 = c^2 \quad \rightarrow \quad 3^2 + b^2 = 5^2$$

$$9 + b^2 = 25 \quad \rightarrow \quad b^2 = 16$$

$$\boldsymbol{b = 4}$$

Now that we have the adjacent side, we can find the cosine.

$$\cos = \frac{adjacent}{hypotenuse} = \frac{4}{5}$$

Answer Choice **A** is correct.

2. In right triangle ABC the sin of $\angle A = \dfrac{a}{c}$, what is the cos of $\angle B$?

   A. $\dfrac{a}{c}$

   B. $\dfrac{b}{c}$

   C. $\dfrac{c}{a}$

   D. $\dfrac{b}{a}$

   E. $\dfrac{c}{b}$

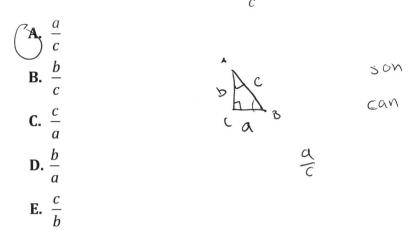

Solve

There's an extra wrinkle to this problem. You've got to know that **the angle makes the side**.

Steps 1 & 2: Draw a Triangle & Label Your Vertexes

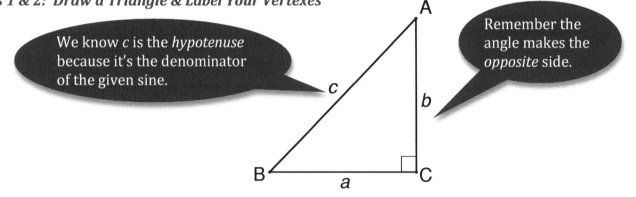

We know c is the *hypotenuse* because it's the denominator of the given sine.

Remember the angle makes the *opposite* side.

Now that we've got the vertexes labeled, it's straightforward to get the cos B.

$$\cos = \frac{adjacent}{hypotenuse} = \frac{a}{c}$$

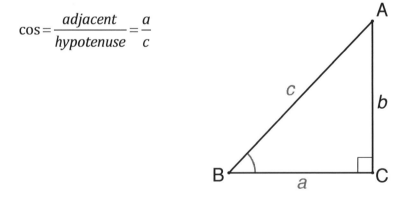

You may notice that sine $\angle A$ = cos $\angle B$. This is always the case with the two acute angles (the angles that aren't the right angle). Because the *opposite* of $\angle A$ is the *adjacent* of $\angle B$, sine will always equal cosine.

Answer Choice **A** is correct.

3. The cosine of angle α is $\dfrac{12}{13}$ and the tan of angle α is $\dfrac{5}{12}$. What is the sine of angle α?

A. $\dfrac{13}{12}$

B. $\dfrac{12}{13}$

C. $\dfrac{5}{13}$

D. $\dfrac{5}{\sqrt{313}}$

E. $\dfrac{12}{\sqrt{313}}$

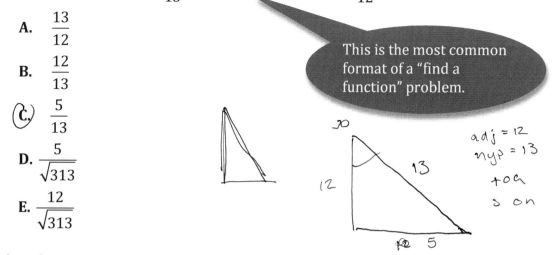

This is the most common format of a "find a function" problem.

Solve

The first thing to notice about this problem type is that you're actually given all three sides of the triangle. While it's not strictly necessary, I recommend you draw the triangle to avoid careless errors.

Let's find our sides first:

$$\cos = \frac{12}{13} = \frac{adjacent}{hypotenuse}, adjacent = 12 \ \& \ hypotenuse = 13$$

$$\tan = \frac{5}{12} = \frac{opposite}{adjacent}, opposite = 5 \ \& \ adjacent = 12$$

Our triangle looks like this:

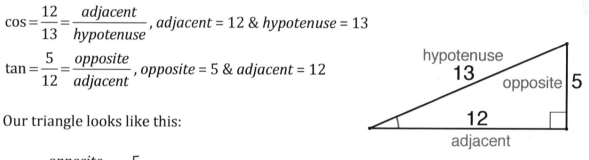

$$\sin = \frac{opposite}{hypotenuse} = \frac{5}{13}$$

Answer Choice **C** is correct.

Wrap Up

What You Need to Know
- ✓ The definitions of sine, cosine, and tangent
- ✓ Trig functions are ratios.
- ✓ Use trig functions as ratios, find other functions *and* solve for a side.
- ✓ The same angle (identical measure) always has the same value for trig functions. The corresponding angles of similar right triangles have identical trig functions.

Videos

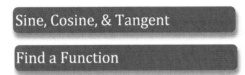

The Strategies
- ✓ Draw your triangle, and label your sides (opposite, adjacent, hypotenuse)
- ✓ Setup your ratios, and work the problems in steps.
- ✓ Use a formal setup, it helps with tricky problems and guarantees you don't miss the easy ones.

Related Topics
- ✓ Arcfunctions

- ✓ Unit Circle

- ✓ Trig Identities

- ✓ Trig Graphs

Trigonometry: Functions

1. For right triangle *ABC* shown below, what is the tan of ∠*B*?

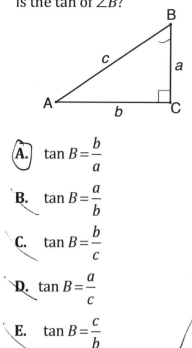

A. $\tan B = \dfrac{b}{a}$

B. $\tan B = \dfrac{a}{b}$

C. $\tan B = \dfrac{b}{c}$

D. $\tan B = \dfrac{a}{c}$

E. $\tan B = \dfrac{c}{b}$

2. For an angle with measure α in a right triangle, $\sin = \dfrac{8}{17}$ and $\tan = \dfrac{8}{15}$. What is the value of $\cos \alpha$?

F. $\dfrac{17}{15}$

G. $\dfrac{15}{17}$

H. $\dfrac{8}{17}$

J. $\dfrac{15}{\sqrt{514}}$

K. $\dfrac{8}{\sqrt{514}}$

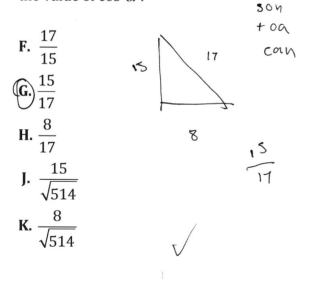

3. In the right triangle shown below, what statement is true about angle *CAB*?

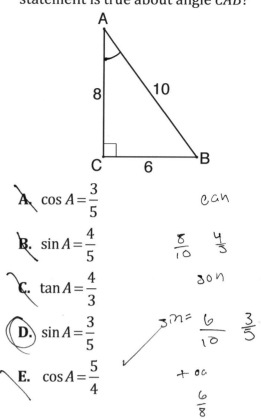

A. $\cos A = \dfrac{3}{5}$

B. $\sin A = \dfrac{4}{5}$

C. $\tan A = \dfrac{4}{3}$

D. $\sin A = \dfrac{3}{5}$

E. $\cos A = \dfrac{5}{4}$

4. The right triangle below has lengths marked. What is the tangent of ∠*A*?

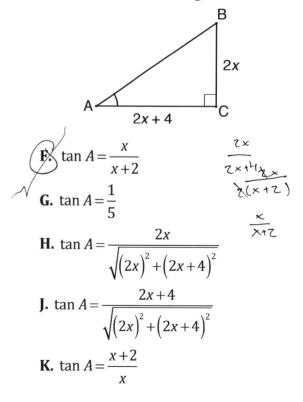

F. $\tan A = \dfrac{x}{x+2}$

G. $\tan A = \dfrac{1}{5}$

H. $\tan A = \dfrac{2x}{\sqrt{(2x)^2 + (2x+4)^2}}$

J. $\tan A = \dfrac{2x+4}{\sqrt{(2x)^2 + (2x+4)^2}}$

K. $\tan A = \dfrac{x+2}{x}$

5. For the right triangle below, what is the sine of $\angle E$?

A. $\dfrac{1}{2}$

B. 2

C. $\dfrac{1}{\sqrt{5}}$

D. $\dfrac{2}{\sqrt{5}}$

E. $\sqrt{5}$

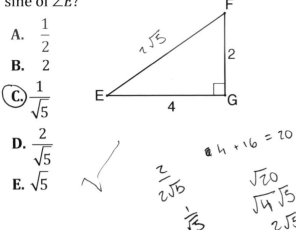

@ $4 + 16 = 20$

$\dfrac{2}{2\sqrt{5}}$ $\dfrac{\sqrt{20}}{\sqrt{4}\sqrt{5}}$

$\dfrac{1}{\sqrt{5}}$ $2\sqrt{5}$

6. For the right triangle below, what is the cosine of $\angle J$?

F. $\dfrac{j^2}{\sqrt{j^2+k^2}}$

G. $\dfrac{k}{\sqrt{j^2+k^2}}$

H. $\dfrac{k}{j+k}$

J. $\dfrac{j}{j+k}$

K. $\dfrac{j}{\sqrt{j^2+k^2}}$

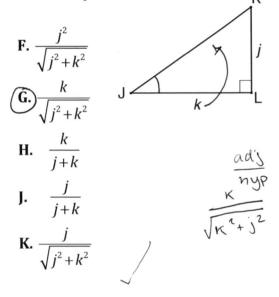

$\dfrac{adj}{hyp}$

$\dfrac{K}{\sqrt{k^2+j^2}}$

7. If f is the longest side of a triangle & $f = 3d$, what is the sine of $\angle EDF$?

A. 3

B. $\dfrac{1}{3}$

C. $\dfrac{1}{2}$

D. $\dfrac{1}{\sqrt{10}}$

E. Cannot be Determined.

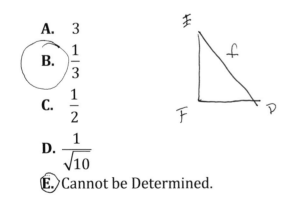

8. For any angle in a right triangle with $\tan = \dfrac{7}{24}$ and $\cos = \dfrac{24}{25}$, what is the sine of the angle?

F. $\sin = \dfrac{7}{24}$

G. $\sin = \dfrac{7}{25}$

H. $\sin = \dfrac{24}{25}$

J. $\sin = \dfrac{7}{\sqrt{1{,}201}}$

K. $\sin = \dfrac{24}{\sqrt{1{,}201}}$

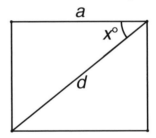

$\dfrac{7}{25}$

9. The rectangle shown below has diagonal d. What is true about angle x?

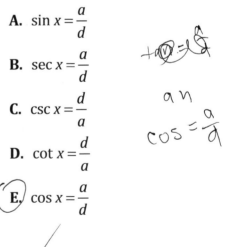

A. $\sin x = \dfrac{a}{d}$

B. $\sec x = \dfrac{a}{d}$

C. $\csc x = \dfrac{d}{a}$

D. $\cot x = \dfrac{d}{a}$

E. $\cos x = \dfrac{a}{d}$

$\tan = \dfrac{o}{a}$

$a n$

$\cos = \dfrac{a}{d}$

Functions: Solutions

1. **For right triangle ABC shown below, what is the tan of $\angle B$?**

Correct Answer A

This is a definition question. You've got to know the definition of tangent and which sides to plug-in.

$$\tan B = \frac{opposite}{adjacent} = \frac{b}{a}$$

Answer choice **A** is correct.

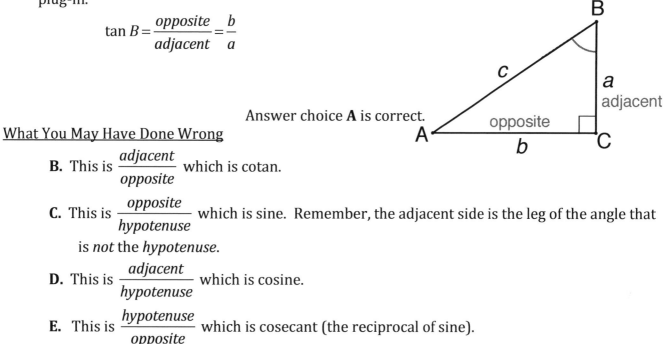

<u>What You May Have Done Wrong</u>

B. This is $\dfrac{adjacent}{opposite}$ which is cotan.

C. This is $\dfrac{opposite}{hypotenuse}$ which is sine. Remember, the adjacent side is the leg of the angle that is *not* the *hypotenuse*.

D. This is $\dfrac{adjacent}{hypotenuse}$ which is cosine.

E. This is $\dfrac{hypotenuse}{opposite}$ which is cosecant (the reciprocal of sine).

2. **For an angle with measure α in a right triangle, $\sin = \dfrac{8}{17}$ and $\tan = \dfrac{8}{15}$. What is the value of cos α?**

Correct Answer G

This is a fairly common setup for finding a function. You don't necessarily need to draw a triangle on this sort of problem, but it's a good idea.

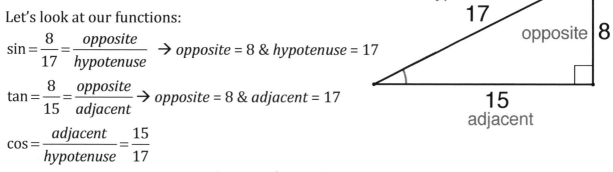

Let's look at our functions:

$\sin = \dfrac{8}{17} = \dfrac{opposite}{hypotenuse}$ → *opposite = 8 & hypotenuse = 17*

$\tan = \dfrac{8}{15} = \dfrac{opposite}{adjacent}$ → *opposite = 8 & adjacent = 17*

$\cos = \dfrac{adjacent}{hypotenuse} = \dfrac{15}{17}$

Answer choice **G** is correct.

<u>What You May Have Done Wrong</u>

F. This is the secant of the angle.

H. This is the sin of the angle.

J. We're given the hypotenuse, so we won't need to use the Pythagorean Theorem.

K. We're given the hypotenuse, so we won't need to use the Pythagorean Theorem.

3. In the right triangle shown below, what statement is true about angle *CAB*?

Correct Answer D

This is a *mark-off* question; the only way to solve it is evaluate each answer choice. Markup your triangle

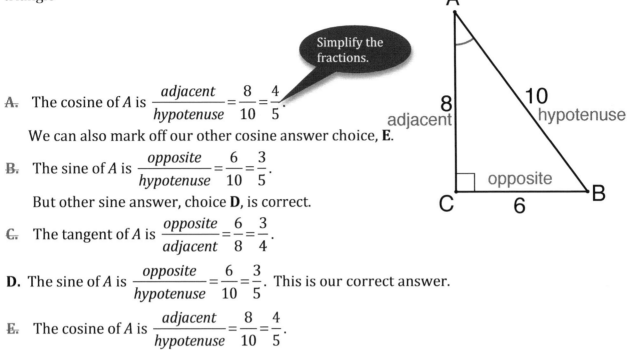

A. The cosine of *A* is $\dfrac{adjacent}{hypotenuse} = \dfrac{8}{10} = \dfrac{4}{5}$.

We can also mark off our other cosine answer choice, **E**.

B. The sine of *A* is $\dfrac{opposite}{hypotenuse} = \dfrac{6}{10} = \dfrac{3}{5}$.

But other sine answer, choice **D**, is correct.

C. The tangent of *A* is $\dfrac{opposite}{adjacent} = \dfrac{6}{8} = \dfrac{3}{4}$.

D. The sine of *A* is $\dfrac{opposite}{hypotenuse} = \dfrac{6}{10} = \dfrac{3}{5}$. This is our correct answer.

E. The cosine of *A* is $\dfrac{adjacent}{hypotenuse} = \dfrac{8}{10} = \dfrac{4}{5}$.

Answer choice **D** is correct

4. The right triangle below has lengths marked. What is the tangent of $\angle A$?

Correct Answer F

A lot of students get thrown off when variables get introduced in sides. The problem is the same. We set up the ratio and solve. In this case, we'll have an extra bit of simplification.

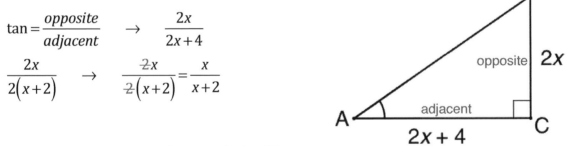

$$\tan = \frac{opposite}{adjacent} \quad \rightarrow \quad \frac{2x}{2x+4}$$

$$\frac{2x}{2(x+2)} \quad \rightarrow \quad \frac{\cancel{2}x}{\cancel{2}(x+2)} = \frac{x}{x+2}$$

Answer choice **F** is correct.

<u>What You May Have Done Wrong:</u>
 G. You improperly cancelled your fraction. You can't reduce 2*x* to 1, because 2*x* is not a factor in the denominator (review <u>fractions</u>)
 H. This is the sine of *A*.
 J. This is the cosine of *A*.

 K. This is the cotan of *A*, $\text{cotan} = \dfrac{adjacent}{opposite}$.

5. **For the right triangle below, what is the sine of $\angle E$?**

This is a define a function question has an extra wrinkle: you've got to find the hypotenuse. It's also got a confusing bit of simplification.

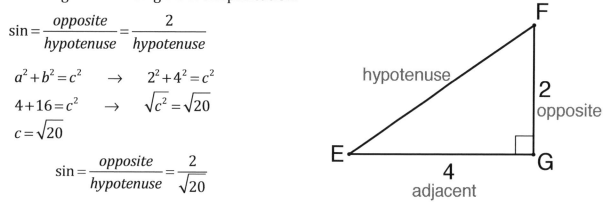

$$\sin = \frac{opposite}{hypotenuse} = \frac{2}{hypotenuse}$$

$$a^2 + b^2 = c^2 \quad \rightarrow \quad 2^2 + 4^2 = c^2$$

$$4 + 16 = c^2 \quad \rightarrow \quad \sqrt{c^2} = \sqrt{20}$$

$$c = \sqrt{20}$$

$$\sin = \frac{opposite}{hypotenuse} = \frac{2}{\sqrt{20}}$$

We aren't done though. We can simplify our denominator (your answer choices should give you a clue).

$$\sqrt{20} \rightarrow \sqrt{4 \cdot 5} \rightarrow 2\sqrt{5}$$

Putting the simplified denominator back in our fraction, we get:

$$\frac{2}{2\sqrt{5}} \rightarrow \frac{\cancel{2}}{\cancel{2}\sqrt{5}} \rightarrow \frac{1}{\sqrt{5}}$$

Answer choice **C** is correct.

<u>What You May Have Done Wrong</u>

    A. This is the tan $\angle E$.

    B. This is the cotan of $\angle E$, $\cotan = \dfrac{adjacent}{opposite}$

    D. This is the cosine of $\angle E$.

    E. This is the cosecant of $\angle E$, $\mathrm{cosec} = \dfrac{hypotenuse}{opposite}$

6. **For the right triangle below, what is the cosine of $\angle J$?**

Correct Answer G

This definition question requires the Pythagorean Theorem. It seems trickier because the sides are variables (instead of numbers) but the steps are the same.

We need to find the hypotenuse.

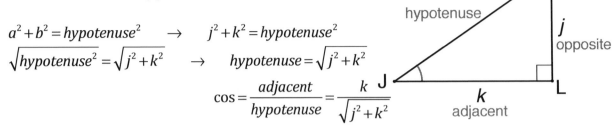

$$a^2 + b^2 = hypotenuse^2 \quad \rightarrow \quad j^2 + k^2 = hypotenuse^2$$

$$\sqrt{hypotenuse^2} = \sqrt{j^2 + k^2} \quad \rightarrow \quad hypotenuse = \sqrt{j^2 + k^2}$$

$$\cos = \frac{adjacent}{hypotenuse} = \frac{k}{\sqrt{j^2 + k^2}}$$

Answer **G** is correct.

<u>What You May Have Done Wrong</u>

F. There's no reason to square j. Remember j is the length of the opposite.

H. $\sqrt{j^2 + k^2}$ does not equal $j + k$. You can't split roots when they are added or subtracted. Also, k should be the numerator.

J. $\sqrt{j^2 + k^2}$ does not equal $j + k$. You can't split roots when they are added or subtracted. Also, k should be the numerator.

K. This is sine of $\angle J$.

7. **If f is the longest side of the triangle, and $f = 3d$, what is the sine of $\angle EDF$?**

Correct Answer B

This is a tricky question. We've got to draw the triangle, correctly label the sides, find the trig function, and do some algebra. First, let's take a look at our triangle. f is our hypotenuse, because it's the longest side. Our function will look like this:

$$\sin = \frac{opposite}{hypotenuse} = \frac{d}{f}$$

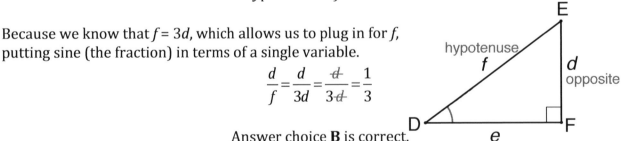

Because we know that $f = 3d$, which allows us to plug in for f, putting sine (the fraction) in terms of a single variable.

$$\frac{d}{f} = \frac{d}{3d} = \frac{\cancel{d}}{3\cancel{d}} = \frac{1}{3}$$

Answer choice **B** is correct.

<u>What You May Have Done Wrong</u>

A. You either calculated cosecant or you had some algebra issues.

C. This was either a guess or a misunderstanding of the triangle.

D. You may have tried to find the hypotenuse using 1 & 3 as side lengths. We don't know those are the side lengths; all we know is that the ratio of the sides is 3:1.

E. This is the answer the ACT *wants you to choose*. The problem is intimidating. But remember, most of the time "Cannot be Determined" is incorrect.

8. **For any angle in a right triangle with** $\tan = \dfrac{7}{24}$ **and** $\cos = \dfrac{24}{25}$ **what is the sine of the angle?**

Correct Answer G

The question tries to confuse you with some awkward wording. "For any angle" doesn't mean anything, it's just one angle in a right triangle that has the tan and cosine given. Define your sides, then (if you need to) draw up a triangle and label the sides. You can pick what ever angle you like for "any angle."

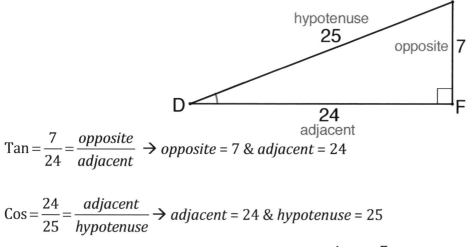

$$\text{Tan} = \frac{7}{24} = \frac{opposite}{adjacent} \rightarrow opposite = 7 \ \& \ adjacent = 24$$

$$\text{Cos} = \frac{24}{25} = \frac{adjacent}{hypotenuse} \rightarrow adjacent = 24 \ \& \ hypotenuse = 25$$

$$\sin = \frac{opposite}{hypotenuse} = \frac{7}{25}$$

Answer **G** is correct.

<u>What You May Have Done Wrong</u>

    F. This is the cotan of the angle.

    H. This is the cosine of the angle (also it's given in the question).

    J. You're given the *hypotenuse*; you don't need to calculate it.

    K. You're given the *hypotenuse*; you don't need to calculate it. Also, the numerator should be 7 (the *opposite*).

9. **The rectangle shown below has diagonal *d*. What is true about angle *x*?**

Correct Answer E

This definition problem is trying to intimidate you. The rectangle makes the problem look more complicated, but the problem is no different from most define a function questions. Historically, the ACT has not required you to know *secant* & *cosecant*, and that is true in this problem. This is a mark-off question.

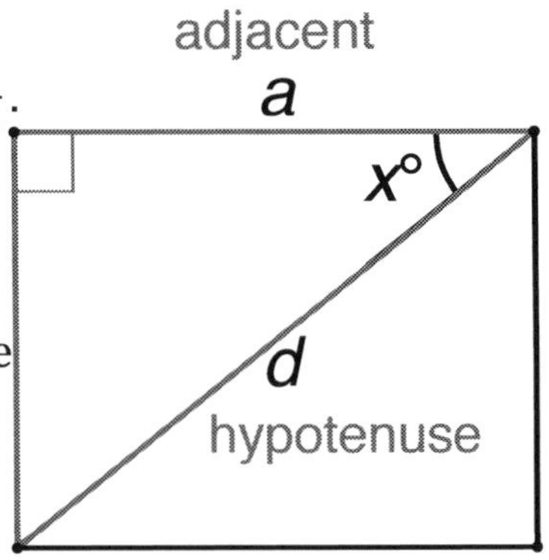

A. $\sin x = \dfrac{a}{d} = \dfrac{adjacent}{hypotenuse}$. This is the *cosine* of *x*. Sine is $\dfrac{opposite}{hypotenuse}$.

At this point I would look for a *cosine* answer and check to see if it's right (it is).

B. $\sec x = \dfrac{a}{d} = \dfrac{adjacent}{hypotenuse}$. Again this is *cosine*. Therefore, even if we

don't know secant, we can mark it off because *secant* won't be the same as *cosine*.

C. $\csc x = \dfrac{d}{a} = \dfrac{hypotenuse}{adjacent}$. If you don't know the definition of *cosecant*, you may want to leave

this answer for now. (It's not right though because $\csc = \dfrac{hypotenuse}{opposite}$).

D. $\cot x = \dfrac{d}{a} = \dfrac{hypotenuse}{adjacent}$. If you don't know the definition of *cotan*, you may want to leave this

answer for now. (It's not right though because $\cot = \dfrac{adjacent}{opposite}$).

E. $\cos x = \dfrac{a}{d} = \dfrac{adjacent}{hypotenuse}$. This is the correct answer.

Answer **E** is correct.

There's a *video* on *Solving for Sides.*

Introduction

The most common trig question is to find the length of a missing side given the measure of an angle and the length of one side. This topic is closely related to the preceding topic, **Finding a Function**.

What You Need to Know
- ✓ The definitions of sine, cosine, and tangent and which one(s) will apply.
- ✓ How to properly label the sides of a right triangle.
- ✓ How to set up and solve ratio problems.

Rules of the Road: Solving for a Side

> **The steps for solving for a side:**
> 1. Decide which function to use. The right function will always include the side we know, and the side we are looking for. Mark-up your triangle.
> 2. Set up your ratios.
> 3. Set your ratios equal, cross-multiply, and solve.

Because the math section of the ACT can be solved without a calculator, we won't *need* to look up functions, but it can be helpful.

Example: Solving for a Side
1. What is the length of side x?

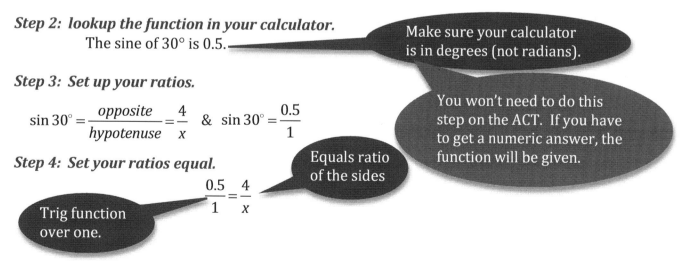

Step 1: Decide on the function & markup your triangle
We've got the hypotenuse and we are looking for the opposite. So, we'll use sine.

Step 2: lookup the function in your calculator.
The sine of 30° is 0.5.

Make sure your calculator is in degrees (not radians).

Step 3: Set up your ratios.

$$\sin 30° = \frac{opposite}{hypotenuse} = \frac{4}{x} \quad \& \quad \sin 30° = \frac{0.5}{1}$$

Step 4: Set your ratios equal.

$$\frac{0.5}{1} = \frac{4}{x}$$

Equals ratio of the sides

You won't need to do this step on the ACT. If you have to get a numeric answer, the function will be given.

Trig function over one.

Step 4: Cross-multiply & solve.

$$\frac{0.5}{1} = \frac{4}{x} \rightarrow 0.5x = 4 \rightarrow x = 8$$

ACT Example: Solving for a Side

1. The length of side $\overline{AB}$ of $\triangle ABC$ is 12. The tan of $\angle C$ is $\dfrac{5}{4}$. How long is side $\overline{CB}$?

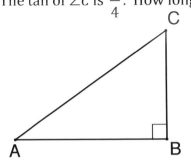

    A. 15
    B. 9.6
    C. 9
    D. 18
    E. 13

Solve

Steps 1 & 2: Decide on the function & markup your triangle
    We're given the function (tan) so the first step is marking up the triangle.

Step 3: Set up your ratios.

$$\text{tan of } \angle C \text{ is } \frac{5}{4} \text{ and } \frac{opposite}{adjacent} = \frac{12}{x}$$

Step 4: Cross-multiply & solve.

$$\frac{5}{4} = \frac{12}{x} \;\rightarrow\; 5x = 48 \;\rightarrow\; x = 9.6$$

Answer choice **B** is correct.

2. Charlie is trying to calculate the height of a building. The angle of elevation from the ground is 42° and Charlie is 50 feet from the building. Which of the expressions gives the length, in feet, of the height of the building?

    A. 50 sin 42°
    B. 50 cos 42°
    C. 50 tan 42°
    D. 75 feet
    E. 33 feet

> These problems can be intimidating. They actually have one less step than other "find the side" problems.

$$\tan 42 = \frac{x}{50}$$

$$x = 45°$$

Solve

Step 1: Decide on the function & markup your triangle

The only trick in setting up your triangle is labeling 50 as the *adjacent* and the building (unknown side) is *opposite*.

Remember, we always want to use a function that includes the side we have (adjacent) and the side we need (opposite). So, we use *tan*.

We can do some marking off, eliminating answers **A**, **B**, and **D** because they do not have *tan*.

Step 2: lookup the function in your calculator.

In this case we won't look up the function. The answer choices all have trig functions in them, so we won't need to find the value of tan 42°.

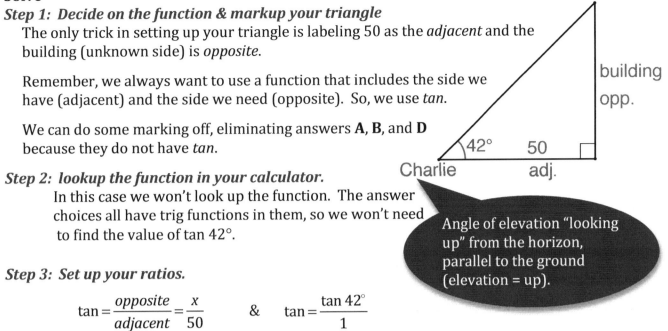

Angle of elevation "looking up" from the horizon, parallel to the ground (elevation = up).

Step 3: Set up your ratios.

$$\tan = \frac{opposite}{adjacent} = \frac{x}{50} \qquad \& \qquad \tan = \frac{\tan 42^\circ}{1}$$

Step 4: Cross-multiply & solve.

$$\frac{\tan 42^\circ}{1} = \frac{x}{50} \quad \rightarrow \quad x = 50 \tan 42^\circ$$

Answer choice **C** is correct.

Wrap Up

What You Need to Know
- ✓ The definitions of sine, cosine, and tangent
- ✓ Trig functions are ratios.
- ✓ Use trig functions as ratios, find other functions *and* solve for a side.
- ✓ The same angle (identical measure) always has the same value for trig functions. The corresponding angles of similar right triangles have identical trig functions.

Videos

> Find the Side

The Strategies
- ✓ Draw your triangle, and label your sides (opposite, adjacent, hypotenuse)
- ✓ Setup your ratios, and work the problems in steps.
- ✓ Use a formal setup, it helps with tricky problems and guarantees you don't miss the easy ones.

Related Topics
- ✓ Arcfunctions
- ✓ Unit Circle
- ✓ Trig Identities
- ✓ Trig Graphs

Trigonometry: Find the Side

1. For ΔDEF below, the length of the hypotenuse is 18 inches. The cosine of angle D is 0.4. How many inches long is $\overline{DF}$?

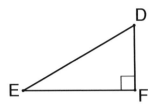

   F. 45 inches
   G. 4 inches
   H. 9.6 inches
   J. 7.2 inches
   K. 2.3 inches

2. Dom is using a sextant to measure the height of a tall flagpole. Sextants measure the angle between the ground and the sun (called the angle of elevation), The angle of elevation is 33°. Dom measures the length of the shadow cast by the flagpole as 32.42 feet. What is the height of the flagpole?

   Note: sin 33°= 0.55, cos 33° = 0.84, & tan 33°=0.65

   F.   21.1 feet
   G. 49.9 feet
   H. 27.2 feet
   J. 17.8 feet
   K. 38.6 feet

3. In triangle *ABC*, angle *B* has a tan of $\frac{3}{4}$ and side *a* is 12 units long. What is the length of *b*?

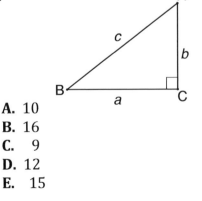

   A. 10
   B. 16
   C.   9
   D. 12
   E.   15

4. A support strut supports horizontal and vertical beams. The beams meet at a ninety-degree angle and have distances and angles as marked. Which expression gives the length of the strut?

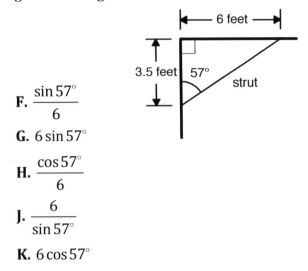

   F. $\dfrac{\sin 57°}{6}$

   G. $6 \sin 57°$

   H. $\dfrac{\cos 57°}{6}$

   J. $\dfrac{6}{\sin 57°}$

   K. $6 \cos 57°$

5. Jake is deep sea diving to attach a cable to a sunken treasure chest. The ship, the HMS Test Guy, is tracking Jake's progress using the length and angle of the cable to calculate Jake's depth. The angle of the cable is the angle from the side of the ship, which is perpendicular to the surface of the ocean. That angle is calculated as 18°. The length of the cable is 190 feet. How deep is Jake?

   Note: sin 72° = 0.95, cos 72° =0.31, tan 18° = 0.33, & sine 18° =0.31

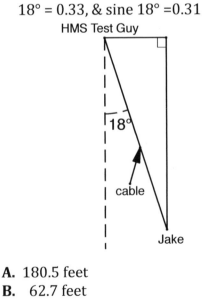

   A. 180.5 feet
   B.   62.7 feet
   C.   64.4 feet
   D. 200 feet
   E. 575.8 feet

Find the Side: Solutions

1. For △*DEF* below, the length of the hypotenuse is 18 inches. The cosine of angle *D* is 0.4.
    How many inches long is $\overline{DF}$?

Correct Answer J

This is a common setup for a solve-for-a-side question. We've got the function defined, so we can skip a couple of steps.

Step 1: *Decide on the function & markup your triangle*

The question determines our choice of function (cosine). But we should still mark-up our triangle.

Step 2: *Set up the ratios.*

We've already got the function cos *D* = 0.4.

$$\cos D = \frac{x}{18} \quad \& \quad \cos D = \frac{0.4}{1}$$

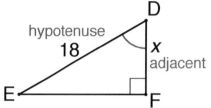

Step 3: *Set your ratios equal, cross-multiply, & solve.*

$$\frac{0.4}{1} = \frac{x}{18} = 7.2 \ inches$$

Answer choice **J** is correct.

<u>What You May Have Done Wrong</u>

F. You set up your proportion backwards (18/*x*). Also, remember that no side can be longer than the hypotenuse.

G. You divided 18 by 4. Review your steps.

H. This is a calculation error. Review your steps.

K. This is a calculation error. Review your steps.

2. **Dom is using a sextant to measure the height of a tall flagpole. Sextants measure the angle between the ground and the sun (called the angle of elevation), The angle of elevation is 33°. Dom measures the length of the shadow cast by the flagpole as 32.42 feet. What is the height of the flagpole?**

   Note: sin 33°= 0.55 cos 33° = 0.84, & tan 33°=0.65

Correct Answer F

This is a common ACT setup. We've got to solve for a side, but to do so; we've got to correctly label the triangle. In this case, it's no big deal, because the angle is marked and the sides are named.

Step 1: Decide on the function & markup your triangle

Since we have the *adjacent* and we need the *opposite* we'll use tangent.

Step 2: Set up your ratios.

We're given the function in the problem tan 33° = 0.65.

$$\tan 33° = \frac{opposite}{adjacent} = \frac{x}{32.42} \quad \& \quad \tan 33° = \frac{0.65}{1}$$

Step 3: Set your ratios equal, cross-multiply, & solve.

$$\frac{0.65}{1} = \frac{x}{32.42} \rightarrow x = (0.65)(32.42) \rightarrow x = 21.1$$

Answer choice **F** is correct.

<u>What You May Have Done Wrong</u>

    G. You flipped one of your ratios or you made a similar error.

    H. You used cosine, instead of tan.

    J. You used sine instead of tan.

    K. You used cosine and you flipped one of your ratios.

3. In triangle *ABC*, angle *B* has a tan of $\frac{3}{4}$ and side *a* is 12 units long. What is the length of *b*?

Correct Answer C

We've got a bit of labeling to do on this "find the side" question.

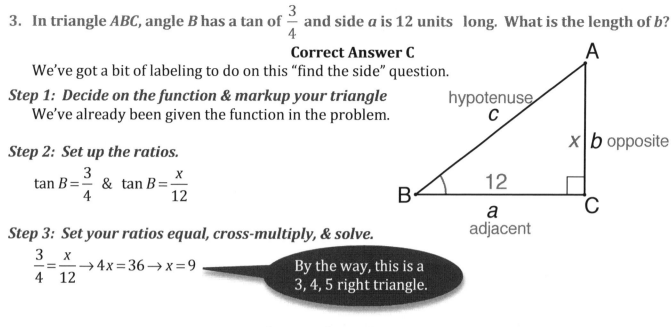

Step 1: Decide on the function & markup your triangle
We've already been given the function in the problem.

Step 2: Set up the ratios.

$$\tan B = \frac{3}{4} \quad \& \quad \tan B = \frac{x}{12}$$

Step 3: Set your ratios equal, cross-multiply, & solve.

$$\frac{3}{4} = \frac{x}{12} \rightarrow 4x = 36 \rightarrow x = 9$$

By the way, this is a 3, 4, 5 right triangle.

Answer choice **C** is correct

<u>What You May Have Done Wrong</u>
   A. You probably made a calculation error or guessed.
   B. You made a mistake in your proportion, dividing 12 by ¾.
   D. You made a calculation error or guessed.
   E. This is the hypotenuse of the triangle; review your steps.

4. A support strut supports horizontal and vertical beams. The beams meet at a ninety-degree angle and have distances and angles as marked. Which expression gives the length of the strut?

Correct Answer J

This is another problem where the question is confusing but the diagram is complete.

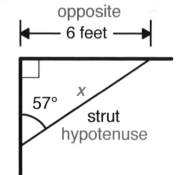

Step 1: Decide on the function & mark-up your triangle
We don't really have anything additional to add to our diagram.
Since we're given *opposite* and we need *hypotenuse*, we'll use sine.

Step 2: Set up the ratios.

$$\sin 57° = \frac{6}{x} \quad \& \quad \sin 57° = \frac{\sin 57°}{1}$$

Step 3: Set your ratios equal, cross-multiply, & solve.

$$\frac{6}{x} = \frac{\sin 57°}{1} \rightarrow x\left(\sin 57°\right) = 6 \rightarrow x = \frac{6}{\sin 57°}$$

Answer choice **J** is correct.

<u>What You May Have Done Wrong:</u>
   F. You flipped a ratio. Review your steps.
   G. You flipped a ratio. Review your steps.
   H. 6 is the opposite side, not the adjacent.
   K. 6 is the opposite side, not the adjacent.

5. **Jake is deep sea diving to attach a cable to a sunken treasure chest. The ship, the HMS Test Guy, is tracking Jake's progress and using the length and angle of the cable to** calculate Jake's depth. The angle of the cable is the angle from the side of the ship, which is perpendicular to the surface of the ocean. That angle is calculated as 18°. The **length of the cable is 190 feet. How deep is Jake?**

Note: $\sin 72° = 0.95$, $\cos 72° = 0.31$, $\tan 18° = 0.33$, & $\sin 18° = 0.31$

Correct Answer A

This is a really long word problem, but don't let the text intimidate you. Label your diagram and go from there.

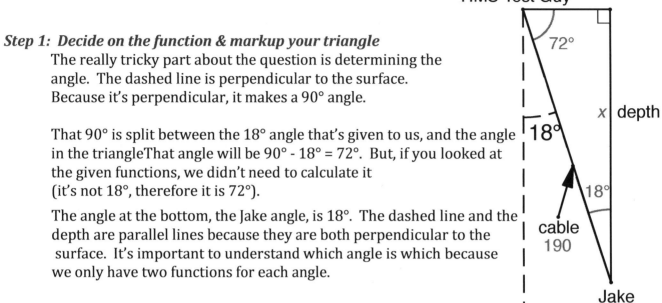

Step 1: Decide on the function & markup your triangle

The really tricky part about the question is determining the angle. The dashed line is perpendicular to the surface. Because it's perpendicular, it makes a 90° angle.

That 90° is split between the 18° angle that's given to us, and the angle in the triangleThat angle will be 90° - 18° = 72°. But, if you looked at the given functions, we didn't need to calculate it (it's not 18°, therefore it is 72°).

The angle at the bottom, the Jake angle, is 18°. The dashed line and the depth are parallel lines because they are both perpendicular to the surface. It's important to understand which angle is which because we only have two functions for each angle.

Here's the trick. Even though you only have two functions for each, you can use your calculator to allow you to use whichever function you prefer. That's the best way to solve this problem, but it's worth talking about the other way. First, we need to identify which functions we can use.For the 18° angle, we've got the length of the *hypotenuse* and we need the length of the

adjacent. Cosine is $\dfrac{adjacent}{hypotenuse}$, but it isn't provided for the 18° angle..

For the 72° angle, we've got the length of the *hypotenuse* and we need the *opposite*, so we'll use sine. Since sine of 72° is provided we can proceed.

We can use *cosine* 18° by using the calculator.

Step 2: Set up the ratios.

$$\sin 72° = \frac{x}{190} \ \& \ \sin 72° = \frac{0.95}{1}$$

Step 3: Set your ratios equal, cross-multiply, & solve.

$$\frac{0.95}{1} = \frac{x}{190} \rightarrow x = (0.95)(190) \rightarrow 180.5$$

Answer choice **A** is correct.

<u>What You May Have Done Wrong</u>

B. You used *tan* instead of sine 72° (or cosine 18°).

C. You used cosine 72° or sine 18°.

D. You used the right function, but flipped a ratio.

E. You used tan, and flipped a ratio.

There's a *video* on *Arc Functions.*

Introduction

Solving for an angle shows up less frequently than *find the side* questions. Like *find a side* questions, these *find an angle* questions test your ability to use functions.

What You Need to Know

- ✓ The definitions of sine, cosine, and tangent
- ✓ How to find a function from the sides of a triangle.
- ✓ How to use the arc functions on your calculator ($\sin^{-1}$, $\cos^{-1}$, $\tan^{-1}$)

Definitions: Arc functions

Arc functions are the *inverse of functions*. Instead of looking up the ratio of the sides, arc functions look up the size of the angle *from* the ratio of the sides.

Rules of the Road: Finding Arc Functions in a Calculator

Steps to finding measure of an angle:

1. Pick a function. You'll want to use a function where both sides are already known
2. Set up your function.
3. Put your function into the correct format.

All ACT problems can be solved without a calculator, so while you won't *need* to look up an angle on the ACT, it can be handy sometimes. To lookup the function in most calculators, including Texas Instruments graphing calculators, follow these steps.

1. Press the second button
2. Press the button of the function you're using (you should see a function^{-1} above the button).
3. Enter the fraction value of the function $\frac{side}{side}$.
4. If your answer is a very small number, your calculator may be in radians. To change a TI graphing calculator from radians press MODE and change the third row from *radians* to *degrees.*

1. Margo is planning a wheelchair ramp for a volunteer project. The ramp will rise 1.5 feet to a doorway and the ramp will extend 10.3 feet. What is the angle of elevation of the ramp?

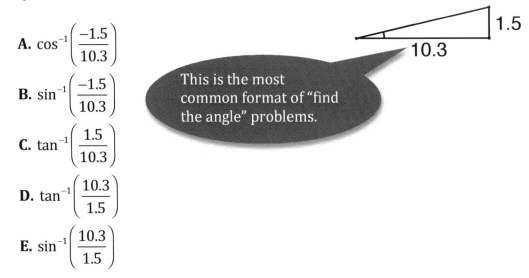

A. $\cos^{-1}\left(\dfrac{-1.5}{10.3}\right)$

B. $\sin^{-1}\left(\dfrac{-1.5}{10.3}\right)$

This is the most common format of "find the angle" problems.

C. $\tan^{-1}\left(\dfrac{1.5}{10.3}\right)$

D. $\tan^{-1}\left(\dfrac{10.3}{1.5}\right)$

E. $\sin^{-1}\left(\dfrac{10.3}{1.5}\right)$

Solve

1. *Pick a function.*

   We've got the opposite and the adjacent, so we'll use *tan*.

2. *Set up your function.*

$$\tan = \frac{opposite}{ajacent} = \frac{1.5}{10.3}$$

3. *Put the function into the proper form*

$$\tan^{-1}\left(\frac{1.5}{10.3}\right) = 8.3$$

Answer Choice **C** is correct.

2. A triangle has sides as marked and a hypotenuse of $\sqrt{185}$. Which of the following expressions will give the measure of angle x?

A. $\tan^{-1}\left(\dfrac{8}{11}\right)$

B. $\tan^{-1}\left(\dfrac{8}{\sqrt{185}}\right)$

C. $\sin^{-1}\left(\dfrac{8}{\sqrt{185}}\right)$

D. $\cos^{-1}\left(\dfrac{8}{\sqrt{185}}\right)$

E. $\cos^{-1}\left(\dfrac{8}{11}\right)$

Solve

In these problems we won't have to look up the function. These are much more like the "find the function" problems. They are usually mark-off problems.

A. $\dfrac{8}{11} = \dfrac{adjacent}{opposite}$, this is cotan not tan.

B. $\dfrac{8}{\sqrt{185}} = \dfrac{adjacent}{hypotenuse}$, this is cosine not tan.

C. $\dfrac{8}{\sqrt{185}} = \dfrac{adjacent}{hypotenuse}$, this is sine not cosine.

D. $\dfrac{8}{\sqrt{185}} = \dfrac{adjacent}{hypotenuse}$, this *is* cosine.

E. $\dfrac{8}{11} = \dfrac{adjacent}{opposite}$, this is cotan, not cosine.

Answer Choice **D** is correct.

Wrap Up

What You Need to Know
- ✓ The definitions of sine, cosine, and tangent
- ✓ How to find a function from the sides of a triangle.
- ✓ How to use the arc functions on your calculator ($\sin^{-1}$, $\cos^{-1}$, $\tan^{-1}$)

Videos

Finding the Angle

The Strategies
- ✓ Follow the same steps as *find a side* questions
- ✓ Your setup will be determined by the sides you know
- ✓ Mark-off most questions, once you've looked at one of the functions (sine, cosine, tangent) evaluate other answer choices containing that function.

Related Topics
- ✓ The Unit Circle

Trigonometry: Arc Functions

1. Duke is measuring dimensions for a large triangular garden he plans to construct. He needs the angle measure, in degrees, of the angle marked. What expression will give the measure of the angle?

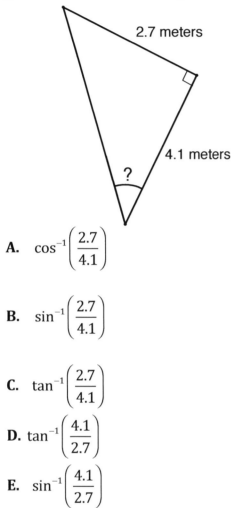

2.7 meters

4.1 meters

?

A. $\cos^{-1}\left(\dfrac{2.7}{4.1}\right)$

B. $\sin^{-1}\left(\dfrac{2.7}{4.1}\right)$

C. $\tan^{-1}\left(\dfrac{2.7}{4.1}\right)$

D. $\tan^{-1}\left(\dfrac{4.1}{2.7}\right)$

E. $\sin^{-1}\left(\dfrac{4.1}{2.7}\right)$

3. Harper is planning a parachute jump from 10,000 feet. If the horizontal distance she covers is 600 feet, which expression gives the angle of elevation (x) of Harper's descent?

10,000

$x°$

600

A. $x° = \cos^{-1}\left(\dfrac{100}{6}\right)$

B. $x° = \tan^{-1}\left(\dfrac{100}{6}\right)$

C. $x° = \cos^{-1}\left(\dfrac{6}{100}\right)$

D. $x° = \sin^{-1}\left(\dfrac{6}{100}\right)$

E. $x° = \tan^{-1}\left(\dfrac{6}{100}\right)$

2. Given the side lengths of the triangle below, what is the measure of angle *CAB*?

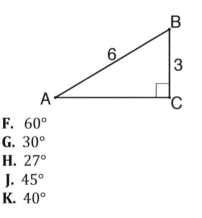

B

6

3

A

C

F. 60°
G. 30°
H. 27°
J. 45°
K. 40°

4. Acute angle *BAC* has a measure of $y°$ and right triangle *ABC* has side lengths of marked. Which expression gives the value of angle *A*?

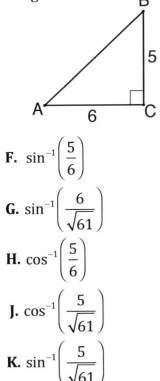

F. $\sin^{-1}\left(\dfrac{5}{6}\right)$

G. $\sin^{-1}\left(\dfrac{6}{\sqrt{61}}\right)$

H. $\cos^{-1}\left(\dfrac{5}{6}\right)$

J. $\cos^{-1}\left(\dfrac{5}{\sqrt{61}}\right)$

K. $\sin^{-1}\left(\dfrac{5}{\sqrt{61}}\right)$

5. In the right triangle shown below, one of the angles has a measure of $\sin^{-1}\left(\dfrac{a}{\sqrt{a^2+b^2}}\right)$.

What is $\tan\left[\sin^{-1}\left(\dfrac{a}{\sqrt{a^2+b^2}}\right)\right]$?

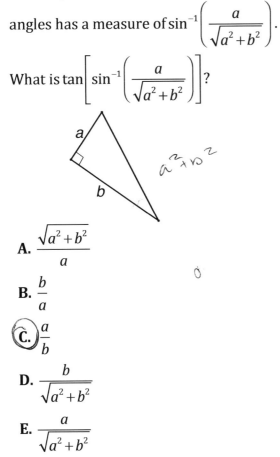

A. $\dfrac{\sqrt{a^2+b^2}}{a}$

B. $\dfrac{b}{a}$

C. $\dfrac{a}{b}$

D. $\dfrac{b}{\sqrt{a^2+b^2}}$

E. $\dfrac{a}{\sqrt{a^2+b^2}}$

6. A circle with center *A* is shown below. The length of radius $\overline{AB}$ is 6 units and the length of $\overline{AC}$ is 5 units.

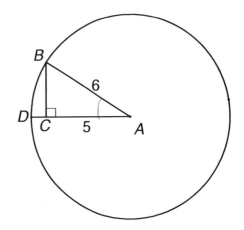

When $\angle BAC$ is measured in degrees, what expression will give the length of minor arc $\overset{\frown}{BD}$?

F. $\dfrac{\pi}{30}\left(\sin^{-1}\left(\dfrac{5}{6}\right)\right)$

G. $\dfrac{15\pi}{6}\left(\cos^{-1}\left(\dfrac{5}{6}\right)\right)$

H. $\dfrac{\pi}{15}\left(\sin^{-1}\left(\dfrac{5}{6}\right)\right)$

J. $\dfrac{\pi}{30}\left(\cos^{-1}\left(\dfrac{5}{6}\right)\right)$

K. $\dfrac{\pi}{15}\left(\tan^{-1}\left(\dfrac{5}{6}\right)\right)$

Arc Functions: Solutions

1. **Duke is measuring dimensions for a large triangular garden he plans to construct. He needs the angle measure, in degrees, of the angle marked. What expression will give the measure of the angle?**

Correct Answer C

This is a *mark-off* question that really asks about the definition of a function. Mark-up your triangle and then all you have to do is check out your answer choices and find the one where the function matches the fraction.

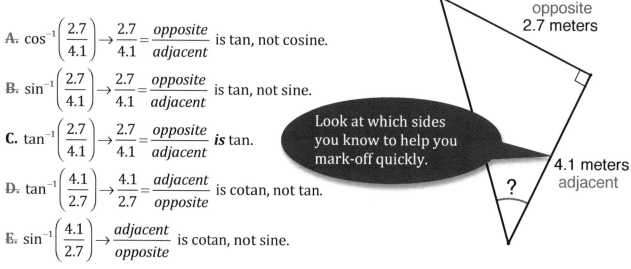

A. $\cos^{-1}\left(\dfrac{2.7}{4.1}\right) \to \dfrac{2.7}{4.1} = \dfrac{opposite}{adjacent}$ is tan, not cosine.

B. $\sin^{-1}\left(\dfrac{2.7}{4.1}\right) \to \dfrac{2.7}{4.1} = \dfrac{opposite}{adjacent}$ is tan, not sine.

C. $\tan^{-1}\left(\dfrac{2.7}{4.1}\right) \to \dfrac{2.7}{4.1} = \dfrac{opposite}{adjacent}$ *is* tan.

D. $\tan^{-1}\left(\dfrac{4.1}{2.7}\right) \to \dfrac{4.1}{2.7} = \dfrac{adjacent}{opposite}$ is cotan, not tan.

E. $\sin^{-1}\left(\dfrac{4.1}{2.7}\right) \to \dfrac{adjacent}{opposite}$ is cotan, not sine.

Look at which sides you know to help you mark-off quickly.

Answer choice C is correct.

<u>What You May Have Done Wrong</u>
All answer choices are discussed above.

2. **Given the side lengths of the triangle below, what is the measure of angle *CAB*?**

Correct Answer G

This question requires you to calculate the measure of the angle. First, markup your triangle and pick a function. Since we have *opposite* & *hypotenuse*, I'll use sine.

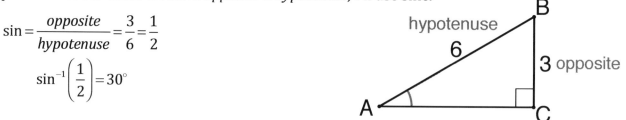

$$\sin = \frac{opposite}{hypotenuse} = \frac{3}{6} = \frac{1}{2}$$

$$\sin^{-1}\left(\frac{1}{2}\right) = 30°$$

It's also a special right triangle, and that's probably the simplest way to solve this problem. A *hypotenuse* twice the length of a *side* means the triangle is a 30°-60°-90° right triangle.

Answer choice G is correct.

<u>What You May Have Done Wrong</u>

F. You used $\cos^{-1}\left(\dfrac{3}{6}\right)$ instead of sine.

H. You used $\tan^{-1}\left(\dfrac{3}{6}\right)$ instead of sine.

J. You may have guessed or made a calculation error.

K. This is either a guess or a calculation error.

3. Harper is planning a parachute jump from 10,000 feet. If the horizontal distance she covers is 600 feet, which expression gives the angle of elevation (x) of Harper's descent?

Correct Answer B

This is a definition question. Don't let the confusing question intimidate you; we have a have a fully labeled diagram. Let's mark-off:

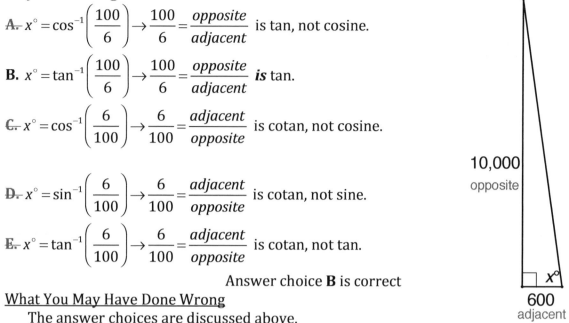

A. $x° = \cos^{-1}\left(\dfrac{100}{6}\right) \rightarrow \dfrac{100}{6} = \dfrac{opposite}{adjacent}$ is tan, not cosine.

B. $x° = \tan^{-1}\left(\dfrac{100}{6}\right) \rightarrow \dfrac{100}{6} = \dfrac{opposite}{adjacent}$ *is* tan.

C. $x° = \cos^{-1}\left(\dfrac{6}{100}\right) \rightarrow \dfrac{6}{100} = \dfrac{adjacent}{opposite}$ is cotan, not cosine.

D. $x° = \sin^{-1}\left(\dfrac{6}{100}\right) \rightarrow \dfrac{6}{100} = \dfrac{adjacent}{opposite}$ is cotan, not sine.

E. $x° = \tan^{-1}\left(\dfrac{6}{100}\right) \rightarrow \dfrac{6}{100} = \dfrac{adjacent}{opposite}$ is cotan, not tan.

Answer choice **B** is correct

<u>What You May Have Done Wrong</u>

The answer choices are discussed above.

4. Acute angle *BAC* has a measure of $y°$ and right triangle *ABC* has side lengths of marked. Which expression gives the value of angle *A*?

Correct Answer K

This is a mark-off question with a little extra wrinkle. We don't have the hypotenuse and, because of the answer choices, we need it.

We actually don't need to calculate the *hypotenuse*. If we look at the answer choices, the only possible value for the *hypotenuse* is $\sqrt{61}$.

$$a^2 + b^2 = c^2 \quad \rightarrow \quad 5^2 + 6^2 = c^2 \quad \rightarrow \quad c = \sqrt{61}$$

If you missed that, the *hypotenuse* can be found by the Pythagorean Theorem. Let's mark-off answers.

F. $\sin^{-1}\left(\dfrac{5}{6}\right) \rightarrow \dfrac{5}{6} = \dfrac{opposite}{adjacent}$ is tan, not sine.

G. $\sin^{-1}\left(\dfrac{6}{\sqrt{61}}\right) \rightarrow \dfrac{6}{\sqrt{61}} = \dfrac{adjacent}{hypotenuse}$ is cosine, not sine.

H. $\cos^{-1}\left(\dfrac{5}{6}\right) \rightarrow \dfrac{5}{6} = \dfrac{opposite}{adjacent}$ is tan, not cosine.

J. $\cos^{-1}\left(\dfrac{5}{\sqrt{61}}\right) \rightarrow \dfrac{5}{\sqrt{61}} = \dfrac{opposite}{hypotenuse}$ is sine, not cosine.

K. $\sin^{-1}\left(\dfrac{5}{\sqrt{61}}\right) \rightarrow \dfrac{5}{\sqrt{61}} = \dfrac{opposite}{hypotenuse}$

Answer choice **K** is correct.

5. In the right triangle shown below, one of the angles has a measure of $\sin^{-1}\left(\dfrac{a}{\sqrt{a^2+b^2}}\right)$.

What is $\tan\left[\sin^{-1}\left(\dfrac{a}{\sqrt{a^2+b^2}}\right)\right]$?

Correct Answer C

This question looks a lot trickier than it is. It's a lot like composition of functions (*Intermediate Algebra: Functions*). Let's talk about what's going on with the question. Arc functions (in this case $\sin^{-1}$) give us the measure of an angle. Then we take the *tan* of that angle.

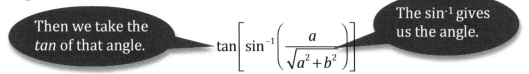

We aren't given the hypotenuse, but from the question we can infer that the hypotenuse is $\sqrt{a^2+b^2}$. Let's decide which angle we're dealing with.

$$\sin = \frac{opposite}{hypotenuse} = \frac{a}{\sqrt{a^2+b^2}}$$

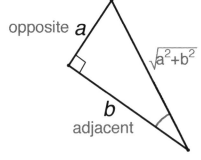

Now we can find the tan of the angle.

$$\tan = \frac{opposite}{adjacent} = \frac{a}{b}$$

Answer choice **C** is correct.

<u>What You May Have Done Wrong</u>
   A. This is the cosecant of the angle, but review your steps.
   B. This is the cotan of the angle. You may have solved for the wrong angle.
   D. This is the cosine of the angle, but review your steps.
   E. This is the sine of the angle, but review your steps.

6. A circle with center A is shown below. The length of radius $\overline{AB}$ is 6 units and the length of $\overline{AC}$ is 5 units. When $\angle BAC$ is measured in degrees, what expression will give the length of minor arc $\overparen{BD}$?

Correct Answer J

This is a tough question, *but if we know which function to use we can mark down to a 50/50.* And, if you think about the size of the arc, the other cosine answer doesn't make sense (the arc would be more than two circles in length). To solve, we've got to deal with two parts: finding the angle & finding the arc.

Let's markup our graph. There's not much to put on the graph other than what we're looking for.

To find the length of an arc, we need to find out what fraction of the circumference is represented.

$$circumference \cdot \frac{angle}{360°}$$

We'll use the arc function in place of the angle.

Let's find the circumference:
$$circumference = 2\pi r$$
$$circumference = 2\pi 6 \rightarrow 12\pi$$

Let's find the angle. We have hypotenuse & adjacent, so we'll use *cosine*.

$$\cos^{-1}\left(\frac{adjacent}{hypotenuse}\right) \rightarrow \cos^{-1}\left(\frac{5}{6}\right)$$

$$circumference \cdot \frac{angle}{360°} \rightarrow 12\pi \cdot \frac{\cos^{-1}\left(\frac{5}{6}\right)}{360°}$$

We'll need to simplify the fraction.

We don't include $\cos^{-1}\left(\frac{5}{6}\right)$ in the simplification because it's a single number, not a fraction.

$$circumference \cdot \frac{angle}{360°} \rightarrow 12\pi \cdot \left(\frac{\cos^{-1}\left(\frac{5}{6}\right)}{360°}\right)$$

$$\frac{12\pi}{360°}\left(\cos^{-1}\left(\frac{5}{6}\right)\right) \rightarrow \frac{\pi}{30}\left(\cos^{-1}\left(\frac{5}{6}\right)\right)$$

Answer choice **J** is correct.

<u>What You May Have Done Wrong</u>
  F. You used the wrong function; it should be *cosine* not *sine*
  G. You flipped your arc fraction and made a calculation error.
  H. You used the wrong function, and you made a mistake in calculating your arc.
  K. You used the wrong function, and you made a mistake in calculating your arc.

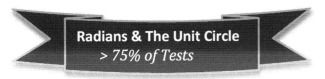

Introduction

Unit circle questions have a few components: a coordinate axis, an angle, radians, and a trig function.

What You Need to Know

- ✓ The definitions of sine, cosine, and tangent
- ✓ How to use and find radians.
- ✓ How to find the function of an angle on a co-ordinate axis, which sides are opposite, adjacent, and hypotenuse.

Definitions: Radians

> **Radians are a way to measure angles by using *arc length*.**
> ***Arc length* is based on *circumference*.**
> 2π radians = 360° (a whole circle)
> π radians = 180° (a semi-circle)

A circle with a radius of 1 (a unit circle) has a circumference of:
$$circumference = 2\pi r \rightarrow circumference = 2\pi(1)$$
$$circumference = 2\pi$$

Any arc of that circle will be a fraction (a portion) of 2π.

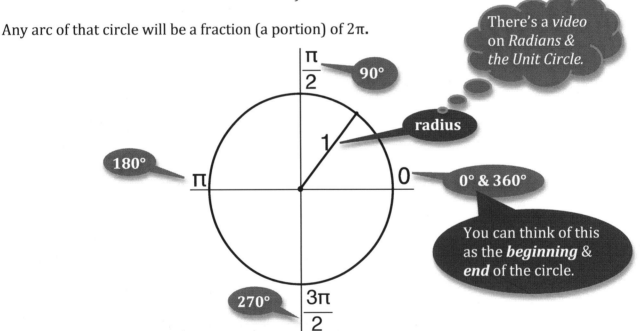

There's a *video* on *Radians & the Unit Circle.*

You can think of this as the **beginning** & **end** of the circle.

measure of angle based on circumference

On Unit Circles

When we deal with angles on the unit circle, the angle has a vertex of the origin (0,0). Angles "start" at the positive x-axis. The angle goes counter-clockwise until it reaches its terminal side, "the end." The terminal side is the leg of the angle that isn't the positive x-axis.

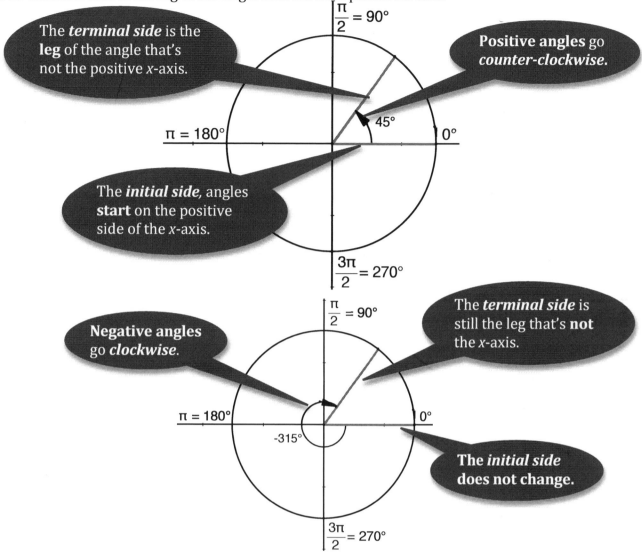

The **terminal side** is the **leg** of the angle that's not the positive x-axis.

Positive angles go *counter-clockwise.*

The **initial side**, angles **start** on the positive side of the x-axis.

Negative angles go *clockwise.*

The **terminal side** is still the leg that's **not** the x-axis.

The **initial side** does not change.

Converting Degrees & Radians

Converting from degrees to radians and vice versa can be useful, particularly if you plan to rely on your calculator for trig problems. You can change the mode on your calculator to output radians or degrees. Be careful, though, because it's easy to forget to switch back.

Changing Degrees to Radians:
1. Divide the angle by 180°
2. Put π in the numerator of the resulting fraction.

Example

Convert 45° to radians. $\dfrac{45°}{180°} \to \dfrac{1\pi}{4} \to \dfrac{\pi}{4}$

Changing Radians to Degrees:
1. Replace π with 180°
2. Multiply by numerator and divide by denominator.

Example

Convert $\dfrac{3\pi}{4}$ radians to degrees. $\dfrac{3\pi}{4} \to \dfrac{3(180°)}{4} \to \dfrac{540°}{4} = 135°$

ACT Example: Angles in the Unit Circle

1. Angle C measures $\frac{7\pi}{2}$ radians from its initial side to its terminal side. Angle D has the same initial side and same terminal side as Angle C. What could be the measure of Angle D?

A. 270°
B. 90°
C. 180°
D. 360°
E. 540°

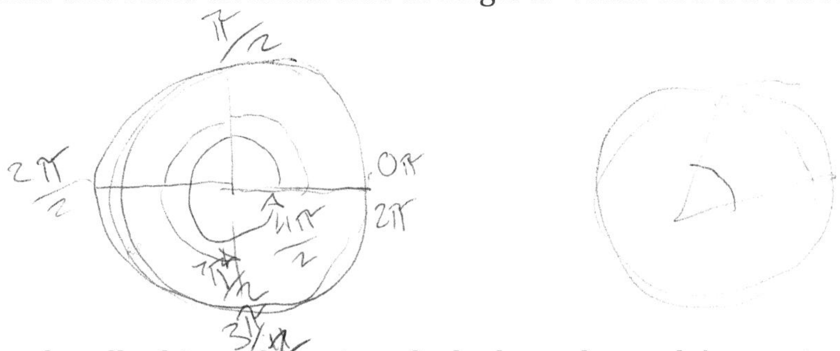

Solve

The easiest way to handle this problem is to find where the angle's terminal side will be on the unit circle. There are two ways to do this. We could subtract 2π radians until we get to an angle less than 2π radians.

$$\frac{7\pi}{2}-\frac{4\pi}{2}=\frac{3\pi}{2}$$

Subtract 2π radians

Now, we've got an angle *less* than 2π radians.

-OR-

$$\frac{7\pi}{2}=\frac{7(180^\circ)}{2}=630^\circ=\frac{3\pi}{2}$$

$$630^\circ-360^\circ=270^\circ$$

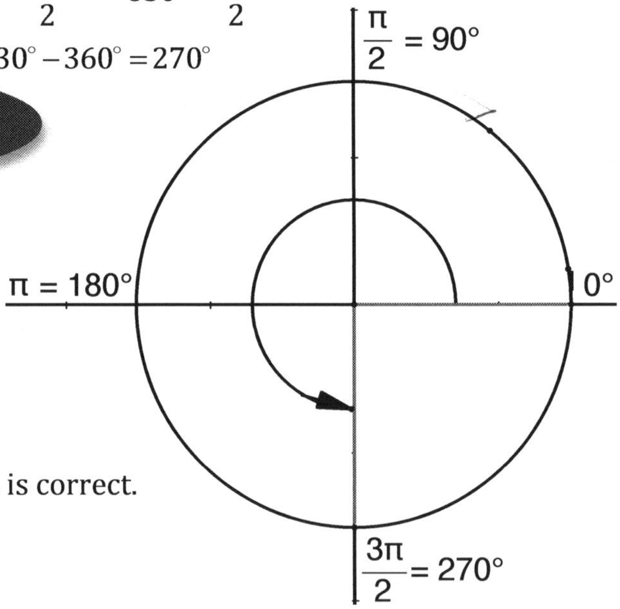

We don't necessarily need to, but we can draw up a unit circleto see the 270° or $\frac{3\pi}{2}$ angle more clearly.

Answer choice **A** is correct.

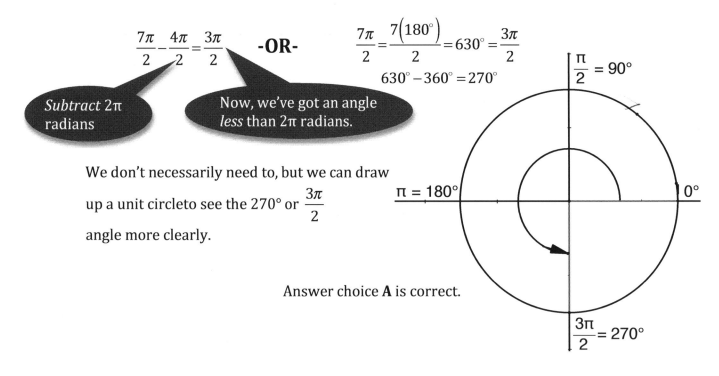

Getting Trig Functions from Unit Circles

We can draw a vertical line (parallel to the *y*-axis) to make a right triangle from the angle. The point where the *terminal side* meets the circle, allows us to determine our side lengths.

The *x*-axis (initial side) is the *adjacent* side. The *hypotenuse* is the *terminal side*. The *opposite side* is the line you draw.

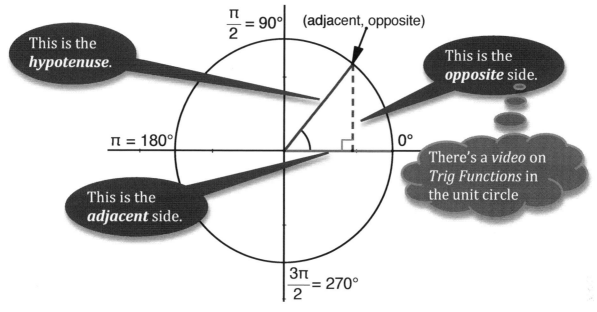

As long as the point is on the unit circle it will have a hypotenuse of 1. So, any point on the unit circle can be defined in three ways.

$$(x, y) \rightarrow (adjacent, opposite) \rightarrow (\cos, \sin)$$

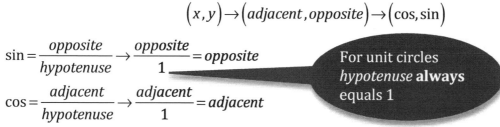

$$\sin = \frac{opposite}{hypotenuse} \rightarrow \frac{opposite}{1} = opposite$$

$$\cos = \frac{adjacent}{hypotenuse} \rightarrow \frac{adjacent}{1} = adjacent$$

For unit circles hypotenuse **always** equals 1

Positive & Negative Values of Trig Functions

We can determine when functions will have positive & negative values based on their identities. **Hypotenuse is a distance (a length) and hypotenuse is *always* positive.**

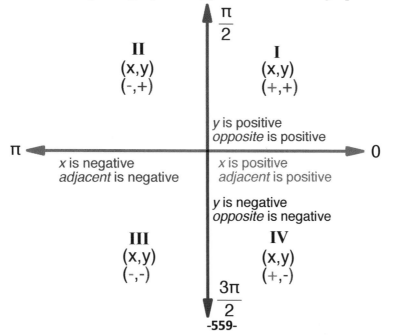

Positive & Negative Values of Trig Functions (cont.)

Function	Definition	When Positive	Quadrants
Sine	$\dfrac{opposite}{hypotenuse} \rightarrow \dfrac{y \; value}{length}$	y positive	I & II
Cosine	$\dfrac{adjacent}{hypotenuse} \rightarrow \dfrac{x \; value}{length}$	x positive	I & IV
Tangent	$\dfrac{opposite}{adjacent} \rightarrow \dfrac{y \; value}{x \; value}$	x & y have same signs	I & III

Hypotenuse is *always* positive.

Rules of the Road: Finding the Sign of Trig Functions

Simple Method
1. Either convert your angle to degrees or shift your calculator into radians.
2. Look up the function in your calculator.

More Complex Method
1. Draw a coordinate axis with radians labeled.
2. Draw the angle (just sketch something) in the correct quadrant. Make a triangle and label your sides.
3. Decide if the sides will be positive or negative, and whether your function will be positive or negative.

Example: Finding the Positive or Negative Value of a Function

1. For the angle $\dfrac{5\pi}{4}$, which functions (sine, cosine, & tangent) are positive?

Solve

Calculator Method
You can also convert radians to degrees.

To convert radians to degrees, plug in 180 for π

$$\frac{5\pi}{4} \rightarrow \frac{5(180°)}{4} \rightarrow \frac{900°}{4} \rightarrow 225°$$

Lookup the value of sine, cosine, and tangent for 225°

$$\sin 225° \approx -0.71$$
$$\cos 225° \approx -0.71$$
$$\tan 225° = 1$$

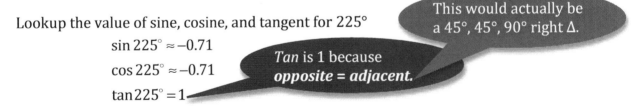

This would actually be a 45°, 45°, 90° right Δ.

Tan is 1 because *opposite = adjacent.*

Or you can convert calculator to radians. Check the sine, cosine and tangent of $\dfrac{5\pi}{4}$ in your calculator.

Example: Finding the Positive or Negative Value of a Function

Unit Circle Method

Because $\dfrac{5\pi}{4}$ is *greater* than π but *less* than $\dfrac{3\pi}{2}$, the angle is in the third quadrant.

In the third quadrant, *opposite* & *adjacent* are both negative.
Hypotenuse is a distance and is always positive.

$$\sin = \frac{opposite}{hypotenuse} = \frac{-}{+} \rightarrow \sin \text{ is negative}$$

$$\cos = \frac{adjacent}{hypotenuse} = \frac{-}{+} \rightarrow \cos \text{ is negative}$$

$$\tan = \frac{opposite}{adjacent} = \frac{-}{-} \rightarrow \tan \text{ is positive}$$

For the angle $\dfrac{5\pi}{4}$ (and any angle in the third quadrant)

only *tan* will be positive. In the third quadrant, *sine* and *cosine* will always be negative.

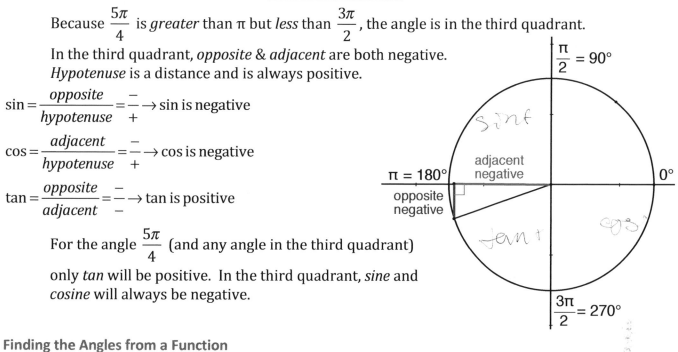

Finding the Angles from a Function

The ACT likes to give you a function and have you solve for both angles that have that function. To do so, you'll need to know how to find the second angle.

In trig class you learned how to calculate reference angles, which is fairly involved, as the procedure changes for each quadrant. The good news, you don't need to calculate reference angles on the ACT.

Rules of the Road: Finding Angles from a Trig Function

1. Figure out which quadrant you're dealing with.
2. Figure out which other quadrant can result in that trig function.

Video on *Finding Angles from a Function*

Example: Finding the Measure of an Angle in a Right Triangle
1. When tan = -0.75, what quadrants will those angles be in?

Solve

When tan is negative, *opposite* and *adjacent* have different signs.

Tan will be negative in quadrants II and IV.

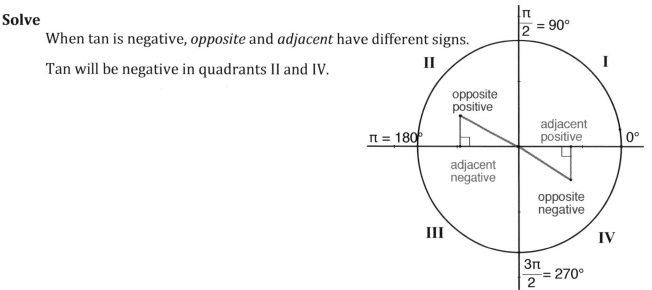

ACT Examples: Finding angles on the Unit Circle

1. When $\sin = 0.534$, which could be true of θ?

A. $\dfrac{\pi}{2} < \theta < \dfrac{5\pi}{6}$

B. $\dfrac{5\pi}{4} < \theta < \dfrac{3\pi}{2}$

C. $\dfrac{7\pi}{6} < \theta < \dfrac{3\pi}{2}$

D. $\dfrac{3\pi}{2} < \theta < \dfrac{5\pi}{3}$

E. $\dfrac{9\pi}{5} < \theta < \dfrac{11\pi}{6}$

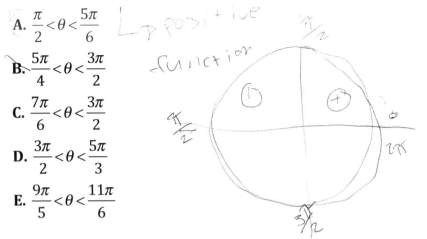

Solve

One way to try this problem is to use the $\sin^{-1}$ function on your calculator. That gives you 32.28° or 0.562 radians. We can run through the answers and see if any of those answers have 0.562 radians in their range. You can enter the radian fractions in your calculator to check them against 0.562 You may want to do some fraction to decimal conversions. To do so, replace π with 180°.

You can go through the answers, but none of them have a range that includes 32.28°. You can't solve this problem with the calculator alone. **We'd have to find the angle by subtracting 32.28 from 180. This works fine, but you'll have to know how to find your reference angle. To find your reference angle, you've got to know your quadrants.**

There's an easier way to do this problem.

ACT Example (cont.): Finding angles on the Unit Circle

Let's figure out in which quadrants sine is positive. Recall that sine is positive whenever *opposite* is positive. *Opposite = y*, so sine will be positive in quadrants I and II.

We can go ahead and mark off answer choices.

A. $\dfrac{\pi}{2} < \theta < \dfrac{5\pi}{6}$ → This is quadrant II

B. $\dfrac{5\pi}{4} < \theta < \dfrac{3\pi}{2}$ → This is quadrant III

C. $\dfrac{7\pi}{6} < \theta < \dfrac{3\pi}{2}$ → This is quadrant III

D. $\dfrac{3\pi}{2} < \theta < \dfrac{5\pi}{3}$ → This is quadrant III

E. $\dfrac{9\pi}{5} < \theta < \dfrac{11\pi}{6}$ → This is quadrant IV

II
sine is positive

I
sine is positive

$\dfrac{\pi}{2}$

y is positive
opposite is positive

π —————→ 0

x is negative
adjacent is negative

x is positive
adjacent is positive

y is negative
opposite is negative

III

IV

$\dfrac{3\pi}{2}$

Answer Choice **A** is correct.

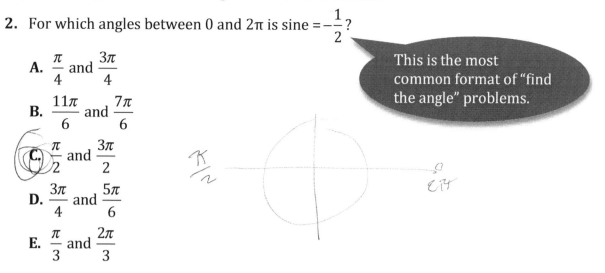

2. For which angles between 0 and 2π is sine $= -\dfrac{1}{2}$?

> This is the most common format of "find the angle" problems.

A. $\dfrac{\pi}{4}$ and $\dfrac{3\pi}{4}$

B. $\dfrac{11\pi}{6}$ and $\dfrac{7\pi}{6}$

C. $\dfrac{\pi}{2}$ and $\dfrac{3\pi}{2}$

D. $\dfrac{3\pi}{4}$ and $\dfrac{5\pi}{6}$

E. $\dfrac{\pi}{3}$ and $\dfrac{2\pi}{3}$

Solve

This problem works backwards. We'll use the sine to find the angle.

Calculator Method

$$\sin\theta = -\frac{1}{2} \rightarrow \sin^{-1}\left(-\frac{1}{2}\right) = -30°$$

> Review *Trig: Arc Functions*

The calculator only gives us one angle, -30°. We'll have to calculate the other angles. Let's start with the positive x-axis, which is equal to both 0° & 360°. We'll add -30 to 360°.

$$360° - 30° = 330°$$

For the other angle, start at the *negative* x-axis (180° AKA π) and subtract -30°.

Now, convert the answers to radians. $180° - \left(-30°\right) \rightarrow 180° + 30° = 210°$

$$\frac{330°}{180°} \rightarrow \frac{11\pi}{6} = \frac{\pi}{6} \quad \& \quad \frac{210°}{180°} \rightarrow \frac{7\pi}{6}$$

But there's an easier way...

Unit Circle Method

We can use marking-off to answer this question. Recall the definition of sine.

$$\sin = \frac{opposite}{hypotenuse} \rightarrow \frac{y}{length}$$

Because *hypotenuse* can never be negative (it's a measure of distance), sine will be negative whenever *y* is negative. That's in quadrants III and IV.

A. $\dfrac{\pi}{4}$ and $\dfrac{3\pi}{4}$ → Both sines are positive.

B. $\dfrac{7\pi}{6}$ and $\dfrac{11\pi}{6}$ → *Both* sines are negative.

C. $\dfrac{\pi}{2}$ and $\dfrac{3\pi}{2}$ → The sine of $\dfrac{\pi}{2}$ is positive.

D. $\dfrac{3\pi}{4}$ and $\dfrac{5\pi}{6}$ → The sine of $\dfrac{3\pi}{4}$ is positive.

E. $\dfrac{\pi}{3}$ and $\dfrac{2\pi}{3}$ → Both sines are positive.

Answer Choice **B** is correct.

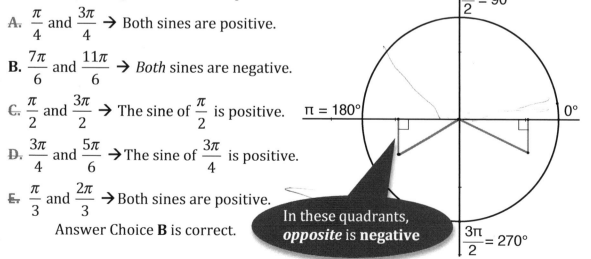

> In these quadrants, *opposite* is **negative**

ACT Example: Finding a Function from a Function

3. Given that $\tan\theta = \dfrac{4}{3}$ and $0° \leq \theta \leq 360°$, what are all possible values of $\sin\theta$?

A. $\dfrac{3}{4}$ only

B. $\dfrac{3}{4}$ and $-\dfrac{3}{4}$

C. $\dfrac{4}{5}$ only

D. $-\dfrac{4}{5}$ only

E. $\dfrac{4}{5}$ and $-\dfrac{4}{5}$

Solve

You could try to solve this using your calculator only, by finding the angle using $\tan^{-1}\left(\dfrac{4}{3}\right) \approx 53.1°$. But you'll be stuck on finding your second angle (unless you want to calculate the reference angle). We know there will be a second angle because tan, like all functions, is positive in two quadrants.

The best way to solve this is to use our coordinate axes. Tan is positive whenever *adjacent* (x) and *opposite* (y) have the same signs.

ow we can draw triangles and find our sines.

$$\tan = \frac{4}{3} = \frac{opposite}{adjacent} = \frac{y}{x} \quad \&$$

$$\tan = \frac{-4}{-3} = \frac{4}{3} = \frac{opposite}{adjacent} = \frac{y}{x}$$

We aren't given the hypotenuse, so we can calculate it using the Pythagorean Theorem or you may recognize that it's a 3,4,5 special right triangle.

Quadrant I has a sine of

$$\frac{opposite}{hypotenuse} = \frac{y}{length} = \frac{4}{5}$$

Quadrant III has a sine of

$$\frac{opposite}{hypotenuse} = \frac{y}{length} = \frac{-4}{5} = -\frac{4}{5}$$

Answer Choice **E** is correct.

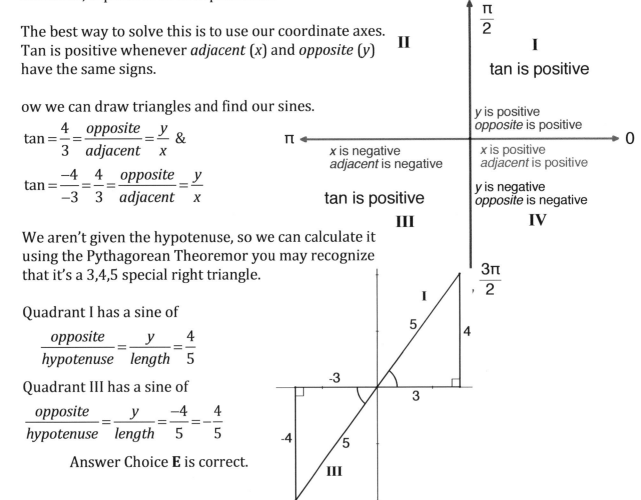

Wrap Up

What You Need to Know
- ✓ The definitions of sine, cosine, and tangent
- ✓ How to use and find radians.
- ✓ How to find the function of an angle on a co-ordinate axis, which sides are opposite, adjacent, and hypotenuse.

Videos

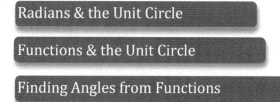

Radians & the Unit Circle

Functions & the Unit Circle

Finding Angles from Functions

The Strategies
- ✓ Draw a triangle. Remember, angles with a vertex of the origin have an *opposite* side of *y* and an *adjacent* side of *x*.
- ✓ Remember that *hypotenuse* is always positive.
- ✓ There are always two angles for any given function, and use quadrants to mark-off answer choices.

Related Topics
- ✓ Trig, Find the Side

- ✓ Trig, Find the Function

- ✓ Trig, Find the Angle

Trigonometry: Unit Circle

1. What are the values of the angle, between 0 and 2π, where $\sin = -\dfrac{1}{2}$?

A. $\dfrac{\pi}{6}$ and $\dfrac{5\pi}{6}$

B. $\dfrac{5\pi}{6}$ and $\dfrac{7\pi}{6}$

C. $\dfrac{5\pi}{6}$ and $\dfrac{11\pi}{6}$

D. $\dfrac{7\pi}{6}$ and $\dfrac{11\pi}{6}$

E. $\dfrac{\pi}{6}, \dfrac{7\pi}{6}$, and $\dfrac{11\pi}{6}$

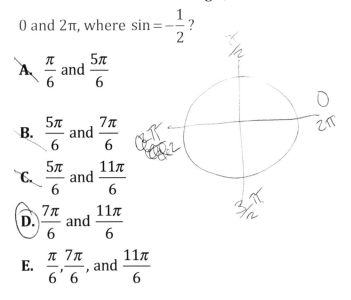

2. If the $\cos\theta = \dfrac{24}{25}$ and $0 \le \theta < 2\pi$, what are all the possible values of $\sin\theta$?

F. $-\dfrac{24}{25}$ and $\dfrac{24}{25}$ only

G. $-\dfrac{24}{25}$ only

H. $-\dfrac{7}{25}$ only

J. $\dfrac{7}{25}$ only

K. $-\dfrac{7}{25}$ and $\dfrac{7}{25}$

3. Angle B measures $\dfrac{11}{2}\pi$ radians measured from the positive x-axis. Angle C has the same initial side and same terminal side as Angle B. Which of the following could be the measure of Angle C?

A. 90°
B. 135°
C. 180°
D. 270°
E. 360°

4. When $\sin A = -\dfrac{5}{13}$ and $\dfrac{3}{2}\pi < A < 2\pi$, then Tan A = ?

F. $\dfrac{13}{12}$

G. $-\dfrac{12}{5}$

H. $-\dfrac{12}{13}$

J. $-\dfrac{5}{12}$

K. $\dfrac{5}{12}$

5. Angle θ has its vertex at (0,0) in the standard (x, y) coordinate plane. The terminal side of this angle passes through the point (8,-6). What is the sin of θ?

A. $-\dfrac{3}{4}$

B. $-\dfrac{3}{5}$

C. $\dfrac{3}{5}$

D. $\dfrac{4}{5}$

E. $-\dfrac{4}{5}$

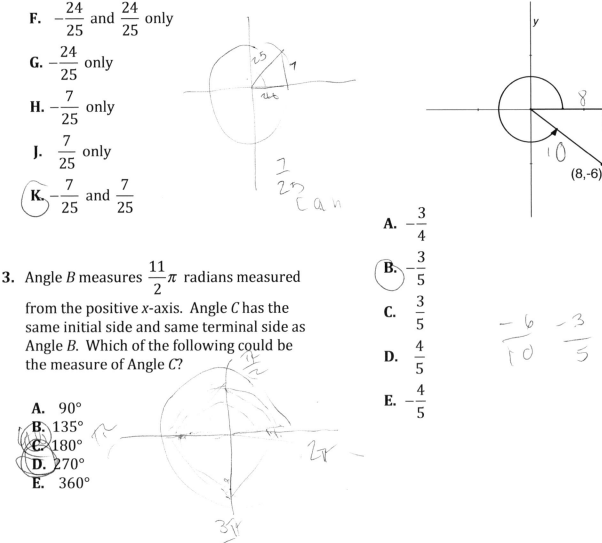

6. What are the values between 0 and 2π where $\tan = 1$?

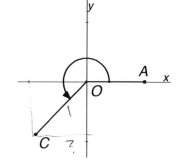

    F. 45° & 135°
    G. 45° & 225°
    H. 135° & 225°
    J. 135° & 315°
    K. 225° & 315°

7. In the standard (x, y) coordinate plane below, the $\angle AOC$ measures 225°. The distance from O to C is 1 unit and A is on the x-axis. What are the coordinates of C?

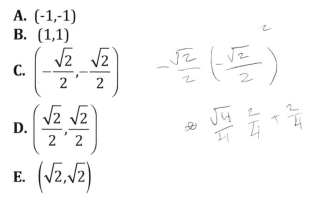

    A. (-1,-1)
    B. (1,1)
    C. $\left(-\dfrac{\sqrt{2}}{2}, -\dfrac{\sqrt{2}}{2} \right)$
    D. $\left(\dfrac{\sqrt{2}}{2}, \dfrac{\sqrt{2}}{2} \right)$
    E. $\left(\sqrt{2}, \sqrt{2} \right)$

8. Points S, T, U, V, are on the unit circle shown below. The center of the unit circle is O, and the positive measure of $\angle UOT$ is θ and the positive measure of $\angle UOS$ is $\dfrac{4}{3}\theta$. Minor arcs $\overset{\frown}{ST}$ and $\overset{\frown}{UV}$ are the same length.

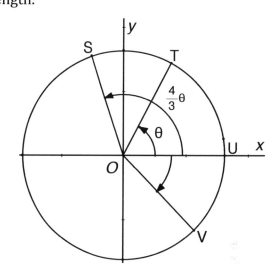

What is the measure of $\angle UOV$ in the direction shown?

    F. $\dfrac{1}{3}\theta$
    G. $-\dfrac{1}{3}\theta$
    H. θ
    J. $-\dfrac{4}{3}\theta$
    K. $\dfrac{4}{3}\theta$

Trigonometry the Unit Circle: Solutions

1. What are the values of the angle, between 0 and 2π, where $\sin = -\dfrac{1}{2}$?

Correct Answer D

This is a common setup for unit circle problems. By requiring both angles, it's a lot harder to use our calculator. The *easiest* way to solve this is to find which quadrants have negative sine values. As a last resort, you could switch your calculator to radians (or convert the answer choices to degrees) and test answer choices.

$$\sin = \frac{opposite}{hypotenuse} \rightarrow \frac{y}{length}$$

Sine is negative when *y* is negative, quadrants **III** & **IV.**

We can now mark-off answers that don't have an angle in quadrant III *and* an angle in quadrant IV.

II $\dfrac{\pi}{2}$ **I**

y is positive
opposite is positive

x is negative
adjacent is negative

x is positive
adjacent is positive

π 0

A. $\dfrac{\pi}{6}$ and $\dfrac{5\pi}{6}$ are in quadrants I & II.

sine is negative   sine is negative

B. $\dfrac{5\pi}{6}$ and $\dfrac{7\pi}{6}$ are in quadrants II & III.

y is negative
opposite is negative

III   **IV**

C. $\dfrac{5\pi}{6}$ and $\dfrac{11\pi}{6}$ are in quadrants II & IV.

$\dfrac{3\pi}{2}$

D. $\dfrac{7\pi}{6}$ and $\dfrac{11\pi}{6}$ are in quadrants III & IV.

E. $\dfrac{\pi}{6}, \dfrac{7\pi}{6}$, and $\dfrac{11\pi}{6}$ are in quadrants I, III, & IV.

Answer choice D is correct.

2. If the $\cos \theta = \dfrac{24}{25}$ and $0 \le \theta < 2\pi$, what are all the possible values of $\sin \theta$?

Correct Answer K

This is the other most common format of unit circle question. There are a couple of tricks to it. **First, there are *always* two angles in the unit circle that have the original function, and those two angles will be in two different quadrants. *You can automatically mark-off any answer that has only one angle.***

All you'll need to do is figure out the sine of a triangle with an *adjacent* of 24 and a *hypotenuse* of 25. To do that, we'll need to find the *opposite* using the Pythagorean Theorem. Using the Pythagorean Theorem...

$$a^2 + b^2 = c^2 \rightarrow 24^2 + b^2 = 25^2 \rightarrow b^2 = 49 \rightarrow b = 7$$

So, the sine of θ will be $\dfrac{7}{25}$ and its other possible value is $-\dfrac{7}{25}$.

<u>Graphically</u>

First, we've got to figure out the quadrants where cosine is positive.

Cosine is defined as $\cos = \dfrac{adjacent}{hypotenuse} \rightarrow \dfrac{x}{length}$. So, cosine is positive when x is positive.

The adjacent side, x, will be positive on the right side of our coordinate plane. So, we're looking at quadrants **I** & **IV**. Let's draw our triangles.

So, the two values for $\sin \theta$ are $\dfrac{7}{25}$ & $-\dfrac{7}{25}$.

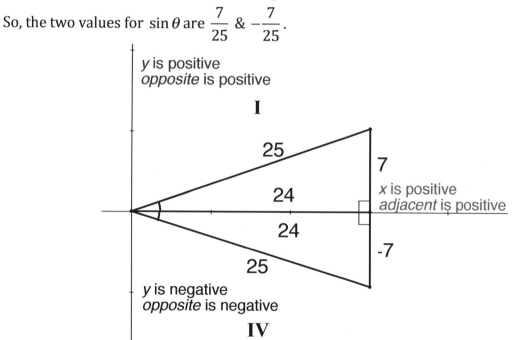

Answer choice **K** is correct.

<u>What You May Have Done Wrong</u>

    F. This is the cosine, and it's given.
    G. This is just the negative of the cosine.
    H. This is one sine of the *two* possible sines.
    J. This is one sine of the *two* possible sines.

3. Angle *B* measures $\dfrac{11}{2}\pi$ radians measured from the positive *x*-axis. Angle *C* has the same initial side and same terminal side as Angle *B*. Which of the following could be the measure of Angle *C*?

Correct Answer D

This question is half about finding the angle and half about the conversion from radians to degrees. You can either convert first or find the angle first; it won't matter. To convert, plug in 180° for π (π radians = 180°).

$$\frac{11\pi}{2} \rightarrow \frac{11\left(180°\right)}{2} = \frac{1,980°}{2} = 990°$$

Now, we need to find an angle less than 360° (2π) that has the same initial side and terminal side. To do that, we subtract 360° (2π) until we have an angle less than 360°.

$$990° - 360° = 630° \rightarrow 630 - 360° = 270°$$

Of course you could have done it the other way around, subtracting 2π from

$$\frac{11\pi}{2} - 2\pi = \frac{7\pi}{2} \rightarrow \frac{7\pi}{2} - 2\pi = \frac{3\pi}{2} \quad \text{and then convert to degrees.}$$

Answer choice **D** is correct

What You May Have Done Wrong

A. You may have made a conversion error, or went clockwise when calculating the angle.
B. This may be a conversion or calculation error.
C. You may have guessed or made a conversion error.
E. You may have guessed or made a conversion error.

4. When $\sin A = -\dfrac{5}{13}$ and $\dfrac{3}{2}\pi < A < 2\pi$, then Tan *A* = ?

Correct Answer J

This is another example of a *find a function* question. In this case, we're only looking at one quadrant (IV) so we'll only have one angle. Since we know it's the fourth quadrant, we can go ahead and draw our triangle.

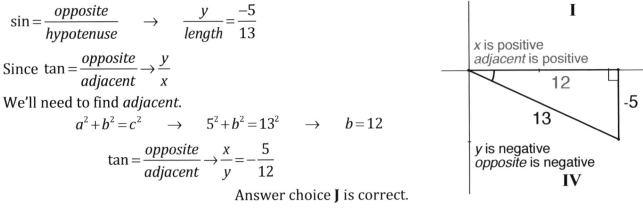

$$\sin = \frac{opposite}{hypotenuse} \quad \rightarrow \quad \frac{y}{length} = \frac{-5}{13}$$

Since $\tan = \dfrac{opposite}{adjacent} \rightarrow \dfrac{y}{x}$

We'll need to find *adjacent*.

$$a^2 + b^2 = c^2 \quad \rightarrow \quad 5^2 + b^2 = 13^2 \quad \rightarrow \quad b = 12$$

$$\tan = \frac{opposite}{adjacent} \rightarrow \frac{x}{y} = -\frac{5}{12}$$

Answer choice **J** is correct.

What You May Have Done Wrong:

F. This is secant $\dfrac{hypotenuse}{adjacent}$ of *A*.

G. This is cosecant $\dfrac{hypotenuse}{opposite}$ of *A*.

H. This is cotan $\dfrac{adjacent}{opposite}$ of *A*.

K. This is cotan, but you also dropped a sign (it's -5).

5. Angle θ has its vertex at (0,0) in the standard (x, y) coordinate plane. The terminal side of this angle passes through the point (8,-6). What is the sine of θ?

Correct Answer B

This is another format of the *find a function* question. We're given a large angle and asked to find to find the sine. They've given us two pieces of information that are important. First, the vertex is (0,0) and second that the point (8,-6) is on the terminal side of the angle. We're ready to draw the triangle and solve.

We'll need to calculate the length of the *hypotenuse*.

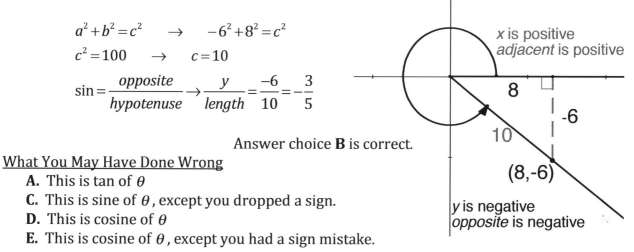

$$a^2 + b^2 = c^2 \quad \rightarrow \quad -6^2 + 8^2 = c^2$$
$$c^2 = 100 \quad \rightarrow \quad c = 10$$
$$\sin = \frac{opposite}{hypotenuse} \rightarrow \frac{y}{length} = \frac{-6}{10} = -\frac{3}{5}$$

x is positive
adjacent is positive

8

-6

10

(8,-6)

y is negative
opposite is negative

Answer choice **B** is correct.

<u>What You May Have Done Wrong</u>
  A. This is tan of θ
  C. This is sine of θ, except you dropped a sign.
  D. This is cosine of θ
  E. This is cosine of θ, except you had a sign mistake.

6. What are the values between 0 and 2π where tan = 1?

Correct Answer G

We're using the function to find the angle, and at first it looks like we may have to convert radians to degrees. Actually, we don't have to convert radians to degrees. The question just asks us for the angles between 0 and 2π, so we just say that the angles need to be between 0° and 360°. Because the answer choices are in degrees, *plugging in answers* works pretty well and it's fast enough. Let's talk about the "proper" way to do the problem.

$$\tan = \frac{opposite}{adjacent} \rightarrow \frac{y}{x}$$

Tan will be positive when x & y have the same sign.

That's quadrants I & III.
We can mark-off any answers
that don't have both I & III or
have angles in other quadrants.

F. 45° & 135° are in quadrants **I & II.**
G. 45° & 225° *are* in quadrants **I & III.**
H. 135° & 225° are in quadrants **II & III.**
J. 135° & 315° are in quadrants **II & IV.**
K. 225° & 315° are in quadrants **III & IV.**

$\frac{\pi}{2}$

II   I

y is positive
opposite is positive

tan is positive

π ← → 0

x is negative x is positive
adjacent is negative   *adjacent* is positive

tan is positive y is negative
                         opposite is negative

III   IV

$\frac{3\pi}{2}$

You could use your calculator to test answers quickly.

Answer **G** is correct.

-571-

7. **In the standard (x, y) coordinate plane below, the $\angle AOC$ measures 225°. The distance from O to A is one unit and A is on the x-axis. What are the coordinates of C?**

Correct Answer C

This is a bit of a twist on the unit circle problem. You can start it by using your calculator and looking up the trig function or make you can make a (special) right triangle. Look up the tan of 225°,

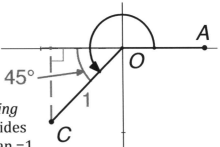

$$\tan 225° = \frac{opposite}{adjacent} = 1.$$

That means the **ratio** of opposite and adjacent is 1, *opposite = adjacent.* It does **not** mean that the sides have lengths of 1 (or -1). *That's the drawback of relying on your calculator.* The ACT wants you to think the sides are 1 and 1. Although an x of -1 and a y -1 will have tan =1,

the distance of $\overline{OC}$ is 1, and therefore that won't work (in the Pythagorean Theorem). Instead, you could draw a triangle and, from the negative x-axis determine that the angle will be 45°. Once you know that the *opposite = adjacent* you can use the Pythagorean theorem to find the side length. The question tells us that $\overline{OC}$ is 1, so our *hypotenuse* will be 1.

Because I know that *opposite = adjacent*, I can say it's $a^2 + a^2$

$$a^2 + b^2 = c^2 \qquad \rightarrow \qquad a^2 + a^2 = 1$$

$$2a^2 = 1 \qquad \rightarrow \qquad a^2 = \frac{1}{2} \qquad \rightarrow \qquad a = \sqrt{\frac{1}{2}}$$

We can rewrite $\sqrt{\frac{1}{2}}$ as $\frac{\sqrt{1}}{\sqrt{2}}$, but we end up with a square root in the denominator. Since we can't have roots in the denominator, we'll have to *rationalize* the fraction.

This doesn't match our answer choices; we'll have to **rationalize** the fraction.

$$\sqrt{\frac{1}{2}} = \frac{\sqrt{1}}{\sqrt{2}} = \frac{1}{\sqrt{2}} \rightarrow \frac{1}{\sqrt{2}} \cdot \frac{\sqrt{2}}{\sqrt{2}} = \frac{\sqrt{2}}{2}$$

Multiply by $\sqrt{2}$ on the top & bottom to get rid of the root in the denominator

But, there's one more step. We've got the length of the *adjacent & opposite* sides, but we need the coordinate points.

So, point *C* is at $\left(-\frac{\sqrt{2}}{2}, -\frac{\sqrt{2}}{2} \right)$.

Because we're on the negative side, subtract.

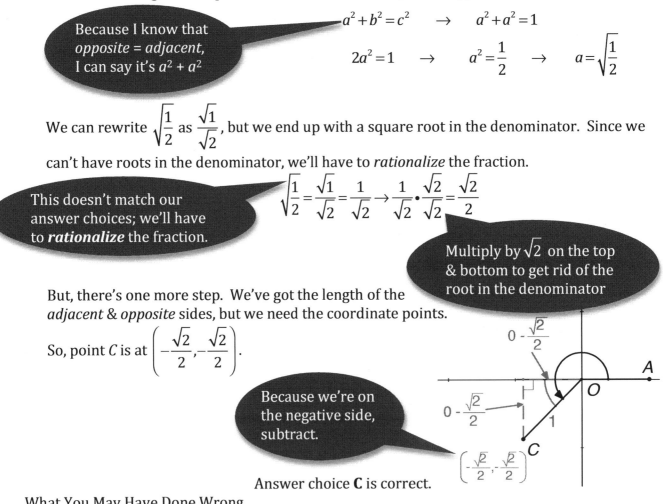

Answer choice **C** is correct.

<u>What You May Have Done Wrong</u>

A. You used the ratio of tan as the length of the sides.

B. You used the ratio of tan as the length of the sides, and you failed to account for what quadrant the point is in.

D. This is so very close to the right answer, but you forgot the find the point.

E. You probably made a math error.

8. Points S, T, U, V, are on the unit circle shown below. The center of the unit circle is O, and the positive measure of $\angle UOT$ is θ and the positive measure of $\angle UOS$ is $\frac{4}{3}\theta$.

Minor arcs $\overset{\frown}{ST}$ and $\overset{\frown}{UV}$ are the same length. What is the measure of $\angle UOV$ in the direction shown?

Correct Answer G

This is a strange definition question. Essentially, they're testing your knowledge of positive and negative angles on the unit circle and some logic. The first thing you should notice is that $\angle UOV$ is moving in the *negative direction* (remember, on the unit circles negative angles go clockwise). We can mark off three answers right away: **F, H, & K.** If you didn't know how to proceed, you'd have a 50/50. Let's mark up our graph and go from there.

Let's find angle $\angle TOS$, $\angle TOS = \frac{4}{3}\theta - \theta \rightarrow \angle TOS = \frac{1}{3}\theta$.

Since $\angle UOV$ has the same measure but moves in the negative direction its measure will be $\angle UOV = -\frac{1}{3}\theta$.

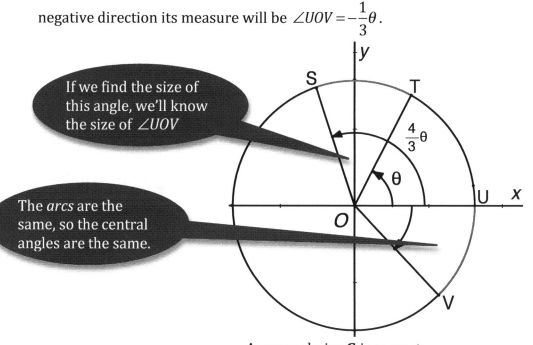

If we find the size of this angle, we'll know the size of $\angle UOV$

The *arcs* are the same, so the central angles are the same.

Answer choice **G** is correct.

What You May Have Done Wrong
   F. This is the right value, but wrong sign. Remember, we're moving in the negative direction.
   H. You may have guessed or marked the wrong arc equal.
   J. You used the entire angle measure $\angle UOS$, but your sign was right.
   K. You used the entire angle measure $\angle UOS$.

Introduction

Trig identities show up as plug-in and definition problems. The ACT does not require you to have these identities memorized. It can be helpful, though, to know that $\sin^2 + \cos^2 = 1$. I am only going to review the most common problem types. But regardless of the identity, the problem will work the same way: identify your sides & angles, plug-in, and solve. **Trig identities questions are just trig based plug-in problems.**

What You Need to Know

- ✓ The *Big Three* Trig Functions: Sine, Cosine, & Tangent
- ✓ How to properly label diagrams
- ✓ How to find the function of an angle on a co-ordinate axis, which sides are opposite, adjacent, and hypotenuse.
- ✓ How to plug in and solve functions.

Definitions: The Pythagorean Identity

On occasion, the ACT asks us about the Pythagorean Identity $\sin^2 + \cos^2 = 1$. You don't *need* to know it, but if you don't you've got to be comfortable *plugging in numbers.*

> The **Pythagorean Theorem** defines a relationship between *sine* and *cosine*. Remember, in the unit circle *hypotenuse* = 1. In the unit circle we can define points three ways
>
> $(x, y) \rightarrow (adjacent, opposite) \rightarrow (\cos, \sin)$
>
> $$a^2 + b^2 = c^2$$
> $$y^2 + x^2 = 1^2$$
> $$\sin^2 + \cos^2 = 1$$

There are other Pythagorean Identities, but $\sin^2 + \cos^2 = 1$, is the only one I'd take the time to learn. I haven't seen the others tested.

1. Angle A is between 0 and $\dfrac{\pi}{2}$. Which of the following is equivalent to the expression

$\dfrac{1-\cos^2 A}{\sin A} - \sin A?$

> There's a *video* on *Pythagorean Identities*

    A. 0
    B. 1
    C. $\cos A$
    D. $\sin^2 A$
    E. Cannot be Determined

Solve

This is a great example of when it's nice, but not necessary, to know the Pythagorean Identity $\sin^2 + \cos^2 = 1$.

Using The Identity

To solve, we'll need to re-arrange the identity to look like the numerator of the fraction.

$$\sin^2 + \cos^2 = 1 \rightarrow \sin^2 A + \cos^2 A = 1 \rightarrow \sin^2 = 1 - \cos^2$$

Now we can plug in $\sin^2$ into our fraction.

$$\dfrac{1-\cos^2 A}{\sin A} - \sin A \rightarrow \dfrac{\sin^2 A}{\sin A} - \sin A$$

> Plug in $\sin^2$

$$\dfrac{\sin^2 A}{\sin A} - \sin A \rightarrow \dfrac{\sin^2 A}{\sin A} - \sin A$$

> Simplify.

$$\sin A - \sin A \rightarrow 0$$

Plugging in Numbers

To solve, pick a measure between $0°$ and $90°$ for angle A. We plug that in for A and solve using our calculator. I'm using $45°$.

$$\dfrac{1-\left(\cos 45°\right)^2}{\sin 45°} - \sin 45° \rightarrow \dfrac{0.5}{0.707} - 0.707 = 0$$

Answer choice **A** is correct.

$\sin^2 + \cos^2 = 1$

Law of Sines & The Law of Cosines

The law of sines and the law of cosines allow you to work with triangles that aren't right triangles. For the ACT, we'll just have to plug-in and solve.

ACT Example: Law of Sines

1. Three ships the *Sophie*, the *Madee*, and the *Taylar* are on lake Michigan. The *Madee* is 7 miles from the *Taylar* and the *Sophie* is 5 miles from the *Madee* and the measure of angle *T* is 42°. What equation would give the measure of angle *S*?

(Note: For a triangle with sides of length a, b, and c that are opposite $\angle A, \angle B, \angle C$, respectively, $\dfrac{\sin A}{a} = \dfrac{\sin B}{b} = \dfrac{\sin C}{c}$.)

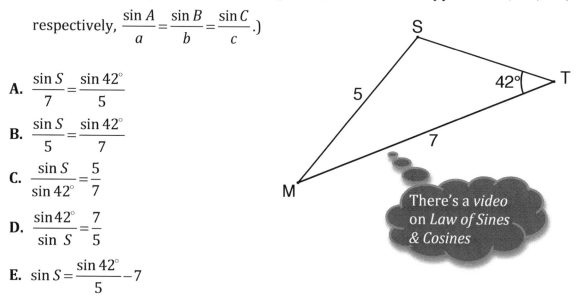

A. $\dfrac{\sin S}{7} = \dfrac{\sin 42°}{5}$

B. $\dfrac{\sin S}{5} = \dfrac{\sin 42°}{7}$

C. $\dfrac{\sin S}{\sin 42°} = \dfrac{5}{7}$

D. $\dfrac{\sin 42°}{\sin S} = \dfrac{7}{5}$

E. $\sin S = \dfrac{\sin 42°}{5} - 7$

Solve

All you've got to do is set-up your equation by plugging in the right numbers. It's actually just like working a ratio problem. Start by writing out your law of sines. Since we're only solving for one side, we don't have to write all three parts of the equation (we can just write two parts).

$$\frac{\sin A}{a} = \frac{\sin B}{b}$$

Let's mark-up our triangle.

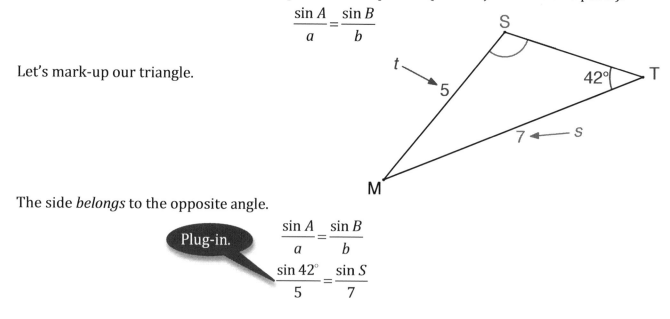

The side *belongs* to the opposite angle.

Plug-in.

$$\frac{\sin A}{a} = \frac{\sin B}{b}$$

$$\frac{\sin 42°}{5} = \frac{\sin S}{7}$$

Answer choice **A** is correct.

1. Alexa is looking at two landmarks, a statue and a tree. The tree is 0.7 miles from Alexa and the statue is 1.8 miles from Alexa. The angle between the line of sight to the statue and the line of sight to the tree is 20°. The distance from the tree to the statue is given by which expression?

   (Note: For a triangle with sides of length a, b, and c that are opposite $\angle A, \angle B, \angle C$, respectively, $c^2 = a^2 + b^2 - 2ab\cos C$.)

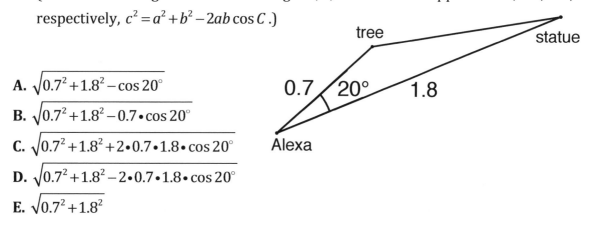

   A. $\sqrt{0.7^2 + 1.8^2 - \cos 20°}$

   B. $\sqrt{0.7^2 + 1.8^2 - 0.7 \cdot \cos 20°}$

   C. $\sqrt{0.7^2 + 1.8^2 + 2 \cdot 0.7 \cdot 1.8 \cdot \cos 20°}$

   D. $\sqrt{0.7^2 + 1.8^2 - 2 \cdot 0.7 \cdot 1.8 \cdot \cos 20°}$

   E. $\sqrt{0.7^2 + 1.8^2}$

Solve

This is another plug-in problem. We've only got one angle, and two sides. The law of cosines requires one angle and two sides.

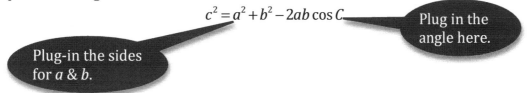

It actually doesn't matter which side we plug in for a and which side we plug in for b. Order doesn't matter in multiplication and addition.

$$c^2 = a^2 + b^2 - 2ab\cos C$$
$$c^2 = 0.7^2 + 1.8^2 - 2 \cdot 0.7 \cdot 1.8 \cdot \cos 20°$$

To find c, we'll need to take the square root of both sides of the equation.

$$c^2 = 0.7^2 + 1.8^2 - 2 \cdot 0.7 \cdot 1.8 \cdot \cos 20°$$
$$c = \sqrt{0.7^2 + 1.8^2 - 2 \cdot 0.7 \cdot 1.8 \cdot \cos 20°}$$

Answer choice **D** is correct.

Secant, Cosecant, & Cotan

The other three trig functions aren't tested commonly. And when they are tested, the definitions are provided (the exception is a long cotangent problem). It's worth knowing, however, how these functions relate to *the big three (sine, cosine, & tangent)*.

What You Need to Know

- ✓ The reciprocal relationship between sine & cosecant, cosine & secant, and tangent & cotangent.
- ✓ The minimum values of *secant* and *cosecant*.
- ✓ That *secant* and *cosecant* can be **undefined**.

Definitions: Secant, Cosecant, & Cotangent

There's a video on sec, csc, & cot.

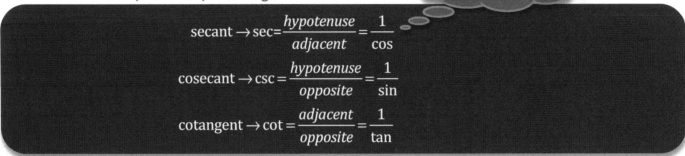

$$\text{secant} \rightarrow \sec = \frac{hypotenuse}{adjacent} = \frac{1}{\cos}$$

$$\text{cosecant} \rightarrow \csc = \frac{hypotenuse}{opposite} = \frac{1}{\sin}$$

$$\text{cotangent} \rightarrow \cot = \frac{adjacent}{opposite} = \frac{1}{\tan}$$

Secant, cosecant, and cotangent are all reciprocals of cosine, sine, and tangent.

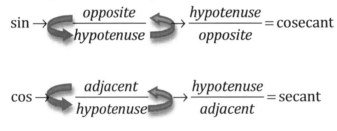

$$\sin \rightarrow \frac{opposite}{hypotenuse} \rightarrow \frac{hypotenuse}{opposite} = \text{cosecant}$$

$$\cos \rightarrow \frac{adjacent}{hypotenuse} \rightarrow \frac{hypotenuse}{adjacent} = \text{secant}$$

$$\tan \rightarrow \frac{opposite}{adjacent} \rightarrow \frac{adjacent}{opposite} = \text{cotan}$$

The Other Three Trig Functions

The other way we commonly see secant, cosecant, and cotangent are in terms of cosine, sine and tangent

$$\text{secant} = \frac{1}{\cos}$$

$$\text{cosecant} = \frac{1}{\sin}$$

$$\text{cotangent} = \frac{1}{\tan}$$

Sine goes with *cosecant*
Cosine goes with *secant*
S goes with *C*
C goes with *S*

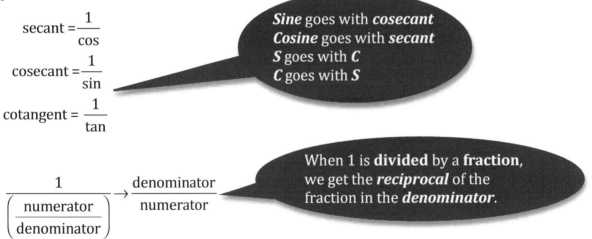

$$\frac{1}{\left(\frac{numerator}{denominator}\right)} \rightarrow \frac{denominator}{numerator}$$

When 1 is **divided** by a **fraction**, we get the *reciprocal* of the fraction in the *denominator*.

The Minimum Values of Secant & Cosecant

Remember that **sine** and **cosine** have a **maximum value** of 1, because *hypotenuse* is in the denominator. By definition, *hypotenuse* is the longest side of a right triangle.

Secant & **cosecant** have a **minimum value** of 1, because *hypotenuse* is in the numerator, and, again, *hypotenuse* is the longest side.

Undefined functions

Sine and **cosine** are *always defined*, because the *hypotenuse* will always have a value that isn't zero.

Tan, **cot**, **sec**, & **csc** can be *undefined*. Why?

$$\tan = \frac{opposite}{adjacent}$$

$$\cot = \frac{adjacent}{opposite}$$

$$\sec = \frac{hypotenuse}{adjacent}$$

$$\csc = \frac{hypotenuse}{opposite}$$

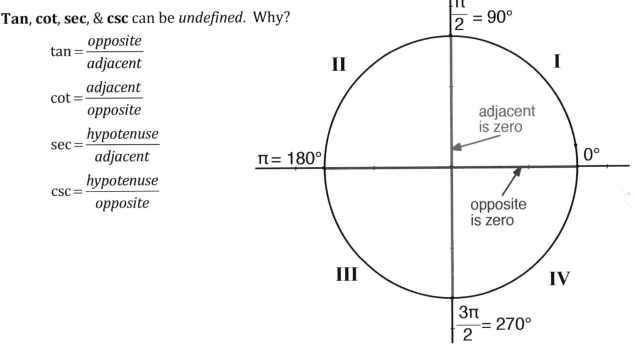

The functions above have *opposite* & *adjacent* in the denominator. Functions with *opposite* in the denominator will be undefined on the *x*-axis, at 0 and 180°.

Functions with *adjacent* in the denominator will be undefined on the *y*-axis, at 90° and 270°.

1. Which of the following trigonometric functions is equivalent to the expression $(\sin\theta)(\cot\theta)$?

Note: $\cot\theta = \dfrac{1}{\tan\theta}$

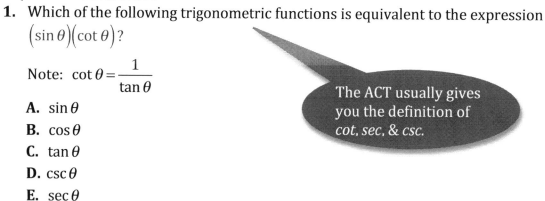

The ACT usually gives you the definition of *cot, sec, & csc.*

A. $\sin\theta$
B. $\cos\theta$
C. $\tan\theta$
D. $\csc\theta$
E. $\sec\theta$

Solve

There aren't many questions that require you to use the other trig functions, and, in general, they'll give you the definition of the function. In this case, we've just got to figure out what function is the product of multiplying *sine* and *cotangent* together.

Sine is defined $\sin\theta = \dfrac{opposite}{hypotenuse}$

Cotangent is defined $\cot\theta = \dfrac{1}{\tan} \rightarrow \dfrac{1}{\dfrac{opposite}{adjacent}} \rightarrow \dfrac{adjacent}{opposite}$

Now, we can multiply *sine & cotangent.*

$$(\sin\theta)(\cot\theta) = \left(\dfrac{opposite}{hypotenuse}\right)\left(\dfrac{adjacent}{opposite}\right) = \dfrac{opposite \cdot adjacent}{hypotenuse \cdot opposite}$$

$$\dfrac{opposite \cdot adjacent}{hypotenuse \cdot opposite} = \dfrac{\cancel{opposite} \cdot adjacent}{hypotenuse \cdot \cancel{opposite}} = \cos\theta$$

Answer choice **B** is correct.

Wrap Up

What You Need to Know
- ✓ The *Big Three* Trig Functions: Sine, Cosine, & Tangent
- ✓ How to properly label diagrams
- ✓ How to find the function of an angle on a co-ordinate axis, which sides are opposite, adjacent, and hypotenuse.
- ✓ How to plug in and solve functions.
- ✓ The reciprocal relationship between sine & cosecant, cosine & secant, and tangent & cotangent.
- ✓ The minimum values of *secant* and *cosecant*.
- ✓ That *secant* and *cosecant* can be **undefined**.

Videos

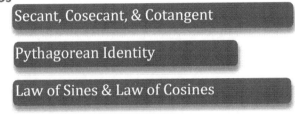

The Strategies
- ✓ You'll almost always be given the definitions of sec,csc, & cot. Cotangent is the only one that has shown up (from what I've seen) without a definition.
- ✓ Don't be intimidated; these are plug-in problems. Either plug in the sides (opposite/adjacent/hypotenuse) or plug in the length of the sides & the angle.

Related Skills
- ✓ Intermediate functions (just in style, not content)

- ✓ Trig: Find the Side & Find the Angle

- ✓ Trig: The Unit Circle

Trigonometry: Identities

1. Which of the following trigonometric functions is equivalent to $\dfrac{\tan\theta}{\sec\theta}$?

   (Note: secant = $\dfrac{1}{\cos}$)

   A. $\cos\theta$
   B. $\sin\theta$
   C. $\tan\theta$
   D. $\cot\theta$
   E. $\sec\theta$

2. What is $\cos\dfrac{5\pi}{12}$ given that $\dfrac{5\pi}{12}=\dfrac{2\pi}{3}-\dfrac{\pi}{4}$ and that

   $\cos(\alpha-\beta)=(\cos\alpha)(\cos\beta)+(\sin\alpha)(\sin\beta)$?

θ	$\sin\theta$	$\cos\theta$
$\dfrac{\pi}{6}$	$\dfrac{1}{2}$	$\dfrac{\sqrt{3}}{2}$
$\dfrac{2\pi}{3}$	$\dfrac{\sqrt{3}}{2}$	$-\dfrac{1}{2}$
$\dfrac{\pi}{4}$	$\dfrac{\sqrt{2}}{2}$	$\dfrac{\sqrt{2}}{2}$

   F. $\dfrac{1}{2}$
   G. $\dfrac{\sqrt{6}-\sqrt{2}}{4}$
   H. $\dfrac{\sqrt{2}+\sqrt{6}}{4}$
   J. $\dfrac{\sqrt{3}}{4}$
   K. $\dfrac{\sqrt{3}-1}{4}$

3. Which of the following trigonometric functions is equivalent to $\dfrac{1}{(\csc A)(\tan A)}$?

   (Note: cosecant = $\dfrac{1}{\sin}$)

   A. $\cot A$
   B. $\cos A$
   C. $\sin A$
   D. $\tan A$
   E. $\sec A$

4. Triangle *HIJ* has sides and an angle as marked. Which equation will give the measure of $\angle HIJ$?

   (Note: For a triangle with sides of length a, b, and c that are opposite $\angle A$, $\angle B$, $\angle C$, respectively, $\dfrac{\sin A}{a}=\dfrac{\sin B}{b}=\dfrac{\sin C}{c}$.)

   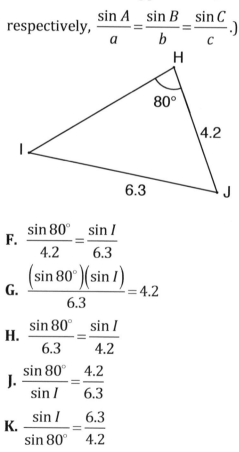

   F. $\dfrac{\sin 80^\circ}{4.2}=\dfrac{\sin I}{6.3}$
   G. $\dfrac{(\sin 80^\circ)(\sin I)}{6.3}=4.2$
   H. $\dfrac{\sin 80^\circ}{6.3}=\dfrac{\sin I}{4.2}$
   J. $\dfrac{\sin 80^\circ}{\sin I}=\dfrac{4.2}{6.3}$
   K. $\dfrac{\sin I}{\sin 80^\circ}=\dfrac{6.3}{4.2}$

5. Angle θ is between 0 & $\dfrac{\pi}{2}$ radians. What is equivalent to

$$\frac{\sqrt{1-\sin^2\theta}}{\cos\theta}+2\left(\sin^2\theta+\cos^2\theta\right)?$$

A. 1

B. 2

C. 3

D. $\dfrac{1-\sin\theta}{\cos\theta}+2$

E. $\sin\theta$

6. Sam is standing on top of a mountain such that her field of vision is circular. The sun is rising in the East and Sam uses it to calculate the angle from the sun to two other mountains, G & H. The angles Sam calculates are marked on the diagram, as well as her distance from mountains G & H. What expression will find the straight-line distance between G & H (line segment $\overline{GH}$)?

(Note: For a triangle with sides of length a, b, and c that are opposite $\angle A, \angle B, \angle C$, respectively,

$c^2 = a^2 + b^2 - 2ab\cos C$.)

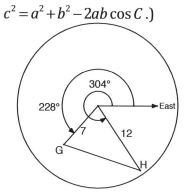

F. $\sqrt{7^2+12^2}$

G. $\sqrt{7^2+12^2+2(7)(12)\cos76°}$

H. $\sqrt{7^2+12^2-2(7)(12)\cos132°}$

J. $\sqrt{7^2+12^2+2(7)(12)\cos132°}$

K. $\sqrt{7^2+12^2-2(7)(12)\cos76°}$

7. Triangle ABC shown below has sides as marked and an angle with measure θ. A similar triangle, DEF has sides that are twice the length of $\triangle ABC$, which expression will give the area of $\triangle DEF$ in terms of a & b?

(Note: The area of a triangle is $\dfrac{1}{2}ab\sin x$,

where a and b are the lengths of the sides that form the interior angle with measure x.)

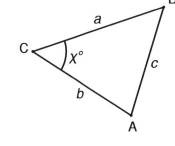

A. $\dfrac{1}{2}ab\sin x$

B. $ab\sin x$

C. $2ab\sin x$

D. $\dfrac{1}{2}ab\sin 2x$

E. $ab\sin 2x$

Trig Identities: Solutions

1. Which of the following trigonometric functions is equivalent to $\dfrac{\tan \theta}{\sec \theta}$?

(Note: secant = $\dfrac{1}{\cos}$)

Correct Answer B

This is a standard format for a question about the *other three* trig functions. We're given the definition of secant, and we're asked to simplify an expression. Start by converting secant into sides:

$$\text{secant} = \frac{1}{\cos} \rightarrow \frac{1}{\dfrac{adjacent}{hypotenuse}} = \frac{hypotenuse}{adjacent}$$

Now we can plug in the sides and simplify.

Flip the bottom fraction & multiply

$$\frac{\tan \theta}{\sec \theta} \rightarrow \frac{\tan \theta}{\dfrac{hypotenuse}{adjacent}} \rightarrow \frac{\dfrac{opposite}{adjacent}}{\dfrac{hypotenuse}{adjacent}}$$

$$\frac{opposite}{adjacent} \cdot \frac{adjacent}{hypotenuse} \rightarrow \frac{opposite \cdot \cancel{adjacent}}{\cancel{adjacent} \cdot hypotenuse}$$

$$\frac{opposite}{hypotenuse} = \sin$$

Answer choice **B** is correct.

<u>What You May Have Done Wrong</u>

    A. Cosine is *adjacent/hypotenuse.* You may have cancelled incorrectly.

    C. Tan is *opposite/adjacent.* Hypotenuse won't cancel.

    D. Cot is *adjacent/opposite.* Hypotenuse won't cancel.

    E. Sec is *hypotenuse/adjacent.* You didn't flip the bottom fraction & you cancelled incorrectly.

2. What is $\cos\dfrac{5\pi}{12}$ given that $\dfrac{5\pi}{12}=\dfrac{2\pi}{3}-\dfrac{\pi}{4}$ and that $\sin(\alpha-\beta)=(\cos\alpha)(\cos\beta)+(\sin\alpha)(\sin\beta)$?

Correct Answer G

This is an *angle difference identity* and it's another plug-in problem (like all trig identities problems). We need to decide what values to use, pull the correct values from the table, plug-in and solve.

Using $\dfrac{5\pi}{12}=\dfrac{2\pi}{3}-\dfrac{\pi}{4}$, we know that $\alpha=\dfrac{2\pi}{3}$ and $\beta=\dfrac{\pi}{4}$ because the angles go in that order.

$$\cos(\alpha-\beta)=(\cos\alpha)(\cos\beta)+(\sin\alpha)(\sin\beta)$$

$$\cos\left(\dfrac{2\pi}{3}-\dfrac{\pi}{4}\right)=\left(\cos\dfrac{2\pi}{3}\right)\left(\cos\dfrac{\pi}{4}\right)+\left(\sin\dfrac{2\pi}{3}\right)\left(\sin\dfrac{\pi}{4}\right)$$

Now, we've got plug in the correct values from the table. We won't need the first row, $\dfrac{\pi}{6}$; it's just there to trick you.

$$\cos\left(\dfrac{2\pi}{3}-\dfrac{\pi}{4}\right)=\left(\cos\dfrac{2\pi}{3}\right)\left(\cos\dfrac{\pi}{4}\right)+\left(\sin\dfrac{2\pi}{3}\right)\left(\sin\dfrac{\pi}{4}\right)$$

θ	$\sin\theta$	$\cos\theta$
$\dfrac{\pi}{6}$	$\dfrac{1}{2}$	$\dfrac{\sqrt{3}}{2}$
$\dfrac{2\pi}{3}$	$\dfrac{\sqrt{3}}{2}$	$-\dfrac{1}{2}$
$\dfrac{\pi}{4}$	$\dfrac{\sqrt{2}}{2}$	$\dfrac{\sqrt{2}}{2}$

$$\cos\left(\dfrac{2\pi}{3}-\dfrac{\pi}{4}\right)=\left(-\dfrac{1}{2}\right)\left(\dfrac{\sqrt{2}}{2}\right)+\left(\dfrac{\sqrt{3}}{2}\right)\left(\dfrac{\sqrt{2}}{2}\right)$$

Now we multiply the fractions and simplify.

$$\cos\left(\dfrac{2\pi}{3}-\dfrac{\pi}{4}\right)=\left(-\dfrac{1\bullet\sqrt{2}}{2\bullet2}\right)+\left(\dfrac{\sqrt{3}\bullet\sqrt{2}}{2\bullet2}\right)$$

$$\cos\left(\dfrac{2\pi}{3}-\dfrac{\pi}{4}\right)=\left(-\dfrac{\sqrt{2}}{4}\right)+\left(\dfrac{\sqrt{6}}{4}\right) \quad \text{Plug-in the values}$$

The fractions have the same denominator, so we can add.

$$\cos\left(\dfrac{2\pi}{3}-\dfrac{\pi}{4}\right)=\dfrac{\sqrt{6}-\sqrt{2}}{4}$$

Answer choice **G** is correct.

<u>What You May Have Done Wrong</u>

F. You may have guessed by using the table or tried to simplify your numerator by subtracting $\sqrt{6}-\sqrt{2}$, which you can't do. You may want to review roots.

H. This is actually the sine of $\dfrac{5\pi}{12}$. You probably made a mistake combining the fractions.

J. You may have tried to simplify the top by incorrectly dividing. Review your steps.

K. You may have improperly tried to simplify the top by factoring out a $\sqrt{2}$. You can do that, actually, but you'd end up with a root in the denominator.

3. **Which of the following trigonometric functions is equivalent to $\dfrac{1}{\left(\csc A\right)\left(\tan A\right)}$? (Note:**

$\text{cosecant} = \dfrac{1}{\sin}$)

Correct Answer B

This is a two-step problem, but the second step is pretty straightforward. First, convert both functions into sides and simplify the denominator.

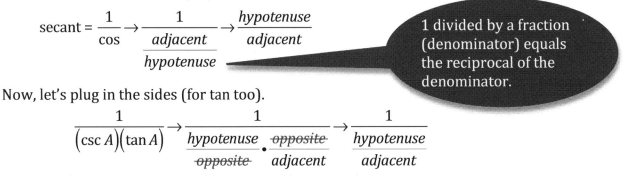

$$\text{secant} = \frac{1}{\cos} \rightarrow \frac{1}{\dfrac{adjacent}{hypotenuse}} \rightarrow \frac{hypotenuse}{adjacent}$$

1 divided by a fraction (denominator) equals the reciprocal of the denominator.

Now, let's plug in the sides (for tan too).

$$\frac{1}{\left(\csc A\right)\left(\tan A\right)} \rightarrow \frac{1}{\dfrac{hypotenuse}{\cancel{opposite}} \cdot \dfrac{\cancel{opposite}}{adjacent}} \rightarrow \frac{1}{\dfrac{hypotenuse}{adjacent}}$$

Whenever we have a lone 1 in the numerator and a fraction in the denominator. We take the reciprocal of the bottom fraction.

$$\frac{1}{\dfrac{hypotenuse}{adjacent}} \rightarrow \frac{adjacent}{hypotenuse} = \cos A$$

Answer choice B is correct

<u>What You May Have Done Wrong</u>
- **A.** Cotan is *adjacent/opposite*. You probably made a mistake cancelling terms.
- **C.** Sine is *opposite/hypotenuse*. You probably made a mistake cancelling terms.
- **D.** Tan is *opposite/adjacent*. You may have made a mistake setting up your problem.
- **E.** Secant is *hypotenuse/adjacent*. You didn't flip your final answer. In general, the answer will *never be* secant, cosecant, or cotangent unless they are defined.

4. Triangle *HIJ* has sides and an angle as marked. Which equation will give the measure of ∠HIJ?

   (Note: For a triangle with sides of length a, b, and c that are opposite ∠A, ∠B, ∠C, respectively, $\frac{\sin A}{a} = \frac{\sin B}{b} = \frac{\sin C}{c}$.)

Correct Answer H

This is a law of sines question that requires us to pair up the angles and the sides and then plug into the identity.

Sides can be labeled in by their opposite angle. For example ∠I will have a side lowercase *i* across from it. We can label our triangle in this way and rewrite the law of sines for the letters in our triangle

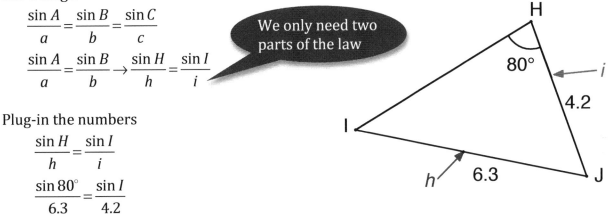

$$\frac{\sin A}{a} = \frac{\sin B}{b} = \frac{\sin C}{c}$$

$$\frac{\sin A}{a} = \frac{\sin B}{b} \rightarrow \frac{\sin H}{h} = \frac{\sin I}{i}$$

We only need two parts of the law

Plug-in the numbers

$$\frac{\sin H}{h} = \frac{\sin I}{i}$$

$$\frac{\sin 80°}{6.3} = \frac{\sin I}{4.2}$$

Answer choice **H** is correct.

What You May Have Done Wrong:

  F. You have the wrong denominators for the angles in the numerator. Sin 80°

  G. This is a compound error. Review your steps.

  J. This should be set up as sine over side. You could set it up this way, but your sides aren't correctly matched with your angles.

  K. This should be set up as sine over side. You could set it up this way, but your sides aren't correctly matched with your angles.

5. Angle θ is between 0 & $\dfrac{\pi}{2}$ radians. What is equivalent to $\dfrac{\sqrt{1-\sin^2\theta}}{\cos\theta}+2\left(\sin^2\theta+\cos^2\theta\right)$?

Correct Answer C

This question is based on the first Pythagorean Identity, $\sin^2+\cos^2=1$. While it's nice to know the identity (and easier), you can pick a number for the angle to solve.

<u>Using the Identity</u>
Substitute when we have function².

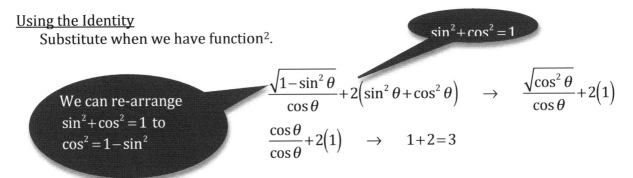

We can re-arrange $\sin^2+\cos^2=1$ to $\cos^2=1-\sin^2$

$\sin^2+\cos^2=1$

$\dfrac{\sqrt{1-\sin^2\theta}}{\cos\theta}+2\left(\sin^2\theta+\cos^2\theta\right) \quad \rightarrow \quad \dfrac{\sqrt{\cos^2\theta}}{\cos\theta}+2(1)$

$\dfrac{\cos\theta}{\cos\theta}+2(1) \quad \rightarrow \quad 1+2=3$

<u>Picking a Number</u>
Pick a number between 0° and 90° for your angle. I'm using 45°.

$$\dfrac{\sqrt{1-\sin^2\theta}}{\cos\theta}+2\left(\sin^2\theta+\cos^2\theta\right)$$

$$\dfrac{\sqrt{1-\sin^2 45°}}{\cos 45°}+2\left(\sin^2 45°+\cos^2 45°\right)$$

Lookup sin 45° & cos 45° and plug into the equation.

$$\dfrac{\sqrt{1-\sin^2 45°}}{\cos 45°}+2\left(\sin^2 45°+\cos^2 45°\right)$$

These are approximate values

$$\dfrac{\sqrt{1-\left(0.707\right)^2}}{0.707}+2\left(\left(0.707\right)^2+\left(0.707\right)^2\right)$$

Solve:

$$\dfrac{\sqrt{1-0.5}}{0.707}+2\left(0.5+0.5\right) \quad \rightarrow \quad \dfrac{\sqrt{0.5}}{0.707}+2(1)$$

$$\dfrac{0.707}{0.707}+2=2+1=3$$

Answer choice **C** is correct.

<u>What You May Have Done Wrong</u>
  A. You may have guessed, or made a compound error.
  B. You may have forgotten to multiply the result of the second parentheses (1) by 3.
  D. You tried to simplify the numerator by splitting the root. You can't split roots when adding or subtracting.
  E. This is either a guess or a compound error.

6. Sam is standing on top of a mountain such that her field of vision is circular. The sun is rising in the East and Sam uses it to calculate the angle from the sun to two other mountains, *G* & *H*. The angles Sam calculates are marked on the diagram, as well as her distance from mountains *G* & *H*. What expression will find the straight-line distance between *G* & *H* (line segment $\overline{GH}$)?

(Note: For a triangle with sides of length a, b, and c that are opposite $\angle A, \angle B, \angle C$, respectively, $c^2 = a^2 + b^2 - 2ab\cos C$.)

Correct Answer K

The long, complicated question is more straightforward than it looks. We've got to find an angle to be able to use the law of cosines (we need cos *C*)

The angle at the center can be found by subtracting the small angle (228°) from the large angle (304°). The difference between the two is our angle
$$304° - 228° = 76°$$

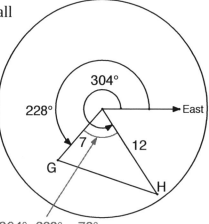

Now that we have our angle, we can start plugging in the sides and the angle.

It won't matter which side (7 or 12) we plug in for *a* and *b* because we are adding and multiplying. Order doesn't matter in addition & multiplication.

Let's go ahead and finish the problem.
$$c^2 = a^2 + b^2 - 2ab\cos C$$
$$c^2 = 7^2 + 12^2 - 2(7)(12)\cos 76°$$
$$c = \sqrt{7^2 + 12^2 - 2(7)(12)\cos 76°}$$

Order doesn't matter in multiplication & addition, so *a* & *b* (7 & 12) are interchangeable.

Answer **K** is correct.

<u>What You May Have Done Wrong</u>
- **F.** This is the Pythagorean theorem, and it won't work because we don't have a right triangle. We need to use the law of cosines.
- **G.** You need to subtract the cosine term, not add it.
- **H.** You calculated the angle incorrectly by subtracting 228° from 360°
- **J.** There are two problems here: the angle is incorrect (it should be 76°) and you're adding the cosine term (you should subtract).

7. Triangle *ABC* shown below has sides as marked and an angle with measure θ. A similar triangle, *DEF* has sides that are twice the length of $\triangle ABC$, which expression will give the area of $\triangle DEF$ in terms of *a & b*?

(Note: The area of a triangle is $\frac{1}{2}ab\sin x$, where *a* and *b* are the lengths of the sides that form the interior angle with measure *x*.)

Correct Answer C

This is a definition question that's really more about similar triangles than it is about the identity. Let's look at our original diagram and create a diagram for $\triangle DEF$.

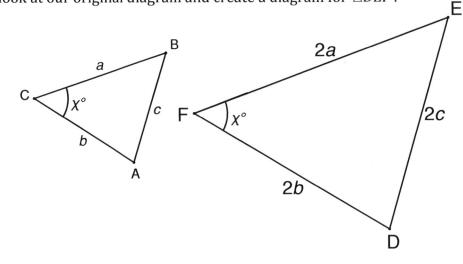

Because the triangles are similar, the interior angles will be the same. The area of $\triangle ABC$ can be represented by the identity, $\frac{1}{2}ab\sin x$.

The sides of $\triangle DEF$ are all twice the length of $\triangle ABC$, so we can label the sides in terms of *a & b*. To find the area, we'll plug the sides into the identity

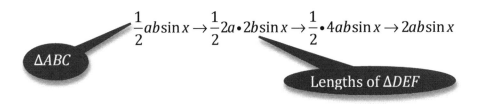

$$\frac{1}{2}ab\sin x \rightarrow \frac{1}{2}2a \cdot 2b\sin x \rightarrow \frac{1}{2} \cdot 4ab\sin x \rightarrow 2ab\sin x$$

Answer choice **C** is correct

What You May Have Done Wrong
  A. This is the area of $\triangle ABC$, triangle $\triangle DEF$ has larger sides and will have a larger area.
  B. You doubled the area of the $\triangle ABC$, which would work if *only one side* was double the length.
  D. Because the triangles are similar, the angles won't change.
  E. Because the triangles are similar, the angles won't change.

Introduction

This is an uncommon topic, but it's worth spending a little time on it—particularly because there's only a few concepts to understand.

What You Need to Know

- ✓ Period, Amplitude, horizontal, & vertical shifts
- ✓ Trig functions are ratios.

Definitions: Periodic Functions (Sine & Cosine)

Sine & Cosine have curves that repeat at regular intervals. What repeats are *y*-values.

Amplitude is how high/low the curve goes from zero. Unless the amplitude is changed, sine and cosine have an amplitude of 1.

Period is how long it takes for a curve to repeat itself. It's usually measured from highest point to highest point (peak to peak) or lowest point to lowest point (trough to trough). Unless the period is changed, cosine and sine have a period of 2π (360°)

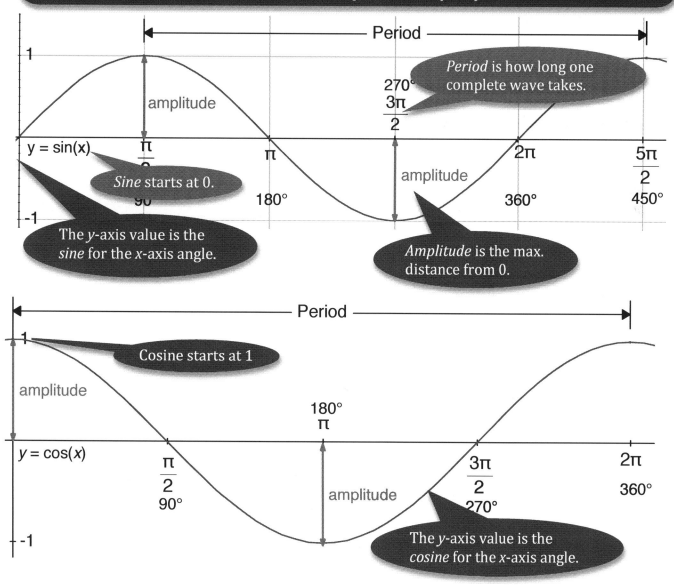

Periodic Functions (Sine & Cosine): Changing Graphs

$y = \sin(x)$ ← This is the unmodified "parent" function. It's got an amplitude of 1

$y = \cos(x)$ and a period of 2π (360°).

$y = 3\sin(x)$ ← By multiplying the *function* we change the amplitude: the bigger the number, the

$y = 3\cos(x)$ bigger the amplitude.

> *Period* stays the same

> This is *cosine*, but *sine* works the same

2

90°
$\frac{\pi}{2}$ 180°
π

3π
$\overline{2}$
270° 2π
360°

$y = \cos(x)$
$y = 3\cos(x)$
$y = \frac{1}{2}\cos(x)$

-2

> As the coefficient in front of the function increases/decreases the *amplitude* increases/decreases

Periodic Functions (Sine & Cosine): Changing Graphs

$y = \sin(x)$ ← This is the unmodified "parent" function.

$y = \cos(x)$

> The *normal* period of a cosine curve is 2π

$y = \sin(2x)$ ← This period is changed. There is an *inverse* relationship between the coefficient in

$y = \cos(2x)$ between the coefficient in front of the x and the period. The larger the coefficient,

the smaller the period, it works like this:

$$y = \cos(2x) \to \frac{2\pi}{2} \to \pi$$

> This is *sine*, but co*sine* works the same

> Divide the *normal* period by the coefficient to find the new period

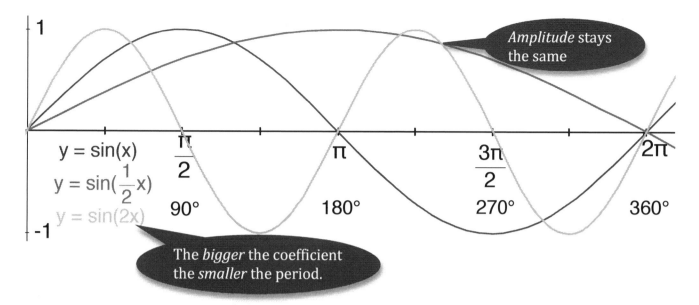

Amplitude stays the same

The *bigger* the coefficient the *smaller* the period.

$y = \sin(x)$
$y = \sin(\frac{1}{2}x)$
$y = \sin(2x)$

Sine & Cosine Phase Shifts

Like other functions, the graphs of trig functions can be shifted up or down.

<u>Vertical Shifts</u>

$y = \sin(x)$ ← This is the unmodified "parent" function. The *midline* is zero.

$y = \cos(x)$

$y = \sin(x) + 1$ ← This function is *shifted up* one. The *midline* is +1.

$y = \cos(x) + 1$

Adding moves the midline up, *subtracting* moves it down

midline

midline

$y = \sin(x)$
$y = \sin(x) + 1$

This is *sine* but *cosine* works the same way

Period & Amplitude don't change

Sine & Cosine Phase Shifts

Trig functions go through horizontal shifts in the same way as other functions. That is, they are sort of backwards. Subtracting moves the function *right* (in the positive direction) and adding moves the function *left* (in the negative direction).

<u>Horizontal Shifts</u>

$y = \sin(x)$ ← This is the unmodified "parent" function. The *sine* is zero at 0°. *Cosine* is 1 at

$y = \cos(x)$ 0°.

$y = \sin\left(x + \dfrac{\pi}{2}\right)$ ← This *sine* is *shifted right* by 90°. At 0° at it is 1. The *cosine* is also *shifted right* by

$y = \cos\left(x + \dfrac{\pi}{2}\right)$ 90°. At 0° it is 0.

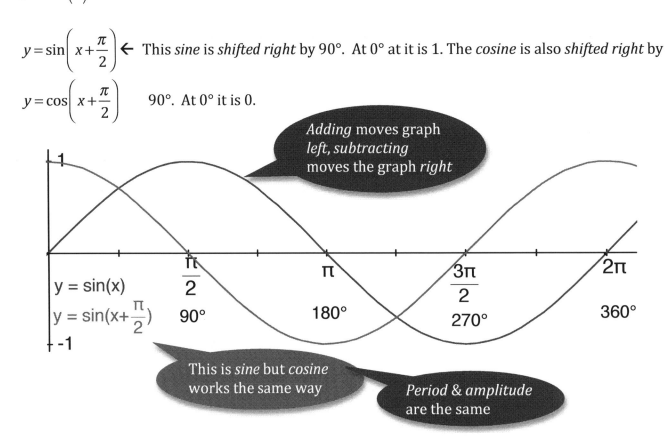

Sine & Cosine Phase Shifts

We can also "flip" the graphs of *sine* and *cosine*.

<u>Flipping Graphs</u>

$y = \sin(x)$ ← This is the unmodified "parent" function. The *sine* is zero at 0°. *Cosine* is 1 at 0°.

$y = \cos(x)$

$y = -\sin(x)$ ← These graphs are *inverted*. Where *cosine* or *sine* would be 1, it's now -1. Where it

$y = -\cos(x)$ would be -1, it's now 1.

y = sin(x)
y = -sin(x)

This is *sine* but *cosine* works the same way

Amplitude & period aren't changed.

The Graphs of Sine & Cosine

You may have seen changes to the graphs of trig functions explained this way.

$$y = a\sin(bx + c) + d$$

$a = amplitude$

$b = period$

$c = horizontal\ shift$

$d = vertical\ shift$

The horizontal and vertical shifts are similar to algebraic functions.

Personally, I've never been wild about that format and I've never seen a good mnemonic way to remember how it works. I think it's easiest to think of it like an algebraic function (like a parabola). The only difference is *amplitude*. Algebraic functions don't really have an amplitude (or a period really) but we can think of period as how fast something moves up/down. If you need or like a way to remember it, try this:

$$y = a\sin(px + h) + v$$

$a = amplitude \rightarrow always$

$p = period \rightarrow please$

$h = horizontal\ shift \rightarrow hungry$

$v = vertical\ shift \rightarrow velociraptors$

The only difference between sine/cosine and tangent is the amplitude of tan does not affect the maximum or minimum. Rather it makes the graph shorter or taller. Numbers below 1 make the graph squatter. Numbers greater than 1 make it more stretched.

1. A trigonometric function with equation $y = a\cos(bx + c) + d$ has real numbers values for a, b, c, d. The function is graphed on the standard (x, y) plane below. The *period* of this function $f(x)$ is the smallest positive number p so that the value of $f(x)$ and $f(x + p)$ are the same for every real number value of x. What is the period of the function?

A. 3
B. 1
C. 2π
D. π
E. $\dfrac{\pi}{2}$

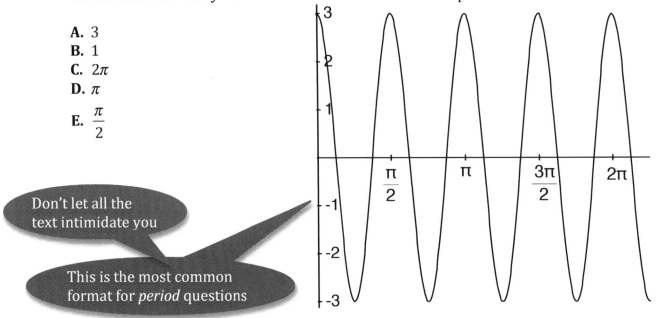

Don't let all the text intimidate you

This is the most common format for *period* questions

Solve

This is the most common format of *period* questions. The text is long and intentionally confusing, and it has a weird equation in the question itself. *All the question asks is "what is the period of the function graphed below?"*

All we need to do is read the graph. Starting at 0, the function repeats returns to its highpoint at $\dfrac{\pi}{2}$.

So, the period is $\dfrac{\pi}{2}$.

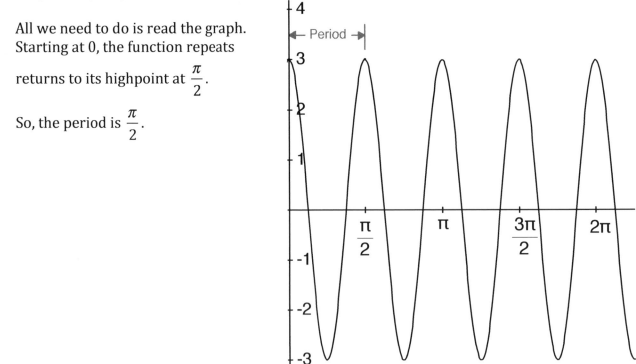

Answer choice **E** is correct.

1. Below are the graphs of functions $y = \sin(x)$ and $y = a\sin(x) + b$, where a and b are real numbers. Which of the following statements about a and b is true?

A. $a < 0$ and $b > 0$
B. $a < 0$ and $b < 0$
C. $a < 0$ and $b = 0$
D. $a > 0$ and $b = 0$
E. $a > 0$ and $b > 0$

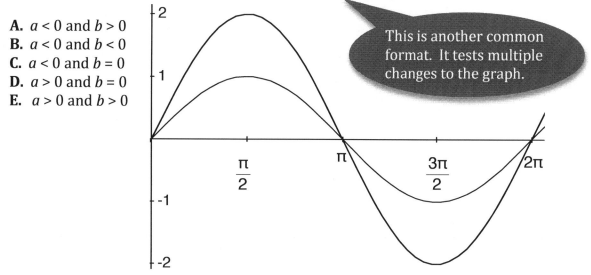

This is another common format. It tests multiple changes to the graph.

Solve

This is another definition question. We're given the graph of our parent function for comparison. Find the difference in the graphs.

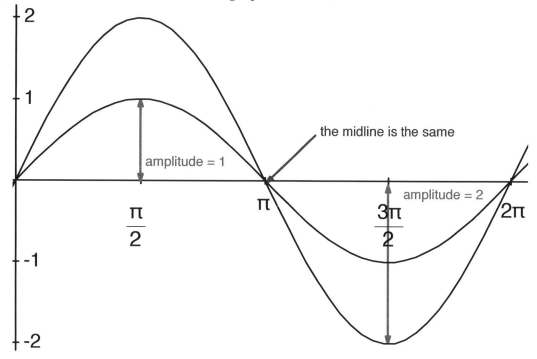

Because both functions the have the x-axis as the midline, we know that $b = 0$. The amplitude, however, does change from 1 to 2. Therefore, $a = 2$ which means $a > 0$.

Answer Choice **D** is correct.

The Graph of Tangent

This is an incredibly infrequent topic on the ACT, showing up only once in all the tests I've reviewed and not at all in either Red Book. As such, I'm going to the discussion of tan short and to the point.

Tangent is a periodic function like *sine & cosine.*

It has vertical asymptotes where it is undefined. Tan is $\dfrac{opposite}{adjacent}$ and is undefined when *adjacent* = 0.

The period of tan lies between the vertical asymptotes and is π. The period starts and ends at the 90° angles of the unit circle, 90° & 270° $\dfrac{\pi}{2}$ & $\dfrac{3\pi}{2}$.

Amplitude is infinite. Unlike *sine & cosine* that have an amplitude of 1 and a range of -1 to 1, tan has infinite amplitude and a range of $-\infty$ to ∞.

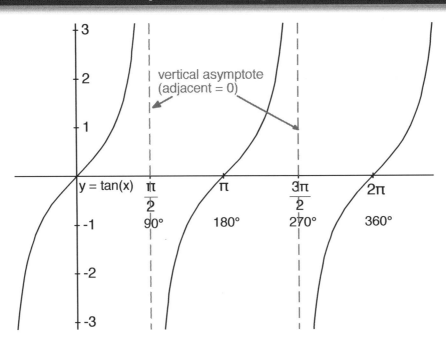

Wrap Up

What You Need to Know
- ✓ Period, Amplitude, horizontal, & vertical shifts
- ✓ Trig functions are ratios.

Videos

The Graphs of Trig Functions

The Strategies
- ✓ You'll want to know amplitude & period. You may want to use *APHV.*
- ✓ Use your gut: don't let the question intimidate you.

Related Skills
- ✓ The graph of algebraic functions

Trigonometry: Graphs

1. What is the amplitude of the function

$$f(x) = 2\sin\left(3x + \frac{\pi}{2}\right)?$$

   A. 2
   B. 3
   C. $\dfrac{\pi}{2}$
   D. 6
   E. π

2. The graph of $y = \tan(x)$ is shown in the standard (x, y) coordinate plane below. What is the period of tan x?

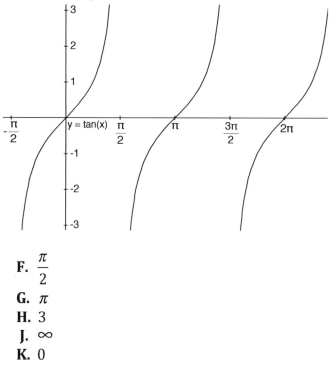

   F. $\dfrac{\pi}{2}$
   G. π
   H. 3
   J. ∞
   K. 0

3. The functions $y = \cos(x)$ and $y = a\cos(x) + b$ are shown below. The functions do *not* have the same maximum or minimum values. One of the following statements about a and b is true, which statement is it?

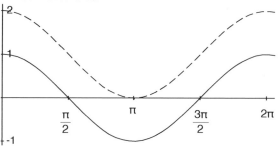

   A. $a > b$
   B. $a = b$
   C. $a < b$
   D. $a < b < 0$
   E. $a > b > 0$

4. The graph of $y = a\cos(bx)$ is shown in the standard (x, y) coordinate axis below. Which one of the values below is equal to b?

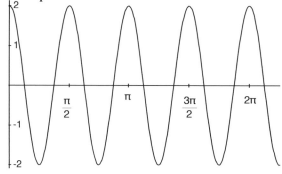

   F. $\dfrac{1}{4}$
   G. $\dfrac{1}{2}$
   H. 1
   J. 2
   K. 4

5. The equations of the two graphs below are $f_1(m) = a_1 \cos(b_1 m)$ and $f_2(m) = a_2 \sin(b_2 m)$, where the constants a_1, a_2, b_1, b_2 are real numbers. Which of the following statements *must* be true about a_1 & a_2?

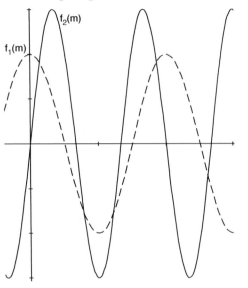

A. $a_1 = a_2$

B. $a_1 < a_2$

C. $a_1 > a_2$

D. $\dfrac{3}{2}(a_1) = a_2$

E. Cannot be Determined

Trig Graphs: Solutions

1. What is the amplitude of the function $f(x)=2\sin\left(3x+\dfrac{\pi}{2}\right)$?

Correct Answer A

This is a definition question. You've got to know which coefficient or constant is amplitude. You could try and graph these and remove numbers until the amplitude changes, but it would be very time consuming.

Amplitude is always first. So, our amplitude will be 2.

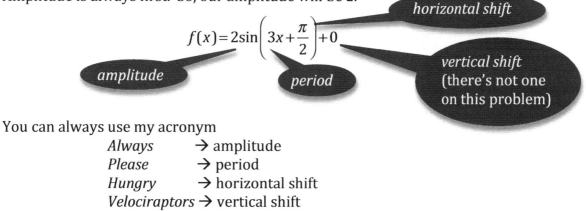

You can always use my acronym

Always	→ amplitude
Please	→ period
Hungry	→ horizontal shift
Velociraptors	→ vertical shift

Some answer choices have you distributing 2 into the parentheses. We'll *never* distribute like that. $\sin\left(3x+\dfrac{\pi}{2}\right)$ is a *single number*.

Answer choice **A** is correct.

What You May Have Done Wrong

 B. This is period not amplitude.
 C. This is the horizontal shift.
 D. This is period *and* you distributed into the sine.
 E. This is horizontal shift *and* you distributed into the sine.

2. **The graph of** $y = \tan(x)$ **is shown in the standard** (x, y) **coordinate plane below. What is the period of tan** x**?**

Correct Answer G

This is a definition question, but you can just read the graph to find the answer. *Period* is how many radians, or degrees, on the *x*-axis before the graph repeats itself, the *y*-axis values.

You can measure the period in a couple of ways: from asymptote to asymptote. Or, you can measure (and I think this is easier) from *x*-intercept to *x*-intercept.

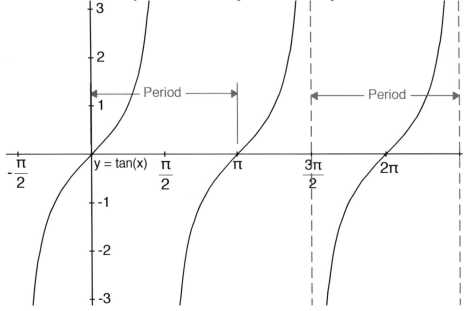

Answer choice **G** is correct.

<u>What You May Have Done Wrong</u>

    F. This is half of the period, or one of the asymptotes.

    H. This is the maximum *y*-value shown, but we're concerned with *y* not *x*. It's also not the maximum amplitude of tan. Tan goes to infinity.

    J. This is the amplitude of tan.

    K. You probably guessed.

3. **The functions** $y = \cos(x)$ **and** $y = a\cos(x) + b$ **are shown below. The functions do not have the same maximum or minimum values. One of the following statements about** a **and** b **is true, which statement is is it?**

Correct Answer B

This is a mark-off question, but we'll have to do some legwork first.

We've got to look at both a and b. Coefficient a is a change in amplitude and coefficient b is a vertical shift. Let's look at the graph:

Because the dashed line function has a range of 2 (it's bottom value is 0 and it's top value is 2), has an amplitude of 1 and a midline of 1. So, the amplitude is unchanged and a = 1. There is a *vertical shift*, as we moved the midline from 0 to 1. So, the value of b = 1.

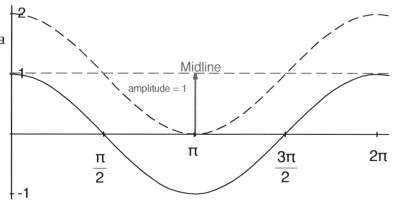

Answer choice **B** is correct

<u>What You May Have Done Wrong</u>
  A. You may have mixed up what a & b represent. Review the steps.
  C. You may have incorrectly thought a was 0.
  D. a and b are both positive and $a = b$.
  E. a and b are both positive (so they are greater than 0) but a is not larger than b.

4. **The graph of** $y = a\cos(bx)$ **is shown in the standard** (x, y) **axis below. Which one of the values below is equal to** b?

Correct Answer K

We need to know that a represents *amplitude* and b represents period. But we also need to know the unmodified amplitude (1) and period of cosine (2π).

Let's look at the graph. The amplitude is 2, but we're interested in period. Recall that the *larger* the number the *smaller* the period. It's an inverse relationship; we divide the unmodified period by b.

$$\frac{2\pi}{b} = \frac{\pi}{2} \rightarrow 4\pi = b\pi \rightarrow b = 4$$

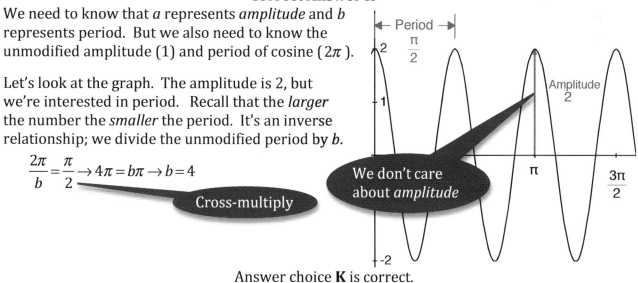

Answer choice **K** is correct.

<u>What You May Have Done Wrong:</u>
  F. b and the period have an inverse relationship.
  G. b and the period have an inverse relationship and you probably thought the standard period of cosine was π.
  H. This is probably a guess.
  J. You probably confused amplitude and period.

5. **The equations of the two graphs below are** $f_1(m) = a_1 \cos(b_1 m)$ **and** $f_2(m) = a_2 \sin(b_2 m)$, **where the constants** a_1, a_2, b_1, b_2 **are real numbers. Which of the following statements is true about** a_1 **&** a_2**?**

Correct Answer B

This is a really complicated way to ask the same sort of question we've been seeing. It's intentionally intimidating, but the procedure is the same. Compare the graphs of the functions; know what the variables represent; and mark-off answer choices. Let's look at the graph:

I have the period marked on the graph (for reference) but we're only interested in the a coefficients, which represent *amplitude*. $f_2(m)$ has the larger *amplitude*.

Let's run though the answer choices:

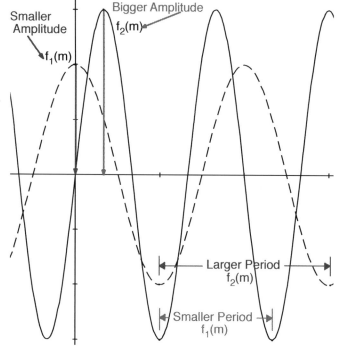

A. $a_1 = a_2$ **cannot** be true. Even though $f_1(m)$ & $f_2(m)$ are different functions, *cosine* & *sine*, they have the same original amplitude. Since the amplitudes are different, a_1 can't equal a_2.

B. $a_1 < a_2$ **is** true. $f_1(m)$ has a smaller amplitude than $f_2(m)$ and therefore a_1 is less than a_2.

C. $a_1 > a_2$ **cannot** be true. $f_1(m)$ has a smaller amplitude than $f_2(m)$ and therefore a_1 cannot be greater than a_2.

D. $a_1 > a_2$ **could** be true. $f_1(m)$ looks like it's about 1.5 times smaller than $f_2(m)$ but without labels on our y-axis, we don't know for sure. The question asks for what **must** be true.

E. Remember, cannot be determined is usually a trap answer. We may not be able to quantify the relationship between a_1 and a_2, but we can determine which one is greater.

Answer choice **B** is correct.

Strategy Section

I talk about strategy throughout the book. You'll find each section has an introduction and general strategy page. Within each section, each topic has strategy notes in the wrap-up, and strategy is discussed in the example problems and the solutions.

The Strategy Section is meant to cover general test taking strategy. I also go into more detail on some of the strategies we see over and over again in the book.

How to Use this Section

Go through the three major strategies that have broad applicability: *marking-off*, *picking numbers*, & *testing answer choices*. Check out the sample problems in each section and pay attention to how the questions are structured.

The way the question is structured dictates what strategy or strategies will work on the problem.

While these are the most important strategies, they don't replace the strategy notes at the end of each topic. You'll find more detailed information for specific question types on the Wrap-Up page of each section and in the example problems in the material.

Section Strategy

What to Do
- ✓ Each question counts the same; make sure you get the easy points.
- ✓ It's better to run out of time with a few questions left than it is to rush through the section. You'll do better guessing on a handful of problems than skipping through and making careless errors.
- ✓ Set up problems. You don't have to know how you're going to finish a problem, just find the first thing to do.
- ✓ Write more. You actually work faster by writing things down; the time you spend "thinking" seems faster than it really is. You'll also get more questions right.
- ✓ Don't skip around. Fill in every bubble, attempt every question, and guess if you need to.
- ✓ Don't get stuck. Every question counts the same, don't sacrifice 3 or 4 questions to maybe get one right.
- ✓ Never, ever leave question unanswered. Bubble every single question. There's no deduction for wrong answers.

Frustration & Confidence

What people don't talk about (and they should) is the psychology of taking the ACT.

Confidence rolls downhill, it gains weight and momentum like an avalanche. Frustration freezes you, makes you panic, and throws off your rhythm. Everyone has questions they don't know or don't feel confident on.

Every single test taker feels unsure at times. Remember that each question is it's own entity: it lives and dies by itself. When you get a hard question, it's just that, a hard question. It doesn't mean that you've reached the end of the questions you know how to solve.

Marking-Off

When to Use
- ✓ Questions that use the word *which*[1]
- ✓ Questions the use *must be, could be, CANNOT be, etc.*
- ✓ Questions with roman numerals (I, II, III...)
- ✓ Questions with solutions containing multiple steps.

The Strategy

A lot of times, we don't have a choice other than marking-off. For example, if I ask, "which jacket do you like best?" You have to be able to see the jackets to make your choice. Other times, you won't need to mark-off, but it's the most efficient way to answer a question.

When you mark-off, **focus on proving things wrong**. The beauty of ACT is that there are two ways to get the correct answer: know/find the right answer or eliminate the wrong answers.

Question Types

There are three major categories of *mark-off* questions.

1. Questions **you've got to mark-off**, including *which, equivalent to, and roman numeral* questions.

2. Questions **you've got to mark-off that have a conditional (*must be, could be*...).**

3. Questions **you can mark-off.**

Questions You *Have* to Mark-Off

On *which* (and some *what* questions), *definition questions, logical operators,* and *roman numeral* questions you'll need to run through the answer choices and mark-off.

Oftentimes, these questions are best handled in parts, do one part then mark-off and repeat.

Example Problems: Questions You *Have* to Mark-Off

1. Erin is running for student government president and wants to do a poll to see what percent of the student body plans to vote for her. She surveys everyone in her homeroom. Which of the following describes Erin's poll?

   A. Randomized census
   B. Nonrandomized census
   C. Randomized experiment
   D. Randomized survey
   E. Nonrandomized survey

It's a which question

And there's no problem to work.

The answers are text.

The *solution* to this problem is in *Pre-Algebra: Data.*

Dissecting the Question

There's no way to handle this problem other than marking off. Here's why:
- ✓ It's a *which* question.
- ✓ There's no problem to work. This is strictly a definition question, and the answer choices are text.

---

[1] All *which* questions are mark-off questions, but some *which* questions just have to be worked all the way through.

2. Which statement is equal to $|x|$?

A. x^2
B. $x^2 - x$
C. x
D. $\sqrt{x^2}$
E. $-|x|$

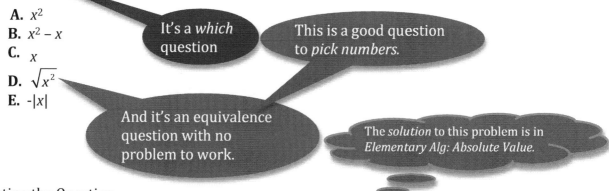

Dissecting the Question

There's no way to handle this problem other than marking off. Here's why:

✓ It's a *which* question.
✓ There's no problem to work. They're asking you what is equivalent to the absolute value of *x*.
✓ This is really a definition question, and it's a great question to *pick numbers* on and then mark-off.

Example Problems: Questions You *Have* to Mark-Off (cont.)

3. Which of the following is equivalent to $\dfrac{x+3}{x+2}$?

A. $\dfrac{2x+4}{2x+6}$

B. $\dfrac{x+6}{x+4}$

C. $\dfrac{4x+12}{4x+6}$

D. $\dfrac{2x^2+6x}{2x^2+8x}$

E. $\dfrac{2x+6}{2x+4}$

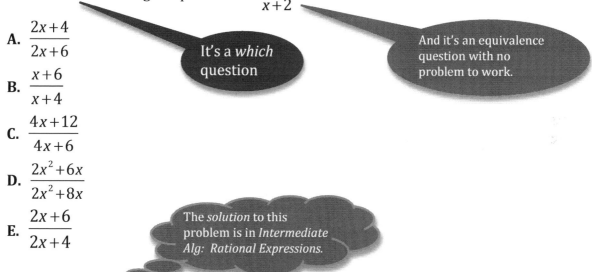

Dissecting the Question

There's no way to handle this problem other than marking off. Here's why:

✓ It's a *which* question.
✓ There's no problem to work. They're asking you what is equivalent to the rational expression given, and there are many possible answers.
✓ If you're not very comfortable with factors (but you really need to be comfortable with them), you could pick numbers on this problem.

4. Which of the following functions will have no real zeroes?

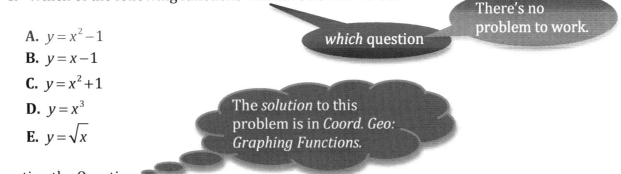

A. $y = x^2 - 1$

B. $y = x - 1$

C. $y = x^2 + 1$

D. $y = x^3$

E. $y = \sqrt{x}$

which question

There's no problem to work.

The *solution* to this problem is in *Coord. Geo: Graphing Functions.*

Dissecting the Question

There's no way to handle this problem other than marking off. Here's why:

✓ It's a definition question. You're defining the concept of real zeroes with equations.

✓ This is a good question to pick numbers on, but I encourage you to know how algebraic functions are shifted.

Example Problems: Must Be, Could Be, or Cannot Be

Try to prove the *opposite*. If a question specifies that something *must be true*, prove that it *could be false*.

1. When *a* is a rational number which *must be false*?

A. *a* is a complex number

B. *a* is an integer

C. *a* is natural number

D. *a* is a fraction

E. When squared, *a* is a negative number.

Logical operator

There's no problem to work.

The answers are text.

The *solution* to this problem is in *Pre-Algebra: Numbers.*

Dissecting the Question

There's no way to handle this problem other than marking off. Here's why:

✓ It's a *must be false question*. To solve, flip each condition, *must be* becomes *could be* and *false* becomes *true*. Mark-off any choice that *could be true*.

✓ There's no problem to work. This is strictly a definition question, and the answer choices are text.

Example Problems: *Must Be, Could Be,* or *Cannot Be* (cont.)

2. If $x \neq y$, which CANNOT be true?

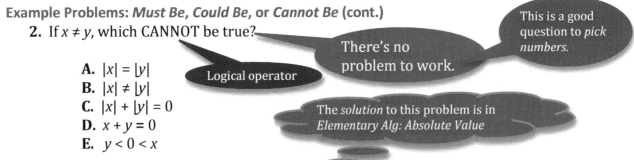

A. $|x| = |y|$

B. $|x| \neq |y|$

C. $|x| + |y| = 0$

D. $x + y = 0$

E. $y < 0 < x$

Logical operator

There's no problem to work.

This is a good question to *pick numbers.*

The *solution* to this problem is in *Elementary Alg: Absolute Value*

Dissecting the Question

There's no way to handle this problem other than marking off. Here's why:

✓ It's a *CANNOT be true* question (which is the same as *must be false*). To solve, flip each condition, *CANNOT be* becomes *could be* and *true* becomes *false*. Mark-off any choice that *could be false*.

✓ There's no problem to work, but if you're not good at conceptual problems, this is a great question to pick numbers on.

3. Which of the matrix products are defined?

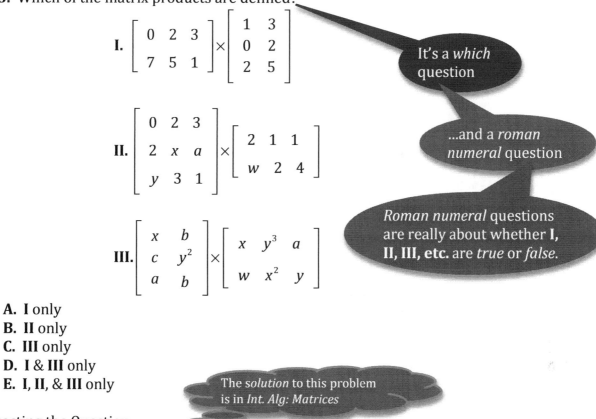

I. $\begin{bmatrix} 0 & 2 & 3 \\ 7 & 5 & 1 \end{bmatrix} \times \begin{bmatrix} 1 & 3 \\ 0 & 2 \\ 2 & 5 \end{bmatrix}$

It's a *which* question

II. $\begin{bmatrix} 0 & 2 & 3 \\ 2 & x & a \\ y & 3 & 1 \end{bmatrix} \times \begin{bmatrix} 2 & 1 & 1 \\ w & 2 & 4 \end{bmatrix}$

...and a *roman numeral* question

III. $\begin{bmatrix} x & b \\ c & y^2 \\ a & b \end{bmatrix} \times \begin{bmatrix} x & y^3 & a \\ w & x^2 & y \end{bmatrix}$

Roman numeral questions are really about whether **I, II, III, etc.** are *true* or *false*.

- **A.** **I** only
- **B.** **II** only
- **C.** **III** only
- **D.** **I & III** only
- **E.** **I, II, & III** only

The *solution* to this problem is in *Int. Alg: Matrices*

<u>Dissecting the Question</u>

There's no way to handle this problem other than marking off. Here's why:

✓ It's a *which* question.

✓ The answer choices are lists, not solutions

✓ When you mark-off on these problems, mark-off using the roman numerals. Test **I**, mark-off answers that either contain it (if **I** isn't correct) or that don't have **I** (if **I** is correct), and them move down the list.

4. A bathtub is filling from the faucet and the drain is closed. The graph below shows the depth of the tube as a function of time since the faucet was turned on. At time 1 exactly *one* of the following events occurred, which of the following could it be?

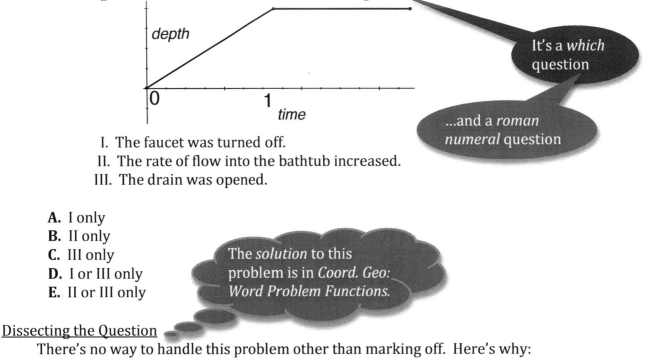

I. The faucet was turned off.
II. The rate of flow into the bathtub increased.
III. The drain was opened.

A. I only
B. II only
C. III only
D. I or III only
E. II or III only

The *solution* to this problem is in *Coord. Geo: Word Problem Functions.*

Dissecting the Question
There's no way to handle this problem other than marking off. Here's why:
   ✓ It's a *which* question.
   ✓ The answer choices are events, not solutions
   ✓ When you mark-off on these problems, mark-off using the roman numerals. Test **I**, mark-off answers that either contain it (if **I** isn't correct) or that don't have **I** (if **I** is correct), and them move down the list.

5. Which of the following CANNOT be two angles of an isosceles triangle?

A. 10° and 140°
B. 30° and 120°
C. 45° and 90°
D. 65° and 50°
E. 55° and 70°

The *solution* to this problem is in *Plane Geo: Triangles.*

Dissecting the Question
There's no way to handle this problem other than marking off. Here's why:
   ✓ It's a *which* question.
   ✓ It's a CANNOT question, so flip the operator, CANNOT becomes *can*. Mark-off any answer choice that *can* be an isosceles triangle.
   ✓ To solve this problem, you've got to go through each answer choice and see if they can add to 180 degrees.

Questions You *Can* Mark-Off

Some questions are easiest when you mark-off, but you don't have to. They tend to be *equivalence questions* or the more open-ended questions where there could be more than one possible answer.

Example Problems: Questions you *can* mark-off

1. An integer, *x*, is subtracted from ten, and the difference is multiplied by four. The result equals the same integer added to four and that sum multiplied by three. Which equation represents this relationship?

   A. $4(x - 10) = 3(x + 4)$
   B. $4x - 10 = 3x + 4$
   C. $4(x - 10) = 3x + 4$
   D. $x(10 - 4) = 3x$
   E. $4(10 - x) = 3(x + 4)$

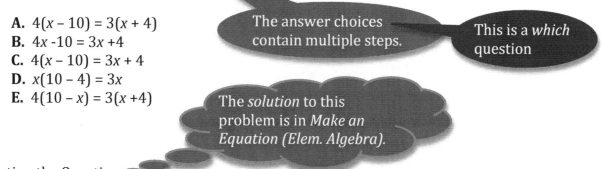

The answer choices contain multiple steps.

This is a *which* question

The *solution* to this problem is in *Make an Equation (Elem. Algebra)*.

<u>Dissecting the Question</u>

This is a *make an equation* problem, and you can solve it by making the whole equation and matching it to the answer choice. But, you can save time, improve accuracy, and increase confidence by marking off. Here's why:

   ✓ *Make an equation* questions work step-by-step. The answer choices reflect each step.
   ✓ If you mark-off as you go you won't need to finish this problem, and that's generally the case.

Example Problems: Questions you *can* mark-off (cont.)

2. Which is equivalent to $(3 - i)(4 + i)$?

   A. $12 - i + i^2$
   B. $13 - i$
   C. $11 + i$
   D. $11 - i$
   E. 7

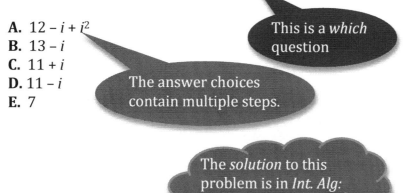

This is a *which* question

The answer choices contain multiple steps.

The *solution* to this problem is in *Int. Alg: Complex Numbers.*

<u>Dissecting the Question</u>

This equivalence problem is another good example of checking at the end of each step. Here's why:

   ✓ This equivalence question has a clear way forward; you're going to have to FOIL the binomials.
   ✓ Because you know what you have to do (FOIL) and FOIL has steps that show up in the answer, you can mark-off after each little step.

3. The equation $y = \dfrac{x}{x^3 - 8}$ is graphed in the standard (x, y) coordinate plane. Where will the function have *no x* coordinate?

A. 0
B. 2
C. -1
D. 1
E. -3

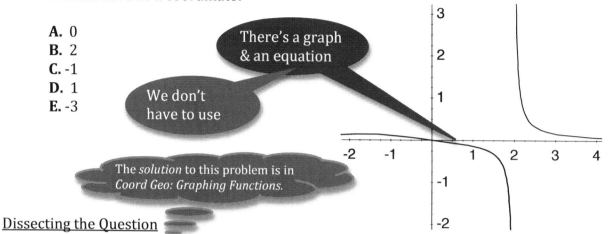

There's a graph & an equation

We don't have to use

The *solution* to this problem is in *Coord Geo: Graphing Functions.*

<u>Dissecting the Question</u>

There are two ways to deal with this problem. You can do it algebraically by knowing how vertical asymptotes work. You can also use the graph and mark-off. Here's why:

✓ While you need a numeric answer, you're given two ways to get there.
✓ Eyeballing the graph and common sense will give you the answer just as fast as doing the algebra.

4. How many diagonals are in the hexagon below?

A. 24
B. 9
C. 18
D. 12
E. 6

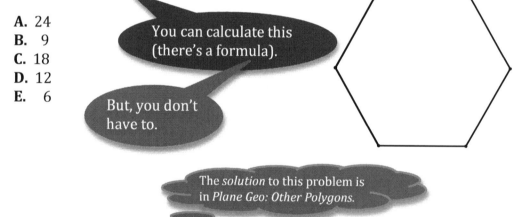

You can calculate this (there's a formula).

But, you don't have to.

The *solution* to this problem is in *Plane Geo: Other Polygons.*

<u>Dissecting the Question</u>

There are two ways to deal with this problem. You can know the formula for the number of diagonals in a hexagon, or use my method of counting from a single vertex. If you didn't know how to do either, you can still get the right answer, so long as you know the definition of a diagonal. Here's why:

✓ Work your way *up* the answer choices by drawing diagonals.
✓ Start drawing diagonals and until you get one over an answer choice. Then mark-off that answer choice.
✓ Common sense should allow you to eliminate the smallest answer choices in this problem.

5. Given that $\tan\theta = \dfrac{4}{3}$ and $0° \leq \theta \leq 360°$, what are all possible values of $\sin\theta$?

A. $\dfrac{3}{4}$ only

B. $\dfrac{3}{4}$ only $-\dfrac{3}{4}$

C. $\dfrac{4}{5}$ only

D. $-\dfrac{4}{5}$ only

E. $\dfrac{4}{5}$ and $-\dfrac{4}{5}$

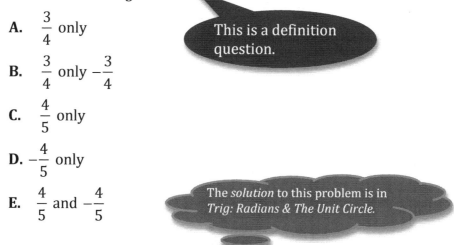

This is a definition question.

The *solution* to this problem is in *Trig: Radians & The Unit Circle.*

Dissecting the Question

There are two ways to deal with this problem. You can find the angles (there's always two) that have a tan of 4/3, or you can use some common sense. Here's why:

✓ If you remember the definition of your functions, you'll realize that neither 4 nor 3 can be in the denominator.

✓ If you remember that there has to be two angles, you can finish the problem.

Picking Numbers

✓ When the question is about *relationships* & *the answer choices are in terms of relationships*

The Strategy

When you aren't worried about getting to a specific quantity, you can pick numbers.

The ACT doesn't ever "require" you to pick numbers, but it can save you some nasty algebra and/or tricky conceptual reasoning. Picking numbers saves time, stress, and build confidence.

To pick numbers, follow the rules (relationships) set out in the question. Use easy numbers, and if two answer choices work, pick a second number, or set of numbers.

Question Types

There are two major categories of *picking numbers* questions. A lot of times these categories overlap. Strategies also overlap, and it's pretty common to *pick numbers* & *mark-off*.

1. Questions **where you're using one equation to evaluate a change or you're relating two things with the same equation.**

2. Questions **with tough algebra you aren't comfortable with.**

Questions that Evaluate a Change or Relationship

If you've got to evaluate a change or compare two things using the same equation, it's often best to pick numbers. You don't have to pick numbers, but it   can save you some really tricky algebra or tough thinking.

Remember, *picking numbers* works when we have a question that's about a relationship and answer choices that are expressed as relationships.

Example Problems: Evaluating a Change or Relationship

1. If $0 > x > y > z$, which of the following expressions has the greatest value?

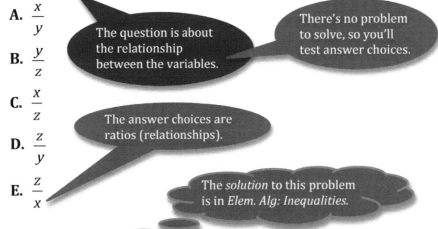

A. $\dfrac{x}{y}$

B. $\dfrac{y}{z}$

C. $\dfrac{x}{z}$

D. $\dfrac{z}{y}$

E. $\dfrac{z}{x}$

The question is about the relationship between the variables.

There's no problem to solve, so you'll test answer choices.

The answer choices are ratios (relationships).

The *solution* to this problem is in *Elem. Alg: Inequalities.*

Dissecting the Question

This question is about negative numbers & inequalities. You can think your way through it, but it's much easier to pick numbers.
✓ Pick easy integers, like -1, -2, & -3.
✓ Now the picking number question has become a testing answer choice question.

2. The flow rate of two special pumps it determined by the impeller speed and the equation $r = \sqrt{\dfrac{2s}{15}}$. If Pump A has a flow rate that is four times Pump B's flow rate, the speed of Pump A's impeller is how many times the speed of Pump B's impeller?

A. 32
B. 16
C. 8
D. 4
E. 2

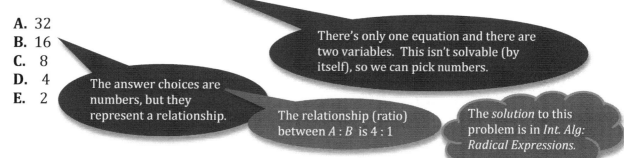

There's only one equation and there are two variables. This isn't solvable (by itself), so we can pick numbers.

The answer choices are numbers, but they represent a relationship.

The relationship (ratio) between $A : B$ is $4 : 1$

The *solution* to this problem is in *Int. Alg: Radical Expressions.*

Dissecting the Question

This question is about the relationship between two different things, and it involves some tricky algebra (setting the equation equal to itself multiplied bya coefficient). It's easiest to pick numbers here—unless you're really good at algebra.

✓ You've got to follow the rules, and make Pump *A*'s number 4 times Pump *B*'s, I'd use 4 & 1.
✓ Plug-in the number you picked for Pump *A* and solve for *s*. Do the same for Pump *B*. Then find the ratio.

3. Below are the graphs of functions $y = \sin(x)$ and $y = a\sin(x) + b$, where a and b are real numbers. Which of the following statements about a and b is true?

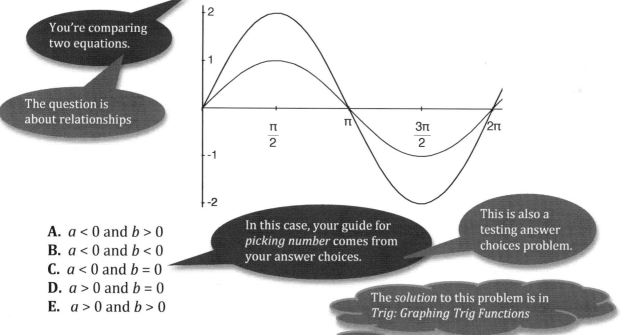

You're comparing two equations.

The question is about relationships

A. $a < 0$ and $b > 0$
B. $a < 0$ and $b < 0$
C. $a < 0$ and $b = 0$
D. $a > 0$ and $b = 0$
E. $a > 0$ and $b > 0$

In this case, your guide for *picking number* comes from your answer choices.

This is also a testing answer choices problem.

The *solution* to this problem is in *Trig: Graphing Trig Functions*

Dissecting the Question

If you don't know the translations of trig functions, you could plug sample numbers into your calculator to test. (Check out *picking numbers* for more).

✓ Graph a regular *sin* function and another one to test.
✓ Try a value for *a* greater than zero, because it's the more common answer.
✓ Try *b* separately because you only want to change one variable at a time.

Tough Algebra Questions

At times, *picking numbers* is the best way to go. Sometimes, it's a strategy that can bail you out on really tough equivalence questions. You should, however, still learn the algebra because those skills are critical.

Example Problems: Tough to Rearrange (cont.)

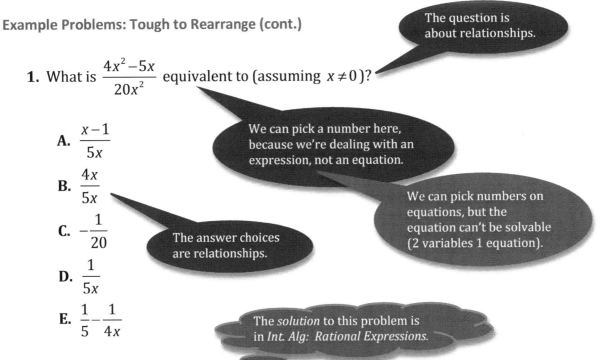

1. What is $\dfrac{4x^2 - 5x}{20x^2}$ equivalent to (assuming $x \neq 0$)?

> The question is about relationships.

> We can pick a number here, because we're dealing with an expression, not an equation.

> We can pick numbers on equations, but the equation can't be solvable (2 variables 1 equation).

A. $\dfrac{x-1}{5x}$

B. $\dfrac{4x}{5x}$

C. $-\dfrac{1}{20}$

> The answer choices are relationships.

D. $\dfrac{1}{5x}$

E. $\dfrac{1}{5} - \dfrac{1}{4x}$

> The *solution* to this problem is in *Int. Alg: Rational Expressions.*

Dissecting the Question

This question isn't that bad, so long as you are really comfortable with fractions/rational expressions. If you aren't, however, it will put you on firmer footing and boost your confidence to pick numbers.

✓ Pick an easy number, like 1.
✓ You're looking to match fractions.

Example Problems: Tough to Rearrange (cont.)

2. If $x = 7 + a$ and $y = 3 - 2a$, which expresses x in terms of y?

A. $x = \dfrac{y-3}{2}$

B. $x = 2y - 11$

C. $x = 7 - \dfrac{y-3}{2}$

> This is a good question to pick numbers on. You have flexibility on what x & y can equal. You aren't looking for a specific answer.

D. $x = 7 + \dfrac{y-3}{2}$

E. $x = 7 + \dfrac{y-3}{2}$

> The *solution* to this problem is in *Elementary Alg: Algebra Operations.*

Dissecting the Question

This question asks the relationship between x & y. To do the algebra, you re-arrange the $y = 3 - 2a$ equation for a, and then plug-in to the other equation.

✓ Pick an easy number for a. I'd pick 1 or zero.
✓ Find the value of y
✓ Find the value of x
✓ Plug in for y in the answer choices and see which equals your x-value.

Testing Answer Choices

When to Use
- ✓ Problems when you can plug the answer choices directly into the question.
- ✓ Problems where you can move "up" or "down" answers based on plugging in.
- ✓ Problems where plugging in a bad answer helps you determine what answer to try next.
- ✓ When you're really stuck.

The Strategy
Use the answer choices as inputs in the question to test whether or not they work. You can do this on a respectable portion of ACT Math problems, but it's often inefficient and error prone. So, be judicious about when you test answers. For most questions, testing answers is a last resort—don't jump on it right away.

You generally want to test answers in two situations

Question Types
Testing answer choices is directly related to *marking off*, and you'll find more example problems in that section.

1. Questions **you're going to mark-off**, including *which, equivalent to, and roman numeral* questions. Those example problems are covered in the section on *marking off*.

2. Questions **where testing answer an answer choice helps you determine what to test next.**

Questions Where Testing Helps You Along
When we have *which*, *equivalent to*, or *roman numeral* questions (and some *what* questions), you'll run through the answer choices and mark-off.

Oftentimes, these questions are best handled in parts, do one part then mark-off and repeat.

1. What is the least common multiple of 8, 10, & 12

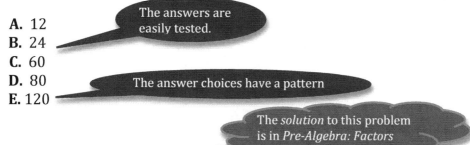

- **A.** 12
- **B.** 24
- **C.** 60
- **D.** 80
- **E.** 120

The answers are easily tested.

The answer choices have a pattern

The *solution* to this problem is in *Pre-Algebra: Factors*

Dissecting the Question
You can solve this problem by using prime factorization or any other method to find least common multiple, or you can test the answer choices.
- ✓ Common sense allows you to eliminate two answers, 12 & 24.
- ✓ Because we want the *least*, we can start at the smallest number, test it, and either stop (if it works) or move up to the next answer choice.

2. What number can you add to both the numerator and the denominator of $\frac{8}{11}$ to equal $\frac{2}{3}$?

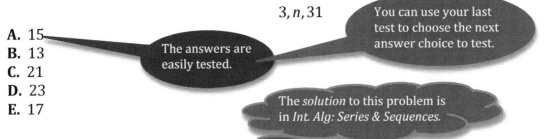

   A. 4
   B. -2
   C. 2
   D. -3
   E. -6

The answers are easily tested.

The solution to this problem is in Elem. Alg: Make an Equation.

Dissecting the Question

   You can solve this problem by making the equation. It's pretty common for people to struggle making equations unless they are plugging in answer choices (even though it's actually the same thing).
   - ✓ You can follow the text to set up the answer choices.
   - ✓ You may, or may not, get a good idea of where to go next depending on how intuitive you are.

Questions Where Testing Helps You Along (cont.)

3. The value of *n* is such that the difference between consecutive numbers in the list is the same. What is the value of *n*?

$$3, n, 31$$

   A. 15
   B. 13
   C. 21
   D. 23
   E. 17

The answers are easily tested.

You can use your last test to choose the next answer choice to test.

The solution to this problem is in Int. Alg: Series & Sequences.

Dissecting the Question

   There's a pretty simple way to solve this, but if you don't remember it, you can easily test the answer choices.
   - ✓ You can follow the text to set up the answer choices.
   - ✓ You can get a feel of the next spot to test by your last plug-in. Some answer choices you may be able to skip altogether.

4. A line passes through points (3,1) and (5,3). What is the equation of the line?

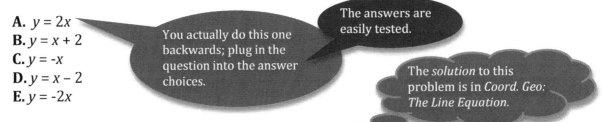

   A. $y = 2x$
   B. $y = x + 2$
   C. $y = -x$
   D. $y = x - 2$
   E. $y = -2x$

The answers are easily tested.

You actually do this one backwards; plug in the question into the answer choices.

The solution to this problem is in Coord. Geo: The Line Equation.

Dissecting the Question

   In my opinion, the easiest way to do this problem is to find the slope. The slope will allow you to mark-off a lot of answer choices. From there, you can deduce which has the right *y*-intercept. But, you could also plug-in.
   - ✓ In this case, plug the given points into equations.
   - ✓ Start with a single point, and run through the answer choices. You'll need to check both points; you can't just stop when one point works.

6 Laws for ACT Math Success

1. **Use your calculator strategically**

   Before you whip out the calculator, know what it is you want the calculator to do. Remember, calculators are no substitute for setting a problem up.

2. **Write more, not less**

   You've got to write stuff down. The ACT rewards setup and caution. It gets you more points and (believe it or not) makes you faster.

3. **The answer choices are your friend**

   The ACT is predictable (more in *How the ACT Handcuffs Itself* at the beginning of the book). Answer choices can tell you what you need to do, they let you mark-off, plug-in numbers, test answer choices. They frame the problem. *Read the question, read the answer choices, and then solve.*

4. **Setup, setup, setup**

   Setup your questions. You won't make as many mistakes, you'll save time, and you'll crack tougher problems.

5. **Bite sized pieces**

   Break questions down into small, easily digestible pieces. You really need to do this on the long word problems that the ACT loves.

6. **Use & draw diagrams**

   If the question describes a picture, draw it. If there's a diagram, transfer the relevant information to the diagram. Lean on the diagram, it can help you rule out nonsensical answers. While the ACT doesn't "draw things to scale" the diagrams are always pretty accurate and you can eyeball good estimates.

Final Thoughts

The ACT & the SAT are important, but only for a short time in your life. They don't have any bearing on what you can do for a career, what you can major in, how smart you are. Don't ever let a test define you.

I hope you've gotten a lot out of this book. I love to hear what you thought about it, so flip the page to leave me a review. Or drop me a line at **Jacob@thetestguy.com**. I'm always excited to talk to students and their families, and I don't charge for it.

Pre-Test Answers

1.	E	Numbers		19.	C	Percents
2.	C	Fractions		20.	E	Percents
3.	C	Fractions		21.	A	Percents
4.	B	Factors		22.	C	Probability
5.	E	Factors		23.	E	Probability
6.	C	Units		24.	A	Probability
7.	E	Units		25.	E	Probability
8.	B	Units		26.	D	Probability
9.	B	Units		27.	E	Combinations
10.	A	Units		28.	A	Combinations
11.	D	Ratios		29.	C	Combinations
12.	C	Ratios		30.	D	Mean & Median
13.	A	Ratios		31.	E	Mean & Median
14.	A	Ratios		32.	E	Mean & Median
15.	A	Percents		33.	B	Data
16.	A	Percents		34.	C	Data
17.	B	Percents		35.	C	Data
18.	B	Percents		36.	E	Data
				37.	C	Decimals
				38.	B	Decimals

Made in the USA
Middletown, DE
18 October 2018